JUSTICE STATISTICS

AN EXTENDED LOOK AT CRIME IN THE UNITED STATES

Edited by
Shana Hertz Hattis

Lanham, MD

Published in the United States of America
by Bernan Press, a wholly owned subsidiary of
The Rowman & Littlefield Publishing Group, Inc.
4501 Forbes Boulevard, Suite 200
Lanham, Maryland 20706

Bernan Press
800-462-6420
www.rowman.com

 ISBN-13: 978-1-59888-785-3
eISBN-13: 978-1-59888-786-0

∞™ The paper used in this publication meets the minimum requirements of
American National Standard for Information Sciences—Permanence of
Paper for Printed Library Materials, ANSI/NISO Z39.48-1992.

Manufactured in the United States of America.

JUSTICE STATISTICS

AN EXTENDED LOOK AT CRIME
IN THE UNITED STATES

Contents

INTRODUCTION

Bernan Press is pleased to present its first-ever comprehensive collection of justice statistics in the United States. This volume provides valuable information compiled by the Department of Justice, including its subsidiaries, the Bureau of Justice Statistics and the Federal Bureau of Investigation.

Justice Statistics: An Extended Look at Crime in the United States is a special edition of *Crime in the United States*. It brings together nine key reports that fall under this category. Topics covered include capital punishment, rape and sexual assault among college-age women, correctional populations, crime in the United States, hate crimes, probation, parole, and law enforcement officers killed and assaulted. Tables in this volume provide a comprehensive account of each of these subjects; for more information, including full-scope methodologies and information about standard errors for each table, please see the full reports at the URLs listed below.

Each section contains statistical tables and figures highlighting the data, as well as a brief summary of the report's methodology and at-a-glance highlights of the most compelling information.

The reports are listed below:

Capital Punishment, 2013, details statistics about inmates condemned to death. The full report can be accessed at http://www.bjs.gov/content/pub/pdf/cp13st.pdf.

Correctional Populations in the United States, 2013, discusses the trends and changes in the incarcerated populations of the country's prisons. The full report is available at http://www.bjs.gov/content/pub/pdf/cpus13st.pdf.

Crime in the United States, 2013, provides an introduction to overall crime trends. This report is more fully presented in

Bernan Press's *Crime in the United States*; however, given the importance of the report in the understanding of justice and crime trends in the United States, its most relevant tables have been included in this volume. New to this book are the expanded offense tables, which are presented here in their entirety. The full report can be accessed at https://www.fbi.gov/about-us/cjis/ucr/crime-in-the-u.s/2013/crime-in-the-u.s.-2013.

Crimes Against Persons with Disabilities, 2009–2013, focuses on nonfatal violent victimizations of persons with disabilities, comparing them to persons who are not disabled. The full report is available at http://www.bjs.gov/content/pub/pdf/capd0913st.pdf.

Hate Crime Statistics, 2013, details the hate crimes committed in the United States throughout 2013. It can be accessed at https://www.fbi.gov/about-us/cjis/ucr/hate-crime/2013.

Jail Inmates at Midyear, 2014, presents estimates of the inmate populations of jails based on various demographic characteristics. The full report can be accesses at http://www.bjs.gov/content/pub/pdf/jim14.pdf.

Law Enforcement Officers Killed and Assaulted, 2013, is the primary resource for data about harm done to law enforcement officers. This volume provides a comprehensive sample of the report; further information can be obtained at https://www.fbi.gov/about-us/cjis/ucr/leoka/2013/leoka-home.

Probation and Parole, 2013, details data about post-release inmates still in the legal system. The report can be accessed at http://www.bjs.gov/content/pub/pdf/ppus13.pdf.

Rape and Sexual Assault Among College-Age Females, 1995–2013, provides a look at these acts in regard to young women throughout the United States. The report can be found at http://www.bjs.gov/content/pub/pdf/rsavcaf9513.pdf.

ABOUT THE EDITOR

Shana Hertz Hattis is an editor with more than a decade of experience in statistical and government research publications. Past titles include *State Profiles: The Population and Economy of Each U.S. State, Housing Statistics of the United States,* and *Crime in the United States.* She earned her bachelor of science in journalism and master of science in education degrees from Northwestern University.

PART 1

Capital Punishment, 2013

HIGHLIGHTS

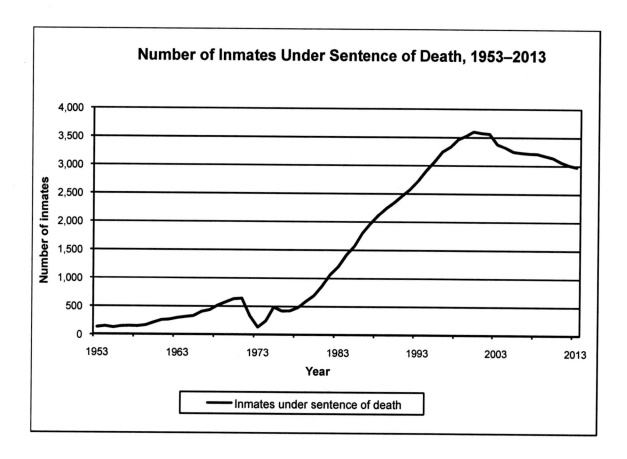

Number of Inmates Under Sentence of Death, 1953–2013

- The 35 states and the Federal Bureau of Prisons held 2,979 inmates under sentence of death on December 31, 2013, which was 32 fewer than at year end 2012.

- Five states (California, Florida, Texas, Pennsylvania, and Alabama) held 60 percent of all inmates on death row on December 31, 2013. The Federal Bureau of Prisons held 56 inmates under sentence of death.

- At year end 2013, approximately 56 percent of death row inmates were White and 42 percent were Black; 98 percent were male and 2 percent were female.

- Nine states executed 39 inmates in 2013; 43 inmates were executed in nine states in 2012.

- Among the 36 jurisdictions with prisoners under sentence of death on December 31, 2013, six jurisdictions had more inmates than a year earlier, 16 had fewer inmates, and 14 had the same number.

Table 1. Capital Offenses, by State, 2013

State	Offense
Alabama	Intentional murder (Ala. Stat. Ann. 13A-5-40(a)(1)-(18)) with 10 aggravating factors (Ala. Stat. Ann. 13A-5-49).
Arizona	First-degree murder, including premeditated murder and felony murder, accompanied by at least 1 of 14 aggravating factors (A.R.S. ẞ 13-703(F)).
Arkansas	Capital murder (Ark. Code Ann. ẞ 5-10-101) with a finding of at least 1 of 10 aggravating circumstances; treason (Ark. Code Ann. ẞ 5-51-201).
California	First-degree murder with special circumstances; sabotage; train wrecking causing death; treason; perjury in a capital case causing execution of an innocent person; fatal assault by a prisoner serving a life sentence.
Colorado	First-degree murder with at least 1 of 17 aggravating factors; first-degree kidnapping resulting in death; treason.
Connecticut[1]	Capital felony with 8 forms of aggravated homicide (C.G.S. ẞ 53a-54b).
Delaware	First-degree murder (11 Del. C. ẞ 636) with at least 1 statutory aggravating circumstance (11 Del. C. ẞ 4209).
Florida	First-degree murder; felony murder; capital drug trafficking; capital sexual battery.
Georgia	Murder with aggravating circumstances; rape, armed robbery, or kidnapping with bodily injury or ransom when the victim dies; aircraft hijacking; treason.
Idaho	First-degree murder with aggravating factors; first-degree kidnapping; perjury resulting in the execution of an innocent person.
Indiana	Murder with 16 aggravating circumstances (IC 35-50-2-9).
Kansas	Capital murder (K.S.A. 21-5401) with 8 aggravating circumstances (K.S.A. 21-6617 and K.S.A. 21-6624).
Kentucky	Capital murder with the presence of at least one statutory aggravating circumstance; capital kidnapping (KRS 532.025).
Louisiana	First-degree murder; treason (La. R.S. 14:30 and 14:113).
Mississippi	Capital murder (Miss. Code Ann. ẞ 97-3-19(2)); aircraft piracy (Miss. Code Ann. ẞ 97-25-55(1)).
Missouri	First-degree murder (565.020 RSMO 2000).
Montana	Capital murder with 1 of 9 aggravating circumstances (Mont. Code Ann. ẞ 46-18-303); aggravated kidnapping; felony murder; capital sexual intercourse without consent (Mont. Code Ann. ẞ 45-5-503).
Nebraska	First-degree murder with a finding of one or more statutory aggravating circumstances.
Nevada	First-degree murder with at least 1 of 15 aggravating circumstances (NRS 200.030, 200.033, and 200.035).
New Hampshire	Murder committed in the course of rape, kidnapping, drug crimes, or home invasion; killing of a police officer, judge, or prosecutor; murder for hire; murder by an inmate while serving a sentence of life without parole (RSA 630:1 and 630:5).
New Mexico[2]	First-degree murder with at least 1 of 7 aggravating factors (NMSA 1978 ẞ 31-20A-5).
New York[3]	First-degree murder with 1 of 13 aggravating factors (NY Penal Law ẞ125.27).
North Carolina	First-degree murder (N.C.G.S. ẞ14-17) with the finding of at least 1 of 11 statutory aggravating circumstances (N.C.G.S. ẞ 15A-2000).
Ohio	Aggravated murder with at least 1 of 10 aggravating circumstances (O.R.C. 2903.01, 2929.02, and 2929.04).
Oklahoma	First-degree murder in conjunction with a finding of at least 1 of 8 statutorily-defined aggravating circumstances.
Oregon	Aggravated murder (ORS 163.095).
Pennsylvania	First-degree murder with 18 aggravating circumstances.
South Carolina	Murder with at least 1 of 12 aggravating circumstances (ẞ 16-3-20(C)(a)).
South Dakota	First-degree murder with 1 of 10 aggravating circumstances.
Tennessee	First-degree murder (Tenn. Code Ann. ẞ 39-13-202) with 1 of 17 aggravating circumstances (Tenn. Code Ann. ẞ 39-13-204).
Texas	Criminal homicide with 1 of 9 aggravating circumstances (Tex. Penal Code ẞ 19.03).
Utah	Aggravated murder (Utah Code Ann. 76-5-202).
Virginia	First-degree murder with 1 of 15 aggravating circumstances (VA Code ẞ 18.2-31(1-15)).
Washington	Aggravated first-degree murder.
Wyoming	First-degree murder; murder during the commission of sexual assault, sexual abuse of a minor, arson, robbery, burglary, escape, resisting arrest, kidnapping, or abuse of a minor under 16 (W.S.A. ẞ 6-2-101(a)).

[1]Connecticut enacted a prospective repeal of its capital statute as of April 25, 2012. Offenders who committed capital offenses prior to that date are eligible for the death penalty.
[2]New Mexico enacted a prospective repeal of its capital statute as of July 1, 2009. Offenders who committed capital offenses prior to that date are eligible for the death penalty.
[3]The New York Court of Appeals has held that a portion of New York's death penalty sentencing statute (CPL 400.27) was unconstitutional (People v. Taylor, 9 N.Y. 3d 129 (2007)). No legislative action has been taken to amend the statute. As a result, capital cases are no longer pursued in New York.

Table 1A. Prisoners Executed Under Civil Authority in the United States, by Year, Region, and Jurisdiction, 1977–2014

(Number.)

Region and jurisdiction	Total	1977	1978	1979	1980	1981	1982	1983	1984	1985	1986	1987	1988	1989	1990	1991	1992	1993	1994
U.S. Total	1,394	1	0	2	0	1	2	5	21	18	18	25	11	16	23	14	31	38	31
Federal	3	0	0	0	0	0	0	0	0	0	0	0	0	0	0	0	0	0	0
State	1,391	1	0	2	0	1	2	5	21	18	18	25	11	16	23	14	31	38	31
Northeast	4	0	0	0	0	0	0	0	0	0	0	0	0	0	0	0	0	0	0
Connecticut	1	0	0	0	0	0	0	0	0	0	0	0	0	0	0	0	0	0	0
Maine	0	0	0	0	0	0	0	0	0	0	0	0	0	0	0	0	0	0	0
Massachusetts	0	0	0	0	0	0	0	0	0	0	0	0	0	0	0	0	0	0	0
New Hampshire	0	0	0	0	0	0	0	0	0	0	0	0	0	0	0	0	0	0	0
New Jersey	0	0	0	0	0	0	0	0	0	0	0	0	0	0	0	0	0	0	0
New York	0	0	0	0	0	0	0	0	0	0	0	0	0	0	0	0	0	0	0
Pennsylvania	3	0	0	0	0	0	0	0	0	0	0	0	0	0	0	0	0	0	0
Rhode Island	0	0	0	0	0	0	0	0	0	0	0	0	0	0	0	0	0	0	0
Vermont	0	0	0	0	0	0	0	0	0	0	0	0	0	0	0	0	0	0	0
Midwest	171	0	0	0	0	1	0	0	0	1	0	0	0	1	5	1	1	4	3
Illinois	12	0	0	0	0	0	0	0	0	0	0	0	0	0	1	0	0	0	1
Indiana	20	0	0	0	0	1	0	0	0	1	0	0	0	0	0	0	0	0	1
Iowa	0	0	0	0	0	0	0	0	0	0	0	0	0	0	0	0	0	0	0
Kansas	0	0	0	0	0	0	0	0	0	0	0	0	0	0	0	0	0	0	0
Michigan	0	0	0	0	0	0	0	0	0	0	0	0	0	0	0	0	0	0	0
Minnesota	0	0	0	0	0	0	0	0	0	0	0	0	0	0	0	0	0	0	0
Missouri	80	0	0	0	0	0	0	0	0	0	0	0	0	1	4	1	1	4	0
Nebraska	3	0	0	0	0	0	0	0	0	0	0	0	0	0	0	0	0	0	1
North Dakota	0	0	0	0	0	0	0	0	0	0	0	0	0	0	0	0	0	0	0
Ohio	53	0	0	0	0	0	0	0	0	0	0	0	0	0	0	0	0	0	0
South Dakota	3	0	0	0	0	0	0	0	0	0	0	0	0	0	0	0	0	0	0
Wisconsin	0	0	0	0	0	0	0	0	0	0	0	0	0	0	0	0	0	0	0
South	1,131	0	0	1	0	0	2	5	21	16	18	24	10	13	17	13	26	30	26
Alabama	56	0	0	0	0	0	0	1	0	0	1	1	0	4	1	0	2	0	0
Arkansas	27	0	0	0	0	0	0	0	0	0	0	0	0	0	2	0	2	0	5
Delaware	16	0	0	0	0	0	0	0	0	0	0	0	0	0	0	0	1	2	1
District of Columbia	0	0	0	0	0	0	0	0	0	0	0	0	0	0	0	0	0	0	0
Florida	89	0	0	1	0	0	0	1	8	3	3	1	2	2	4	2	2	3	1
Georgia	55	0	0	0	0	0	0	1	2	3	1	5	1	1	0	1	0	2	1
Kentucky	3	0	0	0	0	0	0	0	0	0	0	0	0	0	0	0	0	0	0
Louisiana	28	0	0	0	0	0	0	1	5	1	0	8	3	0	1	1	0	1	0
Maryland	5	0	0	0	0	0	0	0	0	0	0	0	0	0	0	0	0	0	1
Mississippi	21	0	0	0	0	0	0	1	0	0	0	2	0	1	0	0	0	0	0
North Carolina	43	0	0	0	0	0	0	0	2	0	1	0	0	0	0	1	1	0	1
Oklahoma	111	0	0	0	0	0	0	0	0	0	0	0	0	0	1	0	2	0	0
South Carolina	43	0	0	0	0	0	0	0	0	1	1	0	0	0	1	1	0	0	0
Tennessee	6	0	0	0	0	0	0	0	0	0	0	0	0	0	0	0	0	0	0
Texas	518	0	0	0	0	0	1	0	3	6	10	6	3	4	4	5	12	17	14
Virginia	110	0	0	0	0	0	1	0	1	2	1	1	1	1	3	2	4	5	2
West Virginia	0	0	0	0	0	0	0	0	0	0	0	0	0	0	0	0	0	0	0
West	85	1	0	1	0	0	0	0	0	1	0	1	1	2	1	0	4	4	2
Alaska	0	0	0	0	0	0	0	0	0	0	0	0	0	0	0	0	0	0	0
Arizona	37	0	0	0	0	0	0	0	0	0	0	0	0	0	0	0	1	2	0
California	13	0	0	0	0	0	0	0	0	0	0	0	0	0	0	0	1	1	0
Colorado	1	0	0	0	0	0	0	0	0	0	0	0	0	0	0	0	0	0	0
Hawaii	0	0	0	0	0	0	0	0	0	0	0	0	0	0	0	0	0	0	0
Idaho	3	0	0	0	0	0	0	0	0	0	0	0	0	0	0	0	0	0	1
Montana	3	0	0	0	0	0	0	0	0	0	0	0	0	0	0	0	0	0	0
Nevada	12	0	0	1	0	0	0	0	0	1	0	0	0	2	1	0	0	0	0
New Mexico	1	0	0	0	0	0	0	0	0	0	0	0	0	0	0	0	0	0	0
Oregon	2	0	0	0	0	0	0	0	0	0	0	0	0	0	0	0	0	0	0
Utah	7	1	0	0	0	0	0	0	0	0	0	1	1	0	0	0	1	0	0
Washington	5	0	0	0	0	0	0	0	0	0	0	0	0	0	0	0	0	1	1
Wyoming	1	0	0	0	0	0	0	0	0	0	0	0	0	0	0	0	1	0	0

Table 1A. Prisoners Executed Under Civil Authority in the United States, by Year, Region, and Jurisdiction, 1977–2014—*Continued*

(Number.)

Region and jurisdiction	1995	1996	1997	1998	1999	2000	2001	2002	2003	2004	2005	2006	2007	2008	2009	2010	2011	2012	2013	2014
U.S. Total	56	45	74	68	98	85	66	71	65	59	60	53	42	37	52	46	43	43	39	35
Federal	0	0	0	0	0	0	2	0	1	0	0	0	0	0	0	0	0	0	0	0
State	56	45	74	68	98	85	64	71	64	59	60	53	42	37	52	46	43	43	39	35
Northeast	2	0	0	0	1	0	0	0	0	0	1	0	0	0	0	0	0	0	0	0
Connecticut	0	0	0	0	0	0	0	0	0	0	1	0	0	0	0	0	0	0	0	0
Maine	0	0	0	0	0	0	0	0	0	0	0	0	0	0	0	0	0	0	0	0
Massachusetts	0	0	0	0	0	0	0	0	0	0	0	0	0	0	0	0	0	0	0	0
New Hampshire	0	0	0	0	0	0	0	0	0	0	0	0	0	0	0	0	0	0	0	0
New Jersey	0	0	0	0	0	0	0	0	0	0	0	0	0	0	0	0	0	0	0	0
New York	0	0	0	0	0	0	0	0	0	0	0	0	0	0	0	0	0	0	0	0
Pennsylvania	2	0	0	0	1	0	0	0	0	0	0	0	0	0	0	0	0	0	0	0
Rhode Island	0	0	0	0	0	0	0	0	0	0	0	0	0	0	0	0	0	0	0	0
Vermont	0	0	0	0	0	0	0	0	0	0	0	0	0	0	0	0	0	0	0	0
Midwest	11	9	10	5	12	5	10	9	7	7	14	6	5	2	7	8	6	5	5	11
Illinois	5	1	2	1	1	0	0	0	0	0	0	0	0	0	0	0	0	0	0	0
Indiana	0	1	1	1	1	0	2	0	2	0	5	1	2	0	1	0	0	0	0	0
Iowa	0	0	0	0	0	0	0	0	0	0	0	0	0	0	0	0	0	0	0	0
Kansas	0	0	0	0	0	0	0	0	0	0	0	0	0	0	0	0	0	0	0	0
Michigan	0	0	0	0	0	0	0	0	0	0	0	0	0	0	0	0	0	0	0	0
Minnesota	0	0	0	0	0	0	0	0	0	0	0	0	0	0	0	0	0	0	0	0
Missouri	6	6	6	3	9	5	7	6	2	0	5	0	0	0	1	0	1	0	2	10
Nebraska	0	1	1	0	0	0	0	0	0	0	0	0	0	0	0	0	0	0	0	0
North Dakota	0	0	0	0	0	0	0	0	0	0	0	0	0	0	0	0	0	0	0	0
Ohio	0	0	0	0	1	0	1	3	3	7	4	5	2	2	5	8	5	3	3	1
South Dakota	0	0	0	0	0	0	0	0	0	0	0	0	1	0	0	0	0	2	0	0
Wisconsin	0	0	0	0	0	0	0	0	0	0	0	0	0	0	0	0	0	0	0	0
South	41	29	60	55	74	76	50	61	57	50	43	44	36	35	45	35	32	31	32	23
Alabama	2	1	3	1	2	4	0	2	3	2	4	1	3	0	6	5	6	0	1	0
Arkansas	2	1	4	1	4	2	1	0	1	1	1	0	0	0	0	0	0	0	0	0
Delaware	1	3	0	0	2	1	2	0	0	0	1	0	0	0	0	0	1	1	0	0
District of Columbia	0	0	0	0	0	0	0	0	0	0	0	0	0	0	0	0	0	0	0	0
Florida	3	2	1	4	1	6	1	3	3	2	1	4	0	2	2	1	2	3	7	8
Georgia	2	2	0	1	0	0	4	4	3	2	3	0	1	3	3	2	4	0	1	2
Kentucky	0	0	1	0	1	0	0	0	0	0	0	0	0	1	0	0	0	0	0	0
Louisiana	1	1	1	0	1	1	0	1	0	0	0	0	0	0	0	1	0	0	0	0
Maryland	0	0	1	1	0	0	0	0	0	1	0	1	0	0	0	0	0	0	0	0
Mississippi	0	0	0	0	0	0	0	0	2	0	0	1	1	0	2	0	3	2	6	0
North Carolina	2	0	0	3	4	1	5	2	7	4	5	4	0	0	0	0	0	0	0	0
Oklahoma	3	2	1	4	6	11	18	7	14	6	4	4	3	2	3	3	2	6	6	3
South Carolina	1	6	2	7	4	1	0	3	0	4	3	1	1	3	2	0	1	0	0	0
Tennessee	0	0	0	0	0	1	0	0	0	0	0	1	2	0	2	0	0	0	0	0
Texas	19	3	37	20	35	40	17	33	24	23	19	24	26	18	24	17	13	15	16	10
Virginia	5	8	9	13	14	8	2	4	2	5	0	4	0	4	3	3	1	0	1	0
West Virginia	0	0	0	0	0	0	0	0	0	0	0	0	0	0	0	0	0	0	0	0
West	2	7	4	8	11	4	4	1	0	2	2	3	1	0	0	3	5	7	2	1
Alaska	0	0	0	0	0	0	0	0	0	0	0	0	0	0	0	0	0	0	0	0
Arizona	1	2	2	4	7	3	0	0	0	0	0	0	1	0	0	1	4	6	2	1
California	0	2	0	1	2	1	1	1	0	0	2	1	0	0	0	0	0	0	0	0
Colorado	0	0	1	0	0	0	0	0	0	0	0	0	0	0	0	0	0	0	0	0
Hawaii	0	0	0	0	0	0	0	0	0	0	0	0	0	0	0	0	0	0	0	0
Idaho	0	0	0	0	0	0	0	0	0	0	0	0	0	0	0	0	1	1	0	0
Montana	1	0	0	1	0	0	0	0	0	0	0	0	1	0	0	0	0	0	0	0
Nevada	0	1	0	1	1	0	1	0	0	2	0	1	0	0	0	0	0	0	0	0
New Mexico	0	0	0	0	0	0	1	0	0	0	0	0	0	0	0	0	0	0	0	0
Oregon	0	1	1	0	0	0	0	0	0	0	0	0	0	0	0	0	0	0	0	0
Utah	0	1	0	0	1	0	0	0	0	0	0	0	0	0	0	1	0	0	0	0
Washington	0	0	0	1	0	0	1	0	0	0	0	0	0	0	0	1	0	0	0	0
Wyoming	0	0	0	0	0	0	0	0	0	0	0	0	0	0	0	0	0	0	0	0

Table 2. Method of Execution, by State, 2013

(Number.)

State	Lethal injection[1]	Electrocution	Lethal gas	Hanging	Firing squad
Total	35	8	3	3	2
Alabama	x	x			
Arizona[2]	x		x		
Arkansas[3]	x	x			
California	x				
Colorado	x				
Connecticut[4]	x				
Delaware[5]	x			x	
Florida	x	x			
Georgia	x				
Idaho	x				
Indiana	x				
Kansas	x				
Kentucky[6]	x	x			
Louisiana	x				
Mississippi	x				
Missouri	x		x		
Montana	x				
Nebraska	x				
Nevada	x				
New Hampshire[7]	x			x	
New Mexico[8]	x				
New York	x				
North Carolina	x				
Ohio	x				
Oklahoma[9]	x	x			x
Oregon	x				
Pennsylvania	x				
South Carolina	x	x			
South Dakota	x				
Tennessee[10]	x	x			
Texas	x				
Utah[11]	x				x
Virginia	x	x			
Washington	x			x	
Wyoming[12]	x		x		

Note: The method of execution of federal prisoners is lethal injection, pursuant to 28 CFR Part 26. For offenses prosecuted under the Violent Crime Control and Law Enforcement Act of 1994, the execution method is that of the state in which the conviction took place (18 U.S.C. 3596).

[1]Maryland repealed the death penalty effective October 1, 2013. The four men who remained under sentence of death were subject to execution by lethal injection until the governor commuted their death sentences to life in prison without parole on December 31, 2014.
[2]Authorizes lethal injection for persons sentenced after November 15, 1992; inmates sentenced before that date may select lethal injection or gas.
[3]Authorizes lethal injection for inmates whose capital offense occurred on or after July 4, 1983; inmates whose offense occurred before that data may select lethal injection or electrocution.
[4]Authorizes lethal injection for inmates whose capital offense occurred prior to April 25, 2012.
[5]Authorizes hanging if lethal injection is held to be unconstitutional by a court of competent jurisdiction.
[6]Authorizes lethal injection for persons sentenced on or after March 31, 1998; inmates sentenced before that data may select lethal injection or electrocution.
[7]Authorizes hanging only if lethal injection cannot be given.
[8]Authorizes lethal injection for inmates whose capital offense occurred prior to July 1, 2009.
[9]Authorizes electrocution if lethal injection is held to be unconstitutional, and firing squad if both lethal injection and electrocution are held to be unconstitutional.
[10]Authorizes lethal injection for inmates whose capital offense occurred after December 31, 1998; inmates whose offense occurred before that date may select electrocution by written waiver.
[11]Authorizes firing squad if lethal injection is held unconstitutional. Inmates who selected execution by firing squad prior to May 3, 2004, may still be entitled to execution by that method.
[12]Authorizes lethal gas if lethal injection is held to be unconstitutional.

Table 3. Federal Capital Offenses, 2013

Statute	Description
8 U.S.C. 1342	Murder related to the smuggling of aliens.
18 U.S.C. 32-34	Destruction of aircraft, motor vehicles, or related facilities resulting in death.
18 U.S.C. 36	Murder committed during a drug-related drive-by shooting.
18 U.S.C. 37	Murder committed at an airport serving international civil aviation.
18 U.S.C. 115(b)(3) [by cross-reference to 18 U.S.C. 1111]	Retaliatory murder of a member of the immediate family of law enforcement officials.
18 U.S.C. 241, 242, 245, 247	Civil rights offenses resulting in death.
18 U.S.C. 351 [by cross-reference to 18 U.S.C. 1111]	Murder of a member of Congress, an important executive official, or a Supreme Court Justice.
18 U.S.C. 794	Espionage.
18 U.S.C. 844(d), (f), (i)	Death resulting from offenses involving transportation of explosives, destruction of government property, or destruction of property related to foreign or interstate commerce.
18 U.S.C. 924(i)	Murder committed by the use of a firearm during a crime of violence or a drug-trafficking crime.
18 U.S.C. 930	Murder committed in a federal government facility.
18 U.S.C. 1091	Genocide.
18 U.S.C. 1111	First-degree murder.
18 U.S.C. 1114	Murder of a federal judge or law enforcement official.
18 U.S.C. 1116	Murder of a foreign official.
18 U.S.C. 1118	Murder by a federal prisoner.
18 U.S.C. 1119	Murder of a U.S. national in a foreign country.
18 U.S.C. 1120	Murder by an escaped federal prisoner already sentenced to life imprisonment.
18 U.S.C. 1121	Murder of a state or local law enforcement official or other person aiding in a federal investigation; murder of a state correctional officer.
18 U.S.C. 1201	Murder during a kidnapping.
18 U.S.C. 1203	Murder during a hostage taking.
18 U.S.C. 1503	Murder of a court officer or juror.
18 U.S.C. 1512	Murder with the intent of preventing testimony by a witness, victim, or informant.
18 U.S.C. 1513	Retaliatory murder of a witness, victim, or informant.
18 U.S.C. 1716	Mailing of injurious articles with intent to kill or resulting in death.
18 U.S.C. 1751 [by cross-reference to 18 U.S.C. 1111]	Assassination or kidnapping resulting in the death of the President or Vice President.
18 U.S.C. 1958	Murder for hire.
18 U.S.C. 1959	Murder involved in a racketeering offense.
18 U.S.C. 1992	Willful wrecking of a train resulting in death.
18 U.S.C. 2113	Bank robbery-related murder or kidnapping.
18 U.S.C. 2119	Murder related to a carjacking.
18 U.S.C. 2245	Murder related to rape or child molestation.
18 U.S.C. 2251	Murder related to sexual exploitation of children.
18 U.S.C. 2280	Murder committed during an offense against maritime navigation.
18 U.S.C. 2281	Murder committed during an offense against a maritime fixed platform.
18 U.S.C. 2332	Terrorist murder of a U.S. national in another country.
18 U.S.C. 2332a	Murder by the use of a weapon of mass destruction.
18 U.S.C. 2340	Murder involving torture.
18 U.S.C. 2381	Treason.
21 U.S.C. 848(e)	Murder related to a continuing criminal enterprise or related murder of a federal, state, or local law enforcement officer.
49 U.S.C. 1472-1473	Death resulting from aircraft hijacking.

Table 4. Prisoners Under Sentence of Death, by Region, Jurisdiction, and Race, 2012 and 2013

(Number.)

Region and jurisdiction	Under sentence of death, 12/31/12			Received under sentence of death, 2013			Removed from death row (excluding executions), 2013[3]			Executed, 2013			Under sentence of death, 12/31/13		
	All races[1]	White[2]	Black[2]	All races[1]	White[2]	Black[2]	All races[1]	White[2]	Black[2]	All races[1]	White[2]	Black[2]	All races[1]	White[2]	Black[2]
U.S. Total..................................	3,011	1,684	1,258	83	49	33	76	44	30	39	26	13	2,979	1,663	1,248
Federal[4]..........................	56	27	28	2	0	2	2	0	2	0	0	0	56	27	28
State	2,955	1,657	1,230	81	49	31	74	44	28	39	26	13	2,923	1,636	1,220
Northeast..............................	204	87	114	4	2	2	7	2	5	0	0	0	201	87	111
Connecticut	10	4	6	0	0	0	0	0	0	0	0	0	10	4	6
New Hampshire......................	1	0	1	0	0	0	0	0	0	0	0	0	1	0	1
New York	0	0	0	0	0	0	0	0	0	0	0	0	0	0	0
Pennsylvania.........................	193	83	107	4	2	2	7	2	5	0	0	0	190	83	104
Midwest	218	115	99	11	8	3	6	2	3	5	5	0	218	116	99
Indiana................................	12	9	3	3	2	1	1	0	1	0	0	0	14	11	3
Kansas	9	6	3	0	0	0	0	0	0	0	0	0	9	6	3
Missouri	45	26	19	3	3	0	1	0	1	2	2	0	45	27	18
Nebraska..............................	11	7	2	0	0	0	0	0	0	0	0	0	11	7	2
Ohio....................................	138	64	72	4	2	2	3	1	1	3	3	0	136	62	73
South Dakota........................	3	3	0	1	1	0	1	1	0	0	0	0	3	3	0
South....................................	1,538	825	693	34	15	18	45	28	16	32	19	13	1,495	793	682
Alabama	191	98	92	5	1	4	5	3	2	1	1	0	190	95	94
Arkansas..............................	38	15	23	0	0	0	1	0	1	0	0	0	37	15	22
Delaware..............................	16	7	9	1	0	1	0	0	0	0	0	0	17	7	10
Florida.................................	402	252	149	15	10	5	12	11	1	7	5	2	398	246	151
Georgia...............................	89	46	43	0	0	0	6	2	4	1	1	0	82	43	39
Kentucky..............................	34	29	5	0	0	0	1	0	1	0	0	0	33	29	4
Louisiana..............................	85	28	56	0	0	0	1	0	1	0	0	0	84	28	55
Maryland..............................	5	1	4	0	0	0	0	0	0	0	0	0	5	1	4
Mississippi	49	20	28	2	2	0	1	0	1	0	0	0	50	22	27
North Carolina	152	66	79	1	0	1	2	1	1	0	0	0	151	65	79
Oklahoma[5]...........................	56	29	24	1	0	0	3	1	1	6	3	3	48	25	20
South Carolina[6]	49	20	29	0	0	0	4	2	2	0	0	0	45	18	27
Tennesseee	79	43	34	0	0	0	4	4	0	0	0	0	75	39	34
Texas..................................	284	166	114	9	2	7	4	4	0	16	8	8	273	156	113
Virginia	9	5	4	0	0	0	1	0	1	1	1	0	7	4	3
West....................................	995	630	324	32	24	8	16	12	4	2	2	0	1,009	640	328
Arizona...............................	125	103	17	4	4	0	5	5	0	2	2	0	122	100	17
California[6]...........................	718	423	263	25	17	8	8	6	2	0	0	0	735	434	269
Colorado..............................	3	0	3	0	0	0	0	0	0	0	0	0	3	0	3
Idaho	12	12	0	0	0	0	0	0	0	0	0	0	12	12	0
Montana	2	2	0	0	0	0	0	0	0	0	0	0	2	2	0
Nevada................................	80	47	32	2	2	0	1	0	1	0	0	0	81	49	31
New Mexico..........................	2	2	0	0	0	0	0	0	0	0	0	0	2	2	0
Oregon................................	36	30	4	0	0	0	2	1	1	0	0	0	34	29	3
Utah....................................	8	6	1	0	0	0	0	0	0	0	0	0	8	6	1
Washington..........................	8	4	4	1	1	0	0	0	0	0	0	0	9	5	4
Wyoming	1	1	0	0	0	0	0	0	0	0	0	0	1	1	0

Note: Counts for year end 2012 have been revised from those reported in Capital Punishment, 2012 - Statistical Tables (NCJ 245789, BJS web, May 2014). Revised counts include 19 inmates who were either reported late to the National Prisoner Statistics program or were not in custody of state correctional authorities on December 31, 2012 (14 in California; 3 in Florida; and 1 each in Pennsylvania and Oregon) and exclude 42 inmates who were relieved of a death sentence before December 31, 2012 (9 each in Pennsylvania and California; 6 each in Georgia and Texas; 4 in Florida; 3 in Tennessee; 2 in Missouri; and 1 each in Ohio, Delaware, and Nevada). Data for December 31, 2012, also include 1 inmate in Pennsylvania who was erroneously reported as being removed from under sentence of death.

[1]Includes American Indians or Alaska Natives; Asians, Native Hawaiians, or other Pacific Islanders; and inmates of Hispanic or Latino origin for whom no other race was identified.

[2]Counts of white and black inmates include persons of Hispanic or Latino origin, which may differ from other tables in this report.

[3]Includes 25 deaths from natural causes (6 each in Florida and California; 2 each in Alabama and Tennessee; and 1 each in Pennsylvania, Missouri, Ohio, North Carolina, South Carolina, Texas, Arizona, Oregon, and the Federal Bureau of Prisons) and 6 deaths from suicide (2 in Arizona; and 1 each in Ohio, Florida, South Carolina, and California).

[4]Excludes persons held under Armed Forces jurisdiction with a military death sentence for murder.

[5]One inmate who was previously in the custody of Tennessee is now being reported in Oklahoma where he is under a separate sentence of death.

[6]One inmate who was previously in the custody of South Carolina is now being reported in California where he is under a separate sentence of death.

Table 5. Demographic Characteristics of Prisoners Under Sentence of Death, 2013

(Number; percent.)

Characteristic	Total year end	Admissions	Removals
Total Inmates	2,979	83	115
Sex			
Male	98.1	100.0	96.5
Female	1.9	0.0	3.5
Race[1]			
White	55.8	59.0	60.9
Black	41.9	39.8	37.4
All other races[2]	2.3	1.2	1.7
Hispanic/Latino origin[3]			
Hispanic/Latino	14.4	18.3	12.1
Non-Hispanic/Latino	85.6	81.7	87.9
Age			
18–19	X	X	X
20–24	0.7	6.0	0.9
25–29	3.4	12.0	3.5
30–34	9.2	20.5	4.3
35–39	13.2	18.1	10.4
40–44	18.3	16.9	17.4
45–49	16.1	7.2	17.4
50–54	16.3	8.4	15.7
55–59	10.6	6.0	10.4
60–64	6.4	2.4	8.7
65 or older	5.8	2.4	11.3
Average age			
Mean	47	39	49
Median	46	38	49
Education[4]			
8th grade or less	13.1	15.7	22.0
9th–11th grade	34.8	23.5	32.0
High school graduate/GED	42.8	47.1	40.0
Any college	9.4	13.7	6.0
Median education level	12th	12th	11th
Marital status[5]			
Married	21.5	22.4	26.5
Divorced/separated	20.0	20.9	27.5
Widowed	3.6	1.5	4.9
Never married	54.8	55.2	41.2

X = Not applicable.
Note: Detail may not sum to total due to rounding.
[1]Percentages for white and black inmates include persons of Hispanic or Latino origin, which may differ from other tables in this report.
[2]At year end 2013, inmates in "all other races" consisted of 21 American Indian or Alaska Natives (AIAN); 42 Asian, Native Hawaiian, or other Pacific Islanders; and 5 self-identified Hispanics or Latinos. During 2013, 1 AIAN inmate was admitted and 2 AIAN inmates were removed.
[3]Calculations exclude count of inmates with unknown Hispanic or Latino origin: 278 at year end, 1 admission, and 8 removals.
[4]Calculations exclude count of inmates with unknown education level: 544 at year end, 32 admissions, and 15 removals.
[5]Calculations exclude count of inmates with unknown marital status: 335 at year end, 16 admissions, and 13 removals.

Table 6. Female Prisoners Under Sentence of Death, by Region, Jurisdiction, and Race, 2012 and 2013

(Number.)

Region and jurisdiction	Under sentence of death, 12/31/12[1]			Received under sentence of death, 2013	Removed from death row (excluding executions), 2013[4]			Executed, 2013[4]	Under sentence of death, 12/31/13		
	All races[2]	White[3]	Black[3]		All races[2]	White[3]	Black[3]		All races[2]	White[3]	Black[3]
U.S. Total..........................	60	41	15	0	3	3	0	1	56	38	14
Federal............................	1	1	0	0	0	0	0	0	1	1	0
State................................	59	40	15	0	3	3	0	1	55	37	14
Northeast..........................	3	1	2	0	0	0	0	0	3	1	2
Pennsylvania....................	3	1	2	0	0	0	0	0	3	1	2
Midwest............................	2	1	1	0	1	1	0	0	1	0	1
Indiana.............................	1	0	1	0	0	0	0	0	1	0	1
Ohio.................................	1	1	0	0	1	1	0	0	0	0	0
South................................	29	19	10	0	1	1	0	1	27	18	9
Alabama..........................	4	3	1	0	0	0	0	0	4	3	1
Florida.............................	5	2	3	0	0	0	0	0	5	2	3
Georgia............................	1	1	0	0	0	0	0	0	1	1	0
Kentucky..........................	1	1	0	0	0	0	0	0	1	1	0
Louisiana.........................	2	1	1	0	0	0	0	0	2	1	1
Mississippi.......................	2	2	0	0	0	0	0	0	2	2	0
North Carolina	3	2	1	0	1	1	0	0	2	1	1
Oklahoma	1	1	0	0	0	0	0	0	1	1	0
Tennesseee......................	1	1	0	0	0	0	0	0	1	1	0
Texas...............................	9	5	4	0	0	0	0	1	8	5	3
West.................................	25	19	2	0	1	1	0	0	24	18	2
Arizona	3	3	0	0	1	1	0	0	2	2	0
California.........................	20	14	2	0	0	0	0	0	20	14	2
Idaho...............................	1	1	0	0	0	0	0	0	1	1	0
Oregon.............................	1	1	0	0	0	0	0	0	1	1	0

[1]Counts of female prisoners under sentence of death at year end 2012 have been revised from those reported in Capital Punishment, 2012 - Statistical Tables (NCJ 245789 BJS web, May 2014). The revised figures exclude 1 female inmate in Texas whose removal from under sentence of death occurred prior to 2012 but was not reported until the 2013 data collection.
[2]Includes American Indians or Alaska Natives; Asians, Native Hawaiians, or other Pacific Islanders; and inmates of Hispanic or Latino origin for whom no other race was identified.
[3]Counts of white and black inmates include persons of Hispanic or Latino origin, which may differ from other tables in this report.
[4]One black female inmate was executed in Texas in 2013.

Table 7. Hispanic or Latino Prisoners Under Sentence of Death, by Region, Jurisdiction, and Race, 2012 and 2013

(Number.)

Region and jurisdiction	Under sentence of death, 12/31/12	Received under sentence of death, 2013	Removed from death row (excluding executions), 2013	Executed, 2013	Under sentence of death, 12/31/13
U.S. Total................................	387	15	10	3	389
Federal................................	8	0	1	0	7
State....................................	379	15	9	3	382
Northeast..............................	20	0	0	0	20
Pennsylvania.......................	20	0	0	0	20
Midwest	9	0	0	0	9
Nebraska.............................	5	0	0	0	5
Ohio....................................	4	0	0	0	4
South....................................	135	2	6	3	128
Alabama	2	0	0	0	2
Delaware.............................	3	0	0	0	3
Florida.................................	33	1	2	0	32
Georgia...............................	3	0	1	0	2
Louisiana.............................	2	0	0	0	2
North Carolina	4	0	0	0	4
Oklahoma	1	0	0	0	1
South Carolina	1	0	0	0	1
Tennesseee..........................	1	0	0	0	1
Texas...................................	85	1	3	3	80
West.....................................	215	13	3	0	225
Arizona	25	1	0	0	26
California.............................	175	12	3	0	184
Idaho...................................	1	0	0	0	1
Nevada................................	8	0	0	0	8
Oregon	3	0	0	0	3
Utah....................................	3	0	0	0	3

Note: Counts of Hispanic or Latino inmates under sentence of death at year end 2012 have been revised from those reported in Capital Punishment, 2012 - Statistical Tables (NCJ 245789, BJS web, May 2014). Revised counts exclude 1 inmate in New Mexico who was erroneously reported as Hispanic or Latino.

Table 8. Criminal History of Prisoners Under Sentence of Death, by Race and Hispanic Origin, 2013

(Percent.)

Characteristic	All races[1]	White[2]	Black[2]	Hispanic
U.S. Total	100.0	100.0	100.0	100.0
Prior felony convictions[3]				
Yes	67.3	63.9	72.6	64.8
No	32.7	36.1	27.4	35.2
Prior homicide convictions[4]				
Yes	9.0	9.0	9.6	6.6
No	91.0	91.0	90.4	93.4
Legal status at time of capital offense[5]				
Charges pending	8.7	9.6	8.7	6.2
Probation	11.4	9.9	12.0	13.8
Parole	16.5	14.1	18.5	18.3
On escape	1.3	1.8	0.8	1.1
Incarcerated	2.7	3.5	2.2	2.0
Other status	0.1	0.1	0.2	0.3
None	59.3	61.0	57.6	58.4

Note: Percentages are based on offenders for whom data were reported. Detail may not sum to total due to rounding.
[1]Includes American Indians or Alaska Natives and Asians, Native Hawaiians, or Other Pacific Islanders.
[2]Excludes persons of Hispanic or Latino origin.
[3]Data were not reported for 217 inmates.
[4]Data were not reported for 36 inmates.
[5]Data were not reported for 292 inmates.

Table 9. Inmates Removed from Under Sentence of Death, by Region, Jurisdiction, and Method of Removal, 2013

(Number.)

Region and jurisdiction	Total	Execution	Other death	Appeals or higher court overturned		
				Capital statute	Conviction	Sentence
U.S. Total	115	39	31	1	12	32
Federal	2	0	1	0	0	1
State	113	39	30	1	12	31
Northeast	7	0	1	0	0	6
Pennsylvania	7	0	1	0	0	6
Midwest	11	5	3	0	0	3
Indiana	1	0	0	0	0	1
Missouri	3	2	1	0	0	0
Ohio	6	3	2	0	0	1
South Dakota	1	0	0	0	0	1
South	77	32	15	0	11	19
Alabama	6	1	2	0	2	1
Arkansas	1	0	0	0	1	0
Florida	19	7	7	0	3	2
Georgia	7	1	0	0	0	6
Kentucky	1	0	0	0	1	0
Louisiana	1	0	0	0	0	1
Mississippi	1	0	0	0	0	1
North Carolina	2	0	1	0	0	1
Oklahoma	9	6	0	0	3	0
South Carolina	4	0	2	0	0	2
Tennesseee	4	0	2	0	0	2
Texas	20	16	1	0	1	2
Virginia	2	1	0	0	0	1
West	18	2	11	1	1	3
Arizona	7	2	3	1	1	0
California	8	0	7	0	0	1
Nevada	1	0	0	0	0	1
Oregon	2	0	1	0	0	1

Table 10. Average Time Between Sentencing and Execution, 1977–2013

(Number; time in months.)

Year[1]	Number executed	Average elapsed time from sentence to execution[2]
Total	1,359	137
1977	1	:
1979	2	:
1981	1	:
1982	2	:
1983	5	:
1984	21	74
1985	18	71
1986	18	87
1987	25	86
1988	11	80
1989	16	95
1990	23	95
1991	14	116
1992	31	114
1993	38	113
1994	31	122
1995	56	134
1996	45	125
1997	74	133
1998	68	130
1999	98	143
2000	85	137
2001	66	142
2002	71	127
2003	65	131
2004	59	132
2005	60	147
2006	53	145
2007	42	153
2008	37	139
2009	52	169
2010	46	178
2011	43	198
2012	43	190
2013	39	186

Note: In 1972, the U.S. Supreme Court invalidated capital punishment statutes in several states (Furman v. Georgia, 408 U.S. 238 (1972)), effecting a moratorium on executions. Executions resumed in 1977 when the Supreme Court found that revisions to several state statutes had effectively addressed the issues previously held unconstitutional (Gregg v. Georgia, 428 U.S. 153 (1976) and its companion cases).
: = Not calculated. A reliable average could not be generated from fewer than 10 cases.
[1] No inmates were executed in 1978 or 1980.
[2] Average time was calculated from the most recent sentencing date.

Table 11. Number of Inmates Executed, by Race and Hispanic Origin, 1977–2013

(Time in months.)

Year[1]	All races	White[2]	Black[2]	Hispanic	All other races[2,3]
Total	1,359	770	464	111	14
1977	1	1	0	0	0
1979	2	2	0	0	0
1981	1	1	0	0	0
1982	2	1	1	0	0
1983	5	4	1	0	0
1984	21	13	8	0	0
1985	18	9	7	2	0
1986	18	9	7	2	0
1987	25	11	11	3	0
1988	11	6	5	0	0
1989	16	6	8	2	0
1990	23	16	7	0	0
1991	14	6	7	1	0
1992	31	17	11	2	1
1993	38	19	14	4	1
1994	31	19	11	1	0
1995	56	31	22	2	1
1996	45	29	14	2	0
1997	74	41	26	5	2
1998	68	40	18	8	2
1999	98	53	33	9	3
2000	85	43	35	6	1
2001	66	45	17	3	1
2002	71	47	18	6	0
2003	65	41	20	3	1
2004	59	36	19	3	1
2005	60	38	19	3	0
2006	53	25	20	8	0
2007	42	22	14	6	0
2008	37	17	17	3	0
2009	52	24	21	7	0
2010	46	28	13	5	0
2011	43	22	16	5	0
2012	43	25	11	7	0
2013	39	23	13	3	0

Note: In 1972, the U.S. Supreme Court invalidated capital punishment statutes in several states (Furman v. Georgia, 408 U.S. 238 (1972)), effecting a moratorium on executions. Executions resumed in 1977 when the Supreme Court found that revisions to several state statutes had effectively addressed the issues previously held unconstitutional (Gregg v. Georgia, 428 U.S. 153 (1976) and its companion cases).
[1] No inmates were executed in 1978 or 1980.
[2] Excludes persons of Hispanic or Latino origin.
[3] Includes American Indians or Alaska Natives, and Asians, Native Hawaiians, or Other Pacific Islanders.

Table 12. Executions and Other Dispositions of Inmates Sentenced to Death, by Race and Hispanic Origin, 1977–2013

(Number; percent.)

Race/Hispanic origin	Number under sentence of death, 1977–2013[1]	Prisoners executed		Prisoners who received other dispensations[2]	
		Number	Percent of total	Number	Percent of total
Total	8,124	1,359	16.7	3,786	46.6
White[3]	3,907	770	19.7	1,843	47.2
Black[3]	3,334	464	13.9	1,635	49.0
Hispanic/Latino	755	111	14.7	255	33.8
All other races[3,4]	128	14	10.9	53	41.4

Note: In 1972, the U.S. Supreme Court invalidated capital punishment statutes in several states (Furman v. Georgia, 408 U.S. 238 (1972)), effecting a moratorium on executions. Executions resumed in 1977 when the Supreme Court found that revisions to several state statutes had effectively addressed the issues previously held unconstitutional (Gregg v. Georgia, 428 U.S. 153 (1976) and its companion cases).
[1] Includes 4 persons sentenced to death prior to 1977 who were still under sentence of death on December 31, 2013; 375 persons sentenced to death prior to 1977 whose death sentence was removed between 1977 and December 31, 2013; and 7,745 persons sentenced to death between 1977 and 2013.
[2] Includes persons removed from under a sentence of death because of statutes struck down on appeal, sentences or convictions vacated, commutations, or death by other than execution.
[3] Excludes persons of Hispanic or Latino origin.
[4] Includes American Indians, Alaska Natives, Asians, Native Hawaiians, and Other Pacific Islanders.

Table 13. Executions, by Jurisdiction and Method, 1977–2013

(Number.)

Jurisdiction	All executions	Lethal injection	Electrocution	Lethal gas	Hanging	Firing squad
U.S. Total............................	1,359	1,184	158	11	3	3
Federal............................	3	3	0	0	0	0
Alabama............................	56	32	24	0	0	0
Arizona............................	36	34	0	2	0	0
Arkansas............................	27	26	1	0	0	0
California............................	13	11	0	2	0	0
Colorado............................	1	1	0	0	0	0
Connecticut............................	1	1	0	0	0	0
Delaware............................	16	15	0	0	1	0
Florida............................	81	37	44	0	0	0
Georgia............................	53	30	23	0	0	0
Idaho............................	3	3	0	0	0	0
Illinois............................	12	12	0	0	0	0
Indiana............................	20	17	3	0	0	0
Kentucky............................	3	2	1	0	0	0
Louisiana............................	28	8	20	0	0	0
Maryland............................	5	5	0	0	0	0
Mississippi............................	21	17	0	4	0	0
Missouri............................	70	70	0	0	0	0
Montana............................	3	3	0	0	0	0
Nebraska............................	3	0	3	0	0	0
Nevada............................	12	11	0	1	0	0
New Mexico............................	1	1	0	0	0	0
North Carolina............................	43	41	0	2	0	0
Ohio............................	52	52	0	0	0	0
Oklahoma............................	108	108	0	0	0	0
Oregon............................	2	2	0	0	0	0
Pennsylvania............................	3	3	0	0	0	0
South Carolina............................	43	36	7	0	0	0
South Dakota............................	3	3	0	0	0	0
Tennessee............................	6	5	1	0	0	0
Texas............................	508	508	0	0	0	0
Utah............................	7	4	0	0	0	3
Virginia............................	110	79	31	0	0	0
Washington............................	5	3	0	0	2	0
Wyoming............................	1	1	0	0	0	0

Note: In 1972, the U.S. Supreme Court invalidated capital punishment statutes in several states (Furman v. Georgia, 408 U.S. 238 (1972)), effecting a moratorium on executions. Executions resumed in 1977, when the Supreme Court found that revisions to several state statutes had effectively addressed the issues previously held unconstitutional (Gregg v. Georgia, 428 U.S. 153 (1976) and its companion cases).

Table 14. Executions, by Jurisdiction, 1930–2013

(Number.)

Jurisdiction	Since 1930	Since 1977
U.S. Total..	5,218	1,359
Texas..	805	508
Georgia	419	53
New York..	329	0
North Carolina..	306	43
California..	305	13
Florida	251	81
Ohio	224	52
South Carolina..	205	43
Virginia..	202	110
Alabama..	191	56
Mississippi..	175	21
Oklahoma..	168	108
Louisiana	161	28
Pennsylvania	155	3
Arkansas..	145	27
Missouri..	132	70
Kentucky..	106	3
Illinois..	102	12
Tennessee	99	6
Arizona..	74	36
New Jersey..	74	0
Maryland..	73	5
Indiana	61	20
Washington	52	5
Colorado	48	1
Nevada	41	12
District of Columbia	40	0
West Virginia	40	0
Federal system	36	3
Delaware	28	16
Massachusetts	27	0
Connecticut..	22	1
Oregon	21	2
Utah	20	7
Iowa	18	0
Kansas..	15	0
Montana	9	3
New Mexico	9	1
Wyoming..	8	1
Nebraska	7	3
Idaho	6	3
South Dakota..	4	3
Vermont	4	0
New Hampshire	1	0

Note: Statistics on executions under civil authority have been collected by the federal government annually since 1930. Excludes 160 executions carried out by military authorities between 1930 and 1961.

Table 15. Prisoners Under Sentence of Death on December 31, 2013, by Jurisdiction and Year of Sentencing, 1974–2013

(Number.)

Jurisdiction	Year of sentence for prisoners under sentence of death, 12/31/13															Under sentence of death, 12/31/13	Average number of years under sentence of death, 12/31/13
	1974–1979	1980–1982	1983–1985	1986–1988	1989–1991	1992–1994	1995–1997	1998–2000	2001–2002	2003–2004	2005–2006	2007–2008	2009–2010	2011–2012	2013		
Total	25	51	116	175	218	315	413	407	188	194	217	204	211	162	83	2,979	14.6
Florida	11	9	17	26	39	45	36	53	15	15	25	30	26	36	15	398	15
California	5	24	37	56	70	88	106	100	38	29	37	37	59	24	25	735	16.1
Texas	4	3	5	12	11	21	26	42	30	34	22	22	15	17	9	273	13
Nevada	1	3	10	7	7	4	20	9	0	3	3	4	6	2	2	81	17.7
Arizona	1	2	4	5	12	14	9	4	1	11	11	11	22	11	4	122	12.4
Georgia	1	2	0	7	5	9	16	15	3	5	5	8	3	3	0	82	15.5
Tennessee	1	1	10	9	9	3	13	8	5	5	1	2	4	4	0	75	18.4
Arkansas	1	0	0	0	1	8	9	5	3	1	2	4	2	1	0	37	14.7
Pennsylvania	0	2	5	18	19	29	24	23	12	8	12	13	8	13	4	190	15.4
Mississippi	0	2	0	0	6	5	4	7	7	2	4	2	6	3	2	50	13
Kentucky	0	1	3	5	2	5	2	7	2	1	3	0	1	1	0	33	18.3
Alabama	0	1	2	7	7	20	25	31	12	13	24	15	14	14	5	190	12.4
Idaho	0	1	0	1	2	1	2	0	0	2	1	0	2	0	0	12	16.2
Ohio	0	0	9	13	12	10	20	18	10	10	7	7	8	8	4	136	15.2
Maryland	0	0	3	0	0	0	1	1	0	0	0	0	0	0	0	5	:
Louisiana	0	0	2	5	2	6	19	19	7	5	5	2	5	7	0	84	14
Missouri	0	0	2	1	3	2	7	5	4	4	5	7	1	1	3	45	12.4
Oklahoma	0	0	2	1	0	2	3	9	3	8	7	9	2	1	1	48	11.1
South Carolina	0	0	2	0	2	0	6	6	5	8	7	6	3	0	0	45	12
Utah	0	0	1	1	2	0	2	1	0	0	0	1	0	0	0	8	:
North Carolina	0	0	1	0	3	33	45	28	10	8	9	4	6	3	1	151	15.1
Montana	0	0	1	0	0	1	0	0	0	0	0	0	0	0	0	2	:
Nebraska	0	0	0	1	0	0	2	0	0	2	3	1	2	0	0	11	11.3
Connecticut	0	0	0	0	3	0	1	0	0	0	1	3	1	1	0	10	11.9
Washington	0	0	0	0	1	0	2	1	2	0	0	0	1	1	1	9	:
Oregon	0	0	0	0	0	5	5	7	2	3	3	2	3	4	0	34	12
Federal	0	0	0	0	0	2	4	4	7	10	11	8	7	1	2	56	9.1
Indiana	0	0	0	0	0	1	1	3	2	1	2	0	1	0	3	14	9.7
South Dakota	0	0	0	0	0	1	0	0	0	0	0	0	0	1	1	3	:
Colorado	0	0	0	0	0	0	1	0	0	0	0	1	1	0	0	3	:
Delaware	0	0	0	0	0	0	1	0	5	3	3	0	1	3	1	17	8.2
New Mexico	0	0	0	0	0	0	1	0	1	0	0	0	0	0	0	2	:
Virginia	0	0	0	0	0	0	0	1	0	0	3	2	0	1	0	7	:
Kansas	0	0	0	0	0	0	0	0	2	2	1	2	1	1	0	9	:
Wyoming	0	0	0	0	0	0	0	0	0	0	1	0	0	0	0	1	:
New Hampshire	0	0	0	0	0	0	0	0	0	0	0	1	0	0	0	1	:

: = Not calculated. A reliable average could not be generated from fewer than 10 cases.
Note: For persons sentenced to death more than once, the numbers are based on the most recent death sentence.

Table 16. Prisoners Sentenced to Death and the Outcome of the Sentence, by Year of Sentencing, 1973–2013

(Number.)

| Year of sentence | Number sentenced | Number of prisoners removed from under sentence of death | | | | | | | | Remaining under sentence of death, 12/31/13 |
| | | Execution | Other death | Appeal or higher courts overturned | | | Sentence commuted | Other/unknown removals | |
				Capital statute	Conviction	Sentence			
Total, 1973–2013	8,466	1,359	509	523	890	1,781	392	33	2,979
1973	42	2	0	14	9	8	9	0	0
1974	149	11	5	65	15	30	22	1	0
1975	298	6	5	171	24	67	21	2	2
1976	232	14	6	136	17	42	15	0	2
1977	137	19	5	40	26	34	7	0	6
1978	183	38	7	21	36	67	8	0	6
1979	150	28	16	2	28	60	6	1	9
1980	172	47	16	4	30	55	12	0	8
1981	223	58	16	0	43	82	12	1	11
1982	265	67	26	0	42	86	12	0	32
1983	252	69	28	1	31	72	15	2	34
1984	286	72	21	2	46	80	13	8	44
1985	258	53	14	1	44	89	15	4	38
1986	301	75	26	1	50	73	14	5	57
1987	288	59	29	7	45	83	10	7	48
1988	287	64	20	1	38	80	14	0	70
1989	255	48	23	0	33	73	13	1	64
1990	250	51	22	2	37	59	18	1	60
1991	267	45	15	2	38	62	11	0	94
1992	283	51	20	0	28	60	23	0	101
1993	290	67	21	3	23	49	15	0	112
1994	311	74	13	10	37	60	15	0	102
1995	310	67	20	6	22	50	14	0	131
1996	315	46	20	4	21	66	15	0	143
1997	266	35	15	3	21	42	11	0	139
1998	295	50	15	4	22	53	9	0	142
1999	279	36	16	8	23	39	10	0	147
2000	223	28	16	4	12	36	9	0	118
2001	153	16	12	3	7	26	2	0	87
2002	166	25	6	3	3	23	5	0	101
2003	151	19	10	1	8	14	1	0	98
2004	138	10	5	1	5	16	5	0	96
2005	140	1	6	0	3	14	1	0	115
2006	123	1	4	0	7	6	3	0	102
2007	126	2	3	2	7	5	2	0	105
2008	120	2	3	0	3	10	3	0	99
2009	118	1	1	1	0	7	1	0	107
2010	114	0	1	0	6	2	1	0	104
2011	85	2	1	0	0	1	0	0	81
2012	82	0	1	0	0	0	0	0	81
2013	83	0	0	0	0	0	0	0	83

Note: In 1972, the U.S. Supreme Court invalidated capital punishment statutes in several states (Furman v. Georgia, 408 U.S. 238 (1972)), effecting a moratorium on executions. Executions resumed in 1977 when the Supreme Court found that revisions to several state statutes had effectively addressed the issues previously held unconstitutional (Gregg v. Georgia, 428 U.S. 153 (1976) and its companion cases). Some inmates executed since 1977 or currently under sentence of death were sentenced prior to 1977. For persons sentenced to death more than once, the numbers are based on the most recent death sentence.

Table 17. Prisoners Sentenced to Death and the Outcome of the Sentence, by Jurisdiction, 1973–2013

(Number; percent.)

Jurisdiction	Total sentenced to death, 1973–2013	Number of prisoners removed from under sentence of death					Remaining under sentence of death, 12/31/13
		Execution	Other death	Sentence/ conviction overturned	Sentence commuted	Other/unknown removals	
U.S. Total........................	8,466	1,359	509	3,194	392	33	2,979
Federal.............................	71	3	1	10	1	0	56
Alabama............................	439	56	36	155	2	0	190
Arizona.............................	307	36	21	120	7	1	122
Arkansas...........................	114	27	3	45	2	0	37
California..........................	1,013	13	92	158	15	0	735
Colorado...........................	22	1	2	15	1	0	3
Connecticut.......................	15	1	0	4	0	0	10
Delaware...........................	60	16	0	26	1	0	17
Florida..............................	1,040	81	72	469	18	2	398
Georgia.............................	325	53	19	160	10	1	82
Idaho...............................	42	3	3	21	3	0	12
Illinois..............................	307	12	15	97	171	12	0
Indiana.............................	103	20	4	57	6	2	14
Kansas..............................	13	0	0	4	0	0	9
Kentucky...........................	83	3	6	39	2	0	33
Louisiana..........................	245	28	6	119	7	1	84
Maryland...........................	53	5	3	36	4	0	5
Massachusetts....................	4	0	0	2	2	0	0
Mississippi........................	197	21	6	117	0	3	50
Missouri............................	186	70	11	57	3	0	45
Montana............................	15	3	2	6	2	0	2
Nebraska...........................	33	3	5	12	2	0	11
Nevada.............................	156	12	15	44	4	0	81
New Hampshire..................	1	0	0	0	0	0	1
New Jersey.........................	52	0	3	33	8	8	0
New Mexico........................	28	1	1	19	5	0	2
New York...........................	10	0	0	10	0	0	0
North Carolina...................	536	43	25	309	8	0	151
Ohio.................................	419	52	26	183	22	0	136
Oklahoma..........................	353	108	17	176	4	0	48
Oregon.............................	63	2	3	24	0	0	34
Pennsylvania......................	417	3	30	188	6	0	190
Rhode Island......................	2	0	0	2	0	0	0
South Carolina....................	204	43	8	105	3	0	45
South Dakota......................	7	3	1	0	0	0	3
Tennessee..........................	225	6	19	117	6	2	75
Texas................................	1,075	508	45	194	55	0	273
Utah.................................	27	7	1	10	1	0	8
Virginia.............................	152	110	6	17	11	1	7
Washington........................	40	5	1	25	0	0	9
Wyoming...........................	12	1	1	9	0	0	1
Percent of inmates sentenced to death, 1973–2013	100.0	16.1	6.0	37.7	4.6	0.4	35.2

Note: In 1972, the U.S. Supreme Court invalidated capital punishment statutes in several states (Furman v. Georgia, 408 U.S. 238 (1972)), effecting a moratorium on executions. Executions resumed in 1977 when the Supreme Court found that revisions to several state statutes had effectively addressed the issues previously held unconstitutional (Gregg v. Georgia, 428 U.S. 153 (1976) and its companion cases). Some inmates executed since 1977 or currently under sentence of death were sentenced prior to 1977. For persons sentenced to death more than once, the numbers are based on the most recent death sentence.

Table 18. Inmates Under Sentence of Death, by Demographic Characteristics, 2013

(Number.)

Characteristic	Total year end	Admissions	Removals
Total Inmates	2,979	83	115
Sex			
Male	2,923	83	111
Female	56	0	4
Race[1]			
White	1,663	49	70
Black	1,248	33	43
All other races[2]	68	1	2
Hispanic origin			
Hispanic	389	15	13
Non-Hispanic	2,312	67	94
Number unknown	278	1	8
Age			
18–19	0	0	0
20–24	21	5	1
25–29	101	10	4
30–34	273	17	5
35–39	392	15	12
40–44	545	14	20
45–49	479	6	20
50–54	487	7	18
55–59	315	5	12
60–64	192	2	10
65 or older	174	2	13
Education			
8th grade or less	318	8	22
9th–11th grade	847	12	32
High school graduate/GED	1,042	24	40
Any college	228	7	6
Unknown	544	32	15
Marital status			
Married	569	15	27
Divorced/separated	530	14	28
Widowed	95	1	5
Never married	1,450	37	42
Unknown	335	16	13

[1]Counts for white and black inmates include persons of Hispanic or Latino origin, which may differ from other tables in this report.
[2]At year end 2013, inmates in "all other races" consisted of 21 American Indian or Alaska Natives (AIAN); 42 Asian, Native Hawaiian, and Other Pacific Islanders; and 5 self-identified Hispanics or Latinos. During 2013, 1 AIAN inmate was admitted and 2 AIAN inmates were removed.

METHODOLOGY

About the Data

Capital punishment information is collected annually as part of the National Prisoner Statistics program (NPS-8). This data series is collected in two parts: data on persons under sentence of death are obtained from the department of corrections in each jurisdiction currently authorizing capital punishment, and the status of death penalty statutes is obtained from the Office of the Attorney General in each of the 50 states, from the U.S. Attorney's Office in the District of Columbia, and from the Federal Bureau of Prisons for the federal government. Data collection forms are available on the BJS website at www.bjs.gov.

NPS-8 covers all persons under sentence of death at any time during the year who were held in a state or federal nonmilitary correctional facility. This includes capital offenders transferred from prison to mental hospitals and those who may have escaped from custody. It excludes persons whose death sentences have been overturned by the court, regardless of their current incarceration status.

The statistics included in this report may differ from data collected by other organizations for various reasons: (1) NPS-8 adds inmates to the population under sentence of death not at sentencing, but at the time they are admitted to a state or federal correctional facility; (2) if inmates entered prison under a death sentence or were reported as being relieved of a death sentence in one year but the court had acted in the previous year, the counts are adjusted to reflect the dates of court decisions (see note on table 4 for the affected jurisdictions); and (3) NPS counts are always for the last day of the calendar year and will differ from counts for more recent periods. All data in this report have been reviewed for accuracy by the data providers in each jurisdiction prior to publication.

Changes to the Death Penalty

One state repealed its capital statute in 2013, and five states revised statutes relating to the death penalty.

As of December 31, 2013, 35 states and the federal government authorized the death penalty (table 1 and table 3). Although New Mexico repealed the death penalty in 2009 (2009 N.M. Laws, ch. 11 § 5) and Connecticut repealed the death penalty in 2012, the repeals were not retroactive, and offenders charged with a capital offense committed prior to the date of the repeal may be eligible for a death sentence. As of December 31, 2013,

New Mexico held two men and Connecticut held 10 men under previously imposed death sentences.

In 2013, the Maryland legislature repealed the death penalty (2013 Maryland Laws, Ch. 156), effective October 1, 2013. The repeal did not affect previously imposed death sentences, and as of December 31, 2013, Maryland held five men under sentence of death. On December 31, 2014, the four remaining death row inmates' sentences were commuted to life in prison without parole.

During 2013, the Arkansas legislature revised a portion of its capital statute pertaining to the selection and administration of drugs in lethal injections (the Method of Execution Act (MEA), Ark. Code Ann. § 5-4-617 (Repl. 2013)). The changes, which created specific steps to be followed by corrections officials when carrying out executions, were made following a decision by the Arkansas Supreme Court declaring the MEA unconstitutional (Hobbs v. Jones (2012 Ark. 293)) and became effective February 20, 2013.

Kansas amended an element of capital murder—intentional and premeditated murder of a child under age 14 during the commission of kidnapping with intent to commit a sex offense—to include "commercial sexual exploitation" in the definition of sex offenses (K.S.A. 2013 Supp. 21-5401, at subsection (b)), effective July 1, 2013. Mississippi added aggravating factors for which the death penalty can be imposed to include murder committed with the intent to influence government by intimidation, coercion, mass destruction or assassination, or to coerce civilians (Miss. Code Ann. § 99-19-101(4) (i)-(j)), effective July 1, 2013.

Texas amended its code of criminal procedure to require DNA analysis of all biological evidence in death penalty cases (Tex. C.C.P. Art. 38.43(i), (j), (k), (l), (m)), effective September 1, 2013. Utah amended its statute to codify that, for defendants younger than age 18 at the time of the offense, aggravated murder is a noncapital first-degree felony punishable as provided by Utah Code Ann. § 76-3-207.7 (Utah Code Ann. § 76-5-202(3)(e)), effective May 14, 2013.

Executions in 2014

Between January 1, 2014, and November 30, 2014, seven states executed 33 inmates, which was two fewer than the number executed during the same period in 2013.

Three states accounted for 82 percent of the executions carried out during this period: Texas executed 10 inmates, Missouri executed nine inmates, and Florida executed eight inmates. Of the 33 executions carried out in the first 11 months of 2014, all were by lethal injection.

Two women were executed during this period in Texas.

For more information, please see the full report at http://www. bjs.gov/index.cfm?ty=pbdetail&iid=5156.

PART 2

Correctional Populations in the United States, 2013

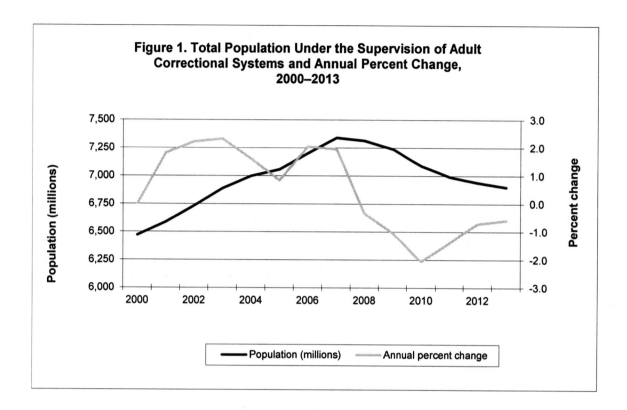

Figure 1. Total Population Under the Supervision of Adult Correctional Systems and Annual Percent Change, 2000–2013

- An estimated 6,899,000 persons were under the supervision of adult correctional systems at the end of 2013, a decline of about 41,500 from 12 months before.

- The correctional population declined 0.6 percent during 2013, down from 0.7 percent in 2012.

- All of the decline in the correctional population during 2013 resulted from decreases in the local jail (down 32,100) and prison (down 13,300) populations.

- Since 2010, the female jail population has been the fastest growing correctional population, increasing by an average of 3.4 percent annually.

- About 1 in 35 adults (2.8 percent) in the United States was under some form of correctional supervision at the end of 2013, unchanged from 2012.

- For the second consecutive year, the community supervision (down 0.6 percent) and incarcerated (down 0.5 percent) populations declined by less than 1 percent.

- While the U.S. prison population increased during 2013 (up 4,300 prisoners), the federal prison population (down 1,900) decreased for the first time since 1980.

- About 1 in 51 adults was on probation or parole at the end of 2013, compared to 1 in 110 adults incarcerated in prison or local jail.

Data in this section have been derived from *Correctional Populations in the United States, 2013*.

Table 1. Estimated Number of Persons Supervised by Adult Correctional Systems, by Correctional Status, Selected Year, 2000, 2005, and 2010–2013

(Number.)

Year	Total correctional population[1]	Community supervision			Incarcerated[1]		
		Total[2,3]	Probation	Parole	Total[1]	Local jail	Prison
2000	6,467,900	4,565,100	3,839,500	725,500	1,945,400	621,100	1,394,200
2005	7,055,800	4,946,800	4,162,500	784,400	2,200,400	747,500	1,525,900
2010	7,088,500	4,887,900	4,055,500	840,700	2,279,100	748,700	1,613,800
2011	6,990,400	4,814,200	3,971,300	853,900	2,252,500	735,600	1,599,000
2012	6,940,500	4,781,300	3,942,800	851,200	2,231,400	744,500	1,570,400
2013	6,899,000	4,751,400	3,910,600	853,200	2,220,300	731,200	1,574,700
Average annual percent change, 2000–2012	0.6	0.4	0.2	1.3	1.1	1.5	1.0
Percent change, 2012–2013	-0.6	-0.6	-0.8	0.2	-0.5	-1.8	0.3

Note: Estimates were rounded to the nearest 100 and may not be comparable to previously published BJS reports due to updated information or rounding. Counts include estimates for nonresponding jurisdictions. All probation, parole, and prison counts are for December 31; jail counts are for the last weekday in June. Detail may not sum to total due to rounding and adjustments made to account for offenders with multiple correctional statuses.
[1]Includes inmates held in local jails or under the jurisdiction of state or federal prisons.
[2]Total was adjusted to account for offenders with multiple correctional statuses.
[3]Includes some offenders held in a prison or jail but who remained under the jurisdiction of a probation or parole agency.

Table 2. U.S. Adult Residents Supervised by Adult Correctional Systems, 2000 and 2005–2013

(Number; rate per 100,000 U.S. adult residents.)

Year	Total correctional population[1]		Community supervision population		Incarcerated population[2]	
	Number supervised (rate)[3]	U.S. adult residents under correctional supervision	Number on probation or parole (rate)	U.S. adult residents on probation or parole	Number incarcerated in prison or local jail (rate)[3]	U.S. adult residents incarcerated in prison or local jail
2000	3,060	1 in 33	2,160	1 in 46	920	1 in 109
2005	3,160	1 in 32	2,210	1 in 45	990	1 in 101
2006	3,190	1 in 31	2,230	1 in 45	1,000	1 in 100
2007	3,210	1 in 31	2,240	1 in 45	1,000	1 in 100
2008	3,160	1 in 32	2,200	1 in 45	1,000	1 in 100
2009	3,100	1 in 32	2,150	1 in 47	980	1 in 102
2010	3,000	1 in 33	2,070	1 in 48	960	1 in 104
2011	2,930	1 in 34	2,010	1 in 50	940	1 in 106
2012	2,870	1 in 35	1,980	1 in 50	920	1 in 108
2013	2,830	1 in 35	1,950	1 in 51	910	1 in 110

Note: Rates were estimated to the nearest 10. Estimates may not be comparable to previously published BJS reports due to updated information or rounding.
[1]Includes offenders in the community under the authority of probation or parole agencies, under the jurisdiction of state or federal prisons, or held in local jails.
[2]Includes inmates under the jurisdiction of state or federal prisons or held in local jails.
[3]Rates were computed using the U.S. adult resident population estimates from the U.S. Census Bureau for January 1 of the following year.

Table 3. Estimated Number of Persons Supervised by Adult Correctional Systems, by Correctional Status, 2010 and 2013

(Number; percent.)

Correctional populations	2010		2013	
	Population	Percent of total population	Population	Percent of total population
Total[1]	7,088,500	100.0	6,899,000	100.0
Probation[2]	4,055,500	57.2	3,910,600	56.7
Parole[2]	840,700	11.9	853,200	12.4
Prison[2]	1,613,800	22.8	1,574,700	22.8
Local jail[3]	748,700	10.6	731,200	10.6
Offenders with multiple correctional statuses[4]	170,300	:	170,800	:

Note: Counts were rounded to the nearest 100 and include estimates for nonresponding jurisdictions. Detail may not sum to total due to rounding and because offenders with multiple correctional statuses were excluded from the total correctional population.
: = Not calculated.
[1]Total was adjusted to account for offenders with multiple correctional statuses.
[2]Population as of December 31.
[3]Population as of the last weekday in June.
[4]Some probationers and parolees on December 31 were held in a prison or jail but still remained under the jurisdiction of a probation or parole agency, and some parolees were also on probation. In addition, some prisoners were held in jail. They were excluded from the total correctional population to avoid double counting. See Table 6.

Table 4. Change in the Number of Persons Supervised by Adult Correctional Systems, 2010 and 2013

(Number; percent.)

Characteristic	2010		2013		2010–2013	
	Change in number	Percent of total change	Change in number	Percent of total change	Change in number	Percent of total change
Total Change[1]	−148,600	100.0	−41,500	100.0	−189,500	100.0
Total increase	16,600	100.0	6,400	100.0	12,500	100.0
Parole	16,600	100.0	4,300	67.2	12,500	100.0
Total decrease	−163,000	100.0	2,100	32.8	−201,500	100.0
Probation	−142,600	87.5	−45,400	100.0	−144,900	71.9
Local jail	−18,700	11.5	−32,100	70.7	−39,100	19.4
Prison	−1,700	1.0	−13,300	29.3	−17,500	8.7
Offenders with mulitple correction statuses[2]	2,200	:	2,500	:	600	:

Note: Estimates were rounded to the nearest 100 and include estimates for nonresponding jurisdictions. Detail may not sum to total due to rounding.
: = Not calculated.
[1]Total change includes the change in the number of offenders with multiple correctional statuses. See Table 6.
[2]Some probationers and parolees on December 31 were held in a prison or jail but still remained under the jurisdiction of a probation or parole agency, and some parolees were also on probation. In addition, some prisoners were held in jail. They were excluded from the total correctional population to avoid double counting. See Table 6.

Table 5. Estimated Number of Persons Supervised by Adult Correctional Systems and Change in the Population, by Sex and Correctional Status, 2000, 2010, and 2013

(Number; percent.)

Year	Total correctional population[1]		Probation		Parole		Local jail		Prison	
	Males	Females	Males	Females	Males	Females	Males	Females	Males	Females
2010	5,389,600	1,078,400	3,003,300	836,200	635,800	89,700	550,200	71,000	1,301,000	93,200
2010	5,824,400	1,264,100	3,081,000	974,500	737,300	103,400	656,400	92,400	1,500,900	112,900
2013	5,642,700	1,256,300	2,948,500	962,100	751,000	102,200	628,900	102,400	1,463,500	111,300
Percent change, 2000–2010										
Total	8.1	17.2	2.6	16.5	16	15.3	19.3	30.1	15.4	21.1
Annual average	0.8	1.6	0.3	1.5	1.5	1.4	1.8	2.6	1.4	1.9
Percent change, 2010–2013										
Total	−3.1	−0.6	−4.3	−1.3	1.9	−1.2	−4.2	10.8	−2.5	−1.4
Annual average	−1.1	−0.2	−1.5	−0.4	0.6	−0.4	−1.4	3.4	−0.8	−0.5

Note: Estimates of probationers, parolees, and prisoners are for December 31; estimates of local jail inmates are for the last weekday in June. Counts were rounded to nearest 100 and include estimates for nonresponding jurisdictions. Detail may not sum to total due rounding and adjustments made to account for persons with multiple correctional statuses.
[1]Total was adjusted to account for offenders with multiple correctional statuses.

Table 6. Estimated Number of Offenders with Multiple Correctional Statuses at Year End, by Correctional Status, 2000–2013

(Number; percent.)

Year	Total	Prisoners held in local jail	Probationers		Parolees		On probation
			Local jail	State or federal prison	Local jail	State or federal prison	
2000	112,500	70,000	20,400	22,100	:	:	:
2001	116,100	72,500	23,400	20,200	:	:	:
2002	122,800	72,600	29,300	20,900	:	:	:
2003	120,400	73,400	25,500	21,500	:	:	:
2004	130,400	74,400	34,400	21,600	:	:	:
2005	164,500	73,100	32,600	22,100	18,300	18,400	:
2006	169,900	77,900	33,900	21,700	20,700	15,700	:
2007	156,400	80,600	19,300	23,100	18,800	14,600	:
2008	178,500	83,500	23,800	32,400	19,300	15,600	3,900
2009	168,100	85,200	21,400	23,100	19,100	14,300	5,000
2010	170,300	83,400	21,300	21,500	21,400	14,400	8,300
2011	169,300	82,100	21,100	22,300	18,000	14,900	11,000
2012	168,200	83,500	21,200	21,600	18,500	10,700	12,700
2013	170,800	85,600	22,400	16,700	21,800	11,800	12,500

Note: Estimates were rounded to the nearest 100 and may not be comparable to previously published BJS reports due to updated information. Detail may not sum to total due to rounding.
: = Not collected or excluded from total correctional population.

Table 7. Estimated Number and Rate of Persons Supervised by Adult Correctional Systems, by Jurisdiction and Correctional Status, 2013

(Number as of 12/31/13; rate per 100,000 adults.) (Number; percent.)

Jurisdiction	Total correctional population[1]	Correctional supervision rate[2]	Community supervision		Incarcerated	
			Number on probation or parole[3]	Community supervision rate[2]	Number in prison or local jail[4]	Incarceration rate[2]
U.S. Total[5]	6,906,200	2,830	4,751,400	1,950	2,227,500	910
Federal[6]	347,000	140	131,900	50	215,100	90
State	6,559,200	2,690	4,619,400	1,900	2,012,400	830
Alabama	115,600	3,100	70,800	1,900	46,000	1,230
Alaska	14,600	2,670	9,500	1,730	5,100	940
Arizona	132,300	2,620	79,200	1,570	55,200	1,090
Arkansas	69,900	3,100	50,200	2,220	22,800	1,010
California	600,400	2,050	381,600	1,300	218,800	750
Colorado	120,700	2,970	89,700	2,210	32,100	790
Connecticut	62,900	2,230	45,400	1,610	17,600	620
Delaware	23,700	3,260	16,700	2,300	7,000	960
District of Columbia	13,700	2,540	12,600	2,330	2,400	450
Florida	389,400	2,490	237,800	1,520	154,500	990
Georgia	624,200	8,290	536,200	7,120	91,600	1,220
Hawaii	28,900	2,630	23,300	2,120	5,600	510
Idaho	45,500	3,820	35,200	2,960	10,200	860
Illinois	222,700	2,250	153,400	1,550	69,300	700
Indiana	179,400	3,580	134,000	2,680	45,400	910
Iowa	45,900	1,930	34,700	1,460	12,700	530
Kansas	37,100	1,710	20,500	940	16,600	760
Kentucky	97,600	2,880	65,900	1,940	32,100	950
Louisiana	115,700	3,280	70,700	2,010	50,100	1,420
Maine	10,500	980	6,700	630	3,800	350
Maryland	74,800	1,620	46,300	1,010	32,700	710
Massachusetts	91,100	1,710	70,000	1,310	21,400	400
Michigan	253,700	3,310	195,200	2,550	60,200	790
Minnesota	123,500	2,970	107,800	2,590	15,700	380
Mississippi	67,400	2,980	38,600	1,710	28,800	1,270
Missouri	114,900	2,460	70,400	1,510	44,500	950
Montana	14,800	1,870	9,500	1,190	6,000	760
Nebraska	23,200	1,640	14,800	1,050	8,500	600
Nevada	37,500	1,750	17,600	820	19,900	930
New Hampshire	11,100	1,050	6,300	590	4,800	460
New Jersey	164,100	2,380	128,100	1,860	37,600	540
New Mexico	34,200	2,170	18,700	1,180	15,500	980
New York	228,100	1,470	151,400	980	81,400	530
North Carolina	156,000	2,050	100,600	1,320	55,300	730
North Dakota	8,100	1,430	5,500	960	2,700	470
Ohio	335,500	3,750	267,400	2,990	69,800	780
Oklahoma[7]	67,700	2,320	**	**	37,900	1,300
Oregon	84,100	2,720	61,100	1,980	22,900	740
Pennsylvania	355,600	3,530	275,800	2,730	85,500	850
Rhode Island	24,600	2,930	23,400	2,790	3,400	400
South Carolina	73,500	1,980	40,900	1,100	32,600	880
South Dakota	14,800	2,310	9,500	1,490	5,300	820
Tennessee	122,500	2,440	77,900	1,550	48,100	960
Texas	711,900	3,640	508,000	2,600	221,800	1,130
Utah	25,200	1,250	14,500	720	12,500	620
Vermont	8,600	1,710	6,900	1,370	2,100	410
Virginia	114,600	1,780	55,800	870	58,800	910
Washington	139,200	2,570	111,100	2,060	29,700	550
West Virginia	20,500	1,390	11,000	750	9,700	660
Wisconsin	98,100	2,200	65,300	1,470	34,800	780
Wyoming	9,700	2,180	6,000	1,340	3,800	840

Note: Counts were rounded to the nearest 100, and rates were rounded to the nearest 10. Detail may not sum to total due to rounding and because offenders with multiple correctional statuses were excluded from the totals. Counts include estimates for nonresponding jurisdictions.
** = Unknown.
[1]Excludes, by jurisdiction, an estimated 85,600 prisoners held in jail, 16,700 probationers in prison, 22,400 probationers in jail, 21,800 parolees in jail, 11,800 parolees in prison, and 12,500 parolees on probation. See table 6.
[2]Rates were computed using the U.S adult state resident population on January 1, 2014.
[3]Excludes, by jurisdiction, an estimated 12,500 parolees on probation.
[4]Excludes, by jurisdiction, an estimated 85,600 prisoners held in local jails. Local jail counts by jurisdiction are based on December 31, 2013. For this reason, the estimates in this table differ from other estimates in the same report issued by BJS.
[5]Total correctional population and total number in prison and jail include local jail counts that are based on December 31, 2013, to produce jurisdiction-level estimates. For this reason, the estimates in this table differ from other estimates in the same report issued by BJS.
[6]Excludes about 11,900 inmates that were held in facilities that were operated by the Federal Bureau of Prisons and functioned as jails.
[7]The Oklahoma state probation agency could not provide the December 31 probation population. The total correctional population includes an estimate of the community supervision population in Oklahoma, including an estimate of the Oklahoma state agency's probation population.

Table 8. Inmates Held in Custody in State or Federal Prisons or in Local Jails, 2000 and 2012–2013

(Number; percent.)

Characteristic	Number of inmates			Average annual change, 2000–2012	Percent change, 2012–2013
	2000	2012	2013		
Inmates in Custody	1,938,500	2,228,400	2,217,000	1.2	-0.5
Federal prisoners[1]	140,100	216,900	215,000	3.6	-0.9
Prisons	133,900	208,000	205,700	3.7	-1.1
Federal facilities	124,500	176,500	173,800	2.9	-1.5
Privately operated facilities	9,400	31,500	31,900	10.1	1.3
Community corrections centers[2]	6,100	8,900	9,300	3.1	4.5
State prisoners	1,177,200	1,267,000	1,270,800	0.6	0.3
State facilities	1,101,200	1,170,200	1,178,700	0.5	0.7
Privately operated facilities	76,100	96,800	92,100	2.0	-4.9
Local jails	621,100	744,500	731,200	1.5	-1.8
Incarceration rate[3]	680	710	700	0.4	-1.4
Adult incarceration rate[4]	920	920	910	0.0	-1.1

Note: Estimates may not be comparable to previously published BJS reports due to updated information. Counts were rounded to the nearest 100 and include estimates for nonresponding jurisdictions. Rates were rounded to the nearest 10. Details may not sum to total due to rounding. Prison counts are for December 31; jail counts are for the last weekday in June. Total includes all inmates held in local jails, state or federal prisons, or privately operated facilities. It does not include inmates held in U.S. territories (Table 9), military facilities (Table 9), in U.S. Immigration and Customs Enforcement facilities, in jails in Indian country (Table 9), or in juvenile facilities.
[1]After 2001, responsibility for sentenced prisoners from the District of Columbia was transferred to the Federal Bureau of Prisons.
[2]Nonsecure, privately operated community corrections centers.
[3]The total number in the custody of local jails, state or federal prisons, or privately operated facilities within the year per 100,000 U.S. residents. Resident population estimates are from the U.S. Census Bureau for January 1 of the following year.
[4]The total number in custody within the year per 100,000 U.S. residents age 18 or older. Adult resident population estimates are from the U.S. Census Bureau for January 1 of the following year.

Table 9. Estimated Number of Inmates Incarcerated by Other Adult Correctional Systems, 2000, 2005, and 2012–2013

(Number; percent.)

Characteristic	Number of inmates				Average annual change, 2000–2012	Percent change, 2012–2013
	2000	2005	2012	2013		
Other Adult Correctional Systems	20,400	19,800	17,600	17,700	-1.2	0.6
Territorial prisons[1]	16,200	15,800	13,800	14,000	-1.3	0.8
Military facilties[2]	2,400	2,300	1,400	1,400	-4.4	
Jails in Indian country[3]	1,800	1,700	2,400	2,300	2.4	-3.3

Note: Estimates were rounded to the nearest 100 and are for December 31. Total excludes inmates held in local jails, under the jurisdiction of state or federal prisons, in U.S. Immigration and Customs Enforcement facilities, or held in juvenile facilities.
[1]The 2012 and 2013 totals include population counts that were estimated for some territories due to nonresponse.
[2]See Prisoners in 2013, NCJ 247282, BJS web, September 2014.
[3]Population counts are for the last weekday in June of each year. The 2005 population was estimated as the 2004 population count because the Survey of Jails in Indian Country was not conducted in 2005 or 2006. See Jails in Indian Country, 2013, NCJ 247017, BJS web, July 2014.

Table 10. Estimated Number of Persons Supervised by Adult Correctional Systems, by Correctional Status, 2000–2013

(Number; percent.)

Year	Total correctional population[1]	Community supervision			Incarcerated[3]		
		Total[1,2]	Probation	Parole	Total[1]	Local jail	Prison
2000	6,467,900	4,565,100	3,839,500	725,500	1,945,400	621,100	1,394,200
2001	6,585,000	4,665,900	3,934,700	731,100	1,962,800	631,200	1,404,000
2002	6,731,100	4,748,300	3,995,200	753,100	2,033,100	665,500	1,440,100
2003	6,887,000	4,847,500	4,074,000	773,500	2,086,500	691,300	1,468,600
2004	6,997,200	4,916,500	4,140,600	775,900	2,136,600	714,000	1,497,100
2005	7,055,800	4,946,800	4,162,500	784,400	2,200,400	747,500	1,525,900
2006	7,199,800	5,035,200	4,237,000	798,200	2,256,600	765,800	1,568,700
2007	7,339,900	5,119,300	4,293,200	826,100	2,296,400	780,200	1,596,800
2008	7,314,400	5,095,200	4,270,900	828,200	2,310,300	785,500	1,608,300
2009	7,237,100	5,017,900	4,198,200	824,100	2,297,700	767,400	1,615,500
2010	7,088,500	4,887,900	4,055,500	840,700	2,279,100	748,700	1,613,800
2011	6,990,400	4,814,200	3,971,300	853,900	2,252,500	735,600	1,599,000
2012	6,940,500	4,781,300	3,942,800	851,200	2,231,400	744,500	1,570,400
2013	6,899,000	4,751,400	3,910,600	853,200	2,220,300	731,200	1,574,700

Note: Estimates were rounded to the nearest 100 and may not be comparable to previously published BJS reports due to updated information or rounding. Counts include estimates for nonresponding jurisdictions. All probation, parole, and prison counts are for December 31; jail counts are for the last weekday in June. Detail may not sum to total due to rounding and adjustments made to account for offenders with multiple correctional statuses.
[1]Total was adjusted to account for offenders with multiple correctional statuses.
[2]Includes some offenders held in a prison or jail but who remained under the jurisdiction of a probation or parole agency.
[3]Includes inmates held in local jails or under the jurisdiction of state or federal prisons.

Methodology

About the Data

The statistics presented in this chapter include data from *Correctional Populations in the United States, 2013*, which itself relies on various Bureau of Justice Statistics (BJS) data collections, each relying on the voluntary participation of federal, state, and local respondents. This report presents statistics on offenders supervised by adult correctional systems in the United States at year end 2013, including offenders supervised in the community on probation or parole and those incarcerated in prison or local jail. The report provides the size and change in the total correctional population during 2013. It details the slowing rate of decline in the population since 2010 and the downward trend in the correctional supervision rate since 2007. It also examines the impact of changes in the community supervision and incarcerated populations on the total correctional population in recent years. Findings cover the size of the male and female correctional populations and compare the rates of change in the populations by correctional status since 2000. Other information comprises correctional populations, including prisoners under military jurisdiction, inmates held by correctional authorities in the U.S. territories and commonwealths, and jail inmates held in Indian country facilities, and estimates of the total correctional population by jurisdiction and correctional status.

For more information about any of the following data collections, or to see the full report, please see http://www.bjs.gov/index.cfm?ty=pbdetail&iid=5177.

Annual Probation Survey and Annual Parole Survey

Administrative data collected from probation and parole agencies in the U.S. Data include the total number of adults on state and federal probation and parole on January 1 and December 31 of each year, the number of adults entering and exiting probation and parole supervision each year, and the characteristics of adults under the supervision of probation and parole agencies. Published data include both national and state-level data. The surveys cover all 50 states, the federal system, and the District of Columbia. They began in 1980 and are conducted annually. Probation data are also available dating back to 1977. Through BJS's National Probation Reports, probation data were collected from 1977 to 1979. Parole data are available dating back to 1975. The parole data from 1975 to 1979 were collected through BJS's Uniform Parole Reports.

Annual Survey of Jails

Collects data from a nationally representative sample of local jails on jail inmate populations, jail capacity, and related information. The collection began in 1982 and has been conducted annually, except for years 1983, 1988, 1993, 1999, and 2005, during which a complete census of U.S. local jails was conducted.

Census of Jails

The 2006 Census of Jail Facilities is part of a series of data collections that study the nation's local jails. To reduce respondent burden and improve data quality and timeliness, the original jail census was split into two parts in 2005: the Census of Jail Inmates (2005) and the Census of Jail Facilities (2006). The Census of Jail Facilities collects information on each facility, including admissions and releases, court orders, programs that offer alternatives to incarceration, counts of inmates on hold for other jurisdictions, use of space and crowding, staffing, inmate work assignments, and education and counseling programs. The census provides the sampling frame for the nationwide Survey of Inmates in Local Jails (SILJ) and the Annual Survey of Jails (ASJ).

Deaths in Custody Reporting Program (DCRP)

Collects inmate death records from each of the nation's 50 state prison systems and approximately 2,800 local jail jurisdictions. In addition, this program collects records of all deaths occurring during the process of arrest. Data are collected directly from state and local law enforcement agencies.

Death records include information on decedent personal characteristics (age, race or Hispanic origin, and sex), decedent criminal background (legal status, offense type, and time served), and the death itself (date, time, location, and cause of death, as well as information on the autopsy and medical treatment provided for any illness or disease).

Data collections covering these populations were developed in annual phases: Annual collection of individual death records from local jail facilities began in 2000, followed by a separate collection for state prison facilities in 2001. Collection of state juvenile correctional agencies began in 2002 but was discontinued in 2006, and collection of arrest-related death records began in 2003. Datasets are produced in an annual format.

National Prisoner Statistics (NPS) Program

Produces annual national and state-level data on the number of prisoners in state and federal prison facilities. Aggregate data are collected on race and sex of prison inmates, inmates held in private facilities and local jails, system capacity, noncitizens, and persons under age 18. Findings are released in the Prisoners series. Data are from the 50 state department of corrections, the Federal Bureau of Prisons, and until 2001, from the District of Columbia (after 2001, felons sentenced under the District of Columbia criminal code were housed in federal facilities).

Survey of Jails in Indian Country

Collects detailed information on confinement facilities, detention centers, jails, and other facilities operated by tribal authorities or the Bureau of Indian Affairs (BIA). Information is gathered on inmate counts, movements, facility operations, and staff. In selected years (1998, 2004, 2007, and 2011), additional information is collected on facility programs and services, such as medical assessments and mental health screening procedures, inmate work assignments, counseling, and educational programs.

Counts Adjusted for Offenders with Multiple Correctional Statuses

Offenders under correctional supervision may have multiple correctional statuses for several reasons. For example, probation and parole agencies may not always be notified immediately of new arrests, jail admissions, or prison admissions; absconders included in a probation or parole agency's population in one jurisdiction may actually be incarcerated in another jurisdiction; persons may be admitted to jail or prison before formal revocation hearings and potential discharge by a probation or parole agency; and persons may be serving separate probation and parole sentences concurrently. In addition, state and federal prisons may hold inmates in county facilities or local jails to reduce crowding in their prisons.

In 1998, through the ASPP, BJS began collecting data on the number of probationers and parolees with multiple correctional statuses and has since expanded on the information collected. In 1999, through the NPS, BJS began collecting data on the number of prisoners under the jurisdiction of state or federal prisons that were held in county facilities or local jails. Table 6 includes adjustments that were made to the total correctional population, total community supervision population, and total incarcerated population estimates presented in this report to exclude offenders with multiple correctional statuses to avoid double counting offenders. The estimates from the ASPP are based on data reported by the probation and parole

agencies that were able to provide the information within the specific reporting year. Because some probation and parole agencies did not provide these data each year, the numbers may underestimate the total number of offenders who had multiple correctional statuses between 2000 and 2013. Due to these adjustments, the sum of correctional statuses in Tables 1, 2, 3, 4, 5 and appendix table 1 will not equal the total correctional population. In addition, the sum of the probation and parole populations for 2008 through 2013 will not yield the total community supervision population because the total was adjusted for parolees who were also on probation. In addition, the sum of the prison and local jail populations for 2000 through 2013 will not equal the total incarcerated population because prisoners held in local jails were excluded from the total.

Adjustments for Nonresponse

Probation, parole, jail, and prison population counts were adjusted to account for nonresponse across the data collections. The methods varied and depended on the type of collection, type of respondent, and availability of information. The local jail population counts that were collected through the 2013 Census of Jails to produce the jurisdiction-level estimates that are reported in appendix table 1 were adjusted for unit and item nonresponse. Nonresponse in the 2013 jail census was minimal as the unit response rate was 92.4% and the item response rate for the December 31, 2013, population total was 99.7%. For jails that did not participate in the census or were unable to provide the 2013 year end count, a sequential hot deck imputation procedure was used to impute values.

Estimates of Males and Females Under Correctional Supervision

The number of males and the number of females on probation or parole were adjusted to account for nonresponse using a ratio adjustment method. For jurisdictions that did not provide data on sex for a portion of their population, the sex distribution of the known portion of the population was used to impute for the unknown portion because it was assumed that the distributions were the same. For states that were unable to provide any data on sex, the state national average was used to impute the number of males and females supervised in those states. Adjusted jurisdiction totals were then aggregated to produce national estimates of the number of males and females on probation and parole. The number of prisoners by sex represents the reported number of males and females under the jurisdiction of state or federal prisons within the reference year. The number of local jail inmates by sex represents the adjusted number of males and females in the custody of local jails within the reference year.

PART 3

Crime in the United States, 2013

HIGHLIGHTS

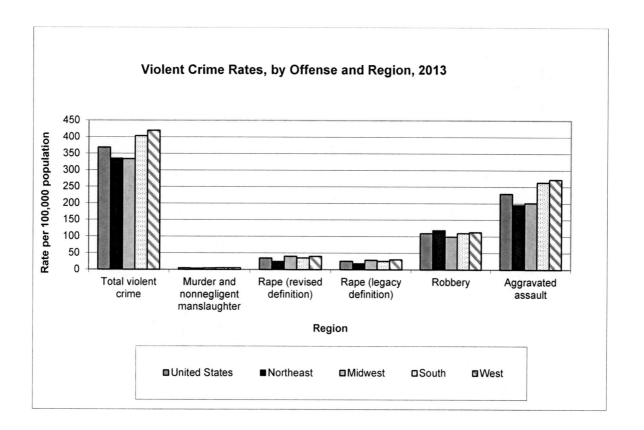

Violent Crime Rates, by Offense and Region, 2013

Rate per 100,000 population

Region

☒United States   ■Northeast   ☒Midwest   ☐South   ☒West

- In 2013, an estimated 1,163,146 violent crimes occurred nationwide, a decrease of 4.2 percent from the 2012 estimate. Aggravated assaults accounted for 62.3 percent of violent crimes reported to law enforcement in 2013.

- In 2013, there were an estimated 8,632,512 property crime offenses in the nation. Of all property crimes in 2013, larceny-theft accounted for 69.6 percent.

- Approximately 48.1 percent of violent crimes and 19.7 percent of property crimes were cleared by arrest or exceptional means in 2013.

- Nationwide, law enforcement made an estimated 11,302,102 arrests in 2013. Of these arrests, 480,360 were for violent crimes, and 1,559,284 were for property crimes. The highest number of arrests were for drug abuse violations (estimated at 1,501,043 arrests).

- A total of 13,051 city and county enforcement agencies provided data on the number of full-time law enforcement employees (sworn officers and civilian personnel) on staff in 2013.

Table 1. Crime in the United States, by Volume and Rate Per 100,000 Inhabitants, 1994–2013

(Number, rate per 100,000 population.)

Year	Population[1]	Violent crime Number	Violent crime Rate	Murder and nonnegligent manslaughter Number	Rate	Rape (legacy definition)[2] Number	Rate	Robbery Number	Rate	Aggravated assault Number	Rate
1994	260,327,021	1,857,670	713.6	23,326	9.0	102,216	39.3	618,949	237.8	1,113,179	427.6
1995	262,803,276	1,798,792	684.5	21,606	8.2	97,470	37.1	580,509	220.9	1,099,207	418.3
1996	265,228,572	1,688,540	636.6	19,645	7.4	96,252	36.3	535,594	201.9	1,037,049	391.0
1997	267,783,607	1,636,096	611.0	18,208	6.8	96,153	35.9	498,534	186.2	1,023,201	382.1
1998	270,248,003	1,533,887	567.6	16,974	6.3	93,144	34.5	447,186	165.5	976,583	361.4
1999	272,690,813	1,426,044	523.0	15,522	5.7	89,411	32.8	409,371	150.1	911,740	334.3
2000	281,421,906	1,425,486	506.5	15,586	5.5	90,178	32.0	408,016	145.0	911,706	324.0
2001[3]	285,317,559	1,439,480	504.5	16,037	5.6	90,863	31.8	423,557	148.5	909,023	318.6
2002	287,973,924	1,423,677	494.4	16,229	5.6	95,235	33.1	420,806	146.1	891,407	309.5
2003	290,788,976	1,383,676	475.8	16,528	5.7	93,883	32.3	414,235	142.5	859,030	295.4
2004	293,656,842	1,360,088	463.2	16,148	5.5	95,089	32.4	401,470	136.7	847,381	288.6
2005	296,507,061	1,390,745	469.0	16,740	5.6	94,347	31.8	417,438	140.8	862,220	290.8
2006	299,398,484	1,435,123	479.3	17,309	5.8	94,472	31.6	449,246	150.0	874,096	292.0
2007	301,621,157	1,422,970	471.8	17,128	5.7	92,160	30.6	447,324	148.3	866,358	287.2
2008	304,059,724	1,394,461	458.6	16,465	5.4	90,750	29.8	443,563	145.9	843,683	277.5
2009	307,006,550	1,325,896	431.9	15,399	5.0	89,241	29.1	408,742	133.1	812,514	264.7
2010[4]	309,330,219	1,251,248	404.5	14,722	4.8	85,593	27.7	369,089	119.3	781,844	252.8
2011	311,587,816	1,206,005	387.1	14,661	4.7	84,175	27.0	354,746	113.9	752,423	241.5
2012	313,914,040	1,214,462	386.9	14,827	4.7	84,376	26.9	354,520	112.9	760,739	242.3
2013	316,128,839	1,163,146	367.9	14,196	4.5	79,770	25.2	345,031	109.1	724,149	229.1

Year	Property crime Number	Rate	Burglary Number	Rate	Larceny-theft Number	Rate	Motor vehicle theft Number	Rate
1994	12,131,873	4,660.2	2,712,774	1,042.1	7,879,812	3,026.9	1,539,287	591.3
1995	12,063,935	4,590.5	2,593,784	987.0	7,997,710	3,043.2	1,472,441	560.3
1996	11,805,323	4,451.0	2,506,400	945.0	7,904,685	2,980.3	1,394,238	525.7
1997	11,558,475	4,316.3	2,460,526	918.8	7,743,760	2,891.8	1,354,189	505.7
1998	10,951,827	4,052.5	2,332,735	863.2	7,376,311	2,729.5	1,242,781	459.9
1999	10,208,334	3,743.6	2,100,739	770.4	6,955,520	2,550.7	1,152,075	422.5
2000	10,182,584	3,618.3	2,050,992	728.8	6,971,590	2,477.3	1,160,002	412.2
2001[3]	10,437,189	3,658.1	2,116,531	741.8	7,092,267	2,485.7	1,228,391	430.5
2002	10,455,277	3,630.6	2,151,252	747.0	7,057,379	2,450.7	1,246,646	432.9
2003	10,442,862	3,591.2	2,154,834	741.0	7,026,802	2,416.5	1,261,226	433.7
2004	10,319,386	3,514.1	2,144,446	730.3	6,937,089	2,362.3	1,237,851	421.5
2005	10,174,754	3,431.5	2,155,448	726.9	6,783,447	2,287.8	1,235,859	416.8
2006	10,019,601	3,346.6	2,194,993	733.1	6,626,363	2,213.2	1,198,245	400.2
2007	9,882,212	3,276.4	2,190,198	726.1	6,591,542	2,185.4	1,100,472	364.9
2008	9,774,152	3,214.6	2,228,887	733.0	6,586,206	2,166.1	959,059	315.4
2009	9,337,060	3,041.3	2,203,313	717.7	6,338,095	2,064.5	795,652	259.2
2010[4]	9,112,625	2,945.9	2,168,459	701.0	6,204,601	2,005.8	739,565	239.1
2011	9,052,743	2,905.4	2,185,140	701.3	6,151,095	1,974.10	716,508	230.0
2012	8,975,438	2,859.2	2,103,787	670.2	6,150,598	1,959.30	721,053	229.7
2013	8,632,512	2,730.7	1,928,465	610.0	6,004,453	1,899.40	699,594	221.3

Note: Although arson data are included in the trend and clearance tables, sufficient data are not available to estimate totals for this offense. Therefore, no arson data are published in this table.
[1]Populations are U.S. Census Bureau provisional estimates as of July 1 for each year except 2000 and 2010, which are decennial census counts.
[2]The figures shown in this column for the offense of rape were estimated using the legacy Uniform Crime Reporting definition of rape. See chapter notes for more detail.
[3]The murder and nonnegligent homicides that occurred as a result of the events of September 11, 2001, are not included in this table.
[4]The crime figures have been adjusted.

Table 1A. Crime in the United States, Percent Change in Volume and Rate Per 100,000 Inhabitants for 2 Years, 5 Years, and 10 Years, 2003–2013

(Percent change.)

Year	Violent crime Number	Rate	Murder and nonnegligent manslaughter Number	Rate	Rape (legacy definition)[1] Number	Rate	Robbery Number	Rate	Aggravated assault Number	Rate	Property crime Number	Rate	Burglary Number	Rate	Larceny-theft Number	Rate	Motor vehicle theft Number	Rate
2003–2013	−14.5	−20.6	−12.1	−18.3	−16.1	−22.1	−14.1	−20.2	−14.5	−20.6	−16.3	−22.3	−10.1	−16.5	−13.4	−19.6	−43.5	−47.5
2008–2013	−12.3	−14.8	−7.8	−10.5	−10.6	−13.2	−15.6	−18.0	−10.9	−13.4	−7.5	−10.2	−12.5	−15.0	−5.3	−8.0	−12.1	−14.6
2012–2013	−4.4	−5.1	−4.4	−5.1	−6.3	−7.0	−2.8	−3.5	−5.0	−5.6	−4.1	−4.8	−8.6	−9.3	−2.7	−3.4	−3.3	−4.0

[1]The figures shown in this column for the offense of rape were estimated using the legacy Uniform Crime Reporting definition of rape. See chapter notes for more detail.

Table 2. Crime in the United States, by Community Type, 2013

(Number, percent, rate per 100,000 population)

Area	Population[1]	Violent crime[2]	Murder and nonnegligent manslaughter	Rape (revised definition)[3]	Rape (legacy definition)[4]	Robbery	Aggravated assault	Property crime	Burglary	Larceny-theft	Motor vehicle theft
United States	316,128,839	1,191,988	14,196	108,612	79,770	345,031	724,149	8,632,512	1,928,465	6,004,453	699,594
Rate per 100,000 inhabitants	X	377.1	4.5	34.4	25.2	109.1	229.1	2,730.7	610.0	1,899.4	221.3
Metropolitan Statistical Areas	269,190,260	X	X	X	X	X	X	X	X	X	X
Area actually reporting (percent)[5]	98.9	1,020,004	12,495	46,965	39,980	330,671	629,873	7,509,668	1,635,957	5,228,622	644,175
Estimated total (percent)	100.0	1,069,788	12,548	90,739	66,640	332,161	634,340	7,579,569	1,650,943	5,280,799	647,827
Rate per 100,000 inhabitants	X	397.4	4.7	33.7	24.8	123.4	235.6	2,815.7	613.3	1,961.7	240.7
Cities Outside Metropolitan Areas	19,062,412	X	X	X	X	X	X	X	X	X	X
Area actually reporting (percent)[5]	92.9	63,185	654	5,256	3,925	8,763	48,512	604,425	129,969	449,937	24,519
Estimated total (percent)	100.0	71,800	714	9,724	7,161	9,581	51,781	651,409	140,654	484,530	26,225
Rate per 100,000 inhabitants	X	376.7	3.7	51.0	37.6	50.3	271.6	3,417.2	737.9	2,541.8	137.6
Nonmetropolitan Counties	27,876,167	X	X	X	X	X	X	X	X	X	X
Area actually reporting (percent)[5]	93.5	45,686	870	5,830	3,537	3,068	35,688	377,843	127,915	225,019	24,160
Estimated total (percent)	100.0	50,400	934	8,149	5,969	3,289	38,028	401,534	136,868	239,124	25,542
Rate per 100,000 inhabitants	X	180.8	3.4	29.2	21.4	11.8	136.4	1,440.4	491.0	857.8	91.6

Note: Although arson data are included in the trend and clearance tables, sufficient data are not available to estimate totals for this offense. Therefore, no arson data are published in this table.
X = Not applicable.
[1] Population figures are U.S. Census Bureau provisional estimates as of July 1, 2013.
[2] The violent crime figures include the offenses of murder, rape (revised definition), robbery, and aggravated assault.
[3] The figures shown in this column for the offense of rape were estimated using the revised Uniform Crime Reporting (UCR) definition of rape. See chapter notes for more detail.
[4] The figures shown in this column for the offense of rape were estimated using the legacy Uniform Crime Reporting (UCR) definition of rape. See chapter notes for more detail.
[5] The percentage reported under "Area actually reporting" is based upon the population covered by agencies providing 3 months or more of crime reports to the FBI.

Table 3. Crime in the United States, Population and Offense Distribution, by Region, 2013

(Percent distribution.)

Region	Population	Violent crime	Murder and nonnegligent manslaughter	Rape (revised definition)[1]	Rape (legacy definition)[2]	Robbery	Aggravated assault	Property crime	Burglary	Larceny-theft	Motor vehicle theft
United States[3]	100.0	100.0	100.0	100.0	100.0	100.0	100.0	100.0	100.0	100.0	100.0
Northeast	17.7	16.1	13.8	12.5	12.6	19.1	15.1	12.7	10.8	13.8	9.0
Midwest	21.4	19.4	21.4	24.8	24.4	19.4	18.8	20.0	19.9	20.3	18.4
South	37.4	41.1	43.8	37.8	37.8	37.6	43.0	42.4	45.2	42.5	34.6
West	23.5	23.5	21.0	24.9	25.3	23.8	23.1	24.8	24.2	23.5	38.1

Note: Although arson data are included in the trend and clearance tables, sufficient data are not available to estimate totals for this offense. Therefore, no arson data are published in this table.
[1] The figures shown in this column for the offense of rape were estimated using the revised Uniform Crime Reporting (UCR) definition of rape. See chapter notes for more detail.
[2] The figures shown in this column for the offense of rape were estimated using the legacy Uniform Crime Reporting (UCR) definition of rape. See chapter notes for more detail.
[3] Because of rounding, the percentages may not add to 100.0.

Table 4. Crime, by Region, Geographic Division, and State, 2012–2013

(Number, rate per 100,000 population, percent.)

Area	Population[1]	Violent crime[2]		Murder and nonnegligent manslaughter		Rape (revised definition)[3]		Rape (legacy definition)[4]		Robbery	
		Number	Rate	Number	Rate	Number	Rate	Number	Rate	Number	Rate
United States[5,6,7,8,9]											
2012	313,873,685	1,217,067	387.8	14,866	4.7	NA	NA	85,141	27.1	355,051	113.1
2013	316,128,839	1,163,146	367.9	14,196	4.5	108,612	34.4	79,770	25.2	345,031	109.1
Percent change	X	–4.4	–5.1	–4.5	–5.2	NA	NA	–6.3	–7.0	–2.8	–3.5
Northeast[5,6,7,8]											
2012	55,771,792	195,891	351.2	2,101	3.8	NA	NA	11,107	19.9	67,737	121.5
2013	55,943,073	187,464	335.1	1,953	3.5	13,623	24.4	10,054	18.0	66,062	118.1
Percent change	X	–4.3	–4.6	–7.0	–7.3	NA	NA	–9.5	–9.8	–2.5	–2.8
New England[5,6,7,8]											
2012	14,563,443	45,245	310.7	323	2.2	NA	NA	3,864	26.5	11,984	82.3
2013	14,618,806	43,740	299.2	310	2.1	5,376	36.8	3,978	27.2	11,977	81.9
Percent change	X	–3.3	–3.7	–4.0	–4.4	NA	NA	+3.0	+2.6	–0.1	–0.4
Connecticut[6]											
2012	3,591,765	10,183	283.5	117	3.3	NA	NA	933	26.0	3,709	103.3
2013	3,596,080	9,153	254.5	86	2.4	955	26.6	668	18.6	3,530	98.2
Percent change	X	–10.1	–10.2	–26.5	–26.6	NA	NA	–28.4	–28.5	–4.8	–4.9
Maine[6,8]											
2012	1,328,501	1,626	122.4	26	2.0	NA	NA	372	28.0	420	31.6
2013	1,328,302	1,615	121.6	24	1.8	447	33.7	344	25.9	335	25.2
Percent change	X	–0.7	–0.7	–7.7	–7.7	NA	NA	–7.5	–7.5	–20.2	–20.2
Massachusetts[6]											
2012	6,645,303	27,047	407.0	121	1.8	NA	NA	1,650	24.8	6,555	98.6
2013	6,692,824	27,038	404.0	137	2.0	2,718	40.6	2,089	31.2	6,706	100.2
Percent change	X	*	–0.7	+13.2	+12.4	NA	NA	+26.6	+25.7	+2.3	+1.6
New Hampshire[7]											
2012	1,321,617	2,841	215.0	15	1.1	NA	NA	486	36.8	471	35.6
2013	1,323,459	2,642	199.6	22	1.7	686	51.8	479	36.2	649	49.0
Percent change	X	–7.0	–7.1	+46.7	+46.5	NA	NA	–1.4	–1.6	+37.8	+37.6
Rhode Island[7]											
2012	1,050,304	2,657	253.0	36	3.4	NA	NA	292	27.8	715	68.1
2013	1,051,511	2,572	244.6	31	2.9	440	41.8	307	29.2	684	65.0
Percent change	X	–3.2	–3.3	–13.9	–14.0	NA	NA	+5.1	+5.0	–4.3	–4.4
Vermont[7]											
2012	625,953	891	142.3	8	1.3	NA	NA	131	20.9	114	18.2
2013	626,630	720	114.9	10	1.6	130	20.7	91	14.5	73	11.6
Percent change	X	–19.2	–19.3	+25.0	+24.9	NA	NA	–30.5	–30.6	–36.0	–36.0
Middle Atlantic[5,7,8]											
2012	41,208,349	150,646	365.6	1,778	4.3	NA	NA	7,243	17.6	55,753	135.3
2013	41,324,267	143,724	347.8	1,643	4.0	8,247	20.0	6,076	14.7	54,085	130.9
Percent change	X	–4.6	–4.9	–7.6	–7.9	NA	NA	–16.1	–16.3	–3.0	–3.3
New Jersey											
2012	8,867,749	25,727	290.1	388	4.4	NA	NA	1,035	11.7	11,385	128.4
2013	8,899,339	25,415	285.6	401	4.5	1,120	12.6	861	9.7	12,082	135.8
Percent change	X	–1.2	–1.6	+3.4	+3.0	NA	NA	–16.8	–17.1	+6.1	+5.7
New York[3]											
2012	19,576,125	79,535	406.3	683	3.5	NA	NA	2,837	14.5	28,633	146.3
2013	19,651,127	76,596	389.8	648	3.3	3,353	17.1	2,577	13.1	27,241	138.6
Percent change	X	–3.7	–4.1	–5.1	–5.5	NA	NA	–9.2	–9.5	–4.9	–5.2
Pennsylvania[7,8]											
2012	12,764,475	45,384	355.5	707	5.5	NA	NA	3,371	26.4	15,735	123.3
2013	12,773,801	41,713	326.6	594	4.7	3,774	29.5	2,638	20.7	14,762	115.6
Percent change	X	–8.1	–8.2	–16.0	–16.0	NA	NA	–21.7	–21.8	–6.2	–6.3
Midwest[5,6,7,8]											
2012	67,321,425	239,436	355.7	3,148	4.7	NA	NA	21,678	32.2	69,716	103.6
2013	67,547,890	225,227	333.4	3,042	4.5	26,929	39.9	19,437	28.8	66,945	99.1
Percent change	X	–5.9	–6.2	–3.4	–3.7	NA	NA	–10.3	–10.6	–4.0	–4.3
East North Central[5,6,7,8]											
2012	46,566,078	172,143	369.7	2,425	5.2	NA	NA	14,918	32.0	56,592	121.5
2013	46,662,180	160,988	345.0	2,309	4.9	18,726	40.1	13,648	29.2	54,137	116.0
Percent change	X	–6.5	–6.7	–4.8	–5.0	NA	NA	–8.5	–8.7	–4.3	–4.5
Illinois[6]											
2012	12,868,192	53,556	416.2	770	6.0	NA	NA	3,581	27.8	19,480	151.4

Table 4. Crime, by Region, Geographic Division, and State, 2012–2013—*Continued*

(Number, rate per 100,000 population, percent.)

Area	Population[1]	Aggravated assault		Property crime		Burglary		Larceny-theft		Motor vehicle theft	
		Number	Rate	Number	Rate	Number	Rate	Number	Rate	Number	Rate
United States[5,6,7,8,9]											
2012	313,873,685	762,009	242.8	9,001,992	2,868.0	2,109,932	672.2	6,168,874	1,965.4	723,186	230.4
2013	316,128,839	724,149	229.1	8,632,512	2,730.7	1,928,465	610.0	6,004,453	1,899.4	699,594	221.3
Percent change	X	−5.0	−5.6	−4.1	−4.8	−8.6	−9.3	−2.7	−3.4	−3.3	−4.0
Northeast[5,6,7,8]											
2012	55,771,792	114,946	206.1	1,161,969	2,083.4	236,761	424.5	855,437	1,533.8	69,771	125.1
2013	55,943,073	109,395	195.5	1,096,709	1,960.4	208,315	372.4	825,630	1,475.8	62,764	112.2
Percent change	X	−4.8	−5.1	−5.6	−5.9	−12.0	−12.3	−3.5	−3.8	−10.0	−10.3
New England[5,6,7,8]											
2012	14,563,443	29,074	199.6	328,658	2,256.7	72,994	501.2	234,804	1,612.3	20,860	143.2
2013	14,618,806	27,475	187.9	307,315	2,102.2	63,966	437.6	223,584	1,529.4	19,765	135.2
Percent change	X	−5.5	−5.9	−6.5	−6.8	−12.4	−12.7	−4.8	−5.1	−5.2	−5.6
Connecticut[6]											
2012	3,591,765	5,424	151.0	77,169	2,148.5	14,787	411.7	55,904	1,556.4	6,478	180.4
2013	3,596,080	4,869	135.4	70,990	1,974.1	12,892	358.5	51,876	1,442.6	6,222	173.0
Percent change	X	−10.2	−10.3	−8.0	−8.1	−12.8	−12.9	−7.2	−7.3	−4.0	−4.1
Maine[6,8]											
2012	1,328,501	808	60.8	33,398	2,514.0	7,476	562.7	24,931	1,876.6	991	74.6
2013	1,328,302	912	68.7	30,447	2,292.2	6,483	488.1	23,050	1,735.3	914	68.8
Percent change	X	+12.9	+12.9	−8.8	−8.8	−13.3	−13.3	−7.5	−7.5	−7.8	−7.8
Massachusetts[6]											
2012	6,645,303	18,721	281.7	143,325	2,156.8	34,635	521.2	99,453	1,496.6	9,237	139.0
2013	6,692,824	18,106	270.5	137,285	2,051.2	30,735	459.2	97,428	1,455.7	9,122	136.3
Percent change	X	−3.3	−4.0	−4.2	−4.9	−11.3	−11.9	−2.0	−2.7	−1.2	−1.9
New Hampshire[7]											
2012	1,321,617	1,869	141.4	32,074	2,426.9	5,988	453.1	25,024	1,893.4	1,062	80.4
2013	1,323,459	1,492	112.7	29,040	2,194.3	4,936	373.0	23,164	1,750.3	940	71.0
Percent change	X	−20.2	−20.3	−9.5	−9.6	−17.6	−17.7	−7.4	−7.6	−11.5	−11.6
Rhode Island[7]											
2012	1,050,304	1,614	153.7	27,039	2,574.4	5,929	564.5	18,478	1,759.3	2,632	250.6
2013	1,051,511	1,550	147.4	25,678	2,442.0	5,607	533.2	17,838	1,696.4	2,233	212.4
Percent change	X	−4.0	−4.1	−5.0	−5.1	−5.4	−5.5	−3.5	−3.6	−15.2	−15.3
Vermont[7]											
2012	625,953	638	101.9	15,653	2,500.7	4,179	667.6	11,014	1,759.6	460	73.5
2013	626,630	546	87.1	13,875	2,214.2	3,313	528.7	10,228	1,632.2	334	53.3
Percent change	X	−14.4	−14.5	−11.4	−11.5	−20.7	−20.8	−7.1	−7.2	−27.4	−27.5
Middle Atlantic[5,7,8]											
2012	41,208,349	85,872	208.4	833,311	2,022.2	163,767	397.4	620,633	1,506.1	48,911	118.7
2013	41,324,267	81,920	198.2	789,394	1,910.2	144,349	349.3	602,046	1,456.9	42,999	104.1
Percent change	X	−4.6	−4.9	−5.3	−5.5	−11.9	−12.1	−3.0	−3.3	−12.1	−12.3
New Jersey											
2012	8,867,749	12,919	145.7	181,481	2,046.5	42,338	477.4	122,662	1,383.2	16,481	185.9
2013	8,899,339	12,071	135.6	167,556	1,882.8	35,873	403.1	117,936	1,325.2	13,747	154.5
Percent change	X	−6.6	−6.9	−7.7	−8.0	−15.3	−15.6	−3.9	−4.2	−16.6	−16.9
New York[3]											
2012	19,576,125	47,382	242.0	375,268	1,917.0	64,389	328.9	293,562	1,499.6	17,317	88.5
2013	19,651,127	46,130	234.7	358,598	1,824.8	56,442	287.2	286,674	1,458.8	15,482	78.8
Percent change	X	−2.6	−3.0	−4.4	−4.8	−12.3	−12.7	−2.3	−2.7	−10.6	−10.9
Pennsylvania[7,8]											
2012	12,764,475	25,571	200.3	276,562	2,166.7	57,040	446.9	204,409	1,601.4	15,113	118.4
2013	12,773,801	23,719	185.7	263,240	2,060.8	52,034	407.3	197,436	1,545.6	13,770	107.8
Percent change	X	−7.2	−7.3	−4.8	−4.9	−8.8	−8.8	−3.4	−3.5	−8.9	−9.0
Midwest[5,6,7,8]											
2012	67,321,425	144,894	215.2	1,873,378	2,782.7	436,009	647.7	1,302,359	1,934.5	135,010	200.5
2013	67,547,890	135,803	201.0	1,729,496	2,560.4	383,297	567.4	1,217,580	1,802.5	128,619	190.4
Percent change	X	−6.3	−6.6	−7.7	−8.0	−12.1	−12.4	−6.5	−6.8	−4.7	−5.1
East North Central[5,6,7,8]											
2012	46,566,078	98,208	210.9	1,291,164	2,772.8	317,592	682.0	880,582	1,891.0	92,990	199.7
2013	46,662,180	90,894	194.8	1,175,272	2,518.7	273,270	585.6	815,378	1,747.4	86,624	185.6
Percent change	X	−7.4	−7.6	−9.0	−9.2	−14.0	−14.1	−7.4	−7.6	−6.8	−7.0
Illinois[6]											
2012	12,868,192	29,725	231.0	332,706	2,585.5	71,100	552.5	235,314	1,828.6	26,292	204.3

Table 4. Crime, by Region, Geographic Division, and State, 2012–2013—*Continued*

(Number, rate per 100,000 population, percent.)

Area	Population[1]	Violent crime[2]		Murder and nonnegligent manslaughter		Rape (revised definition)[3]		Rape (legacy definition)[4]		Robbery	
		Number	Rate	Number	Rate	Number	Rate	Number	Rate	Number	Rate
2013	12,882,135	47,987	372.5	706	5.5	4,263	33.1	3,276	25.4	17,722	137.6
Percent change	X	−10.4	−10.5	−8.3	−8.4	NA	NA	−8.5	−8.6	−9.0	−9.1
Indiana[6]											
2012	6,537,782	22,544	344.8	307	4.7	NA	NA	1,661	25.4	6,601	101.0
2013	6,570,902	22,991	349.9	355	5.4	2,142	32.6	1,646	25.0	7,108	108.2
Percent change	X	+2.0	+1.5	+15.6	+15.1	NA	NA	−0.9	−1.4	+7.7	+7.1
Michigan[7]											
2012	9,882,519	44,962	455.0	701	7.1	NA	NA	4,635	46.9	10,423	105.5
2013	9,895,622	42,536	429.8	631	6.4	6,593	66.6	4,606	46.5	10,105	102.1
Percent change	X	−5.4	−5.5	−10.0	−10.1	NA	NA	−0.6	−0.8	−3.1	−3.2
Ohio[6]											
2012	11,553,031	34,827	301.5	478	4.1	NA	NA	3,813	33.0	15,396	133.3
2013	11,570,808	31,904	275.7	455	3.9	4,041	34.9	2,824	24.4	14,368	124.2
Percent change	X	−8.4	−8.5	−4.8	−5.0	NA	NA	−25.9	−26.1	−6.7	−6.8
Wisconsin[6,8]											
2012	5,724,554	16,254	283.9	169	3.0	NA	NA	1,228	21.5	4,692	82.0
2013	5,742,713	15,570	271.1	162	2.8	1,687	29.4	1,296	22.6	4,834	84.2
Percent change	X	−4.2	−4.5	−4.1	−4.4	NA	NA	+5.5	+5.2	+3.0	+2.7
West North Central[5,6,7]											
2012	20,755,347	67,293	324.2	723	3.5	NA	NA	6,760	32.6	13,124	63.2
2013	20,885,710	64,239	307.6	733	3.5	8,203	39.3	5,789	27.7	12,808	61.3
Percent change	X	−4.5	−5.1	+1.4	+0.8	NA	NA	−14.4	−14.9	−2.4	−3.0
Iowa[7]											
2012	3,075,039	8,167	265.6	49	1.6	NA	NA	901	29.3	962	31.3
2013	3,090,416	8,062	260.9	43	1.4	1,083	35.0	757	24.5	939	30.4
Percent change	X	−1.3	−1.8	−12.2	−12.7	NA	NA	−16.0	−16.4	−2.4	−2.9
Kansas[6]											
2012	2,885,398	10,292	356.7	85	2.9	NA	NA	1,105	38.3	1,493	51.7
2013	2,893,957	9,478	327.5	112	3.9	1,195	41.3	835	28.9	1,350	46.6
Percent change	X	−7.9	−8.2	+31.8	+31.4	NA	NA	−24.4	−24.7	−9.6	−9.8
Minnesota[7]											
2012	5,379,646	12,419	230.9	99	1.8	NA	NA	1,638	30.4	3,475	64.6
2013	5,420,380	12,100	223.2	114	2.1	2,008	37.0	1,403	25.9	3,674	67.8
Percent change	X	−2.6	−3.3	+15.2	+14.3	NA	NA	−14.3	−15.0	+5.7	+4.9
Missouri[7]											
2012	6,024,522	27,189	451.3	390	6.5	NA	NA	1,527	25.3	5,782	96.0
2013	6,044,171	25,509	422.0	371	6.1	2,287	37.8	1,599	26.5	5,484	90.7
Percent change	X	−6.2	−6.5	−4.9	−5.2	NA	NA	+4.7	+4.4	−5.2	−5.5
Nebraska[6]											
2012	1,855,350	4,802	258.8	52	2.8	NA	NA	710	38.3	1,128	60.8
2013	1,868,516	4,712	252.2	57	3.1	801	42.9	616	33.0	1,040	55.7
Percent change	X	−1.9	−2.6	+9.6	+8.8	NA	NA	−13.2	−13.9	−7.8	−8.5
North Dakota[7]											
2012	701,345	1,723	245.7	25	3.6	NA	NA	279	39.8	127	18.1
2013	723,393	1,854	256.3	16	2.2	330	45.6	230	31.8	162	22.4
Percent change	X	+7.6	+4.3	−36.0	−38.0	NA	NA	−17.6	−20.1	+27.6	+23.7
South Dakota[7]											
2012	834,047	2,701	323.8	23	2.8	NA	NA	600	71.9	157	18.8
2013	844,877	2,524	298.7	20	2.4	499	59.1	349	41.3	159	18.8
Percent change	X	−6.6	−7.8	−13.0	−14.2	NA	NA	−41.8	−42.6	+1.3	*
South[5,6,7,9]											
2012	117,253,992	497,113	424.0	6,499	5.5	NA	NA	31,940	27.2	131,951	112.5
2013	118,383,453	477,640	403.5	6,222	5.3	41,028	34.7	30,128	25.4	129,825	109.7
Percent change	X	−3.9	−4.8	−4.3	−5.2	NA	NA	−5.7	−6.6	−1.6	−2.5
South Atlantic[5,7,9]											
2012	61,186,832	255,319	417.3	3,312	5.4	NA	NA	14,741	24.1	71,555	116.9
2013	61,783,647	244,019	395.0	3,194	5.2	19,104	30.9	13,801	22.3	69,577	112.6
Percent change	X	−4.4	−5.3	−3.6	−4.5	NA	NA	−6.4	−7.3	−2.8	−3.7
Delaware[7]											
2012	917,053	5,048	550.5	56	6.1	NA	NA	249	27.2	1,498	163.3
2013	925,749	4,435	479.1	39	4.2	380	41.0	266	28.7	1,226	132.4
Percent change	X	−12.1	−13.0	−30.4	−31.0	NA	NA	+6.8	+5.8	−18.2	−18.9
District of Columbia[7,9]											
2012	633,427	7,866	1,241.8	88	13.9	NA	NA	236	37.3	4,037	637.3
2013	646,449	8,287	1,281.9	103	15.9	395	61.1	276	42.7	4,078	630.8
Percent change	X	+5.4	+3.2	+17.0	+14.7	NA	NA	+16.9	+14.6	+1.0	−1.0

Table 4. Crime, by Region, Geographic Division, and State, 2012–2013—*Continued*

(Number, rate per 100,000 population, percent.)

Area	Population[1]	Aggravated assault		Property crime		Burglary		Larceny-theft		Motor vehicle theft	
		Number	Rate	Number	Rate	Number	Rate	Number	Rate	Number	Rate
2013	12,882,135	26,283	204.0	292,983	2,274.3	58,237	452.1	213,813	1,659.8	20,933	162.5
Percent change	X	−11.6	−11.7	−11.9	−12.0	−18.1	−18.2	−9.1	−9.2	−20.4	−20.5
Indiana[6]											
2012	6,537,782	13,975	213.8	197,994	3,028.5	47,689	729.4	136,668	2,090.4	13,637	208.6
2013	6,570,902	13,882	211.3	187,536	2,854.0	42,909	653.0	130,423	1,984.9	14,204	216.2
Percent change	X	−0.7	−1.2	−5.3	−5.8	−10.0	−10.5	−4.6	−5.1	+4.2	+3.6
Michigan[7]											
2012	9,882,519	29,203	295.5	249,249	2,522.1	65,560	663.4	158,609	1,604.9	25,080	253.8
2013	9,895,622	27,194	274.8	230,334	2,327.6	56,344	569.4	149,423	1,510.0	24,567	248.3
Percent change	X	−6.9	−7.0	−7.6	−7.7	−14.1	−14.2	−5.8	−5.9	−2.0	−2.2
Ohio[6]											
2012	11,553,031	15,140	131.0	370,435	3,206.4	105,312	911.6	245,372	2,123.9	19,751	171.0
2013	11,570,808	14,257	123.2	338,731	2,927.5	91,433	790.2	227,766	1,968.5	19,532	168.8
Percent change	X	−5.8	−6.0	−8.6	−8.7	−13.2	−13.3	−7.2	−7.3	−1.1	−1.3
Wisconsin[6,8]											
2012	5,724,554	10,165	177.6	140,780	2,459.2	27,931	487.9	104,619	1,827.5	8,230	143.8
2013	5,742,713	9,278	161.6	125,688	2,188.7	24,347	424.0	93,953	1,636.0	7,388	128.6
Percent change	X	−8.7	−9.0	−10.7	−11.0	−12.8	−13.1	−10.2	−10.5	−10.2	−10.5
West North Central[5,6,7]											
2012	20,755,347	46,686	224.9	582,214	2,805.1	118,417	570.5	421,777	2,032.1	42,020	202.5
2013	20,885,710	44,909	215.0	554,224	2,653.6	110,027	526.8	402,202	1,925.7	41,995	201.1
Percent change	X	−3.8	−4.4	−4.8	−5.4	−7.1	−7.7	−4.6	−5.2	−0.1	−0.7
Iowa[7]											
2012	3,075,039	6,255	203.4	70,357	2,288.0	17,201	559.4	49,116	1,597.2	4,040	131.4
2013	3,090,416	6,323	204.6	67,800	2,193.9	15,868	513.5	47,686	1,543.0	4,246	137.4
Percent change	X	+1.1	+0.6	−3.6	−4.1	−7.7	−8.2	−2.9	−3.4	+5.1	+4.6
Kansas[6]											
2012	2,885,398	7,609	263.7	91,066	3,156.1	18,874	654.1	65,413	2,267.0	6,779	234.9
2013	2,893,957	7,181	248.1	85,280	2,946.8	17,375	600.4	61,264	2,117.0	6,641	229.5
Percent change	X	−5.6	−5.9	−6.4	−6.6	−7.9	−8.2	−6.3	−6.6	−2.0	−2.3
Minnesota[7]											
2012	5,379,646	7,207	134.0	138,152	2,568.1	25,378	471.7	104,316	1,939.1	8,458	157.2
2013	5,420,380	6,909	127.5	131,195	2,420.4	22,713	419.0	100,516	1,854.4	7,966	147.0
Percent change	X	−4.1	−4.9	−5.0	−5.7	−10.5	−11.2	−3.6	−4.4	−5.8	−6.5
Missouri[7]											
2012	6,024,522	19,490	323.5	199,813	3,316.7	42,510	705.6	140,971	2,340.0	16,332	271.1
2013	6,044,171	18,055	298.7	189,606	3,137.0	38,865	643.0	134,416	2,223.9	16,325	270.1
Percent change	X	−7.4	−7.7	−5.1	−5.4	−8.6	−8.9	−4.6	−5.0	*	−0.4
Nebraska[6]											
2012	1,855,350	2,912	157.0	51,203	2,759.7	8,745	471.3	38,301	2,064.4	4,157	224.1
2013	1,868,516	2,999	160.5	49,018	2,623.4	8,900	476.3	35,655	1,908.2	4,463	238.9
Percent change	X	+3.0	+2.3	−4.3	−4.9	+1.8	+1.1	−6.9	−7.6	+7.4	+6.6
North Dakota[7]											
2012	701,345	1,292	184.2	14,297	2,038.5	2,429	346.3	10,687	1,523.8	1,181	168.4
2013	723,393	1,446	199.9	15,148	2,094.0	2,934	405.6	10,798	1,492.7	1,416	195.7
Percent change	X	+11.9	+8.5	+6.0	+2.7	+20.8	+17.1	+1.0	−2.0	+19.9	+16.2
South Dakota[7]											
2012	834,047	1,921	230.3	17,326	2,077.3	3,280	393.3	12,973	1,555.4	1,073	128.6
2013	844,877	1,996	236.2	16,177	1,914.7	3,372	399.1	11,867	1,404.6	938	111.0
Percent change	X	+3.9	+2.6	−6.6	−7.8	+2.8	+1.5	−8.5	−9.7	−12.6	−13.7
South[5,6,7,9]											
2012	117,253,992	326,723	278.6	3,791,837	3,233.9	948,407	808.8	2,592,195	2,210.8	251,235	214.3
2013	118,383,453	311,465	263.1	3,663,780	3,094.8	871,095	735.8	2,550,709	2,154.6	241,976	204.4
Percent change	X	−4.7	−5.6	−3.4	−4.3	−8.2	−9.0	−1.6	−2.5	−3.7	−4.6
South Atlantic[5,7,9]											
2012	61,186,832	165,711	270.8	1,928,811	3,152.3	470,928	769.7	1,330,920	2,175.2	126,963	207.5
2013	61,783,647	157,447	254.8	1,849,711	2,993.9	430,544	696.9	1,301,807	2,107.0	117,360	190.0
Percent change	X	−5.0	−5.9	−4.1	−5.0	−8.6	−9.5	−2.2	−3.1	−7.6	−8.5
Delaware[7]											
2012	917,053	3,245	353.9	30,707	3,348.4	7,389	805.7	21,880	2,385.9	1,438	156.8
2013	925,749	2,904	313.7	28,379	3,065.5	6,131	662.3	20,916	2,259.4	1,332	143.9
Percent change	X	−10.5	−11.3	−7.6	−8.4	−17.0	−17.8	−4.4	−5.3	−7.4	−8.2
District of Columbia[7,9]											
2012	633,427	3,505	553.3	30,757	4,855.7	3,519	555.5	23,575	3,721.8	3,663	578.3
2013	646,449	3,830	592.5	31,083	4,808.3	3,316	513.0	24,533	3,795.0	3,234	500.3
Percent change	X	+9.3	+7.1	+1.1	−1.0	−5.8	−7.7	+4.1	+2.0	−11.7	−13.5

Table 4. Crime, by Region, Geographic Division, and State, 2012–2013—*Continued*

(Number, rate per 100,000 population, percent.)

Area	Population[1]	Violent crime[2] Number	Violent crime[2] Rate	Murder and nonnegligent manslaughter Number	Murder and nonnegligent manslaughter Rate	Rape (revised definition)[3] Number	Rape (revised definition)[3] Rate	Rape (legacy definition)[4] Number	Rape (legacy definition)[4] Rate	Robbery Number	Robbery Rate
Florida[7]											
2012	19,320,749	94,087	487.0	1,009	5.2	NA	NA	5,260	27.2	23,889	123.6
2013	19,552,860	89,948	460.0	972	5.0	6,760	34.6	4,722	24.1	23,200	118.7
Percent change	X	−4.4	−5.5	−3.7	−4.8	NA	NA	−10.2	−11.3	−2.9	−4.0
Georgia											
2012	9,915,646	37,675	380.0	583	5.9	NA	NA	2,143	21.6	12,502	126.1
2013	9,992,167	35,943	359.7	556	5.6	2,582	25.8	1,984	19.9	12,488	125.0
Percent change	X	−4.6	−5.3	−4.6	−5.4	NA	NA	−7.4	−8.1	−0.1	−0.9
Maryland											
2012	5,884,868	28,086	477.3	373	6.3	NA	NA	1,237	21.0	10,173	172.9
2013	5,928,814	27,734	467.8	381	6.4	1,532	25.8	1,177	19.9	10,048	169.5
Percent change	X	−1.3	−2.0	+2.1	+1.4	NA	NA	−4.9	−5.6	−1.2	−2.0
North Carolina											
2012	9,748,364	34,464	353.5	479	4.9	NA	NA	1,984	20.4	9,392	96.3
2013	9,848,060	33,152	336.6	469	4.8	2,369	24.1	1,821	18.5	9,349	94.9
Percent change	X	−3.8	−4.8	−2.1	−3.1	NA	NA	−8.2	−9.1	−0.5	−1.5
South Carolina[7]											
2012	4,723,417	26,474	560.5	332	7.0	NA	NA	1,712	36.2	4,511	95.5
2013	4,774,839	23,625	494.8	297	6.2	2,171	45.5	1,518	31.8	3,972	83.2
Percent change	X	−10.8	−11.7	−10.5	−11.5	NA	NA	−11.3	−12.3	−11.9	−12.9
Virginia[7]											
2012	8,186,628	15,676	191.5	322	3.9	NA	NA	1,505	18.4	4,718	57.6
2013	8,260,405	15,524	187.9	316	3.8	2,262	27.4	1,581	19.1	4,565	55.3
Percent change	X	−1.0	−1.9	−1.9	−2.7	NA	NA	+5.0	+4.1	−3.2	−4.1
West Virginia[7]											
2012	1,856,680	5,943	320.1	70	3.8	NA	NA	415	22.4	835	45.0
2013	1,854,304	5,371	289.7	61	3.3	653	35.2	456	24.6	651	35.1
Percent change	X	−9.6	−9.5	−12.9	−12.7	NA	NA	+9.9	+10.0	−22.0	−21.9
East South Central[5,6,7]											
2012	18,638,622	80,527	432.0	1,156	6.2	NA	NA	5,474	29.4	18,995	101.9
2013	18,716,202	74,601	398.6	1,037	5.5	6,936	37.1	4,911	26.2	17,610	94.1
Percent change	X	−7.4	−7.7	−10.3	−10.7	NA	NA	−10.3	−10.7	−7.3	−7.7
Alabama[7]											
2012	4,817,528	21,693	450.3	342	7.1	NA	NA	1,296	26.9	5,020	104.2
2013	4,833,722	20,210	418.1	347	7.2	2,044	42.3	1,428	29.5	4,648	96.2
Percent change	X	−6.8	−7.1	+1.5	+1.1	NA	NA	+10.2	+9.8	−7.4	−7.7
Kentucky[6]											
2012	4,379,730	9,852	224.9	201	4.6	NA	NA	1,312	30.0	3,547	81.0
2013	4,395,295	8,737	198.8	167	3.8	1,611	36.7	1,126	25.6	3,246	73.9
Percent change	X	−11.3	−11.6	−16.9	−17.2	NA	NA	−14.2	−14.5	−8.5	−8.8
Mississippi[6]											
2012	2,986,450	7,769	260.1	213	7.1	NA	NA	819	27.4	2,277	76.2
2013	2,991,207	7,999	267.4	195	6.5	930	31.1	715	23.9	2,409	80.5
Percent change	X	+3.0	+2.8	−8.5	−8.6	NA	NA	−12.7	−12.8	+5.8	+5.6
Tennessee[7]											
2012	6,454,914	41,213	638.5	400	6.2	NA	NA	2,047	31.7	8,151	126.3
2013	6,495,978	37,655	579.7	328	5.0	2,351	36.2	1,642	25.3	7,307	112.5
Percent change	X	−8.6	−9.2	−18.0	−18.5	NA	NA	−19.8	−20.3	−10.4	−10.9
West South Central[5,6,7]											
2012	37,428,538	161,267	430.9	2,031	5.4	NA	NA	11,725	31.3	41,401	110.6
2013	37,883,604	159,020	419.8	1,991	5.3	14,988	39.6	11,416	30.1	42,638	112.6
Percent change	X	−1.4	−2.6	−2.0	−3.1	NA	NA	−2.6	−3.8	+3.0	+1.8
Arkansas[7]											
2012	2,949,828	13,851	469.6	174	5.9	NA	NA	1,233	41.8	2,310	78.3
2013	2,959,373	13,191	445.7	159	5.4	1,423	48.1	993	33.6	2,258	76.3
Percent change	X	−4.8	−5.1	−8.6	−8.9	NA	NA	−19.5	−19.7	−2.3	−2.6
Louisiana[6]											
2012	4,602,134	22,839	496.3	489	10.6	NA	NA	1,155	25.1	5,458	118.6
2013	4,625,470	23,609	510.4	498	10.8	1,619	35.0	1,244	26.9	5,548	119.9
Percent change	X	+3.4	+2.8	+1.8	+1.3	NA	NA	+7.7	+7.2	+1.6	+1.1
Oklahoma[6]											
2012	3,815,780	18,102	474.4	220	5.8	NA	NA	1,622	42.5	3,248	85.1
2013	3,850,568	16,484	428.1	195	5.1	2,180	56.6	1,675	43.5	3,031	78.7
Percent change	X	−8.9	−9.8	−11.4	−12.2	NA	NA	+3.3	+2.3	−6.7	−7.5
Texas[6]											
2012	26,060,796	106,475	408.6	1,148	4.4	NA	NA	7,715	29.6	30,385	116.6
2013	26,448,193	105,736	399.8	1,139	4.3	9,766	36.9	7,504	28.4	31,801	120.2
Percent change	X	−0.7	−2.1	−0.8	−2.2	NA	NA	−2.7	−4.2	+4.7	+3.1

Table 4. Crime, by Region, Geographic Division, and State, 2012–2013—*Continued*

(Number, rate per 100,000 population, percent.)

Area	Population[1]	Aggravated assault Number	Aggravated assault Rate	Property crime Number	Property crime Rate	Burglary Number	Burglary Rate	Larceny-theft Number	Larceny-theft Rate	Motor vehicle theft Number	Motor vehicle theft Rate
Florida[7]											
2012	19,320,749	63,929	330.9	632,988	3,276.2	153,563	794.8	442,095	2,288.2	37,330	193.2
2013	19,552,860	61,054	312.3	607,172	3,105.3	138,916	710.5	433,344	2,216.3	34,912	178.6
Percent change	X	−4.5	−5.6	−4.1	−5.2	−9.5	−10.6	−2.0	−3.1	−6.5	−7.6
Georgia											
2012	9,915,646	22,447	226.4	339,473	3,423.6	86,992	877.3	223,875	2,257.8	28,606	288.5
2013	9,992,167	20,915	209.3	334,399	3,346.6	82,258	823.2	225,315	2,254.9	26,826	268.5
Percent change	X	−6.8	−7.5	−1.5	−2.2	−5.4	−6.2	+0.6	−0.1	−6.2	−6.9
Maryland											
2012	5,884,868	16,303	277.0	162,309	2,758.1	33,803	574.4	113,550	1,929.5	14,956	254.1
2013	5,928,814	16,128	272.0	157,913	2,663.5	31,949	538.9	112,546	1,898.3	13,418	226.3
Percent change	X	−1.1	−1.8	−2.7	−3.4	−5.5	−6.2	−0.9	−1.6	−10.3	−10.9
North Carolina											
2012	9,748,364	22,609	231.9	328,594	3,370.8	99,323	1,018.9	213,151	2,186.5	16,120	165.4
2013	9,848,060	21,513	218.4	308,049	3,128.0	90,702	921.0	202,741	2,058.7	14,606	148.3
Percent change	X	−4.8	−5.8	−6.3	−7.2	−8.7	−9.6	−4.9	−5.8	−9.4	−10.3
South Carolina[7]											
2012	4,723,417	19,919	421.7	181,049	3,833.0	45,222	957.4	122,340	2,590.1	13,487	285.5
2013	4,774,839	17,838	373.6	173,049	3,624.2	40,958	857.8	119,511	2,502.9	12,580	263.5
Percent change	X	−10.4	−11.4	−4.4	−5.4	−9.4	−10.4	−2.3	−3.4	−6.7	−7.7
Virginia[7]											
2012	8,186,628	9,131	111.5	178,434	2,179.6	29,651	362.2	139,654	1,705.9	9,129	111.5
2013	8,260,405	9,062	109.7	170,654	2,065.9	26,640	322.5	135,478	1,640.1	8,536	103.3
Percent change	X	−0.8	−1.6	−4.4	−5.2	−10.2	−11.0	−3.0	−3.9	−6.5	−7.3
West Virginia[7]											
2012	1,856,680	4,623	249.0	44,500	2,396.8	11,466	617.6	30,800	1,658.9	2,234	120.3
2013	1,854,304	4,203	226.7	39,013	2,103.9	9,674	521.7	27,423	1,478.9	1,916	103.3
Percent change	X	−9.1	−9.0	−12.3	−12.2	−15.6	−15.5	−11.0	−10.9	−14.2	−14.1
East South Central[5,6,7]											
2012	18,638,622	54,902	294.6	583,536	3,130.8	161,673	867.4	387,973	2,081.6	33,890	181.8
2013	18,716,202	51,043	272.7	553,979	2,959.9	144,636	772.8	376,524	2,011.8	32,819	175.4
Percent change	X	−7.0	−7.4	−5.1	−5.5	−10.5	−10.9	−3.0	−3.4	−3.2	−3.6
Alabama[7]											
2012	4,817,528	15,035	312.1	168,878	3,505.5	47,481	985.6	111,523	2,314.9	9,874	205.0
2013	4,833,722	13,787	285.2	161,993	3,351.3	42,429	877.8	108,993	2,254.8	10,571	218.7
Percent change	X	−8.3	−8.6	−4.1	−4.4	−10.6	−10.9	−2.3	−2.6	+7.1	+6.7
Kentucky[6]											
2012	4,379,730	4,792	109.4	112,800	2,575.5	29,877	682.2	76,199	1,739.8	6,724	153.5
2013	4,395,295	4,198	95.5	103,857	2,362.9	26,213	596.4	71,612	1,629.3	6,032	137.2
Percent change	X	−12.4	−12.7	−7.9	−8.3	−12.3	−12.6	−6.0	−6.4	−10.3	−10.6
Mississippi[6]											
2012	2,986,450	4,460	149.3	83,933	2,810.5	28,084	940.4	51,520	1,725.1	4,329	145.0
2013	2,991,207	4,680	156.5	81,500	2,724.7	24,995	835.6	52,117	1,742.3	4,388	146.7
Percent change	X	+4.9	+4.8	−2.9	−3.1	−11.0	−11.1	+1.2	+1.0	+1.4	+1.2
Tennessee[7]											
2012	6,454,914	30,615	474.3	217,925	3,376.1	56,231	871.1	148,731	2,304.2	12,963	200.8
2013	6,495,978	28,378	436.9	206,629	3,180.9	50,999	785.1	143,802	2,213.7	11,828	182.1
Percent change	X	−7.3	−7.9	−5.2	−5.8	−9.3	−9.9	−3.3	−3.9	−8.8	−9.3
West South Central[5,6,7]											
2012	37,428,538	106,110	283.5	1,279,490	3,418.5	315,806	843.8	873,302	2,333.3	90,382	241.5
2013	37,883,604	102,975	271.8	1,260,090	3,326.2	295,915	781.1	872,378	2,302.8	91,797	242.3
Percent change	X	−3.0	−4.1	−1.5	−2.7	−6.3	−7.4	−0.1	−1.3	+1.6	+0.3
Arkansas[7]											
2012	2,949,828	10,134	343.5	109,389	3,708.3	32,673	1,107.6	70,982	2,406.3	5,734	194.4
2013	2,959,373	9,781	330.5	106,613	3,602.6	30,485	1,030.1	70,450	2,380.6	5,678	191.9
Percent change	X	−3.5	−3.8	−2.5	−2.9	−6.7	−7.0	−0.7	−1.1	−1.0	−1.3
Louisiana[6]											
2012	4,602,134	15,737	342.0	162,673	3,534.7	42,037	913.4	112,764	2,450.3	7,872	171.1
2013	4,625,470	16,319	352.8	165,686	3,582.0	41,184	890.4	115,342	2,493.6	9,160	198.0
Percent change	X	+3.7	+3.2	+1.9	+1.3	−2.0	−2.5	+2.3	+1.8	+16.4	+15.8
Oklahoma[6]											
2012	3,815,780	13,012	341.0	130,969	3,432.3	36,094	945.9	83,131	2,178.6	11,744	307.8
2013	3,850,568	11,583	300.8	126,057	3,273.7	33,348	866.1	81,495	2,116.4	11,214	291.2
Percent change	X	−11.0	−11.8	−3.8	−4.6	−7.6	−8.4	−2.0	−2.9	−4.5	−5.4
Texas[6]											
2012	26,060,796	67,227	258.0	876,459	3,363.1	205,002	786.6	606,425	2,327.0	65,032	249.5
2013	26,448,193	65,292	246.9	861,734	3,258.2	190,898	721.8	605,091	2,287.8	65,745	248.6
Percent change	X	−2.9	−4.3	−1.7	−3.1	−6.9	−8.2	−0.2	−1.7	+1.1	−0.4

Table 4. Crime, by Region, Geographic Division, and State, 2012–2013—*Continued*

(Number, rate per 100,000 population, percent.)

Area	Population[1]	Violent crime[2]		Murder and nonnegligent manslaughter		Rape (revised definition)[3]		Rape (legacy definition)[4]		Robbery	
		Number	Rate	Number	Rate	Number	Rate	Number	Rate	Number	Rate
West[5,6,7,8]											
2012	73,526,476	284,627	387.1	3,118	4.2	NA	NA	20,416	27.8	85,647	116.5
2013	74,254,423	272,815	367.4	2,979	4.0	27,032	36.4	20,151	27.1	82,199	110.7
Percent change	X	−4.1	−5.1	−4.5	−5.4	NA	NA	−1.3	−2.3	−4.0	−5.0
Mountain[5,6,7,8]											
2012	22,611,082	85,702	379.0	875	3.9	NA	NA	8,308	36.7	19,151	84.7
2013	22,881,245	84,139	367.7	938	4.1	11,541	50.4	8,491	37.1	18,588	81.2
Percent change	X	−1.8	−3.0	+7.2	+5.9	NA	NA	+2.2	+1.0	−2.9	−4.1
Arizona[6,8]											
2012	6,551,149	28,077	428.6	358	5.5	NA	NA	2,282	34.8	7,383	112.7
2013	6,626,624	26,892	405.8	357	5.4	3,050	46.0	2,343	35.4	6,702	101.1
Percent change	X	−4.2	−5.3	−0.3	−1.4	NA	NA	+2.7	+1.5	−9.2	−10.3
Colorado[7]											
2012	5,189,458	15,951	307.4	152	2.9	NA	NA	2,122	40.9	3,392	65.4
2013	5,268,367	15,342	291.2	178	3.4	2,934	55.7	2,050	38.9	3,151	59.8
Percent change	X	−3.8	−5.3	+17.1	+15.4	NA	NA	−3.4	−4.8	−7.1	−8.5
Idaho[7]											
2012	1,595,590	3,348	209.8	30	1.9	NA	NA	495	31.0	243	15.2
2013	1,612,136	3,300	204.7	27	1.7	655	40.6	457	28.3	220	13.6
Percent change	X	−1.4	−2.4	−10.0	−10.9	NA	NA	−7.7	−8.6	−9.5	−10.4
Montana[7]											
2012	1,005,494	2,803	278.8	29	2.9	NA	NA	392	39.0	202	20.1
2013	1,015,165	2,444	240.7	22	2.2	410	40.4	287	28.3	204	20.1
Percent change	X	−12.8	−13.6	−24.1	−24.9	NA	NA	−26.8	−27.5	+1.0	*
Nevada											
2012	2,754,354	16,763	608.6	124	4.5	NA	NA	931	33.8	4,918	178.6
2013	2,790,136	16,496	591.2	163	5.8	1,418	50.8	1,090	39.1	5,183	185.8
Percent change	X	−1.6	−2.9	+31.5	+29.8	NA	NA	+17.1	+15.6	+5.4	+4.0
New Mexico											
2012	2,083,540	11,660	559.6	116	5.6	NA	NA	957	45.9	1,847	88.6
2013	2,085,287	12,443	596.7	125	6.0	1,465	70.3	1,126	54.0	1,810	86.8
Percent change	X	+6.7	+6.6	+7.8	+7.7	NA	NA	+17.7	+17.6	−2.0	−2.1
Utah[6]											
2012	2,854,871	5,939	208.0	52	1.8	NA	NA	975	34.2	1,105	38.7
2013	2,900,872	6,070	209.2	49	1.7	1,422	49.0	994	34.3	1,243	42.8
Percent change	X	+2.2	+0.6	−5.8	−7.3	NA	NA	+1.9	+0.3	+12.5	+10.7
Wyoming											
2012	576,626	1,161	201.3	14	2.4	−100.0	NA	154	26.7	61	10.6
2013	582,658	1,152	197.7	17	2.9	187	32.1	144	24.7	75	12.9
Percent change	X	−0.8	−1.8	+21.4	+20.2	NA	NA	−6.5	−7.5	+23.0	+21.7
Pacific[5,6,7,8]											
2012	50,915,394	198,925	390.7	2,243	4.4	NA	NA	12,108	23.8	66,496	130.6
2013	51,373,178	188,676	367.3	2,041	4.0	15,491	30.2	11,660	22.7	63,611	123.8
Percent change	X	−5.2	−6.0	−9.0	−9.8	NA	NA	−3.7	−4.6	−4.3	−5.2
Alaska[7]											
2012	730,307	4,412	604.1	30	4.1	NA		583	79.8	630	86.3
2013	735,132	4,430	602.6	34	4.6	922	125.4	644	87.6	624	84.9
Percent change	X	+0.4	−0.3	+13.3	+12.6	NA	NA	+10.5	+9.7	−1.0	−1.6
California											
2012	37,999,878	160,944	423.5	1,884	5.0	NA	NA	7,837	20.6	56,521	148.7
2013	38,332,521	151,879	396.2	1,746	4.6	9,714	25.3	7,464	19.5	53,640	139.9
Percent change	X	−5.6	−6.5	−7.3	−8.1	NA	NA	−4.8	−5.6	−5.1	−5.9
Hawaii											
2012	1,390,090	3,378	243.0	21	1.5	NA	NA	279	20.1	1,125	80.9
2013	1,404,054	3,444	245.3	21	1.5	385	27.4	296	21.1	1,131	80.6
Percent change	X	+2.0	+0.9	*	−1.0	NA	NA	+6.1	+5.0	+0.5	−0.5
Oregon[6]											
2012	3,899,801	9,638	247.1	91	2.3	NA	NA	1,159	29.7	2,419	62.0
2013	3,930,065	9,546	242.9	80	2.0	1,897	48.3	1,459	37.1	2,397	61.0
Percent change	X	−1.0	−1.7	−12.1	−12.8	NA	NA	+25.9	+24.9	−0.9	−1.7
Washington[6,8]											
2012	6,895,318	20,553	298.1	217	3.1	NA	NA	2,250	32.6	5,801	84.1
2013	6,971,406	19,377	277.9	160	2.3	2,573	36.9	1,797	25.8	5,819	83.5
Percent change	X	−5.7	−6.8	−26.3	−27.1	NA	NA	−20.1	−21.0	+0.3	−0.8

(Number, rate per 100,000 population, percent.)

Area	Population[1]	Aggravated assault		Property crime		Burglary		Larceny-theft		Motor vehicle theft	
		Number	Rate	Number	Rate	Number	Rate	Number	Rate	Number	Rate
West[5,6,7,8]											
2012	73,526,476	175,446	238.6	2,174,808	2,957.9	488,755	664.7	1,418,883	1,929.8	267,170	363.4
2013	74,254,423	167,486	225.6	2,142,527	2,885.4	465,758	627.2	1,410,534	1,899.6	266,235	358.5
Percent change	X	−4.5	−5.5	−1.5	−2.5	−4.7	−5.6	−0.6	−1.6	−0.3	−1.3
Mountain[5,6,7,8]											
2012	22,611,082	57,368	253.7	681,093	3,012.2	148,958	658.8	475,875	2,104.6	56,260	248.8
2013	22,881,245	56,122	245.3	676,136	2,955.0	144,129	629.9	474,704	2,074.6	57,303	250.4
Percent change	X	−2.2	−3.3	−0.7	−1.9	−3.2	−4.4	−0.2	−1.4	+1.9	+0.7
Arizona[6,8]											
2012	6,551,149	18,054	275.6	231,701	3,536.8	52,911	807.7	159,808	2,439.4	18,982	289.8
2013	6,626,624	17,490	263.9	225,243	3,399.1	48,533	732.4	159,272	2,403.5	17,438	263.2
Percent change	X	−3.1	−4.2	−2.8	−3.9	−8.3	−9.3	−0.3	−1.5	−8.1	−9.2
Colorado[7]											
2012	5,189,458	10,285	198.2	139,355	2,685.3	26,163	504.2	101,091	1,948.0	12,101	233.2
2013	5,268,367	9,963	189.1	140,057	2,658.5	25,081	476.1	102,443	1,944.5	12,533	237.9
Percent change	X	−3.1	−4.6	+0.5	−1.0	−4.1	−5.6	+1.3	−0.2	+3.6	+2.0
Idaho[7]											
2012	1,595,590	2,580	161.7	31,825	1,994.6	7,240	453.8	23,203	1,454.2	1,382	86.6
2013	1,612,136	2,596	161.0	30,055	1,864.3	6,640	411.9	21,879	1,357.1	1,536	95.3
Percent change	X	+0.6	−0.4	−5.6	−6.5	−8.3	−9.2	−5.7	−6.7	+11.1	+10.0
Montana[7]											
2012	1,005,494	2,180	216.8	26,102	2,595.9	3,920	389.9	20,484	2,037.2	1,698	168.9
2013	1,015,165	1,931	190.2	25,953	2,556.5	4,064	400.3	20,039	1,974.0	1,850	182.2
Percent change	X	−11.4	−12.3	−0.6	−1.5	+3.7	+2.7	−2.2	−3.1	+9.0	+7.9
Nevada											
2012	2,754,354	10,790	391.7	77,510	2,814.1	22,120	803.1	45,372	1,647.3	10,018	363.7
2013	2,790,136	10,060	360.6	79,177	2,837.7	23,047	826.0	46,132	1,653.4	9,998	358.3
Percent change	X	−6.8	−8.0	+2.2	+0.8	+4.2	+2.9	+1.7	+0.4	−0.2	−1.5
New Mexico											
2012	2,083,540	8,740	419.5	75,094	3,604.2	21,384	1,026.3	48,247	2,315.6	5,463	262.2
2013	2,085,287	9,382	449.9	77,256	3,704.8	21,476	1,029.9	49,875	2,391.8	5,905	283.2
Percent change	X	+7.3	+7.3	+2.9	+2.8	+0.4	+0.3	+3.4	+3.3	+8.1	+8.0
Utah[6]											
2012	2,854,871	3,807	133.4	86,284	3,022.3	13,095	458.7	67,157	2,352.4	6,032	211.3
2013	2,900,872	3,784	130.4	85,586	2,950.4	13,333	459.6	64,788	2,233.4	7,465	257.3
Percent change	X	−0.6	−2.2	−0.8	−2.4	+1.8	+0.2	−3.5	−5.1	+23.8	+21.8
Wyoming											
2012	576,626	932	161.6	13,222	2,293.0	2,125	368.5	10,513	1,823.2	584	101.3
2013	582,658	916	157.2	12,809	2,198.4	1,955	335.5	10,276	1,763.6	578	99.2
Percent change	X	−1.7	−2.7	−3.1	−4.1	−8.0	−9.0	−2.3	−3.3	−1.0	−2.1
Pacific[5,6,7,8]											
2012	50,915,394	118,078	231.9	1,493,715	2,933.7	339,797	667.4	943,008	1,852.1	210,910	414.2
2013	51,373,178	111,364	216.8	1,466,391	2,854.4	321,629	626.1	935,830	1,821.6	208,932	406.7
Percent change	X	−5.7	−6.5	−1.8	−2.7	−5.3	−6.2	−0.8	−1.6	−0.9	−1.8
Alaska[7]											
2012	730,307	3,169	433.9	20,037	2,743.6	2,950	403.9	15,565	2,131.3	1,522	208.4
2013	735,132	3,128	425.5	21,210	2,885.2	2,916	396.7	16,599	2,258.0	1,695	230.6
Percent change	X	−1.3	−1.9	+5.9	+5.2	−1.2	−1.8	+6.6	+5.9	+11.4	+10.6
California											
2012	37,999,878	94,702	249.2	1,049,465	2,761.8	245,767	646.8	635,090	1,671.3	168,608	443.7
2013	38,332,521	89,029	232.3	1,018,907	2,658.1	232,058	605.4	621,557	1,621.5	165,292	431.2
Percent change	X	−6.0	−6.8	−2.9	−3.8	−5.6	−6.4	−2.1	−3.0	−2.0	−2.8
Hawaii											
2012	1,390,090	1,953	140.5	43,419	3,123.5	7,653	550.5	31,901	2,294.9	3,865	278.0
2013	1,404,054	1,996	142.2	42,875	3,053.7	7,533	536.5	31,658	2,254.8	3,684	262.4
Percent change	X	+2.2	+1.2	−1.3	−2.2	−1.6	−2.5	−0.8	−1.7	−4.7	−5.6
Oregon[6]											
2012	3,899,801	5,969	153.1	126,417	3,241.6	22,051	565.4	94,114	2,413.3	10,252	262.9
2013	3,930,065	5,610	142.7	124,737	3,173.9	20,769	528.5	94,106	2,394.5	9,862	250.9
Percent change	X	−6.0	−6.7	−1.3	−2.1	−5.8	−6.5	*	−0.8	−3.8	−4.5
Washington[6,8]											
2012	6,895,318	12,285	178.2	254,377	3,689.1	61,376	890.1	166,338	2,412.3	26,663	386.7
2013	6,971,406	11,601	166.4	258,662	3,710.3	58,353	837.0	171,910	2,465.9	28,399	407.4
Percent change	X	−5.6	−6.6	+1.7	+0.6	−4.9	−6.0	+3.3	+2.2	+6.5	+5.3

Table 4. Crime, by Region, Geographic Division, and State, 2012–2013—*Continued*

(Number, rate per 100,000 population, percent.)

Area	Population[1]	Violent crime[2]		Murder and nonnegligent manslaughter		Rape (revised definition)[3]		Rape (legacy definition)[4]		Robbery	
		Number	Rate	Number	Rate	Number	Rate	Number	Rate	Number	Rate
Puerto Rico											
2012	3,651,545	10,041	275.0	978	26.8	NA	NA	32	0.9	6,298	172.5
2013	3,615,086	9,320	257.8	883	24.4	34	0.9	26	0.7	6,016	166.4
Percent change	X	−7.2	−6.2	−9.7	−8.8	NA	NA	−18.8	−17.9	−4.5	−3.5

Table 4. Crime, by Region, Geographic Division, and State, 2012–2013—*Continued*

(Number, rate per 100,000 population, percent.)

Area	Population[1]	Aggravated assault		Property crime		Burglary		Larceny-theft		Motor vehicle theft	
		Number	Rate	Number	Rate	Number	Rate	Number	Rate	Number	Rate
Puerto Rico											
2012	3,651,545	2,733	74.8	51,679	1,415.3	15,287	418.6	30,545	836.5	5,847	160.1
2013	3,615,086	2,395	66.3	48,851	1,351.3	13,961	386.2	29,360	812.2	5,530	153.0
Percent change	X	−12.4	−11.5	−5.5	−4.5	−8.7	−7.8	−3.9	−2.9	−5.4	−4.5

Note: Although arson data are included in the trend and clearance tables, sufficient data are not available to estimate totals for this offense. Therefore, no arson data are published in this table.
NA = Not available.
X = Not applicable.
* = Less than one-tenth of 1 percent.
[1] Population figures are U.S. Census Bureau provisional estimates as of July 1, 2013.
[2] The violent crime figures include the offenses of murder, rape (legacy definition), robbery, and aggravated assault.
[3] The figures shown in this column for the offense of rape were estimated using the revised Uniform Crime Reporting (UCR) definition of rape. See chapter notes for more detail.
[4] The figures shown in this column for the offense of rape were estimated using the legacy Uniform Crime Reporting (UCR) definition of rape. See chapter notes for more detail.
[5] The crime figures have been adjusted.
[6] Agencies within this state submitted rape data according to both the revised UCR definition of rape and the legacy UCR definition of rape.
[7] This state's agencies submitted rape data according to the revised UCR definition of rape.
[8] Because of changes in the state/local agency's reporting practices, figures are not comparable to previous years' data.
[9] Includes offenses reported by the Zoological Police and the Metro Transit Police.

Table 5. Crime, by State and Area, 2013

(Number, percent, rate per 100,000 population.)

Area	Population	Violent crime[1]	Murder and nonnegligent manslaughter	Rape (revised definition)[2]	Rape (legacy definition)[3]	Robbery	Aggravated assault	Property crime	Burglary	Larceny-theft	Motor vehicle theft
Alabama[4]											
Metropolitan statistical area	3,672,399										
Area actually reporting	96.2%		280	1,454		4,130	10,373	126,932	32,452	86,012	8,468
Estimated total	100.0%	16,664	283	1,507	1,053	4,208	10,666	130,416	33,451	88,269	8,696
Cities outside metropolitan areas	528,341										
Area actually reporting	94.0%		33	282		348	2,022	21,396	5,317	14,897	1,182
Estimated total	100.0%	2,840	35	299	209	367	2,139	22,487	5,605	15,637	1,245
Nonmetropolitan counties	632,982										
Area actually reporting	99.2%		29	236		72	974	9,020	3,347	5,048	625
Estimated total	100.0%	1,322	29	238	166	73	982	9,090	3,373	5,087	630
State total	4,833,722	20,826	347	2,044	1,428	4,648	13,787	161,993	42,429	108,993	10,571
Rate per 100,000 inhabitants		430.8	7.2	42.3	29.5	96.2	285.2	3,351.3	877.8	2,254.8	218.7
Alaska[4]											
Metropolitan statistical area	349,294										
Area actually reporting	100.0%	2,734	15	454	317	569	1,696	14,476	1,523	11,912	1,041
Cities outside metropolitan areas	128,768										
Area actually reporting	96.6%		1	98		33	636	3,606	407	2,950	249
Estimated total	100.0%	795	1	101	71	34	659	3,733	421	3,054	258
Nonmetropolitan counties	257,070										
Area actually reporting	100.0%	1,179	18	367	256	21	773	3,001	972	1,633	396
State total	735,132	4,708	34	922	644	624	3,128	21,210	2,916	16,599	1,695
Rate per 100,000 inhabitants		640.4	4.6	125.4	87.6	84.9	425.5	2,885.2	396.7	2,258.0	230.6
Arizona[5,6]											
Metropolitan statistical area	6,277,606										
Area actually reporting	99.8%		315		1,843	6,567	15,516	213,239	44,933	152,271	16,035
Estimated total	100.0%	24,832	315	2,406	1,843	6,575	15,536	213,617	45,003	152,558	16,056
Cities outside metropolitan areas	123,679										
Area actually reporting	88.4%		36		433	102	1,406	8,420	2,465	4,901	1,054
Estimated total	100.0%	2,378	41	631	490	115	1,591	9,528	2,789	5,546	1,193
Nonmetropolitan counties	225,339										
Area actually reporting	100.0%	389	1	13	10	12	363	2,098	741	1,168	189
State total	6,626,624	27,599	357	3,050	2,343	6,702	17,490	225,243	48,533	159,272	17,438
Rate per 100,000 inhabitants		416.5	5.4	46.0	35.4	101.1	263.9	3,399.1	732.4	2,403.5	263.2
Arkansas[4]											
Metropolitan statistical area	1,803,197										
Area actually reporting	96.1%		100	898		1,852	6,781	69,888	18,297	47,716	3,875
Estimated total	100.0%	9,872	101	928	648	1,865	6,978	71,483	18,856	48,636	3,991
Cities outside metropolitan areas	509,967										
Area actually reporting	92.5%		25	272		316	1,590	20,733	6,846	13,112	775
Estimated total	100.0%	2,382	27	294	205	342	1,719	22,416	7,402	14,176	838
Nonmetropolitan counties	646,209										
Area actually reporting	92.3%		29	186		47	1,001	11,739	3,903	7,052	784
Estimated total	100.0%	1,367	31	201	140	51	1,084	12,714	4,227	7,638	849
State total	2,959,373	13,621	159	1,423	993	2,258	9,781	106,613	30,485	70,450	5,678
Rate per 100,000 inhabitants		460.3	5.4	48.1	33.6	76.3	330.5	3,602.6	1,030.1	2,380.6	191.9
California											
Metropolitan statistical area	37,497,856										
Area actually reporting	99.9%		1,711		7,183	53,239	86,136	998,309	225,528	609,730	163,051
Estimated total	100.0%	150,459	1,711	9,349	7,184	53,247	86,152	998,514	225,576	609,857	163,081
Cities outside metropolitan areas	271,108										
Area actually reporting	100.0%	1,661	15	141	108	244	1,261	10,846	2,848	7,146	852
Nonmetropolitan counties	563,557										
Area actually reporting	100.0%	2,009	20	224	172	149	1,616	9,547	3,634	4,554	1,359
State total	38,332,521	154,129	1,746	9,714	7,464	53,640	89,029	1,018,907	232,058	621,557	165,292
Rate per 100,000 inhabitants		402.1	4.6	25.3	19.5	139.9	232.3	2,658.1	605.4	1,621.5	431.2
Colorado[4]											
Metropolitan statistical area	4,578,645										
Area actually reporting	98.3%		154	2,620		3,073	8,995	126,908	22,739	92,275	11,894
Estimated total	100.0%	14,979	156	2,651	1,852	3,085	9,087	128,078	22,972	93,108	11,998
Cities outside metropolitan areas	327,070										
Area actually reporting	93.8%		14	176		53	516	8,486	1,275	6,897	314
Estimated total	100.0%	809	15	187	131	57	550	9,047	1,359	7,353	335
Nonmetropolitan counties	362,652										
Area actually reporting	97.5%		7	94		9	318	2,860	732	1,933	195
Estimated total	100.0%	438	7	96	67	9	326	2,932	750	1,982	200

Table 5. Crime, by State and Area, 2013—*Continued*

(Number, percent, rate per 100,000 population.)

Area	Population	Violent crime[1]	Murder and nonnegligent manslaughter	Rape (revised definition)[2]	Rape (legacy definition)[3]	Robbery	Aggravated assault	Property crime	Burglary	Larceny-theft	Motor vehicle theft
Colorado (cont.)											
State total	5,268,367	16,226	178	2,934	2,050	3,151	9,963	140,057	25,081	102,443	12,533
Rate per 100,000 inhabitants		308.0	3.4	55.7	38.9	59.8	189.1	2,658.5	476.1	1,944.5	237.9
Connecticut[5]											
Metropolitan statistical area	2,942,348										
Area actually reporting	100.0%	8,879	80	842	571	3,456	4,501	64,527	11,328	47,504	5,695
Cities outside metropolitan areas	116,380										
Area actually reporting	100.0%	148	0	31	26	21	96	2,071	297	1,659	115
Nonmetropolitan counties	537,352										
Area actually reporting	100.0%	413	6	82	71	53	272	4,392	1,267	2,713	412
State total	3,596,080	9,440	86	955	668	3,530	4,869	70,990	12,892	51,876	6,222
Rate per 100,000 inhabitants		262.5	2.4	26.6	18.6	98.2	135.4	1,974.1	358.5	1,442.6	173.0
Delaware[4]											
Metropolitan statistical area	925,749										
Area actually reporting	100.0%	4,547	39	379	265	1,226	2,903	28,378	6,131	20,915	1,332
Cities outside metropolitan areas	None										
Area actually reporting	None										
State total	100.0%	2	0	1	1	0	1	1	0	1	0
Rate per 100,000 inhabitants	925,749	4,549	39	380	266	1,226	2,904	28,379	6,131	20,916	1,332
		491.4	4.2	41.0	28.7	132.4	313.7	3,065.5	662.3	2,259.4	143.9
District of Columbia[4,7]											
Metropolitan statistical area	646,449										
Area actually reporting	100.0%	8,406	103	395	276	4,078	3,830	31,083	3,316	24,533	3,234
Cities outside metropolitan areas	None										
Nonmetropolitan counties	None										
District total	646,449	8,406	103	395	276	4,078	3,830	31,083	3,316	24,533	3,234
Rate per 100,000 inhabitants		1,300.3	15.9	61.1	42.7	630.8	592.5	4,808.3	513.0	3,795.0	500.3
Florida[4]											
Metropolitan statistical area	18,847,207										
Area actually reporting	99.9%	88,501	936	6,543	4,572	22,839	58,183	589,069	133,415	421,479	34,175
Estimated total	100.0%										
Cities outside metropolitan areas	147,373		9	53		185	870	6,505	1,529	4,710	266
Area actually reporting	96.5%	1,158	9	55	37	192	902	6,742	1,585	4,881	276
Estimated total	100.0%										
Nonmetropolitan counties	558,280		25	152		159	1,853	10,690	3,685	6,571	434
Area actually reporting	94.1%	2,327	27	162	113	169	1,969	11,361	3,916	6,984	461
State total	100.0%	91,986	972	6,760	4,722	23,200	61,054	607,172	138,916	433,344	34,912
Rate per 100,000 inhabitants	19,552,860	470.4	5.0	34.6	24.1	118.7	312.3	3,105.3	710.5	2,216.3	178.6
Georgia											
Metropolitan statistical area	8,216,901										
Area actually reporting	99.5%		479		1,647	11,456	16,585	279,224	68,360	186,099	24,765
Estimated total	100.0%	30,818	480	2,154	1,655	11,511	16,673	280,934	68,678	187,372	24,884
Cities outside metropolitan areas	662,073										
Area actually reporting	91.9%		36		181	700	2,179	29,435	6,501	22,199	735
Estimated total	100.0%	3,428	39	256	197	762	2,371	32,025	7,073	24,152	800
Nonmetropolitan counties	1,113,193										
Area actually reporting	91.8%		34		121	197	1,717	19,678	5,972	12,658	1,048
Estimated total	100.0%	2,295	37	172	132	215	1,871	21,440	6,507	13,791	1,142
State total	9,992,167	36,541	556	2,582	1,984	12,488	20,915	334,399	82,258	225,315	26,826
Rate per 100,000 inhabitants		365.7	5.6	25.8	19.9	125.0	209.3	3,346.6	823.2	2,254.9	268.5
Hawaii											
Metropolitan statistical area	1,144,335										
Area actually reporting	100.0%	2,849	12	273	210	1,011	1,553	35,149	5,661	26,292	3,196
Cities outside metropolitan areas	None										
Nonmetropolitan counties	259,719										
Area actually reporting	100.0%	684	9	112	86	120	443	7,726	1,872	5,366	488
State total	1,404,054	3,533	21	385	296	1,131	1,996	42,875	7,533	31,658	3,684
Rate per 100,000 inhabitants		251.6	1.5	27.4	21.1	80.6	142.2	3,053.7	536.5	2,254.8	262.4
Idaho[4]											
Metropolitan statistical area	1,066,771										
Area actually reporting	99.9%		13	474		178	1,774	21,382	4,409	15,890	1,083
Estimated total	100.0%	2,440	13	474	331	178	1,775	21,391	4,411	15,897	1,083
Cities outside metropolitan areas	248,535										
Area actually reporting	100.0%	581	6	98	68	30	447	5,413	1,113	4,078	222
Nonmetropolitan counties	296,830										

Table 5. Crime, by State and Area, 2013—*Continued*

(Number, percent, rate per 100,000 population.)

Area	Population	Violent crime[1]	Murder and nonnegligent manslaughter	Rape (revised definition)[2]	Rape (legacy definition)[3]	Robbery	Aggravated assault	Property crime	Burglary	Larceny-theft	Motor vehicle theft
Idaho (cont.)											
Area actually reporting	100.0%	477	8	83	58	12	374	3,251	1,116	1,904	231
State total	1,612,136	3,498	27	655	457	220	2,596	30,055	6,640	21,879	1,536
Rate per 100,000 inhabitants		217.0	1.7	40.6	28.3	13.6	161.0	1,864.3	411.9	1,357.1	95.3
Illinois[5]											
Metropolitan statistical area	11,373,567										
Area actually reporting	96.8%		672		2,786	17,272	23,387	259,745	50,706	189,093	19,946
Estimated total	100.0%	45,763	680	3,737	2,866	17,502	23,844	266,888	51,966	194,673	20,249
Cities outside metropolitan areas	830,759										
Area actually reporting	86.4%		19		277	166	1,582	17,129	3,712	13,021	396
Estimated total	100.0%	2,458	22	412	321	192	1,832	19,834	4,298	15,077	459
Nonmetropolitan counties	677,809										
Area actually reporting	93.7%		4		83	26	569	5,868	1,849	3,808	211
Estimated total	100.0%	753	4	114	89	28	607	6,261	1,973	4,063	225
State total	12,882,135	48,974	706	4,263	3,276	17,722	26,283	292,983	58,237	213,813	20,933
Rate per 100,000 inhabitants		380.2	5.5	33.1	25.4	137.6	204.0	2,274.3	452.1	1,659.8	162.5
Indiana[5]											
Metropolitan statistical area	5,094,468										
Area actually reporting	88.4%		306		1,300	6,762	11,535	149,461	34,748	102,557	12,156
Estimated total	100.0%	21,194	319	1,852	1,387	6,924	12,099	160,115	36,980	110,263	12,872
Cities outside metropolitan areas	520,960										
Area actually reporting	76.8%		10		108	95	646	13,531	2,236	10,679	616
Estimated total	100.0%	1,137	13	159	141	124	841	17,615	2,911	13,902	802
Nonmetropolitan counties	955,474										
Area actually reporting	73.8%		17		87	44	695	7,236	2,227	4,618	391
Estimated total	100.0%	1,156	23	131	118	60	942	9,806	3,018	6,258	530
State total	6,570,902	23,487	355	2,142	1,646	7,108	13,882	187,536	42,909	130,423	14,204
Rate per 100,000 inhabitants		357.4	5.4	32.6	25.0	108.2	211.3	2,854.0	653.0	1,984.9	216.2
Iowa[4]											
Metropolitan statistical area	1,797,551										
Area actually reporting	97.6%		28	714		820	4,025	47,266	10,301	33,836	3,129
Estimated total	100.0%	5,653	28	723	505	822	4,080	47,750	10,428	34,161	3,161
Cities outside metropolitan areas	601,851										
Area actually reporting	91.3%		6	247		97	1,585	14,008	3,258	10,088	662
Estimated total	100.0%	2,119	7	270	189	106	1,736	15,341	3,568	11,048	725
Nonmetropolitan counties	691,014										
Area actually reporting	87.3%		7	79		10	443	4,112	1,635	2,163	314
Estimated total	100.0%	616	8	90	63	11	507	4,709	1,872	2,477	360
State total	3,090,416	8,388	43	1,083	757	939	6,323	67,800	15,868	47,686	4,246
Rate per 100,000 inhabitants		271.4	1.4	35.0	24.5	30.4	204.6	2,193.9	513.5	1,543.0	137.4
Kansas[5]											
Metropolitan statistical area	1,936,336										
Area actually reporting	99.5%		79	781		1,163	4,998	61,168	11,467	44,275	5,426
Estimated total	100.0%	7,039	79	784	533	1,164	5,012	61,380	11,502	44,438	5,440
Cities outside metropolitan areas	619,820										
Area actually reporting	94.7%		15	296		162	1,519	17,803	3,799	13,191	813
Estimated total	100.0%	2,103	16	312	229	171	1,604	18,793	4,010	13,925	858
Nonmetropolitan counties	337,801										
Area actually reporting	96.0%		16	95		14	542	4,903	1,789	2,785	329
Estimated total	100.0%	696	17	99	73	15	565	5,107	1,863	2,901	343
State total	2,893,957	9,838	112	1,195	835	1,350	7,181	85,280	17,375	61,264	6,641
Rate per 100,000 inhabitants		339.9	3.9	41.3	28.9	46.6	248.1	2,946.8	600.4	2,117.0	229.5
Kentucky[5]											
Metropolitan statistical area	2,555,209										
Area actually reporting	99.7%		95	848		2,737	3,130	76,216	17,632	54,088	4,496
Estimated total	100.0%	6,825	95	851	578	2,744	3,135	76,446	17,680	54,258	4,508
Cities outside metropolitan areas	534,280										
Area actually reporting	96.0%		11	169		315	422	14,792	3,046	11,202	544
Estimated total	100.0%	955	11	176	127	328	440	15,417	3,175	11,675	567
Nonmetropolitan counties	1,305,806										
Area actually reporting	97.4%		59	569		169	607	11,681	5,218	5,531	932
Estimated total	100.0%	1,442	61	584	421	174	623	11,994	5,358	5,679	957
State total	4,395,295	9,222	167	1,611	1,126	3,246	4,198	103,857	26,213	71,612	6,032
Rate per 100,000 inhabitants		209.8	3.8	36.7	25.6	73.9	95.5	2,362.9	596.4	1,629.3	137.2

Table 5. Crime, by State and Area, 2013—*Continued*

(Number, percent, rate per 100,000 population.)

Area	Population	Violent crime[1]	Murder and nonnegligent manslaughter	Rape (revised definition)[2]	Rape (legacy definition)[3]	Robbery	Aggravated assault	Property crime	Burglary	Larceny-theft	Motor vehicle theft
Louisiana[5]											
Metropolitan statistical area	3,853,803										
Area actually reporting	98.8%		453		966	5,050	13,112	140,871	35,041	97,724	8,106
Estimated total	100.0%	20,088	456	1,284	976	5,087	13,261	142,744	35,385	99,191	8,168
Cities outside metropolitan areas	278,847										
Area actually reporting	78.2%		19		84	285	1,254	10,742	2,686	7,761	295
Estimated total	100.0%	2,126	24	134	107	364	1,604	13,738	3,435	9,926	377
Nonmetropolitan counties	492,820										
Area actually reporting	94.3%		17		152	91	1,371	8,676	2,228	5,868	580
Estimated total	100.0%	1,770	18	201	161	97	1,454	9,204	2,364	6,225	615
State total	4,625,470	23,984	498	1,619	1,244	5,548	16,319	165,686	41,184	115,342	9,160
Rate per 100,000 inhabitants		518.5	10.8	35.0	26.9	119.9	352.8	3,582.0	890.4	2,493.6	198.0
Maine[5,6]											
Metropolitan statistical area	779,976										
Area actually reporting	100.0%	1,081	13	250	189	270	548	19,044	3,785	14,734	525
Cities outside metropolitan areas	267,901										
Area actually reporting	100.0%	407	3	117	84	50	237	7,590	1,408	5,980	202
Nonmetropolitan counties	280,425										
Area actually reporting	100.0%	230	8	80	71	15	127	3,813	1,290	2,336	187
State total	1,328,302	1,718	24	447	344	335	912	30,447	6,483	23,050	914
Rate per 100,000 inhabitants		129.3	1.8	33.7	25.9	25.2	68.7	2,292.2	488.1	1,735.3	68.8
Maryland											
Metropolitan statistical area	5,775,247										
Area actually reporting	100.0%	27,579	380	1,499	1,152	9,960	15,740	154,451	31,049	110,069	13,333
Cities outside metropolitan areas	53,189										
Area actually reporting	100.0%	278	0	13	10	71	194	1,716	313	1,382	21
Nonmetropolitan counties	100,378										
Area actually reporting	100.0%	232	1	20	15	17	194	1,746	587	1,095	64
State total	5,928,814	28,089	381	1,532	1,177	10,048	16,128	157,913	31,949	112,546	13,418
Rate per 100,000 inhabitants		473.8	6.4	25.8	19.9	169.5	272.0	2,663.5	538.9	1,898.3	226.3
Massachusetts[5]											
Metropolitan statistical area	6,593,377										
Area actually reporting	98.7%		136		2,016	6,609	17,645	133,596	29,863	94,792	8,941
Estimated total	100.0%	27,297	137	2,659	2,042	6,663	17,838	135,157	30,207	95,912	9,038
Cities outside metropolitan areas	91,728										
Area actually reporting	80.8%		0		38	35	214	1,717	425	1,224	68
Estimated total	100.0%	367	0	59	47	43	265	2,126	526	1,516	84
Nonmetropolitan counties	7,719										
Area actually reporting	100.0%	3	0	0	0	0	3	2	2	0	0
State total	6,692,824	27,667	137	2,718	2,089	6,706	18,106	137,285	30,735	97,428	9,122
Rate per 100,000 inhabitants		413.4	2.0	40.6	31.2	100.2	270.5	2,051.2	459.2	1,455.7	136.3
Michigan[4]											
Metropolitan statistical area	8,089,847										
Area actually reporting	99.2%		596	4,962		9,930	24,679	198,626	48,923	126,298	23,405
Estimated total	100.0%	40,367	597	4,995	3,495	9,973	24,802	200,180	49,238	127,412	23,530
Cities outside metropolitan areas	603,348										
Area actually reporting	90.0%		8	492		69	764	12,790	1,884	10,616	290
Estimated total	100.0%	1,481	9	546	375	77	849	14,215	2,094	11,799	322
Nonmetropolitan counties	1,202,427										
Area actually reporting	96.0%		24	1,010		53	1,482	15,307	4,813	9,807	687
Estimated total	100.0%	2,675	25	1,052	736	55	1,543	15,939	5,012	10,212	715
State total	9,895,622	44,523	631	6,593	4,606	10,105	27,194	230,334	56,344	149,423	24,567
Rate per 100,000 inhabitants		449.9	6.4	66.6	46.5	102.1	274.8	2,327.6	569.4	1,510.0	248.3
Minnesota[4]											
Metropolitan statistical area	4,178,564										
Area actually reporting	99.9%		94	1,514		3,576	5,628	108,013	18,230	82,949	6,834
Estimated total	100.0%	10,813	94	1,514	1,060	3,576	5,629	108,031	18,232	82,964	6,835
Cities outside metropolitan areas	490,171										
Area actually reporting	100.0%	1,118	9	245	169	81	783	13,951	1,962	11,404	585
Nonmetropolitan counties	751,645										
Area actually reporting	100.0%	774	11	249	174	17	497	9,213	2,519	6,148	546
State total	5,420,380	12,705	114	2,008	1,403	3,674	6,909	131,195	22,713	100,516	7,966
Rate per 100,000 inhabitants		234.4	2.1	37.0	25.9	67.8	127.5	2,420.4	419.0	1,854.4	147.0

Table 5. Crime, by State and Area, 2013—*Continued*

(Number, percent, rate per 100,000 population.)

Area	Population	Violent crime[1]	Murder and nonnegligent manslaughter	Rape (revised definition)[2]	Rape (legacy definition)[3]	Robbery	Aggravated assault	Property crime	Burglary	Larceny-theft	Motor vehicle theft
Mississippi[5]											
Metropolitan statistical area	1,361,997										
Area actually reporting	83.9%		74		323	1,363	1,895	36,525	10,137	24,041	2,347
Estimated total	100.0%	4,139	77	460	355	1,441	2,161	40,921	11,410	26,910	2,601
Cities outside metropolitan areas	588,107										
Area actually reporting	67.4%		45		134	538	813	17,725	5,031	11,991	703
Estimated total	100.0%	2,336	67	265	204	798	1,206	26,301	7,465	17,793	1,043
Nonmetropolitan counties	1,041,103										
Area actually reporting	48.9%		25		71	83	642	6,981	2,992	3,625	364
Estimated total	100.0%	1,739	51	205	156	170	1,313	14,278	6,120	7,414	744
State total	2,991,207	8,214	195	930	715	2,409	4,680	81,500	24,995	52,117	4,388
Rate per 100,000 inhabitants		274.6	6.5	31.1	23.9	80.5	156.5	2,724.7	835.6	1,742.3	146.7
Missouri[4]											
Metropolitan statistical area	4,486,519										
Area actually reporting	99.9%		310	1,955		5,176	14,317	150,899	30,232	106,390	14,277
Cities outside metropolitan areas	100.0%	21,763	310	1,956	1,367	5,177	14,320	150,957	30,242	106,435	14,280
Area actually reporting	661,762										
Estimated total	99.7%		17	173		256	2,073	25,737	4,319	20,400	1,018
Nonmetropolitan counties	100.0%	2,527	17	174	122	257	2,079	25,816	4,332	20,463	1,021
Area actually reporting	895,890										
Estimated total	100.0%	1,907	44	157	110	50	1,656	12,833	4,291	7,518	1,024
State total	6,044,171	26,197	371	2,287	1,599	5,484	18,055	189,606	38,865	134,416	16,325
Rate per 100,000 inhabitants		433.4	6.1	37.8	26.5	90.7	298.7	3,137.0	643.0	2,223.9	270.1
Montana[4]											
Metropolitan statistical area	359,094										
Area actually reporting	100.0%	924	5	131	94	143	645	12,945	2,164	9,837	944
Cities outside metropolitan areas	211,218										
Area actually reporting	97.5%		12	166		42	612	6,966	923	5,628	415
Estimated total	100.0%	852	12	170	115	43	627	7,141	946	5,770	425
Nonmetropolitan counties	444,853										
Area actually reporting	94.8%		5	103		17	625	5,562	904	4,202	456
Estimated total	100.0%	791	5	109	78	18	659	5,867	954	4,432	481
State total	1,015,165	2,567	22	410	287	204	1,931	25,953	4,064	20,039	1,850
Rate per 100,000 inhabitants		252.9	2.2	40.4	28.3	20.1	190.2	2,556.5	400.3	1,974.0	182.2
Nebraska[5]											
Metropolitan statistical area	1,195,918										
Area actually reporting	99.3%		53	420		992	2,436	36,568	6,499	26,152	3,917
Estimated total	100.0%	3,988	53	503	422	993	2,439	36,681	6,518	26,238	3,925
Cities outside metropolitan areas	341,308										
Area actually reporting	89.5%		1	128		35	388	8,304	1,414	6,567	323
Estimated total	100.0%	706	1	233	143	39	433	9,277	1,580	7,336	361
Nonmetropolitan counties	331,290										
Area actually reporting	78.7%		2	43		6	100	2,408	631	1,638	139
Estimated total	100.0%	203	3	65	51	8	127	3,060	802	2,081	177
State total	1,868,516	4,897	57	801	616	1,040	2,999	49,018	8,900	35,655	4,463
Rate per 100,000 inhabitants		262.1	3.1	42.9	33.0	55.7	160.5	2,623.4	476.3	1,908.2	238.9
Nevada											
Metropolitan statistical area	2,519,173										
Area actually reporting	100.0%	15,824	143	1,290	991	5,124	9,267	73,425	21,274	42,622	9,529
Cities outside metropolitan areas	47,878										
Area actually reporting	100.0%	282	10	49	38	24	199	1,996	577	1,243	176
Nonmetropolitan counties	223,085										
Area actually reporting	97.9%		10	60		34	582	3,678	1,171	2,220	287
Estimated total	100.0%	718	10	79	61	35	594	3,756	1,196	2,267	293
State total	2,790,136	16,824	163	1,418	1,090	5,183	10,060	79,177	23,047	46,132	9,998
Rate per 100,000 inhabitants		603.0	5.8	50.8	39.1	185.8	360.6	2,837.7	826.0	1,653.4	358.3
New Hampshire[4]											
Metropolitan statistical area	827,519										
Area actually reporting	95.2%		13	367		508	921	17,299	2,813	13,915	571
Estimated total	100.0%	1,850	13	378	264	515	944	17,808	2,888	14,333	587
Cities outside metropolitan areas	442,956										
Area actually reporting	87.1%		8	247		117	407	9,076	1,549	7,259	268
Estimated total	100.0%	894	9	284	198	134	467	10,419	1,778	8,333	308
Nonmetropolitan counties	52,984										
Area actually reporting)	4.5%		0	6		0	13	95	27	66	2
Estimated total	100.0%	105	0	24	17	0	81	813	270	498	45

Table 5. Crime, by State and Area, 2013—*Continued*

(Number, percent, rate per 100,000 population.)

Area	Population	Violent crime[1]	Murder and nonnegligent manslaughter	Rape (revised definition)[2]	Rape (legacy definition)[3]	Robbery	Aggravated assault	Property crime	Burglary	Larceny-theft	Motor vehicle theft
New Hampshire (cont.)											
State total	1,323,459	2,849	22	686	479	649	1,492	29,040	4,936	23,164	940
Rate per 100,000 inhabitants		215.3	1.7	51.8	36.2	49.0	112.7	2,194.3	373.0	1,750.3	71.0
New Jersey											
Metropolitan statistical area	8,899,339										
Area actually reporting	99.7%		400		859	12,059	12,045	167,097	35,779	117,601	13,717
Estimated total	100.0%	25,674	401	1,120	861	12,082	12,071	167,556	35,873	117,936	13,747
Cities outside metropolitan areas	None										
Nonmetropolitan counties	None										
State total	8,899,339	25,674	401	1,120	861	12,082	12,071	167,556	35,873	117,936	13,747
Rate per 100,000 inhabitants		288.5	4.5	12.6	9.7	135.8	135.6	1,882.8	403.1	1,325.2	154.5
New Mexico											
Metropolitan statistical area	1,391,773										
Area actually reporting	93.1%	8,686	69	999	768	1,507	6,111	54,149	14,610	35,010	4,529
Estimated total	100.0%										
Cities outside metropolitan areas	396,083		31		270	251	2,501	17,830	4,508	12,401	921
Area actually reporting	99.0%	3,167	31	355	273	254	2,527	18,012	4,554	12,528	930
Estimated total	100.0%										
Nonmetropolitan counties	297,431		19		64	37	560	3,837	1,741	1,760	336
Area actually reporting	75.3%	929	25	111	85	49	744	5,095	2,312	2,337	446
Estimated total	100.0%	12,782	125	1,465	1,126	1,810	9,382	77,256	21,476	49,875	5,905
State total	2,085,287	613.0	6.0	70.3	54.0	86.8	449.9	3,704.8	1,029.9	2,391.8	283.2
New York											
Metropolitan statistical area	18,238,153										
Area actually reporting	99.4%		626		2,296	26,913	44,671	330,555	50,561	265,122	14,872
Estimated total	100.0%	75,338	627	2,998	2,304	26,959	44,754	332,107	50,808	266,372	14,927
Cities outside metropolitan areas	519,791										
Area actually reporting	95.7%		3		116	209	731	14,041	2,431	11,385	225
Estimated total	100.0%	1,141	3	157	121	218	763	14,665	2,539	11,891	235
Nonmetropolitan counties	893,183										
Area actually reporting	100.0%	893	18	198	152	64	613	11,826	3,095	8,411	320
State total	19,651,127	77,372	648	3,353	2,577	27,241	46,130	358,598	56,442	286,674	15,482
Rate per 100,000 inhabitants		393.7	3.3	17.1	13.1	138.6	234.7	1,824.8	287.2	1,458.8	78.8
North Carolina											
Metropolitan statistical area	7,627,844										
Area actually reporting	98.8%		352		1,403	7,776	16,254	235,075	65,304	158,115	11,656
Estimated total	100.0%	26,427	353	1,841	1,415	7,830	16,403	237,873	65,970	160,141	11,762
Cities outside metropolitan areas	645,472										
Area actually reporting	92.6%		51		173	937	2,529	32,546	8,423	23,035	1,088
Estimated total	100.0%	4,042	55	243	187	1,012	2,732	35,163	9,100	24,888	1,175
Nonmetropolitan counties	1,574,744										
Area actually reporting	94.6%		58		207	480	2,250	33,123	14,788	16,756	1,579
Estimated total	100.0%	3,231	61	285	219	507	2,378	35,013	15,632	17,712	1,669
State total	9,848,060	33,700	469	2,369	1,821	9,349	21,513	308,049	90,702	202,741	14,606
Rate per 100,000 inhabitants		342.2	4.8	24.1	18.5	94.9	218.4	3,128.0	921.0	2,058.7	148.3
North Dakota[4]											
Metropolitan statistical area	354,758										
Area actually reporting	100.0%	1,177	7	198	142	110	862	8,402	1,699	6,182	521
Cities outside metropolitan areas	169,949										
Area actually reporting	98.6%		6	108		46	434	4,834	777	3,445	612
Estimated total	100.0%	602	6	109	72	47	440	4,904	788	3,495	621
Nonmetropolitan counties	198,686										
Area actually reporting	99.3%		3	23		5	143	1,829	444	1,113	272
Estimated total	100.0%	175	3	23	16	5	144	1,842	447	1,121	274
State total	723,393	1,954	16	330	230	162	1,446	15,148	2,934	10,798	1,416
Rate per 100,000 inhabitants		270.1	2.2	45.6	31.8	22.4	199.9	2,094.0	405.6	1,492.7	195.7
Ohio[5]											
Metropolitan statistical area	9,189,827										
Area actually reporting	93.0%		409	2,727		13,349	12,184	267,063	74,511	175,070	17,482
Estimated total	100.0%	30,094	418	3,411	2,377	13,695	12,570	283,543	77,792	187,702	18,049
Cities outside metropolitan areas	1,047,030										
Area actually reporting	83.9%		9	246		446	712	30,023	6,226	23,211	586
Estimated total	100.0%	1,729	11	339	239	531	848	35,766	7,417	27,651	698

Table 5. Crime, by State and Area, 2013—*Continued*

(Number, percent, rate per 100,000 population.)

Area	Population	Violent crime[1]	Murder and nonnegligent manslaughter	Rape (revised definition)[2]	Rape (legacy definition)[3]	Robbery	Aggravated assault	Property crime	Burglary	Larceny-theft	Motor vehicle theft
Ohio (cont.)											
Nonmetropolitan counties	1,333,951										
Area actually reporting	91.8%		24	250		130	770	17,831	5,714	11,396	721
Estimated total	100.0%	1,298	26	291	208	142	839	19,422	6,224	12,413	785
State total	11,570,808	33,121	455	4,041	2,824	14,368	14,257	338,731	91,433	227,766	19,532
Rate per 100,000 inhabitants		286.2	3.9	34.9	24.4	124.2	123.2	2,927.5	790.2	1,968.5	168.8
Oklahoma[5]											
Metropolitan statistical area	2,500,215										
Area actually reporting	100.0%	13,006	156	1,653	1,293	2,700	8,497	90,943	23,527	58,338	9,078
Cities outside metropolitan areas	723,295										
Area actually reporting	100.0%	3,166	21	407	304	292	2,446	27,502	7,002	19,046	1,454
Nonmetropolitan counties	627,058										
Area actually reporting	100.0%	817	18	120	78	39	640	7,612	2,819	4,111	682
State total	3,850,568	16,989	195	2,180	1,675	3,031	11,583	126,057	33,348	81,495	11,214
Rate per 100,000 inhabitants		441.2	5.1	56.6	43.5	78.7	300.8	3,273.7	866.1	2,116.4	291.2
Oregon[5]											
Metropolitan statistical area	3,277,203										
Area actually reporting	99.6%		58		1,197	2,234	4,674	106,257	16,988	80,581	8,688
Estimated total	100.0%	8,537	58	1,548	1,201	2,242	4,689	106,671	17,050	80,905	8,716
Cities outside metropolitan areas	303,728										
Area actually reporting	97.3%		7		159	122	564	12,331	2,127	9,543	661
Estimated total	100.0%	929	7	217	163	125	580	12,678	2,187	9,811	680
Nonmetropolitan counties	349,134										
Area actually reporting	97.0%		15		93	29	331	5,227	1,486	3,289	452
Estimated total	100.0%	518	15	132	95	30	341	5,388	1,532	3,390	466
State total	3,930,065	9,984	80	1,897	1,459	2,397	5,610	124,737	20,769	94,106	9,862
Rate per 100,000 inhabitants		254.0	2.0	48.3	37.1	61.0	142.7	3,173.9	528.5	2,394.5	250.9
Pennsylvania[4,6]											
Metropolitan statistical area	11,277,147										
Area actually reporting	99.4%		553	3,308		14,464	21,664	239,427	46,396	180,021	13,010
Estimated total	100.0%	40,106	553	3,317	2,318	14,496	21,740	240,562	46,574	180,941	13,047
Cities outside metropolitan areas	682,385										
Area actually reporting	97.3%		6	121		168	1,339	11,751	2,091	9,383	277
Estimated total	100.0%	1,679	6	124	87	173	1,376	12,075	2,149	9,641	285
Nonmetropolitan counties	814,269										
Area actually reporting	100.0%	1,064	35	333	233	93	603	10,603	3,311	6,854	438
State total	12,773,801	42,849	594	3,774	2,638	14,762	23,719	263,240	52,034	197,436	13,770
Rate per 100,000 inhabitants		335.4	4.7	29.5	20.7	115.6	185.7	2,060.8	407.3	1,545.6	107.8
Puerto Rico											
Metropolitan statistical area	3,459,216										
Area actually reporting	100.0%	8,986	845	33	25	5,889	2,219	46,957	13,267	28,257	5,433
Cities outside metropolitan areas	155,870										
Area actually reporting	100.0%	342	38	1	1	127	176	1,894	694	1,103	97
Total	3,615,086	9,328	883	34	26	6,016	2,395	48,851	13,961	29,360	5,530
Rate per 100,000 inhabitants		258.0	24.4	0.9	0.7	166.4	66.3	1,351.3	386.2	812.2	153.0
Rhode Island[4]											
Metropolitan statistical area	1,051,511										
Area actually reporting	100.0%	2,678	31	425	297	684	1,538	25,622	5,606	17,809	2,207
Cities outside metropolitan areas	None										
Nonmetropolitan counties	None										
Area actually reporting	100.0%	27	0	15	10	0	12	56	1	29	26
State total	1,051,511	2,705	31	440	307	684	1,550	25,678	5,607	17,838	2,233
Rate per 100,000 inhabitants		257.2	2.9	41.8	29.2	65.0	147.4	2,442.0	533.2	1,696.4	212.4
South Carolina[4]											
Metropolitan statistical area	4,017,846										
Area actually reporting	99.7%		209	1,795		3,440	14,455	144,541	32,985	100,739	10,817
Estimated total	100.0%	19,941	209	1,797	1,256	3,447	14,488	144,952	33,057	101,059	10,836
Cities outside metropolitan areas	208,133										
Area actually reporting	97.8%		37	151		323	1,400	11,953	2,796	8,710	447
Estimated total	100.0%	1,954	38	154	108	330	1,432	12,223	2,859	8,907	457
Nonmetropolitan counties	548,860										
Area actually reporting	100.0%	2,383	50	220	154	195	1,918	15,874	5,042	9,545	1,287
State total	4,774,839	24,278	297	2,171	1,518	3,972	17,838	173,049	40,958	119,511	12,580
Rate per 100,000 inhabitants		508.5	6.2	45.5	31.8	83.2	373.6	3,624.2	857.8	2,502.9	263.5

Table 5. Crime, by State and Area, 2013—*Continued*

(Number, percent, rate per 100,000 population.)

Area	Population	Violent crime[1]	Murder and nonnegligent manslaughter	Rape (revised definition)[2]	Rape (legacy definition)[3]	Robbery	Aggravated assault	Property crime	Burglary	Larceny-theft	Motor vehicle theft
South Dakota[4]											
Metropolitan statistical area	397,651										
Area actually reporting	99.3%		5	267		119	838	9,269	1,971	6,789	509
Estimated total	100.0%	1,232	5	268	194	119	840	9,304	1,979	6,814	511
Cities outside metropolitan areas	216,179										
Area actually reporting	95.8%		7	195		29	977	5,395	1,005	4,060	330
Estimated total	100.0%	1,260	7	203	135	30	1,020	5,633	1,049	4,239	345
Nonmetropolitan counties	231,047										
Area actually reporting	78.0%		6	22		8	106	967	268	635	64
Estimated total	100.0%	182	8	28	20	10	136	1,240	344	814	82
State total	844,877	2,674	20	499	349	159	1,996	16,177	3,372	11,867	938
Rate per 100,000 inhabitants		316.5	2.4	59.1	41.3	18.8	236.2	1,914.7	399.1	1,404.6	111.0
Tennessee[4]											
Metropolitan statistical area	5,003,806										
Area actually reporting	99.4%		274	1,989		6,854	23,330	166,628	39,978	117,086	9,564
Estimated total	100.0%	32,551	275	1,997	1,395	6,867	23,412	167,463	40,121	117,744	9,598
Cities outside metropolitan areas	514,169										
Area actually reporting	100.0%	3,154	17	189	132	331	2,617	22,248	4,697	16,671	880
Nonmetropolitan counties	978,003										
Area actually reporting	100.0%	2,659	36	165	115	109	2,349	16,918	6,181	9,387	1,350
State total	6,495,978	38,364	328	2,351	1,642	7,307	28,378	206,629	50,999	143,802	11,828
Rate per 100,000 inhabitants		590.6	5.0	36.2	25.3	112.5	436.9	3,180.9	785.1	2,213.7	182.1
Texas[5]											
Metropolitan statistical area	23,409,495										
Area actually reporting	99.9%		1,037		6,616	31,004	58,295	789,124	169,961	556,848	62,315
Estimated total	100.0%	99,065	1,037	8,669	6,624	31,020	58,339	789,928	170,112	557,452	62,364
Cities outside metropolitan areas	1,415,777										
Area actually reporting	97.5%		50		521	625	4,394	46,171	11,056	33,426	1,689
Estimated total	100.0%	5,852	51	663	534	637	4,501	47,274	11,325	34,222	1,727
Nonmetropolitan counties	1,622,921										
Area actually reporting	98.1%		50		339	141	2,406	24,073	9,284	13,166	1,623
Estimated total	100.0%	3,081	51	434	346	144	2,452	24,532	9,461	13,417	1,654
State total	26,448,193	107,998	1,139	9,766	7,504	31,801	65,292	861,734	190,898	605,091	65,745
Rate per 100,000 inhabitants		408.3	4.3	36.9	28.4	120.2	246.9	3,258.2	721.8	2,287.8	248.6
Utah[5]											
Metropolitan statistical area	2,588,821										
Area actually reporting	99.8%		37	1,242		1,213	3,270	79,055	12,209	59,737	7,109
Estimated total	100.0%	5,772	37	1,244	879	1,215	3,276	79,240	12,237	59,879	7,124
Cities outside metropolitan areas	136,929										
Area actually reporting	95.8%		4	128		9	229	3,537	544	2,837	156
Estimated total	100.0%	385	4	133	86	9	239	3,693	568	2,962	163
Nonmetropolitan counties	175,122										
Area actually reporting	97.1%		8	44		18	261	2,576	513	1,890	173
Estimated total	100.0%	341	8	45	29	19	269	2,653	528	1,947	178
State total	2,900,872	6,498	49	1,422	994	1,243	3,784	85,586	13,333	64,788	7,465
Rate per 100,000 inhabitants		224.0	1.7	49.0	34.3	42.8	130.4	2,950.4	459.6	2,233.4	257.3
Vermont[4]											
Metropolitan statistical area	214,620										
Area actually reporting	100.0%	257	3	40	28	31	183	5,389	961	4,351	77
Cities outside metropolitan areas	206,762										
Area actually reporting	99.9%		1	49		29	255	5,405	1,099	4,154	152
Nonmetropolitan counties	100.0%	334	1	49	34	29	255	5,411	1,100	4,159	152
Area actually reporting	205,248										
Estimated total	100.0%	168	6	41	29	13	108	3,075	1,252	1,718	105
State total	626,630	759	10	130	91	73	546	13,875	3,313	10,228	334
Rate per 100,000 inhabitants		121.1	1.6	20.7	14.5	11.6	87.1	2,214.2	528.7	1,632.2	53.3
Virginia[4]											
Metropolitan statistical area	7,195,364										
Area actually reporting	99.9%		271	1,887		4,311	7,979	151,579	22,448	121,447	7,684
Estimated total	100.0%	14,453	271	1,888	1,319	4,312	7,982	151,640	22,456	121,497	7,687
Cities outside metropolitan areas	264,175										
Area actually reporting	100.0%	653	9	107	75	153	384	8,260	1,354	6,645	261
Nonmetropolitan counties	800,866										
Area actually reporting	100.0%	1,099	36	267	187	100	696	10,754	2,830	7,336	588
State total	8,260,405	16,205	316	2,262	1,581	4,565	9,062	170,654	26,640	135,478	8,536
Rate per 100,000 inhabitants		196.2	3.8	27.4	19.1	55.3	109.7	2,065.9	322.5	1,640.1	103.3

Table 5. Crime, by State and Area, 2013—*Continued*

(Number, percent, rate per 100,000 population.)

Area	Population	Violent crime[1]	Murder and nonnegligent manslaughter	Rape (revised definition)[2]	Rape (legacy definition)[3]	Robbery	Aggravated assault	Property crime	Burglary	Larceny-theft	Motor vehicle theft
Washington[5,6]											
Metropolitan statistical area	6,256,806										
Area actually reporting	100.0%	18,654	139	2,322	1,611	5,615	10,578	237,420	52,137	158,431	26,852
Cities outside metropolitan areas	294,834										
Area actually reporting	98.6%		10	146		164	606	13,153	3,166	9,051	936
Estimated total	100.0%	939	10	148	109	166	615	13,345	3,212	9,183	950
Nonmetropolitan counties	419,766										
Area actually reporting	100.0%	560	11	103	77	38	408	7,897	3,004	4,296	597
State total	6,971,406	20,153	160	2,573	1,797	5,819	11,601	258,662	58,353	171,910	28,399
Rate per 100,000 inhabitants		289.1	2.3	36.9	25.8	83.5	166.4	3,710.3	837.0	2,465.9	407.4
West Virginia[4]											
Metropolitan statistical area	1,139,033										
Area actually reporting	92.2%		28	438		513	2,350	26,541	6,620	18,624	1,297
Estimated total	100.0%	3,578	29	465	325	549	2,535	28,758	7,042	20,327	1,389
Cities outside metropolitan areas	190,615										
Area actually reporting	71.0%		5	44		39	384	3,272	661	2,515	96
Estimated total	100.0%	665	7	62	43	55	541	4,609	931	3,543	135
Nonmetropolitan counties	524,656										
Area actually reporting	88.2%		22	111		41	994	4,979	1,500	3,133	346
Estimated total	100.0%	1,325	25	126	88	47	1,127	5,646	1,701	3,553	392
State total	1,854,304	5,568	61	653	456	651	4,203	39,013	9,674	27,423	1,916
Rate per 100,000 inhabitants		300.3	3.3	35.2	24.6	35.1	226.7	2,103.9	521.7	1,478.9	103.3
Wisconsin[5,6]											
Metropolitan statistical area	4,236,498										
Area actually reporting	98.1%		143		938	4,706	7,825	99,613	19,037	74,026	6,550
Estimated total	100.0%	14,019	143	1,278	949	4,725	7,873	101,016	19,245	75,179	6,592
Cities outside metropolitan areas	633,490										
Area actually reporting	97.0%		8		209	78	843	15,510	2,043	13,132	335
Estimated total	100.0%	1,204	8	247	216	80	869	15,991	2,106	13,540	345
Nonmetropolitan counties	872,725										
Area actually reporting	98.8%		11		129	29	529	8,574	2,959	5,170	445
Estimated total	100.0%	738	11	162	131	29	536	8,681	2,996	5,234	451
State total	5,742,713	15,961	162	1,687	1,296	4,834	9,278	125,688	24,347	93,953	7,388
Rate per 100,000 inhabitants		277.9	2.8	29.4	22.6	84.2	161.6	2,188.7	424.0	1,636.0	128.6
Wyoming											
Metropolitan statistical area	175,628										
Area actually reporting	100.0%	376	4	40	31	30	302	4,993	818	3,948	227
Cities outside metropolitan areas	244,239										
Area actually reporting	97.1%		4		80	42	452	6,179	823	5,102	254
Estimated total	100.0%	619	4	107	82	43	465	6,363	847	5,254	262
Nonmetropolitan counties	162,791										
Area actually reporting	92.6%		8		29	2	138	1,346	269	995	82
Estimated total	100.0%	200	9	40	31	2	149	1,453	290	1,074	89
State total	582,658	1,195	17	187	144	75	916	12,809	1,955	10,276	578
Rate per 100,000 inhabitants		205.1	2.9	32.1	24.7	12.9	157.2	2,198.4	335.5	1,763.6	99.2

Note: Although arson data are included in the trend and clearance tables, sufficient data are not available to estimate totals for this offense. Therefore, no arson data are published in this table.
[1]The violent crime figures include the offenses of murder, rape (revised definition), robbery, and aggravated assault.
[2]The figures shown in this column for the offense of rape were estimated using the revised Uniform Crime Reporting (UCR) definition of rape. See chapter notes for more detail.
[3]The figures shown in this column for the offense of rape were estimated using the legacy Uniform Crime Reporting (UCR) definition of rape. See chapter notes for more detail.
[4]This state's agencies submitted rape data according to the revised UCR definition of rape.
[5]Agencies within this state submitted rape data according to both the revised UCR definition of rape and the legacy UCR definition of rape.
[6]Because of changes in the state/local agency's reporting practices, figures are not comparable to previous years' data.
[7]Includes offenses reported by the Zoological Police and the Metro Transit Police.

Table 6. Crime, by Selected Metropolitan Statistical Area, 2013

(Number, percent, rate per 100,000 population.)

Area	Population	Violent crime	Murder and nonnegligent manslaughter	Rape[1]	Robbery	Aggravated assault	Property crime	Burglary	Larceny-theft	Motor vehicle theft
Abilene, TX, MSA......................	168,117									
Includes Callahan, Jones, and Taylor Counties										
City of Abilene	119,401	477	1	37	125	314	4,769	1,055	3,460	254
Total area actually reporting	100.0%	560	1	43	128	388	5,522	1,323	3,907	292
Rate per 100,000 inhabitants		333.1	0.6	25.6	76.1	230.8	3,284.6	787.0	2,324.0	173.7
Akron, OH, MSA...........................	703,468									
Includes Portage and Summit Counties										
City of Akron	198,405	1,570	23	160	528	859	9,649	3,096	5,922	631
Total area actually reporting	91.0%	2,003	35	256	660	1,052	18,915	4,798	13,252	865
Estimated total	100.0%	2,091	36	270	695	1,090	20,563	5,122	14,520	921
Rate per 100,000 inhabitants		297.2	5.1	38.4	98.8	154.9	2,923.1	728.1	2,064.1	130.9
Albany, GA, MSA...........................	157,365									
Includes Baker, Dougherty, Lee, Terrell, and Worth Counties										
City of Albany	77,365	749	8	21	183	537	4,661	1,319	3,169	173
Total area actually reporting	96.0%	1,010	9	36	215	750	6,896	1,963	4,658	275
Estimated total	100.0%	1,031	9	37	223	762	7,115	2,010	4,813	292
Rate per 100,000 inhabitants		655.2	5.7	23.5	141.7	484.2	4,521.3	1,277.3	3,058.5	185.6
Albany, OR, MSA...........................	119,155									
Includes Linn County										
City of Albany	51,645	40	0	8	27	5	2,019	252	1,625	142
Total area actually reporting	100.0%	97	1	18	45	33	4,018	750	2,976	292
Rate per 100,000 inhabitants		81.4	0.8	15.1	37.8	27.7	3,372.1	629.4	2,497.6	245.1
Albany-Schenectady-Troy, NY, MSA......................	876,869									
Includes Albany, Rensselaer, Saratoga, Schenectady, and Schoharie Counties										
City of Albany	97,956	791	8	30	227	526	4,090	705	3,243	142
City of Schenectady	66,041	607	8	31	203	365	2,800	769	1,878	153
City of Troy	49,898	371	1	14	145	211	1,985	593	1,305	87
Total area actually reporting	100.0%	2,338	24	131	716	1,467	20,175	3,738	15,787	650
Rate per 100,000 inhabitants		266.6	2.7	14.9	81.7	167.3	2,300.8	426.3	1,800.4	74.1
Albuquerque, NM, MSA......................	902,627									
Includes Bernalillo, Sandoval, Torrance, and Valencia Counties										
City of Albuquerque	558,165	4,325	37	439	1,046	2,803	30,531	7,297	20,229	3,005
Total area actually reporting	89.8%	5,927	50	527	1,183	4,167	36,830	9,466	23,767	3,597
Estimated total	100.0%	6,700	53	573	1,239	4,835	40,471	10,350	26,272	3,849
Rate per 100,000 inhabitants		742.3	5.9	63.5	137.3	535.7	4,483.7	1,146.7	2,910.6	426.4
Alexandria, LA, MSA...........................	154,678									
Includes Grant and Rapides Parishes										
City of Alexandria	48,488	803	6	11	156	630	3,880	1,130	2,561	189
Total area actually reporting	94.5%	1,189	11	46	181	951	7,029	1,967	4,642	420
Estimated total	100.0%	1,228	12	48	188	980	7,387	2,033	4,922	432
Rate per 100,000 inhabitants		793.9	7.8	31.0	121.5	633.6	4,775.7	1,314.3	3,182.1	279.3
Allentown-Bethlehem-Easton, PA-NJ, MSA...........	828,654									
Includes Warren County, NJ and Carbon, Lehigh, and Northampton Counties, PA										
City of Allentown, PA	119,277	628	12	64	329	223	4,324	1,263	2,724	337
City of Bethlehem, PA	75,135	183	4	27	74	78	2,010	365	1,601	44
Total area actually reporting	99.9%	1,536	24	170	540	802	18,173	3,723	13,649	801
Estimated total	100.0%	1,536	24	170	540	802	18,180	3,724	13,655	801
Rate per 100,000 inhabitants		185.4	2.9	20.5	65.2	96.8	2,193.9	449.4	1,647.9	96.7
Altoona, PA, MSA...........................	127,076									
Includes Blair County										
City of Altoona	46,103	131	2	25	29	75	1,035	259	733	43
Total area actually reporting	99.0%	268	2	36	33	197	2,146	393	1,680	73
Estimated total	100.0%	271	2	36	34	199	2,168	396	1,698	74
Rate per 100,000 inhabitants		213.3	1.6	28.3	26.8	156.6	1,706.1	311.6	1,336.2	58.2
Amarillo, TX, MSA...........................	260,305									
Includes Armstrong, Carson, Oldham, Potter, and Randall Counties										
City of Amarillo	196,577	1,286	9	214	242	821	8,154	1,816	5,643	695

Table 6. Crime, by Selected Metropolitan Statistical Area, 2013—*Continued*

(Number, percent, rate per 100,000 population.)

Area	Population	Violent crime	Murder and nonnegligent manslaughter	Rape[1]	Robbery	Aggravated assault	Property crime	Burglary	Larceny-theft	Motor vehicle theft
Amarillo, TX, MSA (cont.)										
Total area actually reporting	100.0%	1,365	9	221	250	885	8,919	1,998	6,178	743
Rate per 100,000 inhabitants		524.4	3.5	84.9	96.0	340.0	3,426.4	767.6	2,373.4	285.4
Ames, IA, MSA..	91,897									
Includes Story County										
City of Ames	61,193	88	0	34	11	43	1,439	224	1,181	34
Total area actually reporting	92.7%	127	0	46	14	67	1,832	310	1,470	52
Estimated total	100.0%	140	0	48	15	77	1,949	331	1,561	57
Rate per 100,000 inhabitants		152.3	0.0	52.2	16.3	83.8	2,120.9	360.2	1,698.6	62.0
Anchorage, AK, MSA	314,553									
Includes Anchorage Municipality and Matanuska-Susitna Borough										
City of Anchorage	299,455	2,435	14	408	522	1,491	12,032	1,318	9,845	869
Total area actually reporting	100.0%	2,497	15	419	528	1,535	13,047	1,398	10,722	927
Rate per 100,000 inhabitants		793.8	4.8	133.2	167.9	488.0	4,147.8	444.4	3,408.6	294.7
Ann Arbor, MI, MSA..	353,189									
Includes Washtenaw County										
City of Ann Arbor	116,799	247	3	48	49	147	2,525	410	2,021	94
Total area actually reporting	100.0%	1,079	11	187	161	720	7,409	1,508	5,525	376
Rate per 100,000 inhabitants		305.5	3.1	52.9	45.6	203.9	2,097.7	427.0	1,564.3	106.5
Anniston-Oxford-Jacksonville, AL, MSA	116,893									
Includes Calhoun County										
City of Anniston	22,648	461	5	39	78	339	1,988	770	1,120	98
City of Oxford	17,121	50	2	6	6	36	910	166	704	40
City of Jacksonville	12,385	35	0	3	10	22	589	137	439	13
Total area actually reporting	100.0%	622	8	64	103	447	4,369	1,366	2,814	189
Rate per 100,000 inhabitants		532.1	6.8	54.8	88.1	382.4	3,737.6	1,168.6	2,407.3	161.7
Appleton, WI, MSA	229,465									
Includes Calumet and Outagamie Counties										
City of Appleton	73,141	176	1	28	14	133	1,304	186	1,088	30
Total area actually reporting	100.0%	285	1	38	19	227	3,178	459	2,651	68
Rate per 100,000 inhabitants		124.2	0.4	16.6	8.3	98.9	1,385.0	200.0	1,155.3	29.6
Athens-Clarke County, GA, MSA.............................	197,437									
Includes Clarke, Madison, Oconee, and Oglethorpe Counties										
City of Athens-Clarke County	120,122	404	2	37	125	240	4,074	967	2,912	195
Total area actually reporting	99.4%	534	2	52	133	347	6,035	1,376	4,388	271
Estimated total	100.0%	537	2	52	134	349	6,080	1,384	4,422	274
Rate per 100,000 inhabitants		272.0	1.0	26.3	67.9	176.8	3,079.5	701.0	2,239.7	138.8
Atlanta-Sandy Springs-Roswell, GA, MSA	5,511,212									
Includes Barrow, Bartow, Butts, Carroll, Cherokee, Clayton, Cobb, Coweta, Dawson, DeKalb, Douglas, Fayette, Forsyth, Fulton, Gwinnett, Haralson, Heard, Henry, Jasper, Lamar, Meriwether, Morgan, Newton, Paulding, Pickens, Pike, Rockdale, Spalding, and Walton Counties										
City of Atlanta	451,020	5,517	84	105	2,363	2,965	27,528	5,938	17,158	4,432
City of Sandy Springs	101,180	186	6	14	105	61	2,739	526	2,063	150
City of Roswell	95,373	144	1	17	72	54	2,107	476	1,556	75
City of Alpharetta	63,442	47	2	2	23	20	1,228	128	1,074	26
Cit of Marietta	58,893	450	5	12	127	306	2,499	457	1,861	181
Total area actually reporting	99.8%	21,396	323	1,074	8,697	11,302	183,047	44,496	119,994	18,557
Estimated total	100.0%	21,444	324	1,077	8,714	11,329	183,570	44,591	120,386	18,593
Rate per 100,000 inhabitants		389.1	5.9	19.5	158.1	205.6	3,330.8	809.1	2,184.4	337.4
Atlantic City-Hammonton, NJ, MSA	276,095									
Includes Atlantic County										
City of Atlantic City	39,482	685	3	9	367	306	2,475	393	2,011	71
City of Hammonton	14,737	8	0	0	1	7	151	47	95	9
Total area actually reporting	100.0%	1,225	8	38	520	659	8,199	1,741	6,226	232
Rate per 100,000 inhabitants		443.7	2.9	13.8	188.3	238.7	2,969.6	630.6	2,255.0	84.0
Augusta-Richmond County, GA-SC, MSA...............	579,933									
Includes Burke, Columbia, Lincoln, McDuffie, and Richmond Counties, GA and Aiken and Edgefield Counties, SC										
Total area actually reporting	98.1%	1,632	32	169	597	834	20,805	5,097	14,032	1,676

Table 6. Crime, by Selected Metropolitan Statistical Area, 2013—*Continued*

(Number, percent, rate per 100,000 population.)

Area	Population	Violent crime	Murder and nonnegligent manslaughter	Rape[1]	Robbery	Aggravated assault	Property crime	Burglary	Larceny-theft	Motor vehicle theft
Augusta-Richmond County, GA-SC, MSA (cont.)										
Estimated total	100.0%	1,672	32	171	612	857	21,255	5,179	14,369	1,707
Rate per 100,000 inhabitants		288.3	5.5	29.5	105.5	147.8	3,665.1	893.0	2,477.7	294.3
Austin-Round Rock, TX, MSA	1,879,235									
Includes Bastrop, Caldwell, Hays, Travis, and Williamson Counties										
City of Austin	859,180	3,123	26	217	763	2,117	41,667	6,550	32,948	2,169
City of Round Rock	108,577	149	2	24	37	86	2,428	297	2,086	45
Total area actually reporting	99.8%	5,091	52	436	999	3,604	59,633	10,017	46,639	2,977
Estimated total	100.0%	5,099	52	437	1,001	3,609	59,731	10,035	46,713	2,983
Rate per 100,000 inhabitants		271.3	2.8	23.3	53.3	192.0	3,178.5	534.0	2,485.7	158.7
Bakersfield, CA, MSA	862,202									
Includes Kern County										
City of Bakersfield	361,859	1,857	24	43	708	1,082	16,814	4,605	9,272	2,937
Total area actually reporting	100.0%	4,969	61	171	1,285	3,452	33,381	10,728	16,851	5,802
Rate per 100,000 inhabitants		576.3	7.1	19.8	149.0	400.4	3,871.6	1,244.3	1,954.4	672.9
Baltimore-Columbia-Towson, MD, MSA	2,771,247									
Includes Anne Arundel, Baltimore, Carroll, Harford, Howard, and Queen Anne's Counties and Baltimore City										
City of Baltimore	622,671	8,725	233	298	3,734	4,460	30,789	7,391	18,946	4,452
Total area actually reporting	100.0%	17,552	278	647	6,303	10,324	83,474	16,662	59,726	7,086
Rate per 100,000 inhabitants		633.4	10.0	23.3	227.4	372.5	3,012.1	601.2	2,155.2	255.7
Bangor, ME, MSA	153,530									
Includes Penobscot County										
City of Bangor	32,744	70	3	10	35	22	1,844	243	1,564	37
Total area actually reporting	100.0%	140	6	23	56	55	4,339	812	3,439	88
Rate per 100,000 inhabitants		91.2	3.9	15.0	36.5	35.8	2,826.2	528.9	2,240.0	57.3
Barnstable Town, MA, MSA	215,847									
Includes Barnstable County										
City of Barnstable	44,837	302	0	18	30	254	1,191	289	835	67
Total area actually reporting	100.0%	941	2	89	78	772	5,203	1,785	3,219	199
Rate per 100,000 inhabitants		436.0	0.9	41.2	36.1	357.7	2,410.5	827.0	1,491.3	92.2
Baton Rouge, LA, MSA[2]	819,681									
Includes Ascension2, East Baton Rouge, East Feliciana, Iberville, Livingston, Pointe Coupee, St. Helena, West Baton Rouge, and West Feliciana2 Parishes										
City of Baton Rouge	230,212	2,127	49	74	974	1,030	11,418	3,264	7,648	506
Total area actually reporting	98.6%	4,120	83	177	1,378	2,482	30,660	7,831	21,810	1,019
Estimated total	100.0%	4,173	84	180	1,388	2,521	31,150	7,921	22,194	1,035
Rate per 100,000 inhabitants		509.1	10.2	22.0	169.3	307.6	3,800.3	966.4	2,707.6	126.3
Bay City, MI, MSA	106,781									
Includes Bay County										
City of Bay City	34,395	217	0	62	21	134	938	210	674	54
Total area actually reporting	100.0%	316	2	119	29	166	2,252	502	1,636	114
Rate per 100,000 inhabitants		295.9	1.9	111.4	27.2	155.5	2,109.0	470.1	1,532.1	106.8
Beaumont-Port Arthur, TX, MSA	406,050									
Includes Hardin, Jefferson, Newton, and Orange Counties										
City of Beaumont	118,177	1,225	16	59	419	731	6,192	1,922	3,987	283
City of Port Arthur	54,032	359	5	18	121	215	2,390	726	1,537	127
Total area actually reporting	100.0%	2,177	35	116	628	1,398	13,641	4,075	8,811	755
Rate per 100,000 inhabitants		536.1	8.6	28.6	154.7	344.3	3,359.4	1,003.6	2,169.9	185.9
Bend-Redmond, OR, MSA	164,183									
Includes Deschutes County										
City of Bend	79,926	182	1	21	22	138	2,267	267	1,913	87
City of Redmond	27,153	87	0	11	15	61	1,067	157	867	43
Total area actually reporting	100.0%	364	3	46	41	274	4,252	632	3,443	177
Rate per 100,000 inhabitants		221.7	1.8	28.0	25.0	166.9	2,589.8	384.9	2,097.1	107.8
Billings, MT, MSA	164,846									
Includes Carbon, Golden Valley, and Yellowstone Counties										
City of Billings	107,802	360	4	39	81	236	5,604	989	4,074	541

Table 6. Crime, by Selected Metropolitan Statistical Area, 2013—*Continued*

(Number, percent, rate per 100,000 population.)

Area	Population	Violent crime	Murder and nonnegligent manslaughter	Rape[1]	Robbery	Aggravated assault	Property crime	Burglary	Larceny-theft	Motor vehicle theft
Billings, MT, MSA (cont.)										
Total area actually reporting	100.0%	439	4	49	84	302	6,591	1,206	4,733	652
Rate per 100,000 inhabitants		266.3	2.4	29.7	51.0	183.2	3,998.3	731.6	2,871.2	395.5
Binghamton, NY, MSA	247,869									
Includes Broome and Tioga Counties										
City of Binghamton	46,304	284	3	19	101	161	2,349	525	1,767	57
Total area actually reporting	100.0%	536	8	55	158	315	6,791	1,323	5,313	155
Rate per 100,000 inhabitants		216.2	3.2	22.2	63.7	127.1	2,739.8	533.7	2,143.5	62.5
Birmingham-Hoover, AL, MSA	1,138,940									
Includes Bibb, Blount, Chilton, Jefferson, St. Clair, Shelby, and Walker Counties										
City of Birmingham	212,001	2,852	63	178	969	1,642	14,157	4,018	8,661	1,478
City of Hoover	84,139	74	2	9	34	29	2,596	344	2,144	108
Total area actually reporting	94.4%	5,822	91	481	1,671	3,579	40,624	10,890	26,788	2,946
Estimated total	100.0%	6,034	93	506	1,712	3,723	42,397	11,366	27,971	3,060
Rate per 100,000 inhabitants		529.8	8.2	44.4	150.3	326.9	3,722.5	997.9	2,455.9	268.7
Bismarck, ND, MSA	124,238									
Includes Burleigh, Morton, Oliver, and Sioux Counties										
City of Bismarck	65,850	194	1	26	15	152	1,730	334	1,289	107
Total area actually reporting	100.0%	494	3	72	22	397	2,862	560	2,081	221
Rate per 100,000 inhabitants		397.6	2.4	58.0	17.7	319.5	2,303.6	450.7	1,675.0	177.9
Blacksburg-Christiansburg-Radford, VA, MSA	179,521									
Includes Floyd, Giles, Montgomery, and Pulaski Counties and Radford City										
City of Blacksburg	42,603	31	0	7	4	20	523	91	417	15
City of Christiansburg	21,581	30	1	13	3	13	545	53	478	14
City of Radford	16,810	91	0	11	7	73	407	75	321	11
Total area actually reporting	100.0%	314	2	79	20	213	3,456	558	2,795	103
Rate per 100,000 inhabitants		174.9	1.1	44.0	11.1	118.6	1,925.1	310.8	1,556.9	57.4
Bloomington, IL, MSA	189,408									
Includes DeWitt and McLean Counties										
City of Bloomington	78,060	399	2	57	59	281	1,901	402	1,446	53
Total area actually reporting	93.3%	583	4	88	94	397	3,699	809	2,801	89
Estimated total	100.0%	610	4	91	102	413	3,946	852	2,995	99
Rate per 100,000 inhabitants		322.1	2.1	48.0	53.9	218.0	2,083.3	449.8	1,581.2	52.3
Bloomington, IN, MSA	163,596									
Includes Monroe and Owen Counties										
City of Bloomington	82,415	275	2	34	78	161	2,606	516	1,942	148
Total area actually reporting	86.9%	407	3	56	87	261	4,135	860	3,062	213
Estimated total	100.0%	426	3	59	90	274	4,406	935	3,239	232
Rate per 100,000 inhabitants		260.4	1.8	36.1	55.0	167.5	2,693.2	571.5	1,979.9	141.8
Bloomsburg-Berwick, PA, MSA	85,071									
Includes Columbia and Montour Counties										
City of Bloomsburg Town	14,563	41	0	9	3	29	231	56	173	2
City of Berwick	10,326	33	0	1	3	29	401	106	284	11
Total area actually reporting	100.0%	214	1	18	11	184	1,492	331	1,129	32
Rate per 100,000 inhabitants		251.6	1.2	21.2	12.9	216.3	1,753.8	389.1	1,327.1	37.6
Boise City, ID, MSA	647,858									
Includes Ada, Boise, Canyon, Gem, and Owyhee Counties										
City of Boise	214,330	600	3	123	45	429	4,741	825	3,703	213
Total area actually reporting	99.9%	1,452	6	313	84	1,049	11,009	2,301	8,179	529
Estimated total	100.0%	1,453	6	313	84	1,050	11,018	2,303	8,186	529
Rate per 100,000 inhabitants		224.3	0.9	48.3	13.0	162.1	1,700.7	355.5	1,263.5	81.7
Boston-Cambridge-Newton, MA-NH, MSA	4,679,143									
Includes the Metropolitan Divisions of Boston, MA; Cambridge-Newton-Framingham, MA; and Rockingham County-Strafford County, NH										
City of Boston, MA	643,799	5,037	39	279	1,868	2,851	17,853	3,096	13,147	1,610
City of Cambridge, MA	107,282	361	2	24	114	221	2,907	401	2,402	104
City of Newton, MA	86,867	74	0	11	18	45	807	205	584	18
City of Framingham, MA	70,753	172	0	4	23	145	1,025	217	735	73
City of Waltham, MA	62,446	141	1	22	28	90	952	212	694	46

Table 6. Crime, by Selected Metropolitan Statistical Area, 2013—*Continued*

(Number, percent, rate per 100,000 population.)

Area	Population	Violent crime	Murder and nonnegligent manslaughter	Rape[1]	Robbery	Aggravated assault	Property crime	Burglary	Larceny-theft	Motor vehicle theft
Boston-Cambridge-Newton, MA-NH, MSA (cont.)										
Total area actually reporting	98.5%	16,394	85	1,286	4,427	10,596	87,219	16,118	65,135	5,966
Estimated total	100.0%	16,586	86	1,308	4,464	10,728	88,451	16,370	66,047	6,034
Rate per 100,000 inhabitants		354.5	1.8	28.0	95.4	229.3	1,890.3	349.9	1,411.5	129.0
Boston, MA, MD	1,942,405									
Includes Norfolk, Plymouth, and Suffolk Counties										
Total area actually reporting	97.3%	9,600	61	640	2,900	5,999	39,680	7,689	29,226	2,765
Estimated total	100.0%	9,770	62	656	2,933	6,119	40,647	7,902	29,920	2,825
Rate per 100,000 inhabitants		503.0	3.2	33.8	151.0	315.0	2,092.6	406.8	1,540.4	145.4
Cambridge-Newton-Framingham, MA, MD	2,313,211									
Includes Essex and Middlesex Counties										
Total area actually reporting	100.0%	6,103	21	456	1,400	4,226	39,326	7,234	29,160	2,932
Rate per 100,000 inhabitants		263.8	0.9	19.7	60.5	182.7	1,700.1	312.7	1,260.6	126.8
Rockingham County-Strafford County, NH, MD	423,527									
Includes Rockingham and Strafford Counties										
Total area actually reporting	96.1%	691	3	190	127	371	8,213	1,195	6,749	269
Estimated total	100.0%	713	3	196	131	383	8,478	1,234	6,967	277
Rate per 100,000 inhabitants		168.3	0.7	46.3	30.9	90.4	2,001.8	291.4	1,645.0	65.4
Boulder, CO, MSA	310,333									
Includes Boulder County										
City of Boulder	102,828	218	0	38	40	140	2,948	612	2,236	100
Total area actually reporting	79.5%	544	0	136	65	343	6,211	1,038	4,922	251
Estimated total	100.0%	658	2	162	74	420	7,079	1,232	5,514	333
Rate per 100,000 inhabitants		212.0	0.6	52.2	23.8	135.3	2,281.1	397.0	1,776.8	107.3
Bowling Green, KY, MSA	163,437									
Includes Allen, Butler, Edmonson, and Warren Counties										
City of Bowling Green	61,130	201	2	59	69	71	2,852	455	2,272	125
Total area actually reporting	100.0%	236	2	72	76	86	3,789	775	2,837	177
Rate per 100,000 inhabitants		144.4	1.2	44.1	46.5	52.6	2,318.3	474.2	1,735.8	108.3
Bremerton-Silverdale, WA, MSA	256,890									
Includes Kitsap County										
City of Bremerton	39,754	227	1	35	55	136	1,946	452	1,354	140
Total area actually reporting	100.0%	707	2	119	105	481	7,569	1,931	5,126	512
Rate per 100,000 inhabitants		275.2	0.8	46.3	40.9	187.2	2,946.4	751.7	1,995.4	199.3
Bridgeport-Stamford-Norwalk, CT, MSA	921,059									
Includes Fairfield County										
City of Bridgeport	147,076	1,397	11	82	584	720	4,464	1,191	2,610	663
City of Stamford	125,876	334	1	28	160	145	1,938	354	1,435	149
City of Norwalk	87,590	239	0	14	61	164	1,728	245	1,377	106
City of Danbury	83,363	108	2	25	53	28	1,257	221	972	64
City of Stratford	52,285	74	0	8	41	25	1,429	251	1,042	136
Total area actually reporting	100.0%	2,252	14	175	943	1,120	14,918	2,955	10,644	1,319
Rate per 100,000 inhabitants		244.5	1.5	19.0	102.4	121.6	1,619.7	320.8	1,155.6	143.2
Brownsville-Harlingen, TX, MSA	419,944									
Includes Cameron County										
City of Brownsville	181,590	473	1	61	136	275	7,838	1,140	6,441	257
City of Harlingen	65,885	264	2	21	59	182	2,584	496	2,012	76
Total area actually reporting	100.0%	1,009	6	126	244	633	14,844	2,761	11,587	496
Rate per 100,000 inhabitants		240.3	1.4	30.0	58.1	150.7	3,534.8	657.5	2,759.2	118.1
Brunswick, GA, MSA[2]	113,744									
Includes Brantley, Glynn,[2] and McIntosh Counties										
City of Brunswick	15,709	162	3	4	38	117	1,110	331	732	47
Total area actually reporting	98.4%		7	19	111		4,346	1,195	2,989	162
Estimated total	100.0%		7	19	113		4,421	1,209	3,045	167
Rate per 100,000 inhabitants			6.2	16.7	99.3		3,886.8	1,062.9	2,677.1	146.8
Buffalo-Cheektowaga-Niagara Falls, NY, MSA	1,135,074									
Includes Erie and Niagara Counties[1]										
City of Buffalo	258,789	3,249	47	145	1,322	1,735	12,491	3,458	8,076	957
City of Cheektowaga Town	78,361	158	0	11	48	99	2,689	345	2,271	73
City of Niagara Falls	49,574	584	3	12	166	403	2,807	746	1,949	112
Total area actually reporting	100.0%	4,883	59	241	1,744	2,839	31,044	6,525	23,046	1,473
Rate per 100,000 inhabitants		430.2	5.2	21.2	153.6	250.1	2,735.0	574.9	2,030.4	129.8

Table 6. Crime, by Selected Metropolitan Statistical Area, 2013—*Continued*

(Number, percent, rate per 100,000 population.)

Area	Population	Violent crime	Murder and nonnegligent manslaughter	Rape[1]	Robbery	Aggravated assault	Property crime	Burglary	Larceny-theft	Motor vehicle theft
Burlington, NC, MSA................................	155,214									
Includes Alamance County										
City of Burlington	51,401	362	0	16	100	246	2,635	546	1,977	112
Total area actually reporting	100.0%	593	3	33	147	410	4,969	1,311	3,433	225
Rate per 100,000 inhabitants		382.1	1.9	21.3	94.7	264.2	3,201.4	844.6	2,211.8	145.0
California-Lexington Park, MD, MSA......................	110,294									
Includes St. Mary's County										
Total area actually reporting	100.0%	242	3	6	62	171	2,489	640	1,730	119
Rate per 100,000 inhabitants		219.4	2.7	5.4	56.2	155.0	2,256.7	580.3	1,568.5	107.9
Canton-Massillon, OH, MSA................................	404,048									
Includes Carroll and Stark Counties										
City of Canton	72,598	673	11	72	357	233	4,253	1,218	2,597	438
City of Massillon	32,159	69	0	14	31	24	975	249	695	31
Total area actually reporting	98.6%	1,073	12	137	479	445	10,670	2,651	7,321	698
Estimated total	100.0%	1,080	12	138	482	448	10,817	2,680	7,434	703
Rate per 100,000 inhabitants		267.3	3.0	34.2	119.3	110.9	2,677.2	663.3	1,839.9	174.0
Cape Coral-Fort Myers, FL, MSA............................	656,243									
Includes Lee County										
City of Cape Coral	163,461	197	3	7	40	147	3,375	803	2,427	145
City of Fort Myers	66,835	752	10	45	185	512	2,279	392	1,726	161
Total area actually reporting	100.0%	2,184	25	150	577	1,432	14,400	3,779	9,808	813
Rate per 100,000 inhabitants		332.8	3.8	22.9	87.9	218.2	2,194.3	575.9	1,494.6	123.9
Cape Girardeau, MO-IL, MSA................................	97,510									
Includes Alexander County, IL, and Bollinger and Cape Girardeau Counties, MO										
City of Cape Girardeau, MO	38,716	258	5	12	85	156	1,990	446	1,487	57
Total area actually reporting	100.0%	478	7	23	100	348	2,981	738	2,136	107
Rate per 100,000 inhabitants		490.2	7.2	23.6	102.6	356.9	3,057.1	756.8	2,190.5	109.7
Carson City, NV, MSA................................	54,937									
Includes Carson City										
Total area actually reporting	100.0%	133	4	0	17	112	924	202	654	68
Rate per 100,000 inhabitants		242.1	7.3	0.0	30.9	203.9	1,681.9	367.7	1,190.5	123.8
Casper, WY, MSA................................	79,993									
Includes Natrona County										
City of Casper	58,688	88	2	7	15	64	2,036	294	1,657	85
Total area actually reporting	100.0%	169	3	11	17	138	2,367	377	1,879	111
Rate per 100,000 inhabitants		211.3	3.8	13.8	21.3	172.5	2,959.0	471.3	2,349.0	138.8
Cedar Rapids, IA, MSA[3]................................	263,588									
Includes Benton, Jones, and Linn Counties										
City of Cedar Rapids	128,642	392	4	46	90	252	4,707	977	3,433	297
Total area actually reporting	87.9%	493	4	68	98	323	5,914	1,302	4,256	356
Estimated total	100.0%	539	4	74	99	362	6,210	1,395	4,435	380
Rate per 100,000 inhabitants		204.5	1.5	28.1	37.6	137.3	2,355.9	529.2	1,682.6	144.2
Chambersburg-Waynesboro, PA, MSA[3].................	151,646									
Includes Franklin County[3]										
City of Chambersburg	20,381	86	0	3	46	37	810	127	660	23
City of Waynesboro[3]	10,650	24	1	3	11	9	242	40	199	3
Total area actually reporting	100.0%	230	4	35	80	111	2,931	528	2,314	89
Rate per 100,000 inhabitants		151.7	2.6	23.1	52.8	73.2	1,932.8	348.2	1,525.9	58.7
Champaign-Urbana, IL, MSA................................	234,223									
Includes Champaign, Ford, and Piatt Counties										
City of Champaign	82,966	654	4	39	119	492	2,275	506	1,698	71
City of Urbana	41,598	141	2	27	66	46	1,605	354	1,211	40
Total area actually reporting	98.2%	1,109	9	116	217	767	5,811	1,385	4,260	166
Estimated total	100.0%	1,118	9	117	220	772	5,896	1,400	4,326	170
Rate per 100,000 inhabitants		477.3	3.8	50.0	93.9	329.6	2,517.3	597.7	1,847.0	72.6
Charleston, North Charleston, SC, MSA.................	710,846									
Includes Berkeley, Charleston, and Dorchester Counties										
City of Charleston	127,206	231	7	29	72	123	3,192	305	2,725	162

Table 6. Crime, by Selected Metropolitan Statistical Area, 2013—*Continued*

(Number, percent, rate per 100,000 population.)

Area	Population	Violent crime	Murder and nonnegligent manslaughter	Rape[1]	Robbery	Aggravated assault	Property crime	Burglary	Larceny-theft	Motor vehicle theft
Charleston North Charleston, SC, MSA (cont.)										
City of North Charleston	103,324	693	13	56	196	428	5,804	892	4,409	503
Total area actually reporting	99.5%	2,539	51	201	502	1,785	22,248	4,396	16,155	1,697
Estimated total	100.0%	2,555	51	202	505	1,797	22,397	4,422	16,271	1,704
Rate per 100,000 inhabitants		359.4	7.2	28.4	71.0	252.8	3,150.8	622.1	2,289.0	239.7
Charlotte-Concord-Gastonia, NC-SC, MSA	2,329,109									
Includes Cabarrus, Gaston, Iredell, Lincoln, Mecklen-burg, Rowan, and Union Counties, NC and Chester, Lancaster, and York Counties, SC										
City of Charlotte-Mecklenburg, NC	837,638	5,093	59	230	1,805	2,999	30,569	6,439	22,274	1,856
City of Concord, NC	82,899	122	7	9	50	56	2,549	414	2,033	102
City of Gastonia, NC	73,049	510	6	22	150	332	3,866	752	2,873	241
City of Rock Hill, SC	68,617	372	4	49	78	241	2,583	396	2,066	121
Total area actually reporting	98.9%	9,347	121	531	2,646	6,049	68,504	15,766	49,171	3,567
Estimated total	100.0%	9,419	122	535	2,665	6,097	69,430	15,963	49,867	3,600
Rate per 100,000 inhabitants		404.4	5.2	23.0	114.4	261.8	2,981.0	685.4	2,141.0	154.6
Charlottesville, VA, MSA	224,663									
Includes Albemarle, Buckingham, Fluvanna, Greene, and Nelson Counties and Charlottesville City										
City of Charlottesville	44,187	211	1	20	63	127	1,471	200	1,218	53
Total area actually reporting	100.0%	430	4	89	97	240	4,287	675	3,439	173
Rate per 100,000 inhabitants		191.4	1.8	39.6	43.2	106.8	1,908.2	300.5	1,530.7	77.0
Chattanooga, TN-GA, MSA	541,195									
Includes Catoosa, Dade, and Walker Counties, GA and Hamilton, Marion, and Sequatchie Counties, TN										
City of Chattanooga, TN	172,286	1,692	18	64	385	1,225	11,468	2,317	8,165	986
Total area actually reporting	100.0%	2,759	22	124	491	2,122	20,946	4,469	14,833	1,644
Rate per 100,000 inhabitants		509.8	4.1	22.9	90.7	392.1	3,870.3	825.8	2,740.8	303.8
Cheyenne, WY, MSA	95,635									
Includes Laramie County										
City of Cheyenne	62,149	133	1	12	12	108	2,065	279	1,698	88
Total area actually reporting	100.0%	198	1	20	13	164	2,626	441	2,069	116
Rate per 100,000 inhabitants		207.0	1.0	20.9	13.6	171.5	2,745.9	461.1	2,163.4	121.3
Chicago-Naperville, Elgin, IL-IN-WI, MSA[4,5]	9,538,161									
Includes the Metropolitan Divisions of Chicago-Naperville, Arlington Heights, IL; Elgin IL; Gary, IN; and Lake County-Kenosha County, IL-WI										
City of Chicago, IL[4,5]	2,720,554		414		11,815		95,908	17,775	65,497	12,636
City of Naperville, IL	144,221	105	0	7	21	77	1,869	225	1,610	34
City of Elgin, IL	110,454	236	3	56	63	114	1,902	351	1,462	89
City of Gary, IN	78,819	883	54	47	327	455	4,719	1,454	2,533	732
City of Arlington Heights, IL	75,978	42	0	7	7	28	800	125	659	16
City of Evanston, IL	75,709	189	1	10	63	115	1,902	361	1,474	67
City of Schaumburg, IL	74,940	71	0	15	30	26	2,176	175	1,928	73
City of Skokie, IL	65,155	157	0	9	58	90	1,575	285	1,221	69
City of Des Plaines, IL	58,975	56	2	7	12	35	791	153	595	43
City of Hoffman Estates, IL	52,422	55	0	16	21	18	548	102	426	20
Total area actually reporting	98.1%		604		15,897		219,689	39,565	161,090	19,034
Estimated total	100.0%		608		15,998		223,102	40,196	163,715	19,191
Rate per 100,000 inhabitants			6.4		167.7		2,339.0	421.4	1,716.4	201.2
Chicago-Naperville-Arlington Heights, IL, MD[4,5]	7,331,456									
Includes Cook, DuPage, Grundy, Kendall, McHenry, and Will Counties										
Total area actually reporting	98.2%		493		14,486		175,167	31,123	127,700	16,344
Estimated total	100.0%		496		14,569		177,733	31,574	129,707	16,452
Rate per 100,000 inhabitants			6.8		198.7		2,424.3	430.7	1,769.2	224.4
Elgin, IL, MD	628,978									
Includes DeKalb and Kane Counties										
Total area actually reporting	97.5%	1,075	9	147	207	712	9,241	1,441	7,549	251
Estimated total	100.0%	1,108	9	150	217	732	9,552	1,496	7,792	264
Rate per 100,000 inhabitants		176.2	1.4	23.8	34.5	116.4	1,518.7	237.8	1,238.8	42.0
Gary, IN, MD	708,116									
Includes Jasper, Lake, Newton, and Porter Counties										

Table 6. Crime, by Selected Metropolitan Statistical Area, 2013—*Continued*

(Number, percent, rate per 100,000 population.)

Area	Population	Violent crime	Murder and nonnegligent manslaughter	Rape[1]	Robbery	Aggravated assault	Property crime	Burglary	Larceny-theft	Motor vehicle theft
Gary, IN, MD (cont.)										
Total area actually reporting	95.5%	2,349	81	141	795	1,332	20,522	4,126	14,337	2,059
Estimated total	100.0%	2,385	82	146	801	1,356	20,995	4,240	14,663	2,092
Rate per 100,000 inhabitants		336.8	11.6	20.6	113.1	191.5	2,964.9	598.8	2,070.7	295.4
Lake County-Kenosha County, IL-WI, MD...........	869,611									
Includes Lake County, IL, and Kenosha County, WI										
Total area actually reporting	99.6%	1,354	21	187	409	737	14,759	2,875	11,504	380
Estimated total	100.0%	1,361	21	188	411	741	14,822	2,886	11,553	383
Rate per 100,000 inhabitants		156.5	2.4	21.6	47.3	85.2	1,704.4	331.9	1,328.5	44.0
Chico, CA, MSA...	222,365									
Includes Butte County										
City of Chico	88,226	299	2	41	95	161	2,572	622	1,568	382
Total area actually reporting	100.0%	634	13	79	148	394	6,223	1,685	3,642	896
Rate per 100,000 inhabitants		285.1	5.8	35.5	66.6	177.2	2,798.6	757.8	1,637.8	402.9
Cincinnati, OH-KY-IN, MSA.......................	2,136,525									
Includes Dearborn, Ohio, and Union Counties, IN; Boone, Bracken, Campbell, Gallatin, Grant, Kenton, and Pendleton Counties, KY; and Brown, Butler, Clermont, Hamilton, and Warren Counties, OH										
City of Cincinnati, OH	296,491	2,826	70	199	1,610	947	17,231	5,467	10,488	1,276
Total area actually reporting	94.1%	5,941	101	666	2,667	2,507	64,608	15,444	46,181	2,983
Estimated total	100.0%	6,094	103	691	2,716	2,584	67,244	16,013	48,133	3,098
Rate per 100,000 inhabitants		285.2	4.8	32.3	127.1	120.9	3,147.4	749.5	2,252.9	145.0
Clarksville, TN-KY, MSA	278,930									
Includes Christian and Trigg Counties, KY, and Montgomery County, TN										
City of Clarksville, TN	145,599	748	6	84	115	543	4,141	1,020	2,965	156
Total area actually reporting	99.7%	1,028	14	133	163	718	6,989	1,818	4,894	277
Estimated total	100.0%	1,030	14	133	164	719	7,013	1,823	4,912	278
Rate per 100,000 inhabitants		369.3	5.0	47.7	58.8	257.8	2,514.3	653.6	1,761.0	99.7
Cleveland, TN, MSA	118,551									
Includes Bradley and Polk Counties										
City of Cleveland	42,735	339	1	27	32	279	2,440	414	1,912	114
Total area actually reporting	100.0%	519	1	37	37	444	3,735	833	2,669	233
Rate per 100,000 inhabitants		437.8	0.8	31.2	31.2	374.5	3,150.5	702.7	2,251.4	196.5
Coeur d'Alene, ID, MSA............................	144,225									
Includes Kootenai County										
City of Coeur d'Alene	46,023	257	0	53	20	184	1,735	359	1,259	117
Total area actually reporting	100.0%	459	3	80	31	345	3,989	916	2,845	228
Rate per 100,000 inhabitants		318.3	2.1	55.5	21.5	239.2	2,765.8	635.1	1,972.6	158.1
College Station-Bryan, TX, MSA	237,174									
Includes Brazos, Burleson, and Robertson Counties										
City of College Station	98,919	379	0	34	37	308	2,230	432	1,750	48
City of Bryan	78,578	358	2	31	75	250	2,311	539	1,683	89
Total area actually reporting	100.0%	881	5	78	122	676	5,900	1,317	4,383	200
Rate per 100,000 inhabitants		371.5	2.1	32.9	51.4	285.0	2,487.6	555.3	1,848.0	84.3
Colorado Springs, CO, MSA......................	678,821									
Includes El Paso and Teller Counties										
City of Colorado Springs	436,108	1,893	26	370	418	1,079	18,175	3,726	12,521	1,928
Total area actually reporting	99.4%	2,496	42	496	463	1,495	22,128	4,755	15,149	2,224
Estimated total	100.0%	2,504	42	498	464	1,500	22,227	4,768	15,228	2,231
Rate per 100,000 inhabitants		368.9	6.2	73.4	68.4	221.0	3,274.4	702.4	2,243.3	328.7
Columbia, MO, MSA	170,724									
Includes Boone County										
City of Columbia	114,587	416	5	67	112	232	4,359	703	3,490	166
Total area actually reporting	100.0%	568	5	78	128	357	5,613	889	4,497	227
Rate per 100,000 inhabitants		332.7	2.9	45.7	75.0	209.1	3,287.8	520.7	2,634.1	133.0
Columbia, SC, MSA	793,289									
Includes Calhoun, Fairfield, Kershaw, Lexington, Richland, and Saluda Counties										
City of Columbia	132,240	952	8	58	331	555	7,989	1,398	5,800	791

Table 6. Crime, by Selected Metropolitan Statistical Area, 2013—*Continued*

(Number, percent, rate per 100,000 population.)

Area	Population	Violent crime	Murder and nonnegligent manslaughter	Rape[1]	Robbery	Aggravated assault	Property crime	Burglary	Larceny-theft	Motor vehicle theft
Columbia, SC, MSA (cont.)										
Total area actually reporting	99.6%	4,572	37	324	836	3,375	28,724	5,905	20,147	2,672
Estimated total	100.0%	4,585	37	325	838	3,385	28,851	5,927	20,246	2,678
Rate per 100,000 inhabitants		578.0	4.7	41.0	105.6	426.7	3,636.9	747.1	2,552.2	337.6
Columbus, GA-AL, MSA............................	315,743									
Includes Russell County, AL, and Chattahoochee, Harris, Marion, and Muscogee Counties, GA										
City of Columbus, GA	201,165	1,022	22	36	481	483	12,475	3,355	8,012	1,108
Total area actually reporting	99.5%	1,298	30	70	530	668	15,502	4,233	9,866	1,403
Estimated total	100.0%	1,304	30	70	532	672	15,566	4,245	9,914	1,407
Rate per 100,000 inhabitants		413.0	9.5	22.2	168.5	212.8	4,930.0	1,344.4	3,139.9	445.6
Columbus, IN, MSA..................................	80,102									
Includes Bartholomew County										
City of Columbus	45,874	82	1	17	19	45	2,124	241	1,754	129
Total area actually reporting	100.0%	148	5	23	21	99	2,674	350	2,142	182
Rate per 100,000 inhabitants		184.8	6.2	28.7	26.2	123.6	3,338.2	436.9	2,674.1	227.2
Corpus Christi, TX, MSA[3]	441,984									
Includes Aransas, Nueces, and San Patricio Counties										
City of Corpus Christi	314,523	1,939	18	147	390	1,384	14,601	2,595	11,519	487
Total area actually reporting	100.0%	2,314	24	198	432	1,660	18,832	3,750	14,382	700
Rate per 100,000 inhabitants		523.5	5.4	44.8	97.7	375.6	4,260.8	848.4	3,254.0	158.4
Corvallis, OR, MSA...................................	86,952									
Includes Benton County										
City of Corvallis	55,218	64	0	10	16	38	1,587	195	1,354	38
Total area actually reporting	100.0%	104	0	13	25	66	2,219	290	1,849	80
Rate per 100,000 inhabitants		119.6	0.0	15.0	28.8	75.9	2,552.0	333.5	2,126.5	92.0
Crestview-Fort Walton Beach-Destin, FL, MSA	252,641									
Includes Okaloosa and Walton Counties										
City of Crestview	22,818	180	0	39	44	97	802	149	612	41
City of Fort Walton Beach	20,568	56	2	3	14	37	661	93	535	33
Total area actually reporting	100.0%	1,044	7	120	125	792	5,929	1,197	4,469	263
Rate per 100,000 inhabitants		413.2	2.8	47.5	49.5	313.5	2,346.8	473.8	1,768.9	104.1
Cumberland, MD-WV, MSA	101,663									
Includes Allegany County, MD, and Mineral County, WV										
City of Cumberland, MD	20,495	160	1	20	44	95	1,341	323	991	27
Total area actually reporting	98.5%	292	4	34	66	188	2,689	624	1,996	69
Estimated total	100.0%	296	4	34	67	191	2,733	631	2,031	71
Rate per 100,000 inhabitants		291.2	3.9	33.4	65.9	187.9	2,688.3	620.7	1,997.8	69.8
Dallas-Fort Worth-Arlington, TX, MSA..................	6,814,175									
Includes the Metropolitan Divisions of Dallas-Plano-Irving and Fort Worth-Arlington										
City of Dallas	1,255,015	8,330	143	543	4,202	3,442	52,274	14,516	30,374	7,384
City of Fort Worth	789,035	4,420	48	523	1,256	2,593	34,272	8,316	23,557	2,399
City of Arlington	378,765	1,837	18	105	562	1,152	15,000	3,181	10,879	940
City of Plano	275,795	389	3	84	106	196	5,930	944	4,730	256
City of Irving	228,367	530	2	24	186	318	6,175	1,137	4,444	594
City of Denton	123,260	338	1	93	52	192	2,777	472	2,203	102
City of Richardson	104,577	128	2	15	60	51	2,758	539	2,068	151
Total area actually reporting	99.9%	22,665	303	2,167	8,225	11,970	206,698	47,750	141,018	17,930
Estimated total	100.0%	22,682	303	2,169	8,229	11,981	206,906	47,789	141,174	17,943
Rate per 100,000 inhabitants		332.9	4.4	31.8	120.8	175.8	3,036.4	701.3	2,071.8	263.3
Dallas-Plano-Irving, TX, MD............................	4,506,295									
Includes Collin, Dallas, Denton, Ellis, Hunt, Kaufman, and Rockwall Counties										
Total area actually reporting	99.9%	14,315	213	1,321	5,981	6,800	130,119	30,888	86,243	12,988
Estimated total	100.0%	14,328	213	1,323	5,984	6,808	130,279	30,918	86,363	12,998
Rate per 100,000 inhabitants		318.0	4.7	29.4	132.8	151.1	2,891.0	686.1	1,916.5	288.4
Fort Worth-Arlington, TX, MD............................	2,307,880									
Includes Hood, Johnson, Parker, Somerville, Tarrant, and Wise Counties										
Total area actually reporting	99.9%	8,350	90	846	2,244	5,170	76,579	16,862	54,775	4,942
Estimated total	100.0%	8,354	90	846	2,245	5,173	76,627	16,871	54,811	4,945
Rate per 100,000 inhabitants		362.0	3.9	36.7	97.3	224.1	3,320.2	731.0	2,375.0	214.3

Table 6. Crime, by Selected Metropolitan Statistical Area, 2013—*Continued*

(Number, percent, rate per 100,000 population.)

Area	Population	Violent crime	Murder and nonnegligent manslaughter	Rape[1]	Robbery	Aggravated assault	Property crime	Burglary	Larceny-theft	Motor vehicle theft
Dalton, GA, MSA..	142,901									
Includes Murray and Whitfield Counties										
City of Dalton	33,475	66	0	7	12	47	1,319	201	1,063	55
Total area actually reporting	98.3%	335	2	32	30	271	3,890	860	2,805	225
Estimated total	100.0%	344	2	33	33	276	3,989	878	2,879	232
Rate per 100,000 inhabitants		240.7	1.4	23.1	23.1	193.1	2,791.4	614.4	2,014.7	162.4
Daphne-Fairhope-Foley, AL, MSA..........................	193,322									
Includes Baldwin County										
City of Daphne	23,204	31	1	3	5	22	526	89	421	16
City of Fairhope	16,847	40	0	6	6	28	678	144	515	19
City of Foley	15,615	55	0	4	10	41	789	111	656	22
Total area actually reporting	100.0%	427	1	48	67	311	4,892	939	3,749	204
Rate per 100,000 inhabitants		220.9	0.5	24.8	34.7	160.9	2,530.5	485.7	1,939.3	105.5
Davenport-Moline-Rock Island, IA-IL, MSA............	383,796									
Includes Henry, Mercer, and Rock Island Counties, IL, and Scott County, IA										
City of Davenport, IA	101,834	654	2	88	167	397	4,248	961	3,048	239
City of Moline, IL	43,172	121	0	8	13	100	1,389	235	1,127	27
City of Rock Island, IL	38,893	200	5	2	32	161	1,006	227	741	38
Total area actually reporting	97.3%	1,366	7	143	241	975	9,411	1,949	7,087	375
Estimated total	100.0%	1,387	7	145	247	988	9,607	1,984	7,240	383
Rate per 100,000 inhabitants		361.4	1.8	37.8	64.4	257.4	2,503.2	516.9	1,886.4	99.8
Dayton, OH, MSA..	802,990									
Includes Greene, Miami, and Montgomery Counties										
City of Dayton	141,167	1,230	28	107	518	577	7,655	2,613	4,427	615
Total area actually reporting	98.0%	2,160	44	326	876	914	26,251	6,840	18,013	1,398
Estimated total	100.0%	2,182	44	330	885	923	26,662	6,921	18,329	1,412
Rate per 100,000 inhabitants		271.7	5.5	41.1	110.2	114.9	3,320.3	861.9	2,282.6	175.8
Decatur, AL, MSA...	154,311									
Includes Lawrence and Morgan Counties										
City of Decatur	56,091	149	5	12	26	106	2,553	569	1,831	153
Total area actually reporting	99.3%	297	7	37	38	215	3,944	1,040	2,665	239
Estimated total	100.0%	301	7	37	39	218	3,990	1,050	2,698	242
Rate per 100,000 inhabitants		195.1	4.5	24.0	25.3	141.3	2,585.7	680.4	1,748.4	156.8
Decatur, IL, MSA..	109,877									
Includes Macon County										
City of Decatur	75,190	351	5	9	84	253	2,369	793	1,512	64
Total area actually reporting	100.0%	422	5	19	87	311	2,806	892	1,832	82
Rate per 100,000 inhabitants		384.1	4.6	17.3	79.2	283.0	2,553.8	811.8	1,667.3	74.6
Deltona-Daytona Beach-Ormond Beach, FL, MSA.	599,128									
Includes Flagler and Volusia Counties										
City of Daytona Beach	62,381	799	4	57	195	543	4,024	745	2,912	367
City of Ormond Beach	38,442	132	0	10	17	105	1,386	259	1,055	72
Total area actually reporting	99.7%	2,345	26	179	455	1,685	18,560	4,129	13,326	1,105
Estimated total	100.0%	2,353	26	180	457	1,690	18,623	4,142	13,372	1,109
Rate per 100,000 inhabitants		392.7	4.3	30.0	76.3	282.1	3,108.4	691.3	2,231.9	185.1
Denver-Aurora-Broomfield, CO, MSA.....................	2,693,369									
Includes Adams, Arapahoe, Broomfield, Clear Creek, Denver, Douglas, Elbert, Gilpin, Jefferson, and Park Counties										
City of Denver	648,981	4,087	40	514	1,132	2,401	23,711	4,918	15,306	3,487
City of Aurora	343,484	1,436	23	224	468	721	10,786	1,981	7,805	1,000
City of Lakewood	146,298	624	6	107	113	398	6,892	872	5,397	623
City of Broomfield	59,424	33	1	12	6	14	1,204	106	1,054	44
Total area actually reporting	99.9%	8,847	99	1,427	2,125	5,196	73,953	12,468	53,444	8,041
Estimated total	100.0%	8,848	99	1,427	2,125	5,197	73,981	12,472	53,466	8,043
Rate per 100,000 inhabitants		328.5	3.7	53.0	78.9	193.0	2,746.8	463.1	1,985.1	298.6
Des Moines-West Des Moines, IA, MSA.................	596,382									
Includes Dallas, Guthrie, Madison, Polk, and Warren Counties										
City of Des Moines	207,391	1,026	11	90	211	714	10,015	2,311	6,854	850

Table 6. Crime, by Selected Metropolitan Statistical Area, 2013—*Continued*

(Number, percent, rate per 100,000 population.)

Area	Population	Violent crime	Murder and nonnegligent manslaughter	Rape[1]	Robbery	Aggravated assault	Property crime	Burglary	Larceny-theft	Motor vehicle theft
Des Moines-West Des Moines, IA, MSA (cont.)										
City of West Des Moines	60,068	90	1	16	12	61	1,658	205	1,377	76
Total area actually reporting	100.0%	1,597	14	159	247	1,177	16,488	3,536	11,762	1,190
Rate per 100,000 inhabitants		267.8	2.3	26.7	41.4	197.4	2,764.7	592.9	1,972.2	199.5
Detroit-Warren-Livonia, MI, MSA	4,296,628									
Includes the Metropolitan Divisions of Detroit-Dearborn-Livonia and Warren-Troy-Farmington Hills										
City of Detroit	699,889	14,504	316	618	4,774	8,796	40,835	11,754	17,188	11,893
City of Warren	134,167	679	3	127	166	383	3,508	887	2,037	584
City of Dearborn	96,012	347	2	33	126	186	3,104	399	2,328	377
City of Livonia	95,220	148	0	18	34	96	1,961	285	1,498	178
City of Troy	82,608	62	0	17	7	38	1,550	222	1,250	78
City of Farmington Hills	81,084	72	1	14	21	36	1,114	245	773	96
City of Southfield	72,755	262	2	39	121	100	2,120	443	1,393	284
City of Taylor	61,836	347	3	49	76	219	2,083	470	1,404	209
City of Novi	57,469	48	2	7	11	28	966	96	833	37
Total area actually reporting	99.8%	24,447	411	2,156	7,052	14,828	110,601	26,182	65,268	19,151
Estimated total	100.0%	24,475	411	2,161	7,058	14,845	110,816	26,226	65,422	19,168
Rate per 100,000 inhabitants		569.6	9.6	50.3	164.3	345.5	2,579.1	610.4	1,522.6	446.1
Detroit-Livonia-Dearborn, MI, MD	1,786,498									
Includes Wayne County										
Total area actually reporting	99.5%	18,691	364	1,117	5,867	11,343	68,184	17,357	35,330	15,497
Estimated total	100.0%	18,719	364	1,122	5,873	11,360	68,399	17,401	35,484	15,514
Rate per 100,000 inhabitants		1,047.8	20.4	62.8	328.7	635.9	3,828.7	974.0	1,986.2	868.4
Warren-Troy-Farmington Hills, MI, MD	2,510,130									
Includes Lapeer, Livingston, Macomb, Oakland, and St. Clair Counties										
Total area actually reporting	100.0%	5,756	47	1,039	1,185	3,485	42,417	8,825	29,938	3,654
Rate per 100,000 inhabitants		229.3	1.9	41.4	47.2	138.8	1,689.8	351.6	1,192.7	145.6
Dothan, AL, MSA	148,166									
Includes Geneva, Henry, and Houston Counties										
City of Dothan	66,588	329	4	16	77	232	2,457	580	1,770	107
Total area actually reporting	98.2%	575	9	61	101	404	4,145	1,103	2,818	224
Estimated total	100.0%	587	9	62	104	412	4,254	1,127	2,896	231
Rate per 100,000 inhabitants		396.2	6.1	41.8	70.2	278.1	2,871.1	760.6	1,954.6	155.9
Dover, DE, MSA	169,725									
Includes Kent County										
City of Dover	37,402	266	1	16	58	191	2,093	88	1,919	86
Total area actually reporting	100.0%	774	4	92	146	532	5,057	769	4,104	184
Rate per 100,000 inhabitants		456.0	2.4	54.2	86.0	313.4	2,979.5	453.1	2,418.0	108.4
Dubuque, IA, MSA	95,753									
Includes Dubuque County										
City of Dubuque	58,313	132	0	14	36	82	1,641	409	1,172	60
Total area actually reporting	100.0%	153	0	16	37	100	1,894	481	1,332	81
Rate per 100,000 inhabitants		159.8	0.0	16.7	38.6	104.4	1,978.0	502.3	1,391.1	84.6
Duluth, MN-WI, MSA	280,163									
Includes Carlton and St. Louis Counties, MN, and Douglas County, WI										
City of Duluth, MN	86,211	342	2	52	72	216	4,283	643	3,484	156
Total area actually reporting	100.0%	654	4	121	115	414	9,537	1,742	7,365	430
Rate per 100,000 inhabitants		233.4	1.4	43.2	41.0	147.8	3,404.1	621.8	2,628.8	153.5
East Stroudsburg, PA, MSA	168,309									
Includes Monroe County										
Total area actually reporting	100.0%	618	8	49	57	504	4,126	1,138	2,886	102
Rate per 100,000 inhabitants		367.2	4.8	29.1	33.9	299.4	2,451.4	676.1	1,714.7	60.6
Eau Claire, WI, MSA	164,463									
Includes Chippewa and Eau Claire Counties										
City of Eau Claire	67,309	123	1	22	14	86	1,570	235	1,287	48
Total area actually reporting	100.0%	205	2	34	23	146	2,775	475	2,212	88
Rate per 100,000 inhabitants		124.6	1.2	20.7	14.0	88.8	1,687.3	288.8	1,345.0	53.5
El Centro, CA, MSA	177,955									
Includes Imperial County										

(Number, percent, rate per 100,000 population.)

Area	Population	Violent crime	Murder and nonnegligent manslaughter	Rape[1]	Robbery	Aggravated assault	Property crime	Burglary	Larceny-theft	Motor vehicle theft
El Centro, CA, MSA (cont.)										
City of El Centro	43,249	144	1	7	54	82	2,039	416	1,499	124
Total area actually reporting	95.5%	517	2	29	102	384	5,698	1,387	3,759	552
Estimated total	100.0%	542	2	30	110	400	5,903	1,435	3,886	582
Rate per 100,000 inhabitants		304.6	1.1	16.9	61.8	224.8	3,317.1	806.4	2,183.7	327.0
Elizabethtown-Fort Knox, KY, MSA..................	150,699									
Includes Hardin, Larue, and Meade Counties										
City of Elizabethtown	29,470	35	0	9	10	16	1,088	182	881	25
Total area actually reporting	100.0%	118	2	35	23	58	2,235	519	1,640	76
Rate per 100,000 inhabitants		78.3	1.3	23.2	15.3	38.5	1,483.1	344.4	1,088.3	50.4
Elmira, NY, MSA	89,040									
Includes Chemung County										
City of Elmira	28,921	81	0	2	29	50	1,027	224	790	13
Total area actually reporting	100.0%	151	0	7	37	107	2,048	351	1,670	27
Rate per 100,000 inhabitants		169.6	0.0	7.9	41.6	120.2	2,300.1	394.2	1,875.6	30.3
El Paso, TX, MSA	842,271									
Includes El Paso and Hudspeth Counties										
City of El Paso	679,700	2,522	10	176	457	1,879	15,558	1,771	12,993	794
Total area actually reporting	100.0%	2,925	12	236	496	2,181	18,331	2,364	15,006	961
Rate per 100,000 inhabitants		347.3	1.4	28.0	58.9	258.9	2,176.4	280.7	1,781.6	114.1
Erie, PA, MSA....................................	280,450									
Includes Erie County										
City of Erie	100,814	457	3	60	175	219	3,208	1,017	2,093	98
Total area actually reporting	99.5%	684	4	89	227	364	6,662	1,707	4,782	173
Estimated total	100.0%	687	4	89	228	366	6,689	1,711	4,804	174
Rate per 100,000 inhabitants		245.0	1.4	31.7	81.3	130.5	2,385.1	610.1	1,713.0	62.0
Eugene, OR, MSA..............................	356,321									
Includes Lane County										
City of Eugene	158,499	402	0	68	195	139	7,920	1,539	5,773	608
Total area actually reporting	99.1%	684	4	104	240	336	13,100	2,537	9,564	999
Estimated total	100.0%	691	4	105	242	340	13,201	2,552	9,643	1,006
Rate per 100,000 inhabitants		193.9	1.1	29.5	67.9	95.4	3,704.8	716.2	2,706.3	282.3
Fairbanks, AK, MSA	34,741									
Includes Fairbanks North Star Borough										
City of Fairbanks	32,505	213	0	34	37	142	1,269	116	1,050	103
Total area actually reporting	100.0%	237	0	35	41	161	1,429	125	1,190	114
Rate per 100,000 inhabitants		682.2	0.0	100.7	118.0	463.4	4,113.3	359.8	3,425.3	328.1
Fargo, ND-MN, MSA..........................	222,166									
Includes Clay County, MN, and Cass County, ND										
City of Fargo, ND	111,101	446	3	71	58	314	3,209	701	2,342	166
Total area actually reporting	100.0%	568	4	93	69	402	5,068	1,098	3,694	276
Rate per 100,000 inhabitants		255.7	1.8	41.9	31.1	180.9	2,281.2	494.2	1,662.7	124.2
Farmington, NM, MSA.........................	127,552									
Includes San Juan County										
City of Farmington	45,820	291	3	49	43	196	1,674	297	1,285	92
Total area actually reporting	100.0%	625	6	94	60	465	2,755	618	1,969	168
Rate per 100,000 inhabitants		490.0	4.7	73.7	47.0	364.6	2,159.9	484.5	1,543.7	131.7
Fayetteville, NC, MSA	378,067									
Includes Cumberland and Hoke Counties										
City of Fayetteville	202,524	1,170	25	65	586	494	12,261	3,279	8,351	631
Total area actually reporting	100.0%	1,853	30	86	767	970	18,564	5,514	12,166	884
Rate per 100,000 inhabitants		490.1	7.9	22.7	202.9	256.6	4,910.2	1,458.5	3,217.9	233.8
Fayetteville-Springdale-Rogers, AR-MO, MSA..................................	488,051									
Includes Benton, Madison, and Washington Counties, AR and McDonald County, MO										
City of Fayetteville, AR	77,900	339	3	33	33	270	3,171	538	2,473	160
City of Springdale, AR	73,939	354	3	77	29	245	2,651	473	2,056	122
City of Rogers, AR	59,787	208	0	31	11	166	1,709	225	1,453	31
City of Bentonville, AR	39,132	61	0	12	2	47	686	117	557	12
Total area actually reporting	98.8%	1,607	12	262	88	1,245	11,410	2,429	8,491	490
Estimated total	100.0%	1,633	12	265	91	1,265	11,619	2,490	8,631	498
Rate per 100,000 inhabitants		334.6	2.5	54.3	18.6	259.2	2,380.7	510.2	1,768.5	102.0

Table 6. Crime, by Selected Metropolitan Statistical Area, 2013—*Continued*

(Number, percent, rate per 100,000 population.)

Area	Population	Violent crime	Murder and nonnegligent manslaughter	Rape[1]	Robbery	Aggravated assault	Property crime	Burglary	Larceny-theft	Motor vehicle theft
Flagstaff, AZ, MSA	136,999									
Includes Coconino County										
City of Flagstaff	67,963	246	1	25	43	177	2,869	220	2,594	55
Total area actually reporting	100.0%	451	3	57	54	337	4,169	473	3,594	102
Rate per 100,000 inhabitants		329.2	2.2	41.6	39.4	246.0	3,043.1	345.3	2,623.4	74.5
Flint, MI, MSA	416,606									
Includes Genesee County										
City of Flint	99,941	1,907	48	145	447	1,267	4,261	1,941	2,000	320
Total area actually reporting	99.9%	3,003	57	341	699	1,906	12,411	4,574	7,053	784
Estimated total	100.0%	3,004	57	341	699	1,907	12,420	4,576	7,059	785
Rate per 100,000 inhabitants		721.1	13.7	81.9	167.8	457.7	2,981.2	1,098.4	1,694.4	188.4
Florence, SC, MSA	207,144									
Includes Darlington and Florence Counties										
City of Florence	37,611	293	2	29	69	193	2,936	456	2,376	104
Total area actually reporting	99.4%	979	11	87	163	718	9,360	2,137	6,690	533
Estimated total	100.0%	984	11	87	164	722	9,410	2,146	6,729	535
Rate per 100,000 inhabitants		475.0	5.3	42.0	79.2	348.5	4,542.7	1,036.0	3,248.5	258.3
Florence-Muscle Shoals, AL, MSA	146,880									
Includes Colbert and Lauderdale Counties										
City of Florence	39,481	207	3	28	56	120	1,807	324	1,380	103
City of Muscle Shoals	13,431	58	0	5	18	35	693	109	539	45
Total area actually reporting	100.0%	520	5	72	93	350	4,327	937	3,103	287
Rate per 100,000 inhabitants		354.0	3.4	49.0	63.3	238.3	2,945.9	637.9	2,112.6	195.4
Fond du Lac, WI, MSA	101,960									
Includes Fond du Lac County										
City of Fond du Lac	43,042	154	1	31	11	111	1,178	126	1,021	31
Total area actually reporting	100.0%	200	1	40	17	142	1,651	250	1,355	46
Rate per 100,000 inhabitants		196.2	1.0	39.2	16.7	139.3	1,619.3	245.2	1,329.0	45.1
Fort Collins-Loveland, CO, MSA	315,907									
Includes Larimer County										
City of Fort Collins	150,066	357	0	57	37	263	3,808	531	3,137	140
Total area actually reporting	100.0%	646	2	138	66	440	6,812	934	5,631	247
Rate per 100,000 inhabitants		204.5	0.6	43.7	20.9	139.3	2,156.3	295.7	1,782.5	78.2
Fort Smith, AR-OK, MSA	280,934									
Includes Crawford, Franklin, and Sebastian Counties, AR and Le Flore and Sequoyah Counties, OK										
City of Fort Smith, AR	87,821	606	4	79	94	429	4,621	975	3,447	199
Total area actually reporting	100.0%	1,122	6	129	116	871	8,739	2,154	6,162	423
Rate per 100,000 inhabitants		399.4	2.1	45.9	41.3	310.0	3,110.7	766.7	2,193.4	150.6
Fort Wayne, IN, MSA	424,081									
Includes Allen, Wells, and Whitley Counties										
City of Fort Wayne	254,820	949	31	95	447	376	9,807	2,396	7,025	386
Total area actually reporting	94.6%	1,109	34	121	496	458	12,131	2,859	8,777	495
Estimated total	100.0%	1,129	34	124	499	472	12,422	2,939	8,967	516
Rate per 100,000 inhabitants		266.2	8.0	29.2	117.7	111.3	2,929.2	693.0	2,114.5	121.7
Fresno, CA, MSA	954,305									
Includes Fresno County										
City of Fresno	508,876	2,552	40	53	903	1,556	22,584	5,223	13,304	4,057
Total area actually reporting	100.0%	4,868	57	163	1,221	3,427	36,698	9,102	21,257	6,339
Rate per 100,000 inhabitants		510.1	6.0	17.1	127.9	359.1	3,845.5	953.8	2,227.5	664.3
Gadsden, AL, MSA	104,345									
Includes Etowah County										
City of Gadsden	36,610	424	6	47	104	267	2,934	830	1,904	200
Total area actually reporting	93.2%	576	8	80	112	376	4,157	1,274	2,601	282
Estimated total	100.0%	607	8	83	119	397	4,442	1,337	2,805	300
Rate per 100,000 inhabitants		581.7	7.7	79.5	114.0	380.5	4,257.0	1,281.3	2,688.2	287.5
Gainesville, FL, MSA	270,523									
Includes Alachua and Gilchrist Counties										
City of Gainesville	126,589	806	6	62	155	583	4,986	742	4,000	244
Total area actually reporting	100.0%	1,466	10	115	238	1,103	8,009	1,548	6,095	366
Rate per 100,000 inhabitants		541.9	3.7	42.5	88.0	407.7	2,960.6	572.2	2,253.0	135.3

Table 6. Crime, by Selected Metropolitan Statistical Area, 2013—*Continued*

(Number, percent, rate per 100,000 population.)

Area	Population	Violent crime	Murder and nonnegligent manslaughter	Rape[1]	Robbery	Aggravated assault	Property crime	Burglary	Larceny-theft	Motor vehicle theft
Gainesville, GA, MSA..........................	187,290									
Includes Hall County										
City of Gainesville	35,111	115	1	21	39	54	1,505	209	1,230	66
Total area actually reporting	100.0%	293	7	45	69	172	4,198	901	3,005	292
Rate per 100,000 inhabitants		156.4	3.7	24.0	36.8	91.8	2,241.4	481.1	1,604.5	155.9
Gettysburg, PA, MSA[3]..........................	101,443									
Includes Adams County										
City of Gettysburg	7,653	27	0	8	8	11	141	28	110	3
Total area actually reporting	99.4%	99	0	25	17	57	1,272	289	943	40
Estimated total	100.0%	100	0	25	17	58	1,283	291	952	40
Rate per 100,000 inhabitants		98.6	0.0	24.6	16.8	57.2	1,264.7	286.9	938.5	39.4
Glens Falls, NY, MSA..........................	128,459									
Includes Warren and Washington Counties										
City of Glens Falls	14,582	22	0	2	3	17	343	50	288	5
Total area actually reporting	100.0%	126	1	16	13	96	2,051	344	1,676	31
Rate per 100,000 inhabitants		98.1	0.8	12.5	10.1	74.7	1,596.6	267.8	1,304.7	24.1
Goldsboro, NC, MSA..........................	125,081									
Includes Wayne County										
City of Goldsboro	37,230	283	5	3	67	208	2,344	571	1,670	103
Total area actually reporting	97.7%	482	8	5	102	367	4,445	1,392	2,831	222
Estimated total	100.0%	489	8	5	104	372	4,545	1,413	2,906	226
Rate per 100,000 inhabitants		390.9	6.4	4.0	83.1	297.4	3,633.6	1,129.7	2,323.3	180.7
Grand Forks, ND-MN, MSA..........................	100,500									
Includes Polk County, MN, and Grand Forks County, ND										
City of Grand Forks, ND	53,625	144	0	30	25	89	1,343	191	1,084	68
Total area actually reporting	100.0%	210	1	54	27	128	2,140	351	1,681	108
Rate per 100,000 inhabitants		209.0	1.0	53.7	26.9	127.4	2,129.4	349.3	1,672.6	107.5
Grand Island, NE, MSA..........................	84,159									
Includes Hall, Hamilton, Howard, and Merrick Counties										
City of Grand Island	50,441	136	1	36	8	91	2,389	526	1,759	104
Total area actually reporting	92.4%	150	1	39	9	101	2,817	665	2,030	122
Estimated total	100.0%	156	1	41	10	104	2,900	680	2,092	128
Rate per 100,000 inhabitants		185.4	1.2	48.7	11.9	123.6	3,445.9	808.0	2,485.8	152.1
Grand Junction, CO, MSA..........................	149,245									
Includes Mesa County										
City of Grand Junction	60,167	262	2	63	48	149	2,552	298	2,141	113
Total area actually reporting	99.5%	464	4	136	54	270	3,830	558	3,087	185
Estimated total	100.0%	465	4	136	54	271	3,847	560	3,101	186
Rate per 100,000 inhabitants		311.6	2.7	91.1	36.2	181.6	2,577.6	375.2	2,077.8	124.6
Grand Rapids-Wyoming, MI, MSA..........................	1,012,133									
Includes Barry, Kent, Montcalm, and Ottawa Counties										
City of Grand Rapids	191,213	1,326	17	82	471	756	6,188	1,621	4,315	252
City of Wyoming	73,786	309	0	59	68	182	1,647	392	1,140	115
Total area actually reporting	99.4%	3,039	24	669	651	1,695	19,641	4,454	14,464	723
Estimated total	100.0%	3,057	24	672	655	1,706	19,779	4,482	14,563	734
Rate per 100,000 inhabitants		302.0	2.4	66.4	64.7	168.6	1,954.2	442.8	1,438.8	72.5
Grants Pass, OR, MSA..........................	83,162									
Includes Josephine County										
City of Grants Pass	34,865	110	1	11	35	63	2,557	477	1,844	236
Total area actually reporting	100.0%	136	3	11	37	85	3,364	772	2,229	363
Rate per 100,000 inhabitants		163.5	3.6	13.2	44.5	102.2	4,045.1	928.3	2,680.3	436.5
Great Falls, MT, MSA..........................	82,197									
Includes Cascade County										
City of Great Falls	58,940	149	0	30	18	101	2,683	393	2,186	104
Total area actually reporting	100.0%	184	0	35	19	130	2,947	451	2,374	122
Rate per 100,000 inhabitants		223.9	0.0	42.6	23.1	158.2	3,585.3	548.7	2,888.2	148.4
Greeley, CO, MSA..........................	268,670									
Includes Weld County										

Table 6. Crime, by Selected Metropolitan Statistical Area, 2013—*Continued*

(Number, percent, rate per 100,000 population.)

Area	Population	Violent crime	Murder and nonnegligent manslaughter	Rape[1]	Robbery	Aggravated assault	Property crime	Burglary	Larceny-theft	Motor vehicle theft
Greeley, CO, MSA (cont.)										
City of Greeley	96,111	491	2	74	68	347	3,219	475	2,558	186
Total area actually reporting	97.6%	782	2	116	81	583	5,139	869	3,930	340
Estimated total	100.0%	795	2	119	83	591	5,297	889	4,056	352
Rate per 100,000 inhabitants		295.9	0.7	44.3	30.9	220.0	1,971.6	330.9	1,509.7	131.0
Green Bay, WI, MSA................................	312,769									
Includes Brown, Kewaunee, and Oconto Counties										
City of Green Bay	105,107	500	2	52	79	367	2,674	575	2,001	98
Total area actually reporting	89.5%	622	2	72	102	446	5,325	947	4,221	157
Estimated total	100.0%	644	2	76	105	461	5,669	1,024	4,474	171
Rate per 100,000 inhabitants		205.9	0.6	24.3	33.6	147.4	1,812.5	327.4	1,430.4	54.7
Greensboro-High Point, NC, MSA........................	742,007									
Includes Guilford, Randolph, and Rockingham Counties										
City of Greensboro	279,343	1,449	27	70	496	856	11,537	2,972	8,063	502
City of High Point	107,261	556	2	30	178	346	4,489	1,206	2,970	313
Total area actually reporting	99.8%	2,554	35	136	795	1,588	25,542	7,241	17,130	1,171
Estimated total	100.0%	2,557	35	136	796	1,590	25,588	7,251	17,164	1,173
Rate per 100,000 inhabitants		344.6	4.7	18.3	107.3	214.3	3,448.5	977.2	2,313.2	158.1
Greenville, NC, MSA................................	174,355									
Includes Pitt County										
City of Greenville	88,018	555	7	20	175	353	3,862	1,157	2,573	132
Total area actually reporting	98.6%	792	11	33	223	525	5,834	1,742	3,891	201
Estimated total	100.0%	799	11	33	225	530	5,923	1,761	3,958	204
Rate per 100,000 inhabitants		458.3	6.3	18.9	129.0	304.0	3,397.1	1,010.0	2,270.1	117.0
Greenville-Anderson-Mauldin, SC, MSA...............	852,405									
Includes Anderson, Greenville, Laurens, and Pickens Counties										
City of Greenville	61,185	455	3	35	118	299	3,261	666	2,384	211
City of Anderson	26,812	278	2	21	43	212	2,417	510	1,767	140
City of Mauldin	24,099	40	0	10	8	22	410	75	302	33
City of Easley	20,115	75	1	4	10	60	1,291	165	1,066	60
Total area actually reporting	99.9%	4,788	46	478	738	3,526	34,269	8,622	23,050	2,597
Estimated total	100.0%	4,793	46	478	739	3,530	34,319	8,631	23,089	2,599
Rate per 100,000 inhabitants		562.3	5.4	56.1	86.7	414.1	4,026.1	1,012.5	2,708.7	304.9
Gulfport-Biloxi-Pascagoula, MS, MSA..................										
Includes Anderson, Greenville, Laurens, and Pickens Counties										
City of Greenville	61,185	455	3	35	118	299	3,261	666	2,384	211
City of Anderson	26,812	278	2	21	43	212	2,417	510	1,767	140
City of Mauldin	24,099	40	0	10	8	22	410	75	302	33
City of Easley	20,115	75	1	4	10	60	1,291	165	1,066	60
Total area actually reporting	99.9%	4,788	46	478	738	3,526	34,269	8,622	23,050	2,597
Estimated total	100.0%	4,793	46	478	739	3,530	34,319	8,631	23,089	2,599
Rate per 100,000 inhabitants		562.3	5.4	56.1	86.7	414.1	4,026.1	1,012.5	2,708.7	304.9
Hagerstown-Martinsburg, MD-WV, MSA...............	257,750									
Includes Washington County, MD and Berkeley County, WV										
City of Hagerstown, MD	40,866	244	5	10	101	128	1,498	375	1,051	72
City of Martinsburg, WV	17,589	70	1	8	27	34	827	97	702	28
Total area actually reporting	100.0%	600	8	48	181	363	5,727	1,332	4,125	270
Rate per 100,000 inhabitants		232.8	3.1	18.6	70.2	140.8	2,221.9	516.8	1,600.4	104.8
Hammond, LA, MSA................................	124,208									
Includes Tangipahoa Parish										
City of Hammond	20,162	251	3	14	77	157	2,305	902	1,322	81
Total area actually reporting	100.0%	1,087	12	57	156	862	6,957	2,421	4,210	326
Rate per 100,000 inhabitants		875.1	9.7	45.9	125.6	694.0	5,601.1	1,949.1	3,389.5	262.5
Hanford-Corcoran, CA, MSA........................	151,256									
Includes Kings County										
City of Hanford	54,425	299	2	10	63	224	1,939	345	1,401	193
City of Corcoran	23,290	71	0	2	10	59	364	103	215	46
Total area actually reporting	100.0%	725	6	35	123	561	3,723	858	2,413	452
Rate per 100,000 inhabitants		479.3	4.0	23.1	81.3	370.9	2,461.4	567.3	1,595.3	298.8

Table 6. Crime, by Selected Metropolitan Statistical Area, 2013—*Continued*

(Number, percent, rate per 100,000 population.)

Area	Population	Violent crime	Murder and nonnegligent manslaughter	Rape[1]	Robbery	Aggravated assault	Property crime	Burglary	Larceny-theft	Motor vehicle theft
Harrisburg-Carlisle, PA, MSA	553,808									
Includes Cumberland, Dauphin, and Perry Counties										
City of Harrisburg	49,753	727	11	56	388	272	2,426	613	1,655	158
City of Carlisle	19,103	48	0	15	19	14	610	60	547	3
Total area actually reporting	99.7%	1,656	18	176	607	855	11,799	2,327	9,079	393
Estimated total	100.0%	1,659	18	176	608	857	11,835	2,333	9,108	394
Rate per 100,000 inhabitants		299.6	3.3	31.8	109.8	154.7	2,137.0	421.3	1,644.6	71.1
Harrisonburg, VA, MSA	129,689									
Includes Rockingham County and Harrisonburg City										
City of Harrisonburg	51,767	106	1	18	16	71	1,367	206	1,126	35
Total area actually reporting	100.0%	166	1	34	17	114	2,022	361	1,603	58
Rate per 100,000 inhabitants		128.0	0.8	26.2	13.1	87.9	1,559.1	278.4	1,236.0	44.7
Hartford-West Hartford-East Hartford, CT, MSA ...	1,023,807									
Includes Hartford, Middlesex, and Tolland Counties										
City of Hartford	124,927	1,473	23	53	557	840	5,036	981	3,416	639
City of West Hartford	63,276	45	0	2	35	8	1,379	176	1,120	83
City of East Hartford	51,275	182	1	31	63	87	1,445	327	998	120
City of Middletown	47,221	60	0	12	22	26	827	87	666	74
Total area actually reporting	100.0%	2,706	35	259	1,046	1,366	22,530	3,998	16,853	1,679
Rate per 100,000 inhabitants		264.3	3.4	25.3	102.2	133.4	2,200.6	390.5	1,646.1	164.0
Hilton Head Island-Bluffton-Beaufort, SC, MSA	196,780									
Includes Beaufort and Jasper Counties										
City of Bluffton	13,047	49	0	2	13	34	379	61	300	18
City of Beaufort	12,918	153	0	6	28	119	804	126	659	19
Total area actually reporting	100.0%	955	6	84	134	731	5,675	1,321	4,077	277
Rate per 100,000 inhabitants		485.3	3.0	42.7	68.1	371.5	2,883.9	671.3	2,071.9	140.8
Hinesville, GA, MSA	82,962									
Includes Liberty and Long Counties										
City of Hinesville	35,311	120	3	8	42	67	1,444	351	1,035	58
Total area actually reporting	100.0%	230	5	16	51	158	2,259	651	1,499	109
Rate per 100,000 inhabitants		277.2	6.0	19.3	61.5	190.4	2,722.9	784.7	1,806.9	131.4
Homosassa Spring, FL, MSA	139,242									
Includes Citrus County										
Total area actually reporting	97.8%	528	5	45	65	413	2,649	631	1,911	107
Estimated total	100.0%	542	5	46	69	422	2,755	653	1,989	113
Rate per 100,000 inhabitants		389.3	3.6	33.0	49.6	303.1	1,978.6	469.0	1,428.4	81.2
Hot Springs, AR, MSA	97,163									
Includes Garland County										
City of Hot Springs	35,551	140	7	25	57	51	3,181	721	2,294	166
Total area actually reporting	100.0%	459	9	70	74	306	5,178	1,547	3,370	261
Rate per 100,000 inhabitants		472.4	9.3	72.0	76.2	314.9	5,329.2	1,592.2	3,468.4	268.6
Houma-Thibodaux, LA, MSA	209,328									
Includes Lafourche and Terrebonne Parishes										
City of Houma	33,717	204	5	16	67	116	1,574	243	1,272	59
City of Thibodaux	14,544	68	1	4	7	56	683	93	577	13
Total area actually reporting	100.0%	626	23	41	130	432	6,740	1,414	5,087	239
Rate per 100,000 inhabitants		299.1	11.0	19.6	62.1	206.4	3,219.8	675.5	2,430.2	114.2
Houston-The Woodlands-Sugar Land, TX, MSA[3]	6,281,279									
Includes Austin, Brazoria, Chambers, Fort Bend, Galveston, Harris, Liberty, Montgomery, and Waller Counties										
City of Houston	2,180,606	20,993	214	618	9,891	10,270	110,919	23,733	73,591	13,595
City of Sugar Land	83,460	108	1	6	35	66	1,613	256	1,311	46
City of Baytown	73,709	285	4	19	126	136	3,653	916	2,373	364
City of Conroe	62,962	216	1	29	60	126	2,071	416	1,550	105
Total area actually reporting	99.9%	35,111	373	1,441	14,656	18,641	219,127	49,637	146,193	23,297
Estimated total	100.0%	35,112	373	1,441	14,656	18,642	219,139	49,639	146,202	23,298
Rate per 100,000 inhabitants		559.0	5.9	22.9	233.3	296.8	3,488.8	790.3	2,327.6	370.9
Huntsville, AL, MSA	434,500									
Includes Limestone and Madison Counties										

Table 6. Crime, by Selected Metropolitan Statistical Area, 2013—*Continued*

(Number, percent, rate per 100,000 population.)

Area	Population	Violent crime	Murder and nonnegligent manslaughter	Rape[1]	Robbery	Aggravated assault	Property crime	Burglary	Larceny-theft	Motor vehicle theft
Huntsville, AL, MSA (cont.)										
City of Huntsville	184,738	1,507	24	87	391	1,005	9,216	1,884	6,629	703
Total area actually reporting	100.0%	2,101	27	187	466	1,421	14,581	3,190	10,393	998
Rate per 100,000 inhabitants		483.5	6.2	43.0	107.2	327.0	3,355.8	734.2	2,391.9	229.7
Idaho Falls, ID, MSA...............	137,561									
Includes Bonneville, Butte, and Jefferson Counties										
City of Idaho Falls	58,188	124	0	31	19	74	1,623	304	1,210	109
Total area actually reporting	100.0%	218	3	48	24	143	2,527	535	1,828	164
Rate per 100,000 inhabitants		158.5	2.2	34.9	17.4	104.0	1,837.0	388.9	1,328.9	119.2
Indianapolis-Carmel-Anderson, IN, MSA...............	1,946,607									
Includes Boone, Brown, Hamilton, Hancock, Hendricks, Johnson, Madison, Marion, Morgan, Putnam, and Shelby Counties										
City of Indianapolis	850,220	10,479	129	656	3,800	5,894	44,606	13,445	26,156	5,005
City of Carmel	84,880	20	0	4	11	5	744	128	573	43
City of Anderson	55,367	200	5	36	103	56	2,664	605	1,829	230
Total area actually reporting	86.8%		141	767	4,056		61,601	16,199	39,292	6,110
Estimated total	100.0%		148	807	4,162		67,521	17,235	43,790	6,496
Rate per 100,000 inhabitants			7.6	41.5	213.8		3,468.7	885.4	2,249.6	333.7
Iowa City, IA, MSA...............	160,439									
Includes Johnson and Washington Counties										
City of Iowa City	70,855	228	0	28	56	144	1,850	357	1,411	82
Total area actually reporting	99.9%	473	0	88	71	314	3,178	576	2,465	137
Estimated total	100.0%	473	0	88	71	314	3,179	576	2,466	137
Rate per 100,000 inhabitants		294.8	0.0	54.8	44.3	195.7	1,981.4	359.0	1,537.0	85.4
Jackson, MI, MSA...............	160,498									
Includes Jackson County										
City of Jackson	33,378	370	4	59	61	246	1,732	433	1,220	79
Total area actually reporting	96.9%	637	5	134	80	418	3,843	869	2,827	147
Estimated total	100.0%	651	5	136	83	427	3,958	892	2,910	156
Rate per 100,000 inhabitants		405.6	3.1	84.7	51.7	266.0	2,466.1	555.8	1,813.1	97.2
Jackson, MS, MSA...............	579,868									
Includes Copiah, Hinds, Madison, Rankin, Simpson, and Yazoo Counties										
City of Jackson	176,039	1,631	50	110	845	626	10,284	3,366	5,864	1,054
Total area actually reporting	83.7%	2,011	57	140	954	860	15,166	4,668	9,167	1,331
Estimated total	100.0%	2,191	58	154	995	984	17,331	5,277	10,615	1,439
Rate per 100,000 inhabitants		377.8	10.0	26.6	171.6	169.7	2,988.8	910.0	1,830.6	248.2
Jackson, TN, MSA...............	130,702									
Includes Chester, Crockett, and Madison Counties										
City of Jackson	67,371	925	11	40	151	723	3,455	815	2,484	156
Total area actually reporting	100.0%	1,209	11	58	168	972	4,775	1,263	3,276	236
Rate per 100,000 inhabitants		925.0	8.4	44.4	128.5	743.7	3,653.3	966.3	2,506.5	180.6
Jacksonville, FL, MSA...............	1,392,914									
Includes Baker, Clay, Duval, Nassau, and St. Johns Counties										
City of Jacksonville	845,745	5,246	93	452	1,424	3,277	33,007	7,069	24,361	1,577
Total area actually reporting	100.0%	6,904	99	583	1,646	4,576	44,974	9,453	33,478	2,043
Rate per 100,000 inhabitants		495.7	7.1	41.9	118.2	328.5	3,228.8	678.6	2,403.5	146.7
Janesville-Beloit, WI, MSA...............	160,586									
Includes Rock County										
City of Janesville	63,603	166	0	41	25	100	1,943	330	1,576	37
City of Beloit	36,817	129	1	16	36	76	1,195	320	830	45
Total area actually reporting	100.0%	368	2	69	70	227	3,986	899	2,969	118
Rate per 100,000 inhabitants		229.2	1.2	43.0	43.6	141.4	2,482.2	559.8	1,848.9	73.5
Jefferson City, MO, MSA...............	150,542									
Includes Callaway, Cole, Moniteau, and Osage Counties										
City of Jefferson City	43,193	200	0	7	36	157	1,446	235	1,162	49
Total area actually reporting	100.0%	426	2	19	54	351	3,243	709	2,418	116
Rate per 100,000 inhabitants		283.0	1.3	12.6	35.9	233.2	2,154.2	471.0	1,606.2	77.1

(Number, percent, rate per 100,000 population.)

Area	Population	Violent crime	Murder and nonnegligent manslaughter	Rape[1]	Robbery	Aggravated assault	Property crime	Burglary	Larceny-theft	Motor vehicle theft
Johnson City, TN, MSA............................	201,439									
Includes Carter, Unicoi, and Washington Counties										
City of Johnson City	64,928	297	2	23	50	222	2,572	399	2,097	76
Total area actually reporting	100.0%	660	7	46	70	537	5,157	1,146	3,828	183
Rate per 100,000 inhabitants		327.6	3.5	22.8	34.7	266.6	2,560.1	568.9	1,900.3	90.8
Johnstown, PA, MSA...............................	140,876									
Includes Cambria County										
City of Johnstown	21,954	129	7	2	44	76	802	277	497	28
Total area actually reporting	100.0%	253	12	15	67	159	2,540	600	1,853	87
Rate per 100,000 inhabitants		179.6	8.5	10.6	47.6	112.9	1,803.0	425.9	1,315.3	61.8
Jonesboro, AR, MSA	125,041									
Includes Craighead and Poinsett Counties										
City of Jonesboro	71,114	313	2	36	58	217	2,995	979	1,930	86
Total area actually reporting	97.4%	440	2	63	65	310	4,321	1,390	2,815	116
Estimated total	100.0%	454	2	64	67	321	4,436	1,423	2,892	121
Rate per 100,000 inhabitants		363.1	1.6	51.2	53.6	256.7	3,547.6	1,138.0	2,312.8	96.8
Joplin, MO, MSA	174,207									
Includes Jasper and Newton Counties										
City of Joplin	49,272	240	1	35	55	149	3,925	617	3,055	253
Total area actually reporting	100.0%	521	4	66	73	378	7,585	1,451	5,639	495
Rate per 100,000 inhabitants		299.1	2.3	37.9	41.9	217.0	4,354.0	832.9	3,237.0	284.1
Kahului-Wailuku-Lahaina, HI, MSA.........................	159,652									
Includes Kalawao and Maui Counties										
Total area actually reporting	100.0%	450	1	45	97	307	5,704	948	4,314	442
Rate per 100,000 inhabitants		281.9	0.6	28.2	60.8	192.3	3,572.8	593.8	2,702.1	276.9
Kankakee, IL, MSA	112,844									
Includes Kankakee and Van Buren Counties										
City of Kankakee	27,286	196	4	23	70	99	1,063	285	743	35
Total area actually reporting	91.2%	342	6	52	84	200	2,667	586	2,009	72
Estimated total	100.0%	362	6	54	90	212	2,860	620	2,160	80
Rate per 100,000 inhabitants		320.8	5.3	47.9	79.8	187.9	2,534.5	549.4	1,914.1	70.9
Kansas City, MO-KS, MSA[1]...................................	2,049,436									
Includes Johnson, Leavenworth, Linn, Miami, and Wyandotte Counties, KS, and Bates, Caldwell, Cass, Clay, Clinton, Jackson, Lafayette, Platte, and Ray Counties, MO										
City of Kansas City, MO	465,514	5,864	99	377	1,662	3,726	24,648	6,412	13,949	4,287
City of Overland Park, KS	180,555	284	2	33	45	204	3,530	404	2,846	280
City of Kansas City, KS	147,618	731	28	83	238	382	7,228	1,617	4,566	1,045
Total area actually reporting	99.9%	9,595	152	861	2,380	6,202	66,618	13,830	44,395	8,393
Estimated total	100.0%	9,601	152	862	2,381	6,206	66,696	13,843	44,456	8,397
Rate per 100,000 inhabitants		468.5	7.4	42.1	116.2	302.8	3,254.4	675.5	2,169.2	409.7
Kennewick-Richland, WA, MSA	273,507									
Includes Benton and Franklin Counties										
City of Kennewick	76,508	240	2	34	43	161	2,478	444	1,876	158
City of Richland	52,465	95	3	17	11	64	1,167	205	927	35
Total area actually reporting	100.0%	603	9	88	88	418	6,236	1,293	4,533	410
Rate per 100,000 inhabitants		220.5	3.3	32.2	32.2	152.8	2,280.0	472.7	1,657.4	149.9
Kingsport-Bristol-Bristol, TN-VA, MSA	309,240									
Includes Hawkins and Sullivan Counties, TN, and Scott and Washington Counties and Bristol City, VA										
City of Kingsport, TN	51,496	267	0	16	31	220	2,657	381	2,151	125
City of Bristol, TN	26,660	96	1	10	8	77	1,124	186	888	50
City of Bristol, VA	17,641	59	0	6	7	46	543	61	462	20
Total area actually reporting	99.5%	972	5	112	73	782	8,271	1,552	6,350	369
Estimated total	100.0%	976	5	113	74	784	8,314	1,558	6,385	371
Rate per 100,000 inhabitants		315.6	1.6	36.5	23.9	253.5	2,688.5	503.8	2,064.7	120.0
Kingston, NY, MSA................................	181,804									
Includes Ulster County										
City of Kingston	23,665	74	1	4	25	44	687	112	565	10
Total area actually reporting	100.0%	294	3	31	52	208	3,281	590	2,636	55
Rate per 100,000 inhabitants		161.7	1.7	17.1	28.6	114.4	1,804.7	324.5	1,449.9	30.3

Table 6. Crime, by Selected Metropolitan Statistical Area, 2013—*Continued*

(Number, percent, rate per 100,000 population.)

Area	Population	Violent crime	Murder and nonnegligent manslaughter	Rape[1]	Robbery	Aggravated assault	Property crime	Burglary	Larceny-theft	Motor vehicle theft
Knoxville, TN, MSA	852,347									
Includes Anderson, Blount, Campbell, Grainger, Knox, Loudon, Morgan, Roane, and Union Counties										
City of Knoxville	183,249	1,541	18	139	415	969	11,438	2,275	8,424	739
Total area actually reporting	96.6%	2,999	30	251	613	2,105	25,895	6,159	18,232	1,504
Estimated total	100.0%	3,103	31	259	626	2,187	26,730	6,302	18,890	1,538
Rate per 100,000 inhabitants		364.1	3.6	30.4	73.4	256.6	3,136.0	739.4	2,216.2	180.4
Kokomo, IN, MSA	83,108									
Includes Howard County										
City of Kokomo	56,878	185	2	18	66	99	2,210	496	1,600	114
Total area actually reporting	100.0%	218	2	18	68	130	2,462	581	1,753	128
Rate per 100,000 inhabitants		262.3	2.4	21.7	81.8	156.4	2,962.4	699.1	2,109.3	154.0
La Crosse-Onalaska, WI-MN, MSA[4]	135,914									
Includes Houston County, MN4 and La Crosse County, WI										
City of La Crosse, WI	51,741	107	1	20	29	57	1,548	305	1,200	43
City of Onalaska, WI	18,408	8	0	0	0	8	429	26	401	2
Total area actually reporting	100.0%	167	2	26	29	110	2,507	443	1,994	70
Rate per 100,000 inhabitants		122.9	1.5	19.1	21.3	80.9	1,844.5	325.9	1,467.1	51.5
Lafayette, LA, MSA	477,151									
Includes Acadia, Iberia, Lafayette, St. Martin, and Vermilion Parishes										
City of Lafayette	123,409	868	8	17	272	571	7,568	1,276	5,995	297
Total area actually reporting	97.7%	2,153	23	83	504	1,543	16,463	3,731	11,720	1,012
Estimated total	100.0%	2,201	24	85	513	1,579	16,915	3,814	12,074	1,027
Rate per 100,000 inhabitants		461.3	5.0	17.8	107.5	330.9	3,545.0	799.3	2,530.4	215.2
Lafayette, West Lafayette, IN, MSA	208,478									
Includes Benton, Carroll, and Tippecanoe Counties										
City of Lafayette	68,173	389	2	35	67	285	3,416	718	2,466	232
City of West Lafayette	30,687	37	0	6	6	25	536	90	430	16
Total area actually reporting	86.5%	489	3	56	81	349	5,232	1,055	3,895	282
Estimated total	100.0%	522	3	60	87	372	5,672	1,158	4,202	312
Rate per 100,000 inhabitants		250.4	1.4	28.8	41.7	178.4	2,720.7	555.5	2,015.6	149.7
Lake Havasu City-Kingman, AZ, MSA	205,099									
Includes Mohave County										
City of Lake Havasu City	52,891	87	1	17	11	58	1,252	285	899	68
City of Kingman	28,400	128	1	11	19	97	1,621	398	1,159	64
Total area actually reporting	97.6%	425	9	34	68	314	6,729	1,833	4,500	396
Estimated total	100.0%	437	9	35	71	322	6,882	1,861	4,616	405
Rate per 100,000 inhabitants		213.1	4.4	17.1	34.6	157.0	3,355.5	907.4	2,250.6	197.5
Lakeland-Winter Haven, FL, MSA	622,846									
Includes Polk County										
City of Lakeland	100,725	460	7	52	143	258	5,410	1,130	4,082	198
City of Winter Haven	35,325	215	2	24	46	143	1,577	353	1,180	44
Total area actually reporting	100.0%	2,287	20	177	396	1,694	18,115	4,929	12,280	906
Rate per 100,000 inhabitants		367.2	3.2	28.4	63.6	272.0	2,908.4	791.4	1,971.6	145.5
Lancaster, PA, MSA[3]	528,698									
Includes Lancaster County										
City of Lancaster	59,370	497	5	53	249	190	2,692	441	2,165	86
Total area actually reporting	100.0%	905	9	132	340	424	9,845	1,741	7,814	290
Rate per 100,000 inhabitants		171.2	1.7	25.0	64.3	80.2	1,862.1	329.3	1,478.0	54.9
Lansing-East Lansing, MI, MSA	466,728									
Includes Clinton, Eaton, and Ingham Counties										
City of Lansing	113,907	1,204	8	127	256	813	3,960	1,268	2,329	363
City of East Lansing	48,506	109	0	31	24	54	799	150	552	97
Total area actually reporting	94.5%	1,815	14	301	366	1,134	9,730	2,368	6,689	673
Estimated total	100.0%	1,893	15	314	383	1,181	10,323	2,488	7,114	721
Rate per 100,000 inhabitants		405.6	3.2	67.3	82.1	253.0	2,211.8	533.1	1,524.2	154.5
Laredo, TX, MSA	262,936									
Includes Webb County										
City of Laredo	247,353	1,027	3	75	207	742	10,482	1,425	8,685	372

Table 6. Crime, by Selected Metropolitan Statistical Area, 2013—*Continued*

(Number, percent, rate per 100,000 population.)

Area	Population	Violent crime	Murder and nonnegligent manslaughter	Rape[1]	Robbery	Aggravated assault	Property crime	Burglary	Larceny-theft	Motor vehicle theft
Laredo, TX, MSA (cont.)										
Total area actually reporting	100.0%	1,133	4	80	211	838	10,879	1,536	8,952	391
Rate per 100,000 inhabitants		430.9	1.5	30.4	80.2	318.7	4,137.5	584.2	3,404.6	148.7
Las Cruces, NM, MSA	215,083									
Includes Dona Ana County										
City of Las Cruces	102,007	332	6	27	74	225	4,349	724	3,454	171
Total area actually reporting	98.3%	686	8	74	89	515	6,242	1,387	4,541	314
Estimated total	100.0%	716	8	76	91	541	6,382	1,421	4,637	324
Rate per 100,000 inhabitants		332.9	3.7	35.3	42.3	251.5	2,967.2	660.7	2,155.9	150.6
Las Vegas-Henderson-Paradise, NV, MSA	2,025,864									
Includes Clark County										
City of Las Vegas Metropolitan Police Department	1,500,455	11,374	97	705	4,072	6,500	47,968	14,785	26,548	6,635
City of Henderson	268,237	367	8	45	160	154	5,358	1,405	3,416	537
Total area actually reporting	100.0%	13,735	116	855	4,716	8,048	61,116	18,568	34,302	8,246
Rate per 100,000 inhabitants		678.0	5.7	42.2	232.8	397.3	3,016.8	916.5	1,693.2	407.0
Lawrence, KS, MSA	113,372									
Includes Douglas County										
City of Lawrence	90,034	338	1	50	74	213	3,625	493	2,959	173
Total area actually reporting	100.0%	371	1	57	75	238	4,152	622	3,334	196
Rate per 100,000 inhabitants		327.2	0.9	50.3	66.2	209.9	3,662.3	548.6	2,940.8	172.9
Lawton, OK, MSA	133,449									
Includes Comanche and Cotton Counties										
City of Lawton	98,548	919	13	80	168	658	5,027	1,485	3,313	229
Total area actually reporting	100.0%	950	13	91	169	677	5,454	1,663	3,541	250
Rate per 100,000 inhabitants		711.9	9.7	68.2	126.6	507.3	4,087.0	1,246.2	2,653.4	187.3
Lebanon, PA, MSA	135,689									
Includes Lebanon County										
City of Lebanon	25,583	103	2	2	62	37	785	139	623	23
Total area actually reporting	100.0%	243	2	14	96	131	2,493	378	2,049	66
Rate per 100,000 inhabitants		179.1	1.5	10.3	70.8	96.5	1,837.3	278.6	1,510.1	48.6
Lewiston, ID-WA, MSA	61,820									
Includes Nez Perce County, ID and Asotin County, WA										
City of Lewiston, ID	32,093	49	0	8	8	33	1,169	264	853	52
Total area actually reporting	100.0%	113	0	11	21	81	2,050	426	1,531	93
Rate per 100,000 inhabitants		182.8	0.0	17.8	34.0	131.0	3,316.1	689.1	2,476.5	150.4
Lewiston-Auburn, ME, MSA	107,469									
Includes Androscoggin County										
City of Lewiston	36,422	89	0	25	20	44	1,217	313	848	56
City of Auburn	22,948	32	0	10	10	12	1,072	197	858	17
Total area actually reporting	100.0%	155	1	46	36	72	2,924	703	2,122	99
Rate per 100,000 inhabitants		144.2	0.9	42.8	33.5	67.0	2,720.8	654.1	1,974.5	92.1
Lexington-Fayette, KY, MSA	489,329									
Includes Bourbon, Clark, Fayette, Jessamine, Scott, and Woodford Counties										
City of Lexington[1]	308,712	946	18	134	467	327	12,447	2,574	9,042	831
Total area actually reporting	99.9%	1,256	24	185	584	463	18,207	3,814	13,376	1,017
Estimated total	100.0%	1,256	24	185	584	463	18,218	3,816	13,384	1,018
Rate per 100,000 inhabitants		256.7	4.9	37.8	119.3	94.6	3,723.1	779.8	2,735.2	208.0
Lima, OH, MSA	105,002									
Includes Allen County										
City of Lima	38,214	366	3	42	78	243	1,932	582	1,255	95
Total area actually reporting	97.3%	397	3	49	86	259	3,495	907	2,443	145
Estimated total	100.0%	402	3	50	88	261	3,567	921	2,499	147
Rate per 100,000 inhabitants		382.8	2.9	47.6	83.8	248.6	3,397.1	877.1	2,380.0	140.0
Lincoln, NE, MSA	313,545									
Includes Lancaster and Seward Counties										
City of Lincoln	267,565	990	5	142	212	631	9,354	1,423	7,625	306
Total area actually reporting	100.0%	1,031	5	152	214	660	10,026	1,547	8,153	326
Rate per 100,000 inhabitants		328.8	1.6	48.5	68.3	210.5	3,197.6	493.4	2,600.3	104.0

Table 6. Crime, by Selected Metropolitan Statistical Area, 2013—*Continued*

(Number, percent, rate per 100,000 population.)

Area	Population	Violent crime	Murder and nonnegligent manslaughter	Rape[1]	Robbery	Aggravated assault	Property crime	Burglary	Larceny-theft	Motor vehicle theft
Little Rock-North Little Rock-Conway, AR, MSA..	723,132									
Includes Faulkner, Grant, Lonoke, Perry, Pulaski, and Saline Counties										
City of Little Rock	197,399	2,777	35	119	944	1,679	15,529	3,794	10,655	1,080
City of North Little Rock	65,398	461	13	11	138	299	3,901	864	2,762	275
City of Conway	64,060	239	1	22	49	167	2,774	367	2,299	108
Total area actually reporting	91.5%	4,685	55	268	1,262	3,100	34,102	8,566	23,279	2,257
Estimated total	100.0%	4,886	56	294	1,270	3,266	35,373	9,031	23,982	2,360
Rate per 100,000 inhabitants		675.7	7.7	40.7	175.6	451.6	4,891.6	1,248.9	3,316.4	326.4
Logan, UT-ID, MSA..................................	129,858									
Includes Franklin County, ID and Cache County, UT										
City of Logan, UT	49,049	35	0	20	0	15	860	138	700	22
Total area actually reporting	100.0%	72	1	33	0	38	1,531	256	1,227	48
Rate per 100,000 inhabitants		55.4	0.8	25.4	0.0	29.3	1,179.0	197.1	944.9	37.0
Longview, TX, MSA..................................	218,274									
Includes Gregg, Rusk, and Upshur Counties										
City of Longview	79,355	440	5	38	148	249	3,291	615	2,481	195
Total area actually reporting	99.5%	901	12	86	189	614	7,179	1,740	5,054	385
Estimated total	100.0%	904	12	86	190	616	7,214	1,747	5,080	387
Rate per 100,000 inhabitants		414.2	5.5	39.4	87.0	282.2	3,305.0	800.4	2,327.4	177.3
Longview, WA, MSA.................................	102,169									
Includes Cowlitz County										
City of Longview	36,374	170	0	38	48	84	2,421	512	1,734	175
Total area actually reporting	100.0%	362	1	101	61	199	4,057	910	2,859	288
Rate per 100,000 inhabitants		354.3	1.0	98.9	59.7	194.8	3,970.9	890.7	2,798.3	281.9
Los Angeles-Long Beach-Anaheim, CA, MSA...........	13,141,130									
Includes the Metropolitan Divisions of Anaheim-Santa Ana-Irvine and Los Angeles-Long Beach-Glendale										
City of Los Angeles	3,878,725	16,524	251	764	7,885	7,624	85,844	15,728	55,734	14,382
City of Long Beach	469,665	2,346	34	103	1,118	1,091	12,999	3,776	6,868	2,355
City of Anaheim	345,320	1,130	11	82	437	600	9,611	1,412	6,518	1,681
City of Santa Ana	332,848	1,121	13	51	463	594	6,425	803	4,163	1,459
City of Irvine	235,830	113	2	12	38	61	3,285	583	2,553	149
City of Glendale	195,366	181	1	8	75	97	3,198	563	2,384	251
City of Torrance	147,534	187	1	16	76	94	2,786	591	1,833	362
City of Pasadena	139,003	434	3	25	162	244	3,779	939	2,553	287
City of Orange	140,304	147	4	8	64	71	2,418	473	1,673	272
City of Costa Mesa	112,538	252	1	46	94	111	3,556	512	2,748	296
City of Burbank	104,727	171	0	13	51	107	2,430	285	1,926	219
City of Carson	93,415	400	3	15	148	234	2,251	514	1,248	489
City of Santa Monica	92,488	324	7	27	120	170	3,544	573	2,806	165
City of Newport Beach	87,639	73	2	7	13	51	2,158	454	1,600	104
City of Tustin	78,836	100	1	6	36	57	1,473	213	1,147	113
City of Monterey Park	61,152	104	0	8	60	36	1,162	316	637	209
City of Gardena	59,703	245	0	16	144	85	1,331	298	726	307
City of Arcadia	57,855	77	0	1	37	39	1,518	376	1,080	62
City of Fountain Valley	56,805	92	0	9	20	63	1,170	262	835	73
Total area actually reporting	100.0%	46,426	594	2,176	18,776	24,880	290,069	58,588	185,313	46,168
Rate per 100,000 inhabitants		353.3	4.5	16.6	142.9	189.3	2,207.3	445.8	1,410.2	351.3
Anaheim-Santa Ana-Irvine, CA, MD..................	3,118,731									
Includes Orange County										
Total area actually reporting	100.0%	6,042	51	424	1,993	3,574	61,650	10,416	44,001	7,233
Rate per 100,000 inhabitants		193.7	1.6	13.6	63.9	114.6	1,976.8	334.0	1,410.9	231.9
Los Angeles-Long Beach-Glendale, CA, MD.......	10,022,399									
Includes Los Angeles County										
Total area actually reporting	100.0%	40,384	543	1,752	16,783	21,306	228,419	48,172	141,312	38,935
Rate per 100,000 inhabitants		402.9	5.4	17.5	167.5	212.6	2,279.1	480.6	1,410.0	388.5
Louisville/Jefferson County, KY-IN, MSA...............	1,257,388									
Includes Clark, Floyd, Harrison, Scott, and Washington Counties, IN, and Bullitt, Henry, Jefferson, Oldham, Shelby, Spencer, and Trimble Counties, KY										
City of Louisville Metro, KY	671,120	3,644	48	160	1,427	2,009	28,780	6,920	19,835	2,025
Total area actually reporting	95.0%		61	262	1,727		42,159	9,801	29,576	2,782
Estimated total	100.0%		62	271	1,741		43,134	10,034	30,252	2,848

(Number, percent, rate per 100,000 population.)

Area	Population	Violent crime	Murder and nonnegligent manslaughter	Rape[1]	Robbery	Aggravated assault	Property crime	Burglary	Larceny-theft	Motor vehicle theft
Louisville/Jefferson County, KY-IN, MSA (cont.)										
Rate per 100,000 inhabitants			4.9	21.6	138.5		3,430.4	798.0	2,405.9	226.5
Lubbock, TX, MSA	300,769									
Includes Crosby, Lubbock, and Lynn Counties										
City of Lubbock	237,875	1,829	5	88	388	1,348	11,557	2,608	8,103	846
Total area actually reporting	100.0%	1,979	9	116	390	1,464	12,775	2,934	8,908	933
Rate per 100,000 inhabitants		658.0	3.0	38.6	129.7	486.8	4,247.4	975.5	2,961.7	310.2
Lynchburg, VA, MSA	256,835									
Includes Amherst, Appomattox, Bedford, and Campbell Counties and Bedford and Lynchburg Cities										
City of Lynchburg	77,757	330	1	36	73	220	1,974	349	1,538	87
Total area actually reporting	100.0%	491	5	83	89	314	4,118	738	3,174	206
Rate per 100,000 inhabitants		191.2	1.9	32.3	34.7	122.3	1,603.4	287.3	1,235.8	80.2
Macon, GA, MSA	232,892									
Includes Bibb, Crawford, Jones, Monroe, and Twiggs Counties										
City of Macon	91,177	583	18	46	231	288	6,800	1,993	4,318	489
Total area actually reporting	99.9%	900	23	72	308	497	11,126	2,876	7,438	812
Estimated total	100.0%	900	23	72	308	497	11,136	2,878	7,445	813
Rate per 100,000 inhabitants		386.4	9.9	30.9	132.3	213.4	4,781.6	1,235.8	3,196.8	349.1
Madera, CA, MSA	152,772									
Includes Madera County										
City of Madera	62,973	568	7	28	107	426	1,855	589	1,010	256
Total area actually reporting	100.0%	1,017	13	59	132	813	3,934	1,454	1,930	550
Rate per 100,000 inhabitants		665.7	8.5	38.6	86.4	532.2	2,575.1	951.7	1,263.3	360.0
Madison, WI, MSA[3]	626,047									
Includes Columbia, Dane, Green, and Iowa Counties										
City of Madison	242,523	884	5	76	296	507	7,729	1,382	6,094	253
Total area actually reporting	99.8%	1,358	11	166	369	812	14,134	2,341	11,360	433
Estimated total	100.0%	1,359	11	166	369	813	14,165	2,345	11,386	434
Rate per 100,000 inhabitants		217.1	1.8	26.5	58.9	129.9	2,262.6	374.6	1,818.7	69.3
Manchester-Nashua, NH, MSA	403,992									
Includes Hillsborough County										
City of Manchester	110,411	747	4	91	295	357	4,194	894	3,141	159
City of Nashua	87,052	182	6	32	61	83	2,248	323	1,857	68
Total area actually reporting	94.1%	1,118	10	177	381	550	9,086	1,618	7,166	302
Estimated total	100.0%	1,137	10	182	384	561	9,330	1,654	7,366	310
Rate per 100,000 inhabitants		281.4	2.5	45.1	95.1	138.9	2,309.5	409.4	1,823.3	76.7
Manhattan, KS, MSA	99,347									
Includes Geary, Pottawatomie, and Riley Counties										
Total area actually reporting	99.3%	191	6	28	20	137	1,729	332	1,324	73
Estimated total	100.0%	192	6	28	20	138	1,745	335	1,336	74
Rate per 100,000 inhabitants		193.3	6.0	28.2	20.1	138.9	1,756.5	337.2	1,344.8	74.5
Mankato-North Mankato, MN, MSA[4]	98,755									
Includes Blue Earth and Nicollet Counties										
City of Mankato[4]	40,360	107	1	18	31	57	1,753	312	1,395	46
City of North Mankato[4]	13,357	22	0	4	2	16	270	65	188	17
Total area actually reporting	100.0%	179	2	37	39	101	2,628	530	1,995	103
Rate per 100,000 inhabitants		181.3	2.0	37.5	39.5	102.3	2,661.1	536.7	2,020.2	104.3
Mansfield, OH, MSA	122,427									
Includes Richland County										
City of Mansfield	46,832	169	0	33	82	54	3,167	982	2,111	74
Total area actually reporting	95.4%	226	1	48	108	69	5,630	1,649	3,861	120
Estimated total	100.0%	233	1	49	111	72	5,777	1,678	3,974	125
Rate per 100,000 inhabitants		190.3	0.8	40.0	90.7	58.8	4,718.7	1,370.6	3,246.0	102.1
McAllen-Edinburg-Mission, TX, MSA	819,252									
Includes Hidalgo County										
City of McAllen	136,169	171	2	6	83	80	5,424	536	4,652	236
City of Edinburg	82,271	277	1	30	50	196	4,292	738	3,299	255
City of Mission	81,360	72	0	4	32	36	2,945	447	2,321	177
Total area actually reporting	100.0%	2,349	22	197	469	1,661	30,267	6,417	22,286	1,564

Table 6. Crime, by Selected Metropolitan Statistical Area, 2013—*Continued*

(Number, percent, rate per 100,000 population.)

Area	Population	Violent crime	Murder and nonnegligent manslaughter	Rape[1]	Robbery	Aggravated assault	Property crime	Burglary	Larceny-theft	Motor vehicle theft
McAllen-Edinburg-Mission, TX, MSA (cont.)										
Rate per 100,000 inhabitants		286.7	2.7	24.0	57.2	202.7	3,694.5	783.3	2,720.3	190.9
Medford, OR, MSA..	207,927									
Includes Jackson County										
City of Medford	76,949	483	1	37	99	346	4,813	575	4,075	163
Total area actually reporting	100.0%	732	4	72	131	525	8,180	1,145	6,739	296
Rate per 100,000 inhabitants		352.0	1.9	34.6	63.0	252.5	3,934.1	550.7	3,241.0	142.4
Memphis, TN-MS-AR, MSA...........................	1,347,803									
Includes Crittenden County, AR; DeSoto, Marshall, Tate, and Tunica Counties; MS, and Fayette, Shelby, and Tipton Counties, TN										
City of Memphis	657,691	10,894	124	437	3,133	7,200	39,804	11,825	25,295	2,684
Total area actually reporting	94.1%	13,260	138	605	3,444	9,073	55,004	15,683	35,897	3,424
Estimated total	100.0%	13,389	139	617	3,468	9,165	56,471	16,117	36,837	3,517
Rate per 100,000 inhabitants		993.4	10.3	45.8	257.3	680.0	4,189.9	1,195.8	2,733.1	260.9
Merced, CA, MSA..	264,498									
Includes Merced County										
City of Merced	81,329	556	5	19	133	399	2,647	644	1,608	395
Total area actually reporting	100.0%	1,555	27	78	231	1,219	8,096	2,097	4,657	1,342
Rate per 100,000 inhabitants		587.9	10.2	29.5	87.3	460.9	3,060.9	792.8	1,760.7	507.4
Miami-Fort Lauderdale-West Pompano Beach, FL, MSA	5,846,679									
Includes the Metropolitan Divisions of Fort Lauderdale-Pompano Beach-Deerfield Beach, Miami-Miami Beach-Kendall, and West Palm Beach-Boca Raton-Delray\ Beach										
City of Miami	418,394	4,945	71	96	2,216	2,562	20,928	3,993	15,021	1,914
City of Fort Lauderdale	172,398	1,456	13	73	701	669	9,650	2,654	6,429	567
City of Pompano Beach	102,510	701	15	29	281	376	4,863	1,024	3,453	386
City of West Palm Beach	103,971	819	7	64	273	475	5,129	1,220	3,580	329
City of Miami Beach	91,433	919	4	53	377	485	9,751	950	8,425	376
City of Boca Raton	88,749	165	4	8	54	99	2,302	464	1,744	94
City of Deerfield Beach	78,203	305	2	28	105	170	2,386	624	1,606	156
City of Delray Beach	62,887	487	0	29	147	311	3,107	588	2,308	211
City of Jupiter	57,826	127	0	7	36	84	1,094	163	864	67
Total area actually reporting	100.0%	31,507	383	1,824	11,062	18,238	215,771	44,416	156,375	14,980
Rate per 100,000 inhabitants		538.9	6.6	31.2	189.2	311.9	3,690.5	759.7	2,674.6	256.2
Fort Lauderdale-Pompano Beach-Deerfield Beach, FL, MD	1,843,375									
Includes Broward County										
Total area actually reporting	100.0%	8,078	80	568	2,981	4,449	63,720	15,934	43,855	3,931
Rate per 100,000 inhabitants		438.2	4.3	30.8	161.7	241.4	3,456.7	864.4	2,379.1	213.3
Miami-Miami Beach-Kendall, FL, MD	2,630,552									
Includes Miami-Dade County										
Total area actually reporting	100.0%	17,247	229	813	6,370	9,835	109,764	18,943	82,490	8,331
Rate per 100,000 inhabitants		655.6	8.7	30.9	242.2	373.9	4,172.7	720.1	3,135.8	316.7
West Palm Beach-Boca Raton-Delray Beach, FL, MD	1,372,752									
Includes Palm Beach County										
Total area actually reporting	100.0%	6,182	74	443	1,711	3,954	42,287	9,539	30,030	2,718
Rate per 100,000 inhabitants		450.3	5.4	32.3	124.6	288.0	3,080.5	694.9	2,187.6	198.0
Midland, TX, MSA	155,778									
Includes Martin and Midland Counties										
City of Midland	122,259	350	5	22	63	260	3,191	568	2,459	164
Total area actually reporting	100.0%	437	6	25	70	336	4,110	788	3,056	266
Rate per 100,000 inhabitants		280.5	3.9	16.0	44.9	215.7	2,638.4	505.8	1,961.8	170.8
Milwaukee-Waukesha-West Allis, WI, MSA...........	1,571,468									
Includes Milwaukee, Ozaukee, Washington, and Waukesha Counties										
City of Milwaukee	600,805	8,194	104	401	3,284	4,405	27,013	6,491	16,138	4,384
City of Waukesha	70,988	90	1	23	25	41	1,327	210	1,079	38
City of West Allis	60,830	196	1	14	104	77	2,851	631	2,128	92
Total area actually reporting	97.3%	9,176	110	526	3,678	4,862	47,226	9,144	33,120	4,962
Estimated total	100.0%	9,226	110	533	3,692	4,891	48,153	9,259	33,908	4,986
Rate per 100,000 inhabitants		587.1	7.0	33.9	234.9	311.2	3,064.2	589.2	2,157.7	317.3

Table 6. Crime, by Selected Metropolitan Statistical Area, 2013—*Continued*

(Number, percent, rate per 100,000 population.)

Area	Population	Violent crime	Murder and nonnegligent manslaughter	Rape[1]	Robbery	Aggravated assault	Property crime	Burglary	Larceny-theft	Motor vehicle theft
Minneapolis-St. Paul-Bloomington, MN-WI, MSA	3,455,982									
Includes Anoka, Carver, Chisago, Dakota, Hennepin, Isanti, Le Sueur, Mille Lacs, Ramsey, Scott, Sherburne, Sibley, Washington, and Wright Counties, MN, and Pierce and St. Croix Counties, WI										
City of Minneapolis, MN	396,206	4,038	36	385	1,856	1,761	19,358	4,601	13,182	1,575
City of St. Paul, MN	294,690	2,200	14	218	716	1,252	10,973	2,769	6,443	1,761
City of Bloomington, MN	87,057	128	1	17	49	61	3,283	193	2,990	100
City of Plymouth, MN	73,684	49	0	21	5	23	1,141	186	903	52
City of Eagan, MN	65,052	37	0	2	14	21	1,287	163	1,087	37
City of Eden Prairie, MN	62,714	39	1	10	7	21	894	83	788	23
Total area actually reporting	99.9%	9,462	87	1,226	3,340	4,809	89,604	15,041	68,577	5,986
Estimated total	100.0%	9,466	87	1,226	3,341	4,812	89,681	15,050	68,642	5,989
Rate per 100,000 inhabitants		273.9	2.5	35.5	96.7	139.2	2,594.9	435.5	1,986.2	173.3
Missoula, MT, MSA..............	112,051									
Includes Missoula County										
City of Missoula	68,877	218	1	32	39	146	2,890	418	2,341	131
Total area actually reporting	100.0%	301	1	47	40	213	3,407	507	2,730	170
Rate per 100,000 inhabitants		268.6	0.9	41.9	35.7	190.1	3,040.6	452.5	2,436.4	151.7
Mobile, AL, MSA[6]..............	414,070									
Includes Mobile County										
City of Mobile6	250,557	1,541	29	88	459	965	13,011	3,207	9,123	681
Total area actually reporting	100.0%	2,426	40	169	658	1,559	18,685	4,953	12,504	1,228
Rate per 100,000 inhabitants		585.9	9.7	40.8	158.9	376.5	4,512.5	1,196.2	3,019.8	296.6
Modesto, CA, MSA..............	524,583									
Includes Stanislaus County										
City of Modesto	204,252	1,704	14	72	450	1,168	9,989	2,251	6,349	1,389
Total area actually reporting	100.0%	2,716	33	126	741	1,816	20,538	5,133	11,936	3,469
Rate per 100,000 inhabitants		517.7	6.3	24.0	141.3	346.2	3,915.1	978.5	2,275.3	661.3
Monroe, LA, MSA..............	178,294									
Includes Ouachita and Union Parishes										
City of Monroe	49,396	516	6	29	147	334	4,371	1,467	2,822	82
Total area actually reporting	97.2%	1,004	17	46	195	746	8,567	2,659	5,679	229
Estimated total	100.0%	1,026	17	47	199	763	8,780	2,698	5,846	236
Rate per 100,000 inhabitants		575.5	9.5	26.4	111.6	427.9	4,924.5	1,513.2	3,278.9	132.4
Monroe, MI, MSA..............	150,897									
Includes Monroe County										
City of Monroe	20,474	110	1	25	23	61	714	151	521	42
Total area actually reporting	94.4%	390	5	104	57	224	3,350	830	2,303	217
Estimated total	100.0%	414	5	108	62	239	3,544	869	2,442	233
Rate per 100,000 inhabitants		274.4	3.3	71.6	41.1	158.4	2,348.6	575.9	1,618.3	154.4
Morgantown, WV, MSA..............	135,362									
Includes Monongalia and Preston Counties										
City of Morgantown	31,406	94	0	18	31	45	681	176	485	20
Total area actually reporting	91.2%	331	1	61	44	225	1,960	463	1,403	94
Estimated total	100.0%	368	1	65	50	252	2,305	518	1,681	106
Rate per 100,000 inhabitants		271.9	0.7	48.0	36.9	186.2	1,702.8	382.7	1,241.9	78.3
Morristown, TN, MSA..............	115,337									
Includes Hamblen and Jefferson Counties										
City of Morristown	29,300	162	2	11	25	124	1,583	134	1,375	74
Total area actually reporting	100.0%	368	2	36	39	291	3,480	658	2,652	170
Rate per 100,000 inhabitants		319.1	1.7	31.2	33.8	252.3	3,017.2	570.5	2,299.3	147.4
Mount Vernon-Anacortes, WA, MSA..............	119,004									
Includes Skagit County										
City of Mount Vernon	32,450	89	1	15	31	42	1,662	258	1,276	128
City of Anacortes	15,980	21	0	6	3	12	559	127	402	30
Total area actually reporting	100.0%	254	4	40	64	146	5,192	1,195	3,659	338
Rate per 100,000 inhabitants		213.4	3.4	33.6	53.8	122.7	4,362.9	1,004.2	3,074.7	284.0
Muncie, IN, MSA..............	117,579									
Includes Delaware County										
City of Muncie	70,059	288	0	29	96	163	3,007	532	2,321	154

Table 6. Crime, by Selected Metropolitan Statistical Area, 2013—*Continued*

(Number, percent, rate per 100,000 population.)

Area	Population	Violent crime	Murder and nonnegligent manslaughter	Rape[1]	Robbery	Aggravated assault	Property crime	Burglary	Larceny-theft	Motor vehicle theft
Muncie, IN, MSA (cont.)										
Total area actually reporting	100.0%	323	0	34	100	189	3,700	700	2,821	179
Rate per 100,000 inhabitants		274.7	0.0	28.9	85.0	160.7	3,146.8	595.3	2,399.2	152.2
Muskegon, MI, MSA	169,764									
Includes Muskegon County										
City of Muskegon	36,658	325	3	47	70	205	1,970	649	1,262	59
Total area actually reporting	100.0%	800	10	159	146	485	6,117	1,337	4,553	227
Rate per 100,000 inhabitants		471.2	5.9	93.7	86.0	285.7	3,603.2	787.6	2,682.0	133.7
Myrtle Beach-Conway-North Myrtle Beach, SC-NC, MSA..................	401,625									
Includes Brunswick County, NC, and Horry County, SC										
City of Myrtle Beach, SC	28,663	475	2	49	186	238	4,575	608	3,497	470
City of Conway, SC	19,121	113	3	11	19	80	880	111	727	42
City of North Myrtle Beach, SC	14,672	120	0	14	20	86	1,568	279	1,153	136
Total area actually reporting	98.3%	1,937	14	229	411	1,283	17,456	4,113	11,943	1,400
Estimated total	100.0%	1,956	14	230	416	1,296	17,696	4,163	12,124	1,409
Rate per 100,000 inhabitants		487.0	3.5	57.3	103.6	322.7	4,406.1	1,036.5	3,018.7	350.8
Napa, CA, MSA.......................................	139,982									
Includes Napa County										
City of Napa	78,761	255	2	26	47	180	1,409	304	975	130
Total area actually reporting	100.0%	417	2	37	83	295	2,574	605	1,732	237
Rate per 100,000 inhabitants		297.9	1.4	26.4	59.3	210.7	1,838.8	432.2	1,237.3	169.3
Naples-Immokalee-Marco Island, FL, MSA	337,025									
Includes Collier County										
City of Naples	20,292	39	0	9	7	23	551	101	438	12
City of Marco Island	16,942	4	0	0	0	4	177	31	145	1
Total area actually reporting	100.0%	785	12	82	114	577	5,236	1,121	3,884	231
Rate per 100,000 inhabitants		232.9	3.6	24.3	33.8	171.2	1,553.6	332.6	1,152.4	68.5
Nashville-Davidson–Murfreesboro–Franklin, TN, MSA....................................	1,745,622									
Includes Cannon, Cheatham, Davidson, Dickson, Hickman, Macon, Maury, Robertson, Rutherford, Smith, Sumner, Trousdale, Williamson, and Wilson Counties										
City of Nashville	635,673	6,612	35	437	1,611	4,529	24,460	5,613	17,650	1,197
City of Murfreesboro	115,587	705	4	54	130	517	4,051	742	3,131	178
City of Franklin	67,465	117	0	19	20	78	988	90	873	25
Total area actually reporting	100.0%	10,405	59	747	2,013	7,586	47,448	10,270	34,923	2,255
Rate per 100,000 inhabitants		596.1	3.4	42.8	115.3	434.6	2,718.1	588.3	2,000.6	129.2
New Bern, NC, MSA	128,857									
Includes Craven, Jones, and Pamlico Counties										
City of New Bern	30,514	120	0	7	43	70	1,567	525	992	50
Total area actually reporting	92.8%	340	1	31	68	240	3,763	1,422	2,207	134
Estimated total	100.0%	354	1	32	70	251	3,929	1,488	2,298	143
Rate per 100,000 inhabitants		274.7	0.8	24.8	54.3	194.8	3,049.1	1,154.8	1,783.4	111.0
New Haven-Milford, CT, MSA	808,809									
Includes New Haven County										
City of New Haven	131,071	1,643	19	76	770	778	6,068	1,082	4,233	753
City of Milford	53,041	42	0	1	23	18	1,555	148	1,302	105
Total area actually reporting	100.0%	3,112	27	156	1,350	1,579	22,735	3,485	16,783	2,467
Rate per 100,000 inhabitants		384.8	3.3	19.3	166.9	195.2	2,810.9	430.9	2,075.0	305.0
New Orleans-Metairie, LA, MSA	1,239,126									
Includes Jefferson, Orleans, Plaquemines, St. Bernard, St. Charles, St. James, St. John the Baptist, and St. Tammany Parishes										
City of New Orleans	377,022	2,965	156	176	1,138	1,495	14,525	3,203	9,179	2,143
Total area actually reporting	100.0%	5,872	235	321	1,805	3,511	39,059	7,853	27,676	3,530
Rate per 100,000 inhabitants		473.9	19.0	25.9	145.7	283.3	3,152.1	633.8	2,233.5	284.9
New York-Newark-Jersey City, NY-NJ-PA, MSA......	19,936,617									
Includes the Metropolitan Divisions of Dutchess County-Putnam County, NY; Nassau County-Suffolk County, NY; Newark, NJ-PA; and New York-Jersey City-White Plains, NY-NJ										
City of New York, NY	8,396,126	52,384	335	1,112	19,170	31,767	141,971	16,606	117,931	7,434

Table 6. Crime, by Selected Metropolitan Statistical Area, 2013—*Continued*

(Number, percent, rate per 100,000 population.)

Area	Population	Violent crime	Murder and nonnegligent manslaughter	Rape[1]	Robbery	Aggravated assault	Property crime	Burglary	Larceny-theft	Motor vehicle theft
New York-Newark-Jersey City, NY-NJ-PA, MSA (cont.)										
City of Newark, NJ	278,246	3,516	112	45	2,433	926	8,965	2,074	3,997	2,894
City of Jersey City, NJ	256,886	1,655	20	35	717	883	4,836	1,052	3,046	738
City of White Plains, NY	57,559	78	1	3	28	46	1,232	77	1,134	21
City of New Brunswick, NJ	56,542	303	3	19	165	116	1,665	546	1,032	87
City of Lakewood Township, NJ	92,664	93	2	5	34	52	998	186	768	44
Total area actually reporting	99.9%	77,703	687	1,915	31,055	44,046	320,027	49,197	249,355	21,475
Estimated total	100.0%	77,802	688	1,920	31,094	44,100	320,962	49,360	250,083	21,519
Rate per 100,000 inhabitants		390.2	3.5	9.6	156.0	221.2	1,609.9	247.6	1,254.4	107.9
Dutchess County-Putnam County, NY, MD.........	397,186									
Includes Dutchess and Putnam Counties										
Total area actually reporting	98.4%	630	12	40	156	422	5,201	910	4,184	107
Estimated total	100.0%	642	12	41	160	429	5,318	927	4,281	110
Rate per 100,000 inhabitants		161.6	3.0	10.3	40.3	108.0	1,338.9	233.4	1,077.8	27.7
Nassau County-Suffolk County, NY, MD............	2,856,018									
Includes Nassau and Suffolk Counties										
Total area actually reporting	99.9%	3,991	51	93	1,714	2,133	40,789	5,944	32,781	2,064
Estimated total	100.0%	3,994	51	93	1,715	2,135	40,816	5,948	32,803	2,065
Rate per 100,000 inhabitants		139.8	1.8	3.3	60.0	74.8	1,429.1	208.3	1,148.6	72.3
Newark, NJ-PA, MD....................................	2,497,536									
Includes Essex, Hunterdon, Morris, Somerset, Sussex, and Union Counties, NJ and Pike County, PA										
Total area actually reporting	100.0%	8,498	177	229	5,022	3,070	42,502	9,249	26,580	6,673
Rate per 100,000 inhabitants		340.3	7.1	9.2	201.1	122.9	1,701.8	370.3	1,064.2	267.2
New York-Jersey City-White Plains, NY-NJ, MD.....	14,185,877									
Includes Bergen, Hudson, Middlesex, Monmouth, Ocean, and Passaic Counties, NJ and Bronx, Kings, New York, Orange, Queens, Richmond, Rockland, and Westchester Counties, NY										
Total area actually reporting	99.7%	64,584	447	1,553	24,163	38,421	231,535	33,094	185,810	12,631
Estimated total	100.0%	64,668	448	1,557	24,197	38,466	232,326	33,236	186,419	12,671
Rate per 100,000 inhabitants		455.9	3.2	11.0	170.6	271.2	1,637.7	234.3	1,314.1	89.3
Niles-Benton Harbor, MI, MSA...............................	155,981									
Includes Berrien County										
City of Niles	11,471	54	0	14	6	34	304	45	241	18
City of Benton Harbor	10,039	225	3	22	60	140	706	304	377	25
Total area actually reporting	98.6%	694	3	143	112	436	4,218	1,108	2,948	162
Estimated total	100.0%	700	3	144	113	440	4,267	1,118	2,983	166
Rate per 100,000 inhabitants		448.8	1.9	92.3	72.4	282.1	2,735.6	716.8	1,912.4	106.4
North Port-Sarasota-Bradenton, FL, MSA..............	728,392									
Includes Manatee and Sarasota Counties										
City of North Port	58,699	108	0	26	15	67	964	264	687	13
City of Sarasota	53,046	413	4	31	151	227	2,742	564	2,023	155
City of Bradenton	51,023	351	9	17	115	210	2,004	438	1,480	86
City of Venice	21,151	37	0	3	4	30	446	95	338	13
Total area actually reporting	100.0%	3,075	20	295	646	2,114	20,615	4,932	14,885	798
Rate per 100,000 inhabitants		422.2	2.7	40.5	88.7	290.2	2,830.2	677.1	2,043.5	109.6
Norwich-New London, CT, MSA............................	146,149									
Includes New London County										
City of Norwich	40,485	130	1	14	29	86	1,002	306	644	52
City of New London	27,738	299	3	23	50	223	791	236	494	61
Total area actually reporting	100.0%	555	4	60	98	393	3,590	787	2,650	153
Rate per 100,000 inhabitants		379.7	2.7	41.1	67.1	268.9	2,456.4	538.5	1,813.2	104.7
Ocala, FL, MSA[5]....................................	337,649									
Includes Marion County										
City of Ocala	57,144	332	6	25	92	209	2,889	530	2,306	53
Total area actually reporting	100.0%	1,453	17	148	170	1,118		1,866		273
Rate per 100,000 inhabitants		430.3	5.0	43.8	50.3	331.1		552.6		80.9
Ocean City, NJ, MSA....................................	96,133									
Includes Cape May County										
City of Ocean City	11,473	12	0	3	3	6	440	88	346	6
Total area actually reporting	100.0%	251	0	22	64	165	3,955	844	3,044	67
Rate per 100,000 inhabitants		261.1	0.0	22.9	66.6	171.6	4,114.1	878.0	3,166.4	69.7

Table 6. Crime, by Selected Metropolitan Statistical Area, 2013—*Continued*

(Number, percent, rate per 100,000 population.)

Area	Population	Violent crime	Murder and nonnegligent manslaughter	Rape[1]	Robbery	Aggravated assault	Property crime	Burglary	Larceny-theft	Motor vehicle theft
Odessa, TX, MSA..................................	147,448									
Includes Ector County										
City of Odessa	108,265	1,080	2	56	143	879	4,374	764	3,147	463
Total area actually reporting	100.0%	1,189	3	58	177	951	6,307	1,165	4,498	644
Rate per 100,000 inhabitants		806.4	2.0	39.3	120.0	645.0	4,277.4	790.1	3,050.6	436.8
Ogden-Clearfield, UT, MSA[2]	620,648									
Includes Box Elder, Davis, Morgan, and Weber Counties										
City of Ogden	85,045	416	2	78	111	225	4,005	578	3,153	274
City of Clearfield	30,433	39	0	12	4	23	630	99	495	36
Total area actually reporting	99.5%	1,013	8	328	184	493			11,547	879
Estimated total	100.0%	1,018	8	329	185	496			11,614	886
Rate per 100,000 inhabitants		164.0	1.3	53.0	29.8	79.9			1,871.3	142.8
Oklahoma City, OK, MSA..	1,315,519									
Includes Canadian, Cleveland, Grady, Lincoln, Logan, McClain, and Oklahoma Counties										
City of Oklahoma City	605,034	4,998	62	450	1,191	3,295	32,479	8,016	20,387	4,076
Total area actually reporting	100.0%	6,617	78	695	1,430	4,414	52,037	12,856	33,747	5,434
Rate per 100,000 inhabitants		503.0	5.9	52.8	108.7	335.5	3,955.6	977.3	2,565.3	413.1
Olympia-Tumwater, WA, MSA	260,949									
Includes Thurston County										
City of Olympia	48,046	131	0	18	38	75	1,789	382	1,284	123
City of Tumwater	18,343	41	0	10	5	26	612	161	421	30
Total area actually reporting	100.0%	518	3	76	101	338	7,008	1,998	4,548	462
Rate per 100,000 inhabitants		198.5	1.1	29.1	38.7	129.5	2,685.6	765.7	1,742.9	177.0
Omaha-Council Bluffs, NE-IA, MSA..........................	893,630									
Includes Harrison, Mills, and Pottawattamie Counties, IA and Cass, Douglas, Sarpy, Saunders, and Washington Counties, NE										
City of Omaha, NE	425,076	2,449	42	184	718	1,505	19,108	3,509	12,519	3,080
City of Council Bluffs, IA	62,021	584	0	75	80	429	4,614	947	3,126	541
Total area actually reporting	99.6%	3,457	47	341	851	2,218	28,936	5,481	19,372	4,083
Estimated total	100.0%	3,462	47	342	851	2,222	29,000	5,492	19,422	4,086
Rate per 100,000 inhabitants		387.4	5.3	38.3	95.2	248.6	3,245.2	614.6	2,173.4	457.2
Orlando-Kissimmee-Sanford, FL, MSA	2,261,201									
Includes Lake, Orange, Osceola, and Seminole Counties										
City of Orlando	253,238	2,316	17	126	573	1,600	16,489	3,485	11,984	1,020
City of Kissimmee	64,617	542	3	36	132	371	2,963	802	2,042	119
City of Sanford	54,972	447	5	36	132	274	3,432	994	2,202	236
Total area actually reporting	99.6%	12,171	89	936	2,776	8,370	77,008	19,883	52,568	4,557
Estimated total	100.0%	12,212	89	939	2,788	8,396	77,335	19,952	52,808	4,575
Rate per 100,000 inhabitants		540.1	3.9	41.5	123.3	371.3	3,420.1	882.4	2,335.4	202.3
Oshkosh-Neenah, WI, MSA	169,484									
Includes Winnebago County										
City of Oshkosh	66,848	155	0	9	23	123	1,421	219	1,163	39
City of Neenah	25,850	41	0	4	3	34	505	55	441	9
Total area actually reporting	100.0%	270	0	20	29	221	2,917	429	2,416	72
Rate per 100,000 inhabitants		159.3	0.0	11.8	17.1	130.4	1,721.1	253.1	1,425.5	42.5
Owensboro, KY, MSA	116,530									
Includes Daviess, Hancock, and McLean Counties										
City of Owensboro	58,304	140	0	47	49	44	2,032	373	1,553	106
Total area actually reporting	100.0%	161	0	56	52	53	2,588	529	1,932	127
Rate per 100,000 inhabitants		138.2	0.0	48.1	44.6	45.5	2,220.9	454.0	1,657.9	109.0
Oxnard-Thousand Oaks-Ventura, CA, MSA	840,678									
Includes Ventura County										
City of Oxnard	202,594	651	15	10	328	298	5,074	974	3,436	664
City of Thousand Oaks	128,884	139	0	7	42	90	1,604	291	1,222	91
City of Ventura	108,204	262	6	21	99	136	4,027	745	3,025	257
City of Camarillo	66,173	73	0	6	25	42	1,130	205	849	76
Total area actually reporting	100.0%	1,629	34	85	607	903	16,400	3,210	11,690	1,500
Rate per 100,000 inhabitants		193.8	4.0	10.1	72.2	107.4	1,950.8	381.8	1,390.5	178.4

Table 6. Crime, by Selected Metropolitan Statistical Area, 2013—*Continued*

(Number, percent, rate per 100,000 population.)

Area	Population	Violent crime	Murder and nonnegligent manslaughter	Rape[1]	Robbery	Aggravated assault	Property crime	Burglary	Larceny-theft	Motor vehicle theft
Palm Bay-Melbourne-Titusville, FL, MSA	550,499									
Includes Brevard County										
City of Palm Bay	104,391	451	3	21	43	384	1,958	517	1,326	115
City of Melbourne	77,277	657	6	61	136	454	3,377	741	2,526	110
City of Titusville	43,989	328	3	32	72	221	1,604	545	903	156
Total area actually reporting	100.0%	2,889	20	277	470	2,122	15,393	3,751	10,952	690
Rate per 100,000 inhabitants		524.8	3.6	50.3	85.4	385.5	2,796.2	681.4	1,989.5	125.3
Panama City, FL, MSA	189,176									
Includes Bay County										
City of Panama City	36,358	322	3	10	65	244	2,299	377	1,803	119
City of Lynn Haven	100.0%	977	8	90	164	715	7,306	1,433	5,551	322
City of Panama City Beach		516.5	4.2	47.6	86.7	378.0	3,862.0	757.5	2,934.3	170.2
Parkersburg-Vienna, WV, MSA	92,396									
Includes Wirt and Wood Counties										
City of Parkersburg	31,207	127	0	21	12	94	1,382	343	982	57
City of Vienna	10,664	10	0	0	0	10	299	18	273	8
Total area actually reporting	96.8%	260	0	36	13	211	2,183	572	1,518	93
Estimated total	100.0%	269	0	37	14	218	2,267	585	1,586	96
Rate per 100,000 inhabitants		291.1	0.0	40.0	15.2	235.9	2,453.6	633.1	1,716.5	103.9
Pensacola-Ferry Pass-Brent, FL, MSA	466,427									
Includes Escambia and Santa Rosa Counties										
City of Pensacola	52,454	389	3	27	69	290	2,613	466	2,035	112
Total area actually reporting	100.0%	2,379	29	197	458	1,695	15,836	3,882	11,099	855
Rate per 100,000 inhabitants		510.0	6.2	42.2	98.2	363.4	3,395.2	832.3	2,379.6	183.3
Peoria, IL, MSA	380,809									
Includes Marshall, Peoria, Stark, Tazewell, and Woodford Counties										
City of Peoria	115,953	784	16	24	275	469	4,415	1,123	3,098	194
Total area actually reporting	93.6%	1,252	21	80	317	834	8,387	2,102	6,007	278
Estimated total	100.0%	1,303	22	85	332	864	8,860	2,185	6,377	298
Rate per 100,000 inhabitants		342.2	5.8	22.3	87.2	226.9	2,326.6	573.8	1,674.6	78.3
Philadelphia-Camden-Wilmington, PA-NJ-DE-MD, MSA	6,036,138									
Includes the Metropolitan Divisions of Camden, NJ; Montgomery County-Bucks County-Chester County, PA; Philadelphia, PA; and Wilmington, DE-MD-NJ										
City of Philadelphia, PA	1,553,153	17,074	247	1,279	7,562	7,986	53,452	10,408	37,253	5,791
City of Wilmington, DE	71,460	1,161	19	24	453	665	3,718	960	2,387	371
Total area actually reporting	99.9%	30,011	426	2,157	11,916	15,512	149,364	28,590	110,507	10,267
Estimated total	100.0%	30,030	426	2,158	11,921	15,525	149,557	28,621	110,663	10,273
Rate per 100,000 inhabitants		497.5	7.1	35.8	197.5	257.2	2,477.7	474.2	1,833.3	170.2
Camden, NJ, MD	1,257,382									
Includes Burlington, Camden, and Gloucester Counties										
Total area actually reporting	100.0%	4,034	84	201	1,516	2,233	29,230	6,597	21,144	1,489
Rate per 100,000 inhabitants		320.8	6.7	16.0	120.6	177.6	2,324.7	524.7	1,681.6	118.4
Montgomery County-Bucks County-Chester County, PA, MD	1,892,483									
Includes Bucks, Chester, and Montgomery Counties										
Total area actually reporting	100.0%	2,800	26	289	875	1,610	33,268	5,620	26,478	1,170
Estimated total										
Rate per 100,000 inhabitants		148.0	1.4	15.3	46.2	85.1	1,757.9	297.0	1,399.1	61.8
Philadelphia, PA, MD	2,114,504									
Includes Delaware and Philadelphia Counties										
Total area actually reporting	99.9%	19,823	278	1,461	8,366	9,718	66,042	12,404	47,178	6,460
Estimated total	100.0%	19,827	278	1,461	8,367	9,721	66,084	12,411	47,212	6,461
Rate per 100,000 inhabitants		937.7	13.1	69.1	395.7	459.7	3,125.3	586.9	2,232.8	305.6
Wilmington, DE-MD-NJ, MD	718,010									
Includes New Castle County, DE; Cecil County, MD; and Salem County, NJ										
Total area actually reporting	100.0%	3,456	40	213	1,074	2,129	21,114	4,579	15,441	1,094
Rate per 100,000 inhabitants		481.3	5.6	29.7	149.6	296.5	2,940.6	637.7	2,150.5	152.4

Table 6. Crime, by Selected Metropolitan Statistical Area, 2013—*Continued*

(Number, percent, rate per 100,000 population.)

Area	Population	Violent crime	Murder and nonnegligent manslaughter	Rape[1]	Robbery	Aggravated assault	Property crime	Burglary	Larceny-theft	Motor vehicle theft
Phoenix-Mesa-Scottsdale, AZ, MSA...................	4,386,981									
Includes Maricopa and Pinal Counties										
City of Phoenix	1,502,139	9,492	118	635	3,233	5,506	60,085	16,747	36,983	6,355
City of Mesa	456,155	1,807	22	203	478	1,104	12,916	2,357	9,607	952
City of Scottsdale	225,523	337	4	37	101	195	5,766	1,093	4,465	208
City of Tempe	168,501	831	3	62	224	542	7,876	1,276	6,113	487
Total area actually reporting	99.9%	17,204	212	1,291	5,055	10,646		32,054	97,294	
Estimated total	100.0%	17,212	212	1,292	5,057	10,651		32,071	97,363	
Rate per 100,000 inhabitants		392.3	4.8	29.5	115.3	242.8		731.0	2,219.4	
Pittsburgh, PA, MSA[3]	2,360,685									
Includes Allegheny, Armstrong, Beaver, Butler, Fayette, Washington, and Westmoreland Counties										
City of Pittsburgh	307,632	2,259	45	78	956	1,180	10,047	2,173	7,258	616
Total area actually reporting	99.0%	6,869	97	363	1,964	4,445	43,408	8,603	33,004	1,801
Estimated total	100.0%	6,913	97	367	1,976	4,473	43,827	8,669	33,343	1,815
Rate per 100,000 inhabitants		292.8	4.1	15.5	83.7	189.5	1,856.5	367.2	1,412.4	76.9
Pittsfield, MA, MSA............................	129,977									
Includes Berkshire County										
City of Pittsfield	43,992	111	0	31	29	51	1,352	481	827	44
Total area actually reporting	91.9%	349	1	72	46	230	3,019	974	1,956	89
Estimated total	100.0%	383	1	75	53	254	3,213	1,017	2,095	101
Rate per 100,000 inhabitants		294.7	0.8	57.7	40.8	195.4	2,472.0	782.4	1,611.8	77.7
Pocatello, ID, MSA............................	84,482									
Includes Bannock County										
City of Pocatello	54,921	195	0	21	27	147	1,776	278	1,415	83
Total area actually reporting	100.0%	242	1	24	30	187	2,490	346	2,044	100
Rate per 100,000 inhabitants		286.5	1.2	28.4	35.5	221.3	2,947.4	409.6	2,419.5	118.4
Portland-South Portland, ME, MSA	518,977									
Includes Cumberland, Sagadahoc, and York Counties										
City of Portland	66,256	177	1	21	85	70	2,612	383	2,160	69
City of South Portland	25,126	60	0	10	13	37	861	113	722	26
Total area actually reporting	100.0%	757	6	152	178	421	11,781	2,270	9,173	338
Rate per 100,000 inhabitants		145.9	1.2	29.3	34.3	81.1	2,270.0	437.4	1,767.5	65.1
Portland-Vancouver-Hillsboro, OR-WA, MSA..........	2,315,358									
Includes Clackamas, Columbia, Multnomah, Washington, and Yamhill Counties, OR and Clark and Skamania Counties, WA										
City of Portland, OR	609,136	2,941	14	234	917	1,776	29,633	4,128	22,216	3,289
City of Vancouver, WA	166,535	593	2	74	146	371	5,933	1,007	3,950	976
City of Hillsboro, OR	96,313	141	0	29	55	57	2,160	311	1,723	126
City of Beaverton, OR	93,551	124	1	20	22	81	1,471	175	1,213	83
Total area actually reporting	99.6%	5,790	32	712	1,696	3,350	68,948	10,955	51,143	6,850
Estimated total	100.0%	5,810	32	715	1,702	3,361	69,261	11,002	51,388	6,871
Rate per 100,000 inhabitants		250.9	1.4	30.9	73.5	145.2	2,991.4	475.2	2,219.4	296.8
Port St. Lucie, FL, MSA	436,841									
Includes Martin and St. Lucie Counties										
City of Port St. Lucie	169,877	303	1	21	40	241	2,461	722	1,666	73
Total area actually reporting	100.0%	1,470	15	87	234	1,134	9,735	2,590	6,740	405
Rate per 100,000 inhabitants		336.5	3.4	19.9	53.6	259.6	2,228.5	592.9	1,542.9	92.7
Prescott, AZ, MSA	214,243									
Includes Yavapai County										
City of Prescott	40,752	124	0	7	11	106	1,085	182	855	48
Total area actually reporting	100.0%	525	3	52	31	439	4,287	894	3,158	235
Rate per 100,000 inhabitants		245.0	1.4	24.3	14.5	204.9	2,001.0	417.3	1,474.0	109.7
Providence-Warwick, RI-MA, MSA........................	1,604,757									
Includes Bristol County, MA and Bristol, Kent, Newport, Providence, and Washington Counties RI										
City of Providence, RI	178,887	1,115	12	97	365	641	7,974	1,828	5,184	962
City of Warwick RI	81,789	93	4	35	15	39	2,015	282	1,648	85
Total area actually reporting	100.0%	5,428	40	683	1,293	3,412	37,865	8,780	26,013	3,072
Rate per 100,000 inhabitants		338.2	2.5	42.6	80.6	212.6	2,359.5	547.1	1,621.0	191.4

(Number, percent, rate per 100,000 population.)

Area	Population	Violent crime	Murder and nonnegligent manslaughter	Rape[1]	Robbery	Aggravated assault	Property crime	Burglary	Larceny-theft	Motor vehicle theft
Provo-Orem, UT, MSA.....................................	561,483									
Includes Juab and Utah Counties										
City of Provo	116,937	160	1	82	21	56	2,810	329	2,373	108
City of Orem	91,438	33	2	13	7	11	2,079	192	1,789	98
Total area actually reporting	100.0%	394	6	154	49	185	10,535	1,296	8,784	455
Rate per 100,000 inhabitants		70.2	1.1	27.4	8.7	32.9	1,876.3	230.8	1,564.4	81.0
Pueblo, CO, MSA...	162,300									
Includes Pueblo County										
City of Pueblo	108,062	1,011	2	165	211	633	7,596	1,900	5,168	528
Total area actually reporting	100.0%	1,063	5	171	219	668	8,835	2,117	6,112	606
Rate per 100,000 inhabitants		655.0	3.1	105.4	134.9	411.6	5,443.6	1,304.4	3,765.9	373.4
Punta Gorda, FL, MSA..................................	163,934									
Includes Charlotte County										
City of Punta Gorda	16,942	21	0	2	2	17	296	36	256	4
Total area actually reporting	100.0%	390	1	39	35	315	3,409	784	2,511	114
Rate per 100,000 inhabitants		237.9	0.6	23.8	21.4	192.2	2,079.5	478.2	1,531.7	69.5
Racine, WI, MSA...	194,711									
Includes Racine County										
City of Racine	78,141	297	1	21	179	96	3,010	1,211	1,704	95
Total area actually reporting	100.0%	354	2	29	197	126	4,802	1,476	3,180	146
Rate per 100,000 inhabitants		181.8	1.0	14.9	101.2	64.7	2,466.2	758.0	1,633.2	75.0
Raleigh, NC, MSA.......................................	1,209,877									
Includes Franklin, Johnston, and Wake Counties										
City of Raleigh	428,993	1,683	12	79	605	987	13,140	3,157	9,278	705
Total area actually reporting	99.3%	2,629	33	152	814	1,630	27,312	6,909	19,134	1,269
Estimated total	100.0%	2,653	33	154	820	1,646	27,625	6,976	19,369	1,280
Rate per 100,000 inhabitants		219.3	2.7	12.7	67.8	136.0	2,283.3	576.6	1,600.9	105.8
Rapid City, SD, MSA...................................	140,926									
Includes Meade and Pennington Counties										
City of Rapid City	70,406	398	2	63	48	285	2,629	578	1,902	149
Total area actually reporting	100.0%	517	2	104	50	361	3,439	811	2,442	186
Rate per 100,000 inhabitants		366.9	1.4	73.8	35.5	256.2	2,440.3	575.5	1,732.8	132.0
Reading, PA, MSA.......................................	413,820									
Includes Berks County										
City of Reading	88,107	743	11	50	328	354	2,799	1,040	1,465	294
Total area actually reporting	99.1%	1,222	11	95	421	695	7,724	1,880	5,368	476
Estimated total	100.0%	1,229	11	96	423	699	7,789	1,890	5,421	478
Rate per 100,000 inhabitants		297.0	2.7	23.2	102.2	168.9	1,882.2	456.7	1,310.0	115.5
Redding, CA, MSA......................................	179,423									
Includes Shasta County										
City of Redding	90,974	705	3	66	131	505	4,380	1,088	2,790	502
Total area actually reporting	100.0%	1,298	7	97	165	1,029	6,280	1,754	3,623	903
Rate per 100,000 inhabitants		723.4	3.9	54.1	92.0	573.5	3,500.1	977.6	2,019.3	503.3
Reno, NV, MSA..	435,223									
Includes Storey and Washoe Counties										
City of Reno	230,486	1,192	7	33	327	825	7,423	1,633	4,909	881
Total area actually reporting	100.0%	1,721	12	85	416	1,208	11,470	2,684	7,542	1,244
Rate per 100,000 inhabitants		395.4	2.8	19.5	95.6	277.6	2,635.4	616.7	1,732.9	285.8
Richmond, VA, MSA....................................	1,242,277									
Includes Amelia, Caroline, Charles City, Chesterfield, Dinwiddie, Goochland, Hanover, Henrico, King William, New Kent, Powhatan, Prince George, and Sussex Counties and Colonial Heights, Hopewell, Petersburg, and Richmond Cities										
City of Richmond	212,830	1,327	37	43	624	623	8,704	1,817	5,949	938
Total area actually reporting	100.0%	3,029	77	249	1,128	1,575	29,761	5,533	22,329	1,899
Rate per 100,000 inhabitants		243.8	6.2	20.0	90.8	126.8	2,395.7	445.4	1,797.4	152.9
Riverside-San Bernardino-Ontario, CA, MSA..........	4,392,057									
Includes Riverside and San Bernardino Counties										
City of Riverside	316,423	1,330	10	78	495	747	10,608	1,978	6,912	1,718

Table 6. Crime, by Selected Metropolitan Statistical Area, 2013—*Continued*

(Number, percent, rate per 100,000 population.)

Area	Population	Violent crime	Murder and nonnegligent manslaughter	Rape[1]	Robbery	Aggravated assault	Property crime	Burglary	Larceny-theft	Motor vehicle theft
Riverside-San Bernardino-Ontario, CA, MSA (cont.)										
City of San Bernardino	214,322	1,949	45	74	794	1,036	9,389	2,673	4,025	2,691
City of Ontario	168,144	453	9	31	167	246	4,507	830	2,586	1,091
City of Corona	160,159	162	9	14	65	74	3,439	644	2,305	490
City of Victorville	121,699	651	9	36	202	404	4,165	1,461	2,067	637
City of Temecula	106,680	91	3	11	39	38	2,848	711	1,897	240
City of Chino	80,704	258	4	7	47	200	2,044	518	1,249	277
City of Redlands	70,282	215	2	15	84	114	3,020	605	2,047	368
Total area actually reporting	100.0%	14,637	219	758	4,736	8,924	122,732	33,572	67,684	21,476
Rate per 100,000 inhabitants		333.3	5.0	17.3	107.8	203.2	2,794.4	764.4	1,541.1	489.0
Roanoke, VA, MSA...	311,327									
Includes Botetourt, Craig, Franklin, and Roanoke Counties and Roanoke and Salem Cities										
City of Roanoke	97,927	457	9	44	142	262	4,444	628	3,636	180
Total area actually reporting	100.0%	742	16	98	173	455	7,609	1,104	6,180	325
Rate per 100,000 inhabitants		238.3	5.1	31.5	55.6	146.1	2,444.1	354.6	1,985.1	104.4
Rochester, MN, MSA.......................................	211,141									
Includes Dodge, Fillmore, Olmsted, and Wabasha Counties										
City of Rochester	109,675	214	0	50	54	110	2,558	429	2,026	103
Total area actually reporting	100.0%	301	0	65	56	180	3,483	714	2,625	144
Rate per 100,000 inhabitants		142.6	0.0	30.8	26.5	85.3	1,649.6	338.2	1,243.2	68.2
Rochester, NY, MSA..	1,084,351									
Includes Livingston, Monroe, Ontario, Orleans, Wayne, and Yates Counties										
City of Rochester	210,562	2,107	42	92	918	1,055	10,051	2,587	6,855	609
Total area actually reporting	99.6%	3,069	52	202	1,209	1,606	26,080	5,609	19,458	1,013
Estimated total	100.0%	3,075	52	202	1,211	1,610	26,151	5,619	19,517	1,015
Rate per 100,000 inhabitants		283.6	4.8	18.6	111.7	148.5	2,411.7	518.2	1,799.9	93.6
Rockford, IL, MSA...	344,806									
Includes Boone and Winnebago Counties										
City of Rockford	150,207	2,065	19	145	394	1,507	7,039	2,001	4,666	372
Total area actually reporting	92.1%	2,394	25	193	440	1,736	9,781	2,630	6,673	478
Estimated total	100.0%	2,452	26	199	457	1,770	10,311	2,723	7,088	500
Rate per 100,000 inhabitants		711.1	7.5	57.7	132.5	513.3	2,990.4	789.7	2,055.6	145.0
Rocky Mount, NC, MSA...................................	151,852									
Includes Edgecombe and Nash Counties										
City of Rocky Mount	57,021	599	4	16	154	425	3,282	992	2,179	111
Total area actually reporting	94.6%	797	16	23	184	574	5,125	1,781	3,142	202
Estimated total	100.0%	819	16	24	190	589	5,416	1,843	3,361	212
Rate per 100,000 inhabitants		539.3	10.5	15.8	125.1	387.9	3,566.6	1,213.7	2,213.3	139.6
Rome, GA, MSA..	96,122									
Includes Floyd County										
City of Rome	36,098	247	2	19	69	157	2,178	413	1,681	84
Total area actually reporting	100.0%	368	4	27	79	258	3,988	875	2,923	190
Rate per 100,000 inhabitants		382.8	4.2	28.1	82.2	268.4	4,148.9	910.3	3,040.9	197.7
Sacramento—Roseville—Arden-Arcade, CA, MSA	2,213,600									
Includes El Dorado, Placer, Sacramento, and Yolo Counties										
City of Sacramento	478,182	3,137	34	95	1,158	1,850	17,980	3,886	11,233	2,861
City of Roseville	126,236	261	1	13	64	183	3,343	482	2,623	238
City of Folsom	73,782	98	0	7	35	56	1,336	240	1,024	72
Total area actually reporting	100.0%	9,207	91	469	2,848	5,799	61,241	14,681	38,144	8,416
Rate per 100,000 inhabitants		415.9	4.1	21.2	128.7	262.0	2,766.6	663.2	1,723.2	380.2
Saginaw, MI, MSA...	198,026									
Includes Saginaw County										
City of Saginaw	50,580	985	29	64	129	763	1,492	746	644	102
Total area actually reporting	100.0%	1,490	38	149	190	1,113	4,306	1,373	2,708	225
Rate per 100,000 inhabitants		752.4	19.2	75.2	95.9	562.0	2,174.5	693.3	1,367.5	113.6
Salem, OR, MSA..	398,927									
Includes Marion and Polk Counties										
City of Salem	158,234	520	7	47	138	328	6,782	983	5,143	656
Total area actually reporting	100.0%	932	14	100	214	604	12,826	2,042	9,640	1,144
Rate per 100,000 inhabitants		233.6	3.5	25.1	53.6	151.4	3,215.1	511.9	2,416.5	286.8

Table 6. Crime, by Selected Metropolitan Statistical Area, 2013—*Continued*

(Number, percent, rate per 100,000 population.)

Area	Population	Violent crime	Murder and nonnegligent manslaughter	Rape[1]	Robbery	Aggravated assault	Property crime	Burglary	Larceny-theft	Motor vehicle theft
Salinas, CA, MSA...................................	430,882									
Includes Monterey County										
City of Salinas	155,742	1,001	24	36	451	490	5,356	1,148	2,720	1,488
Total area actually reporting	100.0%	1,794	47	82	655	1,010	10,940	2,706	6,036	2,198
Rate per 100,000 inhabitants		416.4	10.9	19.0	152.0	234.4	2,539.0	628.0	1,400.8	510.1
Salisbury, MD, MSA.................................	385,257									
Includes Sussex County, DE and Somerset, Wicomico, and Worcester Counties, MD										
City of Salisbury, MD	31,517	326	0	17	99	210	1,806	336	1,420	50
Total area actually reporting	100.0%	1,706	11	176	315	1,204	12,543	3,355	8,793	395
Rate per 100,000 inhabitants		442.8	2.9	45.7	81.8	312.5	3,255.7	870.8	2,282.4	102.5
Salt Lake City, UT, MSA..........................	1,141,757									
Includes Salt Lake and Tooele Counties										
City of Salt Lake City	190,246	1,475	7	204	422	842	13,461	2,068	9,517	1,876
Total area actually reporting	99.9%	4,071	20	654	964	2,433	49,632	7,778	36,235	5,619
Estimated total	100.0%	4,071	20	654	964	2,433	49,644	7,780	36,244	5,620
Rate per 100,000 inhabitants		356.6	1.8	57.3	84.4	213.1	4,348.0	681.4	3,174.4	492.2
San Antonio-New Braunfels, TX, MSA..................	2,271,017									
Includes Atascosa, Bandera, Bexar, Comal, Guadalupe, Kendall, Medina, and Wilson Counties										
City of San Antonio	1,399,725	8,828	72	663	2,192	5,901	79,994	14,850	58,567	6,577
City of New Braunfels	61,651	147	3	16	24	104	2,153	351	1,673	129
Total area actually reporting	99.9%	10,436	105	889	2,429	7,013	100,236	19,289	73,244	7,703
Estimated total	100.0%	10,439	105	889	2,430	7,015	100,269	19,295	73,269	7,705
Rate per 100,000 inhabitants		459.7	4.6	39.1	107.0	308.9	4,415.2	849.6	3,226.3	339.3
San Diego-Carlsbad, CA, MSA.................................	3,206,175									
Includes San Diego County										
City of San Diego	1,349,306	5,303	39	316	1,456	3,492	31,728	6,355	19,230	6,143
City of Carlsbad	110,505	221	1	23	44	153	2,085	525	1,436	124
Total area actually reporting	100.0%	11,177	71	668	3,054	7,384	70,276	13,970	45,034	11,272
Rate per 100,000 inhabitants		348.6	2.2	20.8	95.3	230.3	2,191.9	435.7	1,404.6	351.6
San Francisco-Oakland-Hayward, CA, MSA..........	4,499,119									
Includes the Metropolitan Divisions of Oakland-Hayward-Berkeley, San Francisco-Redwood City-South San Francisco, and San Rafael										
City of San Francisco	833,863	7,064	48	161	4,202	2,653	48,324	5,931	36,527	5,866
City of Oakland	403,887	7,984	90	180	4,922	2,792	25,176	5,058	13,285	6,833
City of Hayward	150,955	589	5	33	333	218	4,844	1,051	2,122	1,671
City of Berkeley	116,217	562	4	26	410	122	5,377	1,055	3,658	664
City of San Leandro	87,490	394	3	26	251	114	3,960	761	2,287	912
City of Redwood City	79,707	190	1	26	66	97	1,871	507	1,138	226
City of San Ramon	74,434	27	0	0	14	13	760	171	485	104
City of Pleasanton	72,975	60	0	3	29	28	1,281	185	979	117
City of Walnut Creek	66,149	78	0	4	31	43	2,161	364	1,634	163
City of South San Francisco	66,157	118	0	5	39	74	1,188	268	739	181
City of San Rafael	58,725	206	0	26	77	103	1,812	366	1,114	332
Total area actually reporting	100.0%	25,131	216	853	13,255	10,807	160,685	30,011	102,174	28,500
Rate per 100,000 inhabitants		558.6	4.8	19.0	294.6	240.2	3,571.5	667.0	2,271.0	633.5
Oakland-Hayward-Berkeley, CA, MD..................	2,660,954									
Includes Alameda and Contra Costa Counties										
Total area actually reporting	100.0%	15,700	155	510	8,339	6,696	91,484	19,520	51,645	20,319
Rate per 100,000 inhabitants		590.0	5.8	19.2	313.4	251.6	3,438.0	733.6	1,940.8	763.6
San Francisco-Redwood City-South San Francisco, CA, MD..................	1,580,707									
Includes San Francisco and San Mateo Counties										
Total area actually reporting	100.0%	8,940	59	295	4,780	3,806	64,189	9,137	47,520	7,532
Rate per 100,000 inhabitants		565.6	3.7	18.7	302.4	240.8	4,060.8	578.0	3,006.2	476.5
San Rafael, CA, MD..........................	257,458									
Includes Marin County										
Total area actually reporting	100.0%	491	2	48	136	305	5,012	1,354	3,009	649
Rate per 100,000 inhabitants		190.7	0.8	18.6	52.8	118.5	1,946.7	525.9	1,168.7	252.1
San Jose-Sunnyvale-Santa Clara, CA, MSA...........	1,914,750									
Includes San Benito and Santa Clara Counties										

Table 6. Crime, by Selected Metropolitan Statistical Area, 2013—*Continued*

(Number, percent, rate per 100,000 population.)

Area	Population	Violent crime	Murder and nonnegligent manslaughter	Rape[1]	Robbery	Aggravated assault	Property crime	Burglary	Larceny-theft	Motor vehicle theft
San Jose-Sunnyvale-Santa Clara, CA, MSA (cont.)										
City of San Jose	992,143	3,215	38	270	1,095	1,812	25,510	5,173	12,411	7,926
City of Sunnyvale	148,160	144	4	16	51	73	2,434	574	1,456	404
City of Santa Clara	120,150	172	0	13	55	104	3,023	461	2,169	393
City of Mountain View	77,399	157	0	13	32	112	1,706	294	1,277	135
City of Milpitas	69,522	93	1	8	56	28	2,067	291	1,491	285
City of Palo Alto	66,964	54	0	4	29	21	1,483	242	1,174	67
City of Cupertino	60,440	41	0	3	23	15	812	179	584	49
Total area actually reporting	100.0%	4,783	57	414	1,533	2,779	45,267	8,960	26,038	10,269
Rate per 100,000 inhabitants		249.8	3.0	21.6	80.1	145.1	2,364.1	467.9	1,359.9	536.3
San Luis Obispo-Paso Robles-Arroyo Grande, CA, MSA.............	276,816									
Includes San Luis Obispo County										
City of San Luis Obispo	46,095	161	0	34	26	101	1,775	328	1,384	63
City of Paso Robles	30,795	103	2	8	6	87	848	211	595	42
City of Arroyo Grande	17,634	31	0	5	4	22	455	137	288	30
Total area actually reporting	100.0%	1,069	5	106	81	877	6,208	1,642	4,167	399
Rate per 100,000 inhabitants		386.2	1.8	38.3	29.3	316.8	2,242.6	593.2	1,505.3	144.1
Santa Cruz-Watsonville, CA, MSA..........................	268,260									
Includes Santa Cruz County										
City of Santa Cruz	62,517	407	4	33	85	285	3,163	552	2,383	228
City of Watsonville	52,076	237	3	20	71	143	1,308	218	824	266
Total area actually reporting	100.0%	1,002	11	78	199	714	8,140	1,640	5,477	1,023
Rate per 100,000 inhabitants		373.5	4.1	29.1	74.2	266.2	3,034.4	611.3	2,041.7	381.3
Santa Maria-Santa Barbara, CA, MSA	434,144									
Includes Santa Barbara County										
City of Santa Maria	102,051	490	3	34	122	331	2,934	647	1,557	730
City of Santa Barbara	90,006	362	2	32	82	246	2,670	459	2,091	120
Total area actually reporting	100.0%	1,416	6	153	285	972	9,824	2,249	6,429	1,146
Rate per 100,000 inhabitants		326.2	1.4	35.2	65.6	223.9	2,262.8	518.0	1,480.8	264.0
Santa Rosa, CA, MSA	494,862									
Includes Sonoma County										
City of Santa Rosa	171,564	541	3	42	105	391	3,506	638	2,559	309
Total area actually reporting	100.0%	1,782	9	126	242	1,405	8,218	1,804	5,693	721
Rate per 100,000 inhabitants		360.1	1.8	25.5	48.9	283.9	1,660.7	364.5	1,150.4	145.7
Savannah, GA, MSA..	366,493									
Includes Bryan, Chatham, and Effingham Counties										
City of Savannah-Chatham Metropolitan	235,200	851	30	49	414	358	8,458	2,125	5,608	725
Total area actually reporting	100.0%	1,158	36	68	500	554	11,236	2,854	7,512	870
Rate per 100,000 inhabitants		316.0	9.8	18.6	136.4	151.2	3,065.8	778.7	2,049.7	237.4
Scranton—Wilkes-Barre—Hazleton, PA, MSA..........	563,315									
Includes Lackawanna, Luzerne, and Wyoming Counties										
City of Scranton	75,732	166	2	18	71	75	2,277	549	1,614	114
City of Wilkes-Barre	41,166	208	12	30	110	56	1,389	317	969	103
City of Hazleton	25,191	83	1	2	26	54	631	242	358	31
Total area actually reporting	96.9%	1,275	24	114	324	813	12,212	2,590	9,105	517
Estimated total	100.0%	1,308	24	117	333	834	12,526	2,639	9,359	528
Rate per 100,000 inhabitants		232.2	4.3	20.8	59.1	148.1	2,223.6	468.5	1,661.4	93.7
Seattle-Tacoma-Bellevue, WA, MSA	3,598,765									
Includes the Metropolitan Divisions of Seattle-Bellevue-Everett and Tacoma-Lakewood										
City of Seattle	642,814	3,758	19	153	1,601	1,985	35,883	7,384	24,189	4,310
City of Tacoma	203,226	1,766	10	144	524	1,088	13,310	3,086	8,200	2,024
City of Bellevue	127,678	125	1	20	48	56	3,949	688	3,013	248
City of Everett	105,129	443	1	42	192	208	6,865	1,129	4,702	1,034
City of Kent	124,359	319	2	58	160	99	5,600	1,061	3,669	870
City of Renton	96,657	254	3	27	101	123	4,938	859	3,396	683
City of Auburn	74,565	293	5	34	110	144	3,944	798	2,474	672
City of Lakewood	59,057	410	2	41	90	277	2,651	674	1,770	207
City of Redmond	57,263	39	0	24	3	12	1,665	193	1,402	70
Total area actually reporting	100.0%	11,643	78	1,136	4,032	6,397	144,789	31,505	94,993	18,291
Rate per 100,000 inhabitants		323.5	2.2	31.6	112.0	177.8	4,023.3	875.4	2,639.6	508.3

Table 6. Crime, by Selected Metropolitan Statistical Area, 2013—*Continued*

(Number, percent, rate per 100,000 population.)

Area	Population	Violent crime	Murder and nonnegligent manslaughter	Rape[1]	Robbery	Aggravated assault	Property crime	Burglary	Larceny-theft	Motor vehicle theft
Seattle-Bellevue-Everett, WA, MD	2,779,025									
Includes King and Snohomish Counties										
Total area actually reporting	100.0%	7,968	53	794	3,082	4,039	110,530	22,959	73,547	14,024
Rate per 100,000 inhabitants		286.7	1.9	28.6	110.9	145.3	3,977.3	826.2	2,646.5	504.6
Tacoma-Lakewood, WA, MD	819,740									
Includes Pierce County										
Total area actually reporting	100.0%	3,675	25	342	950	2,358	34,259	8,546	21,446	4,267
Rate per 100,000 inhabitants		448.3	3.0	41.7	115.9	287.7	4,179.3	1,042.5	2,616.2	520.5
Sebastian-Vero Beach, FL, MSA	141,889									
Includes Indian River County										
City of Sebastian	22,502	55	1	7	5	42	460	77	373	10
City of Vero Beach	15,621	48	1	9	6	32	499	103	388	8
Total area actually reporting	100.0%	419	4	40	41	334	2,983	680	2,215	88
Rate per 100,000 inhabitants		295.3	2.8	28.2	28.9	235.4	2,102.3	479.2	1,561.1	62.0
Sebring, FL, MSA	98,300									
Includes Highlands County										
City of Sebring	10,318	57	2	2	9	44	513	123	378	12
Total area actually reporting	91.1%	349	4	23	52	270	2,960	861	1,960	139
Estimated total	100.0%	388	4	26	63	295	3,268	926	2,186	156
Rate per 100,000 inhabitants		394.7	4.1	26.4	64.1	300.1	3,324.5	942.0	2,223.8	158.7
Sheboygan, WI, MSA	114,951									
Includes Sheboygan County										
City of Sheboygan	48,791	132	1	20	14	97	1,241	187	1,023	31
Total area actually reporting	100.0%	163	1	27	19	116	2,062	261	1,740	61
Rate per 100,000 inhabitants		141.8	0.9	23.5	16.5	100.9	1,793.8	227.1	1,513.7	53.1
Sherman-Denison, TX, MSA	122,729									
Includes Grayson County										
City of Sherman	39,377	120	2	4	21	93	1,316	312	958	46
City of Denison	22,652	94	4	11	15	64	844	145	646	53
Total area actually reporting	99.2%	324	7	26	42	249	3,060	724	2,166	170
Estimated total	100.0%	327	7	26	43	251	3,091	730	2,189	172
Rate per 100,000 inhabitants		266.4	5.7	21.2	35.0	204.5	2,518.6	594.8	1,783.6	140.1
Shreveport-Bossier City, LA, MSA	449,602									
Includes Bossier, Caddo, De Soto, and Webster Parishes										
City of Shreveport	202,189	1,397	26	84	376	911	9,584	2,360	6,720	504
City of Bossier City	65,578	394	6	20	65	303	3,182	473	2,554	155
Total area actually reporting	99.1%	2,377	35	130	462	1,750	15,798	3,541	11,431	826
Estimated total	100.0%	2,394	35	131	465	1,763	15,966	3,572	11,562	832
Rate per 100,000 inhabitants		532.5	7.8	29.1	103.4	392.1	3,551.1	794.5	2,571.6	185.1
Sioux City, IA-NE-SD, MSA	169,444									
Includes Plymouth and Woodbury Counties, IA; Dakota and Dixon Counties, NE; and Union County, SD										
City of Sioux City, IA	82,676	324	3	46	40	235	3,658	604	2,814	240
Total area actually reporting	97.9%	416	4	62	45	305	4,621	816	3,513	292
Estimated total	100.0%	419	4	63	45	307	4,670	826	3,549	295
Rate per 100,000 inhabitants		247.3	2.4	37.2	26.6	181.2	2,756.1	487.5	2,094.5	174.1
Sioux Falls, SD, MSA	241,643									
Includes Lincoln, McCook, Minnehaha, and Turner Counties										
City of Sioux Falls	161,754	636	3	138	67	428	4,930	870	3,796	264
Total area actually reporting	100.0%	705	3	159	68	475	5,720	1,141	4,262	317
Rate per 100,000 inhabitants		291.8	1.2	65.8	28.1	196.6	2,367.1	472.2	1,763.8	131.2
South Bend-Mishawaka, IN-MI, MSA	319,204									
Includes St. Joseph County, IN and Cass County, MI										
City of South Bend, IN	100,711	664	9	93	363	199	4,890	1,468	3,096	326
City of Mishawaka, IN	47,967	136	0	20	61	55	2,704	305	2,259	140
Total area actually reporting	98.0%	966	11	155	444	356	9,595	2,453	6,595	547
Estimated total	100.0%	985	11	158	448	368	9,749	2,483	6,707	559
Rate per 100,000 inhabitants		308.6	3.4	49.5	140.3	115.3	3,054.2	777.9	2,101.2	175.1

Table 6. Crime, by Selected Metropolitan Statistical Area, 2013—*Continued*

(Number, percent, rate per 100,000 population.)

Area	Population	Violent crime	Murder and nonnegligent manslaughter	Rape[1]	Robbery	Aggravated assault	Property crime	Burglary	Larceny-theft	Motor vehicle theft
Spartanburg, SC, MSA	319,563									
Includes Spartanburg County										
City of Spartanburg	37,522	527	3	24	130	370	2,668	490	2,060	118
Total area actually reporting	99.8%	1,479	9	147	292	1,031	10,038	2,559	6,882	597
Estimated total	100.0%	1,481	9	147	292	1,033	10,059	2,563	6,898	598
Rate per 100,000 inhabitants		463.4	2.8	46.0	91.4	323.3	3,147.7	802.0	2,158.6	187.1
Spokane-Spokane Valley, WA, MSA	535,166									
Includes Pend Oreille, Spokane, and Stevens Counties										
City of Spokane	209,524	1,440	11	166	518	745	19,531	3,889	13,352	2,290
City of Spokane Valley	90,835	231	1	35	81	114	5,313	961	3,862	490
Total area actually reporting	100.0%	1,963	20	253	659	1,031	30,755	6,426	20,999	3,330
Rate per 100,000 inhabitants		366.8	3.7	47.3	123.1	192.7	5,746.8	1,200.7	3,923.8	622.2
Springfield, IL, MSA	212,387									
Includes Menard and Sangamon Counties										
City of Springfield	117,351	1,191	4	71	287	829	5,905	1,300	4,439	166
Total area actually reporting	88.6%	1,580	34	153	336	1,057	7,798	1,676	5,334	788
Estimated total	100.0%	1,631	35	158	351	1,087	8,270	1,759	5,703	808
Rate per 100,000 inhabitants		767.9	16.5	74.4	165.3	511.8	3,893.8	828.2	2,685.2	380.4
Springfield, MA, MSA	628,316									
Includes Franklin, Hampden, and Hampshire Counties										
City of Springfield	153,586	1,673	22	89	598	964	7,113	2,360	4,018	735
Total area actually reporting	98.5%	3,251	28	326	907	1,990	18,076	4,779	12,006	1,291
Estimated total	100.0%	3,281	28	329	913	2,011	18,249	4,817	12,130	1,302
Rate per 100,000 inhabitants		522.2	4.5	52.4	145.3	320.1	2,904.4	766.7	1,930.6	207.2
Springfield, MO, MSA	448,011									
Includes Christian, Dallas, Greene, Polk, and Webster Counties										
City of Springfield	163,062	1,894	12	281	395	1,206	14,691	2,313	11,232	1,146
Total area actually reporting	100.0%	2,388	14	340	427	1,607	20,251	3,655	15,113	1,483
Rate per 100,000 inhabitants		533.0	3.1	75.9	95.3	358.7	4,520.2	815.8	3,373.4	331.0
Springfield, OH, MSA	137,153									
Includes Clark County										
City of Springfield	60,012	427	6	46	208	167	4,463	1,304	2,923	236
Total area actually reporting	99.5%	478	6	54	220	198	5,970	1,691	3,997	282
Estimated total	100.0%	478	6	54	220	198	5,987	1,694	4,010	283
Rate per 100,000 inhabitants		348.5	4.4	39.4	160.4	144.4	4,365.2	1,235.1	2,923.7	206.3
State College, PA, MSA	155,409									
Includes Centre County										
City of State College	56,612	41	0	5	13	23	707	101	596	10
Total area actually reporting	100.0%	144	0	37	23	84	2,167	316	1,824	27
Rate per 100,000 inhabitants		92.7	0.0	23.8	14.8	54.1	1,394.4	203.3	1,173.7	17.4
Staunton-Waynesboro, VA, MSA	119,067									
Includes Augusta County and Staunton and Waynesboro Cities										
City of Staunton	24,007	50	1	15	5	29	598	71	510	17
City of Waynesboro	21,175	46	0	15	8	23	688	101	553	34
Total area actually reporting	100.0%	199	2	52	25	120	2,041	341	1,623	77
Rate per 100,000 inhabitants		167.1	1.7	43.7	21.0	100.8	1,714.2	286.4	1,363.1	64.7
St. Cloud, MN, MSA	191,531									
Includes Benton and Stearns Counties										
City of St. Cloud	65,977	250	1	56	46	147	2,842	371	2,308	163
Total area actually reporting	100.0%	322	2	89	50	181	4,667	605	3,812	250
Rate per 100,000 inhabitants		168.1	1.0	46.5	26.1	94.5	2,436.7	315.9	1,990.3	130.5
St. George, UT, MSA[2]	147,923									
Includes Washington County										
City of St. George	76,427	133	1	39	11	82	1,728	475	1,184	69
Total area actually reporting	98.0%	203	2	57	16	128			2,004	111
Estimated total	100.0%	208	2	58	17	131			2,070	118
Rate per 100,000 inhabitants		140.6	1.4	39.2	11.5	88.6			1,399.4	79.8
St. Joseph, MO-KS, MSA	128,425									
Includes Doniphan County, KS and Andrew, Buchanan, and De Kalb Counties, MO										

Table 6. Crime, by Selected Metropolitan Statistical Area, 2013—*Continued*

(Number, percent, rate per 100,000 population.)

Area	Population	Violent crime	Murder and nonnegligent manslaughter	Rape[1]	Robbery	Aggravated assault	Property crime	Burglary	Larceny-theft	Motor vehicle theft
St. Joseph, MO-KS, MSA (cont.)										
City of St. Joseph, MO	77,347	374	1	61	85	227	4,338	805	3,237	296
Total area actually reporting	100.0%	462	2	73	88	299	5,098	1,046	3,722	330
Rate per 100,000 inhabitants		359.7	1.6	56.8	68.5	232.8	3,969.6	814.5	2,898.2	257.0
St. Louis, MO-IL, MSA	2,803,655									
Includes Bond, Calhoun, Clinton, Jersey, Macoupin, Madison, Monroe, and St. Clair Counties, IL and Franklin, Jefferson, Lincoln, St. Charles, St. Louis, and Warren Counties and St. Louis City, MO										
City of St. Louis, MO	318,563	5,077	120	333	1,457	3,167	21,087	4,305	13,452	3,330
City of St. Charles, MO	66,628	113	0	17	27	69	1,770	201	1,502	67
Total area actually reporting	96.7%	11,911	201	961	2,804	7,945	73,094	14,779	52,256	6,059
Estimated total	100.0%	12,103	203	981	2,860	8,059	74,862	15,095	53,631	6,136
Rate per 100,000 inhabitants		431.7	7.2	35.0	102.0	287.4	2,670.2	538.4	1,912.9	218.9
Stockton-Lodi, CA, MSA	708,679									
Includes San Joaquin County										
City of Stockton	299,796	3,622	32	91	1,088	2,411	15,080	4,189	8,748	2,143
City of Lodi	63,639	287	1	11	89	186	2,301	634	1,302	365
Total area actually reporting	100.0%	4,980	47	135	1,477	3,321	28,603	7,538	17,069	3,996
Rate per 100,000 inhabitants		702.7	6.6	19.0	208.4	468.6	4,036.1	1,063.7	2,408.6	563.9
Sumter, SC, MSA....................	108,703									
Includes Sumter County										
City of Sumter	40,928	387	2	13	72	300	2,014	637	1,249	128
Total area actually reporting	100.0%	730	7	51	108	564	3,914	1,382	2,277	255
Rate per 100,000 inhabitants		671.6	6.4	46.9	99.4	518.8	3,600.6	1,271.4	2,094.7	234.6
Syracuse, NY, MSA	661,048									
Includes Madison, Onondaga, and Oswego Counties										
City of Syracuse	143,834	1,192	21	75	400	696	6,473	1,781	4,298	394
Total area actually reporting	100.0%	1,710	28	128	503	1,051	16,397	3,367	12,385	645
Rate per 100,000 inhabitants		258.7	4.2	19.4	76.1	159.0	2,480.5	509.3	1,873.5	97.6
Tallahassee, FL, MSA	378,864									
Includes Gadsden, Jefferson, Leon, and Wakulla Counties										
City of Tallahassee	188,714	1,398	11	160	387	840	8,116	2,082	5,594	440
Total area actually reporting	99.8%	2,203	17	223	454	1,509	12,837	3,252	8,979	606
Estimated total	100.0%	2,206	17	223	455	1,511	12,859	3,257	8,995	607
Rate per 100,000 inhabitants		582.3	4.5	58.9	120.1	398.8	3,394.1	859.7	2,374.2	160.2
Tampa-St. Petersburg-Clearwater, FL, MSA	2,872,186									
Includes Hernando, Hillsborough, Pasco, and Pinellas Counties										
City of Tampa	351,314	2,097	28	78	580	1,411	8,823	1,950	6,320	553
City of St. Petersburg	247,084	2,379	15	155	634	1,575	13,181	2,742	9,315	1,124
City of Clearwater	108,908	618	4	50	177	387	4,316	851	3,284	181
City of Largo	77,913	352	3	47	94	208	2,924	650	2,134	140
Total area actually reporting	100.0%	11,388	123	890	2,607	7,768	78,471	17,794	56,266	4,411
Rate per 100,000 inhabitants		396.5	4.3	31.0	90.8	270.5	2,732.1	619.5	1,959.0	153.6
Terre Haute, IN, MSA	172,996									
Includes Clay, Sullivan, Vermillion, and Vigo Counties										
City of Terre Haute	61,215	177	4	22	54	97	3,261	850	2,130	281
Total area actually reporting	79.0%	258	5	36	61	156	5,092	1,249	3,453	390
Estimated total	100.0%	302	6	41	69	186	5,674	1,383	3,861	430
Rate per 100,000 inhabitants		174.6	3.5	23.7	39.9	107.5	3,279.8	799.4	2,231.8	248.6
Texarkana, TX-AR, MSA	150,224									
Includes Little River and Miller Counties, AR and Bowie County, TX										
City of Texarkana, TX	37,467	329	2	21	71	235	2,300	470	1,725	105
Total area actually reporting	100.0%	839	6	78	120	635	5,887	1,465	4,132	290
Rate per 100,000 inhabitants		558.5	4.0	51.9	79.9	422.7	3,918.8	975.2	2,750.6	193.0
The Villages, FL, MSA...................	104,608									
Includes Sumter County										

Table 6. Crime, by Selected Metropolitan Statistical Area, 2013—*Continued*

(Number, percent, rate per 100,000 population.)

Area	Population	Violent crime	Murder and nonnegligent manslaughter	Rape[1]	Robbery	Aggravated assault	Property crime	Burglary	Larceny-theft	Motor vehicle theft
The Villages, FL, MSA (cont.)										
Total area actually reporting	98.3%	175	2	14	22	137	982	317	612	53
Estimated total	100.0%	183	2	15	24	142	1,045	330	658	57
Rate per 100,000 inhabitants		174.9	1.9	14.3	22.9	135.7	999.0	315.5	629.0	54.5
Toledo, OH, MSA[7]	609,674									
Includes Fulton, Lucas, Ottawa, and Wood Counties										
City of Toledo[7]	283,035	2,902	28	129	962	1,783		5,357		1,064
Total area actually reporting	92.0%	3,165	29	198	1,030	1,908		6,479		1,256
Estimated total	100.0%	3,233	30	209	1,057	1,937		6,728		1,299
Rate per 100,000 inhabitants		530.3	4.9	34.3	173.4	317.7		1,103.5		213.1
Topeka, KS, MSA	234,566									
Includes Jackson, Jefferson, Osage, Shawnee, and Wabaunsee Counties										
City of Topeka	128,009	612	11	33	172	396	6,486	1,238	4,679	569
Total area actually reporting	97.5%	807	13	47	175	572	8,177	1,668	5,832	677
Estimated total	100.0%	819	13	49	176	581	8,307	1,689	5,932	686
Rate per 100,000 inhabitants		349.2	5.5	20.9	75.0	247.7	3,541.4	720.1	2,528.9	292.5
Trenton, NJ, MSA	369,292									
Includes Mercer County										
City of Trenton	84,439	1,122	37	13	525	547	2,321	996	909	416
Total area actually reporting	100.0%	1,518	40	31	685	762	7,491	1,936	4,867	688
Rate per 100,000 inhabitants		411.1	10.8	8.4	185.5	206.3	2,028.5	524.2	1,317.9	186.3
Tucson, AZ, MSA	999,664									
Includes Pima County										
City of Tucson	525,486	3,368	47	216	1,002	2,103	34,587	4,957	27,440	2,190
Total area actually reporting	100.0%	4,334	71	333	1,225	2,705	48,477	7,550	37,897	3,030
Rate per 100,000 inhabitants		433.5	7.1	33.3	122.5	270.6	4,849.3	755.3	3,791.0	303.1
Tulsa, OK, MSA	960,098									
Includes Creek, Okmulgee, Osage, Pawnee, Rogers, Tulsa, and Wagoner Counties										
City of Tulsa	394,498	3,827	60	373	994	2,400	20,978	5,935	12,654	2,389
Total area actually reporting	100.0%	4,962	64	565	1,093	3,240	31,465	8,439	19,762	3,264
Rate per 100,000 inhabitants		516.8	6.7	58.8	113.8	337.5	3,277.3	879.0	2,058.3	340.0
Tuscaloosa, AL, MSA	234,358									
Includes Greene, Hale, and Tuscaloosa Counties										
City of Tuscaloosa	94,126	434	8	44	161	221	4,512	1,165	3,196	151
Total area actually reporting	98.7%	879	16	78	230	555	7,680	1,991	5,335	354
Estimated total	100.0%	892	16	79	233	564	7,801	2,018	5,422	361
Rate per 100,000 inhabitants		380.6	6.8	33.7	99.4	240.7	3,328.7	861.1	2,313.6	154.0
Tyler, TX, MSA	217,202									
Includes Smith County										
City of Tyler	100,033	376	5	43	53	275	4,116	825	3,111	180
Total area actually reporting	99.1%	600	8	56	78	458	6,409	1,568	4,498	343
Estimated total	100.0%	605	8	57	79	461	6,463	1,578	4,539	346
Rate per 100,000 inhabitants		278.5	3.7	26.2	36.4	212.2	2,975.6	726.5	2,089.8	159.3
Utica-Rome, NY, MSA	297,990									
Includes Herkimer and Oneida Counties										
City of Utica	61,686	361	7	27	102	225	2,528	449	1,997	82
City of Rome	32,557	47	4	0	23	20	662	157	470	35
Total area actually reporting	98.5%	661	17	58	146	440	6,507	1,289	5,033	185
Estimated total	100.0%	669	17	58	149	445	6,589	1,301	5,101	187
Rate per 100,000 inhabitants		224.5	5.7	19.5	50.0	149.3	2,211.1	436.6	1,711.8	62.8
Vallejo-Fairfield, CA, MSA	423,574									
Includes Solano County										
City of Vallejo	118,336	1,019	25	30	424	540	5,734	2,972	1,553	1,209
City of Fairfield	108,425	498	3	13	165	317	3,534	735	2,170	629
Total area actually reporting	100.0%	2,001	31	79	718	1,173	13,533	4,666	6,473	2,394
Rate per 100,000 inhabitants		472.4	7.3	18.7	169.5	276.9	3,195.0	1,101.6	1,528.2	565.2
Victoria, TX, MSA	97,898									
Includes Calhoun, Goliad, and Victoria Counties										
City of Victoria	64,979	396	1	53	58	284	2,479	507	1,908	64

Table 6. Crime, by Selected Metropolitan Statistical Area, 2013—*Continued*

(Number, percent, rate per 100,000 population.)

Area	Population	Violent crime	Murder and nonnegligent manslaughter	Rape[1]	Robbery	Aggravated assault	Property crime	Burglary	Larceny-theft	Motor vehicle theft
Victoria, TX, MSA (cont.)										
Total area actually reporting	100.0%	485	3	70	61	351	3,137	717	2,312	108
Rate per 100,000 inhabitants		495.4	3.1	71.5	62.3	358.5	3,204.4	732.4	2,361.6	110.3
Vineland-Bridgeton, NJ, MSA.................	158,281									
Includes Cumberland County										
City of Vineland	60,863	208	1	14	84	109	2,336	594	1,681	61
City of Bridgeton	25,280	340	2	12	165	161	1,186	376	763	47
Total area actually reporting	100.0%	854	4	41	382	427	6,914	1,785	4,939	190
Rate per 100,000 inhabitants		539.5	2.5	25.9	241.3	269.8	4,368.2	1,127.7	3,120.4	120.0
Virginia Beach-Norfolk-Newport News, VA-NC, MSA	1,710,528									
Includes Currituck and Gates Counties, NC and Gloucester, Isle of Wight, James City, Mathews, and York Counties and Chesapeake, Hampton, Newport News, Norfolk, Poquoson, Portsmouth, Suffolk, Virginia Beach, and Williamsburg Cities, VA										
City of Virginia Beach, VA	450,687	730	17	140	304	269	11,226	1,407	9,374	445
City of Norfolk, VA	247,303	1,418	28	134	414	842	10,812	2,039	8,006	767
City of Newport News, VA	181,074	795	15	56	246	478	5,582	991	4,247	344
City of Hampton, VA	136,949	292	22	21	120	129	4,473	722	3,525	226
City of Portsmouth, VA	97,018	590	12	47	177	354	5,355	1,535	3,615	205
Total area actually reporting	99.3%	5,174	118	562	1,534	2,960	51,387	9,025	39,821	2,541
Estimated total	100.0%	5,192	118	563	1,537	2,974	51,598	9,109	39,937	2,552
Rate per 100,000 inhabitants		303.5	6.9	32.9	89.9	173.9	3,016.5	532.5	2,334.8	149.2
Visalia-Porterville, CA, MSA	455,552									
Includes Tulare County										
City of Visalia	127,824	500	8	31	156	305	4,853	1,218	3,016	619
City of Porterville	55,267	194	8	8	44	134	1,506	472	801	233
Total area actually reporting	100.0%	2,151	42	86	438	1,585		4,458	7,870	
Rate per 100,000 inhabitants		472.2	9.2	18.9	96.1	347.9		978.6	1,727.6	
Waco, TX, MSA	258,233									
Includes Falls and McLennan Counties										
City of Waco	127,570	515	4	58	142	311	5,422	1,508	3,751	163
Total area actually reporting	97.9%	873	7	112	179	575	8,495	2,129	6,045	321
Estimated total	100.0%	887	7	114	182	584	8,659	2,160	6,168	331
Rate per 100,000 inhabitants		343.5	2.7	44.1	70.5	226.2	3,353.2	836.5	2,388.5	128.2
Warner Robins, GA, MSA	187,233									
Includes Houston, Peach, and Pulaski Counties										
City of Warner Robins	71,614	364	4	17	138	205	4,213	854	3,191	168
Total area actually reporting	97.0%	700	8	32	185	475	7,077	1,600	5,205	272
Estimated total	100.0%	720	8	33	192	487	7,304	1,641	5,376	287
Rate per 100,000 inhabitants		384.5	4.3	17.6	102.5	260.1	3,901.0	876.4	2,871.3	153.3
Washington-Arlington-Alexandria, DC-VA-MD-WV, MSA	5,943,171									
Includes the Metropolitan Divisions of Silver Spring-Frederick-Rockville, MD and Washington-Arlington-Alexandria, DC-VA-MD-WV										
City of Washington, DC	646,449	7,880	103	393	3,660	3,724	29,569	3,314	23,108	3,147
City of Alexandria, VA	148,519	258	5	21	118	114	2,967	249	2,427	291
City of Frederick, MD	66,709	328	1	7	98	222	1,792	227	1,504	61
Total area actually reporting	99.9%	19,660	222	1,320	8,397	9,721	128,762	17,317	100,443	11,002
Estimated total	100.0%	19,675	222	1,321	8,399	9,733	128,916	17,341	100,567	11,008
Rate per 100,000 inhabitants		331.1	3.7	22.2	141.3	163.8	2,169.1	291.8	1,692.1	185.2
Silver Spring-Frederick-Rockville, MD, MD.........	1,258,323									
Includes Frederick and Montgomery Counties										
Total area actually reporting	100.0%	2,383	14	153	953	1,263	20,394	3,470	15,861	1,063
Rate per 100,000 inhabitants		189.4	1.1	12.2	75.7	100.4	1,620.7	275.8	1,260.5	84.5
Washington-Arlington-Alexandria, DC-VA-MD-WV, MD...	4,684,848									
Includes District of Columbia; Calvert, Charles, and Prince George's Counties, MD; Arlington, Clarke, Culpeper, Fairfax, Fauquier, Loudoun, Prince William, Rapppahannock, Spotsylvania, Stafford, and Warren Counties and Alexandria, Fairfax, Falls Church, Fredericksburg, Manassas, and Manassas Park Cities, VA; and Jefferson County, WV										

Table 6. Crime, by Selected Metropolitan Statistical Area, 2013—*Continued*

(Number, percent, rate per 100,000 population.)

Area	Population	Violent crime	Murder and nonnegligent manslaughter	Rape[1]	Robbery	Aggravated assault	Property crime	Burglary	Larceny-theft	Motor vehicle theft
Washington-Arlington-Alexandria, DC-VA-MD-WV, MD (cont.)										
Total area actually reporting	99.9%	17,277	208	1,167	7,444	8,458	108,368	13,847	84,582	9,939
Estimated total	100.0%	17,292	208	1,168	7,446	8,470	108,522	13,871	84,706	9,945
Rate per 100,000 inhabitants		369.1	4.4	24.9	158.9	180.8	2,316.4	296.1	1,808.1	212.3
Watertown-Fort Drum, NY, MSA	121,663									
Includes Jefferson County										
City of Watertown	28,179	109	0	12	16	81	1,165	169	953	43
Total area actually reporting	97.0%	137	0	14	16	107	2,243	338	1,825	80
Estimated total	100.0%	143	0	14	18	111	2,310	348	1,880	82
Rate per 100,000 inhabitants		117.5	0.0	11.5	14.8	91.2	1,898.7	286.0	1,545.3	67.4
Wausau, WI, MSA	135,041									
Includes Marathon County										
City of Wausau	39,176	85	2	11	13	59	970	217	725	28
Total area actually reporting	98.6%	124	2	17	17	88	2,044	462	1,529	53
Estimated total	100.0%	126	2	17	18	89	2,086	467	1,565	54
Rate per 100,000 inhabitants		93.3	1.5	12.6	13.3	65.9	1,544.7	345.8	1,158.9	40.0
Wichita, KS, MSA	637,215									
Includes Butler, Harvey, Kingman, Sedgwick, and Sumner Counties										
City of Wichita	386,486	3,065	15	244	468	2,338	20,802	3,933	14,885	1,984
Total area actually reporting	99.7%	3,617	22	331	499	2,765	26,310	5,157	18,875	2,278
Estimated total	100.0%	3,621	22	332	499	2,768	26,356	5,165	18,910	2,281
Rate per 100,000 inhabitants		568.3	3.5	52.1	78.3	434.4	4,136.1	810.6	2,967.6	358.0
Wichita Falls, TX, MSA	151,253									
Includes Archer, Clay, and Wichita Counties										
City of Wichita Falls	104,514	401	7	29	124	241	4,558	995	3,277	286
Total area actually reporting	97.7%	509	7	41	132	329	5,348	1,248	3,767	333
Estimated total	100.0%	517	7	42	134	334	5,450	1,267	3,844	339
Rate per 100,000 inhabitants		341.8	4.6	27.8	88.6	220.8	3,603.2	837.7	2,541.4	224.1
Williamsport, PA, MSA	117,439									
Includes Lycoming County										
City of Williamsport	29,536	110	5	10	47	48	1,158	228	902	28
Total area actually reporting	100.0%	201	6	30	59	106	2,547	541	1,949	57
Rate per 100,000 inhabitants		171.2	5.1	25.5	50.2	90.3	2,168.8	460.7	1,659.6	48.5
Wilmington, NC, MSA	266,872									
Includes New Hanover and Pender Counties										
City of Wilmington	110,985	687	7	39	253	388	5,549	1,645	3,569	335
Total area actually reporting	99.1%	960	9	65	296	590	9,450	2,650	6,319	481
Estimated total	100.0%	966	9	65	298	594	9,538	2,669	6,385	484
Rate per 100,000 inhabitants		362.0	3.4	24.4	111.7	222.6	3,574.0	1,000.1	2,392.5	181.4
Winchester, VA-WV, MSA	131,881									
Includes Frederick County and Winchester City, VA, and Hampshire County, WV										
City of Winchester, VA	27,163	89	1	25	29	34	1,006	106	867	33
Total area actually reporting	99.7%	244	3	61	41	139	2,593	404	2,064	125
Estimated total	100.0%	245	3	61	41	140	2,603	406	2,072	125
Rate per 100,000 inhabitants		185.8	2.3	46.3	31.1	106.2	1,973.7	307.9	1,571.1	94.8
Winston-Salem, NC, MSA	651,819									
Includes Davidson, Davie, Forsyth, Stokes, and Yadkin Counties										
City of Winston-Salem	235,811	1,426	15	80	439	892	12,853	3,883	8,359	611
Total area actually reporting	99.3%	2,411	23	141	619	1,628	22,916	7,201	14,651	1,064
Estimated total	100.0%	2,423	23	142	622	1,636	23,074	7,235	14,769	1,070
Rate per 100,000 inhabitants		371.7	3.5	21.8	95.4	251.0	3,539.9	1,110.0	2,265.8	164.2
Worcester, MA-CT, MSA	852,899									
Includes Windham County, CT, and Worcester County, MA										
City of Worcester, MA	183,454	1,750	9	22	483	1,236	6,239	1,916	3,924	399
Total area actually reporting	98.5%	3,562	14	263	688	2,597	16,803	4,331	11,595	877
Estimated total	100.0%	3,602	14	267	696	2,625	17,030	4,381	11,758	891
Rate per 100,000 inhabitants		422.3	1.6	31.3	81.6	307.8	1,996.7	513.7	1,378.6	104.5

Table 6. Crime, by Selected Metropolitan Statistical Area, 2013—*Continued*

(Number, percent, rate per 100,000 population.)

Area	Population	Violent crime	Murder and nonnegligent manslaughter	Rape[1]	Robbery	Aggravated assault	Property crime	Burglary	Larceny-theft	Motor vehicle theft
Yakima, WA, MSA	248,678									
Includes Yakima County										
City of Yakima	93,589	471	9	37	144	281	4,684	1,194	2,896	594
Total area actually reporting	100.0%	719	16	73	191	439	8,365	2,267	4,958	1,140
Rate per 100,000 inhabitants		289.1	6.4	29.4	76.8	176.5	3,363.8	911.6	1,993.7	458.4
York-Hanover, PA, MSA	438,349									
Includes York County										
City of York	43,841	348	12	33	174	129	1,481	486	905	90
City of Hanover	15,362	24	1	1	8	14	505	36	465	4
Total area actually reporting	99.5%	982	19	101	270	592	7,937	1,377	6,299	261
Estimated total	100.0%	986	19	101	271	595	7,980	1,384	6,334	262
Rate per 100,000 inhabitants		224.9	4.3	23.0	61.8	135.7	1,820.5	315.7	1,445.0	59.8
Yuba City, CA, MSA	168,410									
Includes Sutter and Yuba Counties										
City of Yuba City	65,133	174	2	15	39	118	1,980	438	1,210	332
Total area actually reporting	100.0%	516	7	54	85	370	5,081	1,389	2,866	826
Rate per 100,000 inhabitants		306.4	4.2	32.1	50.5	219.7	3,017.0	824.8	1,701.8	490.5
Yuma, AZ, MSA	201,878									
Includes Yuma County										
City of Yuma	96,014	587	5	46	64	472	3,375	805	2,348	222
Total area actually reporting	98.6%	808	12	67	72	657	5,321	1,560	3,379	382
Estimated total	100.0%	816	12	68	74	662	5,413	1,577	3,449	387
Rate per 100,000 inhabitants		404.2	5.9	33.7	36.7	327.9	2,681.3	781.2	1,708.5	191.7
Puerto Rico										
Aguadilla-Isabela, Puerto Rico, MSA	328,531									
Includes Aguada, Aguadilla, Anasco, Isabela, Lares, Moca, Rincon, San Sebastian, and Utuado Municipios										
Total area actually reporting	100.0%	372	36	5	196	135	3,319	1,531	1,680	108
Rate per 100,000 inhabitants		113.2	11.0	1.5	59.7	41.1	1,010.3	466.0	511.4	32.9
Arecibo, Puerto Rico, MSA	195,036									
Includes Arecibo, Camuy, Hatillo, and Quebradillas Municipios										
Total area actually reporting	100.0%	266	27	0	164	75	2,110	759	1,178	173
Rate per 100,000 inhabitants		136.4	13.8	0.0	84.1	38.5	1,081.9	389.2	604.0	88.7
Guayama, Puerto Rico, MSA	82,061									
Includes Arroyo, Guayama, and Patillas Municipios										
Total area actually reporting	100.0%	204	20	1	58	125	1,078	433	615	30
Rate per 100,000 inhabitants		248.6	24.4	1.2	70.7	152.3	1,313.7	527.7	749.4	36.6
Mayaguez, Puerto Rico, MSA	101,172									
Includes Hormigueros and Mayaguez Municipios										
Total area actually reporting	100.0%	217	20	0	112	85	1,699	619	999	81
Rate per 100,000 inhabitants		214.5	19.8	0.0	110.7	84.0	1,679.3	611.8	987.4	80.1
Ponce, Puerto Rico, MSA	333,527									
Includes Guanica, Guyanilla, Juana Diaz, Penuelas, Ponce, Villalba, and Yauco Municipios										
Total area actually reporting	100.0%	655	78	3	361	213	3,261	937	2,140	184
Rate per 100,000 inhabitants		196.4	23.4	0.9	108.2	63.9	977.7	280.9	641.6	55.2
San German, Puerto Rico, MSA	134,623									
Includes Cabo Rojo, Lajas, Sabana Grande, and San German Municipios										
Total area actually reporting	100.0%	121	9	1	46	65	1,155	509	604	42
Rate per 100,000 inhabitants		89.9	6.7	0.7	34.2	48.3	858.0	378.1	448.7	31.2

Table 6. Crime, by Selected Metropolitan Statistical Area, 2013—*Continued*

(Number, percent, rate per 100,000 population.)

Area	Population	Violent crime	Murder and nonnegligent manslaughter	Rape[1]	Robbery	Aggravated assault	Property crime	Burglary	Larceny-theft	Motor vehicle theft
San Juan-Carolina-Caguas, Puerto Rico, MSA	2,284,266									
Includes Aguas Buenas, Aibonito, Barceloneta, Barranquitas, Bayamon, Caguas, Canovanas, Carolina, Catano, Cayey, Ceiba, Ciales, Cidra, Comerio, Corozal, Dorado, Fajardo, Florida, Guaynabo, Gurabo, Humacao, Juncos, Las Piedras, Loiza, Luquillo, Manati, Maunabo, Morovis, Naguabo, Naranjito, Orocovis, Rio Grande, San Juan, San Lorenzo, Toa Alta, Toa Baja, Trujillo Alto, Vega Alta, Vega Baja, and Yabucoa Municipios										
Total area actually reporting	100.0%	7,143	655	15	4,952	1,521	34,335	8,479	21,041	4,815
Rate per 100,000 inhabitants		312.7	28.7	0.7	216.8	66.6	1,503.1	371.2	921.1	210.8

[1]The rape figures in this table are an aggregate total of the data submitted using both the revised and legacy Uniform Crime Reporting (UCR) definitions. See chapter notes for further information.
[2]The FBI determined that the agency's data were overreported. Consequently, those data are not included in this table.
[3]Because of changes in the state/local agency's reporting practices, figures are not comparable to previous years' data.
[4]The data collection methodology for the offense of rape used by Chicago, Illinois does not comply with national UCR Program guidelines. Consequently, its figures for rape and violent crime (of which rape is a part) are not published in this table.
[5]The FBI determined that the agency's data were underreported. Consequently, those data are not included in this table.
[6]The population for the city of Mobile, Alabama, includes 55,819 inhabitants from the jurisdiction of the Mobile County Sheriff's Department.
[7]The FBI determined that the agency did not follow national Uniform Crime Reporting Program guidelines for reporting an offense. Consequently, this figure is not included in this table.

Table 7. Offense Analysis, United States, 2009–2013

(Number.)

Classification	2009	2010	2011	2012[1]	2013
Murder	15,399	14,722	14,661	14,856	14,196
Rape (revised definition)[2]	89,241	85,593	84,175	84,376	X
Rape (legacy definition)[3]	X	X	X	X	108,612
Robbery[4]	408,742	369,089	354,746	355,051	345,031
By location					
Street/highway	174,886	159,307	155,218	154,289	146,472
Commercial house	55,980	48,804	46,156	47,151	45,751
Gas or service station	9,881	8,549	8,539	8,660	8,352
Convenience store	21,983	19,282	18,108	18,180	17,099
Residence	69,280	63,779	60,138	59,979	57,362
Bank	8,829	8,034	7,038	6,666	6,510
Miscellaneous	67,903	61,333	59,549	60,126	63,483
Burglary[4]	2,203,313	2,168,459	2,185,140	2,109,932	1,928,465
Residence (dwelling)	1,599,047	1,602,056	1,628,656	1,571,635	1,425,732
Residence, night	445,983	445,480	442,390	429,662	394,852
Residence, day	819,725	825,163	859,299	832,944	755,178
Residence, unknown	333,339	331,414	326,967	309,028	275,702
Nonresidence (store, office, etc.)	604,266	566,403	556,484	538,297	502,733
Nonresidence, night	255,147	233,765	227,446	220,784	205,639
Nonresidence, day	200,924	192,985	196,461	192,963	183,031
Nonresidence, unknown	148,195	139,652	132,577	124,550	114,063
Larceny-theft (except motor vehicle theft)[4]	6,338,095	6,204,601	6,151,095	6,168,874	6,004,453
By type					
Pocket-picking	26,631	24,231	26,518	29,550	32,345
Purse-snatching	30,493	28,137	27,082	26,407	25,802
Shoplifting	1,149,406	1,064,608	1,077,791	1,147,679	1,196,166
From motor vehicles (except accessories)	1,727,583	1,638,670	1,523,950	1,480,790	1,402,352
Motor vehicle accessories	573,270	549,905	497,980	467,369	438,055
Bicycles	212,362	206,677	216,987	223,786	212,358
From buildings	704,184	699,599	728,050	745,238	738,246
From coin-operated machines	26,085	20,309	19,536	17,240	15,866
All others	1,888,080	1,972,464	2,033,200	2,030,815	1,943,262
By value					
Under $50	2,833,851	2,811,555	2,850,302	2,872,445	2,812,486
$50 to $200	1,443,919	1,421,342	1,399,484	1,398,870	1,339,125
Over $200	2,060,325	1,971,705	1,901,309	1,897,560	1,852,841
Motor vehicle theft	795,652	739,565	716,508	721,053	699,594

[1]The crime figures have been adjusted.
[2]The figures shown in this column for the offense of rape were estimated using the revised Uniform Crime Reporting (UCR) definition of rape. See chapter notes for more detail.
[3]The figures shown in this column for the offense of rape were estimated using the legacy Uniform Crime Reporting (UCR) definition of rape. See chapter notes for more detail.
[4]Because of rounding, the number of offenses may not add to the total.

Table 8. Crime Trends, by Population Group, 2012–2013

(Number, percent change)

Population group	Violent crime	Murder and nonnegligent manslaughter	Forcible rape[1]	Robbery	Aggravated assault	Property crime	Burglary	Larceny-theft	Motor vehicle theft	Arson	Number of agencies	Estimated population, 2013
Total, All Agencies												
2012	1,145,272	14,349	65,733	345,758	719,432	8,507,866	1,992,895	5,816,991	697,980	51,126		
2013	1,095,149	13,716	62,034	335,428	683,971	8,160,228	1,820,544	5,665,392	674,292	44,245	15,232	299,269,511
Percent change	–4.4	–4.4	–5.6	–3.0	–4.9	–4.1	–8.6	–2.6	–3.4	–13.5		
Total, Cities												
2012	919,218	11,198	50,003	303,475	554,542	6,671,809	1,460,169	4,655,398	556,242	38,974		
2013	877,594	10,511	47,606	294,292	525,185	6,434,879	1,335,527	4,557,867	541,485	33,432	11,031	202,966,923
Percent change	–4.5	–6.1	–4.8	–3.0	–5.3	–3.6	–8.5	–2.1	–2.7	–14.2		
Group I (250,000 and over)												
2012	416,885	5,897	15,715	167,168	228,105	2,155,161	493,768	1,401,823	259,570	12,945		
2013	402,988	5,356	15,522	162,815	219,295	2,097,875	454,980	1,395,583	247,312	12,150	77	57,394,814
Percent change	–3.3	–9.2	–1.2	–2.6	–3.9	–2.7	–7.9	–0.4	–4.7	–6.1		
1,000,000 and over (Group I subset)												
2012	166,007	2,255	5,254	74,843	83,655	783,251	166,197	523,397	93,657	3,547		
2013	161,252	1,930	5,356	71,478	82,488	760,143	151,503	521,708	86,932	3,612	10	25,735,804
Percent change	–2.9	–14.4	+1.9	–4.5	–1.4	–3.0	–8.8	–0.3	–7.2	+1.8		
500,000 to 999,999 (Group I subset)												
2012	138,439	1,929	5,833	48,874	81,803	747,008	177,258	481,094	88,656	4,772		
2013	134,216	1,786	5,848	48,375	78,207	733,283	164,283	482,351	86,649	4,466	24	16,780,477
Percent change	–3.1	–7.4	+0.3	–1.0	–4.4	–1.8	–7.3	+0.3	–2.3	–6.4		
250,000 to 499,999 (Group I subset)												
2012	112,439	1,713	4,628	43,451	62,647	624,902	150,313	397,332	77,257	4,626		
2013	107,520	1,640	4,318	42,962	58,600	604,449	139,194	391,524	73,731	4,072	43	14,878,533
Percent change	–4.4	–4.3	–6.7	–1.1	–6.5	–3.3	–7.4	–1.5	–4.6	–12.0		
Group II (100,000 to 249,999)												
2012	154,144	1,788	8,812	50,456	93,088	1,167,627	268,959	793,349	105,319	6,540		
2013	145,408	1,806	7,951	48,590	87,061	1,130,942	246,360	778,577	106,005	5,603	215	32,029,761
Percent change	–5.7	+1.0	–9.8	–3.7	–6.5	–3.1	–8.4	–1.9	+0.7	–14.3		
Group III (50,000 to 99,999)												
2012	116,180	1,162	7,351	34,531	73,136	977,397	215,072	687,344	74,981	5,584		
2013	110,033	1,171	6,972	33,264	68,626	942,519	194,902	673,912	73,705	4,599	471	32,516,218
Percent change	–5.3	+0.8	–5.2	–3.7	–6.2	–3.6	–9.4	–2.0	–1.7	–17.6		
Group IV (25,000 to 49,999)												
2012	85,900	920	6,370	23,082	55,528	836,125	172,406	616,275	47,444	4,538		
2013	80,441	865	6,035	22,462	51,079	806,275	158,056	601,616	46,603	3,489	841	28,988,979
Percent change	–6.4	–6.0	–5.3	–2.7	–8.0	–3.6	–8.3	–2.4	–1.8	–23.1		
Group V (10,000 to 24,999)												
2012	77,759	826	6,011	17,517	53,405	817,630	169,750	608,579	39,301	3,809		
2013	73,998	713	5,587	17,065	50,633	778,955	153,632	586,929	38,394	3,212	1,813	28,865,002
Percent change	–4.8	–13.7	–7.1	–2.6	–5.2	–4.7	–9.5	–3.6	–2.3	–15.7		
Group VI (under 10,000)												
2012	68,350	605	5,744	10,721	51,280	717,869	140,214	548,028	29,627	5,558		
2013	64,726	600	5,539	10,096	48,491	678,313	127,597	521,250	29,466	4,379	7,614	23,172,149
Percent change	–5.3	–0.8	–3.6	–5.8	–5.4	–5.5	–9.0	–4.9	–0.5	–21.2		
Metropolitan Counties												
2012	183,662	2,337	11,357	39,349	130,619	1,461,686	405,229	938,019	118,438	9,151		
2013	177,318	2,386	10,425	38,507	126,000	1,380,837	369,194	901,047	110,596	8,153	1,844	71,774,379
Percent change	–3.5	+2.1	–8.2	–2.1	–3.5	–5.5	–8.9	–3.9	–6.6	–10.9		
Nonmetropolitan Counties[2]												
2012	42,392	814	4,373	2,934	34,271	374,371	127,497	223,574	23,300	3,001		
2013	40,237	819	4,003	2,629	32,786	344,512	115,823	206,478	22,211	2,660	2,357	24,528,209
Percent change	–5.1	+0.6	–8.5	–10.4	–4.3	–8.0	–9.2	–7.6	–4.7	–11.4		
Suburban Areas[3]												
2012	326,107	3,773	21,495	75,543	225,296	3,023,845	709,426	2,112,377	202,042	17,202		
2013	312,046	3,692	20,220	73,494	214,640	2,865,297	642,401	2,030,729	192,167	14,556	8,346	131,056,632
Percent change	–4.3	–2.1	–5.9	–2.7	–4.7	–5.2	–9.4	–3.9	–4.9	–15.4		

[1] The rape figures in this table are based on the legacy Uniform Crime Reporting (UCR) definition of rape. The rape figures shown for 2012 and 2013 include converted National Incident-Based Reporting System rape data and those states/agencies that reported the legacy UCR definition of rape for both years.
[2] Includes state police agencies that report aggregately for the entire state.
[3] Suburban areas include law enforcement agencies in cities with less than 50,000 inhabitants and county law enforcement agencies that are within a Metropolitan Statistical Area. Suburban areas exclude all metropolitan agencies associated with a principal city. The agencies associated with suburban areas also appear in other groups within this table.

Table 9. Rate: Number of Crimes Per 100,000 Population, by Population Group, 2013

(Number, rate.)

Population group	Violent crime		Murder and nonnegligent manslaughter		Rape (revised definition)[1]		Rape (legacy definition)[2]		Robbery		Aggravated assault	
	Number of offenses known	Rate	Number of offenses known	Rate	Number of offenses known	Rate	Number of offenses known	Rate	Number of offenses known	Rate	Number of offenses known	Rate
Total, All Agencies	1,114,351	382.1	13,483	4.6	53,621	39.8	36,209	23.1	329,441	112.9	681,597	233.7
Total, Cities	895,791	449.7	10,346	5.2	37,637	44.0	28,923	25.4	290,331	145.7	528,554	265.3
Group I (250,000 and over)	415,673	734.7	5,282	9.3	10,086	65.7	11,824	28.7	160,525	283.7	227,956	402.9
1,000,000 and over (Group I subset)	172,961	672.1	1,930	7.5	1,279	82.3	6,035	25.0	71,478	277.7	92,239	358.4
500,000 to 999,999 (Group I subset)	132,681	831.1	1,712	10.7	4,584	65.3	3,183	35.6	46,085	288.7	77,117	483.1
250,000 to 499,999 (Group I subset)	110,031	739.5	1,640	11.0	4,223	62.3	2,606	32.2	42,962	288.8	58,600	393.9
Group II (100,000 to 249,999)	147,135	462.9	1,781	5.6	6,540	50.5	4,531	24.1	48,035	151.1	86,248	271.3
Group III (50,000 to 99,999)	111,639	346.2	1,169	3.6	5,909	40.4	3,625	20.6	33,087	102.6	67,849	210.4
Group IV (25,000 to 49,999)	80,625	283.3	827	2.9	5,138	36.3	3,037	21.2	22,060	77.5	49,563	174.1
Group V (10,000 to 24,999)	75,568	268.7	701	2.5	5,331	35.2	2,873	22.1	16,795	59.7	49,868	177.3
Group VI (under 10,000)	65,151	296.0	586	2.7	4,633	34.8	3,033	34.8	9,829	44.7	47,070	213.8
Metropolitan Counties	176,598	256.1	2,337	3.4	10,858	31.7	5,717	16.5	36,566	53.0	121,120	175.7
Nonmetropolitan Counties[3]	41,962	178.5	800	3.4	5,126	34.1	1,569	18.5	2,544	10.8	31,923	135.8
Suburban Areas[4]	312,722	247.0	3,609	2.9	19,718	30.8	11,018	17.6	70,836	55.9	207,541	163.9

Table 9. Rate: Number of Crimes Per 100,000 Population, by Population Group, 2013—*Continued*

Population group	Property crime – Number of offenses known	Property crime – Rate	Burglary – Number of offenses known	Burglary – Rate	Larceny-theft – Number of offenses known	Larceny-theft – Rate	Motor vehicle theft – Number of offenses known	Motor vehicle theft – Rate	Number of agencies	Estimated population, 2013
Total, All Agencies	8,033,404	2,754.2	1,781,179	610.7	5,586,992	1,915.5	665,233	228.1	14,439	291,676,240
Total, Cities	6,368,265	3,196.7	1,311,054	658.1	4,522,141	2,270.0	535,070	268.6	10,444	199,216,695
Group I (250,000 and over)	2,086,616	3,688.0	443,718	784.3	1,398,837	2,472.4	244,061	431.4	76	56,578,450
1,000,000 and over (Group I subset)	760,143	2,953.6	151,503	588.7	521,708	2,027.2	86,932	337.8	10	25,735,804
500,000 to 999,999 (Group I subset)	722,024	4,522.8	153,021	958.5	485,605	3,041.9	83,398	522.4	23	15,964,113
250,000 to 499,999 (Group I subset)	604,449	4,062.6	139,194	935.5	391,524	2,631.5	73,731	495.6	43	14,878,533
Group II (100,000 to 249,999)	1,121,035	3,526.7	243,270	765.3	772,410	2,430.0	105,355	331.4	214	31,786,896
Group III (50,000 to 99,999)	935,283	2,900.3	193,189	599.1	668,768	2,073.8	73,326	227.4	467	32,247,892
Group IV (25,000 to 49,999)	794,193	2,790.2	155,391	545.9	592,993	2,083.3	45,809	160.9	825	28,464,143
Group V (10,000 to 24,999)	767,121	2,727.3	151,190	537.5	578,075	2,055.2	37,856	134.6	1,765	28,127,503
Group VI (under 10,000)	664,017	3,016.6	124,296	564.7	511,058	2,321.7	28,663	130.2	7,097	22,011,811
Metropolitan Counties	1,330,333	1,929.3	357,567	518.6	864,293	1,253.4	108,473	157.3	1,741	68,954,749
Nonmetropolitan Counties[3]	334,806	1,424.4	112,558	478.9	200,558	853.3	21,690	92.3	2,254	23,504,796
Suburban Areas[4]	2,791,140	2,204.6	626,125	494.5	1,976,444	1,561.1	188,571	148.9	7,921	126,607,539

[1]The figures shown in this column for the offense of rape were reported using the revised Uniform Crime Reporting (UCR) definition of rape. See chapter notes for more detail.
[2]The figures shown in this column for the offense of rape were reported using the legacy Uniform Crime Reporting (UCR) definition of rape. See chapter notes for more detail.
[3]Includes state police agencies that report aggregately for the entire state.
[4]Suburban areas include law enforcement agencies in cities with less than 50,000 inhabitants and county law enforcement agencies that are within a Metropolitan Statistical Area. Suburban areas exclude all metropolitan agencies associated with a principal city. The agencies associated with suburban areas also appear in other groups within this table.

Table 10. Rate: Number of Crimes Per 100,000 Inhabitants, by Suburban and Nonsuburban Cities,[1] by Population Group, 2013

(Number, rate.)

Population group	Violent crime		Murder and nonnegligent manslaughter		Rape (revised definition)[2]		Rape (legacy definition)[3]		Robbery		Aggravated assault	
	Number of offenses known	Rate	Number of offenses known	Rate	Number of offenses known	Rate	Number of offenses known	Rate	Number of offenses known	Rate	Number of offenses known	Rate
Total, Suburban Cities	136,124	236.1	1,272	2.2	8,860	29.7	5,301	19.0	34,270	59.4	86,421	149.9
Group IV (25,000 to 49,999)	51,962	233.7	544	2.4	3,054	29.1	1,997	17.0	15,029	67.6	31,338	140.9
Group V (10,000 to 24,999)	47,444	220.0	444	2.1	3,220	28.7	1,744	16.8	12,238	56.7	29,798	138.1
Group VI (under 10,000)	36,718	265.2	284	2.1	2,586	32.0	1,560	27.1	7,003	50.6	25,285	182.6
Total, Nonsuburban Cities	85,220	406.8	842	4.0	6,242	48.9	3,642	44.5	14,414	68.8	60,080	286.8
Group IV (25,000 to 49,999)	28,663	460.3	283	4.5	2,084	57.0	1,040	40.4	7,031	112.9	18,225	292.7
Group V (10,000 to 24,999)	28,124	428.9	257	3.9	2,111	54.0	1,129	42.6	4,557	69.5	20,070	306.1
Group VI (under 10,000)	28,433	348.2	302	3.7	2,047	39.3	1,473	49.7	2,826	34.6	21,785	266.8

Population group	Property crime		Burglary		Larceny-theft		Motor vehicle theft		Number of agencies	Estimated population, 2013
	Number of offenses known	Rate	Number of offenses known	Rate	Number of offenses known	Rate	Number of offenses known	Rate		
Total, Suburban Cities	1,460,807	2,533.8	268,558	465.8	1,112,151	1,929.0	80,098	138.9	6,180	57,652,790
Group IV (25,000 to 49,999)	537,600	2,417.6	101,332	455.7	402,292	1,809.1	33,976	152.8	649	22,236,736
Group V (10,000 to 24,999)	506,939	2,350.2	96,703	448.3	382,131	1,771.6	28,105	130.3	1,340	21,570,172
Group VI (under 10,000)	416,268	3,006.4	70,523	509.3	327,728	2,367.0	18,017	130.1	4,191	13,845,882
Total, Nonsuburban Cities	764,524	3,649.2	162,319	774.8	569,975	2,720.6	32,230	153.8	3,507	20,950,667
Group IV (25,000 to 49,999)	256,593	4,120.4	54,059	868.1	190,701	3,062.3	11,833	190.0	176	6,227,407
Group V (10,000 to 24,999)	260,182	3,967.8	54,487	830.9	195,944	2,988.2	9,751	148.7	425	6,557,331
Group VI (under 10,000)	247,749	3,033.9	53,773	658.5	183,330	2,245.1	10,646	130.4	2,906	8,165,929

[1]Suburban cities include law enforcement agencies in cities with less than 50,000 inhabitants that are within a Metropolitan Statistical Area. Suburban cities exclude all metropolitan agencies associated with a principal city. Nonsuburban cities include law enforcement agencies in cities with less than 50,000 inhabitants that are not associated with a Metropolitan Statistical Area.
[2]The figures shown in this column for the offense of rape were reported using the revised Uniform Crime Reporting (UCR) definition of rape. See chapter notes for more detail.
[3]The figures shown in this column for the offense of rape were reported using the legacy Uniform Crime Reporting (UCR) definition of rape. See chapter notes for more detail.

Table 11. Offense Analysis, Number and Percent Change, 2012–2013

(Number, percent, dollars; 14,230 agencies; 2013 estimated population 289,935,142.)

Classification	Number of offenses, 2013	Percent change from 2012	Percent distribution[1]	Average value (dollars)
Murder	12,404	–3.9	NA	
Rape (Revised Definition)[2]	53,949	NA	NA	
Rape (Legacy Definition)[3]	31,824	NA	NA	
Robbery	301,235	–2.3	100.0	$1,170
By location				
Street/highway	127,880	–3.1	42.5	853
Commercial house	39,944	–0.9	13.3	1,808
Gas or service station	7,292	–1.1	2.4	830
Convenience store	14,929	–3.0	5.0	1,171
Residence	50,081	–3.5	16.6	1,480
Bank	5,684	–0.9	1.9	3,542
Miscellaneous	55,425	–0.2	18.4	961
Burglary	1,743,560	–8.2	100.0	2,322
By location				
Residence (dwelling)	1,289,030	–9.1	73.9	2,315
Residence, night	356,993	–9.4	20.5	1,736
Residence, day	682,770	–9.3	39.2	2,521
Residence, unknown	249,267	–8.1	14.3	2,577
Nonresidence (store, office, etc.)	454,530	–5.7	26.1	2,344
Nonresidence, night	185,922	–6.5	10.7	2,356
Nonresidence, day	165,482	–5.1	9.5	1,957
Nonresidence, unknown	103,126	–5.4	5.9	2,945
Larceny-theft (except motor vehicle theft)	5,392,153	–2.4	100.0	1,259
By type				
Pocket-picking	29,047	+1.1	0.5	514
Purse-snatching	23,171	–1.6	0.4	467
Shoplifting	1,074,188	+4.3	19.9	207
From motor vehicles (except accessories)	1,259,348	–5.0	23.4	937
Motor vehicle accessories	393,385	–6.4	7.3	556
Bicycles	190,703	–4.5	3.5	420
From buildings	662,964	–2.5	12.3	1,384
From coin-operated machines	14,248	–6.4	0.3	448
All others	1,745,099	–3.2	32.4	2,372
By value				
Over $200	2,525,685	–2.3	46.8	2,625
$50 to $200	1,202,569	–3.6	22.3	104
Under $50	1,663,899	–1.7	30.9	21
Motor Vehicle Theft	652,288	–0.3	NA	5,972

NA = Not available.
[1] Because of rounding, the percentages may not add to 100.0.
[2] The figures shown in this column for the offense of rape were reported using the revised Uniform Crime Reporting (UCR) definition of rape. See chapter notes for more detail.
[3] The figures shown in this column for the offense of rape were reported using the legacy Uniform Crime Reporting (UCR) definition of rape. See chapter notes for more detail.

Table 12. Property Stolen and Recovered, by Type and Value, 2013

(Dollars, percent; 13,658 agencies; 2013 estimated population 281,066,647.)

Type of property	Value of property (dollars)		Percent recovered
	Stolen	Recovered	
Total	$10,087,916,015	$2,503,262,060	19.2
Currency, notes, etc.	2,013,267,402	28,453,259	1.4
Jewelry and precious metals	1,743,673,506	88,475,237	5.1
Clothing and furs	304,670,804	33,542,000	11.0
Locally stolen motor vehicles	3,937,054,674	2,159,429,364	54.8
Office equipment	846,233,329	32,167,043	3.8
Televisions, radios, stereos, etc.	665,750,318	32,632,767	4.9
Firearms	154,826,891	13,693,638	8.8
Household goods	422,439,091	114,868,752	27.2
Consumable goods	231,420,776	14,425,417	6.2
Livestock	16,367,591	1,303,936	8.0
Miscellaneous	4,406,114,070	313,240,430	7.1

Table 13. Number and Percent of Offenses Cleared by Arrest or Exceptional Means, by Population Group, 2013

(Number, percent.)

Population group	Violent crime	Murder and nonnegligent manslaughter	Rape (revised definition)[1]	Rape (legacy definition)[2]	Robbery	Aggravated assault	Property crime	Burglary	Larceny-theft	Motor vehicle theft	Arson[3]	Number of agencies	Estimated population, 2013
Total, All Agencies													
Offenses known	1,093,431	13,075	54,598	34,271	319,047	672,440	7,946,255	1,774,472	5,515,119	656,664	43,356	14,943	288,502,854
Percent cleared by arrest	48.1	64.1	40.6	40.0	29.4	57.7	19.7	13.1	22.4	14.2	20.7		
Total Cities													
Offenses known	868,659	9,911	38,571	26,927	277,919	515,331	6,232,236	1,292,660	4,415,748	523,828	32,707	10,799	193,581,763
Percent cleared by arrest	46.3	62.9	37.4	40.0	29.0	56.2	19.7	12.7	22.8	11.3	19.8		
Group I (250,000 and over)													
Offenses known	397,038	4,942	10,656	11,145	151,000	219,295	2,029,407	437,205	1,357,526	234,676	12,231	76	54,674,260
Percent cleared by arrest	42.2	63.0	43.7	39.5	26.8	52.4	14.7	10.0	17.3	8.2	15.1		
1,000,000 and over (Group I subset)													
Offenses known	150,302	1,516	1,279	5,356	59,663	82,488	664,235	133,728	456,211	74,296	3,612	9	23,015,250
Percent cleared by arrest	47.8	79.2	70.4	43.2	30.8	59.4	15.2	10.2	17.9	7.6	11.4		
500,000 to 999,999 (Group I subset)													
Offenses known	136,705	1,786	5,154	3,183	48,375	78,207	760,723	164,283	509,791	86,649	4,466	24	16,780,477
Percent cleared by arrest	38.9	57.2	40.4	36.3	24.6	47.4	13.7	9.5	15.9	8.1	16.5		
250,000 to 499,999 (Group I subset)													
Offenses known	110,031	1,640	4,223	2,606	42,962	58,600	604,449	139,194	391,524	73,731	4,153	43	14,878,533
Percent cleared by arrest	38.7	54.5	39.5	35.6	23.7	49.3	15.5	10.5	18.5	8.9	16.8		
Group II (100,000 to 249,999)													
Offenses known	145,118	1,769	6,540	4,335	47,667	84,807	1,110,662	242,061	763,346	105,255	5,435	209	31,192,769
Percent cleared by arrest	45.2	61.3	34.2	45.2	28.9	54.8	18.2	11.8	21.2	10.7	19.9		
Group III (50,000 to 99,999)													
Offenses known	109,378	1,147	5,982	3,369	32,246	66,634	915,000	189,633	652,727	72,640	4,466	451	31,174,468
Percent cleared by arrest	48.3	57.5	36.7	37.2	31.1	58.1	20.9	13.1	24.3	11.3	21.1		
Group IV (25,000 to 49,999)													
Offenses known	77,991	781	5,195	2,685	21,246	48,084	767,427	151,007	571,330	45,090	3,227	783	27,052,552
Percent cleared by arrest	50.2	65.2	34.0	37.2	33.4	59.8	24.0	14.3	27.3	15.4	23.7		
Group V (10,000 to 24,999)													
Offenses known	73,203	678	5,409	2,450	15,868	48,798	740,642	146,430	557,404	36,808	3,068	1,700	26,946,420
Percent cleared by arrest	54.2	69.0	36.0	42.4	35.9	62.5	26.2	15.9	29.4	18.3	27.1		
Group VI (under 10,000)													
Offenses known	65,931	594	4,789	2,943	9,892	47,713	669,098	126,324	513,415	29,359	4,280	7,580	22,541,294
Percent cleared by arrest	56.2	67.0	34.2	38.4	37.0	63.3	23.8	17.3	25.4	23.4	23.5		
Metropolitan Counties													
Offenses known	181,930	2,343	10,809	5,782	38,492	124,504	1,372,177	366,639	894,885	110,653	8,072	1,858	70,819,193
Percent cleared by arrest	54.3	65.7	48.6	39.7	31.3	62.3	19.6	13.8	21.1	25.9	22.9		
Nonmetropolitan Counties													
Offenses known	42,842	821	5,218	1,562	2,636	32,605	341,842	115,173	204,486	22,183	2,577	2,286	24,101,898
Percent cleared by arrest	59.0	73.9	47.5	41.0	41.9	62.7	18.7	15.8	19.9	23.6	24.8		
Suburban Areas[4]													
Offenses known	313,927	3,545	19,824	10,369	71,201	208,988	2,785,562	628,062	1,968,162	189,338	14,076	8,136	126,228,862
Percent cleared by arrest	54.1	65.2	42.5	40.6	32.9	62.9	21.8	14.7	24.1	22.0	24.1		

[1]The figures shown in this column for the offense of rape were reported using the revised Uniform Crime Reporting (UCR) definition of rape. See chapter notes for more detail.
[2]The figures shown in this column for the offense of rape were reported using the legacy Uniform Crime Reporting (UCR) definition of rape. See chapter notes for more detail.
[3]Not all agencies submit reports for arson to the FBI. As a result, the number of reports the FBI uses to compute the percent of offenses cleared for arson is less than the number it uses to compute the percent of offenses cleared for all other offenses.
[4]Suburban area includes law enforcement agencies in cities with less than 50,000 inhabitants and county law enforcement agencies that are within a Metropolitan Statistical Area. Suburban area excludes all metropolitan agencies associated with a principal city. The agencies associated with suburban areas also appear in other groups within this table.

Table 14. Number of Offenses Cleared by Arrest or Exceptional Means and Percent Involving Persons Under 18 Years of Age, by Population Group, 2013

(Number, percent.)

Population group	Violent crime	Murder and nonnegligent manslaughter	Rape (revised definition)[1]	Rape (legacy definition)[2]	Robbery	Aggravated assault	Property crime	Burglary	Larceny-theft	Motor vehicle theft	Arson[3]	Number of agencies	Estimated population, 2013
Total, All Agencies													
Offenses known	477,735	7,761	18,646	13,687	86,094	351,547	1,429,145	208,967	1,133,743	86,435	8,490	14,330	269,053,710
Percent under 18 years	8.8	3.6	16.9	9.4	13.1	7.4	10.8	9.9	11.1	8.9	27.9		
Total Cities													
Offenses known	375,727	5,896	12,789	10,749	75,979	270,314	1,150,297	151,232	943,231	55,834	6,238	10,478	183,975,386
Percent under 18 years	8.9	3.6	15.9	8.8	13.3	7.4	11.2	10.5	11.4	10.5	29.8		
Group I (250,000 and over)													
Offenses known	161,223	3,002	4,133	4,397	39,286	110,405	285,722	41,668	225,484	18,570	1,800	72	52,805,569
Percent under 18 years	8.9	3.5	15.4	6.6	15.2	6.7	11.2	11.2	11.2	11.3	30.3		
1,000,000 and over (Group I subset)													
Offenses known	71,801	1,200	901	2,314	18,377	49,009	101,185	13,650	81,889	5,646	413	9	23,015,250
Percent under 18 years	8.6	2.7	18.0	4.9	15.6	6.1	9.9	9.6	10.0	8.7	26.6		
500,000 to 999,999 (Group I subset)													
Offenses known	50,807	970	1,791	1,156	11,525	35,365	98,101	14,643	76,709	6,749	723	23	15,934,732
Percent under 18 years	9.5	3.1	16.5	7.7	16.1	7.3	11.9	12.8	11.6	13.8	31.3		
250,000 to 499,999 (Group I subset)													
Offenses known	38,615	832	1,441	927	9,384	26,031	86,436	13,375	66,886	6,175	664	40	13,855,587
Percent under 18 years	8.6	5.0	12.3	9.6	13.2	6.8	12.0	10.9	12.2	11.1	31.5		
Group II (100,000 to 249,999)													
Offenses known	59,153	995	1,866	1,933	12,560	41,799	182,420	25,447	146,686	10,287	1,023	191	28,457,842
Percent under 18 years	8.7	5.0	16.2	7.4	12.0	7.5	12.8	12.2	13.1	10.8	27.9		
Group III (50,000 to 99,999)													
Offenses known	47,460	598	1,899	1,254	8,871	34,838	174,742	22,361	144,834	7,547	903	420	29,118,053
Percent under 18 years	8.8	3.5	14.7	10.4	12.6	7.5	12.7	10.2	13.2	10.9	33.1		
Group IV (25,000 to 49,999)													
Offenses known	35,534	476	1,552	998	6,429	26,079	170,020	18,868	144,740	6,412	726	745	25,674,031
Percent under 18 years	9.0	2.9	17.5	11.1	10.3	8.2	10.8	9.7	11.1	9.1	31.5		
Group V (10,000 to 24,999)													
Offenses known	36,831	444	1,789	1,038	5,338	28,222	183,186	21,925	154,871	6,390	799	1,634	25,893,377
Percent under 18 years	9.2	3.6	18.1	13.1	9.0	8.7	10.3	9.1	10.5	9.7	30.7		
Group VI (under 10,000)													
Offenses known	35,526	381	1,550	1,129	3,495	28,971	154,207	20,963	126,616	6,628	987	7,416	22,026,514
Percent under 18 years	8.7	2.6	14.5	12.2	11.4	8.0	9.2	9.6	9.1	9.0	25.6		
Metropolitan Counties													
Offenses known	78,325	1,280	3,468	2,298	9,103	62,176	217,766	40,476	151,736	25,554	1,633	1,657	61,501,709
Percent under 18 years	9.0	3.5	21.0	11.4	12.1	7.9	9.4	8.9	10.3	5.2	25.7		
Nonmetropolitan Counties													
Offenses known	23,683	585	2,389	640	1,012	19,057	61,082	17,259	38,776	5,047	619	2,195	23,576,615
Percent under 18 years	6.8	3.2	15.9	11.9	4.6	5.7	7.5	7.6	7.2	9.4	15.0		
Suburban Areas[4]													
Offenses known	143,079	1,998	6,268	4,213	19,526	111,074	532,615	77,841	417,021	37,753	3,113	7,711	114,428,508
Percent under 18 years	9.3	3.3	19.5	12.0	11.5	8.4	9.8	9.2	10.2	6.4	28.3		

[1] The figures shown in this column for the offense of rape were reported using the revised Uniform Crime Reporting (UCR) definition of rape. See chapter notes for more detail.
[2] The figures shown in this column for the offense of rape were reported using the legacy Uniform Crime Reporting (UCR) definition of rape. See chapter notes for more detail.
[3] Not all agencies submit reports for arson to the FBI. As a result, the number of reports the FBI uses to compute the percent of offenses cleared for arson is less than the number it uses to compute the percent of offenses cleared for all other offenses.
[4] Suburban area includes law enforcement agencies in cities with less than 50,000 inhabitants and county law enforcement agencies that are within a Metropolitan Statistical Area. Suburban area excludes all metropolitan agencies associated with a principal city. The agencies associated with suburban areas also appear in other groups within this table.

Table 15. Estimated Number of Arrests, 2013

(Number.)

Offense	Arrests
Total[1]	11,302,102
Violent crime[2]	480,360
Murder and nonnegligent manslaughter	10,231
Rape[3]	16,863
Robbery	94,406
Aggravated assault	358,860
Property crime[2]	1,559,284
Burglary	252,629
Larceny-theft	1,231,580
Motor vehicle theft	64,566
Arson	10,509
Other assaults	1,097,741
Forgery and counterfeiting	60,969
Fraud	143,528
Embezzlement	15,730
Stolen property; buying, receiving, possessing	92,691
Vandalism	201,168
Weapons; carrying, possessing, etc.	137,779
Prostitution and commercialized vice	48,620
Sex offenses (except forcible rape and prostitution)	57,925
Drug abuse violations	1,501,043
Gambling	6,024
Offenses against the family and children	101,247
Driving under the influence	1,166,824
Liquor laws	354,872
Drunkenness	443,527
Disorderly conduct	467,993
Vagrancy	25,755
All other offenses	3,282,651
Suspicion	1,096
Curfew and loitering law violations	56,371

[1]Does not include suspicion.
[2]Violent crimes are offenses of murder and nonnegligent manslaughter, forcible rape, robbery, and aggravated assault. Property crimes are offenses of burglary, larceny-theft, motor vehicle theft, and arson.
[3]The rape figures in this table are an aggregate total of the data submitted using both the revised and legacy Uniform Crime Reporting definitions.

Table 16. Number and Rate of Arrests, by Geographic Region, 2013

(Number, rate per 100,000 inhabitants.)

Offense charged	United States total (11,951 agencies; population 245,741,701) Total	Northeast (2,924 agencies; population 44,939,316) Total	Rate	Midwest (3,010 agencies; population 48,866,569) Total	Rate	South (4,215 agencies; population 84,250,091) Total	Rate	West (1,802 agencies; population 67,685,725) Total	Rate
Total[1]	9,445,500	14,91,232	3,292.3	18,26,800	3,889.3	3,604,931	4,352.4	2,522,537	3,718.7
Violent crime[2]	404,037	67,297	148.6	61,941	131.9	129,446	156.3	145,353	214.3
Murder and nonnegligent manslaughter	8,514	1,205	2.7	1,428	3.0	3,435	4.1	2,446	3.6
Rape[3]	13,971	2,409	5.3	2,918	6.2	5,037	6.1	3,607	5.3
Robbery	80,487	17,203	38.0	12,647	26.9	25,749	31.1	24,888	36.7
Aggravated assault	301,065	46,480	102.6	44,948	95.7	95,225	115.0	114,412	168.7
Property crime[2]	1,282,906	2,11,930	467.9	2,55,097	543.1	486,248	587.1	329,631	485.9
Burglary	220,284	34,784	76.8	32,666	69.5	79,732	96.3	73,102	107.8
Larceny-theft	1,000,496	1,68,504	372.0	2,10,144	447.4	388,703	469.3	233,145	343.7
Motor vehicle theft	53,244	7,056	15.6	10,749	22.9	15,059	18.2	20,380	30.0
Arson	8,882	1,586	3.5	1,538	3.3	2,754	3.3	3,004	4.4
Other assaults	930,210	1,67,336	369.4	1,83,609	390.9	375,164	453.0	204,101	300.9
Forgery and counterfeiting	51,987	9,673	21.4	7,461	15.9	22,944	27.7	11,909	17.6
Fraud	118,374	20,812	45.9	20,251	43.1	60,462	73.0	16,849	24.8
Embezzlement	12,429	1,309	2.9	1,894	4.0	6,891	8.3	2,335	3.4
Stolen property; buying, receiving, possessing	75,989	15,146	33.4	13,276	28.3	20,261	24.5	27,306	40.3
Vandalism	177,325	41,276	91.1	37,007	78.8	46,022	55.6	53,020	78.2
Weapons; carrying, possessing, etc.	115,464	15,564	34.4	22,206	47.3	39,940	48.2	37,754	55.7
Prostitution and commercialized vice	43,395	5,381	11.9	5,847	12.4	15,719	19.0	16,448	24.2
Sex offenses (except forcible rape and prostitution)	52,768	8,953	19.8	10,245	21.8	15,460	18.7	18,110	26.7
Drug abuse violations	1,200,538	2,08,351	460.0	2,22,495	473.7	450,386	543.8	319,306	470.7
Gambling	5,976	525	1.2	2,774	5.9	2,112	2.5	565	0.8
Offenses against the family and children	82,121	16,862	37.2	17,664	37.6	35,068	42.3	12,527	18.5
Driving under the influence	987,224	1,40,014	309.1	2,05,543	437.6	318,531	384.6	323,136	476.4
Liquor laws	341,328	43,337	95.7	1,11,281	236.9	92,827	112.1	93,883	138.4
Drunkenness	399,920	35,089	77.5	27,876	59.3	233,492	281.9	103,463	152.5
Disorderly conduct	422,382	1,04,887	231.6	1,23,407	262.7	131,900	159.2	62,188	91.7
Vagrancy	20,900	1,889	4.2	3,570	7.6	5,968	7.2	9,473	14.0
All other offenses (except traffic)	2,666,096	3,56,840	787.8	4,84,204	1,030.9	1,104,223	1,333.2	720,829	1,062.6
Suspicion	1,160	52	0.1	257	0.5	822	1.0	29	0.0
Curfew and loitering law violations	54,131	18,761	41.4	9,152	19.5	11,867	14.3	14,351	21.2

[1]Does not include suspicion.
[2]Violent crimes are offenses of murder and nonnegligent manslaughter, revised and legacy rape, robbery, and aggravated assault. Property crimes are offenses of burglary, larceny-theft, motor vehicle theft, and arson.
[3]The rape figures in this table are an aggregate total of the data submitted using both the revised and legacy Uniform Crime Reporting definitions.

Table 17. Number and Rate of Arrests, by Population Group, 2013

(Number, rate per 100,000 inhabitants.)

Offense charged	Total (12,196 agencies; population 242,925,157)		Total cities (8,659 cities; population 167,355,619)		Group I (65 cities, 250,000 and over; population 44,412,487)		Group II (179 cities, 100,000 to 249,999; population 26,521,279)		Group III (405 cities, 50,000 to 99,999; population 28,114,457)	
	Total	Rate	Total	Rate	Total	Rate	Total	Rate	Total	Rate
Total[2]	9,069,148	3,690.5	6,663,998	3,981.9	1,790,769	4,032.1	1,007,570	3,799.1	1,015,895	3,613.4
Violent crime[3]	392,778	159.8	303,405	181.3	115,377	259.8	51,298	193.4	45,994	163.6
Murder and nonnegligent manslaughter	8,401	3.4	6,167	3.7	2,893	6.5	1,073	4.0	767	2.7
Rape[4]	13,617	5.5	9,956	5.9	3,436	7.7	1,367	5.2	1,465	5.2
Robbery	78,753	32.0	67,460	40.3	30,787	69.3	11,109	41.9	9,552	34.0
Aggravated assault	292,007	118.8	219,822	131.4	78,261	176.2	37,749	142.3	34,210	121.7
Property crime[3]	1,261,124	513.2	1,027,716	614.1	247,849	558.1	163,473	616.4	171,794	611.1
Burglary	203,709	82.9	149,031	89.1	41,146	92.6	27,384	103.3	26,131	92.9
Larceny-theft	996,495	405.5	833,302	497.9	190,742	429.5	127,400	480.4	138,899	494.0
Motor vehicle theft	52,507	21.4	38,841	23.2	14,484	32.6	7,238	27.3	5,701	20.3
Arson	8,413	3.4	6,542	3.9	1,477	3.3	1,451	5.5	1,063	3.8
Other assaults	885,822	360.5	666,195	398.1	192,868	434.3	105,694	398.5	104,566	371.9
Forgery and counterfeiting	48,826	19.9	35,960	21.5	8,738	19.7	5,275	19.9	5,620	20.0
Fraud	113,510	46.2	75,435	45.1	15,282	34.4	9,951	37.5	11,579	41.2
Embezzlement	12,664	5.2	9,682	5.8	2,172	4.9	1,632	6.2	1,599	5.7
Stolen property; buying, receiving, possessing	74,792	30.4	55,382	33.1	14,169	31.9	8,918	33.6	10,627	37.8
Vandalism	162,068	66.0	124,734	74.5	33,186	74.7	18,734	70.6	19,832	70.5
Weapons; carrying, possessing, etc.	112,673	45.9	87,816	52.5	35,012	78.8	13,773	51.9	12,086	43.0
Prostitution and commercialized vice	42,110	17.1	38,619	23.1	27,641	62.2	4,699	17.7	2,560	9.1
Sex offenses (except forcible rape and prostitution)	46,832	19.1	33,349	19.9	11,587	26.1	4,831	18.2	4,857	17.3
Drug abuse violations	1,209,661	492.2	880,503	526.1	276,253	622.0	131,482	495.8	134,791	479.4
Gambling	5,089	2.1	4,225	2.5	3,124	7.0	278	1.0	169	0.6
Offenses against the family and children	78,812	32.1	37,350	22.3	5,980	13.5	7,414	28.0	4,813	17.1
Driving under the influence	918,462	373.8	532,729	318.3	118,787	267.5	72,207	272.3	78,312	278.5
Liquor laws	280,860	114.3	224,739	134.3	45,157	101.7	24,628	92.9	28,760	102.3
Drunkenness	358,036	145.7	307,420	183.7	63,810	143.7	55,929	210.9	54,872	195.2
Disorderly conduct	375,142	152.7	313,717	187.5	70,434	158.6	38,451	145.0	45,243	160.9
Vagrancy	21,633	8.8	19,376	11.6	8,651	19.5	2,528	9.5	3,998	14.2
All other offenses (except traffic)	2,620,320	1,066.3	1,840,531	1,099.8	467,801	1,053.3	282,728	1,066.0	269,527	958.7
Suspicion	844	0.3	484	0.3	0	0.0	0	0.0	164	0.6
Curfew and loitering law violations	47,934	19.5	45,115	27.0	26,891	60.5	3,647	13.8	4,296	15.3

Table 17. Number and Rate of Arrests, by Population Group, 2013—*Continued*

(Number, rate per 100,000 inhabitants.)

Offense charged	Group IV (728 cities, 25,000 to 49,999; population 25,113,552)		Group V (1,520 cities, 10,000 to 24,999; population 24,115,753)		Group VI (5,762 cities, under 10,000; population 19,078,091)		Metropolitan counties (1,374 agencies; population 57,208,460)		Nonmetropolitan counties (1,918 agencies; population 21,177,622)		Suburban areas[1] (6,631 agencies; population 111,178,219)	
	Total	Rate	Total	Rate	Total	Rate	Total	Rate	Total	Rate	Total	Rate
Total[2]	921,571	3,669.6	967,480	4,011.8	960,713	5,035.7	1,699,763	2,971.2	705,387	3,330.8	3,757,710	3,379.9
Violent crime[3]	33,340	132.8	31,838	132.0	25,558	134.0	69,443	121.4	19,930	94.1	136,378	122.7
Murder and nonnegligent manslaughter	566	2.3	510	2.1	358	1.9	1,609	2.8	625	3.0	2,583	2.3
Rape[4]	1,194	4.8	1,341	5.6	1,153	6.0	2,448	4.3	1,213	5.7	4,987	4.5
Robbery	6,849	27.3	5,664	23.5	3,499	18.3	9,895	17.3	1,398	6.6	22,956	20.6
Aggravated assault	24,731	98.5	24,323	100.9	20,548	107.7	55,491	97.0	16,694	78.8	105,852	95.2
Property crime[3]	162,941	648.8	160,573	665.8	121,086	634.7	181,553	317.4	51,855	244.9	508,808	457.7
Burglary	19,069	75.9	19,019	78.9	16,282	85.3	39,089	68.3	15,589	73.6	78,750	70.8
Larceny-theft	139,078	553.8	136,967	568.0	100,216	525.3	130,963	228.9	32,230	152.2	408,402	367.3
Motor vehicle theft	3,970	15.8	3,781	15.7	3,667	19.2	10,155	17.8	3,511	16.6	18,458	16.6
Arson	824	3.3	806	3.3	921	4.8	1,346	2.4	525	2.5	3,198	2.9
Other assaults	91,501	364.3	90,034	373.3	81,532	427.4	161,057	281.5	58,570	276.6	346,497	311.7
Forgery and counterfeiting	5,334	21.2	5,775	23.9	5,218	27.4	9,949	17.4	2,917	13.8	21,671	19.5
Fraud	12,116	48.2	12,356	51.2	14,151	74.2	26,370	46.1	11,705	55.3	53,643	48.2
Embezzlement	1,606	6.4	1,602	6.6	1,071	5.6	2,410	4.2	572	2.7	5,443	4.9
Stolen property; buying, receiving, possessing	8,607	34.3	7,611	31.6	5,450	28.6	15,187	26.5	4,223	19.9	32,653	29.4
Vandalism	18,296	72.9	17,677	73.3	17,009	89.2	28,264	49.4	9,070	42.8	66,003	59.4
Weapons; carrying, possessing, etc.	9,217	36.7	8,352	34.6	9,376	49.1	18,544	32.4	6,313	29.8	38,920	35.0
Prostitution and commercialized vice	1,938	7.7	1,123	4.7	658	3.4	3,338	5.8	153	0.7	6,612	5.9
Sex offenses (except forcible rape and prostitution)	4,249	16.9	3,962	16.4	3,863	20.2	9,740	17.0	3,743	17.7	18,565	16.7
Drug abuse violations	112,495	447.9	110,404	457.8	115,078	603.2	238,806	417.4	90,352	426.6	495,730	445.9
Gambling	94	0.4	169	0.7	391	2.0	724	1.3	140	0.7	996	0.9
Offenses against the family and children	6,506	25.9	6,127	25.4	6,510	34.1	31,135	54.4	10,327	48.8	43,365	39.0
Driving under the influence	76,851	306.0	88,885	368.6	97,687	512.0	228,201	398.9	157,532	743.9	422,322	379.9
Liquor laws	29,378	117.0	36,982	153.4	59,834	313.6	35,940	62.8	20,181	95.3	119,823	107.8
Drunkenness	41,468	165.1	44,714	185.4	46,627	244.4	34,999	61.2	15,617	73.7	125,344	112.7
Disorderly conduct	45,544	181.4	54,137	224.5	59,908	314.0	43,338	75.8	18,087	85.4	157,241	141.4
Vagrancy	2,052	8.2	969	4.0	1,178	6.2	2,026	3.5	231	1.1	5,398	4.9
All other offenses (except traffic)	254,622	1,013.9	280,702	1,164.0	285,151	1,494.7	556,178	972.2	223,611	1,055.9	1,142,346	1,027.5
Suspicion	107	0.4	80	0.3	133	0.7	44	0.1	316	1.5	290	0.3
Curfew and loitering law violations	3,416	13.6	3,488	14.5	3,377	17.7	2,561	4.5	258	1.2	9,952	9.0

[1]Suburban areas include law enforcement agencies in cities with less than 50,000 inhabitants and county law enforcement agencies that are within a Metropolitan Statistical Area. Suburban areas exclude all metropolitan agencies associated with a principal city. The agencies associated with suburban areas also appear in other groups within this table.
[2]Does not include suspicion.
[3]Violent crimes are offenses of murder and nonnegligent manslaughter, forcible rape, robbery, and aggravated assault. Property crimes are offenses of burglary, larceny-theft, motor vehicle theft, and arson.
[4]The rape figures in this table are an aggregate total of the data submitted using both the revised and legacy Uniform Crime Reporting definitions.

Table 18. Ten-Year Arrest Trends, 2004 and 2013

(Number, percent change; 7,858 agencies; 2013 estimated population 192,473,854; 2004 estimated population 178,805,123.)

Offense charged	Total, all ages			Under 18 years of age			18 years of age and over		
	2004	2013	Percent change	2004	2013	Percent change	2004	2013	Percent change
Total[1]	8,402,488	7,120,525	-15.3	1,226,865	666,263	-45.7	7,175,623	6,454,262	-10.1
Violent crime[2]	358,066	312,739	-12.7	53,905	33,667	-37.5	304,161	279,072	-8.2
Murder and nonnegligent manslaughter	7,872	6,695	-15.0	643	492	-23.5	7,229	6,203	-14.2
Rape[3]	15,019	10,471	-30.3	2,414	1,484	-38.5	12,605	8,987	-28.7
Robbery	64,349	61,019	-5.2	14,936	12,340	-17.4	49,413	48,679	-1.5
Aggravated assault	270,826	234,554	-13.4	35,912	19,351	-46.1	234,914	215,203	-8.4
Property crime[2]	998,816	983,307	-1.6	275,169	154,838	-43.7	723,647	828,469	+14.5
Burglary	180,617	163,261	-9.6	49,721	27,960	-43.8	130,896	135,301	+3.4
Larceny-theft	721,769	771,869	+6.9	198,071	117,141	-40.9	523,698	654,728	+25.0
Motor vehicle theft	87,337	41,385	-52.6	22,784	7,367	-67.7	64,553	34,018	-47.3
Arson	9,093	6,792	-25.3	4,593	2,370	-48.4	4,500	4,422	-1.7
Other assaults	769,970	696,659	-9.5	148,743	91,436	-38.5	621,227	605,223	-2.6
Forgery and counterfeiting	71,993	37,884	-47.4	2,988	649	-78.3	69,005	37,235	-46.0
Fraud	196,788	88,245	-55.2	4,622	2,755	-40.4	192,166	85,490	-55.5
Embezzlement	11,995	10,202	-14.9	698	233	-66.6	11,297	9,969	-11.8
Stolen property; buying, receiving, possessing	78,027	58,443	-25.1	13,879	6,354	-54.2	64,148	52,089	-18.8
Vandalism	160,941	128,589	-20.1	61,262	29,676	-51.6	99,679	98,913	-0.8
Weapons; carrying, possessing, etc.	110,697	91,150	-17.7	25,478	12,771	-49.9	85,219	78,379	-8.0
Prostitution and commercialized vice	55,369	35,562	-35.8	1,157	550	-52.5	54,212	35,012	-35.4
Sex offenses (except forcible rape and prostitution)	54,292	35,604	-34.4	10,923	6,249	-42.8	43,369	29,355	-32.3
Drug abuse violations	1,080,301	976,882	-9.6	118,392	75,767	-36.0	961,909	901,115	-6.3
Gambling	6,365	4,400	-30.9	1,099	569	-48.2	5,266	3,831	-27.3
Offenses against the family and children	73,249	60,479	-17.4	3,608	1,668	-53.8	69,641	58,811	-15.6
Driving under the influence	840,325	710,351	-15.5	11,212	4,315	-61.5	829,113	706,036	-14.8
Liquor laws	343,782	206,285	-40.0	71,976	34,283	-52.4	271,806	172,002	-36.7
Drunkenness	363,978	300,708	-17.4	11,117	5,107	-54.1	352,861	295,601	-16.2
Disorderly conduct	364,859	258,950	-29.0	110,374	53,471	-51.6	254,485	205,479	-19.3
Vagrancy	23,137	18,154	-21.5	3,138	545	-82.6	19,999	17,609	-12.0
All other offenses (except traffic)	2,372,952	2,080,548	-12.3	230,539	125,976	-45.4	2,142,413	1,954,572	-8.8
Suspicion	4,249	399	-90.6	535	38	-92.9	3,714	361	-90.3
Curfew and loitering law violations	66,586	25,384	-61.9	66,586	25,384	-61.9	NA	NA	NA

NA = Not available.
[1]Does not include suspicion.
[2]Violent crimes are offenses of murder and nonnegligent manslaughter, forcible rape, robbery, and aggravated assault. Property crimes are offenses of burglary, larceny-theft, motor vehicle theft, and arson.
[3]The rape figures in this table are based on the legacy definition of rape only. The rape figures shown include converted National Incident-Based Reporting System rape data and those states/agencies that reported the legacy definition of rape for both years.

Table 19. Current Year Over Previous Year Arrest Trends, 2012–2013

(Number, percent change; 9,412 agencies; 2013 estimated population 210,277,851; 2012 estimated population 208,777,994.)

Offense charged	Number of persons arrested											
	Total, all ages			Under 15 years of age			Under 18 years of age			18 years of age and over		
	2012	2013	Percent change	2012	2013	Percent change	2012	2013	Percent change	2012	2013	Percent change
Total¹	8,026,954	7,634,314	−4.9	229,577	194,429	−15.3	831,366	702,779	−15.5	7,195,588	6,931,535	−3.7
Violent crime²	343,222	329,703	−3.9	10,306	9,402	−8.8	36,905	33,713	−8.6	306,317	295,990	−3.4
Murder and nonnegligent manslaughter	6,763	6,742	−0.3	47	63	+34.0	425	485	+14.1	6,338	6,257	−1.3
Rape³	11,598	10,967	−5.4	607	572	−5.8	1,607	1,550	−3.5	9,991	9,417	−5.7
Robbery	64,030	62,646	−2.2	2,349	2,325	−1.0	12,408	11,957	−3.6	51,622	50,689	−1.8
Aggravated assault	260,831	249,348	−4.4	7,303	6,442	−11.8	22,465	19,721	−12.2	238,366	229,627	−3.7
Property crime²	1,077,394	1,046,585	−2.9	54,898	45,810	−16.6	192,669	163,822	−15.0	884,725	882,763	−0.2
Burglary	190,916	174,506	−8.6	9,941	8,029	−19.2	36,067	29,715	−17.6	154,849	144,791	−6.5
Larceny-theft	837,404	823,575	−1.7	41,740	34,860	−16.5	146,223	124,844	−14.6	691,181	698,731	+1.1
Motor vehicle theft	42,081	41,650	−1.0	1,567	1,542	−1.6	7,598	6,907	−9.1	34,483	34,743	+0.8
Arson	6,993	6,854	−2.0	1,650	1,379	−16.4	2,781	2,356	−15.3	4,212	4,498	+6.8
Other assaults	782,502	738,781	−5.6	42,078	37,691	−10.4	108,705	96,475	−11.3	673,797	642,306	−4.7
Forgery and counterfeiting	44,624	41,367	−7.3	132	76	−42.4	943	703	−25.5	43,681	40,664	−6.9
Fraud	105,634	98,335	−6.9	573	588	+2.6	3,222	3,070	−4.7	102,412	95,265	−7.0
Embezzlement	11,254	11,349	+0.8	20	26	+30.0	285	260	−8.8	10,969	11,089	+1.1
Stolen property; buying, receiving, possessing	67,623	64,789	−4.2	1,957	1,620	−17.2	8,778	7,122	−18.9	58,845	57,667	−2.0
Vandalism	147,291	133,943	−9.1	14,785	11,648	−21.2	38,254	30,820	−19.4	109,037	103,123	−5.4
Weapons; carrying, possessing, etc.	96,930	93,839	−3.2	5,354	4,520	−15.6	15,528	13,329	−14.2	81,402	80,510	−1.1
Prostitution and commercialized vice	35,645	34,792	−2.4	38	55	+44.7	567	576	+1.6	35,078	34,216	−2.5
Sex offenses (except forcible rape and prostitution)	44,170	38,599	−12.6	3,957	3,368	−14.9	8,003	6,915	−13.6	36,167	31,684	−12.4
Drug abuse violations	991,032	1,005,019	+1.4	15,051	13,387	−11.1	86,818	76,568	−11.8	904,214	928,451	+2.7
Gambling	2,815	2,493	−11.4	33	41	+24.2	262	183	−30.2	2,553	2,310	−9.5
Offenses against the family and children	71,847	69,387	−3.4	717	610	−14.9	2,282	1,894	−17.0	69,565	67,493	−3.0
Driving under the influence	849,335	782,603	−7.9	106	105	−0.9	5,921	4,873	−17.7	843,414	777,730	−7.8
Liquor laws	273,305	226,501	−17.1	4,759	3,632	−23.7	48,790	37,592	−23.0	224,515	188,909	−15.9
Drunkenness	363,894	322,556	−11.4	832	650	−21.9	7,132	5,467	−23.3	356,762	317,089	−11.1
Disorderly conduct	315,394	280,353	−11.1	27,576	22,575	−18.1	70,723	56,989	−19.4	244,671	223,364	−8.7
Vagrancy	19,376	19,141	−1.2	267	145	−45.7	985	590	−40.1	18,391	18,551	+0.9
All other offenses (except traffic)	2,349,757	2,267,608	−3.5	37,642	31,759	−15.6	160,684	135,247	−15.8	2,189,073	2,132,361	−2.6
Suspicion	909	537	−40.9	29	16	−44.8	130	44	−66.2	779	493	−36.7
Curfew and loitering law violations	33,910	26,571	−21.6	8,496	6,721	−20.9	33,910	26,571	−21.6	NA	NA	NA

NA = Not available.
¹Does not include suspicion.
²Violent crimes are offenses of murder and nonnegligent manslaughter, forcible rape, robbery, and aggravated assault. Property crimes are offenses of burglary, larceny-theft, motor vehicle theft, and arson.
³The rape figures in this table are based on the legacy definition of rape only. The rape figures shown include converted National Incident-Based Reporting System rape data and those states/agencies that reported the legacy definition of rape for both years.

Table 20. Full-Time Law Enforcement Employees,[1] by Region and Geographic Division and Population Group, 2013

(Number, rate per 100,000 inhabitants.)

Region/geographic division	Total	Group I (73 cities, 250,000 and over; population 51,744,651)	Group II (193 cities, 100,000 to 249,999; population 28,587,514)	Group III (405 cities, 50,000 to 99,999; population 27,923,876)	Group IV (719 cities, 25,000 to 49,999; population 24,881,626)	Group V (1,597 cities, 10,000 to 24,999; population 25,483,611)
Total						
Number of employees	503,227	175,797	63,410	57,806	53,525	58,127
Average number of employees per 1,000 inhabitants	2.8	3.4	2.2	2.1	2.2	2.3
Northeast						
Number of employees	141,190	63,599	8,446	14,450	17,059	18,043
Average number of employees per 1,000 inhabitants	3.2	5.4	3.0	2.3	2.2	2.1
New England						
Number of employees	33,950	2,704	4,426	6,086	6,841	7,168
Average number of employees per 1,000 inhabitants	2.6	4.2	3.0	2.3	2.2	2.2
Middle Atlantic						
Number of employees	107,240	60,895	4,020	8,364	10,218	10,875
Average number of employees per 1,000 inhabitants	3.5	5.5	2.9	2.3	2.2	2.0
Midwest						
Number of employees	79,766	19,889	8,195	10,919	10,402	13,049
Average number of employees per 1,000 inhabitants	2.4	3.1	2.1	1.8	1.9	2.0
East North Central						
Number of employees	48,115	13,024	4,469	6,838	7,149	7,671
Average number of employees per 1,000 inhabitants	2.4	3.1	2.2	1.9	1.9	2.0
West North Central						
Number of employees	31,651	6,865	3,726	4,081	3,253	5,378
Average number of employees per 1,000 inhabitants	2.4	3.2	2.1	1.7	1.9	2.1
South						
Number of employees	175,764	45,570	27,180	18,377	17,870	20,793
Average number of employees per 1,000 inhabitants	3.3	3.1	2.6	2.6	2.6	2.9
South Atlantic						
Number of employees	88,525	22,199	14,801	9,662	9,002	9,930
Average number of employees per 1,000 inhabitants	3.7	4.0	2.8	2.8	2.8	3.1
East South Central						
Number of employees	31,430	7,256	4,641	2,517	3,576	4,321
Average number of employees per 1,000 inhabitants	3.4	2.9	3.3	2.8	2.6	3.1
West South Central						
Number of employees	55,809	16,115	7,738	6,198	5,292	6,542
Average number of employees per 1,000 inhabitants	2.7	2.5	2.1	2.2	2.4	2.5
West						
Number of employees	106,507	46,739	19,589	14,060	8,194	6,242
Average number of employees per 1,000 inhabitants	2.2	2.5	1.7	1.7	1.7	2.0
Mountain						
Number of employees	35,556	14,983	6,750	3,675	2,953	2,108
Average number of employees per 1,000 inhabitants	2.4	2.6	1.9	2.0	1.9	2.3
Pacific						
Number of employees	70,951	31,756	12,839	10,385	5,241	4,134
Average number of employees per 1,000 inhabitants	2.0	2.4	1.6	1.6	1.7	1.9

Table 20. Full-Time Law Enforcement Employees,[1] by Region and Geographic Division and Population Group, 2013—Continued

(Number, rate per 100,000 inhabitants.)

Region/geographic division	Group VI (6,907 cities, under 10,000; population 21,180,962)	Total city agencies	City population, 2013, estimated	County[2] (3,157 agencies; population 88,882,540)	Total city and county agencies	Total agency population, 2013, estimated	Suburban areas[3] (6,969 agencies; population 117,915,697)
Total							
Number of employees	94,562	9,894	179,802,240	399,183	13,051	268,684,780	434,810
Average number of employees per 1,000 inhabitants	4.5			4.5			3.7
Northeast							
Number of employees	19,593	2,511	43,905,307				
Average number of employees per 1,000 inhabitants	3.1						
New England							
Number of employees	6,725	796	13,004,141				
Average number of employees per 1,000 inhabitants	3.7						
Middle Atlantic							
Number of employees	12,868	1,715	30,901,166				
Average number of employees per 1,000 inhabitants	2.8						
Midwest							
Number of employees	17,312	2,418	33,568,819				
Average number of employees per 1,000 inhabitants	3.2						
East North Central							
Number of employees	8,964	1,247	20,345,551				
Average number of employees per 1,000 inhabitants	3.1						
West North Central							
Number of employees	8,348	1,171	13,223,268				
Average number of employees per 1,000 inhabitants	3.3						
South							
Number of employees	45,974	3,683	53,170,268				
Average number of employees per 1,000 inhabitants	6.5						
South Atlantic							
Number of employees	22,931	1,644	23,704,335				
Average number of employees per 1,000 inhabitants	7.8						
East South Central							
Number of employees	9,119	824	9,149,063				
Average number of employees per 1,000 inhabitants	5.8						
West South Central							
Number of employees	13,924	1,215	20,316,870				
Average number of employees per 1,000 inhabitants	5.5						
West							
Number of employees	11,683	1,282	49,157,846				
Average number of employees per 1,000 inhabitants	5.1						
Mountain							
Number of employees	5,087	519	14,532,260				
Average number of employees per 1,000 inhabitants	4.7						
Pacific							
Number of employees	6,596	763	34,625,586				
Average number of employees per 1,000 inhabitants	5.4						

[1] Full-time law enforcement employees include civilians.
[2] The designation county is a combination of both metropolitan and nonmetropolitan counties.
[3] Suburban areas include law enforcement agencies in cities with less than 50,000 inhabitants and county law enforcement agencies that are within a Metropolitan Statistical Area (see Data Declaration). Suburban areas exclude all metropolitan agencies associated with a principal city. The agencies associated with suburban areas also appear in other groups within this table.

Table 21. Full-Time Law Enforcement Officers, by Region and Geographic Division, and Population Group, 2013

(Number, rate per 100,000 inhabitants.)

Region/geographic division	Total (9,894 cities; population 179,802,240)	Group I (73 cities, 250,000 and over; population 51,744,651)	Group II (193 cities, 100,000 to 249,999; population 28,587,514)	Group III (405 cities, 50,000 to 99,999; population 27,923,876)	Group IV (719 cities, 25,000 to 49,999; population 24,881,626)	Group V (1,597 cities, 10,000 to 24,999; population 25,483,611)
Total						
Number of officers	389,934	133,309	48,284	44,972	42,624	47,120
Average number of officers per 1,000 inhabitants	2.2	2.6	1.7	1.6	1.7	1.8
Northeast						
Number of officers	111,953	46,840	7,165	12,023	14,343	15,317
Average number of officers per 1,000 inhabitants	2.5	4.0	2.5	1.9	1.8	1.7
New England						
Number of officers	28,083	2,131	3,808	5,208	5,722	5,818
Average number of officers per 1,000 inhabitants	2.2	3.3	2.6	1.9	1.8	1.8
Middle Atlantic						
Number of officers	83,870	44,709	3,357	6,815	8,621	9,499
Average number of officers per 1,000 inhabitants	2.7	4.0	2.5	1.9	1.8	1.7
Midwest						
Number of officers	65,308	16,190	6,756	8,888	8,287	10,706
Average number of officers per 1,000 inhabitants	1.9	2.5	1.7	1.5	1.5	1.7
East North Central						
Number of officers	39,878	11,017	3,749	5,587	5,755	6,315
Average number of officers per 1,000 inhabitants	2.0	2.6	1.8	1.6	1.5	1.7
West North Central						
Number of officers	25,430	5,173	3,007	3,301	2,532	4,391
Average number of officers per 1,000 inhabitants	1.9	2.4	1.7	1.4	1.5	1.7
South						
Number of officers	135,928	36,010	20,666	14,103	14,065	16,308
Average number of officers per 1,000 inhabitants	2.6	2.5	2.0	2.0	2.1	2.3
South Atlantic						
Number of officers	68,956	17,098	11,439	7,514	7,184	8,023
Average number of officers per 1,000 inhabitants	2.9	3.1	2.2	2.2	2.3	2.5
East South Central						
Number of officers	24,843	5,965	3,486	1,971	2,884	3,379
Average number of officers per 1,000 inhabitants	2.7	2.4	2.5	2.2	2.1	2.4
West South Central						
Number of officers	42,129	12,947	5,741	4,618	3,997	4,906
Average number of officers per 1,000 inhabitants	2.1	2.0	1.6	1.7	1.8	1.9
West						
Number of officers	76,745	34,269	13,697	9,958	5,929	4,789
Average number of officers per 1,000 inhabitants	1.6	1.8	1.2	1.2	1.3	1.5
Mountain						
Number of officers	24,845	10,128	4,794	2,590	2,172	1,642
Average number of officers per 1,000 inhabitants	1.7	1.8	1.4	1.4	1.4	1.8
Pacific						
Number of officers	51,900	24,141	8,903	7,368	3,757	3,147
Average number of officers per 1,000 inhabitants	1.5	1.8	1.1	1.1	1.2	1.4

Table 21. Full-Time Law Enforcement Officers, by Region and Geographic Division, and Population Group, 2013—*Continued*

(Number, rate per 100,000 inhabitants.)

Region/geographic division	Group VI (6,907 cities, under 10,000; population 21,180,962)	Total city agencies	City population, 2013, estimated	County[1] (3,157 agencies; population 88,882,540)	Total city and county agencies	Total agency population, 2013, estimated	Suburban areas[2] (6,969 agencies; population 117,915,697)
Total							
Number of officers	73,625	9,894	179,802,240	237,008	13,051	268,684,780	287,855
Average number of officers per 1,000 inhabitants	3.5			2.7			2.4
Northeast							
Number of officers	16,265	2,511	43,905,307				
Average number of officers per 1,000 inhabitants	2.5						
New England							
Number of officers	5,396	796	13,004,141				
Average number of officers per 1,000 inhabitants	3.0						
Middle Atlantic							
Number of officers	10,869	1,715	30,901,166				
Average number of officers per 1,000 inhabitants	2.4						
Midwest							
Number of officers	14,481	2,418	33,568,819				
Average number of officers per 1,000 inhabitants	2.7						
East North Central							
Number of officers	7,455	1,247	20,345,551				
Average number of officers per 1,000 inhabitants	2.6						
West North Central							
Number of officers	7,026	1,171	13,223,268				
Average number of officers per 1,000 inhabitants	2.7						
South							
Number of officers	34,776	3,683	53,170,268				
Average number of officers per 1,000 inhabitants	4.9						
South Atlantic							
Number of officers	17,698	1,644	23,704,335				
Average number of officers per 1,000 inhabitants	6.0						
East South Central							
Number of officers	7,158	824	9,149,063				
Average number of officers per 1,000 inhabitants	4.5						
West South Central							
Number of officers	9,920	1,215	20,316,870				
Average number of officers per 1,000 inhabitants	3.9						
West							
Number of officers	8,103	1,282	49,157,846				
Average number of officers per 1,000 inhabitants	3.5						
Mountain							
Number of officers	3,519	519	14,532,260				
Average number of officers per 1,000 inhabitants	3.2						
Pacific							
Number of officers	4,584	763	34,625,586				
Average number of officers per 1,000 inhabitants	3.7						

[1]The designation county is a combination of both metropolitan and nonmetropolitan counties.
[2]Suburban areas include law enforcement agencies in cities with less than 50,000 inhabitants and county law enforcement agencies that are within a Metropolitan Statistical Area. Suburban areas exclude all metropolitan agencies associated with a principal city. The agencies associated with suburban areas also appear in other groups within this table.

Table 22. Full-Time State Law Enforcement Employees, by Selected State, 2013

(Number.)

State/agency	Law enforcement employees	Officers		Civilians	
		Male	Female	Male	Female
Alabama[1]					
Other state agencies	258	197	7	16	38
Alaska					
State Troopers	643	435	19	51	138
Arizona					
Department of Public Safety	1,899	1,051	45	337	466
Arkansas[1]					
Other state agencies	31	29	0	0	2
California					
Highway Patrol	10,623	6,724	512	1,454	1,933
Other state agencies[2]	1,275	938	198	38	101
Colorado					
State Patrol	932	620	49	57	206
Other state agencies	295	51	5	82	157
Connecticut					
State Police	1,661	1,040	89	251	281
Other state agencies	37	27	1	7	2
Delaware					
State Police	924	608	75	102	139
Other state agencies	668	296	103	58	211
Florida					
Highway Patrol	2,335	1,637	209	157	332
Other state agencies	3,304	1,450	216	539	1,099
Georgia[1]					
Other state agencies	1,077	312	84	226	455
Idaho					
State Police	463	246	14	50	153
Illinois					
State Police	2,910	1,570	180	459	701
Other state agencies	221	110	9	65	37
Indiana					
State Police	1,780	1,172	56	233	319
Other state agencies	8	7	0	0	1
Iowa					
Department of Public Safety	896	559	34	150	153
Kansas					
Highway Patrol	768	468	19	113	168
Other state agencies	500	296	17	62	125
Kentucky					
State Police	1,687	953	23	336	375
Other state agencies	366	298	7	38	23
Louisiana					
State Police	1,722	1,095	69	179	379
Maine					
State Police	440	287	24	59	70
Other state agencies[2]	48	20	2	19	7
Maryland					
State Police	2,184	1,377	107	342	358
Other state agencies	1,646	873	135	317	321
Massachusetts					
State Police	2,609	1,970	139	195	305
Other state agencies	336	286	35	6	9

Table 22. Full-Time State Law Enforcement Employees, by Selected State, 2013—*Continued*

(Number.)

State/agency	Law enforcement employees	Officers		Civilians	
		Male	Female	Male	Female
Michigan..					
State Police	2,530	1,505	181	356	488
Minnesota..					
State Patrol	740	482	55	103	100
Other state agencies	60	11	2	39	8
Mississippi[1]......................................					
Other state agencies	74	57	3	2	12
Missouri...					
State Highway Patrol	2,269	1,110	58	497	604
Other state agencies	451	396	33	0	22
Montana..					
Highway Patrol	278	213	10	15	40
Other state agencies	24	16	0	2	6
Nebraska...					
State Patrol	696	427	25	83	161
Nevada..					
Highway Patrol	558	399	46	46	67
New Hampshire.................................					
State Police	508	302	31	58	117
New Jersey					
State Police	3,704	2,352	105	590	657
Other state agencies[2]	29	26	0	1	2
New York...					
State Police	5,489	4,205	399	357	528
Other state agencies	187	160	14	3	10
North Carolina..................................					
Highway Patrol	2,125	1,558	46	313	208
Other state agencies	1,078	682	117	104	175
North Dakota.....................................					
Highway Patrol	194	140	9	13	32
Ohio					
Highway Patrol	2,421	1,466	142	402	411
Other state agencies	397	318	23	17	39
Oklahoma..					
Department of Public Safety	1,400	765	20	272	343
Other state agencies	120	51	7	50	12
Oregon..					
State Police	745	563	43	48	91
Other state agencies	92	68	12	0	12
Pennsylvania					
State Police	6,073	3,957	211	910	995
Other state agencies	379	289	19	44	27
Rhode Island.....................................					
State Police	273	206	21	28	18
Other state agencies	86	64	4	11	7
South Carolina...................................					
Highway Patrol	1,010	805	29	51	125
Other state agencies[2]	1,148	698	139	96	215
South Dakota					
Highway Patrol	244	158	3	52	31
Other state agencies	167	46	4	40	77

Table 22. Full-Time State Law Enforcement Employees, by Selected State, 2013—*Continued*

(Number.)

State/agency	Law enforcement employees	Officers		Civilians	
		Male	Female	Male	Female
Tennessee					
Department of Safety	1,655	779	36	258	582
Other state agencies	1,168	650	148	139	231
Texas					
Department of Public Safety	9,178	3,280	214	1,925	3,759
Utah[1]					
Other state agencies	54	48	5	0	1
Vermont					
State Police	447	246	30	72	99
Other state agencies	120	88	6	9	17
Virginia					
State Police	2,750	1,914	111	245	480
Other state agencies	757	486	60	80	131
Washington					
State Patrol	2,204	966	87	577	574
Other state agencies	141	59	22	16	44
West Virginia					
State Police	1,046	645	20	145	236
Other state agencies	209	165	0	17	27
Wisconsin					
State Patrol	623	414	49	72	88
Other state agencies	376	283	55	17	21
Wyoming					
Highway Patrol	327	177	8	61	81

Note: Caution should be used when comparing data from one state to another. The responsibilities of the various state police, highway patrol, and department of public safety agencies range from full law enforcement duties to traffic patrol only, which can affect the data for the level of employment for agencies as well as the ratio of sworn officers to civilians employed. Any valid comparison must take these factors and the other identified variables affecting crime into consideration.

[1] Police Employee data were not received from the State Police/Highway Patrol/Department of Public Safety for the state.

[2] The total employee count includes employees from agencies that are not represented in other law enforcement employee tables.

Table 23. Murder Victims, by Race and Sex, 2013

(Number.)

Race	Total	Sex		
		Male	Female	Unknown
Total	12,253	9,523	2,707	23
White	5,537	3,879	1,656	2
Black	6,261	5,352	909	0
Other race	308	204	104	0
Unknown race	147	88	38	21
Hispanic or Latino[1]	1,729	1,504	225	0
Not Hispanic or Latino[1]	6,147	5,277	870	0
Unknown[1]	1,670	1,413	250	7

[1]The ethnicity totals are representative of those agencies that provided ethnicity breakdowns. Not all agencies provide ethnicity data, therefore the race and ethnicity totals will not equal.

Table 24. Murder Victims, by Age, Sex, Race, and Ethnicity, 2013

(Number; percent.)
(Single victim/single offender.)

Age	Total	Sex			Race				Ethnicity[2]		
		Male	Female	Unknown	White	Black or African American	Other[1]	Unknown	Hispanic/ Latino	Not Hispanic/ Latino	Unknown
Total	12,253	9,523	2,707	23	5,537	6,261	308	147	1,729	6,147	1,670
Percent distribution[3]	100.0	77.7	22.1	0.2	45.2	51.1	2.5	1.2	18.1	64.4	17.5
Under 18[4]	1,027	715	308	4	492	482	31	22	140	519	124
Under 22[4]	2,603	2,086	511	6	1,005	1,507	54	37	416	1,243	315
18 and over[4]	11,101	8,728	2,368	5	4,986	5,738	277	100	1,577	5,588	1,485
Infant (under 1)	162	96	64	2	110	44	4	4	19	105	22
1 to 4	251	148	102	1	118	113	11	9	26	131	33
5 to 8	78	39	39	0	46	26	4	2	8	40	10
9 to 12	68	42	26	0	35	25	5	3	5	32	11
13 to 16	247	194	52	1	105	134	5	3	41	113	22
17 to 19	911	803	107	1	287	602	13	9	163	400	121
20 to 24	2,249	1,923	324	2	756	1,438	39	16	371	1,056	261
25 to 29	1,746	1,468	278	0	617	1,065	51	13	230	746	237
30 to 34	1,497	1,213	283	1	618	840	32	7	193	757	206
35 to 39	1,101	850	251	0	489	564	36	12	170	554	162
40 to 44	826	618	208	0	413	377	25	11	216	421	116
45 to 49	803	570	233	0	436	340	17	10	94	433	114
50 to 54	689	506	183	0	409	258	20	2	74	398	82
55 to 59	543	384	159	0	335	186	17	5	53	322	79
60 to 64	340	233	107	0	233	89	14	4	25	207	48
65 to 69	214	144	70	0	163	42	5	4	12	136	31
70 to 74	140	86	54	0	102	30	6	2	7	83	21
75 and over	263	126	136	1	206	47	4	6	10	173	33
Unknown	125	80	31	14	59	41	0	25	12	40	61

[1]The ethnicity totals are representative of those agencies that provided ethnicity breakdowns. Not all agencies provide ethnicity data, therefore the race and ethnicity totals will not equal.
[2]Includes American Indian or Alaska Native; Asian; Native Hawaiian or Other Pacific Islander.
[3]Because of rounding, the percentages may not add to 100.0.
[4]Does not include unknown ages.

Table 25. Murder Offenders, by Age, Sex, Race, and Ethnicity, 2013

(Number; percent.)
(Single victim/single offender.)

Age	Total	Sex			Race				Ethnicity[2]		
		Male	Female	Unknown	White	Black or African American	Other[1]	Unknown	Hispanic/ Latino	Not Hispanic/ Latino	Unknown
Total	14,132	9,085	1,085	3,962	4,396	5,375	249	4,112	1,096	2,861	2,909
Percent distribution[3]	100.0	64.3	7.7	28.0	31.1	38.0	1.8	29.1	16.0	41.7	42.4
Under 18[4]	595	558	35	2	209	370	8	8	111	137	51
Under 22[4]	2,669	2,437	221	11	885	1,724	32	28	364	679	181
18 and over[4]	8,863	7,797	1,035	31	4,087	4,435	234	107	932	2,549	702
Infant (under 1)	0	0	0	0	0	0	0	0	0	0	0
1 to 4	0	0	0	0	0	0	0	0	0	0	0
5 to 8	3	3	0	0	0	3	0	0	0	2	0
9 to 12	11	11	0	0	6	5	0	0	0	5	0
13 to 16	288	265	21	2	104	173	5	6	45	64	30
17 to 19	1,227	1,123	102	2	399	808	13	7	183	314	78
20 to 24	2,496	2,237	249	10	899	1,524	46	27	276	667	195
25 to 29	1,541	1,369	168	4	671	799	53	18	178	437	129
30 to 34	1,131	977	151	3	550	535	34	12	139	328	90
35 to 39	701	605	95	1	365	304	21	11	81	205	52
40 to 44	564	473	90	1	317	222	23	2	59	156	45
45 to 49	477	403	73	1	298	155	17	7	30	145	44
50 to 54	415	347	64	4	266	130	13	6	25	136	38
55 to 59	230	201	29	0	146	73	6	5	11	76	21
60 to 64	140	128	12	0	88	43	6	3	10	57	10
65 to 69	104	96	8	0	83	15	3	3	6	37	7
70 to 74	43	40	3	0	36	7	0	0	0	16	4
75 and over	87	77	5	5	68	9	2	8	0	41	10
Unknown	4,674	730	15	3,929	100	570	7	3,997	53	175	2,156

[1]The ethnicity totals are representative of those agencies that provided ethnicity breakdowns. Not all agencies provide ethnicity data, therefore the race and ethnicity totals will not be equal.
[2]Includes American Indian or Alaska Native; Asian; Native Hawaiian or Other Pacific Islander.
[3]Because of rounding, the percentages may not add to 100.0.
[4]Does not include unknown ages.

Table 26. Murder, by Victim/Offender Situations, 2013

(Number; percent.)
(Single victim/single offender.)

Situation	Total	Percent distribution
Total	12,253	100.0
White	5,723	46.7
Black	3,639	29.7
Other race	1,525	12.4
Unknown race	782	6.4
Hispanic or Latino[1]	244	2.0
Not Hispanic or Latino[1]	340	2.8
Unknown[1]		

Table 27. Murder Age of Victim, by Age of Offender, 2013

(Number; percent.)
(Single victim/single offender.)

Age of victim	Total	Age of offender		
		Under 18 years	18 years and over	Unknown
Total	5,723	208	5,218	297
Under 18	533	67	451	15
18 and over	5,133	139	4,714	280
Unknown	57	2	53	2

Note: This table is based on incidents where some information about the offender is known by law enforcement; therefore, when the offender age, sex, and race are all reported as unknown, these data are excluded from the table.

Table 28. Murder, Race, Ethnicity, and Sex of Victim by Race, Ethnicity, and Sex of Offender, 2013

(Number; percent.)
(Single victim/single offender.)

Victim characteristic	Total	Sex			Race				Ethnicity[2]		
		Male	Female	Unknown	White	Black or African American	Other[1]	Unknown	Hispanic/ Latino	Not Hispanic/ Latino	Unknown
Race											
White	3,005	2,661	306	38	3,005	2,509	409	49	532	945	1,528
Black or African American	2,491	2,217	237	37	2,491	189	2,245	20	76	807	1,608
Other race[2]	159	142	13	4	159	32	27	96	10	63	86
Unknown	68	38	7	23	68	25	17	3	3	14	51
Sex											
Male	3,976	3,505	410	61	1,739	2,073	103	61	459	1,253	2,264
Female	1,679	1,515	146	18	991	608	62	18	159	562	958
Unknown	68	38	7	23	25	17	3	23	3	14	51
Ethnicity											
Hispanic or Latino	588	542	41	5	486	87	10	5	439	123	26
Not Hispanic or Latino	1,891	1,708	166	17	877	928	69	17	151	1,671	69
Unknown	3,244	2,808	356	80	1,392	1,683	89	80	31	35	3,178

Note: This table is based on incidents where some information about the offender is known by law enforcement; therefore, when the offender age, sex, and race are all reported as unknown, these data are excluded from the table.
[1] The ethnicity totals are representative of those agencies that provided ethnicity breakdowns. Not all agencies provide ethnicity data, therefore the race and ethnicity totals will not equal.
[2] Includes American Indian or Alaska Native; Asian; Native Hawaiian or Other Pacific Islander.

Table 29. Murder, Types of Weapons Used, Percent Distribution by Region, 2013[1]

(Percent.)

Region	Total, all weapons[2]	Firearms	Knives or cutting instruments	Unknown or other dangerous weapons	Personal weapons (hands, fists,feet, etc.)[3]
Total	100.0	69.0	12.2	13.3	5.6
Northeast	100.0	65.2	15.1	13.8	6.0
Midwest	100.0	72.1	9.3	13.6	4.9
South	100.0	71.4	10.8	12.0	5.8
West	100.0	64.7	15.1	14.6	5.7

[1] Guam and Virgin Islands totals are not included in this table.
[2] Because of rounding, the percentages may not add to 100.0.
[3] Pushed is included in personal weapons.

Table 30. Murder Victims, by Weapon, 2009–2013

(Number.)

Weapons	2009	2010	2011	2012	2013
Total	13,752	13,164	12,795	12,888	12,253
Total firearms	9,199	8,874	8,653	8,897	8,454
Handguns	6,501	6,115	6,251	6,404	5,782
Rifles	351	367	332	298	285
Shotguns	423	366	362	310	308
Other guns	96	93	97	116	123
Firearms, type not stated	1,828	1,933	1,611	1,769	1,956
Knives or cutting instruments	1,836	1,732	1,716	1,604	1,490
Blunt objects (clubs, hammers, etc.)	623	549	502	522	428
Personal weapons (hands, fists, feet, etc.)[1]	817	769	751	707	687
Poison	7	11	5	13	11
Explosives	2	4	6	8	2
Fire	98	78	76	87	94
Narcotics	52	45	33	38	53
Drowning	8	10	15	14	4
Strangulation	122	122	88	90	85
Asphyxiation	84	98	92	106	95
Other weapons or weapons not stated	904	872	858	802	850

[1]Pushed is included in personal weapons.

Table 31. Murder Victims by Age, by Weapon, 2013

(Number.)

Age	Total murder victims	Weapons										
		Firearms	Knives or cutting instruments	Blunt objects (clubs, hammers, etc.)	Personal weapons (hands, fists, feet, etc.)[1]	Poison	Explosives	Fire	Narcotics	Strangulation	Asphyxiation	Other weapon or weapon not stated[2]
Total	12,253	8,454	1,490	428	687	11	2	94	53	85	95	854
Percent distribution[3]	100.0	69.0	12.2	3.5	5.6	0.1	0.0	0.8	0.4	0.7	0.8	7.0
Under 18[4]	1,027	479	77	41	217	1	0	16	8	8	25	155
Under 22[4]	2,603	1,822	195	57	237	1	0	19	14	12	33	213
18 and over[4]	11,101	7,914	1,408	380	450	9	2	75	43	76	68	676
Infant (under 1)	162	9	2	9	82	1	0	1	4	2	6	46
1 to 4	251	28	12	21	107	0	0	6	2	0	10	65
5 to 8	78	27	9	3	15	0	0	5	0	0	3	16
9 to 12	68	37	10	3	5	0	0	4	0	3	2	4
13 to 16	247	197	21	3	3	0	0	0	1	3	4	15
17 to 19	911	777	73	5	11	0	0	1	4	4	4	32
20 to 24	2,249	1,867	204	31	35	1	0	3	7	4	8	89
25 to 29	1,746	1,392	176	32	41	1	0	3	11	12	5	73
30 to 34	1,497	1,158	171	21	44	0	0	4	6	7	6	80
35 to 39	1,101	814	132	36	39	0	0	9	4	6	7	54
40 to 44	826	559	115	32	35	0	0	8	4	13	7	53
45 to 49	803	488	135	28	58	1	0	9	2	8	6	68
50 to 54	689	379	118	47	50	1	1	7	0	8	9	69
55 to 59	543	252	111	55	49	1	1	4	2	2	9	57
60 to 64	340	163	62	31	26	1	0	9	1	3	1	43
65 to 69	214	102	50	20	13	1	0	7	1	2	2	16
70 to 74	140	63	27	20	9	2	0	1	0	0	2	16
75 and over	263	81	57	24	45	0	0	10	2	7	2	35
Unknown	125	61	5	7	20	1	0	3	2	1	2	23

[1]Pushed is included in personal weapons.
[2]Includes drowning.
[3]Because of rounding, the percentages may not add to 100.0.
[4]Does not include unknown ages.

This page intentionally left blank

Table 32. Murder Circumstances, by Relationship, 2013[1]

(Number.)

Circumstances	Total murder victims	Husband	Wife	Mother	Father	Son	Daughter	Brother	Sister
Total	12,253	108	534	128	142	230	148	99	30
Felony type total	1,909	3	28	10	13	20	15	10	4
Rape[2]	20	0	1	0	0	0	0	0	0
Robbery	686	1	0	0	4	0	0	0	0
Burglary	94	0	0	0	0	0	0	0	0
Larceny-theft	16	0	0	0	0	0	0	0	0
Motor vehicle theft	27	0	2	1	2	0	0	0	0
Arson	37	0	0	1	1	0	0	4	2
Prostitution and commercialized vice	13	0	0	0	0	0	0	0	0
Other sex offenses	9	0	0	0	0	0	0	0	0
Narcotic drug laws	386	0	0	0	0	0	1	2	0
Gambling	7	0	0	0	0	0	0	0	0
Other-not specified	614	2	25	8	6	20	14	4	2
Suspected felony type	122	1	5	4	2	2	2	0	1
Other than felony type total:	5,782	89	410	72	102	173	94	72	19
Romantic triangle	69	0	2	0	1	0	0	0	0
Child killed by babysitter	30	0	0	0	0	2	0	0	0
Brawl due to influence of alcohol	93	0	4	1	2	1	1	1	0
Brawl due to influence of narcotics	59	0	1	0	1	0	0	0	0
Argument over money or property	133	0	4	3	0	1	0	3	1
Other arguments	2,889	65	298	46	74	39	14	56	10
Gangland killings	138	0	1	0	0	0	0	0	0
Juvenile gang killings	584	0	0	0	0	0	0	0	0
Institutional killings	15	0	0	0	0	0	0	0	0
Sniper attack	6	0	0	0	0	0	0	0	0
Other-not specified	1,766	24	100	22	24	130	79	12	8
Unknown	4,440	15	91	42	25	35	37	17	6

Table 32. Murder Circumstances, by Relationship, 2013[1]—*Continued*

(Number.)

Circumstances	Other family	Acquaintance	Friend	Boyfriend	Girlfriend	Neighbor	Employee	Employer	Stranger	Unknown
Total	245	2,660	346	137	458	127	6	2	1,281	5,572
Felony type total	31	477	53	9	20	26	2	0	390	798
Rape[2]	2	6	1	0	1	1	0	0	4	4
Robbery	6	151	15	1	1	8	2	0	240	257
Burglary	1	22	1	1	2	3	0	0	23	41
Larceny-theft	2	2	1	0	0	2	0	0	2	7
Motor vehicle theft	4	5	1	0	1	1	0	0	4	6
Arson	2	11	0	1	0	4	0	0	6	5
Prostitution and commercialized vice	0	5	2	0	0	0	0	0	2	4
Other sex offenses	1	4	0	0	0	0	0	0	2	2
Narcotic drug laws	0	146	11	1	2	0	0	0	28	195
Gambling	0	4	0	0	0	0	0	0	0	3
Other-not specified	13	121	21	5	13	7	0	0	79	274
Suspected felony type	2	16	2	0	6	1	0	0	6	72
Other than felony type total:	163	1,644	210	109	348	83	4	2	617	1,571
Romantic triangle	0	36	8	3	9	0	0	0	3	7
Child killed by babysitter	2	25	0	0	0	1	0	0	0	0
Brawl due to influence of alcohol	6	27	14	0	3	1	0	0	21	11
Brawl due to influence of narcotics	1	28	5	1	2	1	0	0	6	13
Argument over money or property	6	59	14	1	6	4	0	0	11	20
Other arguments	98	891	117	90	273	56	2	2	250	508
Gangland killings	0	40	0	0	0	0	0	0	24	73
Juvenile gang killings	0	106	1	0	0	1	0	0	80	396
Institutional killings	0	10	0	0	0	0	0	0	3	2
Sniper attack	0	2	0	0	0	0	0	0	2	2
Other-not specified	50	420	51	14	55	19	2	0	217	539
Unknown	49	523	81	19	84	17	0	0	268	3,131

Note: The relationship categories of husband and wife include both common-law and ex-spouses. The categories of mother, father, sister, brother, son, and daughter include stepparents, stepchildren, and stepsiblings. The category of acquaintance includes homosexual relationships and the composite category of other known to victim.

[1]Relationship is that of victim to offender.

[2]The rape figures in this table are an aggregate total of the data submitted using both the revised and legacy Uniform Crime Reporting definitions.

Table 33. Murder Circumstances, by Weapon, 2013

(Number.)

Circumstances	Total murder victims	Total firearms	Handguns	Rifles	Shotguns	Other guns or type not stated	Knives or cutting instruments	Blunt objects (clubs, hammers, etc.)	Personal weapons (hands, fists, feet, etc.)
Total	12,253	8,454	5,782	285	308	2,079	1,490	428	686
Felony type total	1,909	1,381	1,026	32	36	287	174	79	64
Rape[1]	20	2	2	0	0	0	3	4	6
Robbery	686	536	435	8	10	83	52	39	20
Burglary	94	52	29	2	2	19	24	5	5
Larceny-theft	16	6	4	0	0	2	3	2	2
Motor vehicle theft	27	12	8	0	2	2	4	2	0
Arson	37	1	0	0	0	1	6	1	1
Prostitution and com- mercialized vice	13	7	4	0	0	3	3	0	1
Other sex offenses	9	0	0	0	0	0	3	0	3
Narcotic drug laws	386	327	244	5	8	70	25	4	4
Gambling	7	6	5	0	0	1	1	0	0
Other-not specified	614	432	295	17	14	106	50	22	22
Suspected felony type	122	87	59	2	7	19	15	5	2
Other than felony type total:	5,782	3,673	2,653	164	186	670	922	208	482
Romantic triangle	69	49	36	3	2	8	13	0	1
Child killed by babysitter	30	0	0	0	0	0	0	3	19
Brawl due to influence of alcohol	93	48	33	5	5	5	21	3	13
Brawl due to influence of narcotics	59	35	26	2	1	6	3	2	4
Argument over money or property	133	83	62	4	6	11	25	9	11
Other arguments	2,889	1,747	1,270	80	108	289	616	124	216
Gangland killings	138	117	87	3	1	26	15	0	2
Juvenile gang killings	584	547	428	9	9	101	28	2	2
Institutional killings	15	0	0	0	0	0	0	3	7
Sniper attack	6	6	2	1	0	3	0	0	0
Other-not specified	1,766	1,041	709	57	54	221	201	62	207
Unknown	4,440	3,313	2,044	87	79	1,103	379	136	138

Table 33. Murder Circumstances, by Weapon, 2013—*Continued*

(Number.)

Circumstances	Poison	Pushed or thrown out window	Explosives	Fire	Narcotics	Drowning	Strangulation	Asphyxiation	Other
Total	11	1	2	94	53	4	85	95	850
Felony type total	1	1	0	42	21	0	17	11	118
Rape[1]	0	0	0	0	0	0	1	1	3
Robbery	0	0	0	1	0	0	6	5	27
Burglary	0	0	0	2	0	0	0	1	5
Larceny-theft	0	0	0	0	1	0	2	0	0
Motor vehicle theft	0	0	0	2	0	0	0	0	7
Arson	0	0	0	22	0	0	0	0	6
Prostitution and commercialized vice	0	0	0	0	0	0	1	0	1
Other sex offenses	0	0	0	0	0	0	2	0	1
Narcotic drug laws	0	0	0	1	18	0	0	1	6
Gambling	0	0	0	0	0	0	0	0	0
Other-not specified	1	1	0	14	2	0	5	3	62
Suspected felony type	0	0	0	1	0	0	4	1	7
Other than felony type total:	8	0	2	25	24	4	39	52	343
Romantic triangle	1	0	0	0	0	0	0	2	3
Child killed by babysitter	0	0	0	0	0	0	0	1	7
Brawl due to influence of alcohol	0	0	0	1	0	0	0	2	5
Brawl due to influence of narcotics	0	0	0	0	6	0	0	1	8
Argument over money or property	0	0	0	0	0	0	1	1	3
Other arguments	3	0	1	11	2	2	22	22	123
Gangland killings	0	0	0	0	0	0	0	0	4
Juvenile gang killings	0	0	0	0	0	0	0	0	5
Institutional killings	0	0	0	0	0	0	2	1	2
Sniper attack	0	0	0	0	0	0	0	0	0
Other-not specified	4	0	1	13	16	2	14	22	183
Unknown	2	0	0	26	8	0	25	31	382

[1]The rape figures in this table are an aggregate total of the data submitted using both the revised and legacy Uniform Crime Reporting definitions.

Table 34. Murder Circumstances, 2009–2013

(Number.)

Circumstances	2009	2010	2011	2012	2013
Total	13,752	13,164	12,795	12,888	12,253
Felony type total	2,052	1,974	1,842	1,842	1,909
Rape[1]	24	41	16	16	20
Robbery	857	803	750	656	686
Burglary	110	85	95	91	94
Larceny-theft	13	21	12	15	16
Motor vehicle theft	23	35	23	22	27
Arson	38	35	38	32	37
Prostitution and commercialized vice	6	5	3	6	13
Other sex offenses	10	14	10	13	9
Narcotic drug laws	496	474	397	375	386
Gambling	5	7	8	7	7
Other-not specified	470	454	490	609	614
Suspected felony type	56	68	62	137	122
Other than felony type total:	6,796	6,485	6,056	6,320	5,782
Romantic triangle	88	90	88	98	69
Child killed by babysitter	29	36	38	26	30
Brawl due to influence of alcohol	117	122	113	84	93
Brawl due to influence of narcotics	94	60	121	65	59
Argument over money or property	205	187	156	152	133
Other arguments	3,364	3,280	3,163	3,147	2,889
Gangland killings	177	181	149	152	138
Juvenile gang killings	715	675	526	722	584
Institutional killings	12	17	22	13	15
Sniper attack	1	3	1	1	6
Other-not specified	1,994	1,834	1,679	1,860	1,766
Unknown	4,848	4,637	4,835	4,589	4,440

[1]The rape figures in this table are an aggregate total of the data submitted using both the revised and legacy Uniform Crime Reporting definitions.

Table 35. Murder Circumstances, by Sex of Victim, 2013

(Number.)

Circumstances	Total murder victims	Male	Female	Unknown
Total	12,253	9,523	2,707	23
Felony type total	1,909	1,563	345	1
Rape[1]	20	3	17	0
Robbery	686	605	81	0
Burglary	94	71	23	0
Larceny-theft	16	12	4	0
Motor vehicle theft	27	17	10	0
Arson	37	23	14	0
Prostitution and commercialized vice	13	11	2	0
Other sex offenses	9	2	7	0
Narcotic drug laws	386	352	34	0
Gambling	7	6	1	0
Other-not specified	614	461	152	1
Suspected felony type	122	82	40	0
Other than felony type total:	5,782	4,293	1,485	4
Romantic triangle	69	50	19	0
Child killed by babysitter	30	20	10	0
Brawl due to influence of alcohol	93	74	19	0
Brawl due to influence of narcotics	59	42	17	0
Argument over money or property	133	110	23	0
Other arguments	2,889	2,003	885	1
Gangland killings	138	128	10	0
Juvenile gang killings	584	566	18	0
Institutional killings	15	15	0	0
Sniper attack	6	6	0	0
Other-not specified	1,766	1,279	484	3
Unknown	4,440	3,585	837	18

[1]The rape figures in this table are an aggregate total of the data submitted using both the revised and legacy Uniform Crime Reporting definitions.

Table 36. Justifiable Homicide by Weapon, Law Enforcement,[1] 2009–2013

(Number.)

Year	Total	Total firearms	Handguns	Rifles	Shotguns	Firearms, type not stated	Knives or cutting instruments	Other dangerous weapons	Personal weapons
2009	414	411	326	29	6	50	0	3	0
2010	397	396	323	29	6	38	0	1	0
2011	404	401	305	36	11	49	2	0	1
2012	426	423	339	38	7	39	0	3	0
2013	461	458	332	46	9	71	0	3	0

[1]The killing of a felon by a law enforcement officer in the line of duty.

Table 37. Justifiable Homicide by Weapon, Private Citizen,[1] 2009–2013

(Number.)

Year	Total	Total firearms	Handguns	Rifles	Shotguns	Firearms, type not stated	Knives or cutting instruments	Other dangerous weapons	Personal weapons
2009	266	218	167	9	19	23	30	10	8
2010	285	236	170	8	30	28	33	11	5
2011	270	209	156	13	11	29	49	9	3
2012	315	263	198	20	15	30	35	6	11
2013	281	223	171	5	12	35	35	13	10

[1]The killing of a felon, during the commission of a felony, by a private citizen.

Table 38. Robbery, Location, Percent Distribution Within Region, 2013

(Number.)

Region	Total[1]	Street/highway	Commercial house	Gas or service station	Convenience store	Residence	Bank	Miscellaneous
Total	100.0	42.5	13.3	2.4	5.0	16.6	1.9	18.4
Northeast	100.0	52.7	8.1	2.3	4.8	11.6	2.1	18.3
Midwest	100.0	47.3	11.1	3.7	3.7	15.8	1.9	16.6
South	100.0	36.5	13.6	2.2	5.6	22.8	1.7	17.6
West	100.0	41.5	17.6	2.1	4.8	11.2	2.0	20.7

[1]Because of rounding, the percentages may not add to 100.0.

Table 39. Robbery, Location, Percent Distribution Within Population Group, 2013

(Percent.)

Type	Group I (74 cities, 250,000 and over; population 53,744,776)	Group II (204 cities, 100,000 to 249,999; population 30,349,229)	Group III (456 cities,50,000 to 99,999; population 31,521,356)	Group IV (802 cities, 25,000 to 49,999; population 27,753,171)	Group V (1,713 cities, 10,000 to 24,999; population 27,124,934)	Group VI (7,153 cities, under 10,000; population 22,357,510)	County agencies (3,828 agencies; population 97,084,166)
Total[1]	100.0	100.0	100.0	100.0	100.0	100.0	100.0
Street/highway	51.3	40.3	38.8	34.7	29.5	23.8	31.5
Commercial house	11.5	14.6	14.4	14.6	15.8	13.0	15.3
Gas or service station	1.8	2.4	2.7	3.4	3.7	3.1	3.2
Convenience store	3.4	5.5	6.1	6.9	7.2	7.5	6.3
Residence	15.4	15.5	14.2	15.8	17.3	17.9	23.7
Bank	1.3	1.9	2.5	2.8	3.2	3.0	2.1
Miscellaneous	15.3	19.9	21.4	21.8	23.2	31.7	18.0

[1]Because of rounding, the percentages may not add to 100.0.

Table 40. Robbery, Types of Weapons Used, Percent Distribution Within Region, 2013

(Percent.)

Region	Total all weapons[1]	Armed			Strong arm
		Firearms	Knives or cutting instruments	Other weapons	
Total	100.0	40.0	7.6	8.9	43.6
Northeast	100.0	31.0	9.1	7.9	51.9
Midwest	100.0	44.4	5.5	9.1	41.0
South	100.0	49.0	6.6	8.5	35.9
West	100.0	30.8	9.0	10.1	50.1

[1]Because of rounding, the percentages may not add to 100.0.

Table 41. Aggravated Assault, Types of Weapons Used, Percent Distribution by Region, 2013

(Percent.)

Region	Total all weapons[1]	Firearms	Knives or cutting instruments	Other weapons (clubs, blunt objects, etc.)	Personal weapons (hands, feet, fists, etc.)
Total	100.0	21.6	19.1	32.2	27.0
Northeast	100.0	14.5	22.9	31.0	31.7
Midwest	100.0	24.4	16.8	29.8	28.9
South	100.0	25.0	19.5	33.0	22.5
West	100.0	18.3	17.6	33.2	30.9

[1]Because of rounding, the percentages may not add to 100.0.

Table 42. Larceny-Theft, Percent Distribution Within Region, 2013

(Percent.)

Region	Total[1]	Pocket-picking	Purse snatching	Shoplifting	From motor vehicles (except accessories)	Motor vehicle accessories	Bicycles	From buildings	From coin-operated machines	All others
Total	100.0	0.5	0.4	19.9	23.4	7.3	3.5	12.3	0.3	32.4
Northeast	100.0	1.0	0.5	20.1	20.0	5.0	3.9	17.6	0.2	31.7
Midwest	100.0	0.5	0.4	20.2	19.4	7.8	3.0	15.5	0.2	32.9
South	100.0	0.5	0.4	19.8	22.8	7.9	2.6	10.0	0.3	35.7
West	100.0	0.4	0.4	19.8	28.9	7.2	5.3	11.3	0.3	26.4

[1]Because of rounding, the percentages may not add to 100.0.

Table 43. Motor Vehicle Theft, Percent Distribution Within Region, 2013

(Percent.)

Region	Total[1]	Autos	Trucks and buses	Other vehicles
Total	100.0	73.9	15.2	11.0
Northeast	100.0	85.5	4.4	10.1
Midwest	100.0	76.8	13.0	10.2
South	100.0	65.5	19.8	14.7
West	100.0	77.3	14.5	8.1

[1]Because of rounding, the percentages may not add to 100.0.

Table 44. Arson Rates, by Population Group, 2013

(13,010 agencies; 2013 estimated population 261,746,967; rate per 100,000 inhabitants.)

Population group	Rate per 100,000 inhabitants
Total, All Agencies	15.9
Total Cities	17.9
Group I (250,000 and over)	27.7
1,000,000 and over (Group I subset)	27.6
500,000 to 999,999 (Group I subset)	27.9
250,000 to 499,999 (Group I subset)	27.5
Group II (100,000 to 249,999)	17.6
Group III (50,000 to 99,999)	14.5
Group IV (25,000 to 49,999)	12.2
Group V (10,000 to 24,999)	11.2
Group VI (under 10,000)	20.1
Metropolitan counties	11.8
Nonmetropolitan counties	11.2
Suburban areas[1]	11.5

[1]Suburban areas include law enforcement agencies in cities with less than 50,000 inhabitants and county law enforcement agencies that are within a Metropolitan Statistical Area. Suburban areas exclude all metropolitan agencies associated with a principal city. The agencies associated with suburban areas also appear in other groups within this table.

Table 45. Arson, by Type of Property, 2013

(Number; percent; dollars. 14,365 agencies; 2013 estimated population 259,159,380)

Property classification	Number of arson offenses	Percent distribution[1]	Percent not in use	Average damage (dollars)	Total clearances	Percent of arsons cleared[2]	Percent of clearances under 18
Total	38,795	100.0		$14,390	8,138	21.0	27.9
Total structure	17,790	45.9	16.6	25,761	4,484	25.2	26.7
Single occupancy residential	8,597	22.2	17.9	26,080	2,058	23.9	19.0
Other residential	2,995	7.7	11.3	29,706	871	29.1	18.4
Storage	1,161	3.0	17.4	13,397	233	20.1	28.8
Industrial/manufacturing	161	0.4	23.6	126,606	43	26.7	20.9
Other commercial	1,537	4.0	17.2	43,725	343	22.3	21.9
Community/public	1,655	4.3	15.8	16,287	559	33.8	65.8
Other structure	1,684	4.3	18.6	8,907	377	22.4	33.2
Total mobile	9,238	23.8		7,686	1,026	11.1	11.8
Motor vehicles	8,713	22.5		6,649	945	10.8	10.3
Other mobile	525	1.4		24,903	81	15.4	29.6
Other	11,767	30.3		2,463	2,628	22.3	36.2

[1]Because of rounding, the percentages may not add to 100.0.
[2]Includes arsons cleared by arrest or exceptional means.

Methodology

Submitting Uniform Crime Reporting (UCR) program data to the Federal Bureau of Investigation (FBI) is a collective effort on the part of city, county, state, tribal, and federal law enforcement agencies to present a nationwide view of crime. Law enforcement agencies in 46 states and the District of Columbia voluntarily contribute crime data to the UCR program through their respective state UCR programs. For those states that do not have a state program, local agencies submit crime statistics directly to the FBI. The state UCR programs function as liaisons between local agencies and the FBI. Many states have mandatory reporting requirements, and many state programs collect data beyond the scope of the UCR program to address crime problems specific to their particular jurisdictions. In most cases, state programs also provide direct and frequent service to participating law enforcement agencies, make information readily available for statewide use, and help streamline the national program's operations.

A Note Regarding Rape

In 2013, the FBI UCR Program initiated collection of rape data under a revised definition within the Summary Reporting System. Previously, offense data for forcible rape was collected under the legacy UCR definition: the carnal knowledge of a female forcibly and against her will. Beginning with the 2013 data year, the term "forcible" was removed from the offense title, and the definition was changed. The revised UCR definition of rape is: Penetration, no matter how slight, of the vagina or anus with any body part or object, or oral penetration by a sex organ of another person, without the consent of the victim. Attempts or assaults to commit rape are also included; however, statutory rape and incest are excluded. For more information, please see https://www.fbi.gov/about-us/cjis/ucr/crime-in-the-u.s/2013/crime-in-the-u.s.-2013/rape-addendum/rape_addendum_final.

All rape data submitted in 2013—whether collected under the revised definition or the legacy definition—are presented in this publication. However, because only one year of rape data has been collected under the revised definition, the overview presented here discusses only the legacy definition rape data.

Criteria for State UCR programs

The criteria established for state programs ensure consistency and comparability in the data submitted to the national program, as well as regular and timely reporting. These criteria are:

1. A UCR Program must conform to the FBI UCR Program's submission standards, definitions, specifications, and required deadlines.

2. A UCR Program must establish data integrity procedures and have personnel assigned to assist contributing agencies in quality assurance practices and crime reporting procedures. Data integrity procedures should include crime trend assessments, offense classification verification, and technical specification validation.

3. A UCR Program's submissions must cover more than 50 percent of the law enforcement agencies within its established reporting domain and be willing to cover any and all UCR-contributing agencies that wish to use the UCR Program from within its domain. (An agency wishing to become a UCR Program must be willing to report for all of the agencies within the state.)

4. A UCR Program must furnish the FBI UCR Program with all of the UCR data collected by the law enforcement agencies within its domain.

These requirements do not prohibit the state from gathering other statistical data beyond the national collection.

Data Completeness and Quality

National program staff members contact the state UCR program in connection with crime-reporting matters and, when necessary and approved by the state, they contact individual contributors within the state. To fulfill its responsibilities in connection with the UCR program, the FBI reviews and edits individual agency reports for completeness and quality. Upon request, they conduct training programs within the state on law enforcement record-keeping and crime-reporting procedures. The FBI conducts an audit of each state's UCR data collection procedures once every three years, in accordance with audit standards established by the federal government. Should circumstances develop in which the state program does not comply with the aforementioned requirements, the national program may institute a direct collection of data from law enforcement agencies within the state.

Reporting Procedures

Offenses known and value of property–Law enforcement agencies tabulate the number of Part I offenses reported based on records of all reports of crime received from victims, officers who discover infractions, or other sources, and submit these reports each month to the FBI directly or through their state UCR programs. Part I offenses include murder and nonnegligent manslaughter, forcible rape, robbery, aggravated assault, burglary, larceny-theft, motor vehicle theft, and arson. Each month, law enforcement agencies also submit to the FBI the value of property stolen and recovered in connection with the offenses and detailed information pertaining to criminal homicide.

Unfounded offenses and clearances—When, through investigation, an agency determines that complaints of crimes are unfounded or false, the agency eliminates that offense from its crime tally through an entry on the monthly report. The report also provides the total number of actual Part I offenses, the number of offenses cleared, and the number of clearances that involve only offenders under the age of 18. (Law enforcement can clear crimes in one of two ways: by the arrest of at least one person who is charged and turned over to the court for prosecution or by exceptional means—when some element beyond law enforcement's control precludes the arrest of a known offender.)

Persons arrested—In addition to reporting Part I offenses each month, law enforcement agencies also provide data on the age, sex, and race of persons arrested for Part I and Part II offenses. Part II offenses encompass all crimes, except traffic violations, that are not classified as Part I offenses.

Officers killed or assaulted—Each month, law enforcement agencies also report information to the UCR program regarding law enforcement officers killed or assaulted, and each year they report the number of full-time sworn and civilian law enforcement personnel employed as of October 31.

Hate crimes—At the end of each quarter, law enforcement agencies report summarized data on hate crimes; that is specific offenses that were motivated by an offender's bias against the perceived race, religion, ethnic or national origin, sexual orientation, or physical or mental disability of the victim. Those agencies participating in the UCR program's National Incident-Based Reporting System (NIBRS) submit hate crime data monthly.

Editing Procedures

The UCR program thoroughly examines each report it receives for arithmetical accuracy and for deviations in crime data from month to month and from present to past years that may indicate errors. UCR staff members compare an agency's monthly reports with its previous submissions and with reports from similar agencies to identify any unusual fluctuations in the agency's crime count. Considerable variations in crime levels may indicate modified records procedures, incomplete reporting, or changes in the jurisdiction's geopolitical structure.

Evaluation of trends—Data reliability is a high priority of the FBI, which brings any deviations or arithmetical adjustments to the attention of state UCR programs or the submitting agencies. Typically, FBI staff members study the monthly reports to evaluate periodic trends prepared for individual reporting units. Any significant increase or decrease becomes the subject of a special inquiry. Changes in crime reporting procedures or annexations that affect an agency's jurisdiction can influence the level of reported crime. When this occurs, the FBI excludes the figures for specific crime categories or totals, if necessary, from the trend tabulations.

Training for contributors—In addition to the evaluation of trends, the FBI provides training seminars and instructional materials on crime reporting procedures to assist contributors in complying with UCR standards. Throughout the country, representatives from the national program coordinate with representatives of state programs and law enforcement personnel and hold training sessions to explain the purpose of the program, the rules of uniform classification and scoring, and the methods of assembling the information for reporting. When an individual agency has specific problems with compiling its crime statistics and its remedial efforts are unsuccessful, personnel from the FBI's Criminal Justice Information Services Division may visit the contributor to aid in resolving the problems.

UCR Handbook—The national UCR program publishes the *Uniform Crime Reporting (UCR) Handbook* (revised 2004), which details procedures for classifying and scoring offenses and serves as the contributing agencies' basic resource for preparing reports. The national staff also produces letters to UCR contributors, state program bulletins, and UCR newsletters as needed. These publications provide policy updates and new information, as well as clarification of reporting issues.

The final responsibility for data submissions rests with the individual contributing law enforcement agency. Although the FBI makes every effort through its editing procedures, training practices, and correspondence to ensure the validity of the data it receives, the accuracy of the statistics depends primarily on the adherence of each contributor to the established standards of reporting. Deviations from these established standards that cannot be resolved by the national UCR program may be brought to the attention of the Criminal Justice Information Systems Committees of the International Association of Chiefs of Police and the National Sheriffs' Association.

Population Estimation

For the 2013 population estimates used in this publication, the FBI computed individual rates of growth from one year to the next for every city/town and county using 2010 decennial population counts and 2011 through 2012 population estimates from the U.S. Census Bureau. Each agency's rates of growth were averaged; that average was then applied and added to its 2012 Census population estimate to derive the agency's 2013 population estimate.

Population totals for 2000 and 2010 are from the U.S. Census Bureau's decennial population counts.

NIBRS Conversion

Thirty-three state programs are certified to provide their UCR data in the expanded National Incident-Based Reporting System (NIBRS) format. For presentation in this book, the NIBRS data were converted to the historical Summary Reporting System data. The UCR program staff constructed the NIBRS database to allow for such conversion so that UCR's long-running time series could continue.

Crime Trends

By showing fluctuations from year to year, trend statistics offer the data user an added perspective from which to study crime. Percent change tabulations in this publication are computed only for reporting agencies that provided comparable data for the periods under consideration. The FBI excludes from the trend calculations all figures except those received for common months from common agencies. Also excluded are unusual fluctuations of data that the FBI determines are the result of such variables as improved records procedures, annexations, and so on.

Caution to Users

Data users should exercise care in making any direct comparison between data in this publication and those in prior issues of *Crime in the United States*. Because of differing levels of participation from year to year and reporting problems that require the FBI to estimate crime counts for certain contributors, some data may not be comparable. In addition, this publication may contain updates to data provided in prior years' publications.

For information about the FBI's caution against ranking, including warnings about variables affecting crime and characteristics of jusridictions, please see http://www.fbi.gov/about-us/cjis/ucr/ucr-statistics-their-proper-use.

Offense Estimation

Some tables in this publication contain statistics for the entire United States. Because not all law enforcement agencies provide data for complete reporting periods, the FBI includes estimated crime numbers in these presentations. The FBI estimates data for three areas: Metropolitan Statistical Areas (MSAs), cities outside MSAs, and nonmetropolitan counties; and computes estimates for participating agencies that do not provide 12 months of complete data. For agencies supplying 3 to 11 months of data, the national UCR program estimates for the missing data by following a standard estimation procedure using the data provided by the agency. If an agency has supplied less than three months of data, the FBI computes estimates by using the known crime figures of similar areas within a state and assigning the same proportion of crime volumes to nonreporting agencies. The estimation process considers the following: population size covered by the agency; type of jurisdiction, for example, police department versus sheriff's office; and geographic location.

Estimation of State-Level Data

In response to various circumstances, the FBI calculates estimated offense totals for certain states. For example, some states do not provide forcible rape figures in accordance with UCR guidelines. In addition, problems at the state level have, at times, resulted in no useable data. Also, the conversion of the National Incident-Based Reporting System (NIBRS) data to Summary data has contributed to the need for unique estimation procedures. A summary of state-specific and offense-specific estimation procedures can be found online at http://www.fbi.gov/about-us/cjis/ucr/crime-in-the-u.s/2013/crime-in-the-u.s.-2013/resource-pages/methodology/methodology.

PART 4

Crimes Against Persons with Disabilities, 2009–2013

Animal equipment						
Average number of units per 1,000						
Meat						
Number of officers	70,200	34,200	13,100			130
Average number of officers per 1,000 inhabitants	1.3	1.3	1.2	1.4		
Poultry						
Number of officers	24,195	10,178	4,703	2,100	2,17	160
Average number of officers per 1,000 inhabitants	1.3	1.5	1.4	1.4	1.5	1.4
Profile						
Number of officers	49,744	24,141	8,919	4,936	3,777	3,171
Average number of officers per 1,000 inhabitants	1.3	1.3	1.1	1.4	1.4	1.4

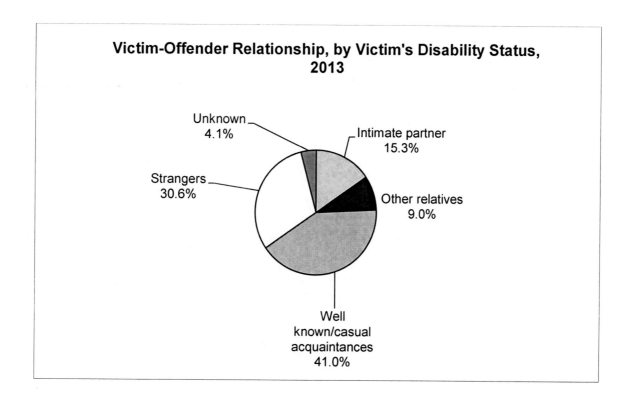

The rate of violent victimization against persons with disabilities (36 per 1,000) was more than twice the age-adjusted rate for persons without disabilities (14 per 1,000) in 2013. Persons with disabilities experienced 1.3 million violent victimizations, accounting for 21 percent of all violent victimizations. Nonfatal violent crimes include rape, sexual assault, robbery, aggravated assault, and simple assault.

- In 2013, for each age group measured except for persons age 65 or older, the rate of violent victimization against persons with disabilities was at least double the rate for those without disabilities. Among persons age 65 or older, there was no statistically significant difference in the rate of violent victimization by disability status (4 per 1,000).

- In 2013, the rate of serious violent victimization for persons with disabilities (14 per 1,000) was more than three times higher than the age-adjusted rate for persons without disabilities (4 per 1,000).

- In 2013, for both males and females, the rate of violent victimization was higher for persons with disabilities than the age-adjusted rate for those without disabilities.

- In 2013, 24 percent of violent crime victims with disabilities believed they were targeted due to their disability, an increase from 2009 (13 percent).

Table 1. Rates of Violent Victimization, by Victim's Disability Status and Age, 2009–2013

(Rate per 1,000 persons.)

Age of victim	Rate per 1,000 persons with disabilities					Rate per 1,000 persons without disabilities				
	2009	2010	2011	2012	2013	2009	2010	2011	2012	2013
Total	28.9	25.1	26.2	34.2	36.0	23.3	20.2	20.0	22.7	22.9
12–15	106.6	69.9	76.8	122.5	166.1	47.8	34.7	29.9	42.7	52.6
16–19	77.1	101.3	122.9	101.8	75.6	37.2	30.9	37.1	40.7	35.0
20–24	103.8	73.8	105.1	100.6	91.0	39.4	32.8	32.1	36.6	31.9
25–34	49.9	39.5	53.7	82.6	66.6	30.3	29.3	27.7	27.9	30.3
35–49	55.8	48.8	41.5	61.0	59.8	19.9	17.2	18.0	22.1	21.3
50–64	25.5	24.1	20.3	27.9	41.5	11.5	11.3	11.2	11.2	11.9
65 or older	2.8	2.5	4.6	5.9	4.1	4.0	3.8	3.2	4.6	4.5

Note: Based on the noninstitutionalized U.S. residential population age 12 or older. Estimates are based on 2-year rolling averages.

Table 2. Rates of Violent Victimization Against Persons With and Without Disabilities, by Type of Crime, 2009–2013

(Rate per 1,000 persons.)

Type of crime	Unadjusted rate per 1,000 persons with disabilities					Age-adjusted rate per 1,000 persons without disabilities[1]				
	2009	2010	2011	2012	2013	2009	2010	2011	2012	2013
Total crime	28.9	25.1	26.2	34.2	36.0	13.6	12.2	11.9	13.6	13.7
Serious violent crime	9.0	9.7	11.4	13.1	14.0	4.1	3.8	3.6	3.9	3.9
Rape/sexual assault	1.3	1.0	1.7	2.3	2.0	0.6	0.5	0.4	0.5	0.6
Robbery	3.9	4.1	4.1	5.1	5.3	1.3	1.3	1.3	1.3	1.3
Aggravated assault	3.8	4.7	5.6	5.8	6.6	2.2	2.0	1.9	2.1	1.9
Simple assault	19.9	15.4	14.8	21.1	22.0	9.5	8.4	8.2	9.8	9.9

Note: Based on the noninstitutionalized U.S. residential population age 12 or older. Estimates are based on 2-year rolling averages.
[1]For each year, rates for persons without disabilities were adjusted using direct standardization with the population with disabilities as the standard population.

Table 3. Rates of Violent Victimization Against Persons With and Without Disabilities, by Victim Characteristics, 2009–2013

(Rate per 1,000 persons.)

Victim characteristic	Unadjusted rate per 1,000 persons with disabilities					Age-adjusted rate per 1,000 persons without disabilities[1]				
	2009	2010	2011	2012	2013	2009	2010	2011	2012	2013
Total	28.9	25.1	26.2	34.2	36.0	13.6	12.2	11.9	13.6	13.7
Sex										
Male	25.9	22.9	25.8	37.0	37.1	15.8	13.7	14.4	16.5	15.8
Female	31.5	27.1	26.6	31.6	35.0	11.8	10.9	9.7	11.2	11.9
Race[2]										
White	28.0	23.9	24.9	34.2	37.5	13.6	12.0	11.7	13.5	13.5
Black	31.7	28.0	25.1	30.2	31.1	19.2	18.7	17.5	21.3	21.7
Other[3]	25.3	14.4	22.1	27.1	15.0	4.8	4.8	4.3	5.0	5.7
Two or more races	54.8	83.4	91.1	78.4	76.4	20.1	16.7	24.3	21.9	21.3
Hispanic/Latino origin[4]										
Hispanic/Latino	19.8	24.9	25.0	28.9	35.9	13.5	11.8	12.3	15.8	15.2
Non-Hispanic/Non-Latino	29.9	25.1	26.4	34.8	35.9	13.7	12.3	11.9	13.5	13.6

Note: Based on the noninstitutionalized U.S. residential population age 12 or older. Estimates are based on 2-year rolling averages.
[1]For each year, rates for persons without disabilities were adjusted using direct standardization with the population with disabilities as the standard population.
[2]Includes persons of Hispanic or Latino origin.
[3]Includes persons identified as American Indian or Alaska Native, Asian, and Native Hawaiian or Other Pacific Islander.
[4]Includes persons of all races.

Table 4. Rates of Violent Victimization Against Persons With Disabilities, by Disability Type, 2009–2013

(Rate per 1,000 persons.)

Disability type	2009	2010	2011	2012	2013
Hearing	16.7	10.6	17.1	20.2	16.9
Vision	28.6	24.9	23.2	25.2	29.8
Ambulatory	20.5	19.7	22.6	30.5	32.2
Cognitive	46.0	43.5	50.5	63.3	66.8
Self-care	18.3	17.8	27.3	27.2	26.0
Independent living	24.4	26.4	25.3	28.6	32.4

Note: Based on the noninstitutionalized U.S. residential population age 12 or older. Estimates are based on 2-year rolling averages. Includes persons with multiple disability types. Age-adjusted rates were not generated by disability types due to differences and limitations with the data for these groups. Rates are per 1,000 persons age 12 or older, except for independent living disability, which is per 1,000 persons age 15 or older.

Table 5. Rates of Serious Violent Victimization Against Persons With Disabilities, by Disability Type, 2009–2013

(Rate per 1,000 persons.)

Disability type	Serious violent victimization				
	2009	2010	2011	2012	2013
Hearing	7.3	4.5	8.2	10.7	8.4
Vision	8.6	12.0	10.5	7.7	11.9
Ambulatory	6.2	8.2	10.5	14.5	14.7
Cognitive	12.4	17.9	23.5	23.6	25.1
Self-care	3.9	7.9	12.3	11.2	9.3
Independent living	6.1	10.2	11.6	12.1	13.6

Note: Based on the noninstitutionalized U.S. residential population age 12 or older. Estimates are based on 2-year rolling averages. Includes persons with multiple disability types. Age-adjusted rates were not generated by disability types due to differences and limitations with the data for these groups. Rates are per 1,000 persons age 12 or older, except for independent living disability, which is per 1,000 persons age 15 or older.

Table 6. Rates of Simple Assault Against Persons With Disabilities, by Disability Type, 2009–2013

(Rate per 1,000 persons.)

Disability type	2009	2010	2011	2012	2013
Hearing	9.4	6.1	8.9	9.4	8.5
Vision	20.0	12.9	12.6	17.5	17.8
Ambulatory	14.2	11.5	12.1	16.0	17.6
Cognitive	33.5	25.6	27.0	39.7	41.6
Self-care	14.4	9.9	15.0	15.9	16.7
Independent living	18.2	16.3	13.7	16.5	18.8

Note: Based on the noninstitutionalized U.S. residential population age 12 or older. Estimates are based on 2-year rolling averages. Includes persons with multiple disability types. Age-adjusted rates were not generated by disability types due to differences and limitations with the data for these groups. Rates are per 1,000 persons age 12 or older, except for independent living disability, which is per 1,000 persons age 15 or older.

Table 7. Rates of Violent Victimization, by Victim's Sex and Disability Type, 2009–2013

(Rate per 1,000 persons.)

Disability type	Rate per 1,000 males					Rate per 1,000 females				
	2009	2010	2011	2012	2013	2009	2010	2011	2012	2013
Hearing	8.9	10.4	19.4	22.3	14.6	27.1	10.7	14.1	17.2	20.2
Vision	32.2	27.7	21.3	23.6	22.7	25.8	22.6	24.7	26.5	35.5
Ambulatory	18.5	19.3	24.6	39.1	38.2	21.8	19.9	21.2	24.5	28.1
Cognitive	44.0	38.0	49.4	65.6	64.6	47.7	48.6	51.5	61.2	68.9
Self-care	19.1	15.1	33.2	34.6	23.6	17.8	19.6	23.1	21.7	27.8
Independent living	25.6	23.4	21.6	29.3	29.1	23.6	28.4	27.7	28.1	34.6

Note: Based on the noninstitutionalized U.S. residential population age 12 or older. Estimates are based on 2-year rolling averages. Includes persons with multiple disability types. Age-adjusted rates were not generated by disability types due to differences and limitations with the data for these groups. Rates are per 1,000 persons age 12 or older, except for independent living disability, which is per 1,000 persons age 15 or older.

Table 8. Percent of Violence Against Persons with Disabilities That Involved Victims with Multiple Disability Types, by Type of Crime, 2009–2013

(Percent.)

Type of crime	2009	2010	2011	2012	2013
Total	41.4	50.7	56.9	52.1	50.5
Serious violent crime	37.3	52.4	60.7	55.6	50.7
Rape/sexual assault	32.1!	47.8	72.5	79.8	68.1
Robbery	27.3	49.4	61.3	51.0	37.0
Aggravated assault	49.3	56.0	56.9	50.1	56.6
Simple assault	43.3	49.7	54.0	49.9	50.3

Note: Based on the noninstituionalized U.S. residential population age 12 or older. Estimates are based on 2-year rolling averages. Persons age 15 or older with multiple disability types have two or more of the following disability types: hearing, vision, ambulatory, cognitive, self-care, and independent living. Persons ages 12 to 14 with multiple disability types have two or more of the following disability types: hearing, vision, ambulatory, cognitive, and self-care.
! = Interpret with caution. Estimate based on 10 or fewer sample cases, or coefficient of variation is greater than 50%.

Table 9. Rates of Violent Victimization, by Number of Disability Types and Type of Crime, 2009–2013

(Rate per 1,000 persons.)

Type of crime	Rate per 1,000 persons with disabilities					Rate per 1,000 persons without disabilities				
	2009	2010	2011	2012	2013	2009	2010	2011	2012	2013
Total	33.3	24.4	22.4	32.5	35.1	24.3	25.9	30.1	35.8	36.9
Serious violent crime	11.1	9.1	8.9	11.6	13.5	6.8	10.4	14	14.7	14.4
Rape/sexual assault	1.7	1	0.9!	0.9!	1.2!	0.8!	0.9	2.4	3.6	2.7
Robbery	5.6	4.1	3.1	4.9	6.6	2.2	4.1	5	5.2	4
Aggravated assault	3.8	4.1	4.8	5.7	5.7	3.8	5.4	6.5	5.8	7.6
Simple assault	22.2	15.2	13.5	21	21.6	17.5	15.5	16.1	21.2	22.5

Note: Based on the noninstitutionalized U.S. residential population age 12 or older. Estimates were based on 2-year rolling averages. Persons age 15 or older with multiple disability types had two or more of the following disability types: hearing, vision, ambulatory, cognitive, self-care, and independent living. Persons ages 12 to 14 with multiple disability types had two or more of the following disability types: hearing, vision, ambulatory, cognitive, and self-care.
! = Interpret with caution. Estimate is based on 10 or fewer sample cases, or coefficient of variation is greater than 50%.

Table 10. Victim-Offender Relationship, by Victim's Disability Status, 2009–2013

(Percent.)

Type of crime	Rate per 1,000 persons with disabilities					Rate per 1,000 persons without disabilities				
	2009	2010	2011	2012	2013	2009	2010	2011	2012	2013
Total	100.0	100.0	100.0	100.0	100.0	100.0	100.0	100.0	100.0	100.0
Intimate partner	22.3	22.0	14.2	15.9	15.3	16.9	16.1	15.3	12.5	11.2
Other relatives	10.5	6.6	11.5	11.5	9.0	5.9	6.6	7.3	6.6	5.6
Well known/casual acquaintances	33.7	38.6	37.9	35.5	41.0	28.5	30.0	29.8	31.1	35.1
Strangers	25.1	24.6	27.2	30.3	30.6	38.0	40.1	38.8	40.3	38.8
Unknown	8.5	8.1	9.2	6.8	4.1	10.8	7.2	8.8	9.5	9.3

Note: Based on the noninstitutionalized U.S. residential population age 12 or older. Estimates are based on 2-year rolling averages.

Table 11. Time Violent Crime Occurred, by Victim's Disability Status, 2009–2013

(Percent.)

Time of crime	Persons with disabilities					Persons without disabilities				
	2009	2010	2011	2012	2013	2009	2010	2011	2012	2013
Total	100.0	100.0	100.0	100.0	100.0	100.0	100.0	100.0	100.0	100.0
Daytime (6 a.m.–6 p.m.)	53.7	57.3	60.7	59.3	57.9	54.1	53.0	53.1	54.2	53.2
Nighttime (6 p.m.–6 a.m.)	38.2	38.9	36.2	34.3	35.0	41.6	42.5	42.9	41.9	43.6
Unknown	8.1	3.9!	3.1	6.4	7.1	4.3	4.5	4.0	3.9	3.2

Note: Based on the noninstitutionalized U.S. residential population age 12 or older. Estimates are based on 2-year rolling averages.
! = Interpet with caution. Estimate is based on 10 or fewer sample cases, or coefficient of variation is greater than 50%.

Table 12. Percent of Violent Crime Reported to Police, by Victim's Disability Status, 2009–2013

(Percent.)

Disability status of victim	2009	2010	2011	2012	2013
Persons with disabilities	54.3	47	47.2	48.6	47.5
Single disability type	49.8	47.5	54.8	53.3	45.9
Multiple disability types	60.7	46.5	41.4	44.2	49.1
Persons without disabilities	43.5	47.5	50.5	45.9	44.2

Note: Based on the noninstitutionalized U.S. residential population age 12 or older. Estimates are based on 2-year rolling averages.

Table 13. Person Who Notified Police of Violent Crime, by Victim's Disability Status, 2009–2013

(Percent.)

Person who contacted police	Persons with disabilities					Persons without disabilities				
	2009	2010	2011	2012	2013	2009	2010	2011	2012	2013
Total	100.0	100.0	100.0	100.0	100.0	100.0	100.0	100.0	100.0	100.0
Respondent	71.3	79.5	72.3	64.2	57.8	60.8	62.9	61.2	57.8	58.4
Other household member	7.2!	3.0!	3.6	3.7	5.7	10.4	9.4	12.3	13.1	9.6
Someone official	8.0	3.4!	2.4!	3.0	7.1	8.1	9.5	8.4	6.7	8.6
Someone else	10.7	8.3	15.8	21.9	22.5	12.4	10.0	9.5	12.0	13.2
Police were at the scene	2.0!	3.9!	2.6!	4.3!	4.0!	5.8	5.7	4.5	6.7	7.9
Offender was a police officer	--!	--!	--!	--!	0.4!	0.9!	1.2!	1.0!	0.2!	0.3!
Some other way	0.7!	1.9!	3.4!	2.9!	2.6!	1.4	1.2	2.4	2.9	2.0
Unknown	--!	--!	--!	--!	--!	0.1!	0.1!	0.7!	0.6!	--!

Note: Based on the noninstitutionalized U.S. residential population age 12 or older. Estimates are based on 2-year rolling averages. Someone official includes a guard, apartment manager, school official, and other officials.
! = Interpret with caution. Estimate is based on 10 or fewer sample cases, or coefficient of variation is greater than 50%.
-- = Less than 0.05%.

Table 14. Reasons for Not Reporting Violent Crime to Police, by Victim's Disability Status, 2009–2013

(Percent.)

Reason for not reporting crime to police	Persons with disabilities					Persons without disabilities				
	2009	2010	2011	2012	2013	2009	2010	2011	2012	2013
Dealt with another way[1]	46.0	34.5	39.2	40.4	43.6	38.9	36.2	38.2	40.8	40.8
Not important enough to respondent[2]	13.2	12.7	15.2	14.0	21.1	23.5	21.6	21.0	23.1	23.5
Insurance wouldn't cover	--!	--!	--!	--!	.02!	0.1!	0.3!	0.4!	0.3!	0.1!
Police couldn't do anything[3]	1.3!	1.9	2.6	2.8	1.8!	3.4	4.2	4.5	3.3	3.1
Police wouldn't help[4]	26.3	36.9	23.2	19.1	19.5	21.8	21.8	17.3	21.3	20.2
Other reason[5]	31.2	35.0	37.4	42.4	38.4	28.8	36.0	35.9	30.2	35.0

Note: Based on the noninstitutionalized U.S. residential population age 12 or older. Estimates are based on 2-year rolling averages. Detail may sum to more than total because more than one response was allowed.
! = Interpret with caution. Estimate is based on 10 or fewer sample cases, or coefficient of variation is greater than 50%.
-- = Less than 0.05%.
[1]Includes reported to another official and private or personal matter.
[2]Includes minor or unsuccessful crime, child offender, and not clear if a crime occurred.
[3]Includes did not find out until too late, could not recover or identify property, and could not find or identify offender.
[4]Includes police would not think it was important enough, police would be inefficient, police would be biased, and offender was a police officer.
[5]Includes did not want to get offender in trouble with the law, was advised not to report to police, afraid of reprisal, too inconvenient, did not know why it was not reported, and other reasons.

Table 15. Percent of Violent Crime Victims Who Received Services from Nonpolice Victim Services Agencies, by Victim's Disability Status, 2009–2013

(Percent.)

Disability status of victim	2009	2010	2011	2012	2013
Persons with disabilities	15.3	11.2	12.3	13.3	12.2
Persons without disabilities	7.3	7.9	7.8	7.2	8.0

Note: Based on the noninstitutionalized U.S. residential population age 12 or older. Estimates are based on 2-year rolling averages.

Table 16. Annual Number of Violent Victimizations, by Victim's Disability Status, 2008–2013

(Number.)

Type of crime	Persons with disabilities						Persons without disabilities					
	2008	2009	2010	2011	2012	2013	2008	2009	2010	2011	2012	2013
Total	999,700	998,400	742,800	1,104,700	1,346,900	1,299,500	5,393,800	4,670,800	4,193,200	4,705,000	5,495,700	4,823,800
Serious violent crime	316,500	304,700	371,200	431,900	508,300	518,000	1,682,200	1,665,200	1,323,600	1,420,100	1,576,300	1,422,000
Rape/sexual assault	56,200	32,400	34,800	82,800	80,100	65,500	293,400	273,200	233,800	161,400	266,700	234,600
Robbery	145,000	125,500	156,800	130,700	233,000	159,100	534,800	509,600	411,700	426,500	508,800	486,500
Aggravated assault	115,200	146,800	179,700	218,400	195,200	293,400	854,000	882,500	678,100	832,200	800,900	700,800
Simple assault	683,300	693,700	371,600	672,800	838,600	781,500	3,711,500	3,005,600	2,869,600	3,284,800	3,919,300	3,401,800

Table 17. U.S. Population, by Disability Status and Demographic Characteristics, 2013

(Number; percent.)

Demographic characteristic	Persons with disabilities		Persons without disabilities	
	Number	Percent of total	Number	Percent of total
Total	37,548,700	14.2	226,131,900	85.8
Sex				
Male	17,921,300	47.7	110,203,500	48.7
Female	19,627,300	52.3	115,928,300	51.3
Race[1]				
White	28,935,400	77.1	168,962,300	74.7
Black/African American	5,119,000	13.6	26,885,100	11.9
Other[2]	2,596,900	6.9	25,024,000	11.1
Two or more races	897,400	2.4	5,260,500	2.3
Hispanic/Latino origin[3]				
Hispanic/Latino	4,268,800	11.4	36,998,900	16.4
Non-Hispanic/Non-Latino	33,279,800	88.6	189,133,000	83.6
Age				
12–15	947,400	2.5	15,718,500	7.0
16–19	936,400	2.5	16,025,800	7.1
20–24	1,325,700	3.5	21,151,000	9.4
25–34	2,516,600	6.7	39,257,100	17.4
35–49	5,442,500	14.5	55,729,000	24.6
50–64	10,618,100	28.3	50,658,600	22.4
65 or older	15,762,000	42.0	27,592,000	12.2
Disability type[4]				
Hearing	10,803,700	28.8	X	X
Vision	7,006,200	18.7	X	X
Ambulatory	20,470,500	54.5	X	X
Cognitive	13,491,500	35.9	X	X
Self-care	7,474,900	19.9	X	X
Independent living[5]	14,005,400	37.3	X	X

Note: Based on the U.S. Census Bureau's ACS PUMS data and the noninstitutionalized U.S. residential population age 12 or older. Numbers rounded to the nearest hundred.
X = Not applicable.
[1]Includes persons of Hispanic or Latino origin.
[2]Includes persons identified as American Indian or Alaska Native and Asian, Native Hawaiian, or other Pacific Islander.
[3]Includes persons of all races.
[4]Because of the allowance of multiple disability types, numbers and percentages sum to more than the total.
[5]Includes persons age 15 or older only.

Table 18. Rates of Violent Victimization Against Persons Without Disabilities, by Type of Crime, 2009–2013

(Rate per 1,000 persons.)

Type of crime	2009	2010	2011	2012	2013
Total	23.3	20.2	20.0	22.7	22.9
Serious violent crime	7.7	6.8	6.2	6.7	6.6
Rape/sexual assault	1.3	1.2	0.9	1.0	1.1
Robbery	2.4	2.1	1.9	2.1	2.2
Aggravated assault	4.0	3.6	3.4	3.6	3.3
Simple assault	15.5	13.4	13.9	16.1	16.2

Note: Based on the noninstitutionalized U.S. residential population age 12 or older. Estimates were based on 2-year rolling averages.

Table 19. Rates of Violent Victimization Against Persons Without Disabilities, by Victim Characteristics, 2009–2013

(Rate per 1,000 persons.)

Victim characteristic	2009	2010	2011	2012	2013
Total crime	23.3	20.2	20.0	22.7	22.9
Sex					
Male	24.8	21.2	22.5	25.9	24.8
Female	21.8	19.3	17.7	19.7	21
Race[1]					
White	24.2	20.4	20.5	23.4	23.4
Black	30.4	29.9	27.3	31.3	30.7
Other[2]	7.2	7.9	7.7	7.8	8.1
Two or more races	29.3	24.4	27.7	28.8	34.7
Hispanic/Latino origin[3]					
Hispanic/Latino	21.1	18.1	18.7	22.9	23.1
Non-Hispanic/Non-Latino	23.6	20.6	20.3	22.7	22.8

Note: Based on the noninstitutionalized U.S. residential population age 12 or older. Estimates were based on 2-year rolling averages.
[1]Includes persons of Hispanic or Latino origin.
[2]Includes persons identified as American Indian or Alaska Native, Asian, and Native Hawaiian or Other Pacific Islander.
[3]Includes persons of all races.

Methodology

About the Data

The use of age-adjusted rates: The differences in age distributions between the two populations must be taken into account when making direct comparisons of the violent victimization rate between persons with and without disabilities. The age distribution of persons with disabilities differs considerably from that of persons without disabilities, and violent crime victimization rates vary significantly with age. According to the U.S. Census Bureau's American Community Survey (ACS), persons with disabilities are generally older than persons without disabilities. For example, about 42% of persons with disabilities were age 65 or older in 2013, compared to 12% of persons without disabilities. The age adjustment standardizes the rate of violence to show what the rate would be if persons without disabilities had the same age distribution as persons with disabilities.

Survey Coverage

The National Crime Victimization Survey (NCVS) is an ongoing data collection conducted by the U.S. Census Bureau for the Bureau of Justice Statistics (BJS). The NCVS is a self-report survey in which interviewed persons are asked about the number and characteristics of victimizations they experienced during the prior 6 months. The NCVS collects information on nonfatal personal crimes (rape or sexual assault, robbery, aggravated and simple assault, and personal larceny) and household property crimes (burglary, motor vehicle theft, and other theft) both reported and not reported to police. In addition to providing annual level and change estimates on criminal victimization, the NCVS is the primary source of information on the nature of criminal victimization incidents. Survey respondents provide information about themselves (e.g., age, sex, race and Hispanic origin, marital status, education level, and income) and whether they experienced a victimization.

The NCVS collects information for each victimization incident about the offender (e.g., age, race and Hispanic origin, sex, and victim–offender relationship), characteristics of the crime (including time and place of occurrence, use of weapons, nature of injury, and economic consequences), whether the crime was reported to police, reasons the crime was or was not reported, and victims' experiences with the criminal justice system. The NCVS is administered to persons age 12 or older from a nationally representative sample of households in the United States. The NCVS defines a household as a group of members who all reside at a sampled address. Persons are considered household members when the sampled address is their usual place of residence at the time of the interview and when they have no usual place of residence elsewhere. Once selected, households remain in the sample for three years, and eligible persons in these households are interviewed every six months either in person or over the phone, for a total of seven interviews. All first interviews are conducted in person with subsequent interviews conducted either in person or by phone. New households rotate into the sample on an ongoing basis to replace outgoing households that have been in the sample for the three-year period. The sample includes persons living in group quarters (such as dormitories, rooming houses, and religious group dwellings) and excludes persons living in military barracks and institutional settings (such as correctional or hospital facilities) and persons who are homeless.

In 2007, the NCVS adopted questions from the U.S. Census Bureau's American Community Survey (ACS) to measure the rate of victimization against people with disabilities. The NCVS does not identify persons in the general population with disabilities. The ACS Subcommittee on Disability Questions developed the disability questions based on questions used in the 2000 Decennial Census and earlier versions of the ACS. The questions identify persons who may require assistance to maintain their independence, be at risk for discrimination, or lack opportunities available to the general population because of limitations related to a prolonged (i.e., 6 months or longer) sensory, physical, mental, or emotional condition. More information about the ACS and the disability questions is available on the U.S. Census Bureau website at http://www.census.gov/acs/www/.

Definitions of Disability Type

Disabilities are classified according to six limitations: hearing, vision, cognitive, ambulatory, self-care, and independent living.

Hearing limitation entails deafness or serious difficulty hearing.

Vision limitation is blindness or serious difficulty seeing, even when wearing glasses.

Cognitive limitation includes serious difficulty in concentrating, remembering, or making decisions because of a physical, mental, or emotional condition.

Ambulatory limitation is difficulty walking or climbing stairs.

Self-care limitation is a condition that causes difficulty dressing or bathing.

Independent living limitation is a physical, mental, or emotional condition that impedes doing errands alone, such as visiting a doctor or shopping.

PART 5

Hate Crime Statistics, 2013

HIGHLIGHTS

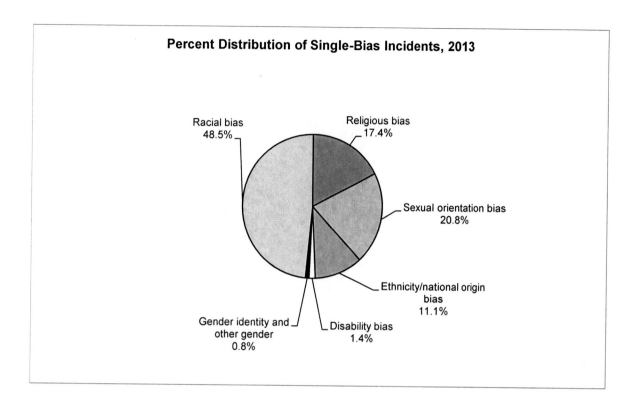

Percent Distribution of Single-Bias Incidents, 2013

Racial bias
48.5%

Religious bias
17.4%

Sexual orientation bias
20.8%

Ethnicity/national origin
bias
11.1%

Gender identity and
other gender
0.8%

Disability bias
1.4%

- In 2013, 1,826 law enforcement agencies reported 5,928 hate crime incidents involving 6,933 offenses.

- There were 5,922 single-bias incidents that involved 6,921 offenses, 7,230 victims, and 5,808 known offenders. Approximately 48.5 percent were racially motivated, 20.8 percent resulted from sexual-orientation bias, 17.4 percent were motivated by religious bias, 11.1 percent stemmed from ethnicity bias, 1.4 percent were prompted by disability bias, 0.5 percent (31 incidents) were motivated by gender-identity bias, and 0.3 percent (18 incidents) resulted from gender bias.

- The six multiple-bias incidents reported in 2013 involved 12 offenses, 12 victims, and six offenders.

- The majority of the 2,424 hate crime offenses that were crimes against property (73.6 percent) were acts of destruction/damage/vandalism.

- The remaining 26.4 percent of crimes against property consisted of robbery, burglary, larceny-theft, motor vehicle theft, arson, and other crime.

- There were 79 offenses defined as crimes against society (e.g., drug or narcotic offenses or prostitution).

Table 1. Incidents, Offenses, Victims, and Known Offenders, by Bias Motivation, 2013

(Number.)

Bias motivation	Incidents	Offenses	Victims[1]	Known offenders[2]
Total	5,928	6,933	7,242	5,814
Single-Bias Incidents	5,922	6,921	7,230	5,808
Race	2,871	3,407	3,563	2,733
Anti-White	653	728	754	680
Anti-Black or African American	1,856	2,263	2,371	1,747
Anti-American Indian or Alaska Native	129	146	159	108
Anti-Asian	135	158	164	130
Anti-Native Hawaiian or Other Pacific Islander	3	3	3	7
Anti-Multiple races, group	95	109	112	61
Religion	1,031	1,163	1,223	682
Anti-Jewish	625	689	737	393
Anti-Catholic	70	74	75	72
Anti-Protestant	35	42	47	17
Anti-Islamic (Muslim)	135	165	167	127
Anti-other religion	117	135	137	44
Anti-multiple religions, group	42	51	53	25
Anti-atheism/agnosticism/etc.	7	7	7	4
Sexual orientation	1,233	1,402	1,461	1,514
Anti-gay (male)	750	849	890	975
Anti-lesbian	160	185	191	174
Anti-lesbian, gay, bisexual, or transgender (mixed group)	277	317	329	324
Anti-heterosexual	21	24	24	20
Anti-bisexual	25	27	27	21
Ethnicity	655	794	821	743
Anti-Hispanic or Latino	331	418	432	418
Anti-Not Hispanic or Latino[3]	324	376	389	325
Disability	83	92	99	77
Anti-physical	22	23	24	23
Anti-mental	61	69	75	54
Gender	18	30	30	20
Anti-male	5	5	5	7
Anti-female	13	25	25	13
Gender Identity	31	33	33	39
Anti-transgender	23	25	25	30
Anti-gender nonconforming	8	8	8	9
Multiple-Bias Incidents[4]	6	12	12	6

[1]The term victim may refer to a person, business, institution, or society as a whole.
[2]The term known offender does not imply that the identity of the suspect is known, but only that an attribute of the suspect has been identified, which distinguishes him/her from an unknown offender.
[3]The term anti-not Hispanic or Latino does not imply the victim was targeted because he/she was not of Hispanic origin, but it refers to other or unspecified ethnic biases that are not Hispanic or Latino.
[4]A multiple-bias incident is an incident in which one or more offense types are motivated by two or more biases.

Table 2. Incidents, Offenses, Victims, and Known Offenders, by Offense Type, 2013

(Number.)

Offense type	Incidents[1]	Offenses	Victims[2]	Known offenders[3]
Total	5,928	6,933	7,242	5,814
Crimes against Persons	3,607	4,430	4,430	4,440
Murder and nonnegligent manslaughter	5	5	5	5
Rape (revised definition)[4]	15	15	15	15
Rape (legacy definition)[5]	6	6	6	10
Aggravated assault	588	734	734	882
Simple assault	1,441	1,720	1,720	2,013
Intimidation	1,528	1,925	1,925	1,494
Other[6]	24	25	25	21
Crimes against Property	2,424	2,424	2,733	1,527
Robbery	126	126	145	261
Burglary	174	174	202	164
Larceny-theft	225	225	246	168
Motor vehicle theft	20	20	21	9
Arson	36	36	40	21
Destruction/damage/vandalism	1,783	1,783	2,011	862
Other[6]	60	60	68	42
Crimes against Society[6]	79	79	79	102

[1]The actual number of incidents is 5,928. However, the column figures will not add to the total because incidents may include more than one offense type, and these are counted in each appropriate offense type category.
[2]The term victim may refer to a person, business, institution, or society as a whole.
[3]The term known offender does not imply that the identity of the suspect is known, but only that an attribute of the suspect has been identified, which distinguishes him/her from an unknown offender. The actual number of known offenders is 5,814. However, the column figures will not add to the total because some offenders are responsible for more than one offense type, and are, therefore, counted more than once in this table.
[4]The figures shown in this row for the offense of rape include only those reported by law enforcement agencies that used the revised Uniform Crime Reporting (UCR) definition of rape.
[5]The figures shown in this row for the offense of rape include only those reported by law enforcement agencies that used the legacy UCR definition of rape.
[6]Includes additional offenses collected in the National Incident-Based Reporting System.

Table 3. Offenses, Known Offender's Race, by Offense Type, 2013

(Number.)

Offense type	Total offenses	Known offender's race						Unknown offender
		White	Black	American Indian/ Alaskan Native	Asian/Pacific Islander	Multiple races, group	Unknown race	
Total	6,718	2,793	992	51	40	229	571	2,042
Crimes against Persons	3,968	2,257	739	40	34	183	248	467
Murder and nonnegligent manslaughter	10	8	1	0	0	0	1	0
Forcible rape	15	6	2	0	0	1	4	2
Aggravated assault	854	533	186	13	2	37	46	37
Simple assault	1,570	834	360	20	19	124	75	138
Intimidation	1,489	857	184	7	13	20	119	289
Other[1]	30	19	6	0	0	1	3	1
Crimes against Property	2,547	456	159	10	4	39	314	1,565
Robbery	126	42	55	1	0	10	7	11
Burglary	142	30	16	0	0	8	24	64
Larceny-theft	258	79	22	1	1	2	36	117
Motor vehicle theft	23	5	0	0	0	0	2	16
Arson	38	12	4	1	3	1	7	10
Destruction/damage/vandalism	1,906	260	57	5	0	18	231	1,335
Other[1]	54	28	5	2	0	0	7	12
Crimes against Society[1]	203	80	94	1	2	7	9	10

[1]Includes additional offenses collected in the National Incident-Based Reporting System.

Table 4. Offenses, Offense Type, by Bias Motivation, 2013

(Number.)

Bias motivation	Total offenses	Crimes against persons						
		Murder and nonnegligent manslaughter	Rape (revised definition)[1]	Rape (legacy definition)[2]	Aggravated assault	Simple assault	Intimidation	Other[3]
Total	6,933	5	15	6	734	1,720	1,925	25
Single-Bias Incidents	6,921	5	15	6	733	1,717	1,922	25
Race	3,407	2	7	0	398	750	1,087	15
Anti-White	728	1	6	0	79	194	155	9
Anti-Black or African American	2,263	1	0	0	288	478	829	2
Anti-American Indian or Alaska Native	146	0	0	0	11	16	26	1
Anti-Asian	158	0	1	0	15	43	43	2
Anti-Native Hawaiian or Other Pacific Islander	3	0	0	0	1	1	1	0
Anti-Multiple races, group	109	0	0	0	4	18	33	1
Religion	1,163	0	1	1	23	134	255	1
Anti-Jewish	689	0	0	0	5	72	152	0
Anti-Catholic	74	0	0	0	0	6	11	0
Anti-Protestant	42	0	0	0	0	0	3	0
Anti-Islamic (Muslim)	165	0	0	1	17	41	53	0
Anti-other religion	135	0	1	0	1	11	26	1
Anti-multiple religions, group	51	0	0	0	0	3	10	0
Anti-atheism/agnosticism/etc.	7	0	0	0	0	1	0	0
Sexual orientation	1,402	2	3	4	193	547	318	1
Anti-gay (male)	849	2	0	0	120	359	188	0
Anti-lesbian	185	0	0	4	24	66	56	0
Anti-lesbian, gay, bisexual, or transgender (mixed group)	317	0	1	0	47	111	58	0
Anti-heterosexual	24	0	1	0	0	6	6	1
Anti-bisexual	27	0	1	0	2	5	10	0
Ethnicity	794	1	1	0	103	241	235	6
Anti-Hispanic or Latino	418	1	1	0	79	118	128	0
Anti-Not Hispanic or Latino[4]	376	0	0	0	24	123	107	6
Disability	92	0	1	0	6	16	21	2
Anti-physical	23	0	1	0	1	5	5	0
Anti-mental	69	0	0	0	5	11	16	2
Gender	30	0	2	0	2	19	2	0
Anti-male	5	0	0	0	1	1	0	0
Anti-female	25	0	2	0	1	18	2	0
Gender Identity	33	0	0	1	8	10	4	0
Anti-transgender	25	0	0	0	8	7	4	0
Anti-gender nonconforming	8	0	0	1	0	3	0	0
Multiple-Bias Incidents[5]	12	0	0	0	1	3	3	0

Table 4. Offenses, Offense Type, by Bias Motivation, 2013—*Continued*

Bias motivation	Crimes against property							Crimes against society[3]
	Robbery	Burglary	Larceny-theft	Motor vehicle theft	Arson	Destruction/damage/vandalism	Other[3]	
Total	126	174	225	20	36	1,783	60	79
Single-Bias Incidents	125	174	225	20	36	1,779	60	79
Race	54	91	126	11	17	759	36	54
Anti-White	24	32	75	6	4	98	17	28
Anti-Black or African American	23	36	16	1	11	557	7	14
Anti-American Indian or Alaska Native	3	16	27	4	0	22	10	10
Anti-Asian	4	6	5	0	2	34	2	1
Anti-Native Hawaiian or Other Pacific Islander	0	0	0	0	0	0	0	0
Anti-Multiple races, group	0	1	3	0	0	48	0	1
Religion	3	29	38	1	17	649	6	5
Anti-Jewish	1	6	11	0	4	437	1	0
Anti-Catholic	0	6	9	0	3	36	1	2
Anti-Protestant	0	6	5	0	3	24	1	0
Anti-Islamic (Muslim)	2	2	2	0	1	43	2	1
Anti-other religion	0	5	4	1	5	78	1	1
Anti-multiple religions, group	0	3	6	0	1	27	0	1
Anti-atheism/agnosticism/etc.	0	1	1	0	0	4	0	0
Sexual orientation	47	30	17	3	2	223	8	4
Anti-gay (male)	30	23	4	0	2	115	6	0
Anti-lesbian	3	0	3	0	0	28	1	0
Anti-lesbian, gay, bisexual, or transgender (mixed group)	13	3	4	2	0	76	1	1
Anti-heterosexual	0	3	2	0	0	2	0	3
Anti-bisexual	1	1	4	1	0	2	0	0
Ethnicity	15	18	23	3	0	132	7	9
Anti-Hispanic or Latino	11	9	7	1	0	55	4	4
Anti-Not Hispanic or Latino[4]	4	9	16	2	0	77	3	5
Disability	3	5	17	1	0	11	3	6
Anti-physical	2	0	6	0	0	2	1	0
Anti-mental	1	5	11	1	0	9	2	6
Gender	0	0	2	1	0	1	0	1
Anti-male	0	0	1	1	0	1	0	0
Anti-female	0	0	1	0	0	0	0	1
Gender Identity	3	1	2	0	0	4	0	0
Anti-transgender	3	1	0	0	0	2	0	0
Anti-gender nonconforming	0	0	2	0	0	2	0	0
Multiple-Bias Incidents[5]	1	0	0	0	0	4	0	0

[1]The figures shown in this column for the offense of rape include only those reported by law enforcement agencies that used the revised Uniform Crime Reporting (UCR) definition of rape.
[2]The figures shown in this column for the offense of rape include only those reported by law enforcement agencies that used the legacy UCR definition of rape.
[3]Includes additional offenses collected in the National Incident-Based Reporting System.
[4]The term anti-not Hispanic or Latino does not imply the victim was targeted because he/she was not of Hispanic origin, but it refers to other or unspecified ethnic biases that are not Hispanic or Latino.
[5]A multiple-bias incident is an incident in which one or more offense types are motivated by two or more biases.

Table 5. Offenses, Known Offender's Race, by Bias Motivation, 2013

(Number.)

Bias motivation	Total offenses	Known offender's race							Known offender's ethnicity[1]				Unknown offender
		White	Black or African American	American Indian or Alaska Native	Asian	Native Hawaiian or Other Pacific Islander	Group of multiple races	Unknown race	Hispanic or Latino	Not Hispanic or Latino	Group of multiple ethnicities	Unknown ethnicity	
Total	6,933	2,963	1,091	50	41	2	199	787	13	173	12	98	1,800
Single-Bias Incidents	6,921	2,955	1,089	50	41	2	199	787	13	173	12	98	1,798
Race	3,407	1,667	446	33	22	1	77	266	5	66	9	35	895
Anti-White	728	176	299	14	4	1	15	43	0	16	3	10	176
Anti-Black or African American	2,263	1,336	85	9	14	0	58	175	4	46	2	19	586
Anti-American Indian or Alaska Native	146	47	31	7	3	0	0	14	0	0	2	4	44
Anti-Asian	158	69	23	0	1	0	3	15	1	3	1	1	47
Anti-Native Hawaiian or Other Pacific Islander	3	2	0	0	0	0	1	0	0	0	0	0	0
Anti-Multiple races, group	109	37	8	3	0	0	0	19	0	1	1	1	42
Religion	1,163	297	68	1	0	0	22	306	1	4	1	9	469
Anti-Jewish	689	143	35	0	0	0	4	236	0	2	0	7	271
Anti-Catholic	74	25	0	0	0	0	2	24	1	1	0	0	23
Anti-Protestant	42	8	0	0	0	0	0	9	0	1	0	0	25
Anti-Islamic (Muslim)	165	67	20	0	0	0	16	17	0	0	1	1	45
Anti-other religion	135	39	4	1	0	0	0	13	0	0	0	0	78
Anti-multiple religions, group	51	15	7	0	0	0	0	6	0	0	0	1	23
Anti-atheism/agnosticism/etc.	7	0	2	0	0	0	0	1	0	0	0	0	4
Sexual orientation	1,402	564	329	7	11	0	75	149	6	36	0	32	267
Anti-gay (male)	849	334	208	4	9	0	51	95	2	19	0	25	148
Anti-lesbian	185	81	41	2	1	0	10	18	0	6	0	3	32
Anti-lesbian, gay, bisexual, or transgender (mixed group)	317	126	73	0	1	0	14	29	3	8	0	2	74
Anti-heterosexual	24	10	3	0	0	0	0	5	0	1	0	2	6
Anti-bisexual	27	13	4	1	0	0	0	2	1	2	0	0	7
Ethnicity	794	365	203	8	3	1	20	53	1	52	2	15	141
Anti-Hispanic or Latino	418	220	97	4	2	1	14	12	1	13	2	2	68
Anti-Not Hispanic or Latino[2]	376	145	106	4	1	0	6	41	0	39	0	13	73
Disability	92	32	21	1	5	0	4	8	0	4	0	0	21
Anti-physical	23	10	7	0	0	0	1	1	0	0	0	0	4
Anti-mental	69	22	14	1	5	0	3	7	0	4	0	0	17
Gender	30	22	4	0	0	0	0	3	0	1	0	2	1
Anti-male	5	2	1	0	0	0	0	2	0	0	0	2	
Anti-female	25	20	3	0	0	0	0	1	0	1	0	0	1
Gender Identity	33	8	18	0	0	0	1	2	0	10	0	5	4
Anti-transgender	25	4	17	0	0	0	0	0	0	9	0	5	4
Anti-gender nonconforming	8	4	1	0	0	0	1	2	0	1	0	0	0
Multiple-Bias Incidents[3]	12	8	2	0	0	0	0	0	0	0	0	0	2

[1]The total number of offenses by the known offender's ethnicity do not equal the total number of offenses by the known offender's race because not all law enforcement agencies that report offender race data also report offender ethnicity data.
[2]The term anti-not Hispanic or Latino does not imply the victim was targeted because he/she was not of Hispanic origin, but it refers to other or unspecified ethnic biases that are not Hispanic or Latino.
[3]In a multiple-bias incident, two conditions must be met: (a) more than one offense type must occur in the incident and (b) at least two offense types must be motivated by different biases.

Table 6. Offenses, Victim Type, by Offense Type, 2013

(Number.)

Offense type	Total offenses	Victim type					
		Individual	Business/ financial institution	Government	Religious organization	Society/ public[1]	Other/ unknown/ multiple
Total	6,933	5,682	307	177	180	79	508
Crimes against persons[2]	4,430	4,430	NA	NA	NA	NA	NA
Crimes against property	2,424	1,252	307	177	180	0	508
Robbery	126	120	1	0	0	0	5
Burglary	174	116	15	0	16	0	27
Larceny-theft	225	145	56	3	8	0	13
Motor vehicle theft	20	17	2	0	0	0	1
Arson	36	16	0	0	9	0	11
Destruction/damage/vandalism	1,783	796	220	172	147	0	448
Other[2]	60	42	13	2	0	0	3
Crimes against society[2]	79	NA	NA	NA	NA	79	NA

NA = Not available.

[1]The victim type *society/public* is collected only in the National Incident-Based Reporting System (NIBRS).

[2]Includes additional offenses collected in the NIBRS.

Table 7. Victims, Offense Type, by Bias Motivation, 2013

(Number.)

Bias motivation	Total victims	Crimes against persons						
		Murder and nonnegligent manslaughter	Rape (revised definition)[1]	Rape (legacy definition)[2]	Aggravated assault	Simple assault	Intimidation	Other[3]
Total	7,242	5	15	6	734	1,720	1,925	25
Single-Bias Incidents	7,230	5	15	6	733	1,717	1,922	25
Race	3,563	2	7	0	398	750	1,087	15
Anti-White	754	1	6	0	79	194	155	9
Anti-Black or African American	2,371	1	0	0	288	478	829	2
Anti-American Indian or Alaska Native	159	0	0	0	11	16	26	1
Anti-Asian	164	0	1	0	15	43	43	2
Anti-Native Hawaiian or Other Pacific Islander	3	0	0	0	1	1	1	0
Anti-Multiple races, group	112	0	0	0	4	18	33	1
Religion	1,223	0	1	1	23	134	255	1
Anti-Jewish	737	0	0	0	5	72	152	0
Anti-Catholic	75	0	0	0	0	6	11	0
Anti-Protestant	47	0	0	0	0	0	3	0
Anti-Islamic (Muslim)	167	0	0	1	17	41	53	0
Anti-other religion	137	0	1	0	1	11	26	1
Anti-multiple religions, group	53	0	0	0	0	3	10	0
Anti-atheism/agnosticism/etc.	7	0	0	0	0	1	0	0
Sexual orientation	1,461	2	3	4	193	547	318	1
Anti-gay (male)	890	2	0	0	120	359	188	0
Anti-lesbian	191	0	0	4	24	66	56	0
Anti-lesbian, gay, bisexual, or transgender (mixed group)	329	0	1	0	47	111	58	0
Anti-heterosexual	24	0	1	0	0	6	6	1
Anti-bisexual	27	0	1	0	2	5	10	0
Ethnicity	821	1	1	0	103	241	235	6
Anti-Hispanic or Latino	432	1	1	0	79	118	128	0
Anti-Not Hispanic or Latino[4]	389	0	0	0	24	123	107	6
Disability	99	0	1	0	6	16	21	2
Anti-physical	24	0	1	0	1	5	5	0
Anti-mental	75	0	0	0	5	11	16	2
Gender	30	0	2	0	2	19	2	0
Anti-male	5	0	0	0	1	1	0	0
Anti-female	25	0	2	0	1	18	2	0
Gender Identity	33	0	0	1	8	10	4	0
Anti-transgender	25	0	0	0	8	7	4	0
Anti-gender nonconforming	8	0	0	1	0	3	0	0
Multiple-Bias Incidents[5]	12	0	0	0	1	3	3	0
Individual Victim Age Total[6]	2,801							
Individual victims 18 and over	2,352							
Individual victims under 18	449							

Table 7. Victims, Offense Type, by Bias Motivation, 2013—*Continued*

Bias motivation	Crimes against property							Crimes against society[3]
	Robbery	Burglary	Larceny-theft	Motor vehicle theft	Arson	Destruction/ damage/ vandalism	Other[3]	
Total	145	202	246	21	40	2,011	68	79
Single-Bias Incidents	144	202	246	21	40	2,007	68	79
Race	60	110	138	12	20	867	43	54
Anti-White	25	36	79	6	4	111	21	28
Anti-Black or African American	25	49	21	1	11	645	7	14
Anti-American Indian or Alaska Native	6	17	30	5	0	24	13	10
Anti-Asian	4	6	5	0	5	37	2	1
Anti-Native Hawaiian or Other Pacific Islander	0	0	0	0	0	0	0	0
Anti-Multiple races, group	0	2	3	0	0	50	0	1
Religion	4	32	40	1	18	702	6	5
Anti-Jewish	1	7	12	0	4	483	1	0
Anti-Catholic	0	6	9	0	3	37	1	2
Anti-Protestant	0	8	5	0	3	27	1	0
Anti-Islamic (Muslim)	3	2	2	0	1	44	2	1
Anti-other religion	0	5	4	1	6	79	1	1
Anti-multiple religions, group	0	3	7	0	1	28	0	1
Anti-atheism/agnosticism/etc.	0	1	1	0	0	4	0	0
Sexual orientation	56	33	18	3	2	269	8	4
Anti-gay (male)	37	26	4	0	2	146	6	0
Anti-lesbian	3	0	4	0	0	33	1	0
Anti-lesbian, gay, bisexual, or transgender (mixed group)	15	3	4	2	0	86	1	1
Anti-heterosexual	0	3	2	0	0	2	0	3
Anti-bisexual	1	1	4	1	0	2	0	0
Ethnicity	17	20	24	3	0	153	8	9
Anti-Hispanic or Latino	13	9	7	1	0	67	4	4
Anti-Not Hispanic or Latino[4]	4	11	17	2	0	86	4	5
Disability	4	6	22	1	0	11	3	6
Anti-physical	3	0	6	0	0	2	1	0
Anti-mental	1	6	16	1	0	9	2	6
Gender	0	0	2	1	0	1	0	1
Anti-male	0	0	1	1	0	1	0	0
Anti-female	0	0	1	0	0	0	0	1
Gender Identity	3	1	2	0	0	4	0	0
Anti-transgender	3	1	0	0	0	2	0	0
Anti-gender nonconforming	0	0	2	0	0	2	0	0
Multiple-Bias Incidents[5]	1	0	0	0	0	4	0	0
Individual Victim Age Total[6]								
Individual victims 18 and over								
Individual victims under 18								

[1]The figures shown in this column for the offense of rape include only those reported by law enforcement agencies that used the revised Uniform Crime Reporting (UCR) definition of rape.
[2]The figures shown in this column for the offense of rape include only those reported by law enforcement agencies that used the legacy UCR definition of rape.
[3]Includes additional offenses collected in the National Incident-Based Reporting System.
[4]The term anti-not Hispanic or Latino does not imply the victim was targeted because he/she was not of Hispanic origin, but it refers to other or unspecified ethnic biases that are not Hispanic or Latino.
[5]A multiple-bias incident is an incident in which one or more offense types are motivated by two or more biases.
[6]The individual victim age total does not equal the total number of victims because a victim can be an individual, a business, an institution, or society as a whole. In addition, not all law enforcement agencies report the ages of individual victims.

Table 8. Incidents, Victim Type, by Bias Motivation, 2013

(Number.)

Bias motivation	Total incidents	Victim type					
		Individual	Business/ financial institution	Government	Religious organization	Society/ public[1]	Other/ unknown/ multiple
Total	5,928	4,696	298	177	171	64	522
Single-Bias Incidents	5,922	4,690	298	177	171	64	522
Race	2,871	2,402	145	107	10	43	164
Religion	1,031	450	87	44	158	5	287
Sexual Orientation	1,233	1,154	25	12	1	4	37
Ethnicity	655	572	35	13	2	5	28
Disability	83	69	4	1	0	6	3
Gender	18	15	1	0	0	1	1
Gender Identity	31	28	1	0	0	0	2
Multiple-Bias Incidents[2]	6	6	0	0	0	0	0

[1]The victim type society/public is collected only in the National Incident-Based Reporting System.
[2]A multiple-bias incident is an incident in which one or more offense types are motivated by two or more biases.

Table 9. Known Offenders,[1] by Known Offender's Race, Ethnicity, and Age, 2013

(Number.)

Race/ethnicity/age	Total
Race	5,814
White	3,046
Black or African American	1,410
American Indian or Alaska Native	49
Asian	40
Native Hawaiian or Other Pacific Islander	3
Group of multiple races[2]	407
Unknown race	859
Ethnicity[3]	368
Hispanic or Latino	12
Not Hispanic or Latino	199
Group of multiple ethnicities[4]	23
Unknown ethnicity	134
Age[3]	2,527
Total known offenders 18 and over	1,719
Total known offenders under 18	808

[1]The term known offender does not imply that the identity of the suspect is known, but only that an attribute of the suspect has been identified, which distinguishes him/her from an unknown offender.
[2]The term group of multiple races is used to describe a group of offenders of varying races.
[3]The total number of known offenders by age and the total number of known offenders by ethnicity do not equal the total number of known offenders by race because not all law enforcement agencies report the age and/or ethnicity of the known offenders.
[4]The term group of multiple ethnicities is used to describe a group of offenders of varying ethnicities.

Table 10. Incidents, Bias Motivation, by Location, 2013

(Number.)

Location	Total incidents	Bias motivation							Multiple-bias incidents[1]
		Race	Religion	Sexual orientation	Ethnicity	Disability	Gender	Gender Identity	
Total	5,928	2,871	1,031	1,233	655	83	18	31	6
Abandoned/condemned structure	2	0	0	1	0	1	0	0	0
Air/bus/train terminal	63	31	5	21	4	0	0	2	0
Arena/stadium/fairgrounds/coliseum	3	1	0	2	0	0	0	0	0
Auto dealership new/used	2	2	0	0	0	0	0	0	0
Bank/savings and loan	11	4	3	1	2	1	0	0	0
Bar/nightclub	121	53	5	44	16	1	1	1	0
Camp/campground	2	1	1	0	0	0	0	0	0
Church/synagogue/temple/mosque	206	13	189	2	2	0	0	0	0
Commercial office building	117	62	17	18	15	3	1	1	0
Community center	1	0	1	0	0	0	0	0	0
Construction site	13	5	3	0	5	0	0	0	0
Convenience store	69	33	10	3	23	0	0	0	0
Daycare facility	3	1	0	1	1	0	0	0	0
Department/discount store	59	29	10	8	10	1	0	1	0
Drug store/Doctor's office/hospital	48	30	11	3	3	0	0	1	0
Farm facility	1	1	0	0	0	0	0	0	0
Field/woods	53	31	5	14	3	0	0	0	0
Gambling facility/casino/race track	3	1	0	0	2	0	0	0	0
Government/public building	107	60	13	15	18	1	0	0	0
Grocery/supermarket	53	32	2	8	10	1	0	0	0
Highway/road/alley/street/sidewalk	1,071	551	92	284	120	15	1	7	1
Hotel/motel/etc.	32	13	6	5	7	1	0	0	0
Industrial site	6	4	0	1	1	0	0	0	0
Jail/prison/penitentiary/corrections facility	71	46	5	14	5	0	1	0	0
Lake/waterway/beach	4	2	2	0	0	0	0	0	0
Liquor store	8	3	0	2	3	0	0	0	0
Park/playground	67	46	7	11	3	0	0	0	0
Parking/drop lot/garage	336	182	28	75	44	0	3	2	2
Rental storage facility	4	1	1	2	0	0	0	0	0
Residence/home	1,865	976	240	397	207	37	2	5	1
Rest area	2	1	0	0	1	0	0	0	0
Restaurant	126	63	9	30	21	1	0	2	0
School/college[2]	234	111	53	45	21	3	1	0	0
School—college/university	100	47	13	23	13	1	1	1	1
School—elementary/secondary	158	92	13	21	27	4	1	0	0
Service/gas station	55	30	6	8	10	0	0	1	0
Shelter—mission/homeless	4	2	0	2	0	0	0	0	0
Shopping mall	9	3	2	2	1	1	0	0	0
Specialty store (TV, fur, etc.)	42	22	6	5	8	1	0	0	0
Tribal lands	4	2	0	0	1	0	0	1	0
Other/unknown	782	276	272	164	48	9	6	6	1
Multiple locations	11	8	1	1	0	1	0	0	0

[1] A multiple-bias incident is an incident in which one or more offense types are motivated by two or more biases.
[2] The location designation School/college has been retained for agencies that have not updated their records management systems to include the new location designations of "School—college/university" and "School—elementary/secondary," which allow for more specificity in reporting.

Table 11. Offenses, Offense Type, by Selected State, 2013

(Number.)

State	Total offenses	Crimes against persons						
		Murder and nonnegligent manslaughter	Rape (revised definition)[1]	Rape (legacy definition)[2]	Aggravated assault	Simple assault	Intimidation	Other[3]
Total	6,933	5	15	6	734	1,720	1,925	25
Alabama	6	0	0		2	2	1	0
Alaska	9	0	0		3	1	3	0
Arizona	212	0	0	1	45	46	61	0
Arkansas	34	1	0		6	4	17	0
California	1,012	1		1	149	239	235	0
Colorado	154	0	2		19	37	48	0
Connecticut	172	0	0	0	9	29	71	0
Delaware	13	0	0		3	3	5	0
District of Columbia	80	0	0		16	37	12	0
Florida	82	0	0		13	21	16	0
Georgia	72	0		0	9	22	31	0
Idaho	37	0	0		9	6	10	0
Illinois	123	0	0	0	28	42	18	0
Indiana	78	0	0	0	13	21	30	0
Iowa	15	0	0		6	1	3	0
Kansas	74	0	0	0	3	21	17	0
Kentucky	209	0	0	0	10	42	68	6
Louisiana	23	0	0	0	1	6	2	0
Maine	28	0	0	0	0	8	13	0
Maryland	58	0		0	13	12	6	0
Massachusetts	393	0	2	0	16	72	177	1
Michigan	399	0	3		54	92	152	0
Minnesota	167	0	2		25	38	63	0
Mississippi	4	0	0	0	0	0	0	1
Missouri	116	1	1		21	29	21	1
Montana	37	0	0		3	11	0	1
Nebraska	39	0	0	0	2	13	3	1
Nevada	80	0		1	14	31	9	0
New Hampshire	23	0	0		1	5	7	0
New Jersey	447	0		0	11	26	259	0
New Mexico	12	0		0	2	3	3	0
New York	655	2		1	28	300	3	0
North Carolina	140	0		0	20	34	37	0
North Dakota	63	0	1		4	22	13	1
Ohio	447	0	1	0	11	62	181	2
Oklahoma	45	0	0	0	2	14	13	0
Oregon	75	0	0	0	7	12	15	0
Pennsylvania	110	0	0		11	12	72	0
Rhode Island	8	0	0	0	0	2	1	0
South Carolina	59	0	0		13	16	12	0
South Dakota	18	0	0		2	7	1	1
Tennessee	245	0	2		36	100	47	8
Texas	161	0	0	1	27	65	29	0
Utah	87	0	0	0	7	12	10	2
Vermont	13	0	0		1	4	2	0
Virginia	126	0	0		6	31	20	0
Washington	344	0	1	1	41	76	86	0
West Virginia	63	0	0		4	12	4	0
Wisconsin	65	0	0	0	7	19	18	0
Wyoming	1	0		0	1	0	0	0

Table 11. Offenses, Offense Type, by Selected State, 2013—*Continued*

State		Crimes against property						Crimes against society[3]
	Robbery	Burglary	Larceny-theft	Motor vehicle theft	Arson	Destruction/ damage/ vandalism	Other[3]	
Total	126	174	225	20	36	1,783	60	79
Alabama	0	0	1	0	0	0	0	0
Alaska	0	1	0	0	0	1	0	0
Arizona	8	5	3	0	0	39	1	3
Arkansas	0	0	1	0	1	4	0	0
California	32	19	3	2	7	324	0	0
Colorado	6	1	3	0	0	37	1	0
Connecticut	0	1	12	0	0	41	1	8
Delaware	0	0	0	0	0	2	0	0
District of Columbia	6	1	1	0	0	7	0	0
Florida	2	2	1	1	0	26	0	0
Georgia	3	0	0	0	0	7	0	0
Idaho	0	0	2	0	0	9	1	0
Illinois	3	2	4	0	1	25	0	0
Indiana	1	2	0	0	0	11	0	0
Iowa	0	1	0	0	0	4	0	0
Kansas	0	2	7	0	0	20	3	1
Kentucky	6	13	10	3	2	40	5	4
Louisiana	0	0	4	0	1	8	1	0
Maine	1	0	0	0	1	4	0	1
Maryland	0	1	1	0	2	23	0	0
Massachusetts	3	6	14	0	0	98	3	1
Michigan	2	10	13	0	3	66	4	0
Minnesota	5	1	1	0	0	32	0	0
Mississippi	0	1	2	0	0	0	0	0
Missouri	3	6	4	3	0	19	4	3
Montana	0	1	8	1	0	11	1	0
Nebraska	0	0	1	0	0	15	2	2
Nevada	4	7	0	0	0	14	0	0
New Hampshire	0	2	0	0	0	8	0	0
New Jersey	2	2	1	0	1	145	0	0
New Mexico	0	0	1	0	0	3	0	0
New York	0	26	8	0	5	282	0	0
North Carolina	3	2	3	0	0	41	0	0
North Dakota	0	1	6	1	0	8	1	5
Ohio	10	22	43	6	1	90	10	8
Oklahoma	1	1	1	0	1	11	1	0
Oregon	0	3	1	0	0	37	0	0
Pennsylvania	0	0	0	0	4	11	0	0
Rhode Island	0	1	0	0	0	4	0	0
South Carolina	0	1	5	0	0	10	2	0
South Dakota	1	1	1	0	0	4	0	0
Tennessee	6	2	4	0	1	30	3	6
Texas	6	1	0	0	0	31	0	1
Utah	0	2	10	2	0	16	2	24
Vermont	0	0	2	0	0	4	0	0
Virginia	1	2	1	0	2	60	2	1
Washington	4	11	26	1	2	76	8	11
West Virginia	4	10	14	0	0	12	3	0
Wisconsin	3	1	2	0	1	13	1	0
Wyoming	0	0	0	0	0	0	0	0

[1] The figures shown in this column for the offense of rape include only those reported by law enforcement agencies that used the revised Uniform Crime Reporting (UCR) definition of rape.
[2] The figures shown in this column for the offense of rape include only those reported by law enforcement agencies that used the legacy UCR definition of rape.
[3] Includes additional offenses collected in the National Incident-Based Reporting System.

Table 12. Agency Hate Crime Reporting, by Selected State and Territory, 2013

(Number.)

State	Number of participating agencies	Population covered	Agencies submitting incident reports	Total number of incidents reported
Total	15,016	295,016,072	1,826	5,928
Alabama	48	1,147,612	4	6
Alaska	33	730,950	1	8
Arizona	81	6,358,545	21	155
Arkansas	265	2,809,536	20	27
California	732	38,324,460	229	843
Colorado	226	5,163,276	48	128
Connecticut	98	3,566,367	48	145
Delaware	58	925,749	11	12
District of Columbia	2	646,449	2	72
Florida	504	19,455,529	41	76
Georgia	499	7,817,674	7	57
Guam[1]	1	0	0	0
Idaho	108	1,611,676	12	32
Illinois	720	12,269,532	38	105
Indiana	134	4,034,953	15	75
Iowa	222	2,958,457	9	10
Kansas	354	2,665,446	30	64
Kentucky	385	4,334,254	77	171
Louisiana	109	3,237,092	6	22
Maine	148	1,328,302	17	25
Maryland	154	5,928,814	20	51
Massachusetts	330	6,496,451	78	350
Michigan	600	9,733,958	141	329
Minnesota	257	4,904,213	39	144
Mississippi	90	1,497,332	2	4
Missouri	621	6,040,074	20	102
Montana	98	1,000,016	12	31
Nebraska	182	1,511,235	10	36
Nevada	5	2,229,342	5	73
New Hampshire	151	1,178,087	16	21
New Jersey	508	8,898,292	140	414
New Mexico	23	888,880	3	12
New York	566	19,515,678	85	615
North Carolina	522	9,845,983	48	118
North Dakota	105	722,021	19	51
Ohio	644	10,376,248	111	370
Oklahoma	328	3,850,568	25	41
Oregon	76	2,301,273	18	66
Pennsylvania	1,375	12,657,821	20	64
Rhode Island	48	1,051,511	7	7
South Carolina	418	4,761,406	39	51
South Dakota	113	767,653	8	13
Tennessee	466	6,495,978	56	196
Texas	1,000	26,304,575	50	132
Utah	131	2,883,607	35	75
Vermont	88	623,447	10	12
Virginia	416	8,258,337	54	119
Virgin Islands[1]	2	0	0	0
Washington	244	6,967,181	80	291
West Virginia	263	1,670,269	17	56
Wisconsin	402	5,691,976	21	50
Wyoming	63	577,987	1	1

[1]The 2012 population estimates were not available at the time of publication.

Table 13. Hate Crime Incidents Per Bias Motivation and Quarter, by Selected State and Agency, 2013

(Number.)

State/agency	Number of incidents per bias motivation							Number of incidents per quarter[1]				Population[2]
	Race	Religion	Sexual orientation	Ethnicity	Disability	Gender	Gender Identity	1st quarter	2nd quarter	3rd quarter	4th quarter	
ALABAMA												
Total	5	0	1	0	0	0	0					
Cities	5	0	1	0	0	0	0					
Florence............................	2	0	0	0	0	0	0	0	1	0	1	39,481
Hoover............................	0	0	1	0	0	0	0	0	1	0	0	84,139
Prattville..........................	2	0	0	0	0	0	0	1	0	1	0	35,154
Tuscaloosa	1	0	0	0	0	0	0	0	0	1	0	94,126
ALASKA												
Total	8	0	0	0	0	0	0					
Cities	8	0	0	0	0							
Anchorage.........................	8	0	0	0	0	0	0	2	3	3	0	299,455
ARIZONA												
Total	73	30	27	24	1	0	0					
Cities	68	27	25	23	1	0	0					
Apache Junction	1	0	0	0	0	0	0	1	0	0		36,626
Avondale..........................	4	0	0	1	0	0	0	1	1	3	0	78,905
Eagar...............................	0	0	0	1	0	0	0	0	1	0	0	5,034
El Mirage..........................	1	0	0	0	0	0	0	0	0	1	0	32,837
Gilbert	1	0	0	0	0	0	0	1	0	0	0	225,232
Glendale...........................	2	3	1	1	0	0	0	2	0	3	2	234,006
Goodyear..........................	0	0	2	0	0	0	0	1		1	0	71,048
Maricopa	1	0	0	0	0	0	0	0	0	0	1	44,871
Mesa	1	1	0	0	0	0	0	2	0	0	0	456,155
Phoenix............................	40	12	14	14	1	0	0	25	21	35		1,502,139
Prescott	0	0	0	1	0	0	0	0	0	0	1	40,752
Scottsdale.........................	0	1	0	1	0	0	0	0	0	0	2	225,523
Tempe..............................	1	0	2	0	0	0	0	2	0	1	0	168,501
Tucson	13	6	6	1	0	0	0	8	8	6	4	525,486
Yuma	3	4	0	3	0	0	0	3	5	0	2	96,014
Universities and Colleges	2	0	1	0	0	0	0					
Northern Arizona University	0	0	1	0	0	0	0	0	0	0	1	25,991
University of Arizona......................	2	0	0	0	0	0	0	2	0	0	0	40,223
Metropolitan Counties	3	3	1	1	0	0	0					
Cochise............................	0	1	0	0	0	0	0	0	0	0	1	
Maricopa	1	1	0	0	0	0	0	0			2	
Pima	1	1	1	0	0	0	0	0	0	0	3	
Yuma	1	0	0	1	0	0	0	0	1	0	1	
ARKANSAS												
Total	17	0	8	2	0	0	0					
Cities	10	0	3	0	0	0	0					
Bentonville........................	1	0	0	0	0	0	0	0	0	1	0	39,132
Berryville..........................	1	0	0	0	0	0	0	0	0	1	0	5,417
Cabot	1	0	0	0	0	0	0	0	0	1	0	24,695
England	1	0	0	0	0	0	0	0	1	0	0	2,806
Fairfield Bay	1	0	0	0	0	0	0	0	0	1	0	2,295
Fort Smith.........................	1	0	1	0	0	0	0	0	0	0	2	87,821
Gurdon.............................	1	0	0	0	0	0	0	1	0	0	0	2,184
Marion..............................	0	0	1	0	0	0	0	0	0	1	0	12,258
North Little Rock	1	0	0	0	0	0	0	0	1	0	0	65,398
Pine Bluff.........................	0	0	1	0	0	0	0	1	0	0	0	46,399
Rogers..............................	1	0	0	0	0	0	0	0	1	0	0	59,787
Sherwood..........................	1	0	0	0	0	0	0	1	0	0	0	29,900
Universities and Colleges	0	0	1	0	0	0	0					
University of Arkansas, Pine Bluff	0	0	1	0	0	0	0	0	0	1	0	2,828
Metropolitan Counties	6	0	3	2	0	0	0					
Crawford...........................	2	0	2	0	0	0	0	0	2	1	1	
Faulkner...........................	1	0	0	1	0	0	0	0	1	0	1	
Lonoke	1	0	0	0	0	0	0	1	0	0	0	
Pulaski	1	0	1	1	0	0	0	1	0	1	1	
Sebastian	1	0	0	0	0	0	0	0	1	0	0	

Table 13. Hate Crime Incidents Per Bias Motivation and Quarter, by Selected State and Agency, 2013 –*Continued*

(Number.)

State/agency	Number of incidents per bias motivation							Number of incidents per quarter[1]				Population[2]
	Race	Religion	Sexual orientation	Ethnicity	Disability	Gender	Gender Identity	1st quarter	2nd quarter	3rd quarter	4th quarter	
ARKANSAS (cont.)												
Nonmetropolitan Counties..........	1	0	1	0	0	0	0					
Greene	1	0	0	0	0	0	0	0	0	1	0	
Pope	0	0	1	0	0	0	0	0	1	0	0	
CALIFORNIA												
Total	374	129	217	115	1	0	7					
Cities	291	117	166	87	1	0	6					
Adelanto............................	1	0	0	1	0	0	0	1	0	1	0	31,165
Agoura Hills........................	2	0	0	0	0	0	0	0	2	0	0	20,762
Alameda.............................	0	1	0	0	0	0	0	0	0	0	1	76,206
Alhambra............................	1	0	0	0	0	0	0	0	0	0	1	84,710
Antioch.............................	2	0	0	0	0	0	0	1	1	0	0	106,447
Arcadia.............................	1	0	0	0	0	0	0	1	0	0	0	57,855
Atascadero..........................	1	0	0	1	0	0	0	0	0	1	1	28,938
Atwater.............................	0	0	0	1	0	0	0	0	1	0	0	28,906
Auburn..............................	1	0	0	0	0	0	0	0	1	0	0	13,779
Azusa...............................	1	0	0	0	0	0	0	0	0	1	0	47,754
Bakersfield.........................	2	1	0	0	0	0	0	0	0	2	1	361,859
Baldwin Park........................	0	0	1	0	0	0	0	0	0	1	0	76,745
Banning.............................	0	0	0	1	0	0	0	0	0	1	0	30,503
Berkeley............................	7	1	4	1	0	0	0	6	2	4	1	116,217
Beverly Hills.......................	0	1	0	0	0	0	0	1	0	0	0	34,780
Brentwood[3]	4	0	0	0	0	0	0	0	1	2	1	54,301
Buena Park[3]	0	0	1	1	0	0	0	0	1	0	1	82,632
Burbank.............................	1	1	2	1	0	0	0	1	2	2	0	104,727
Calabasas...........................	0	2	0	0	0	0	0	1	0	0	1	24,114
Camarillo...........................	2	1	0	0	0	0	0	1	1	1	0	66,173
Campbell............................	1	0	0	0	0	0	0	0	1	0	0	40,549
Carlsbad............................	1	1	0	1	0	0	0	0	0	3	0	110,505
Carson..............................	1	0	0	0	0	0	0	0	0	0	1	93,415
Cerritos............................	3	0	0	0	0	0	0	1	0	0	2	49,816
Chico...............................	1	3	0	0	0	0	0	1	2	0	1	88,226
Chino...............................	2	2	2	3	0	0	0	2	2	3	2	80,704
Chula Vista.........................	3	0	1	0	0	0	0	0	3	0	1	255,073
Citrus Heights......................	1	0	0	0	0	0	0	0	1	0	0	85,337
Claremont...........................	1	1	1	0	0	0	0	2	0	0	1	35,623
Clearlake...........................	1	0	1	0	0	0	0	1	0	0	1	14,951
Clovis..............................	0	1	2	1	0	0	0	0	1	1	2	99,483
Colton..............................	1	0	0	0	0	0	0	0	0	0	1	53,403
Compton.............................	1	0	1	0	0	0	0	0	1	0	1	97,907
Concord.............................	1	0	0	0	0	0	0	0	1	0	0	125,464
Corcoran............................	1	0	0	0	0	0	0	0	0	1	0	23,290
Corona..............................	0	0	0	1	0	0	0	0	0	0	1	160,159
Coronado............................	0	1	0	0	0	0	0	1	0	0	0	23,183
Costa Mesa..........................	1	0	0	0	0	0	0	0	0	0	1	112,538
Covina..............................	0	2	1	0	0	0	0	0	3	0	0	48,524
Cupertino...........................	0	0	0	0	0	0	1	0	0	0	1	60,440
Cypress.............................	0	0	0	1	0	0	0	0	0	1	0	49,067
Daly City...........................	0	2	1	0	0	0	0	1	0	1	1	104,536
Dana Point..........................	0	1	0	0	0	0	0	0	1	0	0	34,262
Davis...............................	2	1	4	1	0	0	0	3	4	0	1	66,126
Duarte..............................	1	0	1	0	0	0	0	1	0	1	0	21,759
El Cajon............................	1	0	0	1	0	0	0	0	1	0	1	102,012
El Cerrito..........................	0	2	1	4	0	0	0	3	1	2	1	24,184
Elk Grove...........................	1	0	0	0	0	0	0	0	0	0	1	160,925
El Monte............................	5	0	0	0	0	0	0	0	3	0	2	115,591
Emeryville..........................	1	0	0	0	0	0	0	0	1	0	0	10,415
Encinitas...........................	2	1	0	1	0	0	0	2	1	1	0	61,433
Escondido...........................	4	1	1	2	0	0	0	2	2	3	1	148,650
Eureka..............................	1	0	1	0	0	0	0	1	1	0	0	26,881
Fairfield...........................	2	0	0	1	0	0	0	1	0	0	2	108,425
Fontana.............................	1	0	0	0	0	0	0	0	1	0	0	203,427
Foster City.........................	1	0	0	0	0	0	0	1	0	0	0	32,652
Fresno..............................	4	0	3	2	0	0	1	3	3	1	3	508,876
Fullerton...........................	0	1	1	0	0	0	0	1	0	0	1	139,676
Galt................................	1	0	0	0	0	0	0	0	0	1	0	24,553
Garden Grove........................	1	0	0	3	0	0	0	0	1	2	1	175,469
Gilroy..............................	0	0	2	0	0	0	0	0	1	1	0	51,240
Glendale............................	1	0	0	0	0	0	0	0	0	1	0	195,366

State/agency	Race	Religion	Sexual orientation	Ethnicity	Disability	Gender	Gender Identity	1st quarter	2nd quarter	3rd quarter	4th quarter	Population[2]
CALIFORNIA (cont.)												
Glendora	1	0	0	0	0	0	0	1	0	0	0	50,893
Gridley	0	0	0	1	0	0	0	1	0	0	0	6,563
Hanford	1	0	1	0	0	0	0	1	0	1	0	54,425
Hawaiian Gardens	4	0	0	0	0	0	0	2	1	1	0	14,437
Hayward	0	1	1	0	0	0	0	0	2	0	0	150,955
Healdsburg	1	0	0	0	0	0	0	1	0	0	0	11,483
Hercules	0	0	0	1	0	0	0	0	0	1	0	24,831
Holtville	0	1	0	0	0	0	0	0	0	0	1	6,022
Huntington Beach	0	0	0	0	0	0	1	0	1	0	0	195,842
Imperial Beach	1	0	1	1	0	0	0	1	1	1	0	26,998
Irvine	0	1	0	0	0	0	0	0	1	0	0	235,830
Jurupa Valley	0	1	0	0	0	0	0	0	0	1	0	98,090
Laguna Beach	0	0	1	0	0	0	0	0	1	0	0	23,313
La Habra	0	1	0	0	0	0	0	0	0	1	0	61,740
Lake Elsinore	0	2	0	0	0	0	0	0	0	2	0	56,232
Lake Forest	2	0	0	0	0	0	0	1	0	0	1	79,336
Lakewood	2	0	0	0	0	0	0	0	1	0	1	81,086
La Mirada	1	2	0	0	0	0	0	1	2	0	0	49,150
Lancaster	3	1	0	1	0	0	0	1	2	1	1	159,792
La Quinta	1	1	0	0	0	0	0	1	0	1	0	39,150
Lemon Grove	1	0	1	0	0	0	0	1	1	0	0	26,156
Lemoore	1	0	0	0	0	0	0	1	0	0	0	24,802
Livermore	0	0	0	1	0	0	0	0	0	1	0	84,350
Lodi	0	0	0	2	0	0	0	0	1	1	0	63,639
Lomita	0	0	0	1	0	0	0	0	1	0	0	20,622
Long Beach	3	1	1	0	0	0	0	3	0	1	1	469,665
Los Alamitos	1	0	0	0	0	0	0	1	0	0	0	11,735
Los Angeles	41	29	33	9	0	0	2	21	40	25	28	3,878,725
Los Gatos	2	0	0	0	0	0	0	0	0	1	1	30,351
Lynwood	1	0	0	0	0	0	0	0	0	0	1	71,077
Malibu	1	0	0	0	0	0	0	0	0	1	0	12,891
Manhattan Beach	1	0	0	0	0	0	0	0	0	0	1	35,930
Manteca	1	1	1	0	0	0	0	1	1	0	1	72,261
Milpitas	1	0	0	0	0	0	0	1	0	0	0	69,522
Modesto	0	1	1	1	0	0	0	2	0	1	0	204,252
Montclair	2	0	0	0	0	0	0	1	0	1	0	37,785
Monterey	1	0	1	0	0	0	0	0	0	1	1	29,338
Moreno Valley	1	0	0	0	0	0	0	0	0	0	1	201,284
Morgan Hill	0	1	0	0	0	0	0	0	0	0	1	39,907
Murrieta[3]	3	1	1	0	0	0	0	2	2	1	0	107,768
National City	2	0	1	0	0	0	0	1	0	1	1	59,637
Newark	2	0	0	1	0	0	0	1	1	0	1	43,950
Newport Beach	0	2	1	0	0	0	0	0	0	2	1	87,639
Norwalk	4	1	0	0	0	0	0	0	4	0	1	106,518
Oakland	4	1	4	2	0	0	0	2	4	3	2	403,887
Oceanside	5	1	1	1	0	0	0	2	4	2	0	172,525
Ontario	1	0	0	0	0	0	0	0	1	0	0	168,144
Orange	1	1	1	0	0	0	0	0	1	2	0	140,304
Oroville	1	0	1	0	0	0	0	0	0	1	1	15,581
Oxnard	0	0	1	0	0	0	0	0	0	0	1	202,594
Pacifica	0	1	0	0	0	0	0	0	0	1	0	38,494
Pacific Grove	0	1	0	0	0	0	0	1	0	0	0	15,518
Palmdale	4	1	3	0	0	0	0	3	1	3	1	156,522
Palm Springs	3	1	4	0	0	0	0	4	1	2	1	46,282
Palo Alto	0	0	0	1	0	0	0	1	0	0	0	66,964
Paramount	2	0	0	0	0	0	0	0	1	0	1	54,868
Pasadena	1	1	0	1	0	0	0	0	0	1	2	139,003
Pico Rivera	0	0	1	1	0	0	0	1	1	0	0	63,710
Pinole	0	0	0	1	0	0	0	0	0	1	0	18,848
Placentia	1	0	0	0	0	0	0	0	0	1	0	52,002
Rancho Cordova	1	0	0	0	0	0	0	1	0	0	0	67,634
Rancho Palos Verdes	0	1	0	0	0	0	0	0	0	0	1	42,542
Red Bluff	2	0	1	0	0	0	0	0	1	0	2	14,170
Redding	5	0	1	2	0	0	0	2	2	3	1	91,035
Redlands	0	2	1	0	0	0	0	0	1	0	2	70,282
Redondo Beach	2	0	1	2	0	0	0	1	2	1	1	67,993
Redwood City	0	1	0	0	0	0	0	1	0	0	0	79,707
Richmond	1	0	2	0	0	0	0	0	0	2	1	107,341
Ridgecrest	0	0	1	0	0	0	0	0	1	0	0	28,537
Riverside	11	1	1	2	0	0	1	7	4	0	5	316,423
Rohnert Park	0	0	0	3	0	0	0	2	0	0	1	41,326

(Number.)

State/agency	Race	Religion	Sexual orientation	Ethnicity	Disability	Gender	Gender Identity	1st quarter	2nd quarter	3rd quarter	4th quarter	Population[2]
	Race	Religion	Sexual orientation	Ethnicity	Disability	Gender	Gender Identity	Number of incidents per quarter[1]				
CALIFORNIA (cont.)												
Rolling Hills Estates	1	0	0	0	0	0	0	0	0	0	1	8,229
Roseville	0	0	1	0	0	0	0	0	1	0	0	126,236
Sacramento	6	2	6	2	0	0	0	2	5	6	3	478,182
Salinas	0	0	1	1	0	0	0	0	0	0	2	155,742
San Bernardino	2	0	0	1	0	0	0	0	0	2	1	214,322
San Diego	18	12	12	1	0	0	0	7	10	17	9	1,349,306
San Dimas	1	0	0	0	0	0	0	1	0	0	0	33,854
San Francisco	7	3	13	1	0	0	0	4	8	8	4	833,863
San Jose	6	2	6	1	0	0	0	7	1	2	5	992,143
San Leandro	3	0	1	1	0	0	0	2	1	2	0	87,490
San Luis Obispo	1	0	1	0	0	0	0	0	0	2	0	46,095
San Mateo	0	0	1	0	0	0	0	0	0	1	0	100,440
Santa Ana	0	0	1	0	0	0	0	0	0	1	0	332,848
Santa Barbara	1	0	1	0	0	0	0	0	0	1	1	90,006
Santa Clara	0	0	2	0	0	0	0	0	0	2	0	120,150
Santa Clarita	2	0	3	0	0	0	0	2	1	1	1	204,951
Santa Cruz	1	0	1	0	0	0	0	1	0	0	1	62,517
Santa Maria	0	0	1	0	0	0	0	0	0	0	1	102,051
Santa Rosa	0	1	2	0	0	0	0	2	1	0	0	171,564
Santee	1	0	1	1	0	0	0	2	0	1	0	55,924
Saratoga	1	0	0	0	0	0	0	0	1	0	0	30,897
Simi Valley	1	1	0	1	0	0	0	1	0	2	0	126,215
Sonora	1	0	0	0	0	0	0	0	0	1	0	4,774
South Gate	0	1	1	0	0	0	0	1	0	1	0	95,591
South Lake Tahoe	0	0	0	1	0	0	0	0	0	1	0	21,243
Stanton	0	0	1	0	0	0	0	0	1	0	0	39,128
Stockton	1	0	1	0	0	0	0	1	0	0	1	299,796
Sunnyvale	1	0	0	0	0	0	0	0	1	0	0	148,160
Taft	0	0	1	0	0	0	0	1	0	0	0	8,839
Tehachapi	1	0	0	1	0	0	0	1	0	1	0	13,607
Temecula	1	0	0	0	0	0	0	0	0	1	0	106,680
Temple City	0	1	0	0	0	0	0	0	0	0	1	36,269
Thousand Oaks	0	1	0	0	0	0	0	0	0	0	1	128,884
Torrance	1	0	0	1	0	0	0	0	0	2	0	147,534
Tracy	4	0	1	1	0	0	0	2	1	3	0	85,174
Turlock	1	0	0	0	0	0	0	0	0	0	1	70,075
Union City	1	0	0	4	0	0	0	1	3	1	0	72,480
Vallejo	1	0	0	1	0	0	0	0	2	0	0	118,336
Ventura	0	1	0	0	0	0	0	1	0	0	0	108,204
Vernon	1	0	0	0	0	0	0	0	1	0	0	115
Victorville	6	0	1	0	0	0	0	2	1	2	2	121,699
Visalia	1	0	1	0	0	0	0	1	1	0	0	127,824
Vista	1	0	1	0	0	0	0	0	1	0	1	96,712
Walnut Creek	1	0	0	0	0	0	0	0	0	0	1	66,149
West Covina	6	0	0	0	0	0	0	3	1	1	1	107,867
West Hollywood	1	0	2	2	0	0	0	1	1	3	0	34,902
Westlake Village	0	2	0	0	0	0	0	2	0	0	0	8,440
Westminster	1	1	1	1	1	0	0	1	1	1	2	91,885
Yorba Linda	1	0	0	0	0	0	0	0	0	0	1	67,492
Yuba City	0	0	0	1	0	0	0	0	0	1	0	65,133
Yucca Valley	1	0	0	0	0	0	0	0	0	1	0	21,214
Universities and Colleges	13	4	10	4	0	0	0					
California State Polytechnic University												
Pomona	0	0	0	1	0	0	0	1	0	0	0	22,156
San Luis Obispo	0	0	1	0	0	0	0	1	0	0	0	18,679
California State University												
Dominguez Hills	1	0	1	0	0	0	0	1	0	1	0	13,933
Long Beach	1	0	0	0	0	0	0	0	1	0	0	36,279
San Bernardino	3	0	0	0	0	0	0	2	0	1	0	18,234
San Jose	2	0	1	1	0	0	0	1	1	1	1	30,448
San Marcos	0	0	1	0	0	0	0	1	0	0	0	10,610
Stanislaus	0	0	1	0	0	0	0	0	0	0	1	8,882
Humboldt State University	0	0	1	0	0	0	0	0	1	0	0	8,116
Marin Community College	0	1	1	0	0	0	0	2	0	0	0	7,058
University of California												
Berkeley	3	2	1	1	0	0	0	1	1	4	1	35,893
Davis	1	0	1	1	0	0	0	0	3	0	0	32,354
Riverside	2	0	0	0	0	0	0	0	1	1	0	20,947
San Diego	0	1	0	0	0	0	0	0	1	0	0	28,294

Table 13. Hate Crime Incidents Per Bias Motivation and Quarter, by Selected State and Agency, 2013–*Continued*

(Number.)

State/agency	\multicolumn{7}{c}{Number of incidents per bias motivation}							\multicolumn{4}{c}{Number of incidents per quarter[1]}				Population[2]
	Race	Religion	Sexual orientation	Ethnicity	Disability	Gender	Gender Identity	1st quarter	2nd quarter	3rd quarter	4th quarter	
CALIFORNIA (cont.)												
Santa Cruz	0	0	1	0	0	0	0	1	0	0	0	17,404
Metropolitan Counties	56	7	36	20	0	0	1					
El Dorado	0	0	1	1	0	0	0	1	0	0	1	
Kern	1	0	1	3	0	0	0	1	3	0	1	
Kings	0	0	1	0	0	0	0	1	0	0	0	
Los Angeles	20	3	17	10	0	0	0	14	10	11	15	
Orange	1	0	0	1	0	0	0	1	0	0	1	
Riverside	3	0	0	0	0	0	0	0	1	1	1	
Sacramento	9	1	3	0	0	0	0	2	3	3	5	
San Bernardino	2	0	1	2	0	0	1	1	0	3	2	
San Diego	6	2	3	2	0	0	0	3	2	3	5	
San Luis Obispo	3	0	1	0	0	0	0	0	0	1	3	
San Mateo	0	0	1	0	0	0	0	0	1	0	0	
Santa Barbara	2	0	2	0	0	0	0	1	2	1	0	
Santa Clara	1	0	1	0	0	0	0	0	2	0	0	
Santa Cruz	1	0	1	1	0	0	0	2	0	1	0	
Shasta	4	0	2	0	0	0	0	3	1	2	0	
Sonoma	1	0	1	0	0	0	0	0	0	2	0	
Ventura	1	1	0	0	0	0	0	0	0	2	0	
Yuba	1	0	0	0	0	0	0	0	0	1	0	
Nonmetropolitan Counties	1	0	1	3	0	0	0					
Alpine	1	0	0	0	0	0	0	1	0	0	0	
Amador	0	0	1	0	0	0	0	0	0	1	0	
Calaveras	0	0	0	1	0	0	0	0	0	1	0	
Lake	0	0	0	2	0	0	0	2	0	0	0	
State Police Agencies	1	0	0	0	0	0	0					
Highway Patrol, Plumas County	1	0	0	0	0	0	0	1	0	0	0	
Other Agencies	12	1	4	1	0	0	0					
Department of Parks and Recreation, Tehachapi District	1	0	0	0	0	0	0	0	0	1	0	
Fontana Unified School District	1	0	0	0	0	0	0	0	0	0	1	
Los Angeles Transportation Services Bureau	2	1	3	0	0	0	0	3	3	0	0	
Port of San Diego Harbor	2	0	0	1	0	0	0	0	1	1	1	
San Francisco Bay Area Rapid Transit												
Alameda County	4	0	0	0	0	0	0	0	2	2	0	
Contra Costa County	1	0	0	0	0	0	0	1	0	0	0	
San Francisco County	1	0	1	0	0	0	0	2	0	0	0	
COLORADO												
Total	54	18	40	15	1	0	0					
Cities	38	14	32	12	1	0	0					
Arvada	2	0	0	0	0	0	0	0	0	1	1	110,792
Aurora	4	0	1	1	0	0	0	1	3	0	2	343,484
Castle Rock	0	0	0	2	0	0	0	0	0	0	2	52,309
Centennial	3	2	1	0	0	0	0	2	2	1	1	104,771
Colorado Springs	3	1	2	1	0	0	0	2	4	1	0	436,108
Commerce City	0	1	0	0	0	0	0	0	0	1	0	49,200
Denver	9	5	15	1	0	0	0	3	13	9	5	648,981
Dillon	0	0	0	1	0	0	0	0	1	0	0	906
Durango	0	0	2	0	0	0	0	1	0	1	0	17,303
Englewood	1	0	0	0	1	0	0	0	0	0	2	31,454
Erie	0	1	0	0	0	0	0	1	0	0	0	19,627
Fountain	2	0	1	0	0	0	0	2	1	0	0	27,163
Glendale	0	1	0	0	0	0	0	1	0	0	0	4,502
Glenwood Springs	0	0	1	0	0	0	0	0	0	1	0	9,715
Golden	0	0	0	1	0	0	0	0	0	0	1	19,334
Grand Junction	4	0	1	0	0	0	0	1	1	2	1	60,167
Greeley	0	0	1	0	0	0	0	0	0	0	1	96,111
Greenwood Village	1	0	0	0	0	0	0	0	1	0	0	14,614
Lafayette	2	0	0	1	0	0	0	0	1	2	0	26,145
Lakewood	1	1	1	1	0	0	0	1	1	0	2	146,298
Littleton	1	0	0	0	0	0	0	1	0	0	0	44,375
Lone Tree	0	0	1	0	0	0	0	0	0	1	0	12,056
Longmont	1	0	1	1	0	0	0	2	1	0	0	89,434

(Number.)

State/agency	Number of incidents per bias motivation							Number of incidents per quarter[1]				Population[2]
	Race	Religion	Sexual orientation	Ethnicity	Disability	Gender	Gender Identity	1st quarter	2nd quarter	3rd quarter	4th quarter	
COLORADO (cont.)												
Loveland	1	0	0	0	0	0	0	0	1	0	0	71,325
Monument	0	1	0	0	0	0	0	0	0	1	0	5,800
Pueblo	2	0	0	0	0	0	0	0	0	1	1	108,062
Rifle	0	0	0	1	0	0	0	1	0	0	0	9,306
Snowmass Village	1	0	0	0	0	0	0	1	0	0	0	2,851
Steamboat Springs	0	0	0	1	0	0	0	0	0	1	0	12,008
Telluride	0	0	1	0	0	0	0	0	0	1	0	2,313
Thornton	0	1	2	0	0	0	0	0	0	1	2	125,775
Westminster	0	0	1	0	0	0	0	1	0	0	0	110,093
Universities and Colleges	1	0	2	0	0	0	0					
Colorado State University, Fort Collins	1	0	0	0	0	0	0	0	0	0	1	30,659
University of Colorado, Boulder	0	0	2	0	0	0	0	0	0	0	2	31,945
Metropolitan Counties	10	2	6	2	0	0	0					
Adams	1	0	1	1	0	0	0	1	0	2	0	
Arapahoe	4	2	2	0	0	0	0	6	0	2	0	
El Paso	2	0	0	0	0	0	0	0	0	1	1	
Larimer	0	0	2	0	0	0	0	0	0	0	2	
Mesa	0	0	0	1	0	0	0	1	0	0	0	
Park	1	0	0	0	0	0	0	0	1	0	0	
Pueblo	1	0	0	0	0	0	0	0	0	1	0	
Weld	1	0	1	0	0	0	0	1	0	1	0	
Nonmetropolitan Counties	4	2	0	1	0	0	0					
Cheyenne	0	0	0	1	0	0	0	1	0	0	0	
Garfield	1	1	0	0	0	0	0	0	1	0	1	
Logan	1	1	0	0	0	0	0	0	0	1	1	
Montezuma	1	0	0	0	0	0	0	1	0	0	0	
Pitkin	1	0	0	0	0	0	0	0	0	0	1	
State Police Agencies	1	0	0	0	0	0	0					
Colorado State Patrol	1	0	0	0	0			0	0	0	1	
CONNECTICUT												
Total	72	20	26	24	3	0	0					
Cities	66	18	21	21	3	0	0					
Bethel	1	0	0	0	0	0	0	1	0	0	0	19,338
Bridgeport	5	1	2	3	0	0	0	2	4	3	2	147,076
Canton	0	0	1	0	0	0	0	0	0	1	0	10,369
Danbury	0	1	1	1	0	0	0		2		1	83,363
Derby	1	0	0	0	0	0	0	0	0	0	1	12,806
East Hampton	0	2	0	0	0	0	0	0	1	0	1	12,934
East Hartford	0	0	1	0	0	0	0	0	1	0	0	51,275
East Windsor	1	0	0	0	0	0	0	0	0	1	0	11,455
Enfield	1	0	0	0	0	0	0			1		44,661
Glastonbury	1	0	0	0	0	0	0	1	0	0	0	34,782
Groton	1	1	0	0	0	0	0	0	1	1	0	9,359
Groton Town	1	0	0	0	1	0	0	0	1	1		29,946
Guilford	0	1	0	0	0	0	0				1	22,409
Hamden	0	1	0	0	0	0	0	0	1	0	0	60,829
Hartford	1	1	2	0	0	0	0	2	1	1	0	124,927
Manchester	7	2	0	1	0	0	0	2	2	4	2	58,304
Meriden	2	0	1	0	0	0	0	1	1		1	60,558
Middletown	5	0	1	1	0	0	0	0	3	1	3	47,221
Milford	4	1	0	0	0	0	0		2	4		53,041
New Britain	0	0	1	0	0	0	0	1				73,134
New Haven	5	0	4	1	0	0	0	3	2	4	1	131,071
Newington	1	2	0	0	0	0	0			1	2	30,612
New London	1	0	2	0	0	0	0	3	0	0	0	27,738
New Milford	0	0	0	1	0	0	0	0	1	0	0	27,743
North Branford	1	0	0	1	0	0	0	2	0	0	0	14,369
Norwalk	1	0	1	1	0	0	0	0	0	3	0	87,590
Norwich	1	0	0	0	0	0	0				1	40,485
Old Saybrook	3	0	0	0	0	0	0	0	1	0	2	10,239
Plainville	0	0	1	0	0	0	0				1	17,850
Plymouth	0	1	1	0	0	0	0	0	1	1	0	12,043
Southington	1	0	0	6	0	0	0	3	2	2	0	43,542
South Windsor	0	1	0	0	0	0	0			1		25,871

Table 13. Hate Crime Incidents Per Bias Motivation and Quarter, by Selected State and Agency, 2013–*Continued*

(Number.)

State/agency	Number of incidents per bias motivation							Number of incidents per quarter[1]				Population[2]
	Race	Religion	Sexual orientation	Ethnicity	Disability	Gender	Gender Identity	1st quarter	2nd quarter	3rd quarter	4th quarter	
CONNECTICUT (cont.)												
Stamford	1	2	2	2	1	0	0	2	2	1	3	125,876
Stratford	1	1	0	1	0	0	0	0	1	1	1	52,285
Suffield	1	0	0	0	0	0	0	0	0	1	0	15,908
Torrington	5	0	0	0	0	0	0	1	3	1	0	35,634
Wallingford	2	0	0	2	0	0	0	1	1	2	0	45,185
Waterbury	6	0	0	0	0	0	0	3	1	2	0	109,763
West Haven	1	0	0	0	0	0	0			1		55,349
Willimantic	1	0	0	0	0	0	0	1	0	0	0	17,839
Winchester	2	0	0	0	0	0	0	2	0	0	0	11,019
Windsor Locks	0	0	0	0	1	0	0	0	1	0	0	12,560
Wolcott	1	0	0	0	0	0	0	0	1	0	0	16,735
Universities and Colleges	5	1	2	1	0	0	0					
Central Connecticut State University	0	0	1	0	0	0	0	0	0	0	1	12,091
Southern Connecticut State University	2	0	0	0	0	0	0	1	1	0	0	11,117
University of Connecticut, Storrs, Avery Point, and Hartford[4]	3	1	0	1	0	0	0	2	1	1	1	
Yale University	0	0	1	0	0	0	0				1	11,906
State Police Agencies	1	1	3	2	0	0	0					
Connecticut State Police	1	1	3	2	0	0	0	2	1	4	0	
DELAWARE												
Total	9	0	3	0	0	0	0					
Cities	5	0	2	0	0	0	0					
Dover	0	0	1	0	0	0	0	0	0	1	0	37,402
Milford	1	0	1	0	0	0	0	0	2	0	0	9,872
Milton	1	0	0	0	0	0	0	1	0	0	0	2,687
New Castle	1	0	0	0	0	0	0	0	0	1	0	5,388
Seaford	1	0	0	0	0	0	0	0	0	1	0	7,241
Smyrna	1	0	0	0	0	0	0	1	0	0	0	10,900
Universities and Colleges	1	0	0	0	0	0	0					
Delaware State University	1	0	0	0	0	0	0	0	1	0	0	4,324
Metropolitan Counties	1	0	0	0	0	0	0					
New Castle County Police Department	1	0	0	0	0	0	0	0	1	0	0	
State Police Agencies	2	0	1	0	0	0	0					
Kent County	1	0	0	0	0	0	0	1	0	0	0	
New Castle County	1	0	0	0	0	0	0	0	1	0	0	
Sussex County	0	0	1	0	0	0	0	0	0	1	0	
DISTRICT OF COLUMBIA												
Total	18	6	32	4	0	0	12					
Cities	18	6	31	3	0	0	12					
Washington	18	6	31	3	0	0	12	19	21	20	10	646,449
Other Agencies	0	0	1	1	0	0	0					
Metro Transit Police	0	0	1	1	0	0	0	0	0	2	0	
FLORIDA												
Total	40	8	20	8	0	0	0					
Cities	24	7	14	4	0	0	0					
Delray Beach	1	0	0	0	0	0	0	0	1	0	0	62,887
Gainesville	2	0	1	0	0	0	0	0	0	0	3	126,589
Hallandale	2	0	1	0	0	0	0	0	1	0	2	38,710
Homestead	2	0	1	0	0	0	0	2	1	0	0	64,024
Jacksonville	5	0	0	0	0	0	0	3	1	1	0	845,745
Jupiter	1	0	1	0	0	0	0	1	1	0	0	57,826
Lake Alfred	0	0	0	1	0	0	0	0	1	0	0	5,148
Largo	0	0	1	0	0	0	0	0	1	0	0	77,913
Melbourne	1	1	0	0	0	0	0	1	0	0	1	77,277
Miramar	0	0	1	0	0	0	0	0	1	0	0	130,926
North Miami	2	1	3	0	0	0	0	3	1	0	2	61,120
North Miami Beach	0	0	1	0	0	0	0	1	0	0	0	43,417

(Number.)

State/agency	Race	Religion	Sexual orientation	Ethnicity	Disability	Gender	Gender Identity	1st quarter	2nd quarter	3rd quarter	4th quarter	Population[2]
FLORIDA (cont.)												
North Port	0	0	1	0	0	0	0	0	1	0	0	58,699
Orlando	1	0	1	0	0	0	0	2	0	0	0	253,238
Palm Bay	0	1	0	1	0	0	0	0	0	0	2	104,391
Panama City	2	0	0	0	0	0	0	0	2	0	0	36,358
Pembroke Pines	0	0	0	1	0	0	0	0	0	1	0	162,064
Pensacola	0	0	1	0	0	0	0	0	1	0	0	52,454
Pompano Beach	1	1	0	1	0	0	0	0	0	0	3	103,971
Port St. Lucie	1	0	0	0	0	0	0	1	0	0	0	169,877
Sanford	0	0	1	0	0	0	0	0	0	1	0	54,972
St. Petersburg	0	1	0	0	0	0	0	0	1	0	0	247,084
Sunrise	1	0	0	0	0	0	0	1	0	0	0	90,274
Tallahassee	1	0	0	0	0	0	0	0	1	0	0	188,714
Venice	0	2	0	0	0	0	0	2	0	0	0	21,151
Weston	1	0	0	0	0	0	0	0	0	0	1	68,369
Metropolitan Counties	16	1	6	4	0	0	0					
Alachua	0	0	0	1	0	0	0	1	0	0	0	
Brevard	0	0	1	0	0	0	0	0	0	1	0	
Charlotte	1	0	0	0	0	0	0	0	0	0	1	
Clay	1	0	0	0	0	0	0	0	0	0	1	
Collier	1	0	0	0	0	0	0	0	0	0	1	
Flagler	2	0	0	0	0	0	0	2	0	0	0	
Hillsborough	0	0	0	1	0	0	0	0	1	0	0	
Lake	1	0	0	0	0	0	0	0	1	0	0	
Manatee	1	0	0	0	0	0	0	0	0	1	0	
Orange	6	0	4	0	0	0	0	6	2	0	2	
Osceola	0	0	0	2	0	0	0	1	0	1	0	
Palm Beach	0	1	0	0	0	0	0	1	0	0	0	
Pasco	1	0	0	0	0	0	0	1	0	0	0	
Santa Rosa	0	0	1	0	0	0	0	1	0	0	0	
Volusia	2	0	0	0	0	0	0	0	1	0	1	
GEORGIA												
Total	29	5	17	5	1	0	0					
Cities	7	1	12	2	1	0	0					
Atlanta	5	1	12	2	1	0	0	8	11	2	0	451,020
Conyers	1	0	0	0	0	0	0	0	0	0	1	15,465
Villa Rica	1	0	0	0	0	0	0	1	0	0	0	14,307
Universities and Colleges	2	1	3	0	0	0	0					
Kennesaw State University	0	0	2	0	0	0	0	1	0	0	1	24,604
University of Georgia	2	1	1	0	0	0	0	1	0	0	3	34,519
Metropolitan Counties	20	3	2	3	0	0	0					
Cobb County Police Department	19	3	2	3	0	0	0	1	12	8	6	
Henry County Police Department	1	0	0	0	0	0	0	0	1	0	0	
IDAHO												
Total	19	6	4	3	0	0	0					
Cities	18	4	4	2	0	0	0					
Boise	8	1	4	0	0	0	0	2	0	7	4	214,330
Caldwell	1	0	0	0	0	0	0	1	0	0	0	48,069
Chubbuck	0	3	0	0	0	0	0	0	0	0	3	14,224
Coeur d'Alene	2	0	0	0	0	0	0	0	1	0	1	46,023
Hailey	0	0	0	1	0	0	0	0	0	1	0	7,915
Montpelier	1	0	0	0	0	0	0	0	0	1	0	2,520
Nampa	3	0	0	1	0	0	0	2	1	1	0	84,634
Payette	2	0	0	0	0	0	0	1	0	0	1	7,442
Twin Falls	1	0	0	0	0	0	0	0	1	0	0	45,378
Metropolitan Counties	0	1	0	1	0	0	0					
Ada	0	1	0	1	0	0	0	0	1	0	1	
Nonmetropolitan Counties	1	1	0	0	0	0	0					
Cassia	0	1	0	0	0	0	0	1	0	0	0	
Shoshone	1	0	0	0	0	0	0	0	0	1	0	
ILLINOIS												
Total	61	7	29	8	0	0	0					

State/agency	Number of incidents per bias motivation							Number of incidents per quarter[1]				Population[2]
	Race	Religion	Sexual orientation	Ethnicity	Disability	Gender	Gender Identity	1st quarter	2nd quarter	3rd quarter	4th quarter	
ILLINOIS (cont.)												
Cities	48	7	27	6	0	0	0					
Aurora	0	0	1	0	0	0	0	0	0	1	0	200,551
Bartlett	0	1	0	1	0	0	0	0	0	1	1	41,733
Berwyn	1	0	0	0	0	0	0	0	1	0	0	56,838
Carol Stream	0	1	0	0	0	0	0	1	0	0	0	40,376
Champaign	1	0	0	0	0	0	0	0	1	0	0	82,966
Chester	1	0	0	0	0	0	0	0	0	1	0	8,448
Chicago	22	2	18	3	0	0	0	11	10	15	9	2,720,554
Crystal Lake	0	1	0	0	0	0	0	0	0	1	0	40,383
De Kalb	1	0	0	0	0	0	0	0	0	1	0	43,765
Dixon	0	0	1	0	0	0	0	0	0	0	1	15,304
Harvey	1	0	0	0	0	0	0	0	0	0	1	25,408
Irving	1	0	0	0	0	0	0	0	1	0	0	485
La Grange	0	1	0	0	0	0	0	0	1	0	0	15,718
Mokena	1	0	0	0	0	0	0	0	1	0	0	19,130
Moline	1	0	0	0	0	0	0	0	0	1	0	43,172
Morton	0	0	1	0	0	0	0	0	0	1	0	16,462
Normal	0	0	1	0	0	0	0	0	0	0	1	54,241
Pekin	2	0	0	0	0	0	0	1	1	0	0	34,085
Peoria	3	0	2	0	0	0	0	2	1	1	1	115,953
Quincy	1	0	0	0	0	0	0	0	0	0	1	40,841
Rockford	2	1	1	0	0	0	0	0	2	2	0	150,209
Roscoe	1	0	0	0	0	0	0	0	1	0	0	10,700
Skokie	2	0	0	1	0	0	0	0	2	0	1	65,155
Springfield	5	0	0	0	0	0	0	0	2	2	1	117,351
St. Charles	0	0	1	1	0	0	0	1	1	0	0	33,433
Sterling	0	0	1	0	0	0	0	1	0	0	0	15,183
Urbana	2	0	0	0	0	0	0	0	0	1	1	41,598
Universities and Colleges	4	0	0	0	0	0	0					
Northwestern University, Evanston	3	0	0	0	0	0	0	1	0	0	2	21,215
University of Illinois, Springfield	1	0	0	0	0	0	0	0	1	0	0	5,048
Metropolitan Counties	8	0	1	2	0	0	0					
Cook	0	0	0	1	0	0	0	0	1	0	0	
Jackson	1	0	0	0	0	0	0	1	0	0	0	
Lake	1	0	0	1	0	0	0	0	0	2	0	
McLean	1	0	0	0	0	0	0	0	0	0	1	
Peoria	2	0	0	0	0	0	0	0	0	0	2	
Sangamon	1	0	1	0	0	0	0	0	0	1	1	
Will	2	0	0	0	0	0	0	0	0	2	0	
Nonmetropolitan Counties	1	0	1	0	0	0	0					
Cumberland	0	0	1	0	0	0	0	0	1	0	0	
Douglas	1	0	0	0	0	0	0	0	0	1	0	
INDIANA												
Total	49	3	13	9	1	0	0					
Cities	41	0	12	8	0	0	0					
Bloomington	8	0	2	0	0	0	0	1	5	3	1	82,415
Fort Wayne	1	0	0	0	0	0	0	0	1	0	0	254,820
Franklin	1	0	0	0	0	0	0	0	0	0	1	24,034
Goshen	0	0	1	0	0	0	0	1		0	0	32,195
Indianapolis	29	0	6	8	0	0	0	8	15	16	4	850,220
Mishawaka	0	0	2	0	0	0	0		1	1		47,967
South Bend	2	0	1	0	0	0	0	1		2		100,711
Universities and Colleges	2	1	1	0	0	0	0					
Ball State University	0	1	0	0	0	0	0	0	1	0	0	21,053
Purdue University	2	0	1	0	0	0	0	1	1	1		40,393
Metropolitan Counties	2	1	0	0	1	0	0					
Elkhart	2	1	0	0	1	0	0	0		3	1	
	4	1	0	1	0	0	0					
State Police Agencies	4	1	0	1	0	0	0					
Henry County	1	1	0	0	0	0	0	2				
Knox County	1	0	0	0	0	0	0				1	
Lake County	1	0	0	0	0	0	0	1				
Monroe County	0	0	0	1	0	0	0		1			

Table 13. Hate Crime Incidents Per Bias Motivation and Quarter, by Selected State and Agency, 2013–*Continued*

(Number.)

State/agency	Number of incidents per bias motivation							Number of incidents per quarter[1]				Population[2]
	Race	Religion	Sexual orientation	Ethnicity	Disability	Gender	Gender Identity	1st quarter	2nd quarter	3rd quarter	4th quarter	
INDIANA (cont.)												
Perry County....................................	1	0	0	0	0	0	0	1				
IOWA												
Total	5	1	3	1	0	0	0					
Cities	2	1	2	1	0	0	0					
Altoona..	0	0	1	0	0	0	0	0	0	1	0	15,683
Ames..	1	0	0	1	0	0	0	0	0	1	1	61,193
Grinnell..	0	0	1	0	0	0	0	0	0	0	1	9,090
Indianola..	0	1	0	0	0	0	0	0	1	0	0	14,993
Waterloo..	1	0	0	0	0	0	0	0	0	0	1	68,255
Universities and Colleges	0	0	1	0	0	0	0					
Iowa State University........................	0	0	1	0	0	0	0	0	1	0	0	30,748
Metropolitan Counties	2	0	0	0	0	0	0					
Mills...	1	0	0	0	0	0	0	0	1	0	0	
Scott..	1	0	0	0	0	0	0	0	0	1	0	
Nonmetropolitan Counties..........	1	0	0	0	0	0	0					
Ida...	1	0	0	0	0	0	0	0	1	0	0	
KANSAS												
Total	38	6	13	5	2	0	0					
Cities	36	5	10	3	1	0	0					
Andover..	0	1	1	0	0	0	0	0	1	1	0	12,188
Arkansas City....................................	2	0	0	0	0	0	0	0	1	0	1	12,322
Belleville...	1	0	0	0	0	0	0	1	0	0	0	1,928
Cheney..	1	0	0	0	0	0	0	0	0	0	1	2,127
Dodge City	1	0	0	0	0	0	0	0	0	1	0	28,265
Gardner..	0	1	0	0	0	0	0	0	1	0	0	20,708
Hays	1	0	1	0	0	0	0	0	2	0	0	21,156
Hutchinson..	3	1	0	0	0	0	0	1	1	1	1	41,909
Iola..	1	0	1	0	0	0	0	0	2	0	0	5,697
Lansing...	2	0	0	0	0	0	0	0	0	2	0	11,688
Larned..	1	0	0	0	0	0	0	0	0	1	0	4,012
Lawrence...	5	2	1	2	0	0	0	1	2	4	3	90,034
Leavenworth......................................	1	0	0	0	0	0	0	1	0	0	0	35,965
Lenexa..	1	0	0	0	0	0	0	0	1	0	0	49,777
Louisburg..	0	0	1	0	0	0	0	1	0	0	0	4,268
McPherson..	1	0	1	0	1	0	0	0	1	2	0	13,245
Mulvane	1	0	0	0	0	0	0	0	0	1	0	6,307
Parsons	2	0	0	0	0	0	0	0	2	0	0	10,278
Pittsburg...	1	0	0	0	0	0	0	0	1	0	0	20,395
Pratt...	1	0	0	0	0	0	0	0	0	0	1	6,900
Protection...	0	0	1	0	0	0	0			1	0	521
Wichita...	10	0	3	1	0	0	0	4	4	4	2	386,486
Metropolitan Counties	1	0	2	2	1	0	0					
Douglas..	0	0	1	1	0	0	0	0	2	0	0	
Leavenworth......................................	0	0	0	0	1	0	0	0	0	1	0	
Riley County Police Department	0	0	1	0	0	0	0	0	0	1	0	
Shawnee...	1	0	0	0	0	0	0	0	0	1	0	
Wyandotte..	0	0	0	1	0	0	0	1	0	0	0	
Nonmetropolitan Counties..........	1	1	1	0	0	0	0					
Ellis..	0	0	1	0	0	0	0	0	1	0	0	
Greenwood	1	0	0	0	0	0	0	0	1	0	0	
Marshall...	0	1	0	0	0	0	0	1	0	0	0	
KENTUCKY												
Total	113	5	31	15	7	0	0					
Cities	87	4	26	12	4	0	0					
Ashland..	3	0	0	0	0	0	0	1	0	2	0	21,432
Bellevue..	0	0	1	0	0	0	0	1	0	0	0	5,918
Berea..	0	1	1	0	0	0	0	0	1	0	1	14,331
Bowling Green..................................	4	0	2	2	0	0	0	1	2	4	1	61,130
Burkesville..	1	0	0	0	0	0	0	0	0	1	0	1,526
Cadiz..	0	0	2	0	0	0	0	0	1	1	0	2,624

Table 13. Hate Crime Incidents Per Bias Motivation and Quarter, by Selected State and Agency, 2013–*Continued*

(Number.)

State/agency	Race	Religion	Sexual orientation	Ethnicity	Disability	Gender	Gender Identity	1st quarter	2nd quarter	3rd quarter	4th quarter	Population[2]
KENTUCKY (cont.)												
Carlisle	1	0	0	0	0	0	0	0	1	0	0	1,956
Carrollton	1	0	0	0	0	0	0	0	0	0	1	3,966
Corbin	2	0	0	0	0	0	0	0	0	1	1	7,257
Covington	3	0	3	3	0	0	0	1	4	2	2	40,766
Cynthiana	1	0	0	0	0	0	0	0	1	0	0	6,305
Danville	0	0	1	0	0	0	0	0	1	0	0	16,388
Elizabethtown	2	0	0	0	0	0	0	0	0	0	2	29,470
Elkton	1	0	0	0	0	0	0	0	1	0	0	2,211
Elsmere	1	0	0	0	0	0	0	1	0	0	0	8,478
Flatwoods	1	0	0	0	0	0	0	0	0	1	0	7,412
Florence	1	0	0	0	2	0	0	1	1	1	0	31,434
Frankfort	1	0	1	1	0	0	0	1	1	0	1	27,680
Georgetown	2	0	0	0	0	0	0	0	0	2	0	30,611
Harrodsburg	1	0	0	0	0	0	0	0	0	1	0	8,301
Hazard	1	0	0	0	0	0	0	0	0	1	0	5,455
Henderson	2	0	0	0	0	0	0	0	0	0	2	28,952
Hillview	0	0	1	0	0	0	0	0	0	1	0	9,465
Hopkinsville	1	0	1	0	0	0	0	0	0	1	1	33,253
Leitchfield	1	0	0	0	0	0	0	0	1	0	0	6,814
Lexington	16	1	5	4	1	0	0	5	10	10	2	308,712
Louisville Metro	7	0	4	0	0	0	0	2	4	3	2	671,120
Ludlow	1	0	0	0	1	0	0	0	2	0	0	4,536
Madisonville	1	0	0	0	0	0	0	1	0	0	0	19,761
Morehead	1	0	0	0	0	0	0	0	0	1	0	6,864
Mount Washington	1	0	0	0	0	0	0	0	0	0	1	9,377
Murray	1	0	1	0	0	0	0	0	1	1	0	18,048
Newport	5	0	0	0	0	0	0	0	1	1	3	15,425
Oak Grove	1	0	0	0	0	0	0	0	0	1	0	7,638
Owensboro	2	0	1	1	0	0	0	1	2	1	0	58,304
Paducah	1	0	0	0	0	0	0	0	0	0	1	25,064
Paris	1	0	0	0	0	0	0	0	0	0	1	9,752
Radcliff	2	0	0	0	0	0	0	0	1	0	1	23,177
Ravenna	1	0	0	0	0	0	0	0	1	0	0	595
Richmond	1	1	1	0	0	0	0	1	1	0	1	32,333
Russellville	1	0	1	0	0	0	0	0	1	1	0	6,949
Shelbyville	4	0	0	0	0	0	0	0	1	2	1	14,743
Shepherdsville	0	1	0	0	0	0	0	0	0	1	0	11,534
Shively	0	0	0	1	0	0	0	1	0	0	0	15,511
St. Matthews	2	0	0	0	0	0	0	0	1	0	1	17,768
Vine Grove	1	0	0	0	0	0	0	1	0	0	0	5,298
Williamsburg	1	0	0	0	0	0	0	1	0	0	0	5,258
Winchester	5	0	0	0	0	0	0	1	2	1	1	18,478
Universities and Colleges	1	0	1	0	0	0	0					
Morehead State University	1	0	0	0	0	0	0	0	0	1	0	11,169
University of Louisville	0	0	1	0	0	0	0	0	0	1	0	21,239
Metropolitan Counties	11	0	2	1	2	0	0					
Boone	3	0	0	1	0	0	0	1	2	0	1	
Bullitt	3	0	1	0	0	0	0	0	2	1	1	
Christian	1	0	0	0	1	0	0	0	1	1	0	
Daviess	0	0	1	0	0	0	0	0	0	1	0	
Hardin	1	0	0	0	0	0	0	0	1	0	0	
Meade	1	0	0	0	1	0	0	2	0	0	0	
Shelby	1	0	0	0	0	0	0	0	1	0	0	
Trigg	1	0	0	0	0	0	0	0	0	0	1	
Nonmetropolitan Counties	8	1	0	1	1	0	0					
Calloway	1	0	0	0	0	0	0	0	0	1	0	
Clay	0	1	0	0	0	0	0	0	0	1	0	
Hopkins	1	0	0	0	0	0	0	0	0	1	0	
Knott	0	0	0	1	0	0	0	0	1	0	0	
Knox	1	0	0	0	0	0	0	0	0	0	1	
Lyon	1	0	0	0	0	0	0	0	1	0	0	
Marshall	1	0	0	0	0	0	0	0	1	0	0	
Nelson	1	0	0	0	0	0	0	0	0	1	0	
Ohio	1	0	0	0	1	0	0	1	1	0	0	
Perry	1	0	0	0	0	0	0	1	0	0	0	
State Police Agencies	6	0	2	0	0	0	0					
Campbellsburg	1	0	0	0	0	0	0	0	1	0	0	

(Number.)

State/agency	Number of incidents per bias motivation							Number of incidents per quarter[1]				Population[2]
	Race	Religion	Sexual orientation	Ethnicity	Disability	Gender	Gender Identity	1st quarter	2nd quarter	3rd quarter	4th quarter	
KENTUCKY (cont.)												
Dry Ridge	0	0	1	0	0	0	0	1	0	0	0	
Frankfort	0	0	1	0	0	0	0	0	0	1	0	
Henderson	1	0	0	0	0	0	0	0	0	0	1	
Madisonville	1	0	0	0	0	0	0	0	0	1	0	
Morehead	1	0	0	0	0	0	0	0	0	1	0	
Pikeville	1	0	0	0	0	0	0	1	0	0	0	
Richmond	1	0	0	0	0	0	0	0	0	1	0	
Other Agencies	0	0	0	1	0	0	0					
Montgomery County School District	0	0	0	1	0	0	0	0	0	0	1	
LOUISIANA												
Total	7	6	8	1	0	0	0					
Cities	1	1	5	1	0	0	0					
New Orleans	1	1	5	1	0	0	0	2	3	3	0	377,022
Universities and Colleges	1	0	0	0	0	0	0					
University of New Orleans	1	0	0	0	0	0	0	1	0		0	10,071
Metropolitan Counties	5	5	3	0	0	0	0					
Ascension	3	1	0	0	0	0	0	0	3	1	0	
Calcasieu	0	4	3	0	0	0	0	4	1	1	1	
Iberia	1	0	0	0	0	0	0	0	0	1	0	
Jefferson	1	0	0	0	0	0	0	0	0	1		
MAINE												
Total	12	3	10	0	0	0	0					
Cities	10	3	9	0	0	0	0					
Auburn	2	0	0	0	0	0	0	0	0	2	0	22,948
Belfast	0	0	1	0	0	0	0	1	0	0	0	6,654
Cape Elizabeth	1	0	0	0	0	0	0	0	1	0	0	9,104
Ellsworth	1	0	0	0	0	0	0	0	1	0	0	7,853
Lewiston	0	0	1	0	0	0	0	0	0	0	1	36,422
Machias[3]	0	0	1	0	0	0	0	0	0	0	1	2,173
Mexico	1	0	0	0	0	0	0	1	0	0	0	2,633
Old Orchard Beach	1	0	0	0	0	0	0	0	1	0	0	8,681
Portland	1	1	0	0	0	0	0	0	1	1	0	66,256
Scarborough	0	0	1	0	0	0	0	0	1	0	0	19,252
Searsport	0	0	1	0	0	0	0	1	0	0	0	2,618
Skowhegan	1	0	2	0	0	0	0	1	0	1	1	8,537
South Portland	1	2	2	0	0	0	0	1	2	2	0	25,126
Wiscasset	1	0	0	0	0	0	0	1	0	0	0	3,673
Metropolitan Counties	0	0	1	0	0	0	0					
Sagadahoc	0	0	1	0	0	0	0	0	1	0	0	
Nonmetropolitan Counties	1	0	0	0	0	0	0					
Waldo	1	0	0	0	0	0	0	0	1	0	0	
State Police Agencies	1	0	0	0	0	0	0					
State Police, Somerset County	1	0	0	0	0	0	0	0	0		1	
MARYLAND												
Total	26	15	7	3	0	0	0					
Cities	3	3	1	1	0	0	0					
Aberdeen	0	1	0	0	0	0	0	0	0	1	0	15,039
Annapolis	0	1	0	0	0	0	0	1	0	0	0	38,649
Baltimore	0	1	0	1	0	0	0	1	0	0	1	622,671
Bel Air	1	0	0	0	0	0	0	1	0	0	0	10,314
Frederick	2	0	0	0	0	0	0	0	0	1	1	66,709
Greenbelt	0	0	1	0	0	0	0	0	1	0	0	23,680
Universities and Colleges	2	0	1	0	0	0	0					
St. Mary's College	1	0	1	0	0	0	0	0	2	0	0	1,933
Towson University	1	0	0	0	0	0	0	0	1	0	0	21,960
Metropolitan Counties	19	8	5	2	0	0	0					
Baltimore County Police Department	3	2	0	0	0	0	0	1	0	2	2	

Table 13. Hate Crime Incidents Per Bias Motivation and Quarter, by Selected State and Agency, 2013–*Continued*

(Number.)

State/agency	\multicolumn{7}{c}{Number of incidents per bias motivation}							\multicolumn{4}{c}{Number of incidents per quarter[1]}				Population[2]
	Race	Religion	Sexual orientation	Ethnicity	Disability	Gender	Gender Identity	1st quarter	2nd quarter	3rd quarter	4th quarter	
MARYLAND (cont.)												
Carroll	2	0	0	0	0	0	0	0	0	2	0	
Charles	0	0	1	0	0	0	0	0	1	0	0	
Frederick	3	2	0	0	0	0	0	3	0	2	0	
Harford	1	0	0	0	0	0	0	0	0	0	1	
Howard County Police Department	4	0	1	1	0	0	0	0	2	2	2	
Montgomery County Police Department	6	4	2	1	0	0	0	3	5	2	3	
Prince George's County Police Department	0	0	1	0	0	0	0	0	1	0	0	
Nonmetropolitan Counties	1	0	0	0	0	0	0					
Garrett	1	0	0	0	0	0	0	0	0	0	1	
State Police Agencies	1	2	0	0	0	0	0					
Frederick County	0	2	0	0	0	0	0	0	1	0	1	
Queen Anne's County	1	0	0	0	0	0	0	1	0	0	0	
Other Agencies	0	2	0	0	0	0	0					
State Fire Marshal	0	2	0	0	0	0	0	0	0	2	0	
MASSACHUSETTS												
Total	146	64	91	42	3	1	3					
Cities	142	57	86	40	3	0	3					
Acton	3	0	0	0	0	0	0	0	2	0	1	22,871
Amesbury	0	1	0	0	0	0	0	0	1	0	0	16,655
Amherst	1	0	0	0	0	0	0	1	0	0	0	39,127
Attleboro	1	0	0	1	0	0	0	0	1	0	1	44,034
Bedford	1	2	0	0	0	0	0	1	0	0	2	13,947
Belmont	0	0	0	1	0	0	0	0	1	0	0	25,421
Beverly	0	1	0	0	0	0	0	0	0	1	0	40,592
Billerica	0	1	0	0	0	0	0	0	0	0	1	41,926
Bolton	0	0	1	0	0	0	0	0	0	1	0	5,060
Boston	73	21	53	15	0	0	3	39	56	40	30	643,799
Braintree	3	0	0	0	0	0	0	0	2	1	0	36,496
Brookline	0	1	0	0	0	0	0	1	0	0	0	59,382
Cambridge	4	3	3	3	0	0	0	6	2	3	2	107,282
Chelsea	1	0	0	0	0	0	0	0	0	0	1	37,454
Danvers	0	1	0	0	0	0	0	1	0	0	0	27,263
Douglas	0	0	1	0	0	0	0	0	1	0	0	8,628
Dover	0	0	1	0	0	0	0	0	0	1	0	5,778
Dracut	4	1	0	0	0	0	0	0	1	2	2	30,533
East Longmeadow	2	0	3	0	0	0	0	0	3	0	2	15,946
Edgartown	1	0	0	0	0	0	0	1	0	0	0	4,252
Fall River	1	0	0	0	0	0	0	1	0	0	0	89,220
Framingham	2	0	0	0	0	0	0	0	0	2	0	70,753
Greenfield	0	0	1	0	0	0	0	0	1	0	0	17,598
Haverhill	2	1	3	2	0	0	0	4	2	1	1	62,249
Kingston	0	1	0	0	0	0	0	0	0	1	0	12,791
Lakeville	0	1	0	0	0	0	0	0	1	0	0	10,939
Lincoln	0	0	1	0	0	0	0	0	0	0	1	6,563
Lowell	0	0	1	1	0	0	0	0	0	1	1	109,449
Lunenburg	1	0	0	0	0	0	0	0	0	0	1	11,149
Lynn	3	2	5	4	2	0	0	1	5	6	4	91,769
Malden	1	2	0	0	0	0	0	0	2	1	0	60,816
Marblehead	1	0	0	0	0	0	0	0	1	0	0	20,209
Marlborough	0	0	0	1	0	0	0	0	0	1	0	39,531
Medford	5	3	0	1	1	0	0	2	4	4	0	57,428
Middleboro	1	0	0	0	0	0	0	0	1	0	0	23,547
Milton	1	2	0	0	0	0	0	0	0	0	3	27,269
Monson	0	0	1	0	0	0	0	0	0	0	1	8,716
Needham	2	0	0	0	0	0	0	0	0	1	1	29,544
New Bedford	0	0	0	1	0	0	0	0	0	1	0	95,156
Newburyport	0	0	1	0	0	0	0	0	0	1	0	17,773
Norton	2	0	0	0	0	0	0	0	0	1	1	19,414
Peabody	0	0	0	2	0	0	0	0	0	2	0	52,178
Pittsfield	0	0	1	0	0	0	0	0	1	0	0	43,992
Plainville	1	0	0	0	0	0	0	1	0	0	0	8,512
Plymouth	9	1	0	0	0	0	0	0	0	6	4	57,893
Provincetown	0	1	0	0	0	0	0	1	0	0	0	2,983
Quincy	6	3	0	4	0	0	0	4	2	4	3	93,490

(Number.)

State/agency	Number of incidents per bias motivation							Number of incidents per quarter[1]				Population[2]
	Race	Religion	Sexual orientation	Ethnicity	Disability	Gender	Gender Identity	1st quarter	2nd quarter	3rd quarter	4th quarter	
MASSACHUSETTS (cont.)												
Randolph	0	0	2	0	0	0	0	0	2	0	0	33,583
Reading	1	0	0	0	0	0	0	0	0	1	0	25,398
Revere	0	2	0	1	0	0	0	0	0	1	2	53,777
Salem	1	0	0	0	0	0	0	0	0	0	1	42,468
Saugus	0	0	1	0	0	0	0	0	0	1	0	27,628
Sharon	0	1	0	0	0	0	0	0	1	0	0	17,935
Shrewsbury	0	0	1	0	0	0	0	0	1	0	0	36,315
Somerville	0	0	1	1	0	0	0	0	0	0	2	77,768
South Hadley	1	0	1	0	0	0	0	0	0	1	1	17,794
Spencer	0	1	0	0	0	0	0	0	0	1	0	11,801
Springfield	1	0	2	1	0	0	0	3	0	0	1	153,586
Stoughton	0	1	0	0	0	0	0	0	1	0	0	28,186
Swampscott	1	0	0	0	0	0	0	1	0	0	0	13,995
Taunton	2	0	0	0	0	0	0	1	0	1	0	56,264
Waltham	0	1	0	1	0	0	0	0	0	1	1	62,446
Watertown	0	0	0	1	0	0	0	0	1	0	0	33,254
Westborough	1	0	0	0	0	0	0	0	0	1	0	18,563
West Boylston	1	0	0	0	0	0	0	0	0	0	1	7,821
West Springfield	0	1	0	0	0	0	0	0	0	1	0	28,647
Williamstown	0	1	0	0	0	0	0	0	0	0	1	7,682
Worcester	1	0	1	0	0	0	0	0	1	1	0	183,454
Universities and Colleges	4	7	5	2	0	1	0					
Boston College	0	0	1	0	0	0	0	1	0	0	0	14,605
Boston University	0	0	0	1	0	0	0	0	0	1	0	32,603
Bridgewater State University	1	0	0	0	0	0	0	0	0	0	1	11,417
Dean College	0	1	0	0	0	0	0	0	0	0	1	1,322
Emerson College	1	0	0	0	0	0	0	0	0	0	1	4,531
Massachusetts College of Liberal Arts	0	0	1	0	0	0	0	1	0	0	0	1,799
Northeastern University	0	1	1	0	0	1	0	0	0	0	3	27,694
Tufts University, Medford	0	1	1	0	0	0	0	0	0	1	1	10,837
University of Massachusetts Amherst	2	3	1	1	0	0	0	3	0	2	2	28,236
Harbor Campus, Boston	0	1	0	0	0	0	0	0	0	0	1	15,874
MICHIGAN												
Total	211	44	49	18	4	3	0					
Cities	161	29	32	12	3	2	0					
Adrian	0	0	1	0	0	0	0	0	1	0		20,759
Albion	1	0	0	0	0	0	0	0	1	0	0	8,524
Alpena	1	1	0	0	0	0	0	2	0	0	0	10,299
Ann Arbor	1	1	1	0	0	0	0	0	3	0	0	116,799
Bangor	0	0	0	0	0	0	1	0	0	0	1	1,857
Bath Township	1	0	0	0	0	0	0	0	0	1	0	11,761
Battle Creek	0	1	0	0	0	0	0	0	0	1	0	61,032
Benton Harbor	3	0	0	0	0	0	0	1	0	2	0	10,039
Benton Township	2	0	0	0	0	0	0	0	0	1	1	14,578
Birmingham	1	1	0	0	0	0	0	1	0	1	0	20,544
Blackman Township	3	0	0	0	0	0	0	0	1	0	2	38,115
Bloomfield Township	1	1	0	0	0	0	0	0	1	1	0	41,791
Brownstown Township	1	0	0	0	0	0	0	0	1	0	0	30,388
Buchanan	1	0	0	0	0	0	0	0	1	0	0	4,419
Buena Vista Township	0	0	1	0	0	0	0	0	0	1	0	8,500
Burton	2	0	0	0	0	0	0	0	1	0	1	29,263
Canton Township	1	1	0	0	0	0	0	0	1	1	0	88,958
Charlotte	1	0	0	0	0	0	0	0	1	0	0	9,046
Chesterfield Township	0	0	0	1	0	0	0	0	0	1	0	43,784
Chocolay Township	0	0	1	0	0	0	0	0	0	1	0	6,029
Clare	1	0	0	0	0	0	0	0	0	1	0	3,095
Clinton Township	4	0	0	0	0	0	0	1	2	0	1	98,071
Coldwater	1	0	2	0	0	0	0	0	2	0	1	10,876
Dearborn	7	2	2	3	0	0	0	7	4	2	1	96,012
Detroit	2	0	1	0	0	0	0	0	0	1	2	699,889
East Grand Rapids	1	0	0	0	0	0	0	0	1	0	0	11,100
Eastpointe	1	0	0	1	0	0	0	0	0	2	0	32,402
Elk Rapids	1	0	0	0	0	0	0	0	1	0	0	1,629
Escanaba	1	0	0	0	0	0	0	0	0	0	1	12,531
Essexville	0	1	0	0	0	0	0	1	0	0	0	3,436
Farmington	1	0	0	0	0	0	0	1	0	0	0	10,514

Table 13. Hate Crime Incidents Per Bias Motivation and Quarter, by Selected State and Agency, 2013–*Continued*

(Number.)

State/agency	Number of incidents per bias motivation							Number of incidents per quarter[1]				Population[2]
	Race	Religion	Sexual orientation	Ethnicity	Disability	Gender	Gender Identity	1st quarter	2nd quarter	3rd quarter	4th quarter	
MICHIGAN (cont.)												
Ferndale...................	0	0	1	0	0	0	0	0	0	1	0	20,104
Flint Township...............	2	0	0	0	0	0	0	0	1	1	0	31,182
Flushing...................	0	0	1	0	0	0	0	0	0	1	0	8,204
Forsyth Township..............	1	0	0	0	0	0	0	0	1	0	0	6,278
Franklin...................	2	0	0	0	0	0	0	0	1	1	0	3,194
Fraser....................	2	0	0	0	0	0	0	0	1	1	0	14,529
Fruitport..................	1	0	0	0	0	0	0	0	0	0	1	1,090
Garden City...............	1	0	0	0	0	0	0	1	0	0	0	27,110
Gerrish Township...........	1	0	0	0	0	0	0	0	1	0	0	2,942
Grand Blanc Township	2	0	0	0	0	0	0	1	0	0	1	36,793
Grand Rapids..............	2	0	1	0	0	0	0	1	2	0	0	191,213
Grandville.................	1	0	1	1	1	0	0	2	0	2	0	15,669
Grayling..................	1	0	0	0	0	0	0	0	0	0	1	1,872
Grosse Pointe Park.........	1	0	0	0	0	0	0	0	0	1	0	11,287
Grosse Pointe Woods........	0	0	0	1	0	0	0	0	1	0	0	15,760
Hamtramck...............	1	0	1	0	0	0	0	0	0	1	1	22,017
Harper Woods	1	0	0	0	0	0	0	0	1	0	0	13,922
Hartford..................	3	0	0	0	0	0	0	1	0	0	2	2,633
Hazel Park................	1	0	0	0	0	0	0	0	0	1	0	16,642
Highland Park	0	1	0	0	0	0	0	0	0	0	1	11,591
Holland...................	1	0	0	1	0	0	0	2	0	0	0	33,354
Huntington Woods	0	2	0	0	0	0	0	2	0	0	0	6,305
Inkster	3	0	0	0	0	0	0	2	0	0	1	24,850
Jackson..................	1	0	0	0	0	0	0	0	0	1	0	33,378
Jonesville.................	1	0	0	0	0	0	0	0	0	0	1	2,231
Kalamazoo................	4	0	0	0	0	0	0	0	3	1	0	75,352
Kentwood.................	2	0	0	0	0	0	0	0	0	1	1	50,016
Lake Orion................	1	0	0	0	0	0	0	0	0	0	1	3,052
Lansing..................	2	1	1	1	0	0	0	0	2	2	1	113,907
Lincoln Township	1	0	0	0	0	0	0	0	0	1	0	14,618
Livonia...................	0	0	1	0	0	0	0	0	0	0	1	95,220
Mackinac Island	0	1	0	0	0	0	0	0	0	1	0	494
Madison Heights...........	4	1	0	0	0	0	0	1	2	1	1	30,080
Madison Township.........	0	1	0	0	0	0	0	1	0	0	0	8,567
Marshall..................	1	0	0	0	0	0	0	0	0	0	1	7,050
Meridian Township.........	4	0	0	0	0	0	0	0	1	2	1	40,609
Midland..................	0	0	2	0	0	0	0	1	1	0	0	42,072
Milan....................	1	0	0	0	0	0	0	0	0	1	0	5,875
Milford...................	0	1	0	0	0	0	0	1	0	0	0	16,170
Monroe..................	2	0	0	0	0	0	0	0	1	1	0	20,474
Mount Morris Township	2	0	0	0	0	0	0	1	0	0	1	20,990
Mount Pleasant............	3	0	1	0	1	0	0	1	2	2	0	26,238
Muskegon	3	0	0	0	0	0	0	2	0	0	1	36,658
Muskegon Heights.........	6	0	0	0	0	0	0	0	3	3	0	10,768
Newaygo	1	0	0	0	0	0	0	0	0	1	0	1,961
Northfield Township.........	1	0	0	0	0	0	0	0	0	0	1	8,387
Northville Township.........	1	0	0	0	0	0	0	1	0	0	0	28,734
Norton Shores.............	1	0	1	0	0	0	0	0	0	2	0	23,834
Novi.....................	1	0	0	0	0	0	0	0	0	1	0	57,469
Ontwa Township-Edwardsburg	1	0	0	0	0	0	0	0	0	1	0	6,585
Owosso	1	0	0	0	0	0	0	1	0	0	0	14,745
Pittsfield Township	1	0	2	0	0	0	0	1	2	0	0	36,091
Portage..................	1	0	0	0	0	0	0	1	0	0	0	47,387
Port Huron................	0	0	2	0	0	0	0	1	0	1	0	29,542
Romeo...................	2	0	0	0	0	0	0	0	0	2	0	3,597
Roseville..................	5	0	1	0	0	0	0	1	3	2	0	47,327
Royal Oak	1	0	0	0	0	0	0	0	0	1	0	58,804
Saginaw..................	4	0	2	0	0	0	0	1	1	2	2	50,580
Saginaw Township	0	1	0	0	0	0	0	0	0	0	1	40,636
Saline....................	1	0	0	0	0	0	0	0	0	0	1	9,028
Sault Ste. Marie	1	1	0	0	0	0	0	0	0	1	1	14,203
Shelby Township	2	0	0	0	0	0	0	0	0	1	1	75,347
Southfield	2	1	0	0	0	0	0	0	2	0	1	72,755
Sparta...................	0	2	0	0	0	0	0	0	1	1	0	4,224
St. Joseph	1	0	0	0	0	0	0	1	0	0	0	8,293
Sumpter Township	1	0	1	0	0	0	0	0	0	0	2	9,310
Taylor....................	1	0	2	0	0	0	0	1	2	0	0	61,836
Three Rivers	1	0	0	0	0	0	0	0	0	0	1	7,712
Traverse City..............	0	0	1	0	0	0	0	0	1	0	0	14,989
Trenton..................	1	0	0	0	0	0	0	0	1	0	0	18,483
Troy.....................	2	1	0	0	0	0	0	0	1	0	2	82,608

(Number.)

State/agency	Number of incidents per bias motivation							Number of incidents per quarter[1]				Population[2]
	Race	Religion	Sexual orientation	Ethnicity	Disability	Gender	Gender Identity	1st quarter	2nd quarter	3rd quarter	4th quarter	
MICHIGAN (cont.)												
Utica	2	0	0	0	0	0	0	0	1	0	1	4,765
Van Buren Township	1	1	0	0	0	0	0	0	1	0	1	28,282
Warren	7	1	0	0	0	1	0	0	0	4	5	134,167
Waterford Township	0	1	0	0	0	0	0	0	0	1	0	72,949
Wayland	0	0	0	0	1	0	0	0	1	0		4,074
Wayne	4	0	0	0	0	0	0	1	1	1	1	17,232
West Bloomfield Township	5	1	1	2	0	0	0	5	2	2	0	65,840
Westland	1	0	0	1	0	0	0	1	0	0	1	82,554
White Lake Township	0	1	0	0	0	0	0	0	0	0	1	30,585
Woodhaven	1	0	0	0	0	0	0	0	0	0	1	12,652
Wyoming	1	1	0	0	0	0	0	1	0	0	1	73,786
Universities and Colleges	4	4	4	1	1	1	0					
Eastern Michigan University	1	0	0	0	0	0	0	0	0	0	1	23,518
Michigan State University	2	0	2	0	0	1	0	1	0	2	2	48,783
Oakland University[3]	0	3	0	1	1	0	0	1	0	3	1	19,740
Saginaw Valley State University	1	0	0	0	0	0	0	0	0	0	1	10,552
University of Michigan, Ann Arbor	0	1	1	0	0	0	0	1	1	0	0	43,426
Western Michigan University	0	0	1	0	0	0	0	0	0	1	0	24,598
Metropolitan Counties	36	9	9	4	0	0	0					
Eaton	0	1	0	0	0	0	0	0	0	0	1	
Ingham	1	0	0	0	0	0	0	1	0	0	0	
Jackson	1	1	0	0	0	0	0	0	0	1	1	
Kent	2	0	1	0	0	0	0	1	2	0	0	
Livingston	1	0	0	0	0	0	0	0	0	1	0	
Macomb	10	1	1	1	0	0	0	2	5	3	3	
Monroe	4	1	1	0	0	0	0	1	3	2	0	
Oakland	7	2	5	3	0	0	0	5	4	5	3	
Ottawa	4	0	0	0	0	0	0	1	2	0	1	
Van Buren	3	0	1	0	0	0	0	1	1	2	0	
Washtenaw	3	3	0	0	0	0	0	0	2	2	2	
Nonmetropolitan Counties	5	0	1	1	0	0	0					
Missaukee	1	0	0	1	0	0	0	0	1	1	0	
Ogemaw	2	0	0	0	0	0	0	0	0	1	1	
Otsego	0	0	1	0	0	0	0	0	0	0	1	
Tuscola	2	0	0	0	0	0	0	0	1	1	0	
State Police Agencies	2	2	3	0	0	0	0					
Cass County	1	0	0	0	0	0	0	0	1	0	0	
Genesee County	1	0	1	0	0	0	0	0	1	0	1	
Jackson County	0	1	0	0	0	0	0	0	0	1	0	
Oakland County	0	1	0	0	0	0	0	1	0	0	0	
Van Buren County	0	0	2	0	0	0	0	0	0	2	0	
Other Agencies	3	0	0	0	0	0	0					
Gerald R. Ford International Airport	1	0	0	0	0	0	0	0	0	0	1	
Huron-Clinton Metropolitan Authority, Lower Huron Metropark	2	0	0	0	0	0	0	0	1	1	0	
MINNESOTA												
Total	83	19	30	11	1	0	0					
Cities	80	19	28	11	1	0	0					
Bemidji	0	0	1	0	0	0	0	0	1	0	0	13,805
Blaine	4	0	0	0	0	0	0	1	2	1	0	60,093
Brooklyn Park	3	0	0	0	0	0	0	1	1	1	0	78,353
Chaska	1	0	0	0	0	0	0		1	0	0	24,158
Columbia Heights	1	0	0	1	0	0	0	1	1	0	0	19,715
Crosby	1	0	0	0	0	0	0	0	1	0	0	2,369
Duluth	1	0	0	0	0	0	0	1	0	0	0	86,211
Eagan	0	2	0	0	0	0	0	0	1	1	0	65,052
Eden Prairie	1	0	0	0	0	0	0	0	0	0	1	62,714
Elk River	1	0	0	0	0	0	0	0	0	0	1	23,351
Faribault	0	0	1	0	0	0	0			1		23,405
Inver Grove Heights	0	1	0	0	0	0	0	1	0	0	0	34,294
Lino Lakes	0	0	1	0	0	0	0		0	0	1	20,910
Mankato	2	2	2	0	0	0	0	0	2	2	2	40,360
Maple Grove	0	0	1	0	0	0	0		1	0	0	65,318

(Number.)

State/agency	Race	Religion	Sexual orientation	Ethnicity	Disability	Gender	Gender Identity	1st quarter	2nd quarter	3rd quarter	4th quarter	Population[2]
MINNESOTA (cont.)												
Marshall	1	0	0	1	0	0	0	1	1	0	0	13,370
Mendota Heights	0	0	1	0	0	0	0	0	0	0	1	11,158
Minneapolis	20	4	11	3	1	0	0	6	13	11	9	396,206
Moorhead	1	0	1	0	0	0	0	0	0	1	1	39,322
Plymouth	3	2	2	0	0	0	0	0	3	4	0	73,684
Rochester	2	0	0	2	0	0	0	0	2	2	0	109,675
Roseville	2	0	1	0	0	0	0	0	2	1	0	34,991
Savage	0	0	1	0	0	0	0	0	1	0	0	28,285
Shakopee	0	0	1	0	0	0	0	1	0	0	0	39,214
Shoreview	0	0	1	0	0	0	0	0	0	1		25,810
Spring Lake Park	0	0	0	1	0	0	0	0	1	0	0	6,458
St. Anthony	1	0	0	0	0	0	0	0	1	0	0	8,445
St. Cloud	6	0	0	2	0	0	0	0	3	3	2	65,977
St. Louis Park	3	4	0	0	0	0	0	1	4	1	1	46,723
St. Paul	24	4	2	0	0	0	0	0	18	11	1	294,690
Wadena	0	0	1	0	0	0	0	1	0	0	0	4,092
Waite Park	0	0	0	1	0	0	0	0	0	1	0	6,683
West St. Paul	1	0	0	0	0	0	0	0	0	1	0	19,761
Woodbury	1	0	0	0	0	0	0	1				65,259
Universities and Colleges	1	0	0	0	0	0	0					
University of Minnesota, Morris	1	0	0	0	0	0	0	0	0	1	0	1,896
Metropolitan Counties	1	0	1	0	0	0	0					
Hennepin	0	0	1	0	0	0	0	0	1	0	0	
Mille Lacs	1	0	0	0	0	0	0	0	1	0	0	
Nonmetropolitan Counties	1	0	1	0	0	0	0					
Mahnomen	0	0	1	0	0	0	0			1		
Rice	1	0	0	0	0	0	0	0	1	0	0	
MISSISSIPPI												
Total	2	0	0	2	0	0	0					
Cities	2	0	0	2	0	0	0					
Biloxi	1	0	0	0	0	0	0	1	0	0	0	44,744
Gulfport	1	0	0	2	0	0	0	2	1	0	0	70,863
MISSOURI												
Total	51	11	27	6	1	4	2					
Cities	44	10	23	6	1	4	2					
Branson	0	0	0	1	0	0	0	0	0	0	1	10,918
Clayton	0	1	0	0	0	0	0	0	1	0	0	15,901
Grandview	1	0	0	0	0	0	0	0	0	1		24,630
Independence	1	0	1	0	0	0	0	1	0	1	0	117,381
Joplin	2	0	0	0	0	0	0	2	0	0	0	49,272
Kansas City	30	7	14	5	1	4	2	13	17	21	12	465,514
Raytown	1	0	0	0	0	0	0	0	0	0	1	29,501
Springfield	1	1	1	0	0	0	0	0	3	0	0	163,062
St. Charles	1	0	0	0	0	0	0	0	1	0	0	66,628
St. Joseph	2	0	0	0	0	0	0	1	0	1	0	77,347
St. Louis	4	1	7	0	0	0	0	3	2	2	5	318,563
University City	1	0	0	0	0	0	0	0	0	1	0	35,186
Universities and Colleges	2	0	0	0	0	0	0					
University of Missouri, Columbia	2	0	0	0	0	0	0	0	0	0	2	34,704
Metropolitan Counties	4	0	3	0	0	0	0					
De Kalb	1	0	0	0	0	0	0	0	0	1	0	
Jefferson	0	0	1	0	0	0	0	0	0	0	1	
St. Charles	2	0	2	0	0	0	0	0	2	2	0	
St. Louis County Police Department	1	0	0	0	0	0	0	0	0	1	0	
Nonmetropolitan Counties	1	1	1	0	0	0	0					
Carroll	0	1	0	0	0	0	0	0	0	0	1	
Henry	0	0	1	0	0	0	0	0	0	0	1	
Laclede	1	0	0	0	0	0	0	0	0	0	1	
MONTANA												
Total	25	2	3	1	0	0	0					

(Number.)

State/agency	Race	Religion	Sexual orientation	Ethnicity	Disability	Gender	Gender Identity	1st quarter	2nd quarter	3rd quarter	4th quarter	Population[2]
MONTANA (cont.)												
Cities	21	2	2	0	0	0	0					
Billings	5	1	1	0	0	0	0	1	2	1	3	107,802
Columbia Falls	1	0	0	0	0	0	0	0	1	0	0	4,721
Great Falls	1	0	0	0	0	0	0	0	0	0	1	58,940
Hamilton	0	1	0	0	0	0	0	0	0	0	1	4,555
Helena	11	0	0	0	0	0	0	11	0	0	0	29,411
Kalispell	2	0	0	0	0	0	0	0	0	2	0	20,665
Missoula	1	0	1	0	0	0	0	1	0	1	0	68,877
Universities and Colleges	1	0	0	0	0	0	0					
Montana State University	1	0	0	0	0	0	0	0	1	0	0	14,269
Metropolitan Counties	2	0	0	1	0	0	0					
Cascade	1	0	0	1	0	0	0	0	0	2	0	
Missoula	1	0	0	0	0	0	0	0	0	1	0	
Nonmetropolitan Counties	1	0	1	0	0	0	0					
Park	0	0	1	0	0	0	0	0	0	0	1	
Silver Bow	1	0	0	0	0	0	0	0	0	1	0	
NEBRASKA												
Total	17	5	8	6	0	0	0					
Cities	14	5	8	5	0	0	0					
Columbus	0	0	1	0	0	0	0	0	0	1	0	22,624
Cozad	0	0	0	1	0	0	0	1		0	0	3,929
Grand Island	0	0	0	2	0	0	0	0	0	2	0	50,441
Kearney	0	1	0	0	0	0	0	0	0	1	0	32,113
Lexington	2	0	0	0	0	0	0	0		0	2	10,204
Lincoln	8	2	4	1	0	0	0	5	3	2	5	267,565
Omaha	4	2	2	1	0	0	0	2	3	3	1	425,076
Sidney	0	0	1	0	0	0	0	1	0			6,831
Metropolitan Counties	0	0	0	1	0	0	0					
Lancaster	0	0	0	1	0	0	0	0	1	0	0	
Nonmetropolitan Counties	3	0	0	0	0	0	0					
Dawson	3	0	0	0	0	0	0	0	0	1	2	
NEVADA												
Total	31	10	25	7	0	0	0					
Cities	31	10	25	7	0	0	0					
Carlin	1	0	0	0	0	0	0				1	2,457
Henderson	1	0	0	0	0	0	0			1		268,237
Las Vegas Metropolitan Police Department	27	9	23	6	0	0	0	16	13	18	18	1,500,455
North Las Vegas	0	0	1	1	0	0	0		1	1		225,632
Reno	2	1	1	0	0	0	0		1	3		232,561
NEW HAMPSHIRE												
Total	11	5	4	1	0	0	0					
Cities	10	5	3	1	0	0	0					
Ashland	1	0	0	0	0	0	0	0	1	0	0	2,056
Bedford	1	0	0	0	0	0	0	0	1	0	0	21,645
Concord	2	1	0	0	0	0	0	0	2	1	0	42,615
Conway	0	0	1	0	0	0	0	1	0	0	0	10,056
Farmington	1	0	0	0	0	0	0	0	0	1	0	6,799
Hampton	1	0	0	0	0	0	0	0	0	1	0	15,067
Hampton Falls	0	0	0	1	0	0	0	0	1	0	0	2,294
Hanover	0	0	1	0	0	0	0	0	1	0	0	11,195
Keene	0	1	0	0	0	0	0	0	0	1	0	23,236
Londonderry	0	1	0	0	0	0	0	0	1	0	0	24,338
Manchester	1	0	0	0	0	0	0	0	0	0	1	110,411
Newbury	0	0	1	0	0	0	0	1	0	0	0	2,110
Pelham	1	2	0	0	0	0	0	2	1	0	0	13,034
Plaistow	1	0	0	0	0	0	0	0	0	0	1	7,620
Windham	1	0	0	0	0	0	0	1	0	0	0	14,092

State/agency	Race	Religion	Sexual orientation	Ethnicity	Disability	Gender	Gender Identity	1st quarter	2nd quarter	3rd quarter	4th quarter	Population[2]
NEW HAMPSHIRE (cont.)												
Universities and Colleges	1	0	1	0	0	0	0					
University of New Hampshire	1	0	1	0	0			1	0	1	0	15,267
NEW JERSEY												
Total	187	121	64	38	4	0	0					
Cities	180	121	61	38	4	0	0					
Aberdeen Township	8	1	2	0	0	0	0	1	6	1	3	18,150
Allenhurst....................................	0	2	0	0	0	0	0	0	0	1	1	493
Asbury Park	1	0	3	0	0	0	0	1	2	1	0	15,779
Bedminster Township	1	1	0	0	0	0	0	0	2	0	0	8,213
Belleville.....................................	0	0	2	0	0	0	0	0	0	1	1	36,229
Brick Township.............................	2	1	0	1	0	0	0	1	2	1	0	75,371
Burlington...................................	0	0	0	0	1	0	0	1	0	0	0	9,865
Burlington Township	0	1	0	0	0	0	0	1	0	0	0	22,750
Caldwell......................................	1	0	0	0	0	0	0	0	0	1	0	7,876
Cinnaminson Township	1	0	0	0	0	0	0	0	0	0	1	16,686
Clark Township	0	1	0	0	0	0	0	0	1	0	0	15,021
Closter..	0	0	1	0	0	0	0	1	0	0	0	8,548
Colts Neck Township......................	3	0	0	0	0	0	0	0	0	2	1	10,075
Cranford Township	0	1	0	0	0	0	0	1	0	0	0	23,165
Delran Township	2	0	0	0	0	0	0	0	1	0	1	16,862
Eastampton Township.....................	0	0	0	1	0	0	0	1	0	0	0	6,103
East Brunswick Township	1	10	2	1	0	0	0	3	4	3	4	48,073
East Hanover Township	0	1	0	0	0	0	0	0	0	0	1	11,350
East Orange.................................	0	1	0	0	0	0	0	0	0	0	1	64,425
East Windsor Township	0	1	0	0	0	0	0	0	0	1	0	27,564
Egg Harbor Township......................	2	0	0	1	0	0	0	0	2	0	1	43,709
Elmwood Park...............................	1	0	0	0	1	0	0	1	1	0	0	20,077
Evesham Township.........................	7	1	0	0	0	0	0	4	3	1	0	45,798
Ewing Township............................	1	0	2	0	0	0	0	0	1	0	2	36,449
Fairview	0	0	0	1	0	0	0	0	0	1	0	14,358
Fanwood	0	1	0	0	0	0	0	0	0	1	0	7,447
Fort Lee	2	0	1	0	0	0	0	2	1	0	0	35,900
Franklin Lakes	0	1	0	1	0	0	0	1	1	0	0	10,746
Franklin Township, Gloucester County.................................	0	1	0	0	0	0	0	0	0	1	0	16,740
Freehold Township	0	1	0	0	0	0	0	1	0	0	0	36,048
Galloway Township........................	0	0	1	0	0	0	0	0	1	0	0	37,304
Glassboro	8	0	2	2	0	0	0	3	2	3	4	19,038
Glen Ridge...................................	0	1	0	0	0	0	0	0	1	0	0	7,626
Gloucester Township......................	2	0	0	0	0	0	0	0	2	0	0	64,440
Green Brook Township	0	2	0	0	0	0	0	1	1	0	0	7,240
Greenwich Township, Warren County.................................	1	0	0	0	0	0	0	0	0	0	1	5,582
Haddonfield.................................	0	1	0	0	0	0	0	0	0	0	1	11,590
Haddon Township.........................	0	0	0	1	0	0	0	0	0	1	0	14,732
Hardyston Township.......................	0	0	1	0	0	0	0	0	0	1	0	8,049
Harrison......................................	0	0	1	0	0	0	0	0	0	0	1	13,975
Harrison Township	1	0	0	0	0	0	0	0	0	1	0	12,616
Highland Park	2	3	3	0	0	0	0	1	4	2	1	14,420
Hightstown..................................	1	1	0	1	0	0	0	0	1	1	1	5,572
Hillsborough Township....................	1	0	0	0	0	0	0	0	1	0	0	39,037
Hoboken......................................	3	3	1	0	0	0	0	1	2	1	3	52,771
Holmdel Township	2	3	0	0	0	0	0	2	2	0	1	16,657
Howell Township...........................	5	6	4	3	0	0	0	2	7	5	4	51,100
Irvington.....................................	0	0	1	0	0	0	0	0	0	1	0	54,246
Jackson Township	2	1	0	0	0	0	0	1	0	0	2	55,817
Jersey City...................................	2	0	2	1	0	0	0	0	3	0	2	256,886
Keansburg	3	0	1	0	0	0	0	1	0	2	1	9,981
Lacey Township.............................	3	0	2	2	1	0	0	1	5	1	1	27,865
Lakewood Township	5	15	0	3	0	0	0	2	6	7	8	92,664
Lawrence Township, Mercer County.	0	0	0	1	0	0	0	0	0	1	0	33,172
Little Egg Harbor Township	3	1	0	2	0	0	0	1	2	0	3	20,412
Little Falls Township	0	0	1	0	0	0	0	0	1	0	0	14,504
Livingston Township.......................	2	0	0	0	0	0	0	0	0	2	0	29,621
Logan Township............................	1	0	0	0	0	0	0	0	0	1	0	6,019
Long Beach Township	0	1	0	0	0	0	0	0	1	0	0	3,068
Lower Township............................	1	0	0	0	0	0	0	0	0	1	0	22,467
Lumberton Township	2	0	0	0	0	0	0	0	0	2	0	12,516

Table 13. Hate Crime Incidents Per Bias Motivation and Quarter, by Selected State and Agency, 2013—*Continued*

(Number.)

State/agency	Race	Religion	Sexual orientation	Ethnicity	Disability	Gender	Gender Identity	1st quarter	2nd quarter	3rd quarter	4th quarter	Population[2]
NEW JERSEY (cont.)												
Mahwah Township	0	1	0	0	0	0	0	0	0	1	0	26,292
Manalapan Township	1	0	0	2	0	0	0	2	0	1	0	39,313
Manasquan	1	2	0	0	0	0	0	1	2	0	0	5,860
Manchester Township	3	0	0	0	0	0	0	0	3	0	0	43,013
Maple Shade Township	1	0	0	0	0	0	0	1	0	0	0	19,291
Margate City	1	0	0	0	0	0	0	0	0	0	1	6,319
Marlboro Township	2	0	0	0	0	0	0	1	1	0	0	40,190
Medford Lakes	0	0	1	0	0	0	0	0	1	0	0	4,196
Medford Township	4	2	1	0	0	0	0	2	1	1	3	23,285
Mendham	0	1	0	0	0	0	0	0	0	0	1	5,029
Middlesex	1	0	0	0	0	0	0	1	0	0	0	13,787
Middletown Township	1	0	0	0	0	0	0	0	1	0	0	66,246
Monroe Township, Middlesex County	8	1	1	1	0	0	0	1	0	2	8	41,356
Montclair	4	2	0	0	0	0	0	2	2	1	1	37,962
Montgomery Township	1	3	0	0	0	0	0	1	1	0	2	22,467
Moorestown Township	1	0	0	0	0	0	0	0	0	1	0	20,706
Morris Township	0	1	0	0	0	0	0	0	0	0	1	22,640
Mount Laurel Township	0	0	0	1	0	0	0	0	0	0	1	41,839
Mount Olive Township	0	0	0	2	0	0	0	0	1	0	1	28,611
Neptune Township	10	0	3	1	0	0	0	0	8	2	4	27,856
Newark	2	0	1	0	0	0	0	0	2	0	1	278,246
New Brunswick	3	1	1	0	0	0	0	3	1	1	0	56,542
New Providence	1	2	0	0	0	0	0	1	2	0	0	12,463
North Brunswick Township	1	0	1	2	0	0	0	1	2	0	1	41,425
Nutley Township	2	1	0	0	0	0	0	0	1	2	0	28,660
Oakland	1	2	2	0	0	0	0	1	2	1	1	12,927
Oceanport	0	1	0	0	0	0	0	0	0	1	0	5,833
Old Bridge Township	1	0	1	0	0	0	0	1	0	1	0	66,528
Palmyra	1	0	0	0	0	0	0	0	0	1	0	7,412
Paramus	0	0	0	1	0	0	0	0	0	0	1	26,628
Parsippany-Troy Hills Township	0	2	0	0	0	0	0	0	0	0	2	53,851
Passaic	2	2	0	1	0	0	0	0	1	2	2	70,445
Paulsboro	1	0	0	0	0	0	0	0	0	0	1	6,034
Pemberton Township	1	0	0	0	0	0	0	0	0	0	1	27,949
Pennsauken Township	0	1	0	0	0	0	0	0	0	0	1	35,788
Pequannock Township	0	1	0	0	0	0	0	0	0	0	1	15,580
Phillipsburg	0	1	0	1	0	0	0	0	0	1	1	14,619
Pine Hill	1	0	0	0	0	0	0	0	0	0	1	10,704
Piscataway Township	0	2	2	0	0	0	0	3	1	0	0	58,259
Pitman	6	1	0	0	0	0	0	1	0	5	1	8,930
Plainsboro Township	0	0	0	0	1	0	0	0	1	0	0	23,256
Point Pleasant	4	1	0	1	0	0	0	1	4	1	0	18,458
Randolph Township	1	0	2	0	0	0	0	0	0	2	1	25,969
Raritan	0	0	2	0	0	0	0	0	0	0	2	7,352
Readington Township	0	1	0	0	0	0	0	0	0	0	1	15,910
Robbinsville Township	2	1	0	0	0	0	0	1	1	1	0	14,046
Runnemede	0	1	0	0	0	0	0	0	0	0	1	8,459
Salem	1	0	0	0	0	0	0	0	0	1	0	5,175
Secaucus	0	2	2	0	0	0	0	0	1	0	3	19,119
Shrewsbury	2	0	0	0	0	0	0	2	0	0	0	3,941
Somerville	0	1	0	0	0	0	0	0	0	1	0	12,174
South Brunswick Township	0	4	1	0	0	0	0	0	1	2	2	44,575
South Orange	1	0	1	0	0	0	0	1	1	0	0	16,297
South Plainfield	1	0	0	1	0	0	0	1	1	0	0	23,789
Spotswood	0	2	0	0	0	0	0	0	1	1	0	8,459
Toms River Township	0	1	0	0	0	0	0	0	0	1	0	92,332
Totowa	1	1	1	0	0	0	0	0	1	2	0	10,985
Trenton	1	0	1	0	0	0	0	0	1	1	0	84,439
Union Beach	0	0	0	1	0	0	0	0	1	0	0	6,198
Union City	0	1	1	0	0	0	0	1	1	0	0	68,254
Verona	0	1	0	0	0	0	0	0	1	0	0	13,429
Vineland	0	1	1	0	0	0	0	0	1	0	1	60,863
Voorhees Township	2	1	0	0	0	0	0	0	2	1	0	29,284
Washington	3	1	0	0	0	0	0	1	0	2	1	6,408
Washington Township, Gloucester County	2	0	0	0	0	0	0	0	1	1	0	48,110
Washington Township, Warren County	0	0	1	0	0	0	0	0	0	0	1	6,493
Watchung	0	1	0	0	0	0	0	0	0	1	0	5,844
Weehawken Township	1	0	1	0	0	0	0	0	1	1	0	12,937

Table 13. Hate Crime Incidents Per Bias Motivation and Quarter, by Selected State and Agency, 2013–Continued

(Number.)

State/agency	Number of incidents per bias motivation							Number of incidents per quarter[1]				Population[2]
	Race	Religion	Sexual orientation	Ethnicity	Disability	Gender	Gender Identity	1st quarter	2nd quarter	3rd quarter	4th quarter	
NEW JERSEY (cont.)												
West Caldwell Township	0	1	0	0	0	0	0	0	0	1	0	10,878
West Deptford Township	3	1	0	1	0	0	0	3	1	1	0	21,497
West Long Branch	0	1	0	0	0	0	0	0	0	1	0	8,660
West Milford Township	3	0	0	0	0	0	0	2	0	1	0	26,095
Woodbridge Township	1	2	0	0	0	0	0	0	2	0	1	100,568
Woodbury	4	1	0	0	0	0	0	0	0	2	3	10,073
Woodbury Heights	1	0	0	0	0	0	0	1	0	0	0	3,026
Woolwich Township	1	0	0	0	0	0	0	0	1	0	0	11,167
Metropolitan Counties	6	0	2	0	0	0	0					
Camden County Police Department	6	0	2	0	0	0	0	0	4	4	0	
	1	0	1	0	0	0	0					
State Police Agencies												
Ocean County	0	0	1	0	0	0	0	0	1	0	0	
Salem County	1	0	0	0	0	0	0	0	1	0	0	
NEW MEXICO												
Total	6	1	4	1	0	0	0					
Cities	6	1	4	1	0	0	0					
Albuquerque	5	1	4	0	0	0	0	2	1	6	1	558,165
Belen	0	0	0	1	0	0	0				1	7,247
Los Lunas	1	0	0	0	0	0	0	0		1		15,252
NEW YORK												
Total	150	294	122	36	2	6	5					
Cities	95	182	107	26	2	4	3					
Albany	1	2	0	0	0	0	0	0	2	1	0	97,956
Amherst Town	3	0	0	0	0	0	0	0	0	1	2	118,296
Batavia	1	0	0	0	0	0	0	0	0	1	0	15,374
Brighton Town	1	0	0	0	0	0	0	1	0	0	0	36,689
Buffalo	11	1	2	2	0	1	0	6	3	4	4	258,789
Canandaigua	1	0	0	0	0	0	0	0	1	0	0	10,470
Clarkstown Town	1	2	0	0	0	0	0	2	1	0	0	80,705
Cohoes	1	0	0	0	0	0	0	0	1	0	0	16,179
Colonie Town	0	0	1	0	0	0	0	0	1	0	0	78,215
Crawford Town	3	4	0	0	0	0	0	0	1	0	6	9,264
Croton-on-Hudson Village	0	0	0	0	0	1	0	0	1	0	0	8,180
Freeport Village	0	0	0	1	0	0	0	1	0	0	0	43,214
Greece Town	3	0	0	0	0	0	0	0	1	2	0	96,667
Hamburg Town	1	0	0	0	0	0	0	1	0	0	0	45,535
Hyde Park Town	1	0	0	0	0	0	0	0	0	1	0	21,397
Ithaca	0	0	1	0	0	0	0	0	1	0		30,433
Jamestown	2	0	0	0	0	0	0	1	0	0	1	30,658
Liberty Village	0	4	0	0	0	0	0	0	0	0	4	4,285
Middletown	1	0	0	0	0	0	0	0	0	1	0	27,809
Monroe Village	0	2	0	0	0	0	0	0	1	0	1	8,544
Mount Vernon	2	0	0	1	0	0	0	1	1	0	1	68,071
Newburgh	0	0	1	1	0	0	0	0	1	0	1	28,571
New Rochelle	1	2	0	0	0	0	0	1	1	1	0	78,800
New York	44	152	99	17	1	0	1	56	84	81	93	8,396,126
Niagara Falls	2	0	0	1	0	0	0	0	2	0	1	49,574
North Syracuse Village	2	0	0	0	0	0	0	0	1	1	0	6,964
Owego Village	0	0	1	0	0	0	0	0	0	1	0	3,818
Poughkeepsie	0	0	0	2	1	0	1	2	1	0	1	30,778
Poughkeepsie Town	2	1	1	0	0	0	0	0	2	1	2	43,866
Ramapo Town	0	1	0	0	0	0	0	0	0	0	1	87,204
Rochester	3	1	0	0	0	0	0	0	2	2	0	210,562
Rockville Centre Village	0	1	0	0	0	0	0	0	1	0	0	24,129
Salamanca	1	0	0	0	0	0	0	0	0	1	0	5,691
Saratoga Springs	1	2	0	0	0	0	0	0	0	1	2	27,081
Scarsdale Village	0	1	0	0	0	0	0	1	0	0	0	17,564
Schodack Town	0	0	0	0	0	1	0	0	0	1	0	11,573
Sleepy Hollow Village	0	2	0	0	0	0	0	0	1	1	0	9,996
Spring Valley Village	1	1	0	0	0	0	0	0	0	1	1	32,288
Troy	1	0	0	0	0	0	0	0	0	1	0	49,898
Tuckahoe Village	0	0	0	1	0	0	0	1	0	0	0	6,578
Utica	1	0	0	0	0	0	0	0	0	1	0	61,686
West Seneca Town	2	0	0	0	0	0	0	0	1	1	0	44,821
Yonkers	1	3	1	0	0	1	1	2	0	3	2	199,134

Table 13. Hate Crime Incidents Per Bias Motivation and Quarter, by Selected State and Agency, 2013 –*Continued*

(Number.)

State/agency	Number of incidents per bias motivation							Number of incidents per quarter[1]				Population[2]
	Race	Religion	Sexual orientation	Ethnicity	Disability	Gender	Gender Identity	1st quarter	2nd quarter	3rd quarter	4th quarter	
NEW YORK (cont.)												
Universities and Colleges	8	9	4	1	0	1	1					
Cornell University..........................	1	0	1	0	0	0	0	0	1	1		21,424
Ithaca College...............................	0	0	0	1	0	0	0	0	1	0	0	6,759
State University of New York												
Binghamton................................	0	2	0	0	0	0	1	0	0	3	1	15,308
Stony Brook	0	2	0	0	0	0	0	0	1	1	0	23,946
State University of New York Agricultural and Technical College												
Alfred	1	0	0	0	0	0	0	0	0	0	1	3,528
Cobleskill	0	0	1	0	0	0	0	0	0	0	1	2,492
Morrisville	0	0	0	0	0	1	0	0	1	0	0	3,095
State University of New York College												
Buffalo..	0	0	1	0	0	0	0	0	1	0	0	11,781
Cortland	2	1	0	0	0	0	0	1	1	0	1	7,098
Fredonia	1	0	0	0	0	0	0	0	1	0	0	5,521
New Paltz....................................	2	0	0	0	0	0	0	0	0	0	2	7,655
Oneonta	0	2	0	0	0	0	0	0	0	1	1	6,041
Oswego	0	1	0	0	0	0	0	1	0	0	0	7,921
Potsdam	1	0	1	0	0	0	0	1	0	0	1	4,224
Purchase	0	1	0	0	0	0	0	0	1	0	0	4,240
Metropolitan Counties	41	79	9	8	0	0	1					
Broome..	1	0	0	0	0	0	0	0	0	0	1	
Erie..	0	0	0	1	0	0	0	0	0	0	1	
Livingston	1	0	0	0	0	0	0	1	0	0	0	
Monroe	1	0	0	0	0	0	0	0	1	0	0	
Nassau	10	28	2	3	0	0	0	9	16	9	9	
Oneida...	1	0	0	0	0	0	0	0	1	0	0	
Putnam..	0	0	0	0	0	0	1	0	0	1	0	
Suffolk County Police Department ..	26	50	7	4	0	0	0	11	33	22	21	
Ulster...	1	0	0	0	0	0	0	0	0	1	0	
Westchester Public Safety	0	1	0	0	0	0	0	0	0	0	1	
Nonmetropolitan Counties..........	1	0	0	0	0	0	0					
St. Lawrence.................................	1	0	0	0	0	0	0	0	1	0	0	
	3	8	2	1	0	1	0					
State Police Agencies..................												
Broome County	0	0	1	0	0	0	0	0	0	0	1	
Dutchess County...........................	0	1	0	0	0	0	0	0	0	1	0	
Franklin County	1	1	0	0	0	0	0	0	1	1	0	
Herkimer County	1	0	0	0	0	0	0	0	1	0	0	
Jefferson County...........................	0	0	1	0	0	0	0	1	0	0	0	
Madison County	0	1	0	0	0	0	0	0	1	0	0	
Nassau County..............................	1	0	0	0	0	0	0	0	1	0	0	
Orange County.............................	0	1	0	0	0	0	0	0	1	0	0	
Otsego County	0	1	0	0	0	0	0	0	0	0	1	
Putnam County.............................	0	0	0	1	0	0	0	0	0	1	0	
Saratoga County...........................	0	1	0	0	0	0	0	0	0	1	0	
Steuben County	0	0	0	0	0	1	0	0	0	0	1	
Ulster County................................	0	1	0	0	0	0	0	0	1	0	0	
Westchester County.......................	0	1	0	0	0	0	0	0	0	0	1	
Other Agencies...........................	2	16	0	0	0	0	0					
New York City Metropolitan Transportation Authority	2	15	0	0	0	0	0	4	5	4	4	
State Park, Long Island Regional......	0	1	0	0	0	0	0	1	0	0		
NORTH CAROLINA												
Total	67	17	23	11	0	0	0					
Cities	51	10	16	8	0	0	0					
Albemarle.....................................	1	0	0	0	0	0	0	0	0	0	1	15,946
Asheboro......................................	1	0	0	0	0	0	0	0	0	0	1	25,665
Asheville.......................................	5	2	2	1	0	0	0	3	0	3	4	86,445
Burlington....................................	1	0	0	0	0	0	0	0	0	0	1	51,401
Carrboro.......................................	1	0	0	0	0	0	0	0	0	0	1	20,709
Chapel Hill....................................	0	0	0	1	0	0	0	0	1	0	0	58,744
Charlotte-Mecklenburg..................	8	4	6	3	0	0	0	10	4	2	5	837,638
Concord..	1	0	0	0	0	0	0	0	1	0	0	82,899

Table 13. Hate Crime Incidents Per Bias Motivation and Quarter, by Selected State and Agency, 2013–*Continued*

(Number.)

State/agency	Race	Religion	Sexual orientation	Ethnicity	Disability	Gender	Gender Identity	1st quarter	2nd quarter	3rd quarter	4th quarter	Population[2]
NORTH CAROLINA (cont.)												
Creedmoor	1	0	0	0	0	0	0	0	0	1	0	4,254
Durham	2	1	3	1	0	0	0	3	0	4	0	242,865
Fayetteville....................	4	1	0	1	0	0	0	2	1	2	1	202,524
Gastonia........................	0	1	0	0	0	0	0	0	1	0	0	73,049
Greensboro.....................	3	0	0	0	0	0	0	0	1	0	2	279,343
Greenville	1	0	0	0	0	0	0	0	1	0	0	88,018
Hickory	0	0	1	0	0	0	0	0	1	0	0	40,109
Huntersville....................	1	0	0	0	0	0	0	0	0	1	0	50,162
King..............................	0	1	0	0	0	0	0	0	1	0	0	6,860
Leland...........................	1	0	1	0	0	0	0	1	0	0	1	15,535
Lilesville	1	0	0	0	0	0	0	0	0	1	0	519
Mint Hill........................	1	0	0	0	0	0	0	0	1	0	0	24,350
Morganton	1	0	0	0	0	0	0	0	1	0	0	16,852
New Bern........................	1	0	0	0	0	0	0	0	1	0	0	30,514
Oxford...........................	1	0	0	0	0	0	0	0	0	0	1	8,607
Raleigh..........................	3	0	0	1	0	0	0	0	2	2	0	428,993
Rocky Mount...................	1	0	1	0	0	0	0	0	1	1	0	57,021
Roxboro.........................	2	0	0	0	0	0	0	0	0	2	0	8,310
Salisbury........................	1	0	0	0	0	0	0	0	0	0	1	33,626
Siler City	2	0	0	0	0	0	0	1	0	1	0	8,243
Thomasville....................	1	0	0	0	0	0	0	0	0	1	0	26,866
Wadesboro......................	1	0	0	0	0	0	0	0	0	1	0	5,673
Wilmington	3	0	1	0	0	0	0	3	0	0	1	110,985
Wilson	0	0	1	0	0	0	0	0	0	0	1	49,737
Wrightsville Beach...........	1	0	0	0	0	0	0	0	1	0	0	2,551
Universities and Colleges	5	0	4	0	0	0	0					
East Carolina University..................	1	0	0	0	0	0	0	0	1	0	0	26,947
North Carolina School of the Arts ...	2	0	0	0	0	0	0	1	0	0	1	880
University of North Carolina												
Greensboro..............................	1	0	2	0	0	0	0	0	0	1	2	18,516
Wilmington...............................	1	0	0	0	0	0	0	0	0	1	0	13,733
Wake Forest University..................	0	0	2	0	0	0	0	1	0	1	0	7,432
Metropolitan Counties	8	5	2	3	0	0	0					
Buncombe.......................	2	0	0	1	0	0	0	0	0	2	1	
Cabarrus.........................	0	0	0	1	0	0	0	0	0	1	0	
Catawba.........................	1	0	0	0	0	0	0	0	0	1	0	
Guilford.........................	0	0	1	0	0	0	0	0	1	0	0	
Iredell	0	5	0	0	0	0	0	0	2	3	0	
New Hanover...................	1	0	1	0	0	0	0	0	1	0	1	
Pitt...............................	4	0	0	1	0	0	0	1	1	2	1	
Nonmetropolitan Counties..........	3	2	1	0	0	0	0					
Rutherford......................	1	2	1	0	0	0	0	0	2	1	1	
Surry.............................	1	0	0	0	0	0	0	0	0	0	1	
Swain	1	0	0	0	0	0	0	0	0	0	1	
NORTH DAKOTA												
Total	27	5	4	10	5	0	0					
Cities	20	4	4	8	1	0	0					
Beulah....	0	0	0	1	0	0	0	1	0	0	0	3,149
Bismarck........................	0	0	1	5	0	0	0	3	0	2	1	65,850
Carrington......................	1	0	0	0	0	0	0	0	0	1	0	2,108
Devils Lake.....................	0	0	1	0	0	0	0	0	0	0	1	7,260
Dickinson.......................	0	1	0	0	0	0	0	0	0	1	0	20,347
Fargo............................	8	2	2	1	1	0	0	2	3	6	3	111,101
Mandan..........................	2	0	0	0	0	0	0	0	0	1	1	19,168
Minot	1	0	0	0	0	0	0	0	0	1	0	44,635
Valley City......................	1	0	0	0	0	0	0	1	0	0	0	6,580
West Fargo	6	1	0	1	0	0	0	1	2	2	3	28,018
Williston	1	0	0	0	0	0	0	0	0	0	1	19,949
Metropolitan Counties	4	1	0	0	0	0	0					
Cass..............................	0	1	0	0	0	0	0	0	0	0	1	
Grand Forks....................	2	0	0	0	0	0	0	0	1	0	1	
Morton...........................	2	0	0	0	0	0	0	0	1	1	0	
Nonmetropolitan Counties..........	3	0	0	2	4	0	0					
Dunn.............................	1	0	0	0	0	0	0	0	0	1	0	

Table 13. Hate Crime Incidents Per Bias Motivation and Quarter, by Selected State and Agency, 2013–*Continued*

(Number.)

State/agency	Race	Religion	Sexual orientation	Ethnicity	Disability	Gender	Gender Identity	1st quarter	2nd quarter	3rd quarter	4th quarter	Population[2]
NORTH DAKOTA (cont.)												
Golden Valley	0	0	0	1	0	0	0	0	0	1	0	
Grant	1	0	0	0	0	0	0	0	0	0	1	
Mountrail	1	0	0	1	3	0	0	0	0	1	4	
Walsh	0	0	0	0	1	0	0	0	0	1	0	
OHIO												
Total	226	17	61	42	24	0	0					
Cities	197	13	51	34	20	0	0					
Akron	5	0	2	1	0	0	0	3	3	2	0	198,405
Alliance	0	0	0	1	0	0	0	0		1		22,144
Ashland	1	0	0	0	0	0	0	1	0	0	0	20,306
Athens	0	0	1	0	0	0	0	1	0	0	0	23,721
Austintown	2	0	0	0	0	0	0	0	1	1	0	36,192
Barberton	3	0	1	0	0	0	0	0	2	1	1	26,245
Bath Township, Summit County	0	0	1	0	0	0	0	0	0	1	0	9,724
Bellefontaine	1	0	0	1	0	0	0	0	1	1	0	13,147
Blue Ash	0	0	1	0	0	0	0	0	0	1	0	12,105
Boardman	1	0	0	0	0	0	0	0	1	0	0	40,277
Bucyrus	0	0	0	1	0	0	0	0	0	0	1	12,007
Butler Township	0	0	0	0	1	0	0	1	0	0	0	7,864
Celina	1	0	1	0	0	0	0	1	1	0	0	10,392
Cincinnati	9	0	1	5	1	0	0	4	0	2	10	296,491
Circleville	1	0	1	0	0	0	0	0	1	0	1	13,491
Clearcreek Township	0	0	0	1	0	0	0	0	0	1	0	14,642
Cleveland	1	0	5	1	0	0	0	1	0	4	2	389,181
Colerain Township	2	0	0	0	0	0	0	0	0	1	1	58,578
Columbus	88	4	17	15	12	0	0	8	22	60	46	816,364
Dayton	5	0	2	1	0	0	0	2	3	1	2	141,167
East Liverpool	1	1	0	0	0	0	0	2	0			11,010
East Palestine	1	0	0	0	0	0	0	0	0	1	0	4,631
Eaton	0	0	1	0	0	0	0	0	0	0	1	8,307
Englewood	0	0	1	0	0	0	0	0	0	1	0	13,455
Fairborn	2	0	0	0	0	0	0	1	0	1	0	32,820
Fairfield	0	1	0	0	0	0	0	0	1	0	0	42,677
Findlay	1	0	1	0	0	0	0	0	1	0	1	41,660
Gahanna	0	0	2	0	0	0	0	0	0	0	2	34,011
Girard	1	0	0	0	0	0	0	0	0	1	0	9,771
Greenhills	1	0	0	0	1	0	0	2	0	0	0	3,591
Grove City	3	0	0	1	0	0	0	1	2	1	0	37,208
Hamilton	0	0	1	0	0	0	0	0	1	0		62,268
Huber Heights	1	1	4	0	2	0	0	1	3	4	0	38,118
Hudson	1	0	0	1	0	0	0	1	0	1	0	22,340
Jackson Township, Stark County	1	0	0	0	0	0	0	0	1	0	0	40,436
Kettering	1	0	0	0	0	0	0	0	1	0	0	55,907
Lancaster	1	0	0	0	0	0	0	0	0	0	1	38,902
Lorain	7	0	0	0	0	0	0	0	5	1	1	63,582
Mansfield	4	0	0	0	0	0	0	0	3	0	1	46,832
Medina	2	0	0	0	0	0	0	2	0	0	0	26,492
Mentor-on-the-Lake	1	0	0	1	0	0	0	0	0	2	0	7,434
Miami Township, Montgomery County	2	0	0	0	0	0	0	0	2	0	0	29,128
Montgomery	2	0	0	0	0	0	0	0	1	1	0	10,305
Montpelier	1	0	0	0	0	0	0	0	0	0	1	4,050
Moraine	0	0	1	1	0	0	0	1	0	0	1	6,317
Mount Vernon	2	0	0	0	0	0	0	1	0	1	0	16,748
Napoleon	1	0	0	0	0	0	0	1	0	0	0	8,663
Nelsonville	1	0	0	0	0	0	0	0	0	1	0	5,334
Niles	1	0	0	0	0	0	0	0	0	1	0	18,950
North Baltimore	1	0	0	0	0	0	0	0	1	0	0	3,492
North Canton	1	0	0	0	0	0	0	0	1	0	0	17,380
North College Hill	2	0	0	0	0	0	0	1	0	1	0	9,340
Norwalk	0	0	1	0	1	0	0	1	1	0	0	16,906
Norwood	1	0	0	2	0	0	0	0	1	1	1	19,052
Ottawa Hills	1	0	0	0	0	0	0	1	0	0	0	4,481
Parma	1	0	0	0	0	0	0	1	0	0	0	80,303
Portsmouth	0	0	2	0	0	0	0	1	1	0	0	20,322
Reynoldsburg	0	1	0	0	0	0	0	0	1	0	0	36,472
Richwood	1	0	0	0	0	0	0	0	1	0	0	2,240
Riverside	2	0	0	0	0	0	0	0	0	1	1	25,115
Solon	1	0	0	0	0	0	0	0	1	0	0	23,105

State/agency	Number of incidents per bias motivation							Number of incidents per quarter[1]				Population[2]
	Race	Religion	Sexual orientation	Ethnicity	Disability	Gender	Gender Identity	1st quarter	2nd quarter	3rd quarter	4th quarter	
OHIO (cont.)												
South Euclid	2	0	0	0	0	0	0	2	0	0	0	21,929
Springfield	3	0	1	0	0	0	0	0	1	3	0	60,012
Springfield Township, Hamilton County	1	0	0	0	0	0	0	1	0	0	0	36,330
Struthers	1	1	0	0	1	0	0	0	2	0	1	10,522
Trotwood	1	0	1	0	0	0	0	0	2	0	0	24,282
Troy	1	0	0	0	0	0	0	0	1	0	0	25,424
Twinsburg	0	1	0	1	0	0	0	0		1	1	18,750
Union Township, Clermont County	1	0	0	0	0	0	0	1	0	0	0	47,066
Upper Arlington	3	0	0	0	0	0	0	0	0	1	2	34,369
Urbana	1	1	0	0	0	0	0	2	0	0	0	11,599
Vandalia	2	0	0	0	0	0	0	0	1	1	0	15,181
Wapakoneta	1	0	0	0	0	0	0	0	0	1	0	9,812
Warren	3	0	0	0	1	0	0	0	3	1	0	40,474
Warren Township	1	0	0	0	0	0	0	0	0	0	1	5,450
Wooster	1	1	0	0	0	0	0	1	1	0	0	26,468
Xenia	3	0	0	0	0	0	0	1	0	1	1	26,038
Youngstown	1	0	0	0	0	0	0	0	0	1	0	64,938
Zanesville	1	1	2	0	0	0	0	1	2	0	1	25,378
Universities and Colleges	5	0	2	0	0	0	0					
Bowling Green State University	1	0	0	0	0	0	0	1	0	0	0	17,286
Capital University	2	0	1	0	0	0	0	0	0	0	3	3,584
Kent State University	0	0	1	0	0	0	0	0	0	1	0	28,602
Ohio State University, Columbus	2	0	0	0	0	0	0	0	2	0	0	56,387
Metropolitan Counties	13	1	6	6	2	0	0					
Butler	3	0	3	0	2	0	0	3	2	1	2	
Clermont	1	0	0	0	0	0	0	0	1	0	0	
Delaware	1	0	0	1	0	0	0	0	0	2	0	
Franklin	0	0	0	2	0	0	0	1	0	1	0	
Fulton	0	0	0	1	0	0	0	0	1	0	0	
Geauga	1	0	0	0	0	0	0	0	1	0	0	
Greene	2	0	1	0	0	0	0	1	2	0	0	
Lorain	1	0	0	0	0	0	0	1	0	0	0	
Lucas	0	1	1	0	0	0	0	1	0	0	1	
Medina	1	0	0	0	0	0	0	0	0		1	
Montgomery	0	0	0	1	0	0	0	1	0	0	0	
Pickaway	1	0	0	0	0	0	0	0	0	1	0	
Richland	1	0	0	0	0	0	0	1	0	0	0	
Stark	1	0	0	1	0	0	0	0	0	1	1	
Trumbull	0	0	1	0	0	0	0	0	1	0	0	
Nonmetropolitan Counties	10	3	2	2	2	0	0					
Ashland	0	0	0	1	0	0	0	0	0	1	0	
Athens	0	0	1	0	0	0	0	0	0	1	0	
Auglaize	1	0	0	0	0	0	0	1	0	0	0	
Hancock	0	0	0	1	0	0	0	0	1	0	0	
Jackson	2	0	0	0	0	0	0	0	0	2	0	
Knox	2	1	0	0	0	0	0	0	2	0	1	
Marion	0	0	1	0	1	0	0	1	0	0	1	
Meigs	0	1	0	0	0	0	0	0	1	0	0	
Ross	2	1	0	0	0	0	0	0	2	0	1	
Shelby	2	0	0	0	0	0	0	0	0	0	2	
Washington	0	0	0	0	1	0	0	1	0	0	0	
Wayne	1	0	0	0	0	0	0	0	0	1	0	
Other Agencies	1	0	0	0	0	0	0					
Cleveland Metropolitan Park District	1	0	0	0	0	0	0	0	0	1	0	
OKLAHOMA												
Total	22	8	7	3	1	0	0					
Cities	20	5	5	3	1	0	0					
Altus	1	0	0	0	0	0	0	0	1	0	0	19,634
Bixby	1	0	0	0	0	0	0	0	1	0	0	23,122
Blanchard	1	0	0	0	0	0	0	1	0	0	0	8,016
Broken Arrow	0	0	0	1	0	0	0	0	0	1	0	102,956
Choctaw	1	0	0	0	0	0	0	1	0	0	0	11,768
Cleveland	0	0	0	1	0	0	0	0	1	0	0	3,224
Elk City	1	0	0	0	0	0	0	1	0	0	0	12,463

(Number.)

State/agency	Number of incidents per bias motivation							Number of incidents per quarter[1]				Population[2]
	Race	Religion	Sexual orientation	Ethnicity	Disability	Gender	Gender Identity	1st quarter	2nd quarter	3rd quarter	4th quarter	
OKLAHOMA (cont.)												
Fairfax	1	0	0	0	0	0	0	1	0	0	0	1,373
Heavener	0	1	0	0	0	0	0	0	0	1	0	3,377
Muskogee	1	1	1	0	0	0	0	1	1	1	0	38,884
Norman	3	1	0	0	0	0	0	2	0	1	1	116,970
Oklahoma City	7	2	2	1	0	0	0	3	4	3	2	605,034
Owasso	1	0	0	0	0	0	0	1	0	0	0	31,973
Sapulpa	0	0	1	0	0	0	0	0	1	0	0	20,857
Sayre	1	0	0	0	0	0	0	0	0	0	1	4,556
Skiatook	0	0	0	0	1	0	0	0	0	0	1	7,751
Talihina	0	0	1	0	0	0	0	0	0	1	0	1,112
Tonkawa	1	0	0	0	0	0	0	0	1	0	0	3,150
Universities and Colleges	0	0	2	0	0	0	0					
Southwestern Oklahoma State University	0	0	1	0	0	0	0	0	0	0	1	5,106
University of Central Oklahoma	0	0	1	0	0	0	0	0	0	0	1	17,211
Metropolitan Counties	0	3	0	0	0	0	0					
Grady	0	1	0	0	0	0	0	0	0	0	1	
Tulsa	0	1	0	0	0	0	0	1	0	0	0	
Wagoner	0	1	0	0	0	0	0	0	1	0	0	
Nonmetropolitan Counties	1	0	0	0	0	0	0					
Roger Mills	1	0	0	0	0	0	0	0	1	0	0	
Tribal Agencies	1	0	0	0	0	0	0					
Tonkawa Tribal	1	0	0	0	0	0	0	0	0	1	0	
OREGON												
Total	32	10	14	9	1	0	0					
Cities	28	8	13	9	1	0	0					
Ashland	1	0	0	0	0	0	0	1	0	0	0	20,455
Beaverton	0	0	1	0	0	0	0				1	93,551
Bend	0	2	0	1	0	0	0	2	0	1	0	79,926
Eugene	6	4	3	2	0	0	0	1	9	1	4	158,499
Newberg-Dundee	0	0	0	1	0	0	0	0	0	1	0	25,647
Newport	0	0	1	0	0	0	0	0	1	0	0	10,029
Portland	1	1	3	1	0	0	0	1	3	2		609,136
Salem	7	1	4	2	0	0	0	9	3	2	0	158,234
Springfield	2	0	0	1	0	0	0	0	1	1	1	60,024
Sutherlin	1	0	0	0	0	0	0	0	1		0	7,747
Tigard	8	0	0	1	0	0	0	2	3	4		50,311
Toledo	2	0	1	0	1	0	0	1	2	1	0	3,461
Metropolitan Counties	2	2	1	0	0	0	0					
Deschutes	1	0	0	0	0	0	0	0	1	0	0	
Jackson	0	1	0	0	0	0	0	0	0	1	0	
Lane	1	0	0	0	0	0	0		1			
Yamhill	0	1	1	0	0	0	0	0	0	1	1	
Nonmetropolitan Counties	2	0	0	0	0	0	0					
Douglas	1	0	0	0	0	0	0	1	0	0	0	
Umatilla	1	0	0	0	0	0	0	0	0	1	0	
PENNSYLVANIA												
Total	44	11	8	1	0	0	0					
Cities	32	5	6	1	0	0	0					
Ferguson Township	0	1	0	0	0	0	0	1	0	0	0	17,807
Johnstown	3	0	0	0	0	0	0	0	1	2	0	21,954
Lancaster	1	0	0	0	0	0	0	0	1	0	0	59,370
Lewistown	0	1	0	0	0	0	0	0	1	0	0	8,370
Northern York Regional	1	0	0	0	0	0	0	1	0	0	0	67,657
Philadelphia	14	1	0	1	0	0	0	3	11	1	1	1,553,153
Pittsburgh	12	0	3	0	0	0	0	1	3	8	3	307,632
Reading	0	0	3	0	0	0	0	1	1	1	0	88,107
Richland Township, Cambria County	1	0	0	0	0	0	0	0	1	0	0	12,581
State College	0	2	0	0	0	0	0	0	0	0	2	56,612
Universities and Colleges	6	3	1	0	0	0	0					

Table 13. Hate Crime Incidents Per Bias Motivation and Quarter, by Selected State and Agency, 2013–*Continued*

(Number.)

State/agency	Race	Religion	Sexual orientation	Ethnicity	Disability	Gender	Gender Identity	1st quarter	2nd quarter	3rd quarter	4th quarter	Population[2]
PENNSYLVANIA (cont.)												
Lehigh University............................	1	0	0	0	0	0	0	0	0	0	1	7,080
Pennsylvania State University..........												
Altoona	1	0	0	0	0	0	0	0	0	1	0	3,863
University Park	4	3	1	0	0	0	0	3	1	2	2	45,783
Metropolitan Counties	1	0	0	0	0	0	0					
Lancaster	1	0	0	0	0	0	0	0	0	1	0	
State Police Agencies..................	5	3	1	0	0	0	0					
Chester County...............	0	1	0	0	0	0	0	1		0	0	
Franklin County	1	0	0	0	0	0	0	1		0	0	
Indiana County	1	0	0	0	0	0	0	0	1		0	
Lancaster County...........................	1	1	0	0	0	0	0	2	0	0	0	
Skippack County..........................	2	0	1	0	0	0	0	0	3	0	0	
Pike County	0	1	0	0	0	0	0	0	0	1	0	
RHODE ISLAND												
Total	4	2	0	1	0	0	0					
Cities	3	2	0	1	0	0	0					
Central Falls......................	1	0	0	0	0	0	0	0	1	0	0	19,404
Johnston...........................	1	0	0	0	0	0	0	1	0	0	0	29,068
Newport	1	0	0	0	0	0	0	0	0	1	0	23,874
Providence	0	0	0	1	0	0	0	1	0	0	0	178,887
Warwick......................	0	1	0	0	0	0	0	0	0	1	0	81,789
West Warwick...................	0	1	0	0	0	0	0	0	0	0	1	28,817
Universities and Colleges	1	0	0	0	0	0	0					
University of Rhode Island..............	1	0	0	0	0	0	0	0	0	1	0	16,451
SOUTH CAROLINA												
Total	33	9	6	3	0	0	0					
Cities	18	7	5	2	0	0	0					
Anderson.........................	1	0	0	0	0	0	0	0	0	0	1	26,812
Belton............................	0	0	1	0	0	0	0	1	0	0	0	4,222
Chapin............................	1	0	0	0	0	0	0	0	0	0	1	1,506
Charleston.......................	2	0	0	0	0	0	0	2	0	0	0	127,206
Clover............................	0	0	1	0	0	0	0	0	0	1	0	5,342
Columbia.........................	1	0	1	0	0	0	0	0	1	1	0	132,240
Dillon............................	0	1	0	0	0	0	0	0	1	0	0	6,627
Forest Acres.....................	1	0	0	0	0	0	0	0	1	0	0	10,516
Georgetown......................	1	0	0	0	0	0	0	0	0	1	0	9,072
Goose Creek......................	1	0	0	0	0	0	0	0	0	1	0	39,425
Greenville	1	0	0	0	0	0	0	0	0	0	1	61,185
Hardeeville......................	0	0	0	1	0	0	0	0	1	0	0	4,064
Hartsville........................	1	0	0	0	0	0	0	0	0	1	0	7,877
Holly Hill........................	1	0	0	0	0	0	0	1	0	0	0	1,259
Honea Path.......................	1	0	0	0	0	0	0	0	0	0	1	3,613
Latta.............................	1	0	0	0	0	0	0	1	0	0	0	1,349
Lexington........................	1	0	0	0	0	0	0	0	1	0	0	19,547
Manning..........................	0	0	1	0	0	0	0	0	0	0	1	4,034
Mauldin..........................	0	0	0	1	0	0	0	0	0	1	0	24,099
Orangeburg.......................	0	0	1	0	0	0	0	0	1	0	0	13,826
Salley............................	1	0	0	0	0	0	0	0	0	1	0	412
St. George	1	0	0	0	0	0	0	1	0	0	0	2,139
Summerville......................	2	0	0	0	0	0	0	1	1	0	0	45,210
Winnsboro........................	0	6	0	0	0	0	0	2	3	0	1	3,428
Universities and Colleges	2	0	0	0	0	0	0					
The Citadel	1	0	0	0	0	0	0	0	0	1	0	3,499
University of South Carolina, Upstate	1	0	0	0	0	0	0	1	0	0	0	5,561
Metropolitan Counties	8	2	1	1	0	0	0					
Berkeley..........................	2	0	0	0	0	0	0	2	0	0	0	
Fairfield..........................	1	0	0	0	0	0	0	0	1	0	0	
Horry County Police Department......	1	0	0	1	0	0	0	1	0	0	1	
Lancaster	0	1	0	0	0	0	0	1	0	0	0	
Lexington.........................	2	0	0	0	0	0	0	1	1	0	0	
Sumter...........................	1	0	1	0	0	0	0	0	0	2	0	

Table 13. Hate Crime Incidents Per Bias Motivation and Quarter, by Selected State and Agency, 2013–*Continued*

(Number.)

State/agency	Number of incidents per bias motivation							Number of incidents per quarter[1]				Population[2]
	Race	Religion	Sexual orientation	Ethnicity	Disability	Gender	Gender Identity	1st quarter	2nd quarter	3rd quarter	4th quarter	
SOUTH CAROLINA (cont.)												
Union	0	1	0	0	0	0	0	0	0	1	0	
York	1	0	0	0	0	0	0	0	1	0	0	
Nonmetropolitan Counties	5	0	0	0	0	0	0					
Chesterfield	1	0	0	0	0	0	0	1	0	0	0	
Colleton	1	0	0	0	0	0	0	0	0	1	0	
Georgetown	1	0	0	0	0	0	0	0	0	0	1	
Hampton	1	0	0	0	0	0	0	0	0	0	1	
Marlboro	1	0	0	0	0	0	0	1	0	0	0	
SOUTH DAKOTA												
Total	10	2	1	0	0	0	0					
Cities	6	1	1	0	0	0	0					
Aberdeen	1	0	0	0	0	0	0	0	0	0	1	26,999
Mitchell	1	0	0	0	0	0	0	0	0	1	0	15,555
Rapid City	0	0	1	0	0	0	0	1	0	0	0	70,406
Sioux Falls	3	1	0	0	0	0	0	1	0	2	1	161,754
Vermillion	1	0	0	0	0	0	0	1	0	0	0	10,892
Nonmetropolitan Counties	4	1	0	0	0	0	0					
Codington	3	0	0	0	0	0	0	1	0	2	0	
Corson	1	0	0	0	0	0	0	0	1	0	0	
Hutchinson	0	1	0	0	0	0	0	1	0	0	0	
TENNESSEE												
Total	59	8	38	81	9	0	1					
Cities	43	4	31	38	8	0	1					
Ashland City	1	0	0	0	0	0	0	0	1	0	0	4,637
Athens	1	0	0	0	0	0	0	0	0	1	0	13,504
Atoka	0	0	0	0	1	0	0	0	0	1	0	8,821
Bristol	1	0	2	1	0	0	0	0	0	0	5	26,660
Burns	1	0	0	0	0	0	0	0	0	1	0	1,469
Chattanooga	2	1	0	0	0	0	0	0	0	2	1	172,286
Clarksville	0	0	5	6	0	0	0	1	2	0	8	145,599
Collegedale	1	0	0	0	0	0	0	0	0	1	0	9,468
Covington	1	0	0	12	4	0	0	3	1	5	8	9,076
Dyersburg	1	0	0	0	0	0	0	0	0	1	0	17,013
Elizabethton	0	0	1	0	0	0	0	0	0	1	0	14,220
Fayetteville	1	0	0	0	0	0	0	0	0	1	0	7,155
Franklin	1	0	0	0	0	0	0	0	0	1	0	67,465
Gatlinburg	0	0	0	1	0	0	0	1	0	0	0	4,074
Graysville	2	0	0	0	0	0	0	0	1	1	0	1,512
Greeneville	0	0	1	0	0	0	0	0	1	0	0	15,015
Humboldt	1	0	0	0	0	0	0	0	0	1	0	8,458
Jackson	0	2	2	0	0	0	0	2	0	1	1	67,371
Johnson City	2	0	0	0	0	0	0	1	1	0	0	64,928
Jonesborough	0	0	0	4	1	0	0	0	0	2	3	5,163
Kingsport	2	0	0	0	0	0	0	0	0	1	1	51,496
Knoxville	0	0	0	2	0	0	0	0	1	1	0	183,249
Manchester	0	0	0	2	0	0	0	1	1	0	0	10,258
Mason	1	0	0	0	0	0	0	0	1	0	0	1,611
McMinnville	0	0	0	1	0	0	0	0	0	0	1	13,595
Memphis	9	0	12	1	1	0	1	6	5	9	4	657,691
Milan	1	0	0	0	0	0	0	0	0	0	1	7,789
Millersville	2	0	1	0	0	0	0	0	0	3	0	6,596
Millington	2	0	0	4	0	0	0	0	2	0	4	10,500
Monterey	0	0	0	1	0	0	0	0	1	0	0	2,829
Mount Carmel	0	0	0	0	1	0	0	0	1	0	0	5,422
Munford	0	0	0	1	0	0	0	0	0	0	1	6,036
Murfreesboro	0	0	1	0	0	0	0	0	0	0	1	115,587
Nashville	4	0	1	1	0	0	0	3	1	1	1	635,673
Oliver Springs	1	1	0	0	0	0	0	0	0	2	0	3,250
Paris	0	0	1	0	0	0	0	0	0	0	1	10,168
Pigeon Forge	0	0	0	1	0	0	0	0	1	0	0	6,023
Rossville	0	0	2	0	0	0	0	0	2	0	0	679
Shelbyville	0	0	1	0	0	0	0	0	0	1	0	20,669
Spring Hill	4	0	0	0	0	0	0	2	2	0	0	31,807
Tullahoma	1	0	0	0	0	0	0	0	0	0	1	18,773
Wartburg	0	0	1	0	0	0	0	0	0	1	0	912

(Number.)

State/agency	Number of incidents per bias motivation							Number of incidents per quarter[1]				Population[2]
	Race	Religion	Sexual orientation	Ethnicity	Disability	Gender	Gender Identity	1st quarter	2nd quarter	3rd quarter	4th quarter	
TENNESSEE (cont.)												
Universities and Colleges	4	1	2	0	0	0	0					
Christian Brothers University	1	0	0	0	0	0	0	0	0	0	1	1,603
Southwest Tennessee Community College	0	0	1	0	0	0	0	0	1	0	0	12,220
Vanderbilt University	3	1	1	0	0	0	0	1	1	0	3	12,710
Metropolitan Counties	12	3	4	39	1	0	0					
Hickman	1	0	1	1	0	0	0	0	0	2	1	
Jefferson	1	0	0	0	0	0	0	0	0	1	0	
Marion...	1	0	0	0	0	0	0	0	0	0	1	
Robertson	0	1	0	0	0	0	0	0	0	0	1	
Shelby...	5	1	3	36	1	0	0	2	7	20	17	
Sullivan	2	1	0	2	0	0	0	1	2	2	0	
Tipton...	2	0	0	0	0	0	0	1	0	1	0	
Nonmetropolitan Counties..........	0	0	1	3	0	0	0					
Bledsoe..	0	0	0	1	0	0	0	0	0	1	0	
Henry...	0	0	0	2	0	0	0	0	0	1	1	
Lake...	0	0	1	0	0	0	0	0	0	1	0	
State Police Agencies...................	0	0	0	1	0	0	0					
Department of Safety.....................	0	0	0	1	0	0	0	1	0	0	0	
TEXAS												
Total	54	7	44	25	2	0	0					
Cities	46	5	41	21	2	0	0					
Austin..	0	0	1	3	0	0	0	2	1	1	0	859,180
Beaumont......................................	3	0	0	0	0	0	0	2	1	0	0	118,177
Bellaire..	0	0	1	0	0	0	0	0	0	1	0	17,617
Bellmead..	2	0	0	0	0	0	0	0	1	0	1	9,950
Benbrook	1	0	0	0	0	0	0	0	0	0	1	22,157
Brownwood....................................	1	0	0	0	0	0	0	0	1	0	0	18,873
Carthage	0	0	1	0	0	0	0	0	0	1	0	6,918
Commerce	1	0	0	0	1	0	0	1	1	0	0	8,267
Corpus Christi.................................	0	0	1	0	0	0	0	0	0	0	1	314,523
Dallas...	3	2	9	4	0	0	0	2	4	9	3	1,255,015
Denison	1	0	0	0	1	0	0	0	1	1	0	22,652
Denton	1	0	0	0	0	0	0	0	1	0	0	123,260
El Paso...	0	0	3	0	0	0	0	2	1	0	0	679,700
Everman	0	0	1	0	0	0	0	1		0	0	6,276
Fort Worth......................................	9	0	2	5	0	0	0	5	1	6	4	789,035
Frisco...	1	1	0	0	0	0	0	0	2	0	0	131,769
Gainesville	1	0	0	0	0	0	0	0	0	1	0	16,089
Garland..	1	0	1	0	0	0	0	1	0	1	0	235,683
Grapevine.......................................	1	0	0	0	0	0	0	0	0	1	0	49,075
Harlingen	1	0	0	0	0	0	0	0	0	1	0	65,885
Houston..	4	0	5	4	0	0	0	4	5	1	3	2,180,606
Lancaster	0	0	1	0	0	0	0	0	0	0	1	38,209
Longview	1	0	0	0	0	0	0	0	0	1	0	81,273
Marble Falls	1	0	0	0	0	0	0	0	0	1	0	6,095
McAllen..	0	0	1	0	0	0	0	0	1	0	0	136,169
McKinney	1	0	1	2	0	0	0	0	1	1	2	146,869
Mercedes..	1	0	0	0	0	0	0	0	0	1	0	16,480
Mineral Wells..................................	0	0	1	0	0	0	0	0	0	0	1	16,717
Pasadena	1	0	0	0	0	0	0	1	0	0	0	153,195
Plano...	1	0	0	1	0	0	0	1	0	0	1	275,795
Richmond	0	0	1	0	0	0	0	1	0	0	0	11,841
San Angelo.....................................	1	0	0	0	0	0	0	1	0	0	0	96,661
San Antonio....................................	3	0	7	1	0	0	0	3	3	3	2	1,399,725
Springtown	0	0	1	0	0	0	0	0	0	1	0	2,698
Temple...	1	0	0	0	0	0	0	0	0	1	0	69,937
Terrell..	1	0	0	0	0	0	0	1	0	0	0	16,233
Tyler..	1	0	3	1	0	0	0	2	1	0	2	100,033
Victoria..	0	2	0	0	0	0	0	0	0	1	1	64,979
Vidor	1	0	0	0	0	0	0	0	0	1	0	10,984
Whitehouse	1	0	0	0	0	0	0	1	0	0	0	7,919
Universities and Colleges	4	1	0	0	0	0	0					
Amarillo College	1	0	0	0	0	0	0	1	0	0	0	11,530

Table 13. Hate Crime Incidents Per Bias Motivation and Quarter, by Selected State and Agency, 2013–*Continued*

(Number.)

State/agency	Race	Religion	Sexual orientation	Ethnicity	Disability	Gender	Gender Identity	1st quarter	2nd quarter	3rd quarter	4th quarter	Population[2]
TEXAS (cont.)												
Southern Methodist University	2	1	0	0	0	0	0	1	1	1	0	10,893
University of Texas, Austin	1	0	0	0	0	0	0	1	0	0	0	52,186
Metropolitan Counties	4	1	2	4	0	0	0					
Collin	0	0	0	1	0	0	0	1	0	0	0	
Goliad	1	0	0	0	0	0	0	0	0	1	0	
Harris	1	1	0	1	0	0	0	1	1	0	1	
Hunt	0	0	0	1	0	0	0	0	0	0	1	
Nueces	1	0	0	0	0	0	0	0	1	0	0	
Travis	1	0	2	1	0	0	0	2	1	0	1	
Other Agencies	0	0	1	0	0	0	0					
Independent School District, Humble	0	0	1	0	0	0	0	1	0		0	
UTAH												
Total	46	10	8	8	2	0	0					
Cities	27	8	4	5	1	0	0					
Bountiful	4	0	0	1	0	0	0	0	1	2	2	42,976
Brigham City	2	0	0	0	0	0	0	1	0	1	0	18,217
Centerville	1	1	0	0	0	0	0	0	2	0	0	16,488
Draper	0	1	0	0	0	0	0	0	0	1	0	44,680
Farmington	2	0	1	0	0	0	0	0	3	0	0	21,582
Grantsville	1	0	0	0	0	0	0	0	0	1	0	9,530
Heber	0	1	0	0	0	0	0	0	1	0	0	12,544
Moab	0	0	0	1	0	0	0	0	1	0	0	5,096
Murray	1	0	0	0	0	0	0	0	0	1	0	48,767
North Salt Lake	0	0	0	0	1	0	0	1	0	0	0	16,815
Pleasant Grove	2	0	0	0	0	0	0	0	0	1	1	34,796
Price	1	0	0	1	0	0	0	2	0	0	0	8,589
Provo	1	0	0	0	0	0	0	0	0	0	1	116,937
Roosevelt	1	0	1	1	0	0	0	0	0	3	0	6,404
Roy	1	1	0	0	0	0	0	0	1	1	0	37,810
Salt Lake City	3	1	1	0	0	0	0	0	3	0	2	190,246
South Jordan	0	1	0	0	0	0	0	0	1	0	0	57,593
South Salt Lake	0	0	1	0	0	0	0	0	0	1	0	24,595
St. George	2	1	0	0	0	0	0	2	1	0	0	76,427
Tooele	0	1	0	0	0	0	0	1	0	0	0	32,241
West Valley	3	0	0	1	0	0	0	1	3	0	0	133,373
Woods Cross	2	0	0	0	0	0	0	0	1	0	1	10,343
Universities and Colleges	3	0	1	0	0	0	0					
University of Utah	3	0	0	0	0	0	0	1	0	0	2	32,388
Utah State University, Logan	0	0	1	0	0	0	0	0	0	0	1	28,786
Metropolitan Counties	6	1	2	0	1	0	0					
Salt Lake County Unified Police Department	0	1	1	0	0	0	0	1	1	0	0	
Tooele	4	0	0	0	1	0	0	1	3	0	1	
Utah	1	0	0	0	0	0	0	1	0	0	0	
Washington	1	0	1	0	0	0	0	0	1	0	1	
Nonmetropolitan Counties	6	1	0	0	0	0	0					
Carbon	3	0	0	0	0	0	0	1	0	2	0	
Emery	0	1	0	0	0	0	0	0	1	0	0	
Summit	1	0	0	0	0	0	0	0	0	1	0	
Uintah	2	0	0	0	0	0	0	0	1	1	0	
State Police Agencies	2	0	1	3	0	0	0					
Utah Highway Patrol	2	0	1	3	0	0	0	2	1	2	1	
Other Agencies	3	0	0	0	0	0	0					
Parks and Recreation	1	0	0	0	0	0	0	0	1	0	0	
Utah Transit Authority	2	0	0	0	0	0	0	0	0	2	0	
VERMONT												
Total	8	1	3	0	0	0	0					
Cities	7	1	2	0	0	0	0					
Bennington	1	0	0	0	0	0	0	0	0	0	1	15,492

Table 13. Hate Crime Incidents Per Bias Motivation and Quarter, by Selected State and Agency, 2013–*Continued*

(Number.)

State/agency	Number of incidents per bias motivation							Number of incidents per quarter[1]				Population[2]
	Race	Religion	Sexual orientation	Ethnicity	Disability	Gender	Gender Identity	1st quarter	2nd quarter	3rd quarter	4th quarter	
VERMONT (cont.)												
Burlington	2	0	1	0	0	0	0	0	1	1	1	42,235
Castleton	0	0	1	0	0	0	0	0	0	0	1	4,649
Colchester	1	0	0	0	0	0	0	0	1	0	0	17,288
Morristown	1	0	0	0	0	0	0	0	0	1	0	5,369
South Burlington	0	1	0	0	0	0	0	0	0	0	1	18,549
Springfield	1	0	0	0	0	0	0	0	0	0	1	9,259
St. Albans	1	0	0	0	0	0	0	0	1	0	0	6,888
Universities and Colleges	1	0	0	0	0	0	0					
University of Vermont	1	0	0	0	0	0	0	0	0	0	1	13,098
State Police Agencies	0	0	1	0	0	0	0					
State Police, St. Albans	0	0	1	0	0	0	0	0	1	0	0	
VIRGINIA												
Total	70	30	12	7	0	0	0					
Cities	30	10	9	2	0	0	0					
Bedford	1	0	1	0	0	0	0	0	0	0	2	5,894
Bristol	0	0	1	0	0	0	0	1	0	0	0	17,641
Charlottesville	1	0	0	0	0	0	0	0	1	0	0	44,187
Chesapeake	4	2	0	0	0	0	0	2	0	2	2	230,577
Christiansburg	1	0	0	0	0	0	0	0	0	0	1	21,581
Danville	0	0	1	0	0	0	0	1	0	0	0	43,133
Farmville	1	0	0	0	0	0	0	0	1	0	0	8,142
Galax	0	0	0	1	0	0	0	0	0	0	1	6,870
Hampton	1	0	1	0	0	0	0	1	0	1	0	136,949
Harrisonburg	3	0	1	0	0	0	0	1	2	0	1	51,767
Hopewell	0	1	0	0	0	0	0	0	0	1	0	22,305
Manassas	1	0	0	0	0	0	0	0	0	1	0	41,512
Manassas Park	0	1	0	0	0	0	0	1	0	0	0	16,332
Newport News	1	1	2	0	0	0	0	0	1	3	0	181,074
Norfolk	3	3	1	0	0	0	0	0	5	1	1	247,303
Poquoson	1	0	0	0	0	0	0	1	0	0	0	12,108
Portsmouth	3	0	0	0	0	0	0	0	0	2	1	97,018
Radford	0	0	1	0	0	0	0	0	1	0	0	16,810
Richmond	0	0	0	1	0	0	0	0	1	0	0	212,830
Roanoke	1	0	0	0	0	0	0	0	1	0	0	97,927
Suffolk	3	0	0	0	0	0	0	0	1	2	0	85,475
Virginia Beach	3	2	0	0	0	0	0	1	1	1	2	450,687
West Point	1	0	0	0	0	0	0	0	1	0	0	3,311
Woodstock	1	0	0	0	0	0	0	0	1	0	0	5,193
Universities and Colleges	3	3	0	2	0	0	0					
Christopher Newport University	1	0	0	0	0	0	0	0	0	1	0	5,186
George Mason University	0	3	0	0	0	0	0	1	0	2	0	32,961
James Madison University	0	0	0	1	0	0	0	1	0	0	0	19,927
University of Richmond	1	0	0	0	0	0	0	0	0	0	1	4,361
Virginia Commonwealth University	0	0	0	1	0	0	0	0	1	0	0	31,445
Virginia Military Institute	1	0	0	0	0	0	0	1	0	0	0	1,664
Metropolitan Counties	31	16	2	3	0	0	0					
Albemarle County Police Department	7	2	0	1	0	0	0	1	5	2	2	
Amherst	1	0	0	0	0	0	0	0	0	1	0	
Appomattox	0	1	0	0	0	0	0	0	0	0	1	
Arlington County Police Department	1	0	1	0	0	0	0	1	0	1	0	
Chesterfield County Police Department	1	1	0	0	0	0	0	2	0	0	0	
Clarke	1	0	0	0	0	0	0	1	0	0	0	
Fairfax County Police Department	7	5	0	1	0	0	0	3	1	5	4	
Fluvanna	1	0	0	1	0	0	0	0	0	1	1	
Gloucester	1	1	0	0	0	0	0	0	0	0	2	
Henrico County Police Department	2	3	0	0	0	0	0	0	4	0	1	
James City County Police Department	0	1	0	0	0	0	0	0	1	0	0	
Loudoun	2	1	0	0	0	0	0	2	0	1	0	
Powhatan	1	0	0	0	0	0	0	1	0	0	0	
Prince George County Police Department	1	0	0	0	0	0	0	0	1	0	0	
Rockingham	1	0	0	0	0	0	0	0	0	1	0	

Table 13. Hate Crime Incidents Per Bias Motivation and Quarter, by Selected State and Agency, 2013–*Continued*

(Number.)

State/agency	Race	Religion	Sexual orientation	Ethnicity	Disability	Gender	Gender Identity	1st quarter	2nd quarter	3rd quarter	4th quarter	Population[2]
VIRGINIA (cont.)												
Spotsylvania	2	1	1	0	0	0	0	3	0	1	0	
York	2	0	0	0	0	0	0	1	0	1	0	
Nonmetropolitan Counties	6	1	0	0	0	0	0					
Carroll	1	0	0	0	0	0	0	0	0	1	0	
Cumberland	1	0	0	0	0	0	0	0	0	0	1	
King George	0	1	0	0	0	0	0	0	0	1	0	
Louisa	1	0	0	0	0	0	0	1	0	0	0	
Orange	2	0	0	0	0	0	0	1	0	0	1	
Westmoreland	1	0	0	0	0	0	0	0	0	0	1	
State Police Agencies	0	0	1	0	0	0	0					
State Police, Buchanan County	0	0	1	0	0	0	0	1	0	0	0	
WASHINGTON												
Total	158	40	49	32	7	4	1					
Cities	131	32	36	23	5	4	1					
Aberdeen	3	0	0	1	0	0	0	1	1	0	2	16,408
Auburn	5	1	0	3	0	0	1	1	1	4	4	74,565
Bellevue	0	1	0	0	0	0	0	1	0	0	0	127,678
Bellingham	4	0	4	2	0	0	0	2	5	3	0	82,645
Burien	0	1	0	0	0	0	0	1	0	0	0	49,822
Cheney	3	0	0	0	0	0	0	1	1	0	1	11,117
Clarkston	1	0	0	0	0	0	0	0	1	0	0	7,295
Covington	0	1	0	0	0	0	0	0	1	0	0	18,526
Des Moines	4	1	0	0	0	0	0	0	1	2	2	30,684
Everett	1	1	2	2	0	0	0	2	1	1	2	105,129
Federal Way	3	4	4	0	0	0	0	1	3	3	4	92,741
Ferndale	1	1	0	0	0	0	0	1	1	0	0	12,173
Fife	0	0	0	1	0	1	0	0	1	1	0	9,380
Granite Falls	1	0	0	0	0	0	0	1	0	0	0	3,435
Hoquiam	1	0	0	0	0	0	0	1	0	0	0	8,472
Kalama	1	0	0	0	0	0	0	0	0	1	0	2,316
Kelso	4	0	0	0	0	0	0	1	1	1	1	11,802
Kenmore	0	0	0	1	0	0	0	1	0	0	0	21,531
Kent[3]	8	0	1	0	0	0	0	0	5	2	2	124,359
Lacey	0	1	0	0	0	0	0	0	0	0	1	44,298
Lakewood	3	0	0	0	0	0	0	1	0	0	2	59,057
Maple Valley	0	0	1	0	0	0	0	0	0	1	0	24,644
Mercer Island	0	1	0	0	0	0	0	0	1	0	0	23,969
Mill Creek	0	0	0	0	0	1	0	0	0	1	0	18,806
Milton	0	0	1	0	0	0	0	0	1	0	0	7,076
Mount Vernon	0	1	0	0	0	0	0	0	0	0	1	32,450
Napavine	1	0	0	0	0	0	0	0	0	0	1	1,766
Normandy Park	2	0	0	0	0	0	0	1	0	1	0	6,556
Oak Harbor	1	0	0	0	0	0	0	0	0	1	0	22,288
Olympia	0	0	0	1	0	0	0	0	0	1	0	48,046
Omak	0	0	1	1	1	0	0	2	1	0	0	4,801
Orting	1	0	0	0	0	0	0	0	0	0	1	6,913
Pacific	1	0	0	0	0	0	0	1	0	0	0	6,911
Pasco	0	0	0	0	1	0	0	0	0	1	0	67,099
Port Townsend	1	1	1	0	0	0	0	1	0	1	1	9,112
Pullman	2	0	0	0	0	0	0	2	0	0	0	31,895
Redmond	1	0	0	0	0	0	0	0	1	0	0	57,263
Renton	10	2	0	1	0	0	0	2	4	2	5	96,657
Seattle	50	14	14	6	3	2	0	19	23	29	18	642,814
Sedro Woolley	1	0	0	0	0	0	0	0	0	1	0	10,652
Shelton	0	0	0	1	0	0	0	0	1	0	0	9,780
Shoreline	2	0	0	0	0	0	0	0	0	0	2	54,762
Spokane	1	0	1	0	0	0	0	1	0	0	1	209,524
Spokane Valley	1	0	0	1	0	0	0	0	1	1	0	90,835
Sunnyside	1	0	0	1	0	0	0	1	0	0	1	16,099
Tacoma	3	0	2	0	0	0	0	2	0	3	0	203,226
Tukwila	1	0	0	0	0	0	0	1	0	0	0	19,765
Tumwater	1	0	0	0	0	0	0	0	0	0	1	18,343
Vancouver	5	0	3	0	0	0	0	2	5	0	1	166,535
Washougal	0	1	0	0	0	0	0	0	0	1	0	14,733
Wenatchee	1	0	0	1	0	0	0	0	0	1	1	32,677
Yakima	1	0	1	0	0	0	0	1	0	0	1	93,589

(Number.)

State/agency	Number of incidents per bias motivation							Number of incidents per quarter[1]				Population[2]
	Race	Religion	Sexual orientation	Ethnicity	Disability	Gender	Gender Identity	1st quarter	2nd quarter	3rd quarter	4th quarter	
WASHINGTON (cont.)												
Universities and Colleges	4	2	2	0	0	0	0					
Eastern Washington University	1	0	0	0	0	0	0	1	0	0	0	12,587
University of Washington	3	2	0	0	0	0	0	0	2	0	3	43,485
Washington State University, Pullman	0	0	1	0	0	0	0	0	0	0	1	27,679
Western Washington University	0	0	1	0	0	0	0	0	1	0	0	14,833
Metropolitan Counties	16	4	9	8	2	0	0					
Benton	0	0	0	0	1	0	0	1	0	0	0	
Chelan	0	2	0	0	0	0	0	0	1	1	0	
Clark	3	0	1	0	0	0	0	1	1	1	1	
Columbia	0	0	0	2	0	0	0	0	2			
Cowlitz	1	0	0	0	0	0	0	0	0	1	0	
King	1	1	1	0	0	0	0	0	1	1	1	
Kitsap	1	0	0	0	0	0	0	0	0	0	1	
Pend Oreille	2	0	1	0	0	0	0	1	0	2	0	
Pierce	2	1	1	2	0	0	0	0	1	4	1	
Skagit	0	0	1	0	0	0	0	0	0	1	0	
Skamania	1	0	0	0	0	0	0	0	0	1	0	
Snohomish	1	0	1	0	0	0	0	0	2	0		
Spokane	1	0	1	3	1	0	0	0	2	1	3	
Stevens	0	0	1	0	0	0	0	0	1	0	0	
Thurston	3	0	1	0	0	0	0	0	1	1	2	
Yakima	0	0	0	1	0	0	0	0	0	0	1	
Nonmetropolitan Counties	6	1	2	1	0	0	0					
Clallam	2	0	0	0	0	0	0	0	0	1	1	
Grant	1	0	0	0	0	0	0	0	0	1	0	
Jefferson	0	1	0	0	0	0	0	1	0	0	0	
Klickitat	0	0	0	1	0	0	0	0	1	0	0	
Lincoln	0	0	1	0	0	0	0	0	1	0	0	
Mason	3	0	0	0	0	0	0	0	0	3	0	
San Juan	0	0	1	0	0	0	0	1	0	0	0	
Other Agencies	1	1	0	0	0	0	0					
Port of Seattle	1	1	0	0	0	0	0	0	0	0	2	
WEST VIRGINIA												
Total	40	6	8	2	0	0	0					
Cities	31	5	5	2	0	0	0					
Barboursville	2	0	0	0	0	0	0	0	1	0	1	4,099
Beckley	3	0	1	0	0	0	0	0	3	1	0	17,593
Buckhannon	1	0	0	0	0	0	0	1	0	0	0	5,649
Charleston	3	3	1	0	0	0	0	1	0	2	4	50,919
Dunbar	0	0	1	0	0	0	0	0	0	0	1	7,834
Fairmont	1	1	0	0	0	0	0	0	2	0	0	18,740
Huntington	4	1	2	1	0	0	0	1	2	5	0	49,172
Martinsburg	1	0	0	0	0	0	0	1	0	0	0	17,589
Morgantown	0	0	0	1	0	0	0	0	0	1	0	31,406
Moundsville	1	0	0	0	0	0	0	0	0	0	1	9,130
Oak Hill	14	0	0	0	0	0	0	0	6	8	0	7,709
Wellsburg	1	0	0	0	0	0	0	0	0	1	0	2,760
Metropolitan Counties	7	0	1	0	0	0	0					
Brooke	4	0	0	0	0	0	0	1	1	2	0	
Fayette	1	0	1	0	0	0	0	0	0	1	1	
Hancock	2	0	0	0	0	0	0	0	0	1	1	
Nonmetropolitan Counties	2	1	2	0	0	0	0					
Harrison	1	1	2	0	0	0	0	0	0	2	2	
McDowell	1	0	0	0	0	0	0	0	1	0	0	
WISCONSIN												
Total	22	5	15	8	0	0	0					
Cities	18	4	11	8	0	0	0					
Algoma	1	1	0	0	0	0	0	0	0	2	0	3,143
Appleton	0	0	2	0	0	0	0	0	2	0	0	73,141
Burlington	1	0	0	0	0	0	0	0	0	0	1	10,502

(Number.)

State/agency	Number of incidents per bias motivation							Number of incidents per quarter[1]				Population[2]
	Race	Religion	Sexual orientation	Ethnicity	Disability	Gender	Gender Identity	1st quarter	2nd quarter	3rd quarter	4th quarter	
WISCONSIN (cont.)												
Fond du Lac	1	0	0	1	0	0	0	0	1	0	1	43,042
Green Bay	1	0	1	0	0	0	0	1	0	1	0	105,107
Janesville	2	0	0	0	0	0	0	0	1	1	0	63,603
La Crosse	0	0	2	0	0	0	0	0	1	1	0	51,741
Madison	3	1	3	5	0	0	0	3	5	2	2	242,523
Merrill	0	0	0	1	0	0	0	0	1	0	0	9,427
Milwaukee	5	1	3	0	0	0	0	1	3	4	1	600,805
Oak Creek	0	1	0	1	0	0	0	2	0	0	0	35,046
River Falls	2	0	0	0	0	0	0	2	0	0	0	15,227
Sparta	1	0	0	0	0	0	0	0	1	0	0	9,623
Wausau	1	0	0	0	0	0	0	1	0	0	0	39,176
Universities and Colleges	0	1	2	0	0	0	0					
University of Wisconsin, Platteville	0	1	2	0	0	0	0	3	0	0	0	8,668
Metropolitan Counties	1	0	0	0	0	0	0					
Dane	1	0	0	0	0	0	0	1	0	0	0	
Nonmetropolitan Counties	3	0	2	0	0	0	0					
Burnett	0	0	1	0	0	0	0	0	0	0	1	
Grant	1	0	0	0	0	0	0	0	1	0	0	
Lincoln	0	0	1	0	0	0	0	1	0	0	0	
Manitowoc	1	0	0	0	0	0	0	0	1	0	0	
Oneida	1	0	0	0	0	0	0	0	1	0	0	
WYOMING												
Total	0	0	0	1	0	0	0					
Cities	0	0	0	1	0	0	0					
Gillette	0	0	0	1	0	0	0	0	0	1	0	31,884

[1]Agencies published in this table indicated that at least one hate crime incident occurred in their respective jurisdictions during the quarter(s) for which they submitted a report to the Hate Crime Statistics Program. Blanks indicate quarters for which agencies did not submit reports.
[2]Population figures are published only for the cities. The figures listed for the universities and colleges are student enrollment and were provided by the United States Department of Education for the 2012 school year, the most recent available. The enrollment figures include full-time and part-time students.
[3]Includes one incident reported with more than one bias motivation.
[4]Student enrollment figures were not available.

Methodology

The Federal Bureau of Investigation (FBI) began the procedures for implementing, collecting, and managing hate crime data after Congress passed the Hate Crime Statistics Act in 1990. This act required the collection of data "about crimes that manifest evidence of prejudice based on race, religion, sexual orientation, or ethnicity." In 1994, the Hate Crime Statistics Act was amended to include bias against persons with disabilities. The Church Arson Prevention Act, which was signed into law in July 1996, removed the sunset clause from the original statute and mandated that the collection of hate crime data become a permanent part of the UCR program. In 2009, Congress further amended the Hate Crime Statistics Act by passing the Matthew Shepard and James Byrd, Jr., Hate Crime Prevention Act. The amendment includes the collection of data for crimes motivated by bias against a particular gender and gender identity, as well as for crimes committed by, and crimes directed against, juveniles.

Definitions

Hate crimes include any crime motivated by bias against race, religion, sexual orientation, ethnicity/national origin, and/or disability. Because motivation is subjective, it is sometimes difficult to know with certainty whether a crime resulted from the offender's bias. Moreover, the presence of bias alone does not necessarily mean that a crime can be considered a hate crime. Only when law enforcement investigation reveals sufficient evidence to lead a reasonable and prudent person to conclude that the offender's actions were motivated, in whole or in part, by his or her bias should an incident be reported as a hate crime.

Data Collection

The UCR (Uniform Crime Reporting) program collects data about both single-bias and multiple-bias hate crimes. A single-bias incident is defined as an incident in which one or more offense types are motivated by the same bias. A multiple-bias incident is defined as an incident in which more than one offense type occurs and at least two offense types are motivated by different biases.

A table with selected places in the United States that did not report hate crimes in 2013 is available at http://www.fbi.gov/about-us/cjis/ucr/hate-crime/2013/tables/14tabledatadecpdf/table_14_hate_crime_zero_data_submitted_per_quarter_by_state_and_agency_2013.xls/view .

Important Note: Rape

In 2013, the FBI UCR Program initiated the collection of rape data under a revised definition and removed the term "forcible" from the offense name. The UCR Program now defines rape as follows:

- Rape (revised): Penetration, no matter how slight, of the vagina or anus with any body part or object, or oral penetration by a sex organ of another person, without the consent of the victim. This includes the offenses of rape, sodomy, and sexual assault with an object.

- Rape (legacy): The carnal knowledge of a female forcibly and against her will.

The offenses of fondling, incest, and statutory rape are included in the Crimes Against Persons, Other category.

Crimes Against Persons, Property, or Society

The UCR program's data collection guidelines stipulate that a hate crime may involve multiple offenses, victims, and offenders within one incident; therefore, the Hate Crime Statistics program is incident-based. According to UCR counting guidelines:

- One offense is counted for each victim in *crimes against persons*

- One offense is counted for each offense type in *crimes against property*

- One offense is counted for each offense type in *crimes against society*

Victims

In the UCR program, the victim of a hate crime may be an individual, a business, an institution, or society as a whole.

Offenders

According to the UCR program, the term *known offender* does not imply that the suspect's identity is known; rather, the term indicates that some aspect of the suspect was identified, thus distinguishing the suspect from an unknown offender. Law enforcement agencies specify the number of offenders and, when possible, the race of the offender or offenders as a group.

Race/Ethnicity

The UCR program uses the following racial designations in its Hate Crime Statistics program: White; Black; American Indian or Alaskan Native; Asian; Native Hawaiian or Other Pacific Islander; and Multiple Races, Group. In addition, the UCR program uses the ethnic designations of Hispanic or Latino and Not Hispanic or Latino.

Agencies that participated in the Hate Crime Statistics program in 2013 represented more than 295 million inhabitants, or 93.2 percent of the nation's population. Their jurisdictions covered 49 states, the District of Columbia, Guam, and the U.S. Virgin Islands. The law enforcement agencies that voluntarily participate in the Hate Crime Statistics program collect details about an offender's bias motivation associated with 11 offense types already being reported to the UCR program: murder and nonnegligent manslaughter, rape, aggravated assault, simple assault, and intimidation (crimes against persons); and robbery, burglary, larceny-theft, motor vehicle theft, arson, and destruction/damage/vandalism (crimes against property). The law enforcement agencies that participate in the UCR program via the National Incident-Based Reporting System (NIBRS) collect data about additional offenses for *crimes against persons* and *crimes against property*. These data appear in the category of other. These agencies also collect hate crime data for the category called *crimes against society*, which includes drug or narcotic offenses, gambling offenses, prostitution offenses, and weapon law violations.

National Volume and Percent Distribution

In 2013, 1,826 law enforcement agencies reported 5,928 hate crime incidents involving 6,933 offenses. Of these, 6,921 were single-bias offenses. An analysis of the single-bias incidents revealed that 48.5 percent were racially motivated, 17.4 percent were motivated by religious bias, 20.8 percent resulted from sexual-orientation bias, 11.1 percent were based on an ethnicity/national origin bias, 0.9 percent were motivated by gender and gender-identity bias, and 1.4 percent were prompted by a disability bias. (Table 1)

The majority of the 3,407 hate crime offenses that were racially motivated resulted from an anti-Black bias (66.4 percent) followed by an anti–White basis (21.4 percent). Bias against people of more than one race accounted for 3.2 percent of offenses, while anti–Asian bias accounted for 4.6 percent of racially motivated offenses, anti–Native Hawaiian and Other Pacific Islander accounted for 0.1 percent of these offenses,

and anti–American Indian or Alaska Native bias accounted for 4.3 percent of these offenses. (Table 1)

Hate crimes motivated by religious bias accounted for 1,163 offenses reported by law enforcement. A breakdown of these offenses revealed 59.2 percent were motivated by anti-Jewish bias, 14.2 percent by anti-Islamic (Muslim) bias, 4.4 percent were anti–multiple religions or groups, 6.4 percent had an anti-Catholic bias, 3.6 percent were anti-Protestant, 0.6 percent were anti-atheism/agnoticism/etc., and the remainder, 11.6 percent, of offenses were based on a bias against other religions—those not specified. (Table 1)

In 2013, more hate crimes (1,402) were committed on the basis of sexual orientation bias than on religious bias. Of the offenses based on sexual orientation, 22.6 percent were classified as having an anti–lesbian, gay, bisexual, or transgender (mixed group) bias; 60.6 percent were classified as having an anti–male homosexual bias; 13.2 percent had an anti–female homosexual basis; 1.9 percent had an anti-bisexual bias; and 1.7 percent had an anti-heterosexual bias. (Table 1)

The majority of the 794 offenses that were committed on the perceived ethnicity or national origin of the victim had an anti–Hispanic or Latino basis (52.6 percent). The remaining 47.4 percent were based on bias against another ethnicity or national origin. (Table 1)

Other hate crime offenses were committed based on disability. The majority (75.0 percent) were classified as anti-mental disability, with the rest (25.0 percent) classified as anti–physical disability. (Table 1)

Of the 33 gender identity bias offenses reported, 25 were anti-transgender and 8 were anti–gender nonconforming. Of the 30 gender bias offenses reported, 25 were anti-female and five were anti-male. (Table 1)

Crimes Against Persons

Law enforcement agencies reported 4,430 hate crime offenses against persons in 2013, up from 3,258 offenses in 2012. Approximately 43.5 percent involved intimidation, 38.8 percent involved simple assault, and 16.6 percent involved aggravated assault. In addition, there were five murders and 21 rapes. (Table 2)

Crimes Against Property

In 2013, hate crime offences against property totaled 2,424. Approximately 73.6 percent of offenses involved destruction/damage or vandalism. The remaining 25.2 percent of crimes against property consisted of robbery, burglary, larceny-theft, motor vehicle theft, arson, and other crimes. (Table 2)

PART 6

Jail Inmates at Midyear, 2014

HIGHLIGHTS

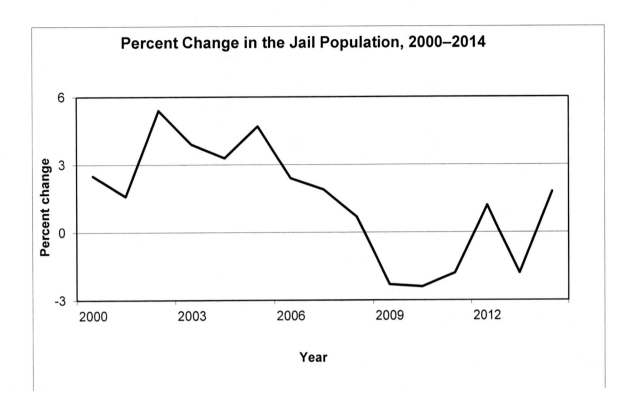

Percent Change in the Jail Population, 2000–2014

- The number of inmates confined in county and city jails was an estimated 744,600 at midyear 2014, which was significantly lower than the peak of 785,500 inmates at midyear 2008.

- At midyear 2014, the jail incarceration rate decreased from a peak of 259 per 100,000 population in 2007 to 234 per 100,000 population.

- An 18.1 percent increase between midyear 2010 and 2014 was noted for the female jail population, while the male population declined 3.2 percent.

- White inmates accounted for 47 percent of the total jail population, Black inmates represented 35 percent of the population, and inmates of Hispanic or Latino ethnicity represented 15 percent of the population.

- Nearly 4,100 juveniles age 17 years or younger were held in local jails at midyear 2014. They accounted for 0.6 percent of the confined population, down from 1.2 percent at midyear 2000.

Table 1. Inmates Confined in Local Jails at Midyear, Average Daily Population, and Incarceration Rates, 2000–2014

(Number; percent.)

Year	Inmates confined at midyear[1]			Average daily population[2]			Jail incarceration rate[3]	
	Total	Year-to-year change Number	Year-to-year change Percent	Total	Year-to-year change Number	Year-to-year change Percent	Adults and juveniles[4]	Adults only
2000	621,149	15,206	2.5	618,319	10,341	1.7	220	292
2001	631,240	10,091	1.6	625,966	7,647	1.2	222	294
2002	665,475	34,235	5.4	652,082	26,116	4.2	231	307
2003	691,301	25,826	3.9	680,760	28,678	4.4	238	315
2004	713,990	22,689	3.3	706,242	25,482	3.7	243	322
2005	747,529	33,539	4.7	733,442	27,200	3.9	252	334
2006	765,819	18,290	2.4	755,320	21,878	3	256	338
2007	780,174	14,355	1.9	773,138	17,818	2.4	259	340
2008	785,533	5,359	0.7	776,573	3,435	0.4	258	338
2009	767,434	-18,099	-2.3	768,135	-8,438	-1.1	250	327
2010	748,728	-18,706	-2.4	748,553	-19,582	-2.5	242	315
2011	735,601	-13,127	-1.8	735,565	-12,988	-1.7	236	307
2012	744,524	8,923	1.2	737,369	1,804	0.2	237	308
2013	731,208	-13,316	-1.8	731,352	-6,017	-0.8	231	299
2014*	744,592	13,384	1.8	738,975	7,623	1	234	302
Average annual change								
2000–2013			1.3			1.3		
2013–2014			1.8			1		

Note: Detail may not sum to total because of rounding. Italics indicate that the difference with comparison year is significant at the 95% confidence level.
* = Comparison year on confined inmates and average daily population.
[1] Number of inmates held on the last weekday in June.
[2] Sum of all inmates in jail each day for a year, divided by the number of days in the year.
[3] Number of inmates confined at midyear per 100,000 U.S. residents.
[4] Juveniles are persons age 17 or younger at midyear.

Table 2. Number of Inmates in Local Jails, by Characteristics, Midyear 2000 and 2005–2014

(Number.)

Characteristic	2000	2005	2006	2007	2008	2009	2010	2011[1]	2012[1]	2013[1]	2014*[1]
Total[2]	621,149	747,529	765,819	780,174	785,533	767,434	748,728	735,601	744,524	731,208	744,592
Sex											
Male	550,162	652,958	666,819	679,654	685,862	673,728	656,360	642,300	645,900	628,900	635,500
Female	70,987	94,571	99,000	100,520	99,670	93,706	92,368	93,300	98,600	102,400	109,100
Adult	613,534	740,770	759,717	773,341	777,829	760,216	741,168	729,700	739,100	726,600	740,400
Male	543,120	646,807	661,164	673,346	678,657	667,039	649,284	636,900	640,900	624,700	631,600
Female	70,414	93,963	98,552	99,995	99,172	93,176	91,884	92,800	98,100	101,900	108,800
Juvenile[3]	7,615	6,759	6,102	6,833	7,703	7,218	7,560	5,900	5,400	4,600	4,200
Held as adult[4]	6,126	5,750	4,835	5,649	6,410	5,846	5,647	4,600	4,600	3,500	3,700
Held as juvenile	1,489	1,009	1,268	1,184	1,294	1,373	1,912	1,400	900	1,100	500
Race/Hispanic origin[5]											
White[6]	260,500	331,000	336,500	338,200	333,300	326,400	331,600	329,400	341,100	344,900	352,800
Black/African American[6]	256,300	290,500	295,900	301,700	308,000	300,500	283,200	276,400	274,600	261,500	263,800
Hispanic/Latino	94,100	111,900	119,200	125,500	128,500	124,000	118,100	113,900	112,700	107,900	110,600
American Indian/Alaska Native[6,7]	5,500	7,600	8,400	8,600	9,000	9,400	9,900	9,400	9,300	10,200	10,400
Asian/Native Hawaiian/Other Pacific Islander[6,7]	4,700	5,400	5,100	5,300	5,500	5,400	5,100	5,300	5,400	5,100	6,000
Two or more races[6]	NC	1,000	700	800	1,300	1,800	800	1,200	1,500	1,600	1,000
Conviction status[5,8]											
Convicted	271,300	284,400	290,000	296,700	291,200	290,100	291,300	289,600	293,100	278,000	277,100
Unconvicted	349,800	463,200	475,800	483,500	494,200	477,300	457,400	446,000	451,400	453,200	467,500

Note: Detail may not sum to total because of rounding. Italics indicate that the difference with comparison year is significant at the 95% confidence level.
NC = Not collected.
* = Comparison year for each characteristic.
[1] Data for 2011–2014 are adjusted for nonresponse and rounded to the nearest 100.
[2] Midyear count is the number of inmates held on the last weekday in June.
[3] Persons age 17 or younger at midyear.
[4] Includes juveniles who were tried or awaiting trial as adults.
[5] Data adjusted for nonresponse and rounded to the nearest 100.
[6] Excludes persons of Hispanic or Latino origin.
[7] Previous reports combined American Indians and Alaska Natives and Asians, Native Hawaiians, and other Pacific Islanders into an Other race category.
[8] Includes juveniles who were tried or awaiting trial as adults.

Table 3. Percent of Inmates in Local Jails, by Characteristics, Midyear 2000 and 2005–2014

(Percent.)

Characteristic	2000	2005	2006	2007	2008	2009	2010	2011	2012	2013	2014
Sex											
Male	88.6	87.3	87.1	87.1	87.3	87.8	87.7	87.3	86.8	86.0	85.3
Female	11.4	12.7	12.9	12.9	12.7	12.2	12.3	12.7	13.2	14.0	14.7
Adult	98.8	99.1	99.2	99.1	99.0	99.1	99.0	99.2	99.3	99.4	99.4
Male	87.4	86.5	86.3	86.3	86.4	86.9	86.7	86.6	86.1	85.4	84.8
Female	11.3	12.6	12.9	12.8	12.6	12.1	12.3	12.6	13.2	13.9	14.6
Juvenile[1]	1.2	0.9	0.8	0.9	1.0	0.9	1.0	0.8	0.7	0.6	0.6
Held as adult[2]	1.0	0.8	0.6	0.7	0.8	0.8	0.8	0.6	0.6	0.5	0.5
Held as juvenile	0.2	0.1	0.2	0.2	0.2	0.2	0.3	0.2	0.1	0.1	0.1
Race/Hispanic origin[3]											
White[3]	41.9	44.3	43.9	43.3	42.5	42.5	44.3	44.8	45.8	47.2	47.4
Black/African American[3]	41.3	38.9	38.6	38.7	39.2	39.2	37.8	37.6	36.9	35.8	35.4
Hispanic/Latino	15.2	15.0	15.6	16.1	16.4	16.2	15.8	15.5	15.1	14.8	14.9
American Indian/Alaska Native[4,5]	0.9	1.0	1.1	1.1	1.1	1.2	1.3	1.3	1.2	1.4	1.4
Asian/Native Hawaiian/Other Pacific Islander[4,5]	0.8	0.7	0.7	0.7	0.7	0.7	0.7	0.7	0.7	0.7	0.8
Two or more races[4]	NC	0.1	0.1	0.1	0.2	0.2	0.1	0.2	0.2	0.2	0.1
Conviction status[5]											
Convicted	44.0	38.0	37.9	38.0	37.1	37.8	38.9	39.4	39.4	38.0	37.2
Unconvicted	56.0	62.0	62.1	62.0	62.9	62.2	61.1	60.6	60.6	62.0	62.8

Note: Percentages are based on the total number of inmates held on the last weekday in June. Detail may not sum to total because of rounding.
NC = Not collected.
[1]Persons age 17 or younger at midyear.
[2]Includes juveniles who were tried or awaiting trial as adults.
[3]Data adjusted for nonresponse,
[4]Excludes persons of Hispanic or Latino origin.
[5]Previous reports combined American Indians and Alaska Natives and Asians, Native Hawaiians, and other Pacific Islanders into an Other race category.

Table 4. Inmates Confined in Local Jails at Midyear, by Size of Jurisdiction, 2013–2014

(Number; percent.)

Jurisdiction size[1]	Inmates confined at midyear[2]		Difference	Percent change	Percent of all inmates	
	2013	2014			2013	2014
Total	731,208	744,592	13,384	1.8	100.0	100.0
49 or fewer	23,545	25,058	1,513	6.4	3.2	3.4
50 to 99	38,970	42,172	3,202	8.2	5.3	5.7
100 to 249	95,031	96,443	1,412	1.5	13.0	13.0
250 to 499	102,362	101,609	-753	-0.7	14.0	13.6
500 to 999	123,155	128,070	4,915	4.0	16.8	17.2
1,000 and over	348,145	351,239	3,094	0.9	47.6	47.2

Note: Detail may not sum to total because of rounding. All comparisons by jurisdiction size are not significant at the 95%-confidence level.
[1]Standardized on the average daily population (ADP) for the 12-month period ending June 30, 2006, the first year in the current Annual Survey of Jails sample. ADP is the sum of all inmates in jail each day for a year, divided by the number of days in the year.
[2]Number of inmates held on the last weekday in June.

Table 5. Rated Capacity of Local Jails and Percent of Capacity Occupied, 2000 and 2005–2014

(Number; percent.)

Year	Rated capacity[1]	Year-to-year change in rated capacity[2]		Percent of capacity occupied[3]	
		Number	Percent	Midyear[4]	Average daily population[5]
2000	677,787	25,466	3.9	92.0	91.2
2005	786,954	33,398	4.1	95.0	93.2
2006	794,984	8,638	1.0	96.3	95.0
2007	810,543	15,863	2.0	96.3	95.4
2008	828,714	18,171	2.2	94.8	93.7
2009	849,895	21,181	2.6	90.3	90.4
2010	857,918	8,023	0.9	87.3	87.3
2011	870,422	12,504	1.5	84.5	84.5
2012	877,396	6,974	0.8	84.9	84.0
2013	872,943	−4,453	−0.5	83.8	83.8
2014*	890,486	17,543	2.0	83.6	83.0
Average annual change					
2000–2013	2.0	17,199			
2013–2014	2.0	17,543			

Note: Italics indicate that the difference with comparison year is significant at the 95% confidence level.
*Comparison year on rated capacity and percent of capacity occupied.
[1]Maximum number of beds or inmates assigned by a rating official to a facility, excluding separate temporary holding areas.
[2]Increase or reduction in the number of beds during the 12 months ending midyear of each year. Number and percentage change for 2000 are calculated using the rated capacity of 652,321 for 1999.
[3]Based on the confined inmate population divided by the rated capacity and multiplied by 100.
[4]Number of inmates held on the last weekday in June.
[5]Sum of all inmates in jail each day for a year, divided by the number of days in the year.

Table 6. Percent of Jail Capacity Occupied at Midyear, by Size of Jurisdiction, 2013–2014

(Percent.)

Jusridiction size	2013	2014
Total	83.8	83.6
49 or fewer	64.4	67
50–99	69.4	74.2
100–249	77.9	78.7
250–499	87.3	86.7
500–999	84.9	85
1,000 or more	87.9	86.5

Note: Number of inmates held on the last weekday in June divided by the rated capacity multiplied by 100. Jurisdiction size is standardized on the average daily population for the 12-month period ending June 30, 2006, the first year in the current Annual Survey of Jails sample. Italics indicate difference with comparison year is significant at the 95% confidence level.

Table 7. Average Daily Jail Population, Admissions, and Turnover Rate, by Size of Jurisdiction, Week Ending June 30, 2013 and 2014

(Number; rate[1])

Jurisdiction size[2]	Average daily population[3]			Estimated number of admissions during last week of June		Weekly turnover rate[1]	
	2013	2014	Difference	2013	2014*	2013	2014*
Total	731,352	738,975	7,623	224,536	218,924	60.2	58.1
49 or fewer	23,301	23,490	189	15,296	12,610	121.1	104.2
50–99	38,721	40,554	1,833	16,315	18,763	83.6	87.2
100–249	93,653	96,200	2,547	32,470	32,087	67.9	65.5
250–499	102,045	99,889	-2,156	35,003	33,527	66.3	65.0
500–999	123,220	125,954	2,734	46,806	35,430	75.5	56.1
1,000 or more	350,412	352,888	2,476	78,645	86,507	44.3	48.5

Note: Detail may not sum to total because of rounding. See Methodology for more detail on estimation procedures. All comparisons by average daily population are not significant at the 95%-confidence level; however, italics indicate that difference with comparison year is significant at the 95% confidence level.
*Comparison year on admissions and weekly turnover rate.
[1]Calculated by adding weekly admissions and releases, dividing by the average daily population (ADP), and multiplying by 100.
[2]Standardized on the ADP for the 12-month period ending June 30, 2006, the first year in the current Annual Survey of Jails sample.
[3]Sum of all inmates in jail each day for a year.

Table 8. Inmate Population in Jail Jurisdictions Reporting on Confined Persons Being Held for U.S. Immigration and Customs Enforcement (ICE), Midyear 2002–2014

(Number; percent.)

Year	Jurisdictions reporting on holdings for ICE[1]	Inmates confined at midyear[2]	Confined persons held at ICE at midyear	
			Number	Percent of all inmates
2002	2,961	626,870	12,501	2.0
2003	2,940	637,631	13,337	2.1
2004	2,962	673,807	14,120	2.1
2005	2,824	703,084	11,919	1.7
2006	2,784	698,108	13,598	1.9
2007	2,713	683,640	15,063	2.2
2008	2,699	704,278	20,785	3.0
2009	2,643	685,500	24,278	3.5
2010	2,531	622,954	21,607	3.5
2011	2,758	672,643	22,049	3.3
2012	2,716	690,337	22,870	3.3
2013	2,685	673,707	17,241	2.6
2014	2,634	654,730	16,384	2.5

Note: Data are based on the reported data and were not estimated for survey item nonresponse. Comparisons were not tested due to changing coverage each year.
[1]Not all jurisdictions reported on holdings for ICE.
[2]Number of inmates held on the last weekday in June in jails reporting complete data or the number of inmates held for ICE.

Table 9. Persons Under Jail Supervision, by Confinement Status and Type of Program, Midyear 2000 and 2006–2014

(Number.)

Confinement status and type of program	2000	2006	2007	2008	2009	2010	2011	2012	2013	2014*
Total	*687,033*	*826,041*	*848,419*	*858,385*	837,647	809,360	798,417	808,622	790,649	808,070
Held in jail[1]	621,149	765,819	*780,174*	*785,533*	767,434	748,728	735,601	744,524	731,208	744,592
Supervised outside of a jail facility[2]	65,884	60,222	68,245	72,852	70,213	60,632	62,816	64,098	59,441	63,478
Weekend programs[3]	*14,523*	*11,421*	10,473	12,325	*11,212*	9,871	*11,369*	10,351	10,950	9,698
Electronic monitoring	*10,782*	*10,999*	13,121	13,539	*11,834*	12,319	*11,950*	13,779	*12,023*	14,223
Home detention[4]	332	807	512	498	738	736	809	*2,129*	*1,337*	646
Day reporting	3,969	4,841	*6,163*	*5,758*	*6,492*	5,552	5,200	3,890	3,683	4,413
Community service	13,592	14,667	15,327	*18,475*	*17,738*	14,646	11,680	14,761	13,877	14,331
Other pretrial supervision	*6,279*	*6,409*	*11,148*	*12,452*	*12,439*	9,375	10,464	7,738	7,542	8,634
Other work programs[5]	8,011	*8,319*	7,369	5,808	5,912	4,351	7,165	7,137	*5,341*	7,003
Treatment programs[6]	*5,714*	*1,486*	2,276	2,259	2,082	1,799	2,449	2,164	2,002	2,100
Other	2,682	*1,273*	*1,857*	1,739	*1,766*	1,983	*1,731*	2,149	2,687	2,430

Note: Italics indicate difference with comparison year is significant at the 95% confidence level.
*Comparison year by status and program.
[1]Number of inmates held on the last weekday in June.
[2]Number of persons under jail supervision but not confined on the last weekday in June. Excludes persons supervised by a probation or parole agency.
[3]Offenders serve their sentences of confinement on weekends only (i.e., Friday to Sunday).
[4]Includes only persons without electronic monitoring.
[5]Includes persons in work release programs, work gangs, and other alternative work programs.
[6]Includes persons in drug, alcohol, mental health, and other medical treatment.

Table 10. Number of Inmates in Local Jails, by Characteristics, Midyear 2000 and 2005–2014

(Number.)

Characteristic	2000	2005	2006	2007	2008	2009	2010	2011	2012	2013	2014
Male	547,624	652,958	666,819	679,654	685,862	673,728	650,341	633,171	636,708	602,193	617,842
Female	70,659	94,571	99,000	100,520	99,670	93,706	91,521	91,923	97,190	98,015	106,081
Adult	610,703	740,770	759,717	773,341	777,829	760,216	734,372	719,253	728,547	695,817	719,857
Male	540,614	646,807	661,164	673,346	678,657	667,039	643,331	627,777	631,802	598,228	614,102
Female	70,089	93,963	98,552	99,995	99,172	93,176	91,042	91,476	96,745	97,589	105,754
Juvenile	7,580	6,759	6,102	6,833	7,703	7,218	7,490	5,840	5,351	4,391	4,067
Held as adult	6,126	5,750	4,835	5,649	6,410	5,846	5,596	4,490	4,489	3,366	3,581
Held as juvenile	1,454	1,009	1,268	1,184	1,294	1,373	1,895	1,350	862	1,025	485
Race/Hispanic origin											
White	236,969	315,598	323,474	327,864	320,111	289,606	274,907	298,663	304,762	297,745	314,846
Black/African American	233,078	276,959	284,412	292,457	295,747	266,638	234,738	250,577	245,376	225,751	235,436
Hispanic/Latino	85,612	106,707	114,564	121,660	123,376	109,998	97,869	103,274	100,682	93,133	98,714
American Indian/Alaska Native	4,974	7,270	8,052	8,347	8,638	8,328	8,223	8,527	8,292	8,793	9,285
Asian/Native Hawaiian/Other Pacific Islander	4,304	5,130	4,940	5,181	5,267	4,785	4,225	4,776	4,826	4,386	5,388
Two or more races	NC	975	633	754	1,237	1,563	689	1,070	1,320	1,419	906
Conviction status											
Convicted	245,698	270,712	280,914	289,098	272,291	250,920	234,566	250,464	248,800	234,134	240,944
Unconvicted	316,728	440,873	460,837	470,960	462,052	412,914	368,411	385,631	383,152	381,588	406,565

NC = Not collected.

Methodology

About the Report

This report presents estimates of the number of jail inmates at midyear 2014 by sex, race, Hispanic origin, and conviction status. It provides estimates of year-to-year changes from midyear 2000 to midyear 2014 in the number of inmates held, average daily population, rated capacity of local jails, and percent of capacity occupied. It also includes statistics, by jurisdiction size, on changes in the number of inmates, number of admissions, and weekly turnover rate between 2013 and 2014. Estimates and standard errors are based on data collected from the *Annual Survey of Jails*.

For more information, please see http://www.bjs.gov/index. cfm?ty=pbdetail&iid=5299.

Terms and Definitions

Admissions: Persons who are officially booked and housed in jails by formal legal document and the authority of the courts or some other official agency. Jail admissions include persons sentenced to weekend programs and those who are booked into the facility for the first time. Excluded from jail admissions are inmates re-entering the facility after an escape, work release, medical appointment or treatment facility appointment, and bail and court appearances. BJS collects jail admissions for the last seven days in June.

Average daily population (ADP): The average is derived by the sum of inmates in jail each day for a year, divided by the number of days in the year (i.e., between July 1, 2013, and June 30, 2014).

Average annual change: The mean average change across a 12-month time period.

Calculating annual admissions: BJS collects the number of jail admissions during the last seven days in June. Annual jail admissions are calculated by multiplying weekly admissions by the sum of 365 days divided by seven days.

Calculating weekly jail turnover rate: This rate is calculated by adding admissions and releases and dividing by the average daily population.

Inmates confined at midyear: The number of inmates held in custody on the last weekday in June.

Jail incarceration rate: The number of inmates held in the custody of local jails, per 100,000 U.S. residents.

Percent of capacity occupied: This percentage is calculated by taking the number of inmates (midyear or average daily population), dividing by the rated capacity, and multiplying by 100.

Rated capacity: The number of beds or inmates assigned by a rating official to a facility, excluding separate temporary holding areas.

Releases: Persons released after a period of confinement (e.g., sentence completion, bail or bond releases, other pretrial releases, transfers to other jurisdictions, and deaths). Releases include those persons who have completed their weekend program and who are leaving the facility for the last time. Excluded from jail releases are temporary discharges including work release, medical appointment or treatment center, court appearance, furlough, day reporting, and transfers to other facilities within the jail's jurisdiction.

Standard errors and tests of significance: As with any survey, the ASJ estimates are subject to error arising from sampling rather than using a complete enumeration of the jail population. A common way to express this sampling variability is to construct a 95% confidence interval around each survey estimate. Typically, multiplying the standard error by 1.96 and then adding or subtracting the result from the estimate produces the confidence interval. This interval expresses the range of values that could result among 95% of the different samples that could be drawn.

Under jail supervision but not confined: This classification includes all persons in community-based programs operated by a jail facility. These programs include electronic monitoring, house arrest, community service, day reporting, and work programs. The classification excludes persons on pretrial release and who are not in a community-based program run by the jail, as well as persons under supervision of probation, parole, or other agencies; inmates on weekend programs; and inmates who participate in work release programs and return to the jail at night.

Weekend programs: Offenders in these programs are allowed to serve their sentences of confinement only on weekends (i.e., Friday to Sunday).

About the Data

In years between the complete census of local jails, the Bureau of Justice Statistics (BJS) conducts the Annual Survey of Jails (ASJ). ASJ uses a stratified probability sample of jail jurisdictions to estimate the number and characteristics of local inmates nationwide. The 2014 ASJ sample consisted of 891 jail jurisdictions, represented by 942 jail facilities (referred to as reporting units). This sample represents about 2,750 jail jurisdictions nationwide.

Local jail jurisdictions include counties (parishes in Louisiana) or municipal governments that administer one or more local jails. In the sampling design, the jail jurisdictions nationwide were grouped into 10 strata. The 10 strata were defined by the interaction of two variables: the jail jurisdiction average daily population (ADP) in 2005, and whether in 2005 the jurisdiction held at least one juvenile. For 8 of the 10 strata, a random sample of jail jurisdictions was selected. For the remaining two strata, all jurisdictions were included in the sample. One stratum consisted of all jails (70) that were operated jointly by two or more jurisdictions (referred to as multi-jurisdictional jails). The other stratum (referred to as certainty stratum) consisted of all jail jurisdictions (267) that held juvenile inmates at the time of the 2005 Census of Jail Inmates and had an ADP of 500 or more inmates during the 12 months ending June 30, 2005; or held only adult inmates and had an ADP of 750 or more.

The sampling design used for the 2014 ASJ is the same as the design used for the 2013 ASJ. The 2013 ASJ differed from the 2006–2012 ASJs in that it included in the sample, with a probability of one, all California jail jurisdictions in response to the two enacted laws—AB 109 and AB 117 by the California State Legislature and governor—to reduce the number of inmates housed in state prisons starting October 1, 2011. The inclusion of all California jail jurisdictions resulted in an additional 21 jail jurisdictions (for a total sample size of 891 jurisdictions). Since the enactment of the two laws in recent years, the California jail population has experienced changes in size that cannot be compared to the changes of any other state in the U.S. For this reason, the California jail jurisdictions were put in separate strata so that they could represent only California jurisdictions. The same sampling design was adopted for the California jurisdictions. BJS obtained data from sampled jail jurisdictions by mailed and web-based survey questionnaires. After follow-up phone calls and facsimiles, the item response rate for jails that responded to the survey was nearly 100% for critical items, such as the number of inmates confined, ADP, and rated capacity. (See appendix tables 1 to 7 for standard errors associated with reported estimates from the 2014 ASJ.) Response rate, nonresponse adjustment, and out-of-scope jail facilities

The 2014 ASJ sample initially comprised 942 reporting units. However, 12 units were out-of-scope for the 2014 data collection because they had closed either permanently or temporarily, which resulted in a sample of 930 active respondents. Ninety-three percent (or 878) of the 930 active individual reporting units responded to the 2014 data collection, and 52 active individual reporting units did not respond to the survey. BJS implemented nonresponse weight adjustment procedures to account for unit nonresponse, as it did in 2011 to 2013.

PART 7

Law Enforcement Officers Killed and Assaulted, 2013

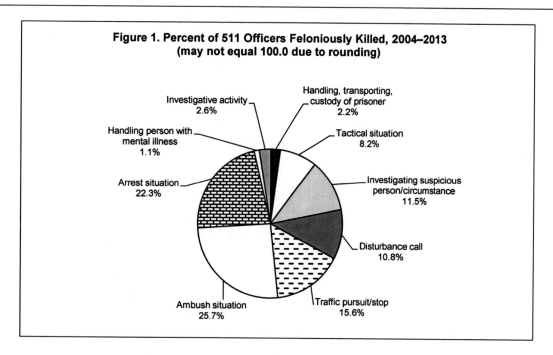

Figure 1. Percent of 511 Officers Feloniously Killed, 2004–2013
(may not equal 100.0 due to rounding)

Investigative activity
2.6%

Handling, transporting,
custody of prisoner
2.2%

Handling person with
mental illness
1.1%

Tactical situation
8.2%

Arrest situation
22.3%

Investigating suspicious
person/circumstance
11.5%

Disturbance call
10.8%

Ambush situation
25.7%

Traffic pursuit/stop
15.6%

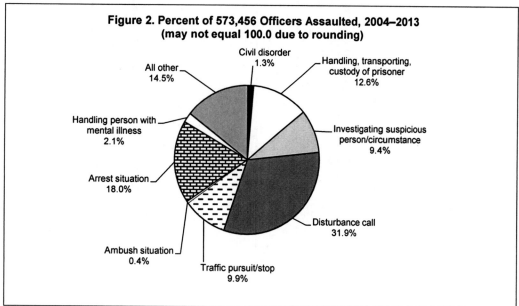

Figure 2. Percent of 573,456 Officers Assaulted, 2004–2013
(may not equal 100.0 due to rounding)

Civil disorder
1.3%

All other
14.5%

Handling, transporting,
custody of prisoner
12.6%

Handling person with
mental illness
2.1%

Investigating suspicious
person/circumstance
9.4%

Arrest situation
18.0%

Disturbance call
31.9%

Ambush situation
0.4%

Traffic pursuit/stop
9.9%

- In 2013, 27 law enforcement officers died from injuries incurred in the line of duty during felonious incidents. Of the officers feloniously killed, 16 were employed by city police departments, including four who were members of law enforcement agencies in cities with 250,000 or more inhabitants.

- The average age of the officers who died in 2013 was 39 years old. The slain officers' average length of law enforcement service was 13 years.

- In 2013, 49 law enforcement officers died as the result of accidents that occurred in the line of duty. Accidental line-of-duty deaths of law enforcement officers occurred in 22 states.

- Law enforcement agencies reported that 49,851 officers were assaulted while performing their duties in 2013.

- In addition to the two officers who were killed in the line of duty, the U.S. Department of Homeland Security employed 588 of the federal officers who were assaulted, and 122 of these officers were injured.

Table 1. Law Enforcement Officers Feloniously Killed, by Region, Geographic Division, and State, 2004–2013

(Number.)

Area	Total	2004	2005	2006	2007	2008	2009	2010	2011	2012	2013
Number of Victim Officers	511	57	55	48	58	41	48	56	72	49	27
Northeast	58	8	5	7	7	3	7	3	10	6	2
New England	9	1	1	1	2	0	0	1	0	2	1
Connecticut	1	1	0	0	0	0	0	0	0	0	0
Maine	0	0	0	0	0	0	0	0	0	0	0
Massachusetts	4	0	0	0	1	0	0	1	0	1	1
New Hampshire	3	0	0	1	1	0	0	0	0	1	0
Rhode Island	1	0	1	0	0	0	0	0	0	0	0
Vermont	0	0	0	0	0	0	0	0	0	0	0
Middle Atlantic	49	7	4	6	5	3	7	2	10	4	1
New Jersey	6	0	0	1	2	0	1	0	2	0	0
New York	18	4	2	3	2	0	0	0	4	2	1
Pennsylvania	25	3	2	2	1	3	6	2	4	2	0
Midwest	90	10	10	6	9	9	5	10	21	6	4
East North Central	58	9	3	5	8	6	2	8	12	2	3
Illinois	15	1	0	2	1	3	2	4	1	0	1
Indiana	9	2	0	1	3	0	0	0	2	0	1
Michigan	17	4	1	1	1	1	0	3	4	1	1
Ohio	14	1	2	1	2	2	0	1	4	1	0
Wisconsin	3	1	0	0	1	0	0	0	1	0	0
West North Central	32	1	7	1	1	3	3	2	9	4	1
Iowa	2	0	0	0	0	0	0	0	1	0	1
Kansas	7	0	2	1	0	0	1	0	1	2	0
Minnesota	7	0	2	0	0	0	1	2	1	1	0
Missouri	12	1	3	0	1	3	0	0	3	1	0
Nebraska	0	0	0	0	0	0	0	0	0	0	0
North Dakota	1	0	0	0	0	0	0	0	1	0	0
South Dakota	3	0	0	0	0	0	1	0	2	0	0
South	238	27	28	22	32	20	21	22	29	22	15
South Atlantic	112	10	13	11	14	13	7	11	18	10	5
Delaware	2	0	0	0	0	0	1	0	1	0	0
District of Columbia	2	1	0	1	0	0	0	0	0	0	0
Florida	34	3	2	3	6	3	3	4	6	2	2
Georgia	19	1	5	2	0	2	0	5	3	1	0
Maryland	7	1	1	0	2	1	0	1	0	0	1
North Carolina	18	3	1	0	3	2	3	1	2	3	0
South Carolina	10	1	1	0	3	2	0	0	2	1	0
Virginia	14	0	3	4	0	3	0	0	3	0	1
West Virginia	6	0	0	1	0	0	0	0	1	3	1
East South Central	49	8	9	4	3	2	5	4	6	5	3
Alabama	17	5	1	2	1	0	4	1	1	2	0
Kentucky	6	0	2	0	1	1	0	0	0	1	1
Mississippi	14	0	6	1	0	0	0	3	1	1	2
Tennessee	12	3	0	1	1	1	1	0	4	1	0
West South Central	77	9	6	7	15	5	9	7	5	7	7
Arkansas	6	0	0	1	1	0	1	2	1	0	0
Louisiana	23	6	2	2	5	2	0	3	0	2	1
Oklahoma	4	0	1	1	0	0	2	0	0	0	0
Texas	44	3	3	3	9	3	6	2	4	5	6
West	104	9	10	11	9	9	13	18	10	9	6
Mountain	41	3	4	4	4	2	2	11	5	5	1
Arizona	18	2	1	0	3	2	0	5	3	2	0
Colorado	8	0	1	2	0	0	1	1	2	1	0
Idaho	1	0	0	0	1	0	0	0	0	0	0
Montana	2	0	0	0	0	0	0	2	0	0	0
Nevada	3	0	0	1	0	0	0	1	0	1	0
New Mexico	5	1	2	1	0	0	1	0	0	0	0
Utah	4	0	0	0	0	0	0	2	0	1	1
Wyoming	0	0	0	0	0	0	0	0	0	0	0
Pacific	63	6	6	7	5	7	11	7	5	4	5
Alaska	2	0	0	0	0	0	0	2	0	0	0
California	44	5	6	6	4	3	5	5	3	2	5
Hawaii	1	0	0	0	1	0	0	0	0	0	0
Oregon	4	0	0	0	0	2	0	0	2	0	0
Washington	12	1	0	1	0	2	6	0	0	2	0
Puerto Rico and other outlying areas	21	3	2	2	1	0	2	3	2	6	0
American Samoa	0	0	0	0	0	0	0	0	0	0	0
Guam	0	0	0	0	0	0	0	0	0	0	0
Mariana Islands	0	0	0	0	0	0	0	0	0	0	0
Puerto Rico	19	2	2	2	1	0	2	3	2	5	0
U.S. Virgin Islands	2	1	0	0	0	0	0	0	0	1	0

Table 2. Law Enforcement Officers Feloniously Killed, by Population Group/Agency Type, 2004–2013

(Number.)

Area	Total	2004	2005	2006	2007	2008	2009	2010	2011	2012	2013
Number of Victim Officers	511	57	55	48	58	41	48	56	72	49	27
Group I (cities 250,000 and over)	110	15	12	8	12	12	15	13	13	6	4
Group II (cities 100,000–249,999)	47	6	6	4	9	1	3	3	9	4	2
Group III (cities 50,000–99,999)	36	4	4	2	5	1	4	3	9	2	2
Group IV (25,000–49,999)	30	2	2	3	2	5	1	6	4	2	3
Group V (cities 10,000–24,999)	31	5	2	3	3	3	3	2	5	3	2
Group VI (cities under 10,000)	53	7	10	3	5	0	6	5	10	4	3
Metropolitan counties	97	8	6	15	11	9	8	9	14	11	6
Nonmetropolitan counties	41	4	4	3	4	4	4	6	4	5	3
State agencies	34	3	5	4	6	3	1	5	0	5	2
Federal agencies	11	0	2	1	0	3	1	1	2	1	0
Puerto Rico and other outlying areas	21	3	2	2	1	0	2	3	2	6	0

Table 3. Law Enforcement Officers Feloniously Killed, by Time of Incident, 2004–2013

(Number.)

Time of day	Total	2004	2005	2006	2007	2008	2009	2010	2011	2012	2013
Number of Victim Officers	511	57	55	48	58	41	48	56	72	49	27
Total A.M. hours	223	20	21	17	24	24	21	23	36	24	13
12:01 a.m.–2 a.m.	61	5	4	5	13	9	3	7	7	5	3
2:01 a.m.–4 a.m.	38	2	4	4	4	4	1	4	9	3	3
4:01 a.m.–6 a.m.	21	2	1	3	0	2	2	3	2	3	3
6:01 a.m.–8 a.m.	21	0	2	2	2	0	5	2	5	3	0
8:01 a.m.–10 a.m.	31	4	5	0	1	4	8	1	3	4	1
10:01 a.m.–noon	51	7	5	3	4	5	2	6	10	6	3
Total P.M. hours	284	37	34	30	34	17	27	33	36	22	14
12:01 p.m.–2 p.m.	38	9	1	5	6	0	5	2	5	2	3
2:01 p.m.–4 p.m.	44	4	7	4	6	4	3	4	6	3	3
4:01 p.m.–6 p.m.	33	1	4	5	2	2	3	4	8	3	1
6:01 p.m.–8 p.m.	47	6	6	4	7	4	3	4	5	6	2
8:01 p.m.–10 p.m.	62	10	6	5	9	2	10	10	3	5	2
10:01 p.m.–midnight	60	7	10	7	4	5	3	9	9	3	3
Not reported	4	0	0	1	0	0	0	0	0	3	0

Table 4. Law Enforcement Officers Feloniously Killed, by Day of Incident, 2004–2013

(Number.)

Day of the week	Total	2004	2005	2006	2007	2008	2009	2010	2011	2012	2013
Number of Victim Officers	511	57	55	48	58	41	48	56	72	49	27
Sunday	60	3	9	2	4	6	9	5	13	7	2
Monday	59	4	8	11	4	1	5	6	12	5	3
Tuesday	70	3	7	3	7	7	6	11	11	10	5
Wednesday	70	8	5	11	8	6	4	12	8	5	3
Thursday	91	11	10	11	10	7	7	11	9	9	6
Friday	79	14	9	5	12	8	4	6	11	5	5
Saturday	82	14	7	5	13	6	13	5	8	8	3

Table 5. Law Enforcement Officers Feloniously Killed, by Month of Incident, 2004–2013

(Number.)

Month	Total	2004	2005	2006	2007	2008	2009	2010	2011	2012	2013
Number of Victim Officers	511	57	55	48	58	41	48	56	72	49	27
January	47	4	6	1	6	8	1	4	9	6	2
February	41	6	3	6	5	4	1	4	3	4	5
March	47	6	6	5	8	0	6	5	9	1	1
April	42	6	6	2	2	1	8	1	9	4	3
May	36	1	6	6	7	2	0	7	3	3	1
June	46	7	3	4	4	6	6	4	6	4	2
July	44	5	4	0	6	4	7	7	8	2	1
August	56	8	7	7	5	4	4	4	7	8	2
September	41	5	3	5	7	6	4	1	1	5	4
October	30	3	2	6	4	1	2	5	5	1	1
November	27	2	7	1	0	1	4	6	2	4	0
December	54	4	2	5	4	4	5	8	10	7	5

Table 6. Law Enforcement Officers Feloniously Killed, by Age Group of Victim Officer, 2004–2013

(Number.)

Age group	Total	2004	2005	2006	2007	2008	2009	2010	2011	2012	2013
Number of Victim Officers	511	57	55	48	58	41	48	56	72	49	27
Under 25	23	3	2	1	7	2	1	3	2	2	0
25–30	89	9	9	9	7	7	9	12	17	8	2
31–35	114	12	15	10	17	7	8	13	11	12	9
36–40	101	9	9	17	8	11	11	9	12	8	7
41–45	69	6	12	3	4	3	13	7	10	7	4
46–50	55	6	7	3	7	4	3	5	13	6	1
51–55	33	6	1	4	5	5	0	1	4	5	2
56–60	17	3	0	0	1	2	3	4	3	0	1
Over 60	7	1	0	1	2	0	0	2	0	0	1
Not reported	3	2	0	0	0	0	0	0	0	1	0
Average age (years)	38	39	37	38	38	39	38	38	38	38	39

Table 7. Law Enforcement Officers Feloniously Killed, by Years of Service of Victim Officer, 2004–2013

(Number.)

Years of service	Total	2004	2005	2006	2007	2008	2009	2010	2011	2012	2013
Number of Victim Officers	511	57	55	48	58	41	48	56	72	49	27
Less than 1	9	2	2	0	2	0	0	1	0	2	0
1–5	150	14	20	16	17	15	13	22	17	12	4
6–10	139	16	10	13	17	11	12	13	24	13	10
11–15	73	8	7	9	7	6	9	6	8	5	8
16–20	61	5	9	4	7	2	6	9	8	10	1
21–25	38	2	5	4	5	4	3	1	12	1	1
26–30	27	6	2	1	3	3	4	1	1	4	2
More than 30	10	2	0	1	0	0	0	3	2	1	1
Not reported	4	2	0	0	0	0	1	0	0	1	0
Average years of service	11	12	10	11	10	10	12	10	12	12	13

Table 8. Law Enforcement Officers Feloniously Killed, by Profile of Victim Officer, Averages, 1994–2013

(Number.)

Characteristic	2013	5-year averages		10-year averages	
		2004–2008	2009–2013	1994–2003	2004–2013
Age	39	38	38	36	38
Years of service	13	11	12	10	11
Height	5'10"	5'10"	5'11"	5'11"	5'11"
Weight[1]	198	198	206		202

Note: The deaths of the 72 law enforcement officers that resulted from the events of September 11, 2001, are not included in this table.
[1]Prior to 1995, data on weight were not collected.

Table 9. Law Enforcement Officers Feloniously Killed, by Race and Sex of Victim Officer, 2004–2013

(Number.)

Characteristic	Total	2004	2005	2006	2007	2008	2009	2010	2011	2012	2013
Number of Victim Officers	511	57	55	48	58	41	48	56	72	49	27
Race											
White	438	46	47	41	48	30	42	48	68	43	25
Black	63	10	8	5	9	10	3	7	3	6	2
Asian/Pacific Islander	5	1	0	1	1	0	1	1	0	0	0
American Indian/Alaska Native	5	0	0	1	0	1	2	0	1	0	0
Sex											
Male	487	54	54	45	58	37	47	54	69	44	25
Female	24	3	1	3	0	4	1	2	3	5	2

Table 10. Law Enforcement Officers Feloniously Killed, by Victim Officer's Use of Weapon During Incident, 2004–2013

(Number.)

Characteristic	Total	2004	2005	2006	2007	2008	2009	2010	2011	2012	2013
Number of Victim Officers	511	57	55	48	58	41	48	56	72	49	27
Fired own weapon	119	11	15	11	11	11	12	17	18	7	6
Attempted to use own weapon	74	9	6	7	17	4	9	7	10	2	3
Did not attempt to use own weapon	251	30	24	22	25	14	18	20	43	37	18
Use of weapon not required	67	7	10	8	5	12	9	12	1	3	0

Table 11. Law Enforcement Officers Feloniously Killed, by Victim Officer's Weapon Stolen[1] by Offender, 2004–2013

(Number.)

Characteristic	Total	2004	2005	2006	2007	2008	2009	2010	2011	2012	2013
Number of Victim Officers	511	57	55	48	58	41	48	56	72	49	27
Total, weapon stolen	54	8	9	4	4	5	7	7	5	3	2
Killed with own weapon	18	4	5	0	2	1	1	4	1	0	0
Killed with weapon other than own	35	4	4	4	2	4	5	3	4	3	2
Killed with weapon, information not reported	1	0	0	0	0	0	1	0	0	0	0
Total, weapon not stolen	452	48	46	43	53	35	41	48	67	46	25
Killed with own weapon	15	3	1	1	0	3	1	2	2	1	1
Killed with weapon other than own	437	45	45	42	53	32	40	46	65	45	24
Killed with weapon, information not reported	0	0	0	0	0	0	0	0	0	0	0
Total, weapon stolen, information not reported	5	1	0	1	1	1	0	1	0	0	0
Killed with own weapon	0	0	0	0	0	0	0	0	0	0	0
Killed with weapon other than own	2	0	0	0	1	0	0	1	0	0	0
Killed with weapon, information not reported	3	1	0	1	0	1	0	0	0	0	0

Note: Weapon is inclusive of all weapon types that may be issued to a law enforcement officer.
[1]The term "stolen" indicates the weapon was taken from the scene of the incident.

Table 12. Law Enforcement Officers Feloniously Killed with Own Weapons, by Victim Officer's Type of Weapon, 2004–2013

(Number.)

Type of weapon	Total	2004	2005	2006	2007	2008	2009	2010	2011	2012	2013
Number of Victim Officers Killed with Own Weapon	33	7	6	1	2	4	2	6	3	1	1
Total, handgun	31	6	6	1	2	4	2	5	3	1	1
.357 caliber	1	1	0	0	0	0	0	0	0	0	0
.357 magnum	1	1	0	0	0	0	0	0	0	0	0
.38 caliber	2	0	0	0	0	1	0	0	1	0	0
.40 caliber	15	1	5	1	1	3	1	1	2	0	0
.45 caliber	3	1	1	0	0	0	0	1	0	0	0
9 millimeter	8	2	0	0	1	0	1	3	0	0	1
Not reported	1	0	0	0	0	0	0	0	0	1	0
Rifle, total	1	1	0	0	0	0	0	0	0	0	0
.22 caliber	1	1	0	0	0	0	0	0	0	0	0
Shotgun, total	1	0	0	0	0	0	0	1	0	0	0
12 gauge	1	0	0	0	0	0	0	1	0	0	0

Table 13. Law Enforcement Officers Feloniously Killed, by Population Group/Agency Type, by Type of Assignment, 2013

(Number.)

Area	Total	2-officer vehicle	1-officer vehicle Alone	1-officer vehicle Assisted	Foot patrol Alone	Foot patrol Assisted	Other[1] Alone	Other[1] Assisted	Off duty
Number of Victim Officers	27	2	8	6	0	0	1	8	2
Group I (cities 250,000 and over)	4	2	0	2	0	0	0	0	0
Group II (cities 100,000–249,999)	2	0	0	0	0	0	0	2	0
Group III (cities 50,000–99,999)	2	0	0	0	0	0	0	2	0
Group IV (25,000–49,999)	3	0	2	1	0	0	0	0	0
Group V (cities 10,000–24,999)	2	0	0	1	0	0	0	0	1
Group VI (cities under 10,000)	3	0	1	1	0	0	0	1	0
Metropolitan counties	6	0	2	0	0	0	0	3	1
Nonmetropolitan counties	3	0	1	1	0	0	1	0	0
State agencies	2	0	2	0	0	0	0	0	0
Federal agencies	0	0	0	0	0	0	0	0	0
Puerto Rico and other outlying areas	0	0	0	0	0	0	0	0	0

[1]Includes detectives, officers on special assignments, undercover officers, and officers on other types of assignments not listed.

Table 14. Law Enforcement Officers Feloniously Killed, by Circumstance at Scene of Incident, 2004–2013

(Number.)

Circumstance	Total	2004	2005	2006	2007	2008	2009	2010	2011	2012	2013
Number of Victim Officers	511	57	55	48	58	41	48	56	72	49	27
Disturbance call	58	10	7	8	5	1	6	6	7	4	4
Disturbance (bar fight, person with firearm, etc.)	29	1	2	6	3	1	4	2	5	2	3
Domestic disturbance (family quarrel, etc.)	29	9	5	2	2	0	2	4	2	2	1
Arrest situation	120	13	8	12	17	9	8	14	23	10	6
Burglary in progress/pursuing burglary suspect	11	2	1	0	1	2	1	3	0	1	0
Robbery in progress/pursuing robbery suspect	46	7	4	6	7	1	3	6	5	4	3
Drug-related matter	7	0	0	2	1	1	0	1	0	2	0
Attempting other arrest	56	4	3	4	8	5	4	4	18	3	3
Civil disorder (mass disobedience, riot, etc.)	0	0	0	0	0	0	0	0	0	0	0
Handling, transporting, custody of prisoner	12	1	1	1	1	1	2	1	1	3	0
Investigating suspicious person/circumstance	62	7	7	6	4	7	4	8	5	9	5
Ambush situation	111	15	8	10	16	6	15	15	15	6	5
Entrapment/premeditation	36	6	4	1	9	1	6	2	2	4	1
Unprovoked attack	75	9	4	9	7	5	9	13	13	2	4
Investigative activity (surveillance, search, interview, etc.)	14	0	4	0	1	2	0	2	1	3	1
Handling person with mental illness	6	2	2	1	0	0	0	0	0	1	0
Traffic pursuit/stop	84	6	15	8	11	8	8	7	11	8	2
Felony vehicle stop	30	0	5	0	5	5	2	3	6	4	0
Traffic violation stop	54	6	10	8	6	3	6	4	5	4	2
Tactical situation (barricaded offender, hostage taking, high-risk entry, etc.)	44	3	3	2	3	7	5	3	9	5	4

Table 15. Law Enforcement Officers Feloniously Killed, by Circumstance at Scene of Incident, by Region, 2013

(Number.)

Circumstance	Total	Northeast	Midwest	South	West	Puerto Rico and other outlying areas
Number of Victim Officers	27	2	4	15	6	0
Disturbance call	4	1	0	3	0	0
Disturbance (bar fight, person with firearm, etc.)	3	1	0	2	0	0
Domestic disturbance (family quarrel, etc.)	1	0	0	1	0	0
Arrest situation	6	0	1	2	3	0
Burglary in progress/pursuing burglary suspect	0	0	0	0	0	0
Robbery in progress/pursuing robbery suspect	3	0	1	2	0	0
Drug-related matter	0	0	0	0	0	0
Attempting other arrest	3	0	0	0	3	0
Civil disorder (mass disobedience, riot, etc.)	0	0	0	0	0	0
Handling, transporting, custody of prisoner	0	0	0	0	0	0
Investigating suspicious person/circumstance	5	0	1	3	1	0
Ambush situation	5	1	0	2	2	0
Entrapment/premeditation	1	0	0	1	0	0
Unprovoked attack	4	1	0	1	2	0
Investigative activity (surveillance, search, interview, etc.)	1	0	0	1	0	0
Handling person with mental illness	0	0	0	0	0	0
Traffic pursuit/stop	2	0	1	1	0	0
Felony vehicle stop	0	0	0	0	0	0
Traffic violation stop	2	0	1	1	0	0
Tactical situation (barricaded offender, hostage taking, high-risk entry, etc.)	4	0	1	3	0	0

Table 16. Law Enforcement Officers Feloniously Killed, by Circumstance at Scene of Incident, by Region, 2004–2013

(Number.)

Circumstance	Total	Northeast	Midwest	South	West	Puerto Rico and other outlying areas
Number of Victim Officers	511	58	90	238	104	21
Disturbance call	58	8	10	31	7	2
Disturbance (bar fight, person with firearm, etc.)	29	3	8	12	4	2
Domestic disturbance (family quarrel, etc.)	29	5	2	19	3	0
Arrest situation	120	18	20	54	19	9
Burglary in progress/pursuing burglary suspect	11	1	2	6	1	1
Robbery in progress/pursuing robbery suspect	46	12	8	15	5	6
Drug-related matter	7	0	0	4	1	2
Attempting other arrest	56	5	10	29	12	0
Civil disorder (mass disobedience, riot, etc.)	0	0	0	0	0	0
Handling, transporting, custody of prisoner	12	1	1	8	0	2
Investigating suspicious person/circumstance	62	4	14	28	14	2
Ambush situation	111	13	21	52	23	2
Entrapment/premeditation	36	5	7	16	6	2
Unprovoked attack	75	8	14	36	17	0
Investigative activity (surveillance, search, interview, etc.)	14	1	3	3	4	3
Handling person with mental illness	6	0	2	2	2	0
Traffic pursuit/stop	84	8	11	42	22	1
Felony vehicle stop	30	3	4	18	5	0
Traffic violation stop	54	5	7	24	17	1
Tactical situation (barricaded offender, hostage taking, high-risk entry, etc.)	44	5	8	18	13	0

Table 17. Law Enforcement Officers Feloniously Killed, by Type of Weapon, 2004–2013

(Number.)

Type of weapon	Total	2004	2005	2006	2007	2008	2009	2010	2011	2012	2013
Number of Victim Officers	511	57	55	48	58	41	48	56	72	49	27
Total firearms	474	54	50	46	56	35	45	55	63	44	26
Handgun	345	36	42	36	39	25	28	38	50	33	18
Rifle	87	13	3	8	8	6	15	15	7	7	5
Shotgun	40	5	5	2	8	4	2	2	6	3	3
Type of firearm not reported	2	0	0	0	1	0	0	0	0	1	0
Knife or other cutting instrument	3	1	0	0	0	0	0	0	1	1	0
Bomb	2	0	0	0	0	2	0	0	0	0	0
Blunt instrument	0	0	0	0	0	0	0	0	0	0	0
Personal weapons	4	0	0	0	0	0	0	0	2	2	0
Vehicle	28	2	5	2	2	4	3	1	6	2	1
Other	0	0	0	0	0	0	0	0	0	0	0

Table 18. Law Enforcement Officers Feloniously Killed, by Number of Victim Officers Wearing Uniform, Body Armor, or Holster, 2004–2013

(Number.)

Characteristic	Total	2004	2005	2006	2007	2008	2009	2010	2011	2012	2013
Number of Victim Officers	511	57	55	48	58	41	48	56	72	49	27
Wearing uniform	397	42	43	32	41	31	40	47	61	40	20
Wearing body armor	330	32	34	27	36	32	36	38	51	25	19
In uniform	297	29	32	22	33	26	32	35	46	24	18
Not in uniform	32	3	2	4	3	6	4	3	5	1	1
Wearing uniform not reported	1	0	0	1	0	0	0	0	0	0	0
Wearing holster	468	53	49	43	52	37	45	53	67	42	27
In uniform	390	42	43	32	40	30	39	46	59	39	20
Not in uniform	77	11	6	10	12	7	6	7	8	3	7
Wearing uniform not reported	1	0	0	1	0	0	0	0	0	0	0

Table 19. Law Enforcement Officers Feloniously Killed, Age Group of Known Offender, 2004–2013

(Number.)

Age group	Total	2004	2005	2006	2007	2008	2009	2010	2011	2012	2013
Number of Known Offenders	565	61	56	59	66	42	45	80	76	52	28
Under 18	28	3	2	4	7	3	2	1	5	1	0
18–24	176	19	19	26	26	8	11	24	20	14	9
25–30	125	12	15	9	10	10	6	23	19	14	7
31–35	73	8	8	7	6	4	9	12	9	5	5
36–40	45	6	2	2	4	5	5	8	7	4	2
41–45	43	6	2	6	3	7	4	6	3	6	0
46–50	23	0	6	1	2	3	1	0	5	2	3
51–55	19	2	0	2	3	1	2	3	4	1	1
56–60	13	3	0	1	2	1	0	2	4	0	0
Over 60	7	2	2	0	0	0	1	1	0	1	0
Not reported	13	0	0	1	3	0	4	0	0	4	1
Average age	31	31	30	28	28	32	32	31	32	31	30

Table 20. Law Enforcement Officers Feloniously Killed, by Profile of Known Offender, Averages, 1994–2013

(Number.)

Characteristic	2013	5-year averages		10-year averages	
		2004–2008	2009–2013	1994–2003	2004–2013
Age	30	30	31	28	31
Height	5'9"	5'10"	5'10"	5'10"	5'10"
Weight[1]	177	178	180		179

Note: The 14 known offenders involved in the events of September 11, 2001, are not included in this table.
[1]Prior to 1995, data on weight were not collected.

Table 21. Law Enforcement Officers Feloniously Killed, by Race and Sex of Known Offender, 2004–2013

(Number.)

Characteristic	Total	2004	2005	2006	2007	2008	2009	2010	2011	2012	2013
Number of Known Offenders	565	61	56	59	66	42	45	80	76	52	28
Race											
White	289	27	36	25	35	20	24	32	44	31	15
Black	243	34	20	31	26	21	17	39	28	16	11
Asian/Pacific Islander	9	0	0	0	4	1	0	2	1	1	0
American Indian/Alaska Native	7	0	0	0	0	0	0	4	2	1	0
Not reported	17	0	0	3	1	0	4	3	1	3	2
Sex											
Male	551	61	56	58	65	40	43	78	74	50	26
Female	13	0	0	1	1	2	2	2	2	2	1
Not reported	1	0	0	0	0	0	0	0	0	0	1

Table 22. Law Enforcement Officers Feloniously Killed, by Status of Known Offender at Time of Incident, 2004–2013

(Number.)

Characteristic	Total	2004	2005	2006	2007	2008	2009	2010	2011	2012	2013
Number of Known Offenders	565	61	56	59	66	42	45	80	76	52	28
Under judicial supervision											
Total	149	16	25	15	19	11	13	19	17	8	6
Probation	66	8	11	5	10	3	7	9	7	4	2
Parole	50	4	10	5	7	5	3	8	4	2	2
Halfway house	3	1	1	0	0	0	0	0	1	0	0
Escapee from penal institution	6	0	2	3	0	0	0	1	0	0	0
Conditional release, pending criminal prosecution	23	2	1	2	2	3	3	1	5	2	2
Not reported	1	1	0	0	0	0	0	0	0	0	0
Known to agency as:											
User of controlled substance	110	12	18	9	9	11	10	19	13	6	3
Dealer of controlled substance	78	10	13	11	9	5	5	7	9	5	4
Possessor of controlled substance	80	10	12	7	12	9	2	12	9	5	2
Use of controlled substance											
Under influence	61	4	9	5	8	3	1	11	8	11	1
Not under influence	99	13	10	8	14	10	9	10	15	5	5
Unknown to victim officer's agency	363	44	37	40	41	28	26	54	48	25	20
Not reported	42	0	0	6	3	1	9	5	5	11	2
Use of alcohol											
Intoxicated/under influence	56	7	6	4	11	2	2	7	7	7	3
Not intoxicated/under influence	116	12	15	10	11	12	11	16	16	9	4
Unknown to victim officer's agency	350	42	35	39	41	27	23	52	48	24	19
Not reported	43	0	0	6	3	1	9	5	5	12	2
Known to agency as having prior mental disorders	38	9	3	4	4	2	3	2	7	2	2
Relationship between victim officer and offender											
Through law enforcement	65	9	11	5	6	5	3	8	11	4	3
Through non-law enforcement	7	2	0	1	1	0	0	1	0	0	2
No known relationship	453	50	45	46	56	36	33	66	60	39	22
Unknown to victim officer's agency	1	0	0	1	0	0	0	0	0	0	0
Not reported	39	0	0	6	3	1	9	5	5	9	1

Table 23. Law Enforcement Officers Feloniously Killed, by Criminal History of Known Offender, 2004–2013

(Number.)

Characteristic	Total	2004	2005	2006	2007	2008	2009	2010	2011	2012	2013
Number of Known Offenders	565	61	56	59	66	42	45	80	76	52	28
Prior criminal arrest	464	49	53	43	60	36	33	71	64	35	20
Convicted on prior criminal charge	357	39	41	31	46	24	28	55	52	28	13
Received juvenile conviction on prior criminal charge	97	15	8	9	14	6	8	10	19	6	2
Received parole/probation on prior criminal charge	285	34	34	22	39	18	26	41	44	18	9
Prior arrest for											
Crime of violence	262	30	25	26	32	16	23	44	37	17	12
Murder	20	2	1	3	2	1	2	7	1	1	0
Drug law violation	240	27	26	27	38	19	13	39	27	16	8
Assaulting an officer/resisting arrest	128	15	12	11	20	6	9	20	23	8	4
Weapons violation	226	25	21	25	29	14	18	40	33	14	7

Table 24. Law Enforcement Officers Feloniously Killed, by Disposition of Known Offender, 2002–2011

(Number.)

Disposition	2002–2006	2007–2011	2002–2011
Number of Known Offenders	298	309	607
Fugitive	0	4	4
Arrested and charged	216	203	419
Guilty of murder	158	104	262
Received death sentence	49	20	69
Received life imprisonment	87	60	147
Received prison term (ranging from 5 years to 198 years)	22	24	46
Guilty of lesser offense related to murder	21	18	39
Guilty of crime other than murder	12	11	23
Acquitted/dismissed/nolle prosequi	14	21	35
Indeterminate charge and sentence	0	1	1
Committed to psychiatric institution	6	3	9
Case pending/disposition unknown	4	44	48
Died in custody prior to sentencing	1	1	2
Not arrested	82	102	184
Justifiably killed	55	63	118
Justifiably killed by victim officer	19	19	38
Justifiably killed by person(s) other than victim officer	36	44	80
Committed suicide	23	33	56
Murdered while at large	0	0	0
Died under other circumstance	4	3	7
Other	0	3	3

Table 25. Law Enforcement Officers Accidentally Killed, by Region, Geographic Division, and State, 2004–2013

(Number.)

Area	Total	2004	2005	2006	2007	2008	2009	2010	2011	2012	2013
Number of Victim Officers	636	82	67	66	83	68	48	72	53	48	49
Northeast	75	10	7	5	6	11	6	8	8	9	5
New England	17	0	2	1	2	1	2	3	2	4	0
Connecticut	4	0	0	1	0	1	0	2	0	0	0
Maine	1	0	0	0	0	0	0	0	1	0	0
Massachusetts	11	0	2	0	2	0	2	1	1	3	0
New Hampshire	0	0	0	0	0	0	0	0	0	0	0
Rhode Island	1	0	0	0	0	0	0	0	0	1	0
Vermont	0	0	0	0	0	0	0	0	0	0	0
Middle Atlantic	58	10	5	4	4	10	4	5	6	5	5
New Jersey	15	1	3	1	2	2	0	4	1	1	0
New York	27	5	1	2	2	3	3	1	5	2	3
Pennsylvania	16	4	1	1	0	5	1	0	0	2	2
Midwest	95	15	13	14	11	5	9	14	7	3	4
East North Central	68	12	9	14	5	5	6	7	3	3	4
Illinois	21	5	3	6	1	0	0	3	0	1	2
Indiana	15	2	3	2	2	2	2	2	0	0	0
Michigan	12	3	3	2	0	0	2	0	1	0	1
Ohio	14	1	0	3	2	2	1	1	2	1	1
Wisconsin	6	1	0	1	0	1	1	1	0	1	0
West North Central	27	3	4	0	6	0	3	7	4	0	0
Iowa	2	0	0	0	1	0	0	0	1	0	0
Kansas	3	0	0	0	1	0	0	2	0	0	0
Minnesota	2	1	0	0	1	0	0	0	0	0	0
Missouri	18	2	4	0	3	0	2	4	3	0	0
Nebraska	1	0	0	0	0	0	1	0	0	0	0
North Dakota	0	0	0	0	0	0	0	0	0	0	0
South Dakota	1	0	0	0	0	0	0	1	0	0	0
South	319	39	30	26	46	32	21	39	27	28	31
South Atlantic	142	16	12	11	22	14	12	16	16	14	9
Delaware	1	1	0	0	0	0	0	0	0	0	0
District of Columbia	2	0	0	0	1	0	0	1	0	0	0
Florida	34	8	3	2	8	4	1	4	1	2	1
Georgia	32	3	3	3	3	3	2	3	6	4	2
Maryland	15	2	0	0	2	3	0	3	2	3	0
North Carolina	19	2	1	0	4	2	3	0	4	2	1
South Carolina	13	0	3	1	1	1	2	2	1	0	2
Virginia	24	0	2	5	2	1	3	3	2	3	3
West Virginia	2	0	0	0	1	0	1	0	0	0	0
East South Central	52	9	4	6	6	4	4	6	3	3	7
Alabama	19	4	2	1	3	2	1	0	2	1	3
Kentucky	5	0	0	2	1	0	0	1	0	1	0
Mississippi	13	1	0	1	2	1	2	2	0	0	4
Tennessee	15	4	2	2	0	1	1	3	1	1	0
West South Central	125	14	14	9	18	14	5	17	8	11	15
Arkansas	10	0	2	1	0	2	1	0	0	0	4
Louisiana	21	1	2	2	4	0	1	3	3	2	3
Oklahoma	13	0	3	1	0	3	1	1	0	2	2
Texas	81	13	7	5	14	9	2	13	5	7	6
West	135	15	14	20	19	17	12	11	10	8	9
Mountain	59	5	3	9	10	6	8	4	4	6	4
Arizona	20	3	2	4	2	2	1	1	2	1	2
Colorado	8	1	1	0	2	0	0	0	0	4	0
Idaho	2	0	0	0	0	0	2	0	0	0	0
Montana	6	0	0	2	1	1	1	0	1	0	0
Nevada	6	1	0	0	1	1	2	0	0	0	1
New Mexico	10	0	0	1	4	1	2	1	0	0	1
Utah	5	0	0	1	0	1	0	2	0	1	0
Wyoming	2	0	0	1	0	0	0	0	1	0	0
Pacific	76	10	11	11	9	11	4	7	6	2	5
Alaska	1	0	0	0	0	0	0	0	0	0	1
California	61	7	10	9	7	11	3	6	5	2	3
Hawaii	6	2	0	1	0	0	0	0	1	2	0
Oregon	1	0	0	0	1	0	0	0	0	0	0
Washington	7	1	1	1	1	0	1	1	0	0	1
Puerto Rico and other outlying areas	12	3	3	1	1	3	0	0	1	0	0
American Samoa	0	0	0	0	0	0	0	0	0	0	0
Guam	1	0	0	0	1	0	0	0	0	0	0
Mariana Islands	0	0	0	0	0	0	0	0	0	0	0
Puerto Rico	10	3	3	1	0	2	0	0	1	0	0
U.S. Virgin Islands	1	0	0	0	0	1	0	0	0	0	0

Table 26. Law Enforcement Officers Accidentally Killed, by Population Group/Agency Type, 2004–2013

(Number.)

Area	Total	2004	2005	2006	2007	2008	2009	2010	2011	2012	2013
Number of Victim Officers	636	82	67	66	83	68	48	72	53	48	49
Group I (cities 250,000 and over)	69	12	4	7	4	10	4	9	5	9	4
Group II (cities 100,000–249,999)	42	4	4	6	7	5	3	3	3	3	4
Group III (cities 50,000–99,999)	34	3	2	3	6	4	3	2	5	1	5
Group IV (25,000–49,999)	38	5	7	2	5	2	1	6	3	6	1
Group V (cities 10,000–24,999)	22	2	4	2	4	3	1	2	0	1	3
Group VI (cities under 10,000)	61	9	8	5	8	8	4	4	7	2	6
Metropolitan counties	143	20	15	19	19	14	10	13	11	12	10
Nonmetropolitan counties	62	9	6	4	6	5	11	9	3	4	5
State agencies	118	9	12	15	14	13	10	19	12	6	8
Federal agencies	35	6	2	2	9	1	1	5	3	4	2
Puerto Rico and other outlying areas	12	3	3	1	1	3	0	0	1	0	0

Table 27. Law Enforcement Officers Feloniously Killed, by Time of Incident, 2004–2013

(Number.)

Time of day	Total	2004	2005	2006	2007	2008	2009	2010	2011	2012	2013
Number of Victim Officers	636	82	67	66	83	68	48	72	53	48	49
Total A.M. hours	223	20	21	17	24	24	21	23	36	24	13
12:01 a.m.–2 a.m.	61	5	4	5	13	9	3	7	7	5	3
2:01 a.m.–4 a.m.	38	2	4	4	4	4	1	4	9	3	3
4:01 a.m.–6 a.m.	21	2	1	3	0	2	2	3	2	3	3
6:01 a.m.–8 a.m.	21	0	2	2	2	0	5	2	5	3	0
8:01 a.m.–10 a.m.	31	4	5	0	1	4	8	1	3	4	1
10:01 a.m.–noon	51	7	5	3	4	5	2	6	10	6	3
Total P.M. hours	284	37	34	30	34	17	27	33	36	22	14
12:01 p.m.–2 p.m.	38	9	1	5	6	0	5	2	5	2	3
2:01 p.m.–4 p.m.	44	4	7	4	6	4	3	4	6	3	3
4:01 p.m.–6 p.m.	33	1	4	5	2	2	3	4	8	3	1
6:01 p.m.–8 p.m.	47	6	6	4	7	4	3	4	5	6	2
8:01 p.m.–10 p.m.	62	10	6	5	9	2	10	10	3	5	2
10:01 p.m.–midnight	60	7	10	7	4	5	3	9	9	3	3
Not reported	4	0	0	1	0	0	0	0	0	3	0

Table 28. Law Enforcement Officers Accidentally Killed, by Time of Incident, 2004–2013

(Number.)

Time of day	Total	2004	2005	2006	2007	2008	2009	2010	2011	2012	2013
Number of Victim Officers	636	82	67	66	83	68	48	72	53	48	49
Total A.M. hours	291	39	32	26	37	32	23	39	22	25	16
12:01 a.m.–2 a.m.	72	8	9	5	8	10	8	10	5	6	3
2:01 a.m.–4 a.m.	71	14	7	5	9	7	2	8	9	5	5
4:01 a.m.–6 a.m.	39	2	9	4	3	5	4	4	3	4	1
6:01 a.m.–8 a.m.	33	4	0	5	2	3	3	5	3	5	3
8:01 a.m.–10 a.m.	36	6	4	2	8	3	2	4	1	4	2
10:01 a.m.–noon	40	5	3	5	7	4	4	8	1	1	2
Total P.M. hours	340	43	34	40	46	36	25	32	31	23	30
12:01 p.m.–2 p.m.	58	7	6	9	10	6	4	4	6	3	3
2:01 p.m.–4 p.m.	53	11	4	3	7	5	3	5	6	5	4
4:01 p.m.–6 p.m.	48	4	5	10	6	4	3	3	7	2	4
6:01 p.m.–8 p.m.	41	6	9	3	3	3	3	5	4	2	3
8:01 p.m.–10 p.m.	65	3	5	6	12	7	8	6	3	5	10
10:01 p.m.–midnight	75	12	5	9	8	11	4	9	5	6	6
Not reported	5	0	1	0	0	0	0	1	0	0	3

Table 29. Law Enforcement Officers Accidentally Killed, by Day of Incident, 2004–2013

(Number.)

Day of the week	Total	2004	2005	2006	2007	2008	2009	2010	2011	2012	2013
Number of Victim Officers	636	82	67	66	83	68	48	72	53	48	49
Sunday	90	15	7	12	11	10	5	11	7	6	6
Monday	70	9	3	4	6	12	8	8	7	7	6
Tuesday	85	14	6	12	11	8	5	7	10	5	7
Wednesday	82	8	18	7	17	7	7	8	2	2	6
Thursday	94	13	7	11	11	11	9	10	10	8	4
Friday	117	12	13	14	16	11	7	17	7	8	12
Saturday	98	11	13	6	11	9	7	11	10	12	8

Table 30. Law Enforcement Officers Accidentally Killed, by Month of Incident, 2004–2013

(Number.)

Month	Total	2004	2005	2006	2007	2008	2009	2010	2011	2012	2013
Number of Victim Officers	636	82	67	66	83	68	48	72	53	48	49
January	47	4	2	6	2	7	9	8	4	4	1
February	44	5	3	6	6	6	4	9	4	1	0
March	45	4	6	5	6	3	2	3	8	3	5
April	49	7	2	6	14	0	5	6	1	3	5
May	67	13	4	4	9	6	6	4	8	4	9
June	54	5	5	3	8	4	3	15	5	4	2
July	58	14	8	4	4	3	3	3	5	8	6
August	48	5	5	8	6	8	4	4	3	2	3
September	58	10	10	5	3	9	2	6	4	6	3
October	74	9	10	7	14	9	4	10	2	4	5
November	45	2	5	8	7	9	2	1	3	5	3
December	47	4	7	4	4	4	4	3	6	4	7

Table 31. Law Enforcement Officers Accidentally Killed, by Age Group of Victim Officer, 2004–2013

(Number.)

Age group	Total	2004	2005	2006	2007	2008	2009	2010	2011	2012	2013
Number of Victim Officers	636	82	67	66	83	68	48	72	53	48	49
Under 25	34	2	4	1	10	2	7	2	2	2	2
25–30	132	19	14	21	11	17	13	15	10	6	6
31–35	120	15	20	15	20	11	8	15	3	9	4
36–40	112	13	13	10	15	14	7	13	11	6	10
41–45	86	14	5	9	9	10	4	5	8	13	9
46–50	67	8	4	2	10	6	7	8	9	8	5
51–55	41	5	2	4	2	4	2	6	5	3	8
56–60	28	4	4	2	5	3	0	5	2	1	2
Over 60	12	2	1	2	1	1	0	2	3	0	0
Not reported	4	0	0	0	0	0	0	1	0	0	3
Average age (years)	38	39	37	36	37	38	35	39	41	40	41

Table 32. Law Enforcement Officers Accidentally Killed, by Years of Service of Victim Officer, 2004–2013

(Number.)

Years of service	Total	2004	2005	2006	2007	2008	2009	2010	2011	2012	2013
Number of Victim Officers	636	82	67	66	83	68	48	72	53	48	49
Less than 1	29	4	3	3	4	3	2	4	2	2	2
1–5	203	27	26	24	32	19	20	24	13	9	9
6–10	165	19	15	20	24	18	12	18	13	14	12
11–15	70	7	6	5	7	9	4	8	7	9	8
16–20	79	12	8	9	8	9	4	8	6	8	7
21–25	35	5	5	1	4	3	2	2	5	3	5
26–30	27	4	1	1	1	3	4	4	3	3	3
More than 30	25	4	3	3	2	3	0	4	4	0	2
Not reported	3	0	0	0	1	1	0	0	0	0	1
Average years of service	11	11	10	10	9	11	9	11	13	12	13

Table 33. Law Enforcement Officers Accidentally Killed, by Profile of Victim Officer, Averages, 1994–2013

(Number.)

Characteristic	2013	5-year averages		10-year averages	
		2004–2008	2009–2013	1994–2003	2004–2013
Age	41	37	39	37	38
Years of service	13	10	12	10	11
Height	5'11"	5'11"	5'11"	5'11"	5'11"
Weight[1]	226	199	210		204

[1]Prior to 1995, data on weight were not collected.

Table 34. Law Enforcement Officers Accidentally Killed, by Race and Sex of Victim Officer, 2004–2013

(Number.)

Characteristic	Total	2004	2005	2006	2007	2008	2009	2010	2011	2012	2013
Number of Victim Officers	636	82	67	66	83	68	48	72	53	48	49
Race											
White	548	75	59	59	70	59	44	60	45	36	41
Black	66	5	7	4	8	7	4	8	7	10	6
Asian/Pacific Islander	12	2	1	3	1	1	0	1	1	2	0
American Indian/Alaska Native	2	0	0	0	0	0	0	2	0	0	0
Not reported	8	0	0	0	4	1	0	1	0	0	2
Sex											
Male	604	76	64	64	79	61	48	67	50	46	49
Female	32	6	3	2	4	7	0	5	3	2	0

Table 35. Law Enforcement Officers Accidentally Killed, by Circumstance at Scene of Incident, 2004–2013

(Number.)

Circumstance	Total	2004	2005	2006	2007	2008	2009	2010	2011	2012	2013
Number of Victim Officers	636	82	67	66	83	68	48	72	53	48	49
Automobile accident	368	48	39	38	49	39	34	45	30	23	23
Motorcycle accident	58	10	4	8	6	6	3	7	4	6	4
Aircraft accident	21	3	2	3	3	2	1	2	1	3	1
Struck by vehicle	101	10	11	13	12	13	7	11	5	10	9
Traffic stop, roadblock, etc.	33	3	5	4	7	1	3	4	3	2	1
Directing traffic, assisting motorist, etc.	68	7	6	9	5	12	4	7	2	8	8
Accidental shooting	31	4	4	4	4	2	2	3	4	2	2
Crossfire, mistaken for subject, firearm mishap	23	2	2	3	4	2	2	1	3	2	2
Training session	3	1	1	0	0	0	0	1	0	0	0
Self-inflicted, cleaning mishap (not apparent or confirmed suicide)	5	1	1	1	0	0	0	1	1	0	0
Drowning	13	3	2	0	2	1	0	0	3	0	2
Fall	15	1	3	0	1	0	0	1	2	3	4
Other accidental	29	3	2	0	6	5	1	3	4	1	4

Table 36. Law Enforcement Officers Accidentally Killed, by Circumstance at Scene of Incident, by Type of Assignment, 2013

(Number.)

Circumstance	Total	2-officer vehicle	1-officer vehicle		Foot patrol		Other[1]		Off duty
			Alone	Assisted	Alone	Assisted	Alone	Assisted	
Number of Victim Officers	49	5	18	3	0	0	6	13	4
Automobile accident	23	3	14	1	0	0	4	1	0
Wearing seatbelt	8	2	5	0	0	0	0	1	0
Not wearing seatbelt[2]	14	1	9	1	0	0	3	0	0
Seatbelt usage not reported	1	0	0	0	0	0	1	0	0
Motorcycle accident	4	0	3	0	0	0	0	1	0
Aircraft accident	1	0	0	0	0	0	1	0	0
Struck by vehicle	9	2	1	1	0	0	1	2	2
Traffic stop, roadblock, etc.	1	0	0	0	0	0	0	1	0
Directing traffic, assisting motorist, etc.	8	2	1	1	0	0	1	1	2
Accidental shooting	2	0	0	0	0	0	0	1	1
Crossfire, mistaken for subject, firearm mishap	2	0	0	0	0	0	0	1	1
Training session	0	0	0	0	0	0	0	0	0
Self-inflicted, cleaning mishap (not apparent or confirmed suicide)	0	0	0	0	0	0	0	0	0
Drowning	2	0	0	0	0	0	0	2	0
Fall	4	0	0	1	0	0	0	3	0
Other accidental	4	0	0	0	0	0	0	3	1

[1]Includes detectives, officers on special assignments, undercover officers, and officers on other types of assignments not listed.
[2]Three of the 14 victim officers not wearing seatbelts were seated in parked patrol vehicles at the time of the incidents.

Table 37. Law Enforcement Officers Assaulted, by Region and Geographic Division, 2013

(Number; rate.)

Characteristic	Total (excluding DC, IL, MT)	Rate per 100 officers	Assaults with injury	Rate per 100 officers	Number of reporting agencies	Population covered	Number of officers employed
Number of Victim Officers	49,851	9.3	14,565	2.7	11,468	247,084,964	533,895
Northeast	6,556	5.6	2,469	2.1	2,393	46,009,689	118,051
New England	1,614	8.5	602	3.2	594	8,536,751	19,013
Middle Atlantic	4,942	5.0	1,867	1.9	1,799	37,472,938	99,038
Midwest	6,277	8.9	2,049	2.9	2,702	37,006,086	70,710
East North Central	2,696	7.5	942	2.6	1,109	19,389,249	35,976
West North Central	3,581	10.3	1,107	3.2	1,593	17,616,837	34,734
South	22,402	10.3	5,767	2.7	4,647	96,252,982	217,527
South Atlantic	14,580	11.4	3,098	2.4	2,196	52,235,029	127,709
East South Central	2,837	8.8	993	3.1	977	14,430,213	32,248
West Soiuth Central	4,985	8.7	1,676	2.9	1,474	29,587,740	57,570
West	14,616	11.5	4,280	3.4	1,726	67,816,207	127,607
Mountain	4,206	11.9	1,181	3.3	605	18,344,218	35,367
Pacific	10,410	11.3	3,099	3.4	1,121	49,471,989	92,240

Table 38. Law Enforcement Officers Assaulted, by Population Group, 2013

(Number; rate.)

Characteristic	Total	Rate per 100 officers	Assaults with injury	Rate per 100 officers	Number of reporting agencies	Population covered	Number of officers employed
Number of Victim Officers	49,851	9.3	14,565	2.7	11,468	247,084,964	533,895
Group I (cities 250,000 and over)	12,677	10.3	3,301	2.7	68	48,611,483	123,078
Group II (cities 100,000–249,999)	6,429	15.2	2,140	5.1	183	27,210,633	42,375
Group III (cities 50,000–99,999)	5,513	13.9	1,715	4.3	396	27,359,925	39,587
Group IV (cities 25,000–49,999)	3,575	10.2	1,101	3.1	626	21,660,578	35,037
Group V (cities 10,000–24,999)	3,588	9.1	1,081	2.7	1,361	21,745,796	39,513
Group VI (cities under 10,000)[1]	3,645	5.9	1,276	2.0	5,689	18,094,947	62,274
Metropolitan counties[1]	12,585	8.2	3,374	2.2	1,321	62,385,317	153,889
Nonmetropolitan counties[1]	1,839	4.8	577	1.5	1,824	20,016,285	38,142

[1]Includes universities and colleges, state police agencies, and/or other agencies to which no population is attributed.

Table 39. Law Enforcement Officers Assaulted, by Time of Incident, Number of Assaults, and Percent Distribution, 2004–2013

(Number; percent.)

Characteristic	Total	Percent distribution	2004		2005		2006		2007		2008	
			Total	Percent distribution	Total	Percent distribution	Total	Percent distribution	Total	Percent distribution	Total	Percent distribution
Total Number of Victim Officers	573,456	100.0	59,692	100.0	57,820	100.0	59,396	100.0	61,257	100.0	61,087	100.0
Total A.M. hours	231,939	40.4	24,355	40.8	23,070	39.9	23,964	40.3	24,488	40.0	24,637	40.3
12:01 a.m.–2 a.m.	87,404	15.2	8,932	15.0	8,325	14.4	8,823	14.9	9,318	15.2	9,585	15.7
2:01 a.m.–4 a.m.	54,549	9.5	5,781	9.7	5,438	9.4	5,505	9.3	5,862	9.6	5,879	9.6
4:01 a.m.–6 a.m.	20,620	3.6	2,183	3.7	2,048	3.5	2,169	3.7	2,157	3.5	2,114	3.5
6:01 a.m.–8 a.m.	14,536	2.5	1,626	2.7	1,549	2.7	1,548	2.6	1,476	2.4	1,480	2.4
8:01 a.m.–10 a.m.	23,859	4.2	2,589	4.3	2,518	4.4	2,621	4.4	2,489	4.1	2,376	3.9
10:01 a.m.–noon	30,971	5.4	3,244	5.4	3,192	5.5	3,298	5.6	3,186	5.2	3,203	5.2
Total P.M. hours	341,517	59.6	35,337	59.2	34,750	60.1	35,432	59.7	36,769	60.0	36,450	59.7
12:01 p.m.–2 p.m.	34,635	6.0	3,627	6.1	3,532	6.1	3,599	6.1	3,659	6.0	3,558	5.8
2:01 p.m.–4 p.m.	42,590	7.4	4,500	7.5	4,268	7.4	4,508	7.6	4,464	7.3	4,286	7.0
4:01 p.m.–6 p.m.	51,418	9.0	5,305	8.9	5,366	9.3	5,307	8.9	5,573	9.1	5,274	8.6
6:01 p.m.–8 p.m.	60,839	10.6	6,067	10.2	6,160	10.7	6,309	10.6	6,372	10.4	6,611	10.8
8:01 p.m.–10 p.m.	72,114	12.6	7,570	12.7	7,276	12.6	7,487	12.6	7,825	12.8	7,853	12.9
10:01 p.m.–midnight	79,921	13.9	8,268	13.9	8,148	14.1	8,222	13.8	8,876	14.5	8,868	14.5

Characteristic	2009		2010		2011		2012		2013	
	Total	Percent distribution	Total	Percent distribution	Total	Percent distribution	Total	Percent distribution	Total	Percent distribution
Total Number of Victim Officers	58,364	100.0	56,491	100.0	55,631	100.0	53,867	100.0	49,851	100.0
Total A.M. hours	23,586	40.4	22,807	40.4	22,703	40.8	22,056	40.9	20,273	40.7
12:01 a.m.–2 a.m.	9,323	16.0	8,829	15.6	8,555	15.4	8,188	15.2	7,526	15.1
2:01 a.m.–4 a.m.	5,653	9.7	5,390	9.5	5,293	9.5	5,212	9.7	4,536	9.1
4:01 a.m.–6 a.m.	2,082	3.6	1,987	3.5	2,126	3.8	1,973	3.7	1,781	3.6
6:01 a.m.–8 a.m.	1,389	2.4	1,428	2.5	1,438	2.6	1,367	2.5	1,235	2.5
8:01 a.m.–10 a.m.	2,192	3.8	2,291	4.1	2,213	4.0	2,272	4.2	2,298	4.6
10:01 a.m.–noon	2,947	5.0	2,882	5.1	3,078	5.5	3,044	5.7	2,897	5.8
Total P.M. hours	34,778	59.6	33,684	59.6	32,928	59.2	31,811	59.1	29,578	59.3
12:01 p.m.–2 p.m.	3,414	5.8	3,307	5.9	3,297	5.9	3,395	6.3	3,247	6.5
2:01 p.m.–4 p.m.	4,232	7.3	4,361	7.7	4,145	7.5	4,083	7.6	3,743	7.5
4:01 p.m.–6 p.m.	5,315	9.1	5,045	8.9	4,826	8.7	4,839	9.0	4,568	9.2
6:01 p.m.–8 p.m.	6,269	10.7	6,088	10.8	6,032	10.8	5,603	10.4	5,328	10.7
8:01 p.m.–10 p.m.	7,337	12.6	7,195	12.7	6,808	12.2	6,684	12.4	6,079	12.2
10:01 p.m.–midnight	8,211	14.1	7,688	13.6	7,820	14.1	7,207	13.4	6,613	13.3

Note: Assault figures published in prior years' editions of Law Enforcement Officers Killed and Assaulted have been updated for inclusion in this table. Because of rounding, percentages may not add to 100.0

Table 40. Law Enforcement Officers Assaulted, by Type of Weapon and Percent Injured, 2004–2013

(Number; percent.)

Characteristic	Total	Percent injured	Firearm Total	Firearm Percent injured	Knife or other cutting instrument Total	Knife or other cutting instrument Percent injured	Other dangerous weapon Total	Other dangerous weapon Percent injured	Personal weapons Total	Personal weapons Percent injured	Number of reporting agencies	Population covered	Number of officers employed
Total Number of Victim Officers	573,456	26.9	21,783	9.3	9,820	12.7	80,382	23.9	461,471	28.6			
2004	59,692	27.8	2,114	9.0	1,123	12.8	8,645	25.6	47,810	29.4	10,589	226,273,199	501,462
2005	57,820	27.4	2,157	8.7	1,059	11.5	8,379	24.6	46,225	29.1	10,119	222,873,755	489,393
2006	59,396	26.7	2,290	9.5	1,055	12.7	8,611	23.6	47,440	28.4	10,596	227,360,586	504,147
2007	61,257	25.9	2,216	8.7	1,028	10.5	8,692	22.2	49,321	27.6	10,973	234,734,286	523,944
2008	61,087	26.0	2,292	8.3	958	13.0	8,466	22.8	49,371	27.7	10,835	238,730,830	541,906
2009	58,364	26.0	2,007	8.1	886	12.4	7,966	23.5	47,505	27.4	11,691	245,925,716	560,387
2010	56,491	26.5	1,925	11.1	918	12.1	7,413	23.8	46,235	27.8	11,826	248,726,641	557,884
2011	55,631	26.6	2,240	9.0	1,003	15.0	7,856	22.4	44,532	28.5	12,031	254,534,862	539,282
2012	53,867	27.7	2,276	9.9	909	13.1	7,435	24.2	43,247	29.6	11,794	250,150,500	525,217
2013	49,851	29.2	2,266	10.9	881	14.6	6,919	27.0	39,785	31.0	11,468	247,084,964	533,895

Note: Assault figures published in prior years' editions of Law Enforcement Officers Killed and Assaulted have been updated for inclusion in this table.

Table 41. Law Enforcement Officers Assaulted, by Region, Geographic Division, and State, by Type of Weapon, 2013

(Number.)

Characteristic	Total	Firearm	Knife or other cutting instrument	Other dangerous weapon	Personal weapons	Number of reporting agencies	Population covered	Number of officers employed
Total Number of Victim Officers	49,851	2,266	881	6,919	39,785	11,468	247,084,964	533,895
Northeast..............................	6,556	224	80	722	5,530	2,393	46,009,689	118,051
New England	1,614	22	19	173	1,400	594	8,536,751	19,013
Connecticut	678	11	7	67	593	101	3,596,080	8,500
Maine...............................	187	1	1	20	165	179	1,327,788	1,980
Massachusetts....................	64	0	0	8	56	30	759,993	2,713
New Hampshire...................	249	5	4	17	223	149	1,177,151	2,228
Rhode Island	368	5	3	52	308	48	1,051,511	2,434
Vermont............................	68	0	4	9	55	87	624,228	1,158
Middle Atlantic	4,942	202	61	549	4,130	1,799	37,472,938	99,038
New Jersey	1,806	42	19	193	1,552	481	8,147,691	21,770
New York	962	28	8	117	809	367	17,626,887	57,696
Pennsylvania......................	2,174	132	34	239	1,769	951	11,698,360	19,572
Midwest	6,277	295	122	806	5,054	2,702	37,006,086	70,710
East North Central.................	2,696	124	57	350	2,165	1,109	19,389,249	35,976
Illinois[1]								
Indiana...........................	924	34	5	64	821	97	2,928,732	4,506
Michigan..........................	921	54	36	175	656	581	9,685,674	16,689
Ohio..............................	183	6	1	10	166	59	1,222,947	2,519
Wisconsin	668	30	15	101	522	372	5,551,896	12,262
West North Central	3,581	171	65	456	2,889	1,593	17,616,837	34,734
Iowa..............................	470	8	16	86	360	226	2,939,034	4,439
Kansas	34	2	0	3	29	91	316,242	971
Minnesota........................	389	8	4	66	311	316	5,336,155	8,743
Missouri..........................	2,291	144	33	260	1,854	551	5,895,986	14,327
Nebraska.........................	162	9	3	24	126	198	1,644,449	3,330
North Dakota	131	0	0	9	122	103	721,183	1,468
South Dakota	104	0	9	8	87	108	763,788	1,456
South..................................	22,402	963	378	3,164	17,897	4,647	96,252,982	217,527
South Atlantic	14,580	504	192	1,829	12,055	2,196	52,235,029	127,709
Delaware..........................	452	4	6	100	342	54	924,670	2,339
District of Columbia[1]								
Florida............................	6,056	196	88	828	4,944	338	17,645,414	42,225
Georgia...........................	1,223	48	11	123	1,041	335	7,535,889	19,554
Maryland..........................	2,319	39	30	195	2,055	151	4,588,155	14,812
North Carolina	2,094	83	33	149	1,829	316	8,204,794	18,988
South Carolina	658	60	15	126	457	344	4,611,730	11,369
Virginia...........................	1,240	51	7	185	997	410	7,056,714	15,400
West Virginia......................	538	23	2	123	390	248	1,667,663	3,022
East South Central	2,837	220	101	608	1,908	977	14,430,213	32,248
Alabama..........................	295	4	4	91	196	210	3,553,040	7,316
Kentucky..........................	738	21	10	122	585	285	3,632,555	6,451
Mississippi........................	100	7	1	11	81	45	918,552	2,227
Tennessee........................	1,704	188	86	384	1,046	437	6,326,066	16,254
West South Central	4,985	239	85	727	3,934	1,474	29,587,740	57,570
Arkansas..........................	60	0	4	16	40	224	2,718,606	5,501
Louisiana..........................	786	25	10	290	461	19	1,160,791	3,809
Oklahoma.........................	662	16	6	128	512	322	3,831,626	7,040
Texas.............................	3,477	198	65	293	2,921	909	21,876,717	41,220
West	14,616	784	301	2,227	11,304	1,726	67,816,207	127,607
Mountain..........................	4,206	373	125	647	3,061	605	18,344,218	35,367
Arizona	2,295	217	37	333	1,708	81	6,231,658	11,555
Colorado..........................	995	98	54	160	683	212	5,079,366	11,527
Idaho.............................	235	11	4	33	187	107	1,610,592	2,706
Montana[1]								
Nevada............................	354	38	18	90	208	34	2,785,500	4,898
New Mexico.......................	21	0	2	2	17	23	128,099	291
Utah..............................	242	8	10	20	204	88	1,946,664	2,979
Wyoming..........................	64	1	0	9	54	60	562,339	1,411
Pacific.............................	10,410	411	176	1,580	8,243	1,121	49,471,989	92,240
Alaska............................	403	26	8	58	311	31	724,166	1,284
California	8,388	352	134	1,291	6,611	681	38,324,460	76,290
Hawaii[2]	40	0	1	5	34	1	159,652	353
Oregon............................	542	5	8	64	465	179	3,739,465	5,740
Washington........................	1,037	28	25	162	822	229	6,524,246	8,573

[1]Data for the District of Columbia, Illinois, and Montana were not available for inclusion in this table.
[2]Data represents the number of assaults on officers reported by the Maui Police Department.

Table 42. Law Enforcement Officers Assaulted, by Circumstance at Scene of Incident, by Type of Weapon and Percent Distribution, 2013

(Number; percent.)

Circumstance	Total	Percent distribution	Firearm		Knife or other cutting instrument		Other dangerous weapon		Personal weapons	
			Total	Percent distribution	Total	Percent distribution	Total	Percent distribution	Total	Percent distribution
Total Number of Victim Officers	49,851	100.0	2,266	4.5	881	1.8	6,919	13.9	39,785	79.8
Disturbance call	15,531	100.0	842	5.4	377	2.4	1,418	9.1	12,894	83.0
Burglary in progress/pursuing burglary suspect	791	100.0	64	8.1	19	2.4	180	22.8	528	66.8
Robbery in progress/pursuing robbery suspect	445	100.0	80	18.0	6	1.3	101	22.7	258	58.0
Attempting other arrest	8,107	100.0	244	3.0	119	1.5	886	10.9	6,858	84.6
Civil disorder (mass disobedience, riot, etc.)	506	100.0	15	3.0	5	1.0	76	15.0	410	81.0
Handling, transporting, custody of prisoner	6,397	100.0	27	0.4	29	0.5	607	9.5	5,734	89.6
Investigating suspicious person/circumstance	4,691	100.0	270	5.8	123	2.6	699	14.9	3,599	76.7
Ambush situation	234	100.0	67	28.6	9	3.8	42	17.9	116	49.6
Handling person with mental illness	1,319	100.0	69	5.2	62	4.7	133	10.1	1,055	80.0
Traffic pursuit/stop	4,335	100.0	248	5.7	20	0.5	1,507	34.8	2,560	59.1
All other	7,495	100.0	340	4.5	112	1.5	1,270	16.9	5,773	77.0

Note: Because of rounding, percentages may not add to 100.0

Table 43. Federal Officers Killed and Assaulted, by Department and Agency, by Number of Victim Officers and Known Offenders, 2012 and 2013

(Number; percent.)

Department/agency	Victim officers		Known offenders	
	2012	2013	2012	2013
Total Number of Victim Officers/Known Offenders	1,858	1,774	1,215	1,177
U.S. Capitol Police	4	13	4	9
U.S. Department of Homeland Security	658	590	87	70
U.S. Customs and Border Protection (CBP)	607	555	43	48
CBP, Office of Air and Marine[1,2]	9	27		
CBP, Office of Border Patrol[1,2]	555	468		
CBP, Office of Field Operations	43	60	43	48
U.S. Immigration and Customs Enforcement[3]	12		15	
U.S. Secret Service	39	35	29	22
U.S. Department of the Interior	861	875	788	842
Bureau of Indian Affairs	716	806	671	776
Bureau of Land Management	5	5	4	5
National Park Service	137	59	109	57
U.S. Fish and Wildlife Service (FWS)	3	5	4	4
FWS, National Wildlife Refuge System	2	5	2	4
FWS, Office of Law Enforcement	1	0	2	0
U.S. Department of Justice	329	293	331	253
Bureau of Alcohol, Tobacco, Firearms and Explosives	20	14	21	14
Federal Bureau of Investigation	24	31	25	19
U.S. Drug Enforcement Administration	0	7	0	13
U.S. Marshals Service	285	241	285	207
U.S. Department of the Treasury				
Internal Revenue Service	2	0	1	0
Treasury Inspector General for Tax Administration	2	0	1	0
	0	0	0	0
U.S. Postal Inspection Service	4	3	4	3

[1] For 2012, known offender data were not reported by the CBP, Office of Air and Marine and Office of Border Patrol.
[2] For 2013, known offender data were not reported by the CBP, Office of Air and Marine and Office of Border Patrol.
[3] For 2013, data were not reported by the U.S. Immigration and Customs Enforcement.

Table 44. Federal Officers Killed and Assaulted, by Department and Agency, by Extent of Injury to Victim Officer, 2009–2013

(Number; percent.)

Department/agency	2009			2010			2011			2012			2013		
	Killed	Injured	Not injured	Killed	Injured	Not injured	Killed	Injured	Not injured	Killed	Injured	Not injured	Killed	Injured	Not injured
Total Number of Victim Officers/Known Offenders	1	181	1,625	1	351	1,534	3	254	1,432	1	206	1,096	4	292	1,478
U.S. Capitol Police	0	9	10	0	1	9	0	8	13	0	1	3	0	6	7
U.S. Department of Homeland Security	1	6	1,196	1	144	858	1	90	745	0	20	83	2	122	466
U.S. Customs and Border Protection (CBP)	1	1	1,183	1	141	846	0	82	720	0	12	40	2	121	432
CBP, Office of Air and Marine[1,2]				0	0	27	0	0	25	0	0	9	0	0	27
CBP, Office of Border Patrol[1,2]	1	0	1,166	1	133	754	0	71	628				2	98	368
CBP, Office of Field Operations	0	1	17	0	8	65	0	11	67	0	12	31	0	23	37
U.S. Immigration and Customs Enforcement[3]	0	2	0	0	2	1	1	4	0	0	6	6			
U.S. Secret Service	0	3	13	0	1	11	0	4	25	0	2	37	0	1	34
U.S. Department of the Interior	0	127	366	0	130	520	0	113	423	1	151	709	1	106	768
Bureau of Indian Affairs	0	102	292	0	114	430	0	88	337	0	112	604	1	94	711
Bureau of Land Management	0	1	9	0	0	4	0	0	7	0	0	5	0	0	5
National Park Service	0	24	61	0	14	84	0	25	76	1	37	99	0	12	47
U.S. Fish and Wildlife Service (FWS)	0	0	4	0	2	2	0	0	3	0	2	1	0	0	5
FWS, National Wildlife Refuge System	0	0	4	0	2	0	0	0	3	0	1	1	0	0	5
FWS, Office of Law Enforcement	0	0	0	0	0	2	0	0	0	0	1	0	0	0	0
U.S. Department of Justice	0	35	48	0	73	135	2	41	246	0	32	297	1	58	234
Bureau of Alcohol, Tobacco, Firearms and Explosives	0	1	34	0	3	21	0	2	22	0	0	20	0	2	12
Federal Bureau of Investigation	0	6	14	0	7	7	0	7	22	0	2	22	0	11	20
U.S. Drug Enforcement Administration	0	0	0	0	4	1	0	0	0	0	0	0	1	0	6
U.S. Marshals Service	0	28	0	0	59	106	2	32	202	0	30	255	0	45	196
U.S. Department of the Treasury	0	1	2	0	1	8	0	0	0	0	2	0	0	0	0
Internal Revenue Service	0	0	2	0	0	8	0	0	0	0	2	0	0	0	0
Treasury Inspector General for Tax Administration	0	1	0	0	1	0	0	0	0	0	0	0	0	0	0
U.S. Postal Inspection Service	0	3	3	0	2	4	0	2	5	0	0	4	0	0	3

[1]Prior to 2010, data were not collected from the CBP, Office of Air and Marine.
[2]For 2012, extent of injury data for 555 victim officers were not reported by the CBP, Office of Border Patrol.
[3]For 2013, data were not reported by the U.S. Immigration and Customs Enforcement.

Methodology

When an officer is killed in the line of duty, the FBI gathers data about circumstances pertaining to the death. The data come from various sources:

- City, university and college, county, state, tribal, and federal law enforcement agencies participating in the Uniform Crime Reporting Program may report line-of-duty deaths that occur in their jurisdictions

- FBI field offices report line-of-duty deaths of law enforcement officers that occur in the United States and its outlying areas

- Several nonprofit organizations, such as the Concerns of Police Survivors and the National Law Enforcement Officers Memorial Fund, which provide various services to the families of fallen officers, also furnish information about line-of-duty deaths

When the FBI receives notification of a line-of-duty death, the Law Enforcement Officers Killed and Assaulted (LEOKA) Program's staff works with FBI field offices to contact the fallen officer's employing agency and request additional details about the fatal incident. The LEOKA staff also obtains criminal history data from the FBI's Interstate Identification Index about individuals who are identified in connection with line-of-duty felonious deaths.

The data in *Law Enforcement Officers Killed and Assaulted* pertain to felonious deaths, accidental deaths, and assaults of duly sworn city, university and college, county, state, tribal, and federal law enforcement officers who, at the time of the incident, met the following criteria:

- They were working in an official capacity, whether on or off duty

- They had full arrest powers

- They ordinarily wore/carried a badge and a firearm

- They were paid from governmental funds set aside specifically for payment of sworn law enforcement representatives

Officers who died are included if their deaths are directly related to injuries received during the incidents.

The FBI publishes *Law Enforcement Officers Killed and Assaulted* each year to provide information about officers who were killed, feloniously or accidentally, and officers who were assaulted while performing their duties. The FBI collects these data through the Uniform Crime Reporting (UCR) Program.

Data Considerations

When reviewing the tables, charts, and summaries presented in this publication, readers should be aware of certain features of the Law Enforcement Officers Killed and Assaulted (LEOKA) data collection process that could affect their interpretation of the information.

- The data in the tables and charts reflect the number of victim officers, not the number of incidents or weapons used

- The UCR Program considers any parts of the body that can be used as weapons (such as hands, fists, or feet) to be personal weapons and designates them as such in its data

- Law enforcement agencies use a different methodology for collecting and reporting data about officers who were killed than the methodology used for those who were assaulted. As a result, information about officers killed and information about officers assaulted reside in two separate databases, and the data are not comparable

- Because the information in the tables of this publication is updated each year, the FBI cautions readers against making comparisons between the data in this publication and those in prior editions

History

Beginning in 1937, the FBI's UCR Program collected and published statistics on law enforcement officers killed in the line of duty in its annual publication, *Crime in the United States*. Statistics regarding assaults on officers were added in 1960. In June 1971, executives from the law enforcement conference, "Prevention of Police Killings," called for an increase in the FBI's involvement in preventing and investigating officers' deaths. In response to this directive, the UCR Program expanded its collection of data to include more details about the incidents in which law enforcement officers were killed and assaulted.

Using this comprehensive set of data, the FBI began in 1972 to produce two reports annually, the *Law Enforcement Officers Killed Summary* and the *Analysis of Assaults on Federal Officers*. These two reports were combined in 1982 to create the annual publication, *Law Enforcement Officers Killed and Assaulted*.

PART 8

Probation and Parole, 2013

HIGHLIGHTS

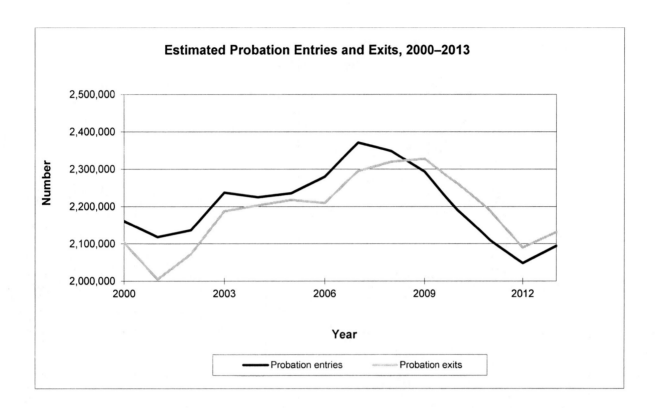

- At year end 2013, an estimated 4,751,400 adults were under community supervision—down about 29,900 offenders from year end 2012.

- Approximately 1 in 51 adults in the United States was under community supervision at year end 2013.

- Between year end 2012 and 2013, the adult probation population declined by about 32,200 offenders, falling to an estimated 3,910,600 offenders at year end 2013.

- The adult parole population increased by about 2,000 offenders between year end 2012 and 2013, to about 853,200 offenders at year end 2013.

- In 2013, 75 percent of adults on probation were male.

Supplementary Table 1. Adults on Parole in the United States, 1975–2012

(Number.)

State	1975	1976	1977	1978	1979	1980	1981	1982	1983	1984	1985	1986	1987	1988	1989	1990	1991 [1]	1992	1993
U.S. Total[2,3]	143,164	146,999	173,632	177,847	217,697	222,036	226,174	224,604	246,440	266,992	300,203	326,259	362,748	407,596	456,803	531,407	590,442	658,601	676,100
Federal	16,750	15,408	23,857	21,280	25,930	23,652	21,342	21,273	16,325	16,854	17,064	17,496	18,846	20,451	21,422	21,693	21,555	39,912	55,710
State[2,3]	126,414	131,591	149,775	156,567	191,767	198,384	204,832	203,331	230,115	250,138	283,139	308,763	343,902	387,145	435,381	509,714	568,887	618,689	620,390
Northeast	32,502	34,014	34,504	35,985	42,158	45,359	46,096	48,361	54,110	54,419	82,849	88,327	90,879	104,680	110,749	128,946	147,792	163,875	167,337
Connecticut	1,593	1,673	2,909	2,099	1,983	1,932	2,184	1,311	1,287	868	695	603	466	371	322	291	509	483	1,000
Maine	683	780	652	432	321	213	204	144	135	122	--	--	--	--	--	--	36	39	38
Massachusetts	3,718	3,729	3,571	4,247	4,412	4,071	3,405	4,303	5,039	4,447	4,496	3,998	4,018	4,333	4,688	4,720	4,944	4,645	4,370
New Hampshire	459	494	529	442	431	441	479	471	471	455	453	539	421	461	477	522	576	623	777
New Jersey	8,293	8,397	7,173	7,386	7,817	8,911	9,706	10,514	12,287	12,206	13,385	14,064	15,709	18,463	20,062	23,298	26,282	36,120	35,775
New York	10,238	11,175	10,196	11,310	17,168	19,652	19,865	21,062	23,489	24,212	28,289	29,325	31,244	33,962	36,885	42,837	47,834	50,004	52,186
Pennsylvania[4,5,6]	7,276	7,582	9,239	9,512	9,437	9,589	9,738	9,982	10,726	11,371	34,785	39,008	38,398	46,466	47,702	56,657	66,893	71,062	72,100
Rhode Island	242	184	235	202	220	257	244	327	371	394	402	453	423	442	393	321	345	483	536
Vermont	--	--	--	355	369	293	271	247	305	344	344	337	200	182	220	300	373	416	555
Midwest	13,827	16,517	21,264	23,500	35,032	36,635	36,739	41,491	46,588	46,967	41,722	43,114	46,747	51,062	55,773	65,693	71,525	76,017	79,852
Illinois[7]	--	--	--	--	8,532	9,507	8,244	11,866	11,556	11,383	11,421	12,311	13,744	14,369	14,550	17,671	23,213	23,304	24,177
Indiana	1,733	1,708	1,920	1,997	2,059	2,028	2,155	2,678	2,954	2,900	2,797	3,273	3,071	3,411	3,456	3,778	3,125	2,899	2,891
Iowa[8]	470	524	631	641	717	639	785	1,050	1,556	1,662	1,971	1,929	1,966	1,945	1,900	2,111	2,081	2,065	2,339
Kansas	--	1,067	1,179	1,305	2,341	2,200	2,400	2,105	2,036	1,997	2,282	2,360	2,676	3,497	5,089	5,751	6,204	6,297	7,141
Michigan	3,866	4,183	5,171	6,580	7,293	6,227	6,585	7,251	8,939	9,365	6,639	5,703	6,342	7,677	9,890	11,901	12,275	13,436	14,015
Minnesota	1,879	1,934	2,011	2,051	1,633	1,534	1,633	1,479	1,498	1,418	1,364	1,437	1,444	1,639	1,699	1,873	1,702	1,901	1,834
Missouri	1,210	1,387	1,327	1,564	1,613	2,395	2,970	2,556	3,330	4,366	4,485	5,229	6,423	7,207	7,545	9,196	10,333	11,671	12,264
Nebraska	--	--	400	345	412	292	255	309	364	361	246	304	459	447	490	632	702	697	815
North Dakota	122	135	123	139	133	127	129	161	170	159	166	159	133	134	138	116	122	107	90
Ohio	4,400	5,452	6,479	6,829	7,461	8,849	8,471	8,616	10,327	9,065	6,509	6,147	5,988	5,991	6,464	7,945	6,738	7,407	6,997
South Dakota	147	127	213	215	190	198	259	295	399	438	415	408	492	617	510	620	851	673	674
Wisconsin	--	--	1,810	1,834	2,648	2,639	2,853	3,125	3,459	3,853	3,427	3,854	4,009	4,128	4,042	4,099	4,179	5,560	6,615
South[3]	49,542	50,395	56,203	60,955	77,826	77,167	81,775	82,403	89,367	102,128	110,894	124,304	141,609	156,696	183,715	215,773	237,436	253,958	257,202
Alabama[5]	3,321	2,165	1,940	2,129	2,726	2,547	2,361	2,266	1,985	2,194	2,425	3,038	3,456	4,701	5,724	5,970	6,858	6,934	6,729
Arkansas	2,209	2,424	2,228	2,397	2,496	2,855	2,918	3,061	3,417	3,463	3,891	4,023	3,932	3,840	3,657	3,971	3,460	3,460	4,036
Delaware	--	--	--	--	582	619	624	621	718	830	864	978	1,100	1,093	1,013	1,283	991	1,120	914
District of Columbia	2,160	1,627	1,316	1,990	2,485	3,045	3,281	2,638	2,348	2,696	3,504	2,980	3,659	3,949	4,915	5,346	5,398	6,294	6,591
Florida	4,206	4,537	5,129	5,984	10,554	8,823	6,620	5,974	6,359	5,661	4,214	3,478	2,873	2,562	2,318	2,064	8,155	14,021	17,567
Georgia	3,175	3,234	3,533	3,341	3,323	3,169	2,652	4,897	6,677	7,246	8,538	10,421	10,917	11,308	17,437	22,646	23,375	23,020	20,790
Kentucky	4,532	4,993	6,986	8,036	8,138	8,120	8,996	3,430	3,722	3,567	3,694	3,370	3,338	3,443	3,133	3,183	3,345	3,684	4,148
Louisiana	2,079	1,946	2,348	2,235	2,107	1,819	1,913	1,961	1,963	3,087	3,346	4,166	7,243	7,387	9,177	8,877	10,331	12,192	14,463
Maryland[6]	5,129	5,141	5,077	5,598	6,508	6,436	6,132	6,024	6,076	7,046	7,308	7,494	8,063	9,225	9,862	11,192	12,350	13,058	13,858
Mississippi	646	834	1,509	2,004	2,213	2,292	2,734	2,914	3,207	3,108	3,392	3,454	3,456	3,177	3,349	3,478	3,292	2,357	1,730
North Carolina	6,022	5,801	5,323	6,400	7,034	6,496	6,875	6,910	5,074	3,892	3,184	3,322	4,646	6,191	7,559	9,883	13,258	14,415	17,284
Oklahoma[9]	2,040	2,002	1,721	1,635	2,081	2,232	2,299	1,858	1,922	1,880	1,625	1,670	1,762	1,455	1,993	3,236	3,511	2,758	2,503
South Carolina[10]	1,610	1,850	2,236	2,494	2,798	3,124	3,306	3,175	3,338	3,441	3,261	3,066	3,469	3,626	3,386	3,543	4,154	5,325	5,790
Tennessee	--	--	--	--	3,098	3,097	3,280	3,303	3,563	6,524	7,899	8,600	9,263	9,529	10,511	11,327	9,931	11,819	11,279
Texas	9,780	10,745	12,649	12,538	16,191	17,235	21,662	26,274	32,131	40,783	47,471	57,509	67,308	77,827	91,294	109,726	118,092	121,141	116,637
Virginia[5,6,11]	2,278	2,750	3,787	3,669	5,025	4,783	5,637	6,487	6,268	5,986	5,640	5,767	6,283	6,576	7,444	9,048	9,897	11,372	11,504
West Virginia	355	346	421	505	467	475	485	610	599	724	638	968	841	807	943	1,000	1,038	988	1,379
West	30,543	30,665	37,804	36,127	36,751	39,223	40,222	31,076	40,050	46,624	47,674	53,018	64,667	74,707	85,144	99,302	112,134	124,839	115,999
Alaska[5]	--	--	117	105	110	93	101	101	104	147	155	119	435	489	533	568	568	710	685
Arizona	--	1,047	962	1,018	1,531	1,093	1,319	1,527	1,684	1,660	1,717	2,034	2,224	1,669	2,048	2,711	2,900	3,588	4,017
California[8,12]	18,539	16,820	17,050	14,069	14,111	15,253	16,080	18,913	25,462	30,645	30,127	33,172	41,333	49,364	57,515	67,562	78,724	87,725	80,845
Colorado	2,937	2,975	2,070	1,752	941	927	1,096	1,202	1,520	1,709	2,003	1,827	1,680	1,743	1,974	2,396	2,306	2,634	2,731
Hawaii	534	540	519	477	452	514	491	421	457	526	716	921	1,012	1,108	1,287	1,425	1,479	1,393	1,541
Idaho	221	230	458	449	449	420	396	409	421	381	483	531	865	247	238	243	397	788	837
Montana[5]	422	533	477	589	690	758	642	658	691	691	634	668	624	671	752	811	617	677	704
Nevada	380	502	632	805	849	1,052	1,172	1,065	1,082	1,187	1,313	1,529	1,598	2,100	2,417	2,850	2,987	3,246	3,398
New Mexico[5]	655	794	765	829	699	884	1,094	1,206	1,079	1,194	1,092	1,147	1,194	1,230	1,151	1,224	1,414	1,331	1,281
Oregon	1,337	1,636	1,890	2,257	2,384	2,639	1,751	1,344	1,558	1,764	1,894	1,973	1,988	3,790	5,794	8,023	10,149	12,505	13,687
Utah	502	390	510	568	616	767	773	939	1,216	1,115	1,169	1,094	1,137	1,218	1,277	1,561	1,809	1,988	2,185
Washington[5]	4,972	5,130	12,271	13,092	13,819	14,669	15,102	3,047	4,403	5,253	6,039	7,666	10,211	10,745	9,832	9,615	8,395	7,850	3,720
Wyoming[6]	44	68	83	117	100	154	205	244	373	352	332	337	366	333	326	313	389	404	368

Note: The Annual Parole Survey collects population counts for January 1 and December 31 of the reporting year. Because some agencies update their year end population counts during the following reporting year, BJS has historically used this information to update the annual counts in this spreadsheet. While the 2012 data represents the population count on December 31, 2012, the 2011 data reflect the updated population counts reported for January 1, 2012. The 2010 data reported here represent the updated counts received for January 1, 2011, etc. This differs with how data were prepared for the reports "Probation and Parole in the United States, 2012" and Probation and Parole in the United States, 2011", in which the population for each year represents that reported for December 31 of that year, for the purpose of making comparisons within the same reporting year. Probation and Parole in the United States, 2012, and earlier reports in this series are available on the BJS website at http://www.bjs.gov/index.cfm?ty=pbse&sid=42. See "Methodology" in the 2012 report for a summary of of how reporting changes have affected the counts of the number of adults on parole, 2000-2012.

** = Not known.

-- = Not reported.

[1]The Annual Parole Survey was not conducted in 1991. The January 1, 1992 population counts were used as estimates of the December 31, 1991 population counts.

[2]Includes an estimated 75,057 parolees under supervision in Pennsylvania in 2003 (i.e., January 1, 2004) due to a change in reporting county parole counts. See footnotes 4 and 5.

[3]Includes an estimated 3,100 parolees under supervision in Oklahoma in 2006 (i.e., January 1, 2007) because the state was unable to provide data for the 2007 reporting year. See footnote 6. Includes an estimated 4,700 parolees under supervision in Virginia in 2007 (i.e., January 1, 2008) because the state was unable to provide data for January 1, 2008. See footnote 7.

[4]Due to a change in reporting county parole counts, the 2003 (i.e., January 1, 2004) estimated total for Pennsylvania based on reporting methods comparable to 2004 was 75,057.

[5]See "Methodology" in "Probation and Parole in the United States, 2009" (http://www.ojp.usdoj.gov/bjs/pub/pdf/ppus09.pdf) for a discussion of changes in reporting methods between 2000 and 2009.

[6]See "Methodology" in "Probation and Parole in the United States, 2010" (http://www.ojp.usdoj.gov/bjs/pub/pdf/ppus10.pdf) for a discussion of changes in reporting methods between 2009 and 2010.

Supplementary Table 1. Adults on Parole in the United States, 1975–2012—*Continued*

(Number.)

State	1994	1995	1996	1997	1998	1999	2000	2001	2002	2003	2004	2005	2006	2007	2008	2009	2010	2011	2012
U.S. Total[2,3]	690,371	679,421	679,733	694,787	696,385	714,457	723,898	732,333	750,934	769,925	771,852	780,616	799,875	821,177	829,560	837,818	840,598	851,662	851,158
Federal	61,430	51,461	59,235	63,512	67,169	71,005	76,069	78,113	83,063	86,567	89,589	86,852	88,993	91,395	97,010	100,598	103,804	106,955	110,739
State[2,3]	628,941	627,960	620,498	631,275	629,216	643,452	647,829	654,220	667,871	683,358	682,263	693,764	710,882	729,782	732,550	737,220	736,794	744,707	740,419
Northeast	173,882	175,207	154,959	162,782	162,006	164,539	159,653	162,971	174,591	152,488	154,309	152,033	152,744	155,192	149,391	170,985	169,673	165,754	171,182
Connecticut	1,146	1,233	1,083	996	1,396	1,526	1,868	2,126	2,186	2,343	2,552	2,571	2,567	2,177	2,328	2,873	2,894	2,561	2,793
Maine	40	55	57	67	33	28	28	31	32	32	32	34	31	32	31	32	32	21	21
Massachusetts	4,755	5,256	4,836	4,596	4,489	4,304	3,703	3,718	3,951	3,597	3,854	3,579	3,435	3,121	3,113	3,253	3,212	2,264	2,106
New Hampshire	835	785	1,066	1,083	1,141	944	944	953	963	1,199	1,212	1,402	1,621	1,653	1,661	1,883	1,973	2,204	2,167
New Jersey	41,802	37,867	14,545	16,903	13,218	12,968	11,709	11,931	12,576	13,248	13,880	13,874	14,405	15,055	15,532	15,356	15,613	15,306	14,987
New York	53,832	55,568	57,137	59,670	59,548	57,956	57,858	56,719	55,990	55,853	54,524	53,533	53,001	53,669	52,225	49,950	48,542	47,243	46,222
Pennsylvania[4,5,6]	70,355	73,234	75,013	78,264	81,001	85,666	82,345	86,238	97,712	102,244	76,989	75,678	76,386	78,107	72,951	96,014	95,870	94,581	101,351
Rhode Island	525	591	573	526	432	397	331	355	384	363	344	302	332	442	469	537	505	505	498
Vermont	592	618	649	677	748	750	867	900	797	796	922	1,060	966	936	1,081	1,087	1,032	1,069	1,037
Midwest	82,478	86,598	89,090	89,860	94,110	101,697	103,331	104,705	114,173	122,678	127,338	131,283	131,638	138,287	141,415	139,094	134,085	132,790	132,922
Illinois[7]	26,695	29,541	30,064	30,348	30,432	31,833	30,196	30,148	35,458	35,008	34,277	34,576	34,917	35,086	33,683	33,162	26,009	26,208	27,456
Indiana	3,409	3,200	3,580	4,044	4,258	4,539	4,917	5,339	5,877	7,019	6,627	7,295	8,205	10,375	10,653	10,989	10,912	10,154	10,153
Iowa[8]	3,696	2,340	2,200	2,037	2,194	2,514	2,763	2,614	2,787	2,974	3,325	3,560	3,578	3,546	3,159	3,259	4,180	4,446	5,151
Kansas	6,291	6,094	6,004	6,150	6,025	5,909	3,829	3,991	3,990	4,145	4,525	4,666	4,886	4,842	4,958	5,010	5,063	5,254	5,126
Michigan	12,846	13,862	14,609	14,351	15,331	15,541	15,753	16,501	17,648	20,233	20,924	19,978	18,486	21,131	22,523	24,374	24,486	22,598	19,113
Minnesota	1,904	2,117	2,377	2,446	2,995	3,151	3,072	3,156	3,577	3,596	3,676	4,007	4,445	4,756	5,093	5,435	5,812	5,841	6,006
Missouri	12,592	13,001	13,087	12,514	10,366	11,448	12,563	12,864	13,533	15,830	17,400	18,374	18,815	18,656	19,212	18,857	21,085	21,140	20,672
Nebraska	771	661	688	688	624	568	476	530	574	648	801	662	797	800	846	823	941	1149	1383
North Dakota	94	114	100	116	174	152	110	117	148	225	246	302	372	340	386	363	428	440	429
Ohio	6,453	7,432	6,331	6,803	11,304	15,776	18,248	17,885	17,853	18,427	18,882	19,512	17,603	18,390	19,119	14,575	12,076	12,344	14,649
South Dakota	662	688	725	823	1,125	1,322	1,481	1,437	1,640	1,944	2,217	2,444	2,767	2,812	2,720	2,748	2,799	2,764	2,761
Wisconsin	7,065	7,548	9,325	9,540	9,282	8,944	9,923	10,123	11,088	12,629	14,438	15,907	16,767	17,553	19,063	19,499	20,294	20,452	20,023
South[3]	253,731	240,478	241,668	236,743	223,922	222,916	225,955	224,269	219,849	224,995	229,775	235,061	238,484	240,465	248,104	252,764	259,135	264,763	273,819
Alabama[5]	7,235	7,793	4,966	6,356	5,221	4,875	5,484	5,663	5,309	6,950	7,745	7,795	7,508	7,790	8,042	8,429	9,006	8,601	8,616
Arkansas	5,224	4,685	5,459	5,719	6,979	7,752	8,659	11,357	12,128	13,180	13,476	16,666	18,057	18,617	19,687	21,077	21,363	23,670	23,372
Delaware	1,029	1,033	591	591	572	634	579	530	551	529	539	600	544	535	551	519	560	553	601
District of Columbia	6,574	6,340	7,120	7,761	7,055	5,103	5,332	4,506	5,297	4,861	5,253	4,926	5,341	5,417	5,767	5,992	6,348	6,153	5,883
Florida	20,573	11,197	9,243	8,477	6,487	6,418	5,982	5,891	5,223	5,098	4,484	4,785	4,790	4,654	4,528	4,323	4,093	4,203	4,538
Georgia	17,505	19,434	21,146	21,915	20,482	22,003	21,556	20,809	20,822	21,161	23,344	22,851	22,958	23,111	23,448	23,709	24,723	25,489	24,761
Kentucky	4,380	4,257	4,621	4,233	4,508	4,868	4,614	4,885	5,968	7,744	8,255	10,162	11,755	13,097	12,377	12,601	13,495	13,699	14,419
Louisiana	17,112	19,028	19,082	19,927	18,759	20,716	22,860	23,330	23,049	23,743	24,219	24,072	23,832	24,085	24,636	23,607	26,105	27,092	28,946
Maryland[6]	14,795	15,748	16,246	15,763	15,528	15,007	13,666	13,415	13,271	13,742	14,351	14,271	14,351	13,856	13,220	13,195	13,195	13,237	13,633
Mississippi	1,519	1,510	1,326	1,378	1,489	1,356	1,596	1,788	1,816	1,816	1,758	1,970	1,899	2,015	2,922	5,426	6,434	7,127	6,804
North Carolina	20,159	18,501	12,358	8,148	5,806	4,389	3,352	2,954	2,805	2,677	2,882	3,101	3,236	3,311	3,409	3,544	3,621	3,744	4,359
Oklahoma[9]	2,604	2,356	2,159	1,928	1,532	1,527	1,825	3,406	3,573	4,047	4,329	4,329	**	2,929	3,073	2,970	2,627	2,459	2,310
South Carolina[10]	6,077	5,545	5,036	4,813	4,404	4,612	4,378	4,161	3,491	3,242	3,237	3,072	2,766	2,289	6,583	6,419	6,299	6,315	6,116
Tennessee	9,353	8,851	8,934	8,693	7,605	7,328	8,093	8,074	7,949	7,957	8,223	8,630	9,570	10,481	10,464	11,556	12,083	12,138	13,138
Texas	108,563	103,089	112,594	109,437	109,820	109,310	111,719	107,688	103,068	102,271	102,072	101,916	100,053	101,748	102,921	104,943	104,763	105,996	112,288
Virginia[5,6,11]	9,649	10,188	9,918	10,710	6,700	5,860	5,148	4,873	4,530	4,834	4,392	4,499	7,201	/	4,471	2,565	2,624	2,244	1,983
West Virginia	1,380	923	869	894	975	1,158	1,112	939	999	1,143	1,216	1,416	1,523	1,830	2,005	1,889	1,796	2,043	2,052
West	118,850	125,677	134,781	141,890	149,178	154,300	158,890	162,275	159,258	183,197	170,841	175,387	188,016	195,838	193,640	174,377	173,901	181,400	162,496
Alaska[5]	412	459	642	472	478	498	525	522	900	927	949	973	1,527	1,539	1,714	1,923	2,089	1,777	1,882
Arizona	4,351	4,109	3,785	3,378	3,742	3,715	3,474	5,143	4,587	5,367	5,728	6,213	6,463	6,755	7,537	8,186	7,998	7,708	7,460
California[8,12]	85,082	91,807	99,578	104,412	108,424	114,046	117,647	117,903	113,185	110,338	110,262	111,744	118,592	123,764	120,753	106,371	105,134	111,703	89,287
Colorado	2,463	3,024	3,294	4,139	5,204	5,263	5,500	5,733	6,215	6,559	7,383	8,196	9,551	11,014	11,654	11,655	11,014	10,775	11,458
Hawaii	1,650	1,689	1,733	1,827	2,009	2,252	2,504	2,608	2,525	2,240	2,296	2,119	2,308	2,015	1,904	1,831	1,850	1,706	1,632
Idaho	931	619	692	820	1,309	1,317	1,409	1,657	1,961	2,329	2,370	2,482	2,732	3,114	3,361	3,447	3,956	4,047	3,848
Montana[5]	710	744	771	755	667	549	621	710	845	815	810	703	844	966	1,062	1,007	986	958	950
Nevada	3,529	2,863	3,216	3,463	4,055	3,847	4,056	4,025	3,971	4,126	3,610	3,518	3,824	3,653	3,908	4,186	4,964	5,332	5,379
New Mexico[5]	1,078	1,366	1,426	1,626	1,773	1,630	1,670	1,562	1,962	2,328	2,469	2,831	3,517	3,527	3,724	3,157	3,146	2,958	5,078
Oregon	14,264	15,019	15,800	16,815	17,270	17,273	17,579	18,290	19,090	19,456	20,515	21,189	22,031	22,196	21,962	22,117	22,260	22,463	22,872
Utah	2,417	2,700	2,920	3,281	3,424	3,252	3,231	3,410	3,352	3,229	3,246	3,242	3,342	3,572	3,566	3,185	2,925	2,933	2,993
Washington[5]	1,650	875	560	480	375	200	160	155	95	24905	10,640	11,568	12,611	13,017	11,768	6,563	6,956	8,422	8,895
Wyoming[6]	313	403	364	422	448	458	514	557	570	578	563	609	674	706	727	749	623	618	762

[7]The state was unable to provide data for the 2011 reporting year. Data on the number of parolees at midyear 2011 were used as an estimate for the December 31, 2011 population. See "Parole: Explanatory notes" in Probation and Parole in the United States, 2011, http://www.bjs.gov/content/pub/pdf/ppus11.pdf, for more information.

[8]See "Methodology" in Probation and Parole in the United States, 2011, http://www.bjs.gov/content/pub/pdf/ppus11.pdf, for information on reporting changes in 2011.

[9]The state was unable to provide data for the 2007 reporting year. The January 1, 2007 population in each jurisdiction was used to update the December 31, 2006 population in each jurisdiction; however, Oklahoma reported 3,072 parolees under supervision on December 31, 2006.

[10]The count for 2008 is based on updated estimates for 2009 using the revised methodology first used for 2010. (The count for December 31, 2008, represents the revised estimate for January 1, 2009.) The count for 2009 is also based on the revised methodology as it has been updated using the data received for January 1, 2010. These data are not comparable to those reported for 2007. See "Methodology" in "Probation and Parole in the United States, 2010" (http://www.ojp.usdoj.gov/bjs/pub/pdf/ppus10.pdf) for a discussion of changes in reporting methods between the data originally reported for 2009 and the revised methodology used for 2010.

[11]The state was unable to provide data for January 1, 2008. The January 1, 2008 population in each jurisdiction was used to update the December 31, 2007, population in each jurisdiction; however, Virginia reported 6,850 parolees under supervision on December 31, 2007 but data are not comparable to 2008 data due to a change in reporting methods. For more details, see "Methodology" in "Probation and Parole in the United States, 2008" http://www.ojp.usdoj.gov/bjs/pub/pdf/ppus08.pdf.

[12]Includes 12,979 parolees on post-release community supervision (PRCS) for 2011; and 32,948 on PRCS for 2012. See "Probation and Parole in the United States, 2012," for more information.

Supplementary Table 2. Adults on Probation in the United States, 1977–2012

(Number.)

State	1977	1978	1979	1980	1981	1982	1983	1984	1985	1986	1987	1988	1989	1990	1991[1]	1992	1993	1994	1995
U.S. Total[2,3]	816,525	899,305	1,080,385	1,118,097	1,225,934	1,378,668	1,582,947	1,740,948	1,968,712	2,114,821	2,247,158	2,386,427	2,522,125	2,670,234	2,728,472	2,811,611	2,903,061	2,981,022	3,077,861
Federal	46,665	45,472	42,441	45,369	46,711	49,134	50,226	52,351	55,378	57,337	60,382	61,029	59,106	58,222	55,236	46,485	48,358	42,309	35,457
State[2,3]	769,860	853,833	1,037,944	1,072,728	1,179,223	1,329,534	1,532,721	1,688,597	1,913,334	2,057,484	2,186,776	2,325,398	2,463,019	2,612,012	2,673,236	2,765,126	2,854,703	2,938,713	3,042,404
Northeast[2]	258,125	282,196	271,007	198,394	219,631	237,660	265,772	287,728	366,040	395,836	413,808	438,691	449,418	466,006	489,947	481,594	486,827	526,375	538,941
Connecticut	17,136	17,189	19,917	22,981	24,778	33,061	40,041	46,681	36,805	41,304	43,659	46,086	42,842	46,640	47,523	48,567	50,904	53,453	54,507
Maine	2,348	2,489	2,394	2,419	2,978	3,040	3,495	4,368	4,451	4,620	4,605	6,059	6,851	7,549	6,943	8,942	8,712	8,638	8,641
Massachusetts[4,5]	98,661	114,633	103,947	19,562	21,633	21,787	22,160	23,141	86,597	94,945	97,571	92,353	88,529	72,459	54,172	48,312	47,154	46,670	43,680
New Hampshire	1,891	1,936	1,721	1,663	2,261	2,263	2,323	3,126	3,096	3,583	2,827	2,948	2,991	3,146	4,126	4,104	4,125	4,323	4,347
New Jersey	31,981	32,183	31,641	29,239	35,326	38,186	41,740	44,208	47,483	51,359	53,827	57,903	64,398	72,341	98,331	108,093	109,576	125,299	126,759
New York	51,801	53,896	55,427	63,691	69,583	72,047	81,570	90,011	99,183	107,337	112,461	125,256	136,686	145,266	157,653	152,013	155,932	163,613	168,012
Pennsylvania[4,5,6]	47,751	52,322	48,179	50,238	53,623	56,548	63,684	64,310	75,591	78,985	85,084	92,296	89,491	97,327	99,425	89,944	88,180	99,524	106,823
Rhode Island	4,080	4,895	5,111	5,501	6,049	6,501	6,495	7,147	7,536	8,174	8,181	9,824	12,231	15,366	16,138	15,585	16,186	18,179	18,850
Vermont	2,476	2,653	2,670	3,100	3,400	4,227	4,264	4,736	5,298	5,529	5,593	5,966	5,399	5,912	5,636	6,034	6,058	6,676	7,322
Midwest	118,891	126,370	169,594	226,827	234,175	245,386	290,181	347,357	408,880	444,241	475,162	510,253	538,994	567,839	564,926	589,858	620,125	642,546	675,380
Illinois[5]	51,258	52,704	60,875	63,360	65,922	61,549	58,512	63,477	74,156	76,203	82,332	90,736	93,944	95,699	74,846	76,125	78,464	104,664	109,489
Indiana[7]	14,155	16,560	16,227	18,650	21,404	21,404	30,401	36,004	42,800	50,806	56,978	60,184	61,777	68,683	76,365	79,850	82,705	83,177	95,267
Iowa[8]	7,911	7,375	8,005	8,815	9,850	10,625	11,672	11,924	12,063	12,584	12,745	13,099	13,722	13,895	12,488	14,084	15,376	15,902	16,579
Kansas	7,833	8,421	9,513	8,984	11,762	13,175	13,607	15,576	16,204	17,125	18,059	19,580	21,675	22,183	23,314	23,994	24,255	17,256	16,547
Michigan[5]	--	--	24,337	25,320	26,751	27,517	52,778	70,948	99,365	102,653	110,241	115,132	122,459	133,439	136,855	135,012	139,753	142,640	141,436
Minnesota	--	--	2,924	27,000	19,578	24,320	27,745	31,440	32,986	38,901	44,363	56,901	58,648	59,323	71,407	72,938	75,961	81,972	83,778
Missouri	10,611	11,643	13,460	17,400	19,149	21,637	24,174	23,574	26,081	33,819	40,766	42,728	44,158	42,322	35,138	32,629	36,000	36,295	41,728
Nebraska[5]	6,077	6,278	7,146	7,980	6,759	9,964	10,935	10,763	10,720	11,265	11,511	11,411	12,627	14,654	14,838	15,386	15,483	18,639	13,895
North Dakota	704	719	761	930	1,098	1,159	1,367	1,517	1,544	1,616	1,504	1,644	1,731	1,829	1,920	1,989	2,036	2,320	
Ohio	3,554	3,783	4,062	25,000	30,540	32,435	36,225	58,194	66,810	72,339	68,769	70,088	78,299	83,380	83,668	94,129	103,377	90,190	103,327
South Dakota	--	1,504	3,764	4,300	1,302	1,998	1,530	1,514	2,249	2,354	2,594	2,585	2,757	3,160	2,700	3,367	3,637	3,874	3,745
Wisconsin	16,788	17,383	18,520	19,088	20,060	19,603	21,235	22,426	23,877	24,648	25,188	26,305	27,284	29,370	31,478	40,424	43,125	45,901	47,269
South[3]	202,318	238,061	376,381	421,765	471,410	539,693	670,156	730,682	789,702	854,043	892,243	929,936	984,909	1,042,012	1,064,635	1,135,326	1,180,579	1,214,375	1,248,608
Alabama[4]	10404	10,496	10,883	10,985	13,021	14,229	15,732	16,338	16,520	21,371	23,406	25,301	25,519	27,686	30,022	31,188	31,460	31,284	33,410
Arkansas	545	671	741	2,400	2,262	3,384	6,800	8,238	9,268	12,700	14,609	15,931	15,552	15,983	12,858	16,928	19,606	22,397	
Delaware	3,507	3,567	3,748	3,762	3,893	4,626	5,419	6,373	7,139	7,985	9,398	9,576	9,701	12,223	13,243	14,887	15,571	15,507	16,124
District of Columbia[4]	4,965	5,386	5,430	6,562	7,178	7,584	9,602	10,319	11,777	12,307	13,750	11,296	10,132	9,742	10,474	10,607	8,264	11,306	10,414
Florida	34,342	35,699	38,862	38,906	44,962	57,074	95,994	118,318	130,399	139,859	155,194	165,475	192,731	210,781	189,746	200,471	235,805	247,014	243,736
Georgia[4,5]	34,979	36,203	39,288	58,450	66,473	78,097	91,183	90,057	94,461	109,485	110,484	121,559	125,147	134,840	155,006	153,154	145,230	140,694	142,954
Kentucky	--	4,966	5,392	12,400	12,615	14,516	14,450	15,004	6,594	6,841	7,181	7,398	8,062	7,482	9,828	10,750	11,689	11,417	11,499
Louisiana	11,104	12,444	12,908	15,120	15,880	20,377	24,494	26,733	26,638	27,677	30,313	31,218	32,295	30,191	30,861	30,468	32,434	33,604	33,753
Maryland[4,5]	28,736	33,893	37,851	41,661	48,068	52,603	61,481	64,827	67,138	69,134	72,816	78,619	84,456	82,898	77,988	82,948	80,208	76,940	71,029
Mississippi	3,485	4,648	4,234	4,864	5,668	6,304	6,293	6,570	6,636	6,458	6,752	6,854	7,333	8,221	9,309	8,031	9,219	9,042	9,595
North Carolina	33,450	36,290	37,556	36,467	40,335	44,274	45,863	52,600	56,207	58,644	62,940	67,164	72,325	77,829	83,911	86,371	86,212	90,418	97,921
Oklahoma[9]	12,776	14,443	17,880	14,360	13,306	14,749	16,012	18,809	21,480	22,740	23,477	23,341	24,240	24,411	25,384	25,902	25,738	26,285	27,866
South Carolina[10]	18,167	18,309	19,056	20,589	19,170	16,981	16,599	17,043	17,979	21,110	24,959	26,260	31,623	32,287	32,871	35,587	38,658	40,005	39,821
Tennessee	5,858	6,669	7,654	9,130	9,716	10,101	23,318	23,598	26,205	26,291	26,403	28,282	30,906	32,719	33,966	38,614	35,293	34,896	36,485
Texas	--	--	120,890	131,996	151,811	177,270	217,350	235,568	269,909	290,074	289,690	288,906	291,156	308,357	320,295	360,702	378,531	396,276	421,213
Virginia[5]	--	10,045	10,601	11,463	14,326	14,813	16,387	16,690	17,447	17,126	16,450	17,945	19,085	21,303	22,710	23,510	23,619	24,089	24,264
West Virginia	--	4,332	3,407	2,650	2,726	2,711	3,179	3,597	3,905	4,241	4,421	4,811	4,646	5,059	6,163	5,688	5,720	5,992	6,127
West	190,526	207,206	220,962	225,742	254,007	306,795	306,612	322,830	348,712	363,364	405,563	446,518	489,698	536,155	553,728	558,348	567,172	555,417	579,475
Alaska	846	928		1,181	1,314	1,816	1,791	2,064	2,606	2,885	2,941	2,994	3,335	3,599	3,744	3,014	3,214	2,899	3,481
Arizona	--	--	10,894	12,584	14,289	14,949	15,757	16,687	18,068	20,283	23,158	25,446	27,340	30,397	31,972	34,647	35,534	34,365	40,614
California	149,587	153,113	150,566	151,085	152,563	167,633	180,474	195,864	210,449	218,526	239,985	265,580	284,437	305,700	309,077	300,635	302,645	277,655	280,545
Colorado[4]	10,571	12,080	13,424	12,238	13,419	14,603	15,580	16,693	17,612	16,335	22,981	23,230	28,037	31,111	32,430	33,700	35,111	39,065	42,687
Hawaii	2,686	2,872	3,283	4,331	4,974	5,725	6,092	6,686	7,986	8,404	8,882	10,704	10,960	11,667	12,317	10,038	11,053	13,088	12,957
Idaho[8]	2,831	3,037	2,757	2,038	2,675	2,955	3,163	3,151	3,414	3,770	4,146	3,587	4,025	4,377	3,921	4,075	4,749	5,770	5,308
Montana	1,772	1,830	2,043	1,945	2,369	2,371	2,471	2,471	2,637	2,943	3,168	3,275	3,459	4,052	3,579	3,948	5,572	5,656	4,318
Nevada	2,722	3,337	4,073	4,989	5,671	4,733	5,095	5,226	5,365	5,518	5,338	7,032	7,065	7,700	8,153	8,533	8,826	9,410	8,634
New Mexico[4]	--	1,817	2,072	2,794	3,360	3,854	4,050	3,926	4,130	4,175	5,310	5,312	5,660	6,294	6,831	6,921	8,367	8,063	8,524
Oregon	--	7,366	9,524	12,201	14,211	18,106	20,067	21,452	23,000	23,402	24,079	27,320	31,878	37,631	40,041	39,019	37,902	38,086	39,725
Utah	5,189	6,327	6,542	6,889	7,346	8,605	8,035	7,721	6,330	5,620	5,833	5,595	5,524	5,830	6,290	6,671	7,348	7,714	8,562
Washington[4]	12,560	13,183	13,776	12,527	30,759	60,142	42,245	39,181	45,399	49,663	57,825	64,257	74,918	84,817	92,247	103,837	103,615	110,279	120,466
Wyoming[5]	1,762	1,316	1,122	940	1,057	1,303	1,792	1,708	1,716	1,840	1,917	2,186	3,060	2,980	3,126	3,310	3,236	3,367	3,654

Supplementary Table 2. Adults on Probation in the United States, 1977–2012—*Continued*

(Number.)

State	1996	1997	1998	1999	2000	2001	2002	2003	2004	2005	2006	2007	2008	2009	2010	2011	2012
U.S. Total[2,3]	3,164,996	3,296,513	3,670,441	3,779,922	3,826,209	3,931,731	4,024,067	4,120,012	4,143,792	4,166,757	4,215,361	4,234,471	4,238,590	4,125,033	4,053,115	3,981,090	3,942,776
Federal	34,247	33,532	33,390	32,843	31,669	31,562	31,330	30,601	28,602	25,473	24,465	23,422	22,483	22,587	22,514	22,455	21,837
State[2,3]	3,130,749	3,262,981	3,637,051	3,747,079	3,794,540	3,900,169	3,992,737	4,089,411	4,115,190	4,141,284	4,190,896	4,211,049	4,216,107	4,102,446	4,030,601	3,958,635	3,920,939
Northeast[2]	551,727	561,707	572,832	574,264	573,280	591,948	629,503	689,053	702,654	699,933	700,556	712,413	719,328	593,162	584,149	565,273	557,620
Connecticut	55,978	55,989	55,000	55,070	47,636	49,352	50,984	52,192	54,067	52,835	54,314	57,498	56,155	55,553	52,937	49,257	47,736
Maine	7,753	7,178	6,953	7,524	7,788	8,939	9,446	9,855	8,907	8,052	7,919	7,854	7,504	7,316	7,278	7,159	6,942
Massachusetts[4,5]	44,858	46,430	46,567	46,267	45,233	44,119	131,319	166,464	163,719	167,960	172,383	180,866	184,079	76,249	72,049	68,615	68,673
New Hampshire	4,414	4,876	5,175	3,629	3,629	3,665	3,702	3,987	4,285	4,615	4,590	4,650	4,549	4,600	4,347	4,119	4,088
New Jersey	125,881	130,565	129,377	128,984	130,610	132,846	134,290	130,303	143,315	139,091	133,158	129,750	127,560	124,176	120,115	114,611	114,886
New York	174,406	181,105	178,612	183,068	186,955	193,074	132,966	126,138	124,853	125,314	122,359	121,614	118,814	121,182	116,658	113,071	107,747
Pennsylvania[4,5,6]	110,532	108,230	121,094	118,770	121,176	125,928	130,786	137,206	167,692	167,520	172,184	176,987	186,973	171,329	179,297	177,851	177,777
Rhode Island	20,446	19,648	21,049	21,753	20,922	24,759	25,914	25,929	26,085	25,613	26,017	26,137	26,754	25,924	25,164	24,518	23,818
Vermont	7,459	7,686	9,005	9,199	9,331	9,266	10,096	9,810	9,731	8,933	7,632	7,057	6,940	6,833	6,304	6,072	5,953
Midwest	708,886	746,286	849,703	876,139	896,061	907,701	937,378	943,026	958,730	975,228	998,775	1,015,046	1,014,735	998,903	996,065	973,778	963,635
Illinois[5]	115,503	119,481	131,850	134,270	139,029	141,508	141,544	144,454	143,871	143,136	141,000	142,790	144,904	130,910	131,910	125,442	124,507
Indiana[7]	93,509	96,752	104,624	105,071	109,251	104,116	114,209	118,773	121,675	117,960	128,655	129,608	130,178	131,635	131,881	124,967	121,145
Iowa[8]	15,386	16,834	18,447	19,675	21,147	22,061	19,970	21,413	22,408	23,404	22,622	22,776	22,958	23,163	29,004	29,828	29,333
Kansas	15,732	16,339	17,219	16,785	15,992	15,250	15,217	14,740	14,439	15,010	15,518	16,131	16,263	17,236	17,402	17,353	17,021
Michigan[5]	147,598	165,449	170,997	170,041	170,276	170,967	174,577	179,486	176,630	180,290	181,024	181,295	175,421	185,416	194,082	185,984	178,597
Minnesota	90,202	94,920	100,818	113,265	115,906	120,720	122,692	110,046	113,121	118,878	126,616	127,152	127,963	121,313	111,544	107,423	108,157
Missouri	42,368	46,301	49,992	52,493	53,299	55,767	54,584	54,543	54,848	53,614	55,098	56,251	57,360	57,805	57,434	56,912	55,470
Nebraska[5]	14,363	16,439	16,527	20,462	21,483	20,847	16,468	18,412	17,994	18,468	18,731	18,910	19,606	17,583	16,320	15,876	14,260
North Dakota	2,599	2,700	2,726	2,783	2,847	2,970	3,229	3,566	3,749	4,085	4,320	4,496	4,266	4,206	4,339	4,563	4,764
Ohio	116,321	113,493	178,830	184,246	189,375	195,213	215,186	218,239	230,758	240,706	244,512	257,809	260,577	256,084	250,021	252,901	256,853
South Dakota	3,548	3,730	3,441	3,790	4,214	4,462	5,088	5,236	5,372	5,308	5,661	5,641	6,146	6,602	6,540	6,819	7,200
Wisconsin	51,757	53,848	54,232	53,258	53,242	53,820	54,614	54,118	53,865	54,369	55,018	52,187	49,093	46,950	45,588	45,710	46,328
South[3]	1,272,488	1,306,375	1,503,679	1,556,545	1,573,215	1,619,937	1,623,038	1,652,705	1,667,198	1,685,782	1,719,489	1,701,976	1,713,042	1,761,825	1,739,810	1,731,606	1,706,122
Alabama[4]	37,865	38,720	40,379	40,595	40,178	40,627	39,713	39,660	36,799	48,607	46,367	51,745	53,250	49,953	53,265	60,913	57,993
Arkansas	25,178	28,294	28,698	28,505	28,409	28,119	27,377	28,164	28,771	30,735	31,166	31,440	30,939	30,642	29,820	31,039	30,122
Delaware	16,528	18,837	20,030	20,976	20,052	19,995	20,201	18,921	18,725	18,462	16,958	16,696	17,216	16,831	16,313	16,195	15,641
District of Columbia[4]	9,740	10,043	11,234	12,129	10,664	9,663	9,389	7,116	7,585	7,006	6,670	8,073	7,706	8,055	8,641	8,706	8,266
Florida	237,117	239,694	283,965	291,631	296,139	292,842	291,315	286,769	278,606	279,613	272,242	276,254	279,057	267,448	252,783	245,040	240,869
Georgia[4,5]	143,457	149,963	278,669	307,686	321,407	360,037	367,349	402,694	423,547	414,409	432,436	379,204	389,901	453,887	464,773	457,217	442,061
Kentucky	11,689	12,093	17,594	18,988	19,620	22,794	24,480	28,869	32,619	37,030	36,396	48,749	51,424	54,947	49,274	56,140	54,511
Louisiana	35,375	35,453	33,028	35,118	35,854	35,744	36,257	36,813	38,231	38,366	38,145	39,006	40,025	42,259	43,825	42,753	41,298
Maryland[4,5]	70,553	74,612	78,051	81,286	81,523	80,708	81,982	77,875	76,676	75,593	94,100	98,470	100,958	95,017	88,181	96,359	96,640
Mississippi	10,376	10,997	11,530	13,427	15,118	15,435	16,633	19,116	20,375	23,864	24,107	21,623	22,267	24,276	26,793	29,466	30,768
North Carolina	102,483	105,416	105,227	105,095	105,949	110,676	112,900	113,161	111,537	111,626	110,419	111,446	109,678	106,581	104,228	100,479	96,070
Oklahoma[9]	28,090	28,790	29,093	28,075	30,969	30,269	29,881	28,326	28,404	28,996	**	27,527	27,940	27,067	25,657	24,448	25,506
South Carolina[10]	42,417	43,095	46,482	48,585	44,632	44,399	41,574	40,354	38,941	39,308	43,284	41,685	35,165	33,876	32,917	33,362	34,945
Tennessee	37,002	35,836	38,924	39,596	40,682	40,889	42,712	44,359	47,099	48,631	52,057	55,908	57,605	58,493	59,655	61,852	64,430
Texas	429,329	438,232	443,688	446,685	441,848	443,682	434,486	431,981	428,836	430,301	431,967	434,306	428,014	426,208	418,479	408,472	405,473
Virginia[5]	29,620	30,002	30,576	32,098	33,955	37,882	40,359	41,663	43,470	45,589	48,144	51,954	53,614	57,876	56,654	50,566	52,956
West Virginia	5,669	6,298	6,511	6,070	6,216	6,176	6,430	6,864	6,977	7,646	7,668	7,890	8,283	8,409	8,552	8,599	8,573
West	597,648	648,613	710,837	740,131	751,984	780,583	802,818	804,627	786,608	780,341	772,076	781,614	769,002	748,556	710,577	687,978	693,562
Alaska	3,999	4,212	4,274	4,547	4,779	4,803	5,229	5,406	5,547	5,680	6,111	6,528	6,689	6,739	6,914	6,955	7,173
Arizona	40,607	44,813	51,329	56,960	59,810	63,073	66,485	65,554	70,532	71,115	73,265	76,830	82,212	78,243	80,910	75,409	72,452
California	286,526	304,531	324,427	332,414	343,145	350,768	358,121	374,701	384,852	388,260	346,495	334,671	325,069	311,728	298,322	297,917	297,728
Colorado[4]	42,688	45,499	45,502	48,733	50,460	55,218	57,328	55,297	57,779	56,438	63,032	77,634	74,123	78,432	76,100	76,164	77,793
Hawaii	14,027	15,401	15,711	15,707	15,525	15,581	16,772	20,165	16,113	16,825	18,598	19,426	19,097	19,469	20,874	22,316	22,211
Idaho[8]	5,855	6,367	31,172	36,436	35,103	35,670	31,361	42,375	44,579	43,712	48,609	48,663	49,513	56,975	39,172	29,203	31,606
Montana	4,473	4,683	5,358	5,906	6,108	6,248	6,703	6,914	7,634	8,316	8,763	9,106	10,422	10,091	9,983	9,875	9,874
Nevada	9,760	11,670	12,561	11,787	12,189	12,416	12,290	12,159	12,645	12,616	13,208	13,461	13,337	12,300	11,834	11,637	11,321
New Mexico[4]	8,903	8,905	10,397	9,878	10,461	10,263	16,287	15,899	17,725	14,982	17,878	20,774	20,883	20,086	19,622	19,852	21,381
Oregon	42,292	43,980	44,809	44,777	46,023	46,063	45,397	43,415	43,324	43,606	43,988	42,471	40,921	39,607	38,753	37,468	37,128
Utah	9,306	9,519	9,482	9,397	9,800	10,292	10,646	10,339	10,267	10,083	10,417	10,801	11,030	11,481	11,560	11,912	11,394
Washington[4]	125,780	145,547	151,990	159,748	154,466	165,711	171,603	147,741	111,193	103,882	116,487	115,891	110,268	98,053	91,337	84,229	88,339
Wyoming[5]	3,432	3,486	3,825	3,841	4,115	4,477	4,596	4,662	4,418	4,826	5,225	5,358	5,438	5,352	5,196	5,041	5,162

Note: The Annual Probation Survey collects population counts for January 1 and December 31 of the reporting year. Because some agencies update their year end population counts during the following reporting year, BJS has historically used this information to update the annual counts in this spreadsheet. While the 2012 data represents the population count on December 31, 2012, the 2011 data reflect the updated population counts reported for January 1, 2012. The 2010 data reported here represent the updated counts received for January 1, 2011, etc. This differs with how data were prepared for the reports "Probation and Parole in the United States, 2012" and Probation and Parole in the United States, 2011", in which the population for each year represents that reported for December 31 of that year, for the purpose of making comparisons within the same reporting year. Probation and Parole in the United States, 2012, and earlier reports in this series are available on the BJS website at http://www.bjs.gov/index.cfm?ty=pbse&sid=42. See "Methodology" in the 2012 report for a summary of of how reporting changes have affected the counts of the number of adults on probation, 2000-2012.

** = Not known.

-- = Not reported.

[1]The Annual Probation Survey was not conducted in 1991. The January 1, 1992 population counts were used as estimates of the December 31, 1991 population counts.

[2]Includes an estimated 164,375 probationers under supervision in Pennsylvania in 2003 (i.e., January 1, 2004) due to a change in reporting county probation counts. See footnotes 4 and 5.

[3]Includes an estimated 26,000 probationers under supervision in Oklahoma in 2006 (i.e., January 1, 2007) because the state agency was unable to provide data for the 2007 reporting year.

[4]See "Methodology" in "Probation and Parole in the United States, 2009" (http://www.ojp.usdoj.gov/bjs/pub/pdf/ppus09.pdf) for a discussion of changes in reporting methods between 2000 and 2009.

[5]See "Methodology" in "Probation and Parole in the United States, 2010" (http://www.ojp.usdoj.gov/bjs/pub/pdf/ppus10.pdf) for a discussion of changes in reporting methods between 2009 and 2010.

[6]Due to a change in reporting county probation counts, the 2003 (i.e., January 1, 2004) estimated total for Pennsylvania based on reporting methods comparable to 2004 was 164,375.

[7]The December 31, 1981 population was used as an estimate for 1982.

[8]See "Methodology" in Probation and Parole in the United States, 2011, http://www.bjs.gov/content/pub/pdf/ppus11.pdf, for information on reporting changes in 2011.

[9]The state agency was unable to provide data for the 2007 reporting year. Two localities in Oklahoma reported an estimated 1,363 probationers under supervision in 2006 (i.e., January 1, 2007). The January 1, 2007 population in each jurisdiction was used to update the December 31, 2006 population in each jurisdiction; however, Oklahoma's state agency and two localities reported an estimated 27,415 probationers under supervision on December 31, 2006.

[10]The count for 2008 is based on updated estimates for 2009 using the revised methodology first used for 2010. (The count for December 31, 2008, represents the revised estimate for January 1, 2009.) The count for 2009 is also based on the revised methodology as it has been updated using the data received for January 1, 2010. These data are not comparable to those reported for 2007. See "Methodology" in "Probation and Parole in the United States, 2010" (http://www.ojp.usdoj.gov/bjs/pub/pdf/ppus10.pdf) for a discussion of changes in reporting methods between the data originally reported for 2009 and the revised methodology used for 2010.

Table 1. U.S. Adult Residents on Community Supervision, Probation, and Parole, 2000–2013

(Number; percent.)

Year	Community supervision population	Probation	Parole
2000	4,565,100	3,839,500	725,500
2001	4,665,900	3,934,700	731,100
2002	4,748,300	3,995,200	753,100
2003	4,847,500	4,074,000	773,500
2004	4,916,500	4,140,600	775,900
2005	4,946,800	4,162,500	784,400
2006	5,035,200	4,237,000	798,200
2007	5,119,300	4,293,200	826,100
2008	5,095,200	4,271,000	828,200
2009	5,017,900	4,198,200	824,100
2010	4,887,900	4,055,500	840,700
2011	4,814,200	3,971,300	853,900
2012	4,781,300	3,942,800	851,200
2013	4,751,400	3,910,600	853,200
Average annual percent change, 2000–2012	0.4	0.2	1.3
Percent change, 2012–2013	-0.6	-0.8	0.2

Note: Counts rounded to the nearest 100. Detail may not sum to total due to rounding. Counts based on most recent data and may differ from previously published statistics. Reporting methods for some probation agencies changed over time.

Table 2. U.S. Adult Residents on Community Supervision, Probation, and Parole, 2000, 2005–2013

(Number; rate.)

Year	Number per 100,000 U.S. adult residents			U.S. adult residents on:		
	Community supervision[1]	Probation	Parole	Community supervision[2]	Probation	Parole
2000	2,162	1,818	344	1 in 46	1 in 55	1 in 291
2005	2,215	1,864	351	1 in 45	1 in 54	1 in 285
2006	2,228	1,875	353	1 in 45	1 in 53	1 in 283
2007	2,239	1,878	361	1 in 45	1 in 53	1 in 277
2008[3]	2,203	1,846	358	1 in 45	1 in 54	1 in 279
2009	2,147	1,796	353	1 in 47	1 in 56	1 in 284
2010	2,067	1,715	355	1 in 48	1 in 58	1 in 281
2011	2,014	1,662	357	1 in 50	1 in 60	1 in 280
2012	1,980	1,633	353	1 in 50	1 in 61	1 in 284
2013	1,950	1,605	350	1 in 51	1 in 62	1 in 286

Note: Detail may not sum to total due to rounding. Rates based on most recent data and may differ from previously published statistics. Rates based on the community supervision, probation, and parole population counts as of December 31 of the reporting year and the estimated U.S. adult resident population on January 1 of each subsequent year.
[1]Includes adults on probation and adults on parole. For 2008 to 2013, detail may not sum to total because the community supervision rate was adjusted to exclude parolees who were also on probation.
[2]Includes adults on probation and parole.
[3]See Methodology for estimating change in population counts.

Table 3. Rate of Probation Exits, by Type of Exit, 2008–2013

(Rate per 100 probationers; months.)

Type of exit	2008	2009	2010	2011	2012	2013
Total exit rate[1]	55	55	55	55	53	54
Completion	35	36	36	36	36	36
Incarceration[2]	9	9	9	9	8	8
Absconder	2	2	1	1	1	1
Discharged to custody, detainer, or warrant	--	--	--	--	--	--
Other unsatisfactory[3]	6	6	6	5	5	6
Transferred to another probation agency	--	--	--	--	--	--
Death	--	--	--	--	--	--
Other[4]	2	2	2	2	2	2
Estimated mean time served on probation (months)[5]	22	22	22	22	22	22

Note: Detail may not sum to total due to rounding. Rates based on most recent data and may differ from previously published statistics.
-- = Less than 0.5 per 100 probationers.
[1]The ratio of the number of probationers exiting supervision during the year to the average daily probation population (i.e., average of the January 1 and December 31 populations within the reporting year).
[2]Includes probationers who were incarcerated for a new offense and those who had their current probation sentence revoked (e.g., violating a condition of supervision).
[3]Includes probationers discharged from supervision who failed to meet all conditions of supervision, including some with only financial conditions remaining, some who had their probation sentence revoked but were not incarcerated because their sentence was immediately reinstated, and other types of unsatisfactory exits. Includes some early terminations and expirations of sentence.
[4]Includes, but not limited to, probationers who were discharged from supervision through a legislative mandate because they were deported or transferred to the jurisdiction of Immigration and Customs Enforcement; were transferred to another state through an interstate compact agreement; had their sentence dismissed or overturned by the court through an appeal; had their sentence administratively closed, deferred, or terminated by the court; were awaiting a hearing; and were released on bond.
[5]Calculated as the inverse of the exit rate times 12 months.

Table 4. Probationers Who Exited Supervision, by Type of Exit, 2008–2013

(Percent; number.)

Type of exit	2008	2009	2010	2011	2012	2013
Total	100.0	100.0	100.0	100.0	100.0	100.0
Completion	63.0	65.0	65.0	66.0	68.0	66.0
Incarceration[1]	17.0	16.0	16.0	16.0	15.0	15.0
Absconder	4.0	3.0	3.0	2.0	3.0	3.0
Discharged to custody, detainer, or warrant	1.0	1.0	1.0	1.0	1.0	—
Other unsatisfactory[2]	10.0	10.0	11.0	9.0	9.0	11.0
Transferred to another probation agency	1.0	—	1.0	1.0	1.0	1.0
Death	1.0	1.0	1.0	1.0	1.0	1.0
Other[3]	4.0	4.0	4.0	4.0	4.0	3.0
Estimated number[4]	2,320,100	2,327,800	2,261,300	2,189,100	2,089,800	2,131,300

Note: Detail may not sum to total due to rounding. Percents based on most recent data and may differ from previously published statistics. Percents based on probationers with known type of exit. Reporting methods for some probation agencies changed over time.
— = Less than 0.5%.
[1]Includes probationers who were incarcerated for a new offense and those who had their current probation sentence revoked (e.g., violating a condition of supervision).
[2]Includes probationers discharged from supervision who failed to meet all conditions of supervision, including some with only financial conditions remaining, some who had their probation sentence revoked but were not incarcerated because their sentence was immediately reinstated, and other types of unsatisfactory exits. Includes some early terminations and expirations of sentence.
[3]Includes, but not limited to, probationers who were discharged from supervision through a legislative mandate because they were deported or transferred to the jurisdiction of Immigration and Customs Enforcement; were transferred to another state through an interstate compact agreement; had their sentence dismissed or overturned by the court through an appeal; had their sentence administratively closed, deferred, or terminated by the court; were awaiting a hearing; and were released on bond.
[4]Counts rounded to the nearest 100. Calculated as the inverse of the exit rate times 12 months. Includes estimates for nonreporting agencies.

Table 5. California Adult Probation Population, 2010 and 2013

(Percent; number.)

Characteristic	Probation entries	Probation exits	December 31 probation
2010 population	149,029	167,883	292,874
2013 population	170,803	166,655	294,057

Characteristic	Percent change		
Percent change of population			
Probation entries	14.6		
Probation exits	-0.7		
Year end probation population	0.4		

Table 6. Rate of Parole Exits, by Type of Exit, 2008–2013

(Rate per 100 parolees; months.)

Type of exit	2008	2009	2010	2011	2012	2013
Total exit rate[1]	69	70	67	63	58	54
Completion	34	35	35	33	34	33
Returned to incarceration	24	24	22	20	15	16
With new sentence	6	6	6	5	5	5
With revocation	17	17	16	13	8	10
Other/unknown	1	1	1	2	2	2
Absconder	7	6	6	6	6	1
Other unsatisfactory[2]	1	1	1	1	1	1
Transferred to another state	1	1	1	1	1	1
Death	1	1	1	1	1	1
Other[3]	1	2	1	2	1	1
Estimated mean time served on parole (months)[4]	17	17	18	19	21	22

Note: Detail may not sum to total due to rounding. Rates based on most recent data and may differ from previously published statistics. See Methodology. Rates based on parolees with known type of exit.
[1]The ratio of the number of parolees exiting supervision during the year to the average daily parole population (i.e., average of the January 1 and December 31 populations within the reporting year).
[2]Includes parolees discharged from supervision who failed to meet all conditions of supervision, including some who had their parole sentence revoked but were not incarcerated because their sentence was immediately reinstated, and other types of unsatisfactory exits. Includes some early terminations and expirations of sentence reported as unsatisfactory exits.
[3]Includes, but not limited to, parolees who were discharged from supervision because they were deported or transferred to the jurisdiction of Immigration and Customs Enforcement, had their sentence terminated by the court through an appeal, or were transferred to another state through an interstate compact agreement and discharged to probation supervision.
[4]Calculated as the inverse of the exit rate times 12 months.

Table 7. Parolees on Probation Excluded from the January 1 and December 31 Community Supervision Populations, 2008–2013

(Number.)

Year	January 1st[1]	December 31st
2008	3,562	3,905
2009	3,905	4,959
2010	8,259	8,259
2011	8,259	10,958
2012	10,958	12,672
2013	12,672	12,511

Note: Counts based on most recent data and may differ from previously published statistics.
[1]For 2008–2009 and 2011–2013, data were based on the count as of December 31 of the prior reporting year. For 2010, the count as of December 31, 2010, was used as a proxy because additional states reported these data in 2010.

Table 8. Change in the Number of Adults on Probation, Based on Reporting Changes, 2000–2012

(Number.)

Year	December 31st probation population	Change[1]
2000	3,839,532	-13,323
2001	3,934,713	-2,982
2002	3,995,165	28,902
2003	4,073,987	18,856
2004	4,140,638	3,154
2005	4,162,495	4,262
2006	4,237,023	-21,662
2007	4,293,163	-58,692
2008	4,270,917	-32,327
2009	4,198,155	-73,122
2010	4,055,514	-2,399
2011	3,971,319	9,771
2012	3,942,776	3,019
Total change, year end 2000–2012	71,115	-136,543

Note: Counts based on most recent data and may differ from previously published statistics.
[1]Calculated as the difference between the December 31 probation population in the reporting year and the January 1 probation population in the following year.

Table 9. Change in the Number of Adults on Parole, Based on Reporting Changes, 2000–2012

(Number.)

Year	December 31st probation population	Change[1]
2000	725,527	-1,629
2001	731,147	1,186
2002	753,141	-2,207
2003	773,498	23,614
2004	775,875	-4,023
2005	784,354	-3,738
2006	798,219	1,656
2007	826,097	-4,920
2008	828,169	1,391
2009	824,115	13,703
2010	840,676	-78
2011	853,852	-2,190
2012	851,158	-11,607
Total change, year end 2000–2012	127,688	11,158

Note: Counts based on most recent data and may differ from previously published statistics.
[1]Calculated as the difference between the December 31 probation population in the reporting year and the January 1 probation population in the following year.

Table 10. Adults Under Community Supervision, 2013

(Number; percent.)

Jurisdiction	Community supervision population, 1/1/13[1]	Entries		Exits		Community supervision population, 12/31/13[1]	Change, 2013		Number under community supervision per 100,000 adult residents, 12/31/13[3]
		Reported	Imputed[2]	Reported	Imputed[2]		Number	Percent	
U.S. Total......................	4,772,700	2,464,400	2,559,500	2,445,200	2,588,700	4,751,400	-21,300	-0.4	1,950
Federal..........................	130,400	59,000	59,000	57,500	57,500	131,900	1,500	1.2	54
State.............................	4,642,300	2,405,400	2,500,500	2,387,700	2,531,200	4,619,400	-22,800	-0.5	1,895
Alabama.........................	71,000	23,200	23,200	23,400	23,400	70,800	-200	-0.3	1,896
Alaska[4]	9,200	1,100	2,800	800	2,500	9,500	300	3.5	1,728
Arizona..........................	79,900	39,000	39,000	38,900	38,900	79,200	-700	-0.9	1,570
Arkansas........................	52,300	17,800	17,800	20,300	20,300	50,200	-2,100	-4.1	2,223
California.......................	390,100	195,400	230,800	188,100	234,200	381,600	-8,500	-2.2	1,301
Colorado[4,5]	89,300	62,700	63,200	62,300	62,800	89,700	400	0.5	2,209
Connecticut	50,600	23,900	23,900	27,700	27,700	45,400	-5,200	-10.3	1,608
Delaware........................	16,200	13,600	13,600	13,200	13,200	16,700	500	2.8	2,299
District of Columbia........	13,500	6,900	6,900	7,900	7,900	12,600	-900	-6.9	2,326
Florida[4,5]	245,100	171,500	180,500	177,600	187,100	237,800	-7,300	-3.0	1,521
Georgia[6]	536,200	305,000	305,000	304,500	304,500	536,200	-100	--	7,117
Hawaii...........................	23,900	5,800	5,800	6,300	6,300	23,300	-600	-2.3	2,116
Idaho.............................	34,800	11,300	11,300	11,700	11,700	35,200	400	1.1	2,957
Illinois	152,000	88,400	88,400	86,900	86,900	153,400	1,500	1.0	1,552
Indiana	133,400	93,000	93,000	92,400	92,400	134,000	600	0.5	2,677
Iowa..............................	34,300	20,100	20,100	19,700	19,700	34,700	400	1.2	1,462
Kansas	22,100	24,900	24,900	26,500	26,500	20,500	-1,600	-7.4	942
Kentucky[4]	72,100	42,100	42,100	28,300	48,300	65,900	-6,200	-8.6	1,943
Louisiana	69,700	30,900	30,900	29,900	29,900	70,700	1,000	1.4	2,006
Maine............................	7,000	3,200	3,200	3,400	3,400	6,700	-200	-3.2	631
Maryland	46,800	38,200	38,200	36,200	36,200	46,300	-400	-0.9	1,006
Massachusetts	70,800	76,300	76,300	77,100	77,100	70,000	-900	-1.2	1,313
Michigan[4,5]	202,100	109,800	125,000	111,300	129,000	195,200	-6,900	-3.4	2,545
Minnesota	111,900	52,900	52,900	57,000	57,000	107,800	-4,200	-3.7	2,590
Mississippi......................	37,600	12,700	12,700	11,700	11,700	38,600	1,000	2.7	1,707
Missouri.........................	76,400	39,500	39,500	45,400	45,400	70,400	-6,000	-7.8	1,511
Montana	9,200	4,400	4,400	4,300	4,300	9,500	300	2.8	1,194
Nebraska........................	14,500	12,200	12,200	11,900	11,900	14,800	300	2.3	1,048
Nevada..........................	16,700	9,500	9,500	8,600	8,600	17,600	900	5.5	823
New Hampshire	6,300	4,300	4,300	4,300	4,300	6,300	/	:	593
New Jersey.....................	129,600	47,700	47,700	49,100	49,100	128,100	-1,400	-1.1	1,856
New Mexico[4]	19,400	7,300	9,700	6,700	9,700	18,700	-700	-3.5	1,184
New York........................	156,400	53,900	53,900	58,900	58,900	151,400	-5,000	-3.2	979
North Carolina	99,900	64,600	64,600	62,400	62,400	100,600	700	0.7	1,323
North Dakota..................	5,200	4,200	4,200	4,000	4,000	5,500	200	4.6	959
Ohio[4,5]	271,700	135,800	149,300	140,700	162,100	267,400	-4,300	-1.6	2,989
Oklahoma[5]	..	..	..	..	..	..	..	..	..
Oregon..........................	59,700	23,200	23,200	21,800	21,800	61,100	1,400	2.3	1,981
Pennsylvania	254,500	152,100	152,100	130,900	130,900	275,800	21,200	8.3	2,734
Rhode Island[4]	24,300	400	5,100	400	5,900	23,400	-900	-3.5	2,791
South Carolina................	40,100	16,000	16,000	15,300	15,300	40,900	800	2.1	1,102
South Dakota..................	9,500	4,300	4,300	4,200	4,200	9,500	/	:	1,489
Tennessee	77,100	31,000	31,000	32,300	32,300	77,900	800	1.0	1,550
Texas.............................	515,100	191,600	191,600	198,600	198,600	508,000	-7,100	-1.4	2,597
Utah..............................	14,400	7,600	7,600	7,500	7,500	14,500	100	0.8	717
Vermont	7,000	4,100	4,100	4,200	4,200	6,900	-100	-1.5	1,365
Virginia	54,400	29,400	29,400	29,800	29,800	55,800	1,400	2.6	869
Washington[4,5]	100,400	53,800	57,400	45,800	56,700	111,100	10,800	10.7	2,056
West Virginia[4]	10,500	1,900	3,200	2,700	2,700	11,000	500	4.8	748
Wisconsin.......................	64,500	29,300	29,300	28,600	28,600	65,300	800	1.2	1,468
Wyoming........................	5,600	3,400	3,400	3,000	3,000	6,000	400	6.3	1,338

Note: Counts rounded to the nearest 100. Detail may not sum to total due to rounding. Counts based on most recent data and may differ from previously published statistics. Due to nonresponse or incomplete data, the community supervision population for some jurisdictions on December 31, 2013, does not equal the population on January 1, 2013, plus entries, minus exits.
-- = Less than 0.05%.
: = Not calculated.
.. = Not known.
/ = Not reported.
[1]The January 1 population excludes 12,672 offenders and the December 31 population excludes 12,511 offenders under community supervision who were on both probation and parole.
[2]Reflects reported data, excluding jurisdictions for which data were unavailable.
[3]Computed using the estimated U.S. adult resident population in each jurisdiction on January 1, 2014.
[4]Data for entries and exits were estimated for nonreporting agencies.
[5]See <http://www.bjs.gov/index.cfm?ty=pbdetail&iid=5135> for more detail.
[6]Probation counts include private agency cases and may overstate the number of persons under supervision.

Table 11. Adults on Probation, 2013

(Number; percent.)

Jurisdiction	Probation population, 1/1/13	Entries		Exits		Probation population, 12/31/13	Change, 2013		Number on probation per 100,000 adult residents, 12/31/13[2]
		Reported	Imputed[1]	Reported	Imputed[1]		Number	Percent	
U.S. Total....................	3,945,795	2,034,375	2,094,100	2,033,860	2,131,300	3,910,647	-35,148	-0.9	1,605
Federal.........................	21,698	9,800	9,800	10,822	10,822	20,676	-1,022	-4.7	8
State.............................	3,924,097	2,024,575	2,084,300	2,023,038	2,120,400	3,889,971	-34,126	-0.9	1,596
Alabama.......................	62,368	20,741	20,741	21,308	21,308	61,801	-567	-0.9	1,655
Alaska[3].......................	7,154	..	1,700	..	1,713	7,167	13	0.2	1,308
Arizona........................	72,452	27,048	27,048	27,173	27,173	71,527	-925	-1.3	1,418
Arkansas......................	29,946	8,547	8,547	9,600	9,600	29,289	-657	-2.2	1,298
California.....................	294,993	170,803	170,803	166,655	166,655	294,057	-936	-0.3	1,003
Colorado[3,4]	77,793	53,991	54,500	53,011	53,500	78,843	1,050	1.3	1,942
Connecticut	47,798	21,554	21,554	25,162	25,162	42,723	-5,075	-10.6	1,515
Delaware	15,641	13,049	13,049	12,651	12,651	16,039	398	2.5	2,209
District of Columbia......	8,051	5,411	5,411	6,111	6,111	7,351	-700	-8.7	1,362
Florida[3,4]	240,607	165,208	174,200	171,448	181,000	233,128	-7,479	-3.1	1,491
Georgia[4,5]	515,896	290,462	290,462	291,881	291,881	514,477	-1,419	-0.3	6,829
Hawaii	22,211	4,957	4,957	5,592	5,592	21,576	-635	-2.9	1,958
Idaho...........................	30,978	9,435	9,435	9,038	9,038	31,375	397	1.3	2,634
Illinois	124,507	60,179	60,179	60,824	60,824	123,862	-645	-0.5	1,253
Indiana	123,250	83,459	83,459	83,036	83,036	123,673	423	0.3	2,471
Iowa	29,333	16,421	16,421	16,453	16,453	29,301	-32	-0.1	1,233
Kansas	17,021	21,255	21,255	21,830	21,830	16,446	-575	-3.4	756
Kentucky[3]	57,720	31,876	31,876	18,569	38,569	51,027	-6,693	-11.6	1,505
Louisiana	42,753	14,836	14,836	15,543	15,543	42,046	-707	-1.7	1,192
Maine	6,942	3,209	3,209	3,432	3,432	6,719	-223	-3.2	629
Maryland	41,123	34,766	34,766	32,982	32,982	40,716	-407		884
Massachusetts	68,673	73,505	73,505	74,394	74,394	67,784	-889	-1.3	1,273
Michigan[3,4]	183,031	99,214	114,435	100,105	117,802	176,795	-6,236	-3.4	2,305
Minnesota	105,923	46,948	46,948	51,109	51,109	101,762	-4,161	-3.9	2,446
Mississippi...................	30,768	9,574	9,574	8,667	8,667	31,675	907	2.9	1,402
Missouri.......................	55,700	25,618	25,618	30,290	30,290	51,028	-4,672	-8.4	1,094
Montana	8,295	3,793	3,793	3,766	3,766	8,472	177	2.1	1,066
Nebraska......................	13,077	10,447	10,447	9,979	9,979	13,545	468	3.6	960
Nevada	11,321	5,448	5,448	4,667	4,667	12,102	781	6.9	565
New Hampshire	4,088	2,759	2,759	2,853	2,853	3,994	-94	-2.3	379
New Jersey....................	114,594	41,451	41,451	42,814	42,814	113,231	-1,363	-1.2	1,639
New Mexico[3]	16,925	6,294	8,700	5,956	8,900	16,696	-229	-1.4	1,057
New York......................	110,204	32,320	32,320	36,115	36,115	106,409	-3,795	-3.4	688
North Carolina	96,070	56,843	56,843	57,623	57,623	94,442	-1,628	-1.7	1,242
North Dakota...............	4,791	3,173	3,173	3,066	3,066	4,898	107	2.2	860
Ohio[3,4]	257,058	127,348	140,800	134,424	155,800	250,630	-6,428	-2.5	2,802
Oklahoma[4]..................	..	..	..	..	..[4]	..	..	..	
Oregon.........................	36,990	14,272	'4,272	13,371	13,371	37,891	901	2.4	1,228
Pennsylvania	162,225	94,442	94,442	84,697	84,697	171,970	9,745	6.0	1,705
Rhode Island[3]	23,818	..	4,600	..	5,500	22,988	-830	-3.5	2,737
South Carolina.............	34,625	13,923	13,923	12,723	12,723	35,825	1,200	3.5	964
South Dakota...............	6,744	2,698	2,698	2,490	2,490	6,952	208	3.1	1,084
Tennessee	64,129	25,790	25,790	27,586	27,586	64,216	87	0.1	1,278
Texas...........................	405,653	156,509	156,509	162,507	162,507	399,655	-5,998	-1.5	2,043
Utah............................	11,379	5,646	5,646	5,822	5,822	11,203	-176	-1.5	554
Vermont	5,955	3,539	3,539	3,703	3,703	5,791	-164	-2.8	1,148
Virginia	53,607	28,831	28,831	29,262	29,262	54,020	413	0.8	841
Washington[3,4]	85,270	47,883	51,500	34,818	45,700	95,217	9,947	11.7	1,762
West Virginia[3]	8,465	..	1,300	1,294	1,294	8,465	0	0.0	574
Wisconsin	45,777	22,741	22,741	21,760	21,760	46,758	981	2.1	1,051
Wyoming	4,899	2,824	2,824	2,516	2,516	5,207	308	6.3	1,165

Note: Counts based on most recent data and may differ from previously published statistics. Counts may not be actual, as reporting agencies may provide estimates on some or all detailed data. Due to nonresponse or incomplete data, the probation population for some jurisdictions on December 31, 2013, does not equal the population on January 1, 2013, plus entries, minus exits. Reporting methods for some probation agencies changed over time, and probation coverage was expanded in 1998 and 1999.

.. = Not known.

[1]Detail may not sum to total due to rounding. Reflects reported data, excluding jurisdictions for which data were unavailable.

[2]Computed using the estimated U.S. adult resident population in each jurisdiction on January 1, 2014.

[3]Data for entries and exits were estimated for nonreporting agencies.

[4]See <http://www.bjs.gov/index.cfm?ty=pbdetail&iid=5135> for more detail.

[5]Includes private agency cases and may overstate the number of persons under supervision.

Table 12. Characteristics of Adults on Probation, 2000, 2012, and 2013

(Percent.)

Characteristic	2000	2012	2013
Total	100.0	100.0	100.0
Sex			
Male	78.0	76.0	75.0
Female	22.0	24.0	25.0
Race/Hispanic origin[1]			
White	54.0	54.0	54.0
Black/African American	31.0	30.0	30.0
Hispanic/Latino	13.0	13.0	14.0
American Indian/Alaska Native	1.0	1.0	1.0
Asian/Native Hawaiian/Other Pacific Islander	1.0	1.0	1.0
Two or more races	NA	NA	--
Status of supervision			
Active	76.0	72.0	69.0
Residential/other treatment program	NA	1.0	1.0
Financial conditions remaining	NA	1.0	1.0
Inactive	9.0	7.0	6.0
Absconder	9.0	10.0	9.0
Supervised out of jurisdiction	3.0	3.0	2.0
Warrant status	NA	3.0	9.0
Other	3.0	3.0	3.0
Type of offense			
Felony	52.0	53.0	55.0
Misdemeanor	46.0	45.0	43.0
Other infractions	2.0	2.0	2.0
Most serious offense			
Violent	NA	19.0	19.0
Domestic violence	NA	4.0	4.0
Sex offense	NA	3.0	3.0
Other violent offense	NA	12.0	12.0
Property	NA	28.0	29.0
Drug	24.0	25.0	25.0
Public order	24.0	17.0	17.0
DWI/DUI	18.0	15.0	14.0
Other traffic offense	6.0	2.0	2.0
Other[2]	52.0	11.0	10.0

Note: Detail may not sum to total due to rounding. Counts based on most recent data and may differ from previously published statistics. Characteristics based on probationers with known type of status.
-- = Less than 0.5%.
NA = Not available.
[1]Excludes persons of Hispanic or Latino origin, unless specified.
[2]Includes violent and property offenses in 2000 because those data were not collected separately.

Table 13. Adults on Parole, 2013

(Number; percent.)

Jurisdiction	Parole population, 1/1/13	Entries		Exits		Parole population, 12/31/13	Change, 2013		Number on parole per 100,000 adult residents, 12/31/13[2]
		Reported	Imputed[1]	Reported	Imputed[1]		Number	Percent	
U.S. Total....................	839,551	430,018	465,500	411,305	457,500	853,215	13,664	1.6	350
Federal........................	108,679	49,212	49,212	46,665	46,665	111,226	2,547	2.3	46
State............................	730,872	380,806	416,200	364,640	410,800	741,989	11,117	1.5	304
Alabama	8,616	2,428	2,428	2,062	2,062	8,982	366	4.2	241
Alaska	2,000	1,103	1,103	800	800	2,303	303	15.2	420
Arizona	7,460	11,929	11,929	11,753	11,753	7,636	176	2.4	151
Arkansas....................	23,227	9,238	9,238	10,660	10,660	21,709	-1,518	-6.5	962
California[3,4,5]	95,120	24,559	60,000	21,396	67,600	87,532	-7,588	-8.0	298
Colorado...................	11,458	8,716	8,716	9,328	9,328	10,846	-612	-5.3	267
Connecticut	2,793	2,367	2,367	2,520	2,520	2,640	-153	-5.5	94
Delaware...................	601	579	579	523	523	657	56	9.3	90
District of Columbia ...	5,928	1,467	1,467	1,772	1,772	5,623	-305	-5.1	1,042
Florida[3,4]...................	4,538	6,252	6,252	6,107	6,107	4,683	145	3.2	30
Georgia[4,5]..................	24,673	14,565	14,565	12,627	12,627	26,611	1,938	7.9	353
Hawaii	1,659	802	802	680	680	1,738	79	4.8	158
Idaho	3,848	1,897	1,897	2,674	2,674	3,851	3	0.1	323
Illinois	27,456	28,236	28,236	26,106	26,106	29,586	2,130	7.8	299
Indiana......................	10,153	9,574	9,574	9,387	9,387	10,340	187	1.8	207
Iowa	5,151	3,675	3,675	3,231	3,231	5,595	444	8.6	235
Kansas	5,126	3,600	3,600	4,661	4,661	4,065	-1,061	-20.7	187
Kentucky[3].................	14,416	10,267	10,267	9,761	9,761	14,922	506	3.5	440
Louisiana...................	27,092	16,058	16,058	14,406	14,406	28,744	1,652	6.1	815
Maine	21	1	1	1	1	21	/	:	2
Maryland	5,648	3,403	3,403	3,239	3,239	5,623	-25	-0.4	122
Massachusetts...........	2,130	2,785	2,785	2,749	2,749	2,166	36	1.7	41
Michigan[3,4]..............	19,113	10,539	10,539	11,213	11,213	18,439	-674	-3.5	240
Minnesota.................	6,006	5,918	5,918	5,927	5,927	5,997	-9	-0.1	144
Mississippi.................	6,804	3,106	3,106	3,009	3,009	6,901	97	1.4	305
Missouri	20,679	13,863	13,863	15,141	15,141	19,401	-1,278	-6.2	416
Montana	943	608	608	530	530	1,021	78	8.3	128
Nebraska...................	1,383	1,764	1,764	1,901	1,901	1,246	-137	-9.9	88
Nevada......................	5,379	4,085	4,085	3,942	3,942	5,522	143	2.7	258
New Hampshire..........	2,167	1,496	1,496	1,407	1,407	2,256	89	4.1	214
New Jersey................	14,987	6,266	6,266	6,335	6,335	14,918	-69	-0.5	216
New Mexico[3].............	2,468	1,038	1,038	762	762	2,010	-458	-18.6	127
New York	46,222	21,570	21,570	22,753	22,753	45,039	-1,183	-2.6	291
North Carolina	4,359	7,723	7,723	4,800	4,800	7,171	2,812	64.5	94
North Dakota	427	1,051	1,051	917	917	561	134	31.4	99
Ohio[3,4]......................	14,653	8,450	8,450	6,306	6,306	16,797	2,144	14.6	188
Oklahoma[4]...............	2,310	908	908	664	664	2,554	244	10.6	87
Oregon	22,755	8,930	8,930	8,439	8,439	23,246	491	2.2	753
Pennsylvania	92,315	57,654	57,654	46,167	46,167	103,802	11,487	12.0	1,029
Rhode Island[3]	481	408	408	430	430	459	-22	-4.6	55
South Carolina	6,000	2,105	2,105	2,549	2,549	5,556	-444	-7.4	150
South Dakota............	2,761	1,570	1,570	1,716	1,716	2,595	-166	-6.0	405
Tennessee..................	12,981	5,229	5,229	4,761	4,761	13,657	676	5.2	272
Texas........................	112,288	35,076	35,076	36,062	36,062	111,302	-986	-0.9	569
Utah.........................	2,986	1,929	1,929	1,632	1,632	3,283	297	9.9	162
Vermont....................	1,037	568	568	510	510	1,095	58	5.6	217
Virginia	1,891	534	534	568	568	1,800	-91	-4.8	28
Washington[3,4]............	15,091	5,870	5,870	11,017	11,017	15,908	817	5.4	294
West Virginia[3]	2,052	1,917	1,917	1,416	1,416	2,553	501	24.4	173
Wisconsin	20,491	6,592	6,592	6,832	6,832	20,251	-240	-1.2	455
Wyoming	729	538	538	491	491	776	47	6.4	174

Note: Counts based on most recent data and may differ from previously published statistics. Counts may not be actual, as reporting agencies may provide estimates on some or all detailed data. Due to nonresponse or incomplete data, the parole population for some jurisdictions on December 31, 2013, does not equal the population on January 1, 2013, plus entries, minus exits.
: = Not calculated.
/ = Not reported.
[1]Detail may not sum to total due to rounding. Reflects reported data, excluding jurisdictions for which data were unavailable.
[2]Computed using the estimated U.S. adult resident population in each jurisdiction on January 1, 2014.
[3]Data for entries and exits were estimated when data was incomplete.
[4]See <http://www.bjs.gov/index.cfm?ty=pbdetail&iid=5135> for more detail.
[5]Includes post-release community supervision and mandatory supervision parolees: 38,781 on January 1, 2013; and 24,559 entries, 21,393 exits, and 41,947 on December 31, 2013.

Table 14. Adults Entering Parole, by Type of Entry, 2013

(Number.)

Jurisdiction	Total reported	Discretionary[1]	Mandatory[2]	Reinstatement[3]	Term of supervised release	Other[4]	Parole population, 1/1/13
U.S. Total......................	430,018	183,899	109,768	13,060	85,972	4,782	32,537
Federal...........................	49,212	361	862	69	47,920	0	0
State...............................	380,806	183,538	108,906	12,991	38,052	4,782	32,537
Alabama	2,428	..	..	..	..	..	2,428
Alaska[5]...........................	1,103	..	..	..	..	..	1,103
Arizona	11,929	146	117	144	10,576	946	0
Arkansas........................	9,238	5,912	1,224	2,102	0	0	0
California.......................	24,559	..	..	..	..	..	24,559
Colorado........................	8,716	3,668	2,793	2,047	0	208	0
Connecticut	2,367	1,344	..	..	1,023	0	0
Delaware	579	..	..	..	..	..	579
District of Columbia	1,467	253	0	0	1,214	0	0
Florida...........................	6,252	38	5,569	0	640	5	0
Georgia..........................	14,565	14,565	0	0	0	0	0
Hawaii	802	791	0	11	0	0	0
Idaho[5]............................	1,897	1,408	~	489	~	~	0
Illinois	28,236	13	26,729	257	~	778	459
Indiana	9,574	0	9,574	0	0	~	0
Iowa	3,675	3,675	0	0	0	0	0
Kansas	3,600	0	9	106	3,433	52	0
Kentucky........................	10,267	6,724	3,543	0	0	0	0
Louisiana.......................	16,058	616	15,105	307	14	16	0
Maine	1	0	0	1	0	0	0
Maryland[5]	3,403	..	..	..	..	..	3,403
Massachusetts................	2,785	2,444	0	229	112	0	0
Michigan........................	10,539	9,174	629	736	~	0	0
Minnesota......................	5,918	0	5,918	0	0	~	0
Mississippi.....................	3,106	2,596	0	510	0	0	0
Missouri	13,863	10,869	834	1,222	~	938	0
Montana	608	608	0	0	0	0	0
Nebraska........................	1,764	1,723	0	41	0	0	0
Nevada...........................	4,085	2,814	1,125	146	~	0	0
New Hampshire	1,496	773	0	586	~	133	4
New Jersey.....................	6,266	4,226	2,040	~	0	0	0
New Mexico....................	1,038	..	955	83	..	..	0
New York........................	21,570	5,624	7,036	~	8,174	736	0
North Carolina	7,723	33	441	~	7,249	~	0
North Dakota	1,051	1,051	0	0	0	0	0
Ohio	8,450	91	8,138	221	0	0	0
Oklahoma......................	908	908	..	..	..	..	0
Oregon	8,930	1,354	7,520	6	9	41	0
Pennsylvania[5]	57,654	54,749	0	2,905	0	0	0
Rhode Island	408	408	~	~	~	~	0
South Carolina	2,105	773	1,332	0	0	0	0
South Dakota.................	1,570	472	942	~	~	154	2
Tennessee	5,229	4,990	7	221	0	11	0
Texas.............................	35,076	33,737	509	369	0	461	0
Utah	1,929	1,764	0	33	0	132	0
Vermont[5]	568	320	~	180	~	68	0
Virginia	534	156	378	0	0	0	0
Washington	5,870	193	5,677	0	0	0	0
West Virginia	1,917	1,917	0	0	0	0	0
Wisconsin	6,592	119	762	0	5,608	103	0
Wyoming	538	499	0	39	0	0	0

Note: Detail may not sum to total due to rounding. Counts based on most recent data and may differ from previously published statistics.
~ = Not applicable.
.. = Not known.
[1]Includes offenders entering due to a parole board decision.
[2]Includes offenders whose release from prison was not decided by a parole board, offenders entering due to determinate sentencing, good-time provisions, and emergency releases.
[3]Includes offenders returned to parole after serving time in a prison due to a parole violation. Depending on the reporting jurisdiction, reinstatement entries may include only parolees who were origi-nally released from prison through a discretionary release, only those originally released through a mandatory release, or a combination of both types. May also include those originally released through a term of supervised release.
[4]Includes parolees who were transferred from another state, placed on supervised release from jail, released to a drug transition program, released from a boot camp operated by the Department of Corrections, and released from prison through a conditional medical or mental health release to parole. Also includes absconders who were returned to parole supervision, on pretrial supervision, under supervision due to a suspended sentence, and others.
[5]Some or all detailed data were estimated for type of sentence.

Table 15. Characteristics of Adults on Parole, 2000, 2012, and 2013

(Percent.)

Characteristic	2000	2012	2013
Total	100.0	100.0	100.0
Sex			
Male	88.0	89.0	88.0
Female	12.0	11.0	12.0
Race/Hispanic origin[1]			
White	38.0	41.0	43.0
Black/African American	40.0	40.0	38.0
Hispanic/Latino	21.0	17.0	17.0
American Indian/Alaska Native	1.0	1.0	1.0
Asian/Native Hawaiian/Other Pacific Islander	--	1.0	1.0
Two or more races	NA	--	--
Status of supervision			
Active	83.0	82.0	84.0
Inactive	4.0	5.0	5.0
Absconder	7.0	6.0	6.0
Supervised out of state	5.0	4.0	4.0
Financial conditions remaining	NA	--	--
Other	1.0	3.0	1.0
Maximum sentence to incarceration			
Less than 1 year	3.0	5.0	5.0
1 year or more	97.0	95.0	95.0
Most serious offense			
Violent	NA	29.0	29.0
Sex offense	NA	9.0	10.0
Other violent offense	NA	20.0	20.0
Property	NA	22.0	22.0
Drug	NA	33.0	32.0
Weapon	NA	4.0	4.0
Other[2]	NA	13.0	13.0

Note: Detail may not sum to total due to rounding. Counts based on most recent data and may differ from previously published statistics. Characteristics based on parolees with known type of status.
-- = Less than 0.5%.
NA = Not available.
[1]Excludes persons of Hispanic or Latino origin, unless specified.
[2]Includes public order offenses.

Table 16. Adults Exiting Parole, by Type of Exit, 2013

(Number.)

Jurisdiction	Total reported	Completion	Returned to incarceration With new sentence	Returned to incarceration With revocation	To receive treatment	Other/ unknown	Absconder	Other unsatisfactory[1]	Death	Other[2]	Unknown or not reported
U.S. Total...............	411,305	234,691	33,499	67,462	2,820	9,482	7,552	4,779	5,126	13,760	32,134
Federal......................	46,665	26,153	1,946	10,085	5	97	1,443	1,443	634	28	4,831
State.........................	364,640	208,538	31,553	57,377	2,815	9,385	6,109	3,336	4,492	13,732	27,303
Alabama	2,062	1,552	213	121	..	0	132	..	14	30	0
Alaska[3]...................	800	..	..	..	..	..	..	..	..	..	800
Arizona....................	11,753	8,427	193	2,979	0	0	0	0	57	97	0
Arkansas.................	10,660	3,651	1,373	5,352	0	0	90	24	170	0	0
California.................	21,396	..	..	..	..	..	..	..	..	..	21,396
Colorado.................	9,328	4,480	3,811	867	0	~	~	~	62	108	0
Connecticut............	2,520	1,392	..	..	..	996	132	0	..	0	0
Delaware	523	331	..	..	..	..	..	85	2	105	0
District of Columbia..	1,772	828	0	0	0	394	0	308	53	189	0
Florida.....................	6,107	3,973	376	750	0	0	0	0	31	766	211
Georgia....................	12,627	10,092	353	557	5	1,217	113	0	103	187	0
Hawaii	680	431	1	232	0	0	0	0	16	0	0
Idaho[3].....................	2,674	673	~	~	~	1,646	333	~	22	~	0
Illinois	26,106	14,476	1,945	7,081	~	~	835	0	79	1,017	673
Indiana....................	9,387	2,775	720	2,078	0	0	1,633	0	64	2,117	0
Iowa	3,231	1,831	79	479	0	0	0	812	27	3	0
Kansas	4,661	3,832	174	0	0	246	169	0	21	219	0
Kentucky.................	9,761	5,326	376	3,212	0	749	0	0	96	2	0
Louisiana.................	14,406	7,259	654	992	~	1,379	~	833	178	3,111	0
Maine	1	0	0	1	0	0	0	0	0	0	0
Maryland[3]	3,239	..	..	..	..	..	..	..	..	..	3,239
Massachusetts........	2,749	2,086	101	541	0	0	0	0	21	0	0
Michigan..................	11,213	7,646	1,388	2,029	~	~	~	~	150	~	0
Minnesota...............	5,927	3,127	353	2,433	0	0	0	~	14	0	0
Mississippi...............	3,009	1,802	..	..	..	664	3	..	23	41	476
Missouri	15,141	6,554	1,257	3,726	844	1,280	1,251	~	206	~	23
Montana	530	304	9	208	0	0	0	0	9	0	0
Nebraska[3]	1,901	1,295	82	508	0	0	1	0	6	2	7
Nevada	3,942	2,877	253	250	~	473	41	0	48	0	0
New Hampshire	1,407	621	..	786	~	~	..	~	..	..	0
New Jersey..............	6,335	4,436	112	1,631	0	0	~	0	113	43	0
New Mexico............	762	439	..	..	..	..	66	169	30	58	0
New York.................	22,753	11,817	1,408	7,327	1,962	0	0	~	239	~	0
North Carolina	4,800	3,652	323	239	~	0	504	41	41	~	0
North Dakota.........	917	657	35	200	..	0	16	..	5	0	4
Ohio	6,306	4,292	1,281	112	0	0	172	0	120	329	0
Oklahoma...............	664	573	33	42	..	..	..	..	16	..	0
Oregon	8,439	4,813	890	1,744	4	~	2	717	124	25	120
Pennsylvania[3].........	46,167	29,954	5,261	4,457	0	0	534	155	583	5,223	0
Rhode Island	430	292	36	95	..	0	0	0	7	0	0
South Carolina	2,549	2,060	122	288	0	0	0	45	34	0	0
South Dakota.........	1,716	871	75	710	~	5	0	~	14	0	41
Tennessee	4,761	2,646	1,157	818	0	0	0	0	140	0	0
Texas.......................	36,062	27,471	5,938	811	..	322	..	..	1,214	..	306
Utah	1,632	306	211	928	0	0	0	125	24	38	0
Vermont[3]	510	318	80	94	~	14	~	0	4	0	0
Virginia	568	255	174	63	0	0	20	0	30	22	4
Washington	11,017	10,861	..	..	..	0	0	0	156	0	0
West Virginia	1,416	825	12	508	0	0	59	0	12	0	0
Wisconsin	6,832	4,050	656	2,015	0	~	0	0	111	0	0
Wyoming	491	309	38	113	0	0	3	22	3	0	3

Note: Detail may not sum to total due to rounding. Counts based on most recent data and may differ from previously published statistics.
~ = Not applicable.
.. = Not known.
[1]Includes parolees discharged from supervision who failed to meet all conditions of supervision, had their parole sentence rescinded, had their parole sentence revoked but were not returned to incarceration because their sentence was immediately reinstated, and other types of unsatisfactory exits. Includes some early terminations and expirations of sentence.
[2]Includes 3,543 parolees who were transferred to another state and 10,217 parolees who exited for other reasons. Other reasons include, but not limited to, parolees who were deported or transferred to the jurisdiction of Immigration and Customs Enforcement, had their sentence terminated by the court through an appeal, and were transferred to another state through an interstate compact agreement or discharged to probation supervision.
[3]Some or all data were estimated for type of exit.

Table 17. Percent of Parole Exits, by Type of Exit, 2008–2013

(Percent; number.)

Type of exit	2008	2009	2010	2011	2012	2013
Total	100.0	100.0	100.0	100.0	100.0	100.0
Completion	49.0	51.0	52.0	52.0	58.0	62.0
Returned to incarceration	36.0	34.0	33.0	32.0	25.0	30.0
With new sentence	9.0	9.0	9.0	9.0	8.0	9.0
With revocation	25.0	24.0	23.0	21.0	14.0	18.0
Other/unknown	1.0	1.0	1.0	2.0	3.0	3.0
Absconder	11.0	9.0	9.0	9.0	11.0	2.0
Other unsatisfactory[1]	2.0	2.0	2.0	2.0	2.0	1.0
Transferred to another state	1.0	1.0	1.0	1.0	1.0	1.0
Death	1.0	1.0	1.0	1.0	1.0	1.0
Other[2]	1.0	3.0	1.0	3.0	3.0	3.0
Estimated number[3]	568,000	575,600	562,500	532,500	496,100	457,500

Note: Detail may not sum to total due to rounding. Counts based on most recent data and may differ from previously published statistics. Percents based on parolees with known type of exit
[1]Includes parolees discharged from supervision who failed to meet all conditions of supervision, including some who had their parole sentence revoked but were not incarcerated because their sentence was immediately reinstated, and other types of unsatisfactory exits. Includes some early terminations and expirations of sentence reported as unsatisfactory exits.
[2]Includes, but not limited to, parolees who were discharged from supervision through a legislative mandate because they were deported or transferred to the jurisdiction of Immigration and Customs Enforcement, had their sentence terminated by the court through an appeal, and were transferred to another state through an interstate compact agreement or discharged to probation supervision.
[3]Estimates rounded to the nearest 100. Includes estimates for nonreporting agencies.

Methodology

About the Data

The Bureau of Justice Statistics' (BJS) Annual Probation Survey and Annual Parole Survey began in 1980 and collect data from probation and parole agencies in the United States that supervise adults. In these data, adults are persons subject to the jurisdiction of an adult court or correctional agency. Juveniles prosecuted as adults in a criminal court are considered adults. Juveniles under the jurisdiction of a juvenile court or correctional agency are excluded from these data.

The National Criminal Justice Information and Statistics Service of the Law Enforcement Assistance Administration, BJS's predecessor agency, began a statistical series on parole in 1976 and on probation in 1979. The two surveys collect data on the total number of adults supervised in the community on January 1 and December 31 each year, the number of entries and exits to supervision during the reporting year, and characteristics of the population at year end.

Both surveys cover all 50 states, the District of Columbia, and the federal system. BJS depends on the voluntary participation of state central reporters and separate state, county, and court agencies for these data. During 2013, Westat (Rockville, MD) served as BJS's collection agent for the 50 states and the District of Columbia. Data for the federal system were provided directly to BJS from the Office of Probation and Pretrial Services, Administrative Office of the United States Courts through the Federal Justice Statistics Program.

Probation

The 2013 Annual Probation Survey was sent to 468 respondents: 33 central state reporters; 435 separate state, county, or court agencies, including the state probation agency in Pennsylvania, which also provided data for 65 counties in Pennsylvania; the District of Columbia; and the federal system. The states with multiple reporters were Alabama (3), Arizona (2), Colorado (8), Florida (41), Georgia (2), Idaho (2), Kentucky (3), Michigan (134), Missouri (2), Montana (4), New Mexico (2), Ohio (187), Oklahoma (3), Pennsylvania (2), Tennessee (3), Washington (33), and West Virginia (2). Two localities in Colorado, five in Florida, 13 in Michigan, nine in Ohio, and two in Washington did not provide data for the 2013 collection. For these localities, the agency's most recent December 31 population was used to estimate the January 1 and December 31, 2013, populations. The largest respondent in Oklahoma, composing the majority of the state's probation population, provided limited estimates for the 2013 collection that were used in the state and national totals but not used to estimate Oklahoma state populations.

Parole

The 2013 Annual Parole Survey was sent to 54 respondents: 50 central state reporters; one municipal agency in Alabama; the state parole agency in Pennsylvania, which also provided data for 65 counties in Pennsylvania; the District of Columbia; and the federal system. In this report, federal parole includes a term of supervised release from prison, mandatory release, parole, military parole, and special parole. A term of supervised release is ordered at the time of sentencing by a federal judge, and it is served after release from a federal prison sentence. Definitional differences exist between parole reported here and in other BJS statistical series. Additional information about the data collection instruments is available on the BJS website at www.bjs.gov.

In a given data collection year, respondents are asked to provide both the January 1 and December 31 population counts. At times, the January 1 count differs greatly from the December 31 count of the prior year. The difference reported may result from administrative changes, such as implementing new information systems, resulting in data review and cleanup; reconciling probationer records; reclassifying offenders, including those on probation to parole and offenders on dual community supervision statuses; and including certain probation populations not previously reported (e.g., supervised for an offense of driving while intoxicated or under the influence, some probationers who had absconded, and some on an inactive status). The cumulative discrepancies between the year end and beginning year (for the year following) between 2000 and 2012 in the probation population counts resulted in an overall decline of about 136,543 probationers (table 8). Discrepancies between the year end and following year parole population count resulted in an increase of about 11,158 parolees between 2000 and 2012.

The number of probation agencies included in the survey expanded in 1998 and continued to expand through 1999 to include misdemeanor probation agencies in a few states that fell within the scope of this survey. For a discussion of this expansion, see *Probation and Parole in the United States, 2010* (NCJ 236019, BJS web, November 2011).

Technically, the change in the probation and parole populations from the beginning of the year to the end of the year should equal the difference between entries and exits during the year. However, those numbers may not be equal. Some probation and parole information systems track the number of cases that enter and exit community supervision, not the number of offenders. This means that entries and exits may include case counts as opposed to counts of offenders, while the beginning and year end population counts represent individuals. Additionally, all of the data on entries and exits may not have been logged into the information systems, or the information systems may not have fully processed all of the data before the data were submitted to BJS. At the national level, 2,014 probationers were the difference between the change in the probation population measured by the difference between January 1 and December 31, 2013, populations and the difference between probation entries and exits during 2013. For parole, 5,702 parolees were the difference between the change in the parole population measured by the difference between January 1 and December 31, 2013, populations and the difference between parole entries and exits during 2013. The percentage change reported in appendix tables 1, 2, and 4 were calculated as the difference between the January 1 and December 31 populations within the reporting year. In figures 1, 2, and 3, the annual percentage change was based on the difference between the December 31 populations for each year. As previously discussed, jurisdiction counts reported for January 1 may be different from December 31 counts reported in the previous year. As a result, the direction of change based on year end data could be in the opposite direction of the within- year change.

PART 9

Rape and Sexual Assault Among College-Age Females, 1995–2013

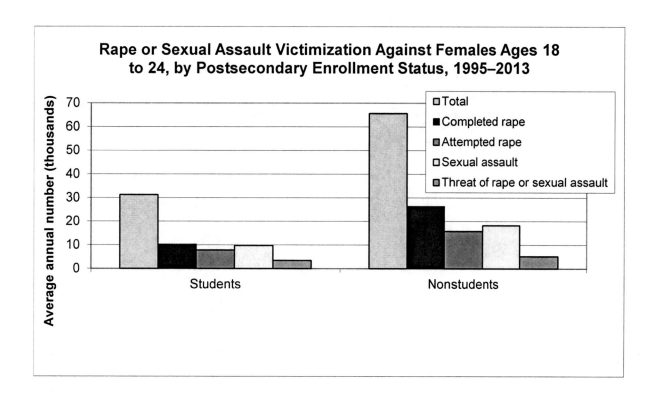

Rape or Sexual Assault Victimization Against Females Ages 18 to 24, by Postsecondary Enrollment Status, 1995–2013

- From 1995–2013, the rate of rape and sexual assault was 1.2 times higher for nonstudents (7.6 per 1,000 population) than for students (6.1 per 1,000 population).

- For both college students and nonstudents, the offender was known to the victim in about 80 percent of victimizations.

- Over half (51 percent) of the student rape and sexual assault victimizations occurred while victims were pursuing leisure activities away from home, in contrast to nonstudents who

were engaged in other activities at home (50 percent) when the victimization occurred.

- The offender had a weapon in more than 1 in 10 rape and sexual assault victimizations against both students and nonstudents.

- Rape and sexual assault victimizations of students (80 percent) were more likely to go unreported to police than nonstudent victimizations (67 percent).

Table 1. Rape or Sexual Assault Victimization Against Females Ages 18 to 24, by Postsecondary Enrollment Status, 1995–2013

(Number; rate.)

Characteristic	Students[1]		Nonstudents[3]		Ratio of nonstudent to student rate
	Average annual number	Rate[2]	Average annual number	Rate[4]	
Total	31,302	6.1	65,668	7.6	1.2
Completed rape	10,237	2.0	26,369	3.1	1.5
Attempted rape	7,864	1.5	15,792	1.8	1.2
Sexual assault	9,714	1.9	18,260	2.1	1.1
Threat of rape or sexual assault	3,488	0.7	5,247	0.6	0.9

Note: Detail may not sum to total due to rounding. Excludes a small number of female victims ages 18 to 24 with unknown enrollment status (less than 1%). The average annual population was 5,130,004 for students and 8,614,853 for nonstudents. Nonstudent total and completed rape rate estimates are significantly different from student estimates at the 95% confidence level. Nonstudent total average annual number estimates are significantly different from student estimates at the 90% confidence level.
[1]Includes females ages 18 to 24 enrolled part time or full time in a post-secondary institution (college or university, trade school, or vocational school).
[2]Per 1,000 female students ages 18 to 24.
[3]Includes females ages 18 to 24 not enrolled in a post-secondary institution.
[4]Per 1,000 females ages 18 to 24 not enrolled in a post-secondary institution.

Table 2. Rate of Violent Victimization Among College-Age Females, 1995–2013

(Number; rate.)

Characteristic	Students[1]	Nonstudents[2]	Ratio of nonstudent to student rate
Violent Crime	31,302	65,668	1.2
Serious Crime	10,237	26,369	1.5
Rape and sexual assault	7,864	15,792	1.2
Robbery	9,714	18,260	1.1
Aggravated assault			
Simple Assault	3,488	5,247	0.9

Note: Excludes a small percentage of females ages 18 to 24 with unknown enrollment status (less than 1%). Nonstudent estimates are significantly different from student estimates at the 95% confidence level.
[1]Per 1,000 females ages 18 to 24 enrolled part time or full time in a post-secondary institution (i.e., college or university, trade school, or vocational school).
[2]Per 1,000 females ages 18 to 24 not enrolled in a post-secondary institution.

Table 3. Rape or Sexual Assault Victimization, by Sex of Victim and Postsecondary Enrollment Status, 1995–2013

(Number; percent; rate.)

Sex of victim	Students[1]			Nonstudents[3]			Ratio of nonstudent to student rate
	Average annual number	Percent of victimizations	Rate[2]	Average annual number	Percent of victimizations	Rate[2]	
Male	6,544	17.0	1.4	2,866	4.0	0.3	0.2
Female	31,302	83.0	6.1	65,668	96.0	7.6	1.2

Note: Excludes a small percentage of victims with unknown enrollment status (less than 1%). Nonstudent estimates for percentages of victimizations and rate of victimizations are significantly different from student estimates at the 95% confidence level.
[1]Includes victims ages 18 to 24 enrolled part time or full time in a post-secondary institution (i.e., college or university, trade school, or vocational school).
[2]Per 1,000 persons ages 18 to 24.
[3]Includes victims ages 18 to 24 not enrolled in a post-secondary institution.

Table 4. Location, Victim Activity, and Time of Day of the Rape/Sexual Assault Victimization Among Females Ages 18 to 24, by Postsecondary Enrollment Status, 1995–2013

(Percent.)

Characteristic	Students[1]	Nonstudents[2]
Location Where Crime Occurred	100.0	100.0
At or near victim's home[3]	38.0	50.0*
At or near home of friend/relative/acquaintance		
Commercial place/parking lot or garage	16.0	15.0
School[4]	4.0!	2.0!
Open areas/public transportation/other[5]	13.0	16.0
Activity Where Crime Occurred	100.0	100.0
Traveling to or from other place/shopping or errands/leisure activity away from home	51.0	29.0*
Sleeping/other activities at home[3]	31.0	50.0*
Working or traveling to work	10.0!	16.0**
Attending school or traveling to school[4]	5.0!	2.0!**
Other/unknown	3.0!	4.0
Time of Day	100.0	100.0
Daytime (6 a.m. – 6 p.m.)	33.0	35.0
Night (6 p.m. – 6 a.m.)	65.0	64.0
Unknown	3.0!	1.0!

Note: Detail may not sum to total due to rounding. Excludes a small percentage of female victims ages 18 to 24 with unknown enrollment status (less than 1%).
! = Interpret with caution; estimate based on 10 or fewer sample cases, or coefficient of variation is greater than 50%.
* = Nonstudent estimates are significantly different from student estimates at the 95% confidence level.
** = Nonstudent estimates are significantly different from student estimates at the 90% confidence level.
[1]Includes female victims ages 18 to 24 enrolled part time or full time in a post-secondary institution (i.e., college or university, trade school, or vocational school).
[2]Includes female victims ages 18 to 24 not enrolled in a post-secondary institution.
[3]In the NCVS, the victim's home is defined as the location of residence at the time of the interview.
[4]Includes schools at any educational level regardless of whether the victim was a student at the location.
[5]Includes locations such as an apartment yard; a park, field, or playground not on school property; a location on the street other than that immediately adjacent to home of the victim, a relative, or friend; in a station or depot for bus or train; on a plane; or in an airport.

Table 5. Rape or Sexual Assault Victimization Among College-Age Females, by Postsecondary Enrollment Status, 1995–2013

(Percent.)

Characteristic	Students[1]	Nonstudents[2]
Involving Weapons	100.0	100.0
No weapon	82.0	84.0
Weapon	11.0	12.0
Don't know	7.0	4.0
Involving Injuries	100.0	100.0
No injury	43.0	37.0
Injury	57.0	63.0
Treatment of Injuries[3]	100.0	100.0
No treatment	60.0	63.0
Any treatment	40.0	37.0

Note: Detail may not sum to total due to rounding. Excludes a small percentage of female victims ages 18 to 24 with unknown enrollment status (less than 1%). Students/weapon data entry should be interpreted with caution; estimate based on 10 or fewer sample cases, or coefficient of variation is greater than 50%.
[1]Includes females ages 18 to 24 enrolled part time or full time in a post-secondary institution (i.e., college or university, trade school, or vocational school).
[2]Includes female victims ages 18 to 24 not enrolled in a post-secondary institution.
[3]Includes female victims ages 18 to 24 who were injured during the victimization.

Table 6. Rape or Sexual Assault Victimization Among College-Age Females, 1995–2013

(Percent.)

Victim-offender relationship	Students[1]	Nonstudents[2]
Stranger	22.0	20.0
Nonstranger	78.0	80.0
Intimate partner[3]	24.0	34.0*
Relative	2.0!	1.0!
Well-known/casual acquaintance	50.0	37.0*

Note: Detail may not sum to total due to rounding. Excludes a small percentage of victimizations in which the victim-offender relationship, number of offenders, or victim enrollment status was unknown
! = Interpret with caution; estimate based on 10 or fewer sample cases, or coefficient of variation is greater than 50%.
* = Nonstudent estimates are significantly different from student estimates at the 95% confidence level.
[1]Includes female victims ages 18 to 24 enrolled part time or full time in a post-secondary institution (i.e., college or university, trade school, or vocational school).
[2]Includes female victims ages 18 to 24 not enrolled in a post-secondary institution.
[3]Includes former or current spouse, boyfriend, or girlfriend.

Table 7. Perceived Offender Characteristics in Rape and Sexual Assault Victimizations Against Females Age 18 to 24, by Postsecondary Enrollment Status of Victim, 1995–2013

(Percent.)

Offender characteristics	Students[1]	Nonstudents[2]
Number of offenders		
One	95.0	92.0
Two or more	5.0!	5.0
Unknown	--!	3.0!
Age[3]		
18–20	17.0	13.0
21–29	51.0	53.0
30 or older	23.0	23.0
Mixed group	2.0!	3.0
Unknown	7.0	7.0
Sex		
Male	97.0	91.0*
Female	1.0!	3.0!*
	2.0!	5.0!*
Race[4]		
White	63.0	60.0
Black	19.0	22.0
Other/mixed group[5]	10.0	12.0
Unknown	8.0	7.0
Alcohol/drug use		
Yes	47.0	40.0
No	25.0	36.0*
Don't know/unknown	28.0	24.0

-- = Less than 0.5%.
! = Interpret with caution; estimate based on 10 or fewer sample cases, or coefficient of variation is greater than 50%.
* = Nonstudent estimates are significantly different from student estimates at the 95% confidence level.
[1]Includes female victims ages 18 to 24 enrolled part time or full time in a post-secondary institution (i.e., college or university, trade school, or vocational school).
[2]Includes female victims ages 18 to 24 not enrolled in a post-secondary institution.
[3]Detail may not sum to total due to small portion of offenders age 17 or younger.
[4]Prior to 2012, victims were not asked about perceived Hispanic origin of offenders, so Hispanic offenders make up an unknown portion of the white, black, and other race of offender categories.
[5]American Indian, Alaska Native, Asian, Native Hawaiian, and other Pacific Islander, persons of two or more races, and mixed groups that may include persons of any race.

Table 8. Rape or Sexual Assault Victimizations Against Females Ages 18 to 24 Reported and Not Reported to Police and Reasons for Not Reporting, by Postsecondary Enrollment Status, 1995–2013

(Percent.)

Characteristic	Students[1]	Nonstudents[2]
Reported[3]	20.0	32.0*
Not reported	80.0	67.0*
Reason for not reporting		
Reported to different official	4.0!	14.0*
Personal matter	26.0	23.0
Not important enough to respondent	12.0	5.0*
Police would not or could not do anything to help	9.0	19.0*
Did not want to get offender in trouble with law	10.0	10.0
Advised not to report	--!	1.0!
Fear of reprisal	20.0	20.0
Other reason	31.0	35.0

Note: Detail may not sum to total due to multiple reasons for not reporting. About 0.4% of student and 0.6% of nonstudent victims did not know or did not report whether the victimization was reported to police.
-- = Less than 0.5%.
! = Interpret with caution; estimate based on 10 or fewer sample cases, or coefficient of variation is greater than 50%.
* = Nonstudent estimates are significantly different from student estimates at the 95% confidence level.
[1]Includes female victims ages 18 to 24 enrolled part time or full time in a post-secondary institution (i.e., college or university, trade school, or vocational school).
[2]Includes female victims ages 18 to 24 not enrolled in a post-secondary institution.
[3]Includes only reports to the police, not to other officials or administrators. The NCVS does not collect information on victim reporting to parties other than law enforcement.

Table 9. Receipt of Assistance from a Victim Service Agency Among Female Rape or Sexual Assault Victims Ages 18 to 24, by Postsecondary Enrollment Status, 1995–2013

(Percent.)

Characteristics	Students[1]	Nonstudents[2]
Received assistance	16.0	18.0
Did not receive assistance	83.0	82.0

Note: Detail does not sum to total due to a small percentage of victims who did not know whether assistance was received. Excludes a small percentage of female victims ages 18 to 24 with unknown enrollment status (less than 1%).
[1]Includes female victims ages 18 to 24 enrolled part time or full time in a post-secondary institution (i.e., college or university, trade school, or vocational school).
[2]Includes female victims ages 18 to 24 not enrolled in a post-secondary institution.

Table 10. Rate of Rape and Sexual Assault Against Female Victims Ages 18 to 24, by Demographic Characteristics and Postsecondary Enrollment Status, 1995–2013

(Number; rate.)

Victim characteristic	Students[1]	Nonstudents[2]	Ratio of nonstudent to student rate
Age			
18–19	6.6	10.4*	1.6
20–21	5.8	8.9*	1.5
22–24	6.0	5.4	0.9
Race/Hispanic origin			
White[3]	6.7	9.2*	1.4
Black[3]	6.4	6.2	1.0
Hispanic	4.5	4.5	1.0
Other[3,4]	3.7!	5.9	1.6
Region[5]			
Northeast	5.2	4.1	0.8
Midwest	8.3	11.0	1.3
South	4.7	6.5**	1.4
West	5.9	8.0	1.4
Location of residence			
Urban	6.6	6.5**	1.3
Suburban	6.0	6.3	1.0
Rural	4.6	8.8*	1.9

Note: Detail may not sum to total due to rounding.
! = Interpret with caution; estimate based on 10 or fewer sample cases, or coefficient of variation is greater than 50%.
* = Nonstudent estimates are significantly different from student estimates at the 95% confidence level.
** = Nonstudent estimates are significantly different from student estimates at the 90% confidence level.
[1]Per 1,000 females ages 18 to 24 enrolled part time or full time in a post-secondary institution (i.e., college or university, trade school, or vocational school).
[2]Per 1,000 females ages 18 to 24 not enrolled in a post-secondary institution.
[3]Excludes persons of Hispanic or Latino origin.
[4]Includes American Indian, Alaska Native, Asian, Native Hawaiian, and other Pacific Islander, and persons of two or more races.
[5]Includes data from 1996 through 2013 because information about region was not collected prior to 1996.

Table 11. Number of Female Students Ages 18 to 24 Enrolled in Postsecondary Institutions According to the NCVS and NCES, 1997–2011

(Number; rate.)

Year	Estimate	Lower confidence level	Upper confidence level	Integrated Postsecondary Education Data System
1997	4,090,000	3,687,000	4,494,000	4,409,000
1998	4,122,000	3,755,000	4,489,000	4,571,000
1999	4,498,000	4,028,000	4,967,000	4,769,000
2000	4,441,000	4,035,000	4,847,000	4,959,000
2001	4,513,000	4,028,000	4,997,000	5,186,000
2002	4,874,000	4,292,000	5,456,000	5,467,000
2003	5,074,000	4,610,000	5,538,000	5,602,000
2004	5,139,000	4,606,000	5,671,000	5,713,000
2005	5,217,000	4,680,000	5,755,000	5,683,000
2006	5,297,000	4,783,000	5,810,000	5,864,000
2007	5,611,000	5,136,000	6,087,000	5,994,000
2008	5,658,000	5,195,000	6,121,000	6,208,000
2009	5,781,000	5,320,000	6,241,000	6,580,000
2010	6,262,000	5,781,000	6,743,000	6,685,000
2011	6,222,000	5,710,000	6,735,000	6,723,000

Methodology

Survey Coverage

The National Crime Victimization Survey (NCVS) is an annual data collection conducted by the U.S. Census Bureau for the Bureau of Justice Statistics (BJS). The NCVS is a self-report survey in which interviewed persons are asked about the number and characteristics of victimizations experienced during the prior six months. The NCVS collects information on non-fatal personal crimes (rape or sexual assault, robbery, aggravated and simple assault, and personal larceny) and household property crimes (burglary, motor vehicle theft, and other theft) both reported and not reported to police. In addition to providing annual level and change estimates on criminal victimization, the NCVS is the primary source of information on the nature of criminal victimization incidents.

Survey respondents provide information about themselves (e.g., age, sex, race and Hispanic origin, marital status, education level, and income) and whether they experienced a victimization. The NCVS collects information for each victimization incident about the offender (e.g., age, sex, race and Hispanic origin, and victim–offender relationship), characteristics of the crime (including time and place of occurrence, use of weapons, nature of injury, and economic consequences), whether the crime was reported to police, reasons the crime was or was not reported, and victim experiences with the criminal justice system. The NCVS is administered to persons age 12 or older from a nationally representative sample of households in the United States. The NCVS defines a household as a group of persons who all reside at a sampled address. Persons are considered household members when the sampled address is their usual place of residence at the time of the interview and when they have no usual place of residence elsewhere. Once selected, households remain in the sample for three years, and eligible persons in these households are interviewed every six months either in person or over the phone for a total of seven interviews.

All first interviews are conducted in person with subsequent interviews conducted either in person or by phone. New households rotate into the sample on an ongoing basis to replace outgoing households that have been in the sample for the three-year period. The sample includes persons living in group quarters, such as dormitories, rooming houses, and religious group dwellings, and excludes persons living in military barracks and institutional settings such as correctional or hospital facilities, and persons who are homeless.

NCVS Measurement of Rape and Sexual Assault

This report focuses on rape and sexual assault victimizations, including completed, attempted, and threatened rape or sexual assault. Because of the sensitive nature of the topic, measuring the extent of these victimizations is often difficult, and best practices are still being determined. For the NCVS, survey respondents are asked to respond to a series of questions about the nature and characteristics of their victimization. The NCVS classifies victimizations as rape or sexual assault, even if other crimes, such as robbery or assault, occur at the same time. The NCVS then uses the following rape and sexual assault definitions:

- Rape is the unlawful penetration of a person against the will of the victim, with use or threatened use of force, or attempting such an act. Rape includes psychological coercion and physical force, and forced sexual intercourse means vaginal, anal, or oral penetration by the offender. Rape also includes incidents where penetration is from a foreign object (e.g., a bottle), victimizations against males and females, and both heterosexual and homosexual rape. Attempted rape includes verbal threats of rape.

- Sexual assault is defined across a wide range of victimizations separate from rape or attempted rape. These crimes include attacks or attempted attacks usually involving unwanted sexual contact between a victim and offender. Sexual assault may or may not involve force and includes grabbing or fondling. The measurement of rape and sexual assault presents many challenges. Victims may not be willing to reveal or share their experiences with an interviewer. The level and type of sexual violence reported by victims is sensitive to how items are worded, which definitions are used, the data collection mode, and a variety of other factors related to the interview process. In addition, the legal definitions of rape and sexual assault vary across jurisdictions. The NCVS presents one approach to measuring and enumerating these incidents as well as other forms of violence and property crime.

Comparison Of NCVS and National Center for Education Statistics Student Population Statistics

This report focused on females ages 18 to 24, which account for about 32% of the total population enrolled in post-secondary institutions. To assess whether the NCVS estimates of the college student population accurately reflect the actual population of students, NCVS weighted counts of enrolled students were compared to data collected through the National Center for Education Statistics' (NCES) Integrated Post-Secondary Education Data System (IPEDS).

From 1997 to 2011, the years of available NCES data, the NCVS estimates of the female population of college students were significantly lower than the NCES estimates in 9 of the 15 years (table 11). In the years in which the NCVS estimate differed from the IPEDS population count, the NCVS female student population was about 10% lower.

Nonresponse and Weighting Adjustments

In 2013, 90,630 households and 160,040 persons age 12 or older were interviewed for the NCVS. Each household was interviewed twice during the year. The response rate was 84% for households and 88% for eligible persons. Victimizations that occurred outside of the United States were excluded from this report. In 2013, less than 1% of the unweighted victimizations occurred outside of the United States and were excluded from the analyses. Estimates in this report use data from the 1995 to 2013 NCVS data files, weighted to produce annual estimates of victimization for persons age 12 or older living in U.S. households. Because the NCVS relies on a sample rather than a census of the entire U.S. population, weights are designed to inflate sample point estimates to known population totals and to compensate for survey nonresponse and other aspects of the sample design. The NCVS data files include both person and household weights. Person weights provide an estimate of the population represented by each person in the sample. Household weights provide an estimate of the U.S. household population represented by each household in the sample. After proper adjustment, both household and person weights are also typically used to form the denominator in calculations of crime rates.

Victimization weights used in this analysis account for the number of persons present during an incident and for high-frequency repeat victimizations (i.e., series victimizations). Series victimizations are similar in type but occur with such frequency that a victim is unable to recall each individual event or describe each event in detail. Survey procedures allow NCVS interviewers to identify and classify these similar victimizations as series victimizations and to collect detailed information on only the most recent incident in the series.

The weight counts series incidents as the actual number of incidents reported by the victim, up to a maximum of 10 incidents. Including series victimizations in national rates results in large increases in the level of violent victimization; however, trends in violence are generally similar, regardless of whether series victimizations are included. In 2013, series incidents accounted for about 1% of all victimizations and 4% of all violent victimizations. Weighting series incidents as the number of incidents up to a maximum of 10 incidents produces more reliable estimates of crime levels, while the cap at 10 minimizes the effect of extreme outliers on rates. Additional information on the series enumeration is detailed in the report Methods for Counting High-Frequency Repeat Victimizations in the National Crime Victimization Survey (NCJ 237308, BJS web, April 2012).

APPENDIX: SOURCES FOR TABLES

Part 1. Capital Punishment, 2013

1   Bureau of Justice Statistics, National Prisoner Statistics Program (NPS-8), 2013.
1A Bureau of Justice Statistics, National Prisoner Statistics Program (NPS-8), 2013.
2   Bureau of Justice Statistics, National Prisoner Statistics Program (NPS-8), 2013
3   Bureau of Justice Statistics, National Prisoner Statistics Program (NPS-8), 2013
4   Bureau of Justice Statistics, National Prisoner Statistics Program (NPS-8), 2013.
5   Bureau of Justice Statistics, National Prisoner Statistics Program (NPS-8), 2013.
6   Bureau of Justice Statistics, National Prisoner Statistics Program (NPS-8), 2013.
7   Bureau of Justice Statistics, National Prisoner Statistics Program (NPS-8), 2013.
8   Bureau of Justice Statistics, National Prisoner Statistics Program (NPS-8), 2013.
9   Bureau of Justice Statistics, National Prisoner Statistics Program (NPS-8), 2013.
10 Bureau of Justice Statistics, National Prisoner Statistics Program (NPS-8), 2013.
11 Bureau of Justice Statistics, National Prisoner Statistics Program (NPS-8), 2013.
12 Bureau of Justice Statistics, National Prisoner Statistics Program (NPS-8), 2013.
13 Bureau of Justice Statistics, National Prisoner Statistics Program (NPS-8), 2013.
14 Bureau of Justice Statistics, National Prisoner Statistics Program (NPS-8), 2013.
15 Bureau of Justice Statistics, National Prisoner Statistics Program (NPS-8), 2013.
16 Bureau of Justice Statistics, National Prisoner Statistics Program (NPS-8), 2013.
17 Bureau of Justice Statistics, National Prisoner Statistics Program (NPS-8), 2013.
18 Bureau of Justice Statistics, National Prisoner Statistics Program (NPS-8), 2013.

Part 2. Correctional Populations in the United States, 2013

1   Bureau of Justice Statistics, Annual Surveys of Probation and Parole, Annual Survey of Jails, Census of Jail Inmates, and National Prisoner Statistics Program, 2000, 2005, and 2010–2013.
2   Adult correctional population estimates are based on the Bureau of Justice Statistics, Annual Surveys of Probation and Parole, Annual Survey of Jails, Census of Jail Inmates, and National Prisoner Statistics Program, 2000, 2005–2013. The adult resident population estimates are based on the U.S. Census Bureau, National Intercensal Estimates, 2000, and 2005–2012, and unpublished adult resident population estimates on January 1, 2013 and January 1, 2014.
3   Bureau of Justice Statistics, Annual Surveys of Probation and Parole, Annual Survey of Jails, and National Prisoner Statistics Program, 2010 and 2013
4   Bureau of Justice Statistics, Annual Surveys of Probation and Parole, Annual Survey of Jails, and National Prisoner Statistics Program, 2010 and 2013.
5   Bureau of Justice Statistics, Annual Surveys of Probation and Parole, Annual Survey of Jails, and National Prisoner Statistics Program, 2000, 2010, and 2013.
6   Bureau of Justice Statistics, Annual Surveys of Probation and Parole, and National Prisoner Statistics Program, 2000–2013.
7   Bureau of Justice Statistics, Annual Surveys of Probation and Parole, Deaths in Custody Reporting Program - Annual Summary on Inmates under Jail Jurisdiction, and National Prisoner Statistics Program, 2013. The adult resident population estimates are based on unpublished U.S. adult state resident populations on January 1, 2014.
8   Bureau of Justice Statistics, Annual Survey of Jails, and National Prisoner Statistics Program, 2000 and 2012–2013. The total and adult resident population estimates are based on U.S. Census Bureau National Intercensal Estimates, 2001, and unpublished total and adult resident population estimates on January 1, 2013, and January 1, 2014.
9   Bureau of Justice Statistics, National Prisoner Statistics Program, and Survey of Jails in Indian Country, 2000, 2005, and 2012–2013.
    Bureau of Justice Statistics, Annual Surveys of Probation and Parole, Annual Survey of Jails, Census of Jail Inmates, and
10 National Prisoner Statistics Program, 2000–2013.

Part 3. Crime in the United States, 2013

  1 United States Department of Justice, Federal Bureau of Investigation, Uniform Crime Reports.
  2 United States Department of Justice, Federal Bureau of Investigation, Uniform Crime Reports.
  3 United States Department of Justice, Federal Bureau of Investigation, Uniform Crime Reports.
  4 United States Department of Justice, Federal Bureau of Investigation, Uniform Crime Reports.
  5 United States Department of Justice, Federal Bureau of Investigation, Uniform Crime Reports.
  6 United States Department of Justice, Federal Bureau of Investigation, Uniform Crime Reports.
  7 United States Department of Justice, Federal Bureau of Investigation, Uniform Crime Reports.
  8 United States Department of Justice, Federal Bureau of Investigation, Uniform Crime Reports.
  9 United States Department of Justice, Federal Bureau of Investigation, Uniform Crime Reports.
10 United States Department of Justice, Federal Bureau of Investigation, Uniform Crime Reports.
11 United States Department of Justice, Federal Bureau of Investigation, Uniform Crime Reports.
12 United States Department of Justice, Federal Bureau of Investigation, Uniform Crime Reports.
13 United States Department of Justice, Federal Bureau of Investigation, Uniform Crime Reports.
14 United States Department of Justice, Federal Bureau of Investigation, Uniform Crime Reports.
15 United States Department of Justice, Federal Bureau of Investigation, Uniform Crime Reports.
16 United States Department of Justice, Federal Bureau of Investigation, Uniform Crime Reports.
17 United States Department of Justice, Federal Bureau of Investigation, Uniform Crime Reports.
18 United States Department of Justice, Federal Bureau of Investigation, Uniform Crime Reports.
19 United States Department of Justice, Federal Bureau of Investigation, Uniform Crime Reports.
20 United States Department of Justice, Federal Bureau of Investigation, Uniform Crime Reports.
21 United States Department of Justice, Federal Bureau of Investigation, Uniform Crime Reports.
22 United States Department of Justice, Federal Bureau of Investigation, Uniform Crime Reports.
23 United States Department of Justice, Federal Bureau of Investigation, Uniform Crime Reports.
24 United States Department of Justice, Federal Bureau of Investigation, Uniform Crime Reports.
25 United States Department of Justice, Federal Bureau of Investigation, Uniform Crime Reports.
26 United States Department of Justice, Federal Bureau of Investigation, Uniform Crime Reports.
27 United States Department of Justice, Federal Bureau of Investigation, Uniform Crime Reports.
28 United States Department of Justice, Federal Bureau of Investigation, Uniform Crime Reports.
29 United States Department of Justice, Federal Bureau of Investigation, Uniform Crime Reports.
30 United States Department of Justice, Federal Bureau of Investigation, Uniform Crime Reports.
31 United States Department of Justice, Federal Bureau of Investigation, Uniform Crime Reports.
32 United States Department of Justice, Federal Bureau of Investigation, Uniform Crime Reports.
33 United States Department of Justice, Federal Bureau of Investigation, Uniform Crime Reports.
34 United States Department of Justice, Federal Bureau of Investigation, Uniform Crime Reports.
35 United States Department of Justice, Federal Bureau of Investigation, Uniform Crime Reports.
36 United States Department of Justice, Federal Bureau of Investigation, Uniform Crime Reports.
37 United States Department of Justice, Federal Bureau of Investigation, Uniform Crime Reports.
38 United States Department of Justice, Federal Bureau of Investigation, Uniform Crime Reports.
39 United States Department of Justice, Federal Bureau of Investigation, Uniform Crime Reports.
40 United States Department of Justice, Federal Bureau of Investigation, Uniform Crime Reports.
41 United States Department of Justice, Federal Bureau of Investigation, Uniform Crime Reports.
42 United States Department of Justice, Federal Bureau of Investigation, Uniform Crime Reports.
43 United States Department of Justice, Federal Bureau of Investigation, Uniform Crime Reports.
44 United States Department of Justice, Federal Bureau of Investigation, Uniform Crime Reports.
45 United States Department of Justice, Federal Bureau of Investigation, Uniform Crime Reports.

Part 4. Crimes Against Persons with Disabilities, 2009–2013

1 Bureau of Justice Statistics, National Crime Victimization Survey, 2008–2013; and U.S. Census Bureau, American Community Survey, 2008–2013.

2 Bureau of Justice Statistics, National Crime Victimization Survey, 2008–2013; and U.S. Census Bureau, American Community Survey, 2008–2013.

3 Bureau of Justice Statistics, National Crime Victimization Survey, 2008–2013; and U.S. Census Bureau, American Community Survey, 2008–2013.

4 Bureau of Justice Statistics, National Crime Victimization Survey, 2008–2013; and U.S. Census Bureau, American Community Survey, 2008–2013.

5 Bureau of Justice Statistics, National Crime Victimization Survey, 2008–2013; and U.S. Census Bureau, American Community Survey, 2008–2013.

6 Bureau of Justice Statistics, National Crime Victimization Survey, 2008–2013; and U.S. Census Bureau, American Community Survey, 2008–2013.

7 Bureau of Justice Statistics, National Crime Victimization Survey, 2008–2013; and U.S. Census Bureau, American Community Survey, 2008–2013.

8 Bureau of Justice Statistics, National Crime Victimization Survey, 2008–2013.

9 Bureau of Justice Statistics, National Crime Victimization Survey, 2008–2013; and U.S. Census Bureau, American Community Survey, 2008–2013.

10 Bureau of Justice Statistics, National Crime Victimization Survey, 2008–2013.

11 Bureau of Justice Statistics, National Crime Victimization Survey, 2008–2013.

12 Bureau of Justice Statistics, National Crime Victimization Survey, 2008–2013.

13 Bureau of Justice Statistics, National Crime Victimization Survey, 2008–2013.

14 Bureau of Justice Statistics, National Crime Victimization Survey, 2008–2013.

15 Bureau of Justice Statistics, National Crime Victimization Survey, 2008–2013.

16 Bureau of Justice Statistics, National Crime Victimization Survey, 2008–2013.

17 U.S. Census Bureau, American Community Survey, 2013.

18 Bureau of Justice Statistics, National Crime Victimization Survey, 2008–2013; and U.S. Census Bureau, American Community Survey, 2008–2013.

19 Bureau of Justice Statistics, National Crime Victimization Survey, 2008–2013; and U.S. Census Bureau, American Community Survey, 2008–2013.

Part 5. Hate Crime Statistics, 2013

1 Federal Bureau of Investigation, Hate Crime Statistics, 2013.

2 Federal Bureau of Investigation, Hate Crime Statistics, 2013.

3 Federal Bureau of Investigation, Hate Crime Statistics, 2013.

4 Federal Bureau of Investigation, Hate Crime Statistics, 2013.

5 Federal Bureau of Investigation, Hate Crime Statistics, 2013.

6 Federal Bureau of Investigation, Hate Crime Statistics, 2013.

7 Federal Bureau of Investigation, Hate Crime Statistics, 2013.

8 Federal Bureau of Investigation, Hate Crime Statistics, 2013.

9 Federal Bureau of Investigation, Hate Crime Statistics, 2013.

10 Federal Bureau of Investigation, Hate Crime Statistics, 2013.

11 Federal Bureau of Investigation, Hate Crime Statistics, 2013.

12 Federal Bureau of Investigation, Hate Crime Statistics, 2013.

13 Federal Bureau of Investigation, Hate Crime Statistics, 2013.

Part 6. Jail Inmates at Midyear, 2014

1   Bureau of Justice Statistics, Annual Survey of Jails, midyear 2000–2004 and midyear 2006–2014; and Census of Jail Inmates, midyear 2005.

2   Bureau of Justice Statistics, Annual Survey of Jails, midyear 2000 and midyear 2006–2014; and Census of Jail Inmates, midyear 2005.

3   Bureau of Justice Statistics, Annual Survey of Jails, midyear 2000 and midyear 2006–2014; and Census of Jail Inmates, midyear 2005.

4   Bureau of Justice Statistics, Annual Survey of Jails, midyear 2013–2014.

5   Bureau of Justice Statistics, Annual Survey of Jails, midyear 2000 and midyear 2006–2014; and Census of Jail Inmates, midyear 2005.

6   Bureau of Justice Statistics, Annual Survey of Jails, midyear 2013–2014.

7   Bureau of Justice Statistics, Annual Survey of Jails, midyear 2013–2014

8   Bureau of Justice Statistics, Annual Survey of Jails, midyear 2002–2004 and midyear 2006–2014; and Census of Jail Inmates, midyear 2005.

9   Bureau of Justice Statistics, Annual Survey of Jails, midyear 2000 and midyear 2006–2014.

10   Bureau of Justice Statistics, Annual Survey of Jails, midyear 2000 and midyear 2006–2014; and Census of Jail Inmates, midyear 2005.

Part 7. Law Enforcement Officers Killed and Assaulted, 2013

1   United States Department of Justice, Federal Bureau of Investigation, Uniform Crime Reports.

2   United States Department of Justice, Federal Bureau of Investigation, Uniform Crime Reports.

3   United States Department of Justice, Federal Bureau of Investigation, Uniform Crime Reports.

4   United States Department of Justice, Federal Bureau of Investigation, Uniform Crime Reports.

5   United States Department of Justice, Federal Bureau of Investigation, Uniform Crime Reports.

6   United States Department of Justice, Federal Bureau of Investigation, Uniform Crime Reports.

7   United States Department of Justice, Federal Bureau of Investigation, Uniform Crime Reports.

8   United States Department of Justice, Federal Bureau of Investigation, Uniform Crime Reports.

9   United States Department of Justice, Federal Bureau of Investigation, Uniform Crime Reports.

10   United States Department of Justice, Federal Bureau of Investigation, Uniform Crime Reports.

11   United States Department of Justice, Federal Bureau of Investigation, Uniform Crime Reports.

12   United States Department of Justice, Federal Bureau of Investigation, Uniform Crime Reports.

13   United States Department of Justice, Federal Bureau of Investigation, Uniform Crime Reports.

14   United States Department of Justice, Federal Bureau of Investigation, Uniform Crime Reports.

15   United States Department of Justice, Federal Bureau of Investigation, Uniform Crime Reports.

16   United States Department of Justice, Federal Bureau of Investigation, Uniform Crime Reports.

17   United States Department of Justice, Federal Bureau of Investigation, Uniform Crime Reports.

18   United States Department of Justice, Federal Bureau of Investigation, Uniform Crime Reports.

19   United States Department of Justice, Federal Bureau of Investigation, Uniform Crime Reports.

20   United States Department of Justice, Federal Bureau of Investigation, Uniform Crime Reports.

21   United States Department of Justice, Federal Bureau of Investigation, Uniform Crime Reports.

22   United States Department of Justice, Federal Bureau of Investigation, Uniform Crime Reports.

23   United States Department of Justice, Federal Bureau of Investigation, Uniform Crime Reports.

24   United States Department of Justice, Federal Bureau of Investigation, Uniform Crime Reports.

25   United States Department of Justice, Federal Bureau of Investigation, Uniform Crime Reports.

26   United States Department of Justice, Federal Bureau of Investigation, Uniform Crime Reports.

27   United States Department of Justice, Federal Bureau of Investigation, Uniform Crime Reports.

28   United States Department of Justice, Federal Bureau of Investigation, Uniform Crime Reports.

29   United States Department of Justice, Federal Bureau of Investigation, Uniform Crime Reports.

30   United States Department of Justice, Federal Bureau of Investigation, Uniform Crime Reports.

31   United States Department of Justice, Federal Bureau of Investigation, Uniform Crime Reports.

32   United States Department of Justice, Federal Bureau of Investigation, Uniform Crime Reports.

33   United States Department of Justice, Federal Bureau of Investigation, Uniform Crime Reports.

34   United States Department of Justice, Federal Bureau of Investigation, Uniform Crime Reports.

35 United States Department of Justice, Federal Bureau of Investigation, Uniform Crime Reports.
36 United States Department of Justice, Federal Bureau of Investigation, Uniform Crime Reports.
37 United States Department of Justice, Federal Bureau of Investigation, Uniform Crime Reports.
38 United States Department of Justice, Federal Bureau of Investigation, Uniform Crime Reports.
39 United States Department of Justice, Federal Bureau of Investigation, Uniform Crime Reports.
40 United States Department of Justice, Federal Bureau of Investigation, Uniform Crime Reports.
41 United States Department of Justice, Federal Bureau of Investigation, Uniform Crime Reports.
42 United States Department of Justice, Federal Bureau of Investigation, Uniform Crime Reports.
43 United States Department of Justice, Federal Bureau of Investigation, Uniform Crime Reports.
44 United States Department of Justice, Federal Bureau of Investigation, Uniform Crime Reports.

Part 8. Probation and Parole, 2013

Supp. Table 1 BJS, Annual Parole Survey data series (CJ-7)
Supp. Table 2 BJS, Annual Probation Survey data series (CJ-8)
 1 Bureau of Justice Statistics, Annual Probation Survey and Annual Parole Survey, 2000–2013.
    Bureau of Justice Statistics, Annual Probation Survey and Annual Parole Survey, 2000, 2005–2013; and U.S. Census
 2 Bureau, National Intercensal Estimates, 2001, 2005–2010, and Population Estimates, January 1, 2011–2014.
 3 Bureau of Justice Statistics, Annual Probation Survey and Annual Parole Survey, 2008–2013.
 4 Bureau of Justice Statistics, Annual Probation Survey, 2008–2013.
 5 Bureau of Justice Statistics, Annual Probation Survey, 2010 and 2013.
 6 Bureau of Justice Statistics, Annual Parole Survey, 2008–2013.
 7 Bureau of Justice Statistics, Annual Probation Survey and Annual Parole Survey, 2008–2013.
 8 Bureau of Justice Statistics, Annual Parole Survey, 2000–2012.
 9 Bureau of Justice Statistics, Annual Parole Survey, 2000–2012.
10 Bureau of Justice Statistics, Annual Probation Survey and Annual Parole Survey, 2013.
11 Bureau of Justice Statistics, Annual Probation Survey and Annual Parole Survey, 2013.
12 Bureau of Justice Statistics, Annual Probation Survey, 2000, 2012, and 2013.
13 Bureau of Justice Statistics, Annual Parole Survey, 2013.
14 Bureau of Justice Statistics, Annual Parole Survey, 2013.
15 Bureau of Justice Statistics, Annual Parole Survey, 2000, 2012, and 2013.
16 Bureau of Justice Statistics, Annual Parole Survey, 2013.
17 Bureau of Justice Statistics, Annual Parole Survey, 2008–2013.

Part 9. Rape and Sexual Assault Among College-Age Females, 1995–2013

 1 Bureau of Justice Statistics, National Crime Victimization Survey, 1995–2013.
 2 Bureau of Justice Statistics, National Crime Victimization Survey, 1995–2013.
 3 Bureau of Justice Statistics, National Crime Victimization Survey, 1995–2013.
 4 Bureau of Justice Statistics, National Crime Victimization Survey, 1995–2013.
 5 Bureau of Justice Statistics, National Crime Victimization Survey, 1995–2013.
 6 Bureau of Justice Statistics, National Crime Victimization Survey, 1995–2013.
 7 Bureau of Justice Statistics, National Crime Victimization Survey, 1995–2013.
 8 Bureau of Justice Statistics, National Crime Victimization Survey, 1995–2013.
 9 Bureau of Justice Statistics, National Crime Victimization Survey, 1995–2013.
10 Bureau of Justice Statistics, National Crime Victimization Survey, 1995–2013.
11 Bureau of Justice Statistics, National Crime Victimization Survey, 1997–2011; and National Center for Education Statistics, Integrated Post-Secondary Education Data System, 1997–2011.

INDEX

CPSIA information can be obtained
at www.ICGtesting.com
Printed in the USA
FFOW03n0055151015
17714FF

9 781598 887853